Mark Siegel

Sailor Twain

or The Mermaid in the Hudson

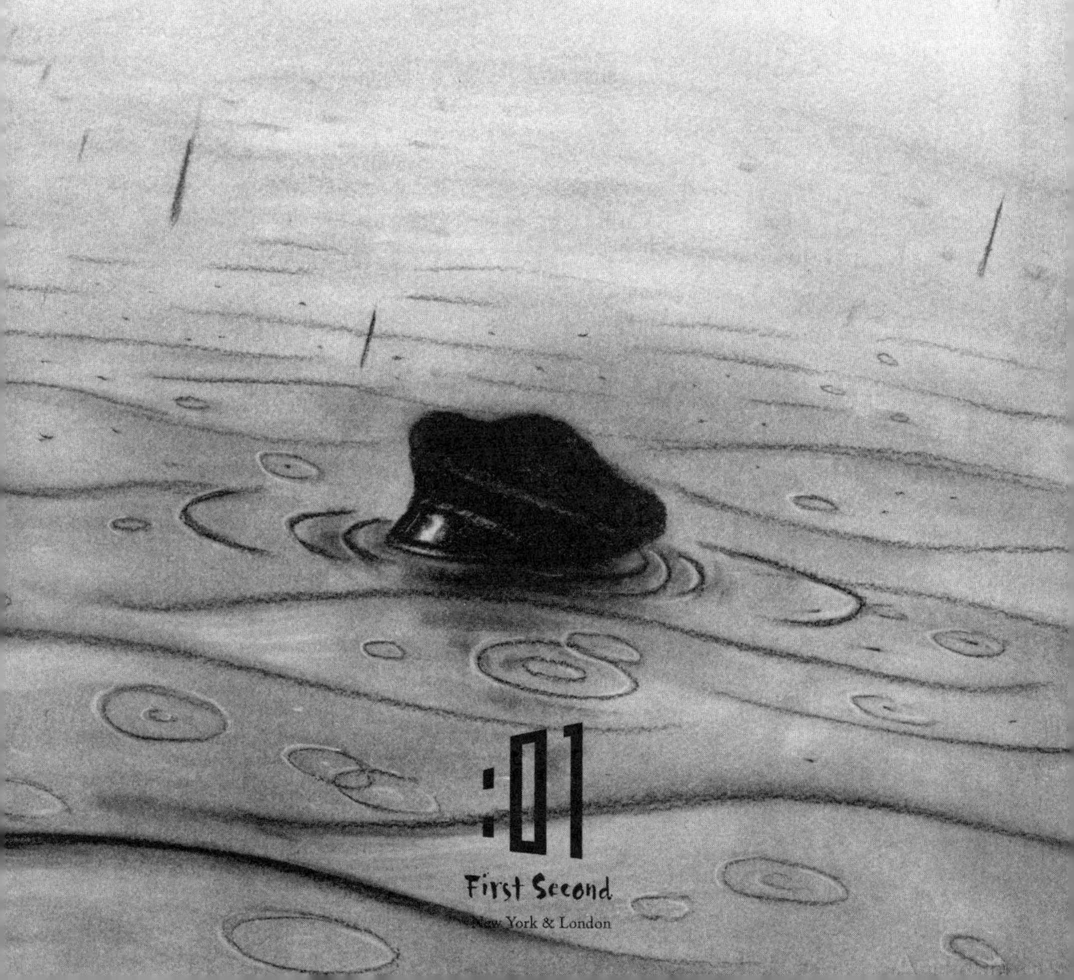

:01
First Second
New York & London

For Edward and Marie-Claire Siegel

Mon front est rouge encor du baiser de la Reine;
J'ai rêvé dans la grotte où nage la sirène . . .

Gérard de Nerval, *El Desdichado*

CONTENTS

Overture: 5

PART I: TWAIN'S SECRET

Chapter 1: THE FRENCHMAN'S STEAMBOAT 21

Chapter 2: AN UNLIKELY SURVIVOR. 35

Chapter 3: A PRAYER DOWN BELOW .47

Chapter 4: THE MERMAID IN THE HUDSON 61

Chapter 5: BEAVERTON'S NEW BOOK 75

Chapter 6: LAFAYETTE'S LETTER 97

Chapter 7: SOUTH'S PROMISE 105

Chapter 8: PEARL'S SONG 121

Chapter 9: THREE PRISONERS 137

Chapter 10: THE CURE FOR MERMAIDS 155

Chapter 11: SOUTH OF THE NORTH RIVER 167

Chapter 12: THE MISSING MUSE. 191

PART II: CAMOMILLE

Chapter 1:   THE BEAVERTON REVELATION 209

Chapter 2:   INK STAINS 229

Chapter 3:   "THE DAME'S AUDACIOUS" 235

Chapter 4:   ECLIPSE 239

Chapter 5:   SEVENING 257

Chapter 6:   ENTICEMENT 263

Chapter 7:   THE STRAINS OF ABSENCE 281

Chapter 8:   TWAIN DREAMS 285

PART III: WORLD'S END

Chapter 1:   IN THE OTHER REALM 293

Chapter 2:   THE LOST BROTHER 305

Chapter 3:   A LADY BEGUILED 312

Chapter 4:   THE CHAINED HEART 335

PART IV: SAILOR TWAIN

Chapter 1:   THE TWAIN SHALL MEET 312

Chapter 2:   THE SIREN'S WRATH 379

Coda: 393

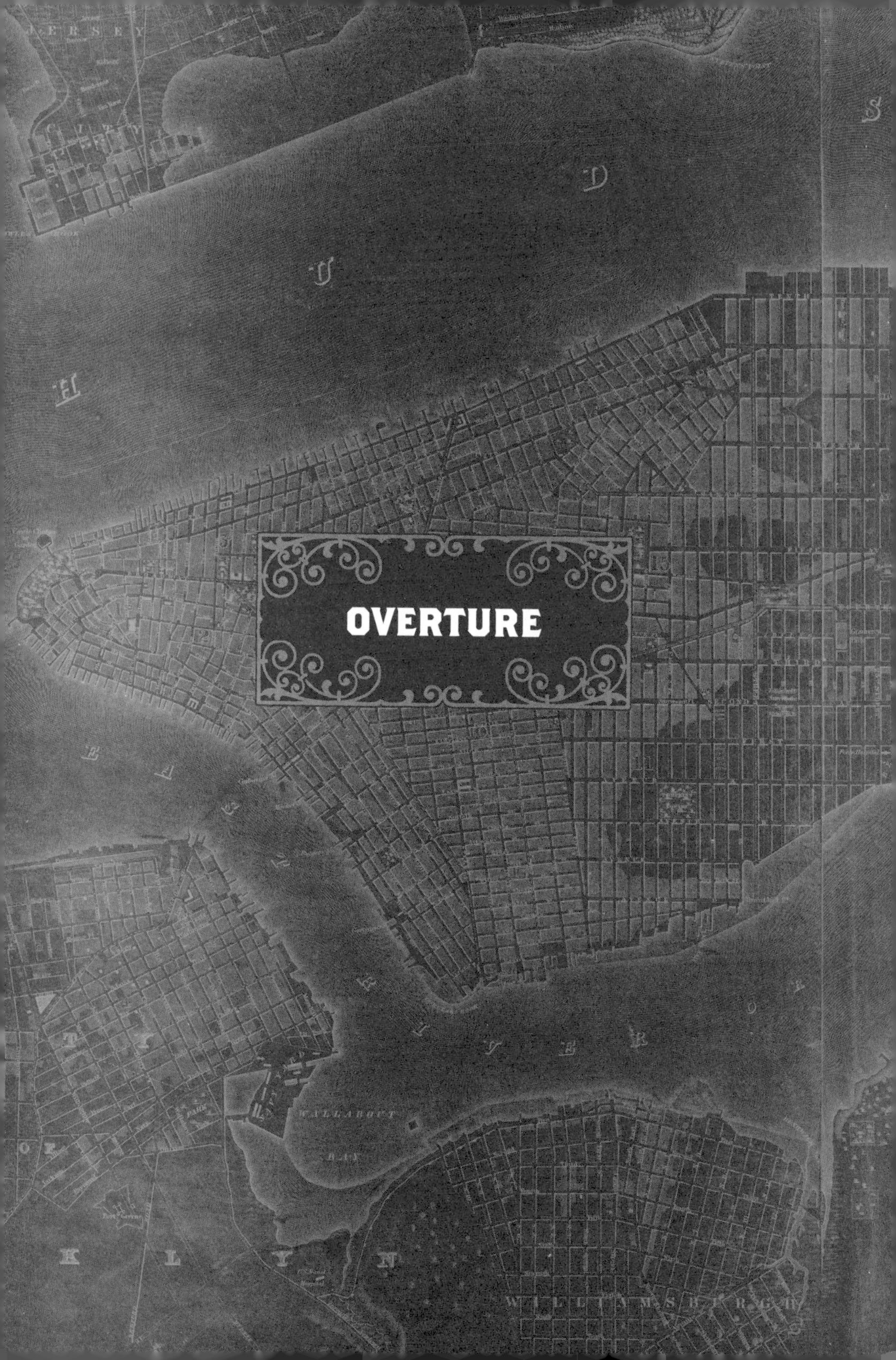
JERSEY
WALLABOUT
BAY

OVERTURE

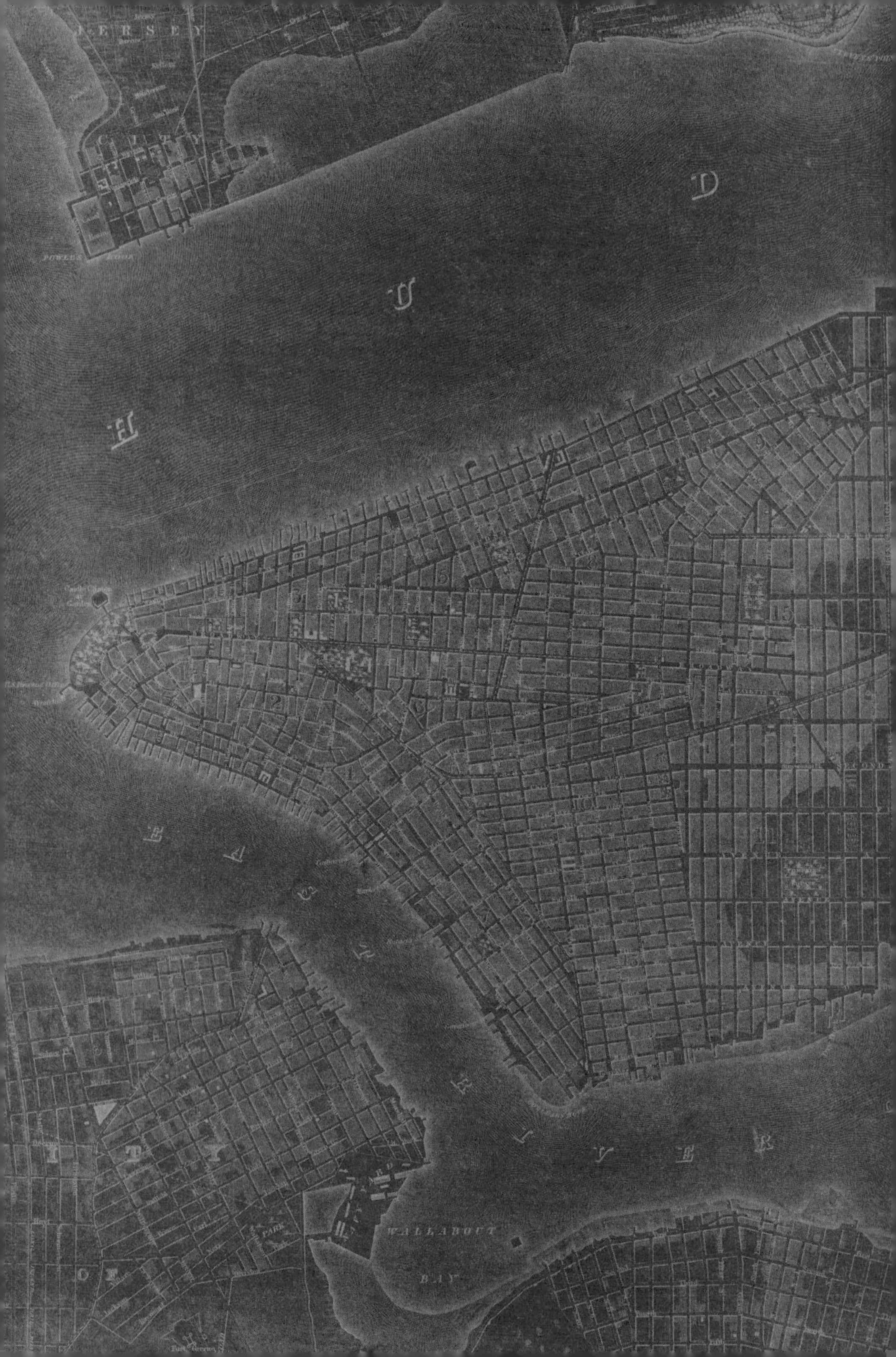
JERSEY
WALLABOUT
BAY

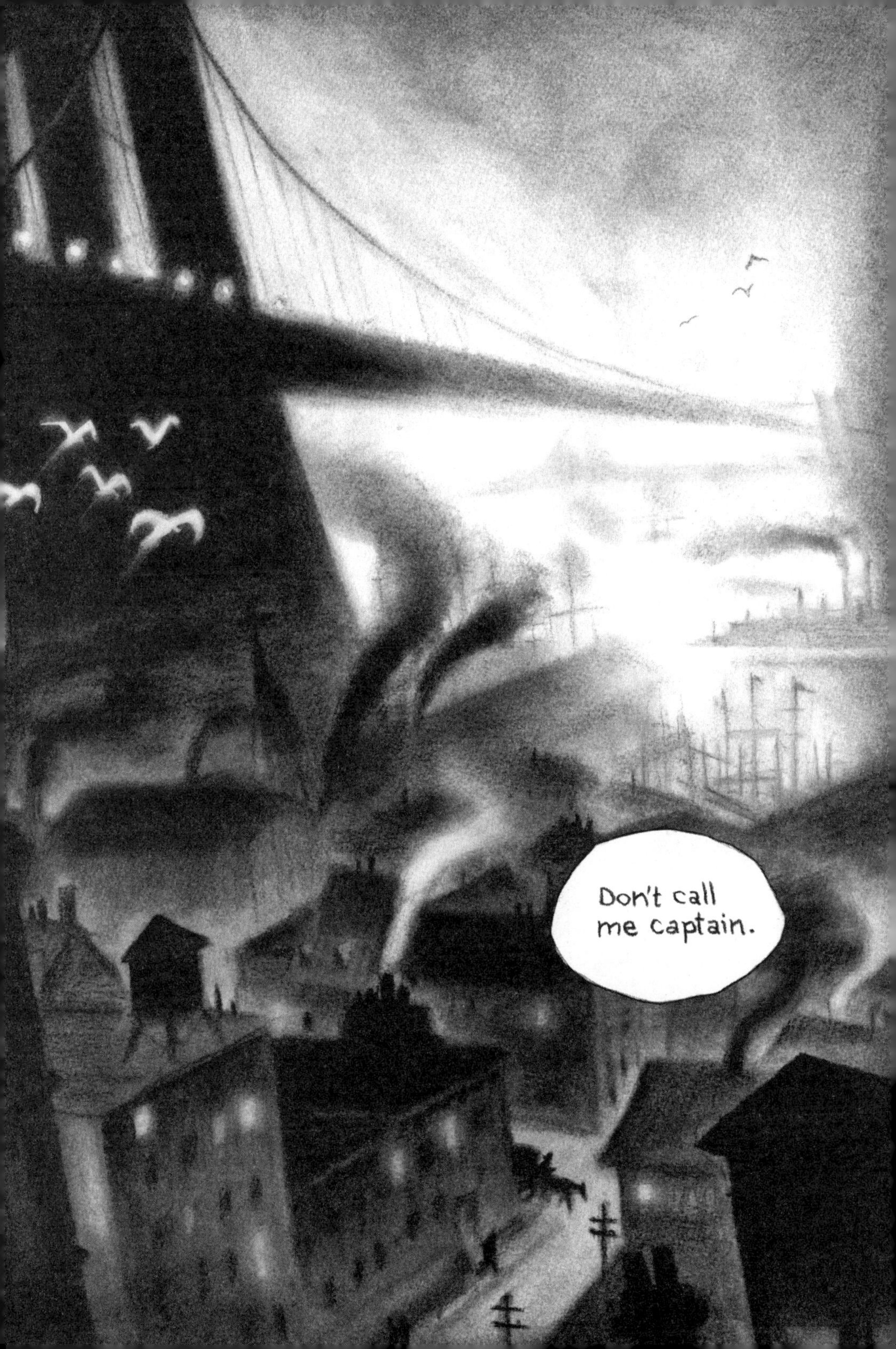
Don't call me captain.

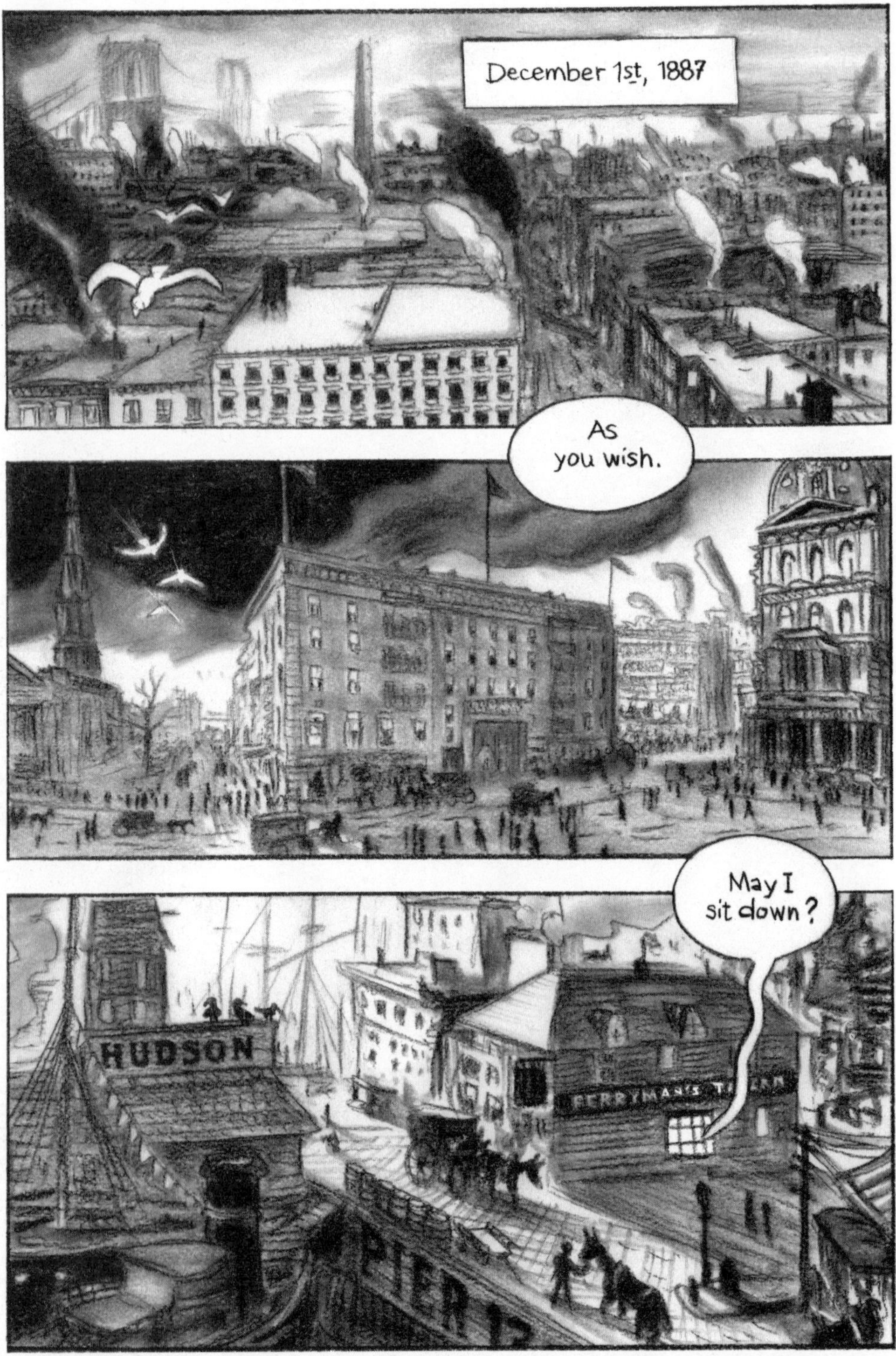
December 1st, 1887
As you wish.
May I sit down?
HUDSON

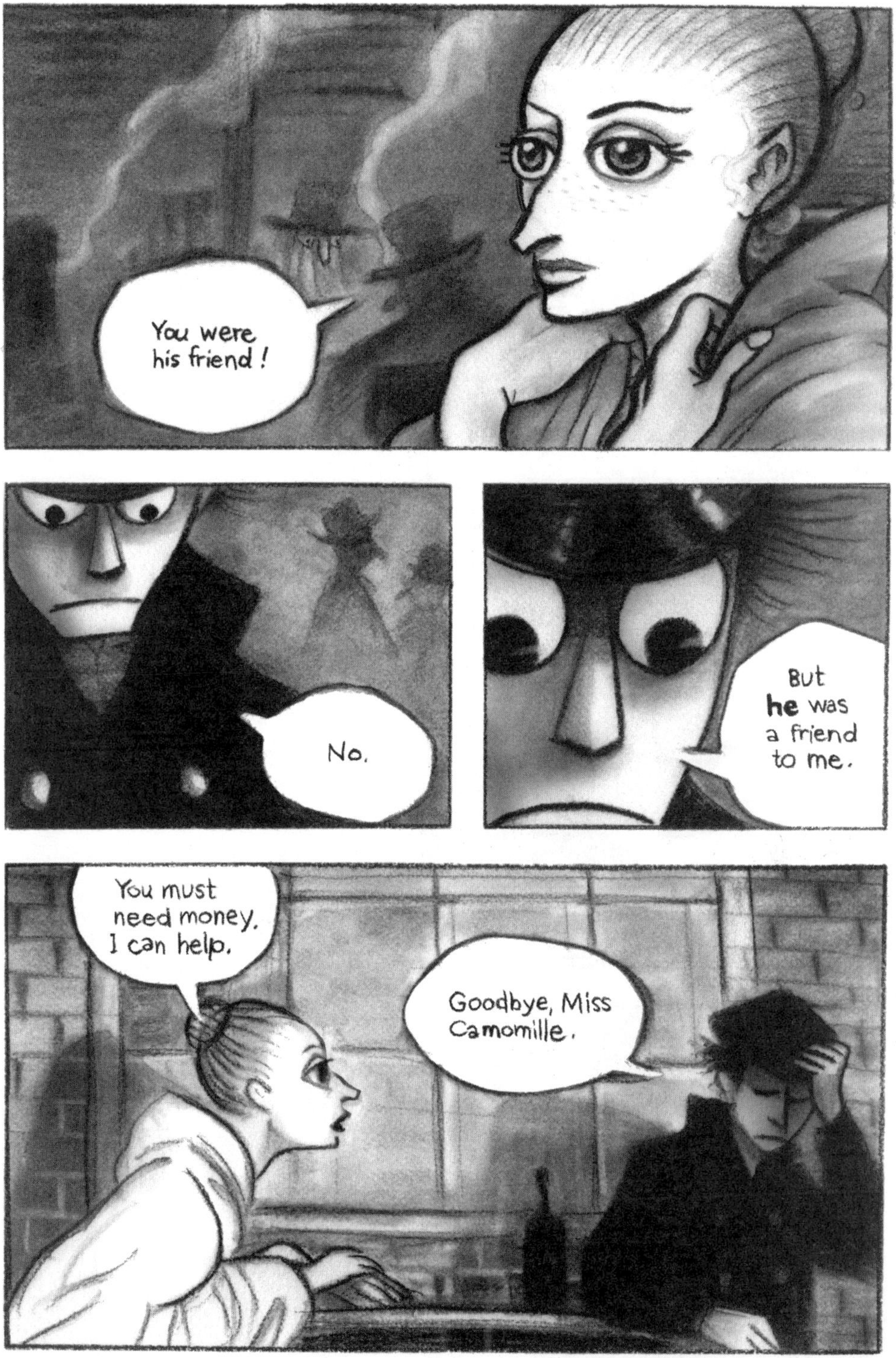
You were his friend!
No.
But he was a friend to me.
You must need money. I can help.
Goodbye, Miss Camomille.

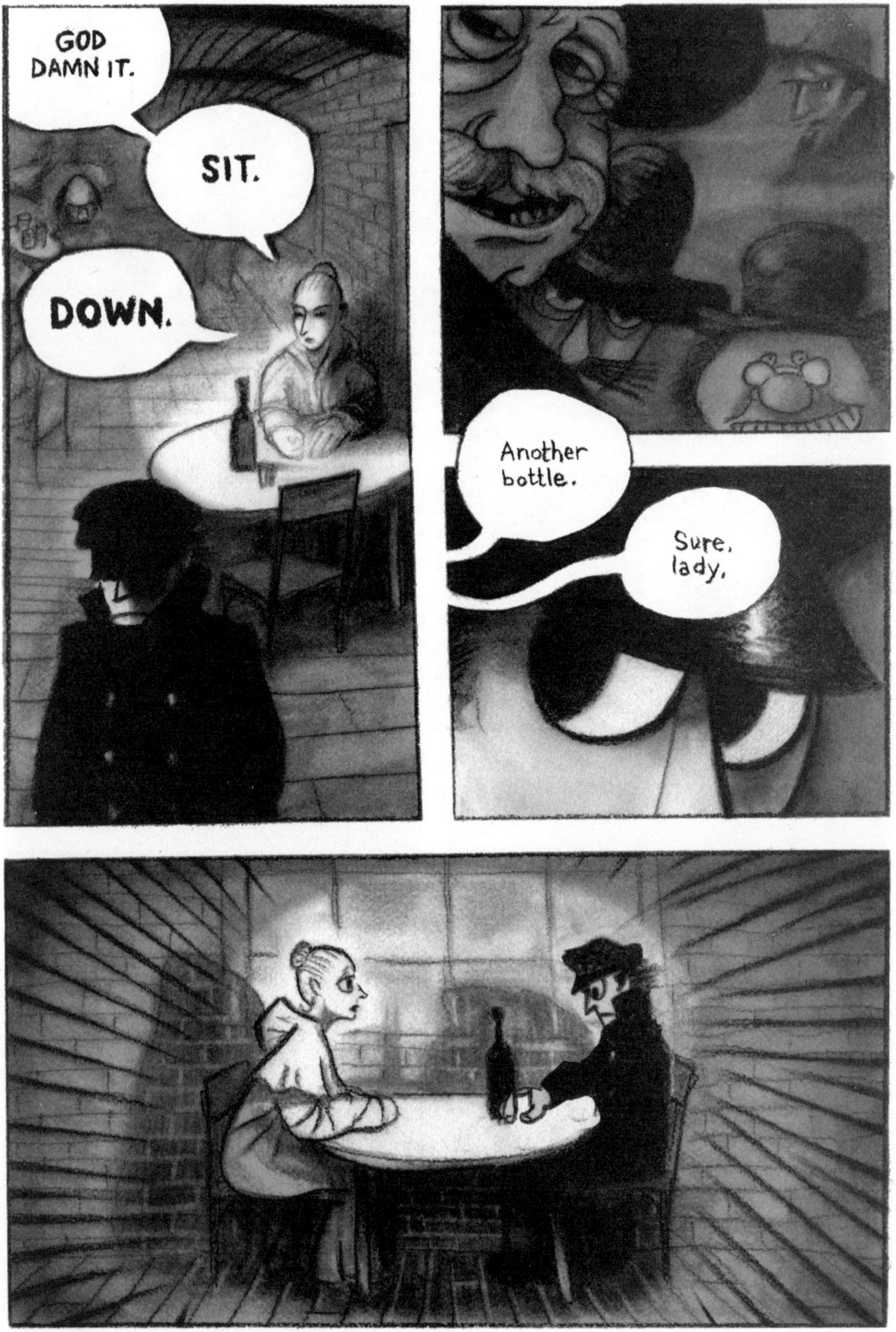
GOD DAMN IT.
SIT.
DOWN.
Another bottle.
Sure, lady.

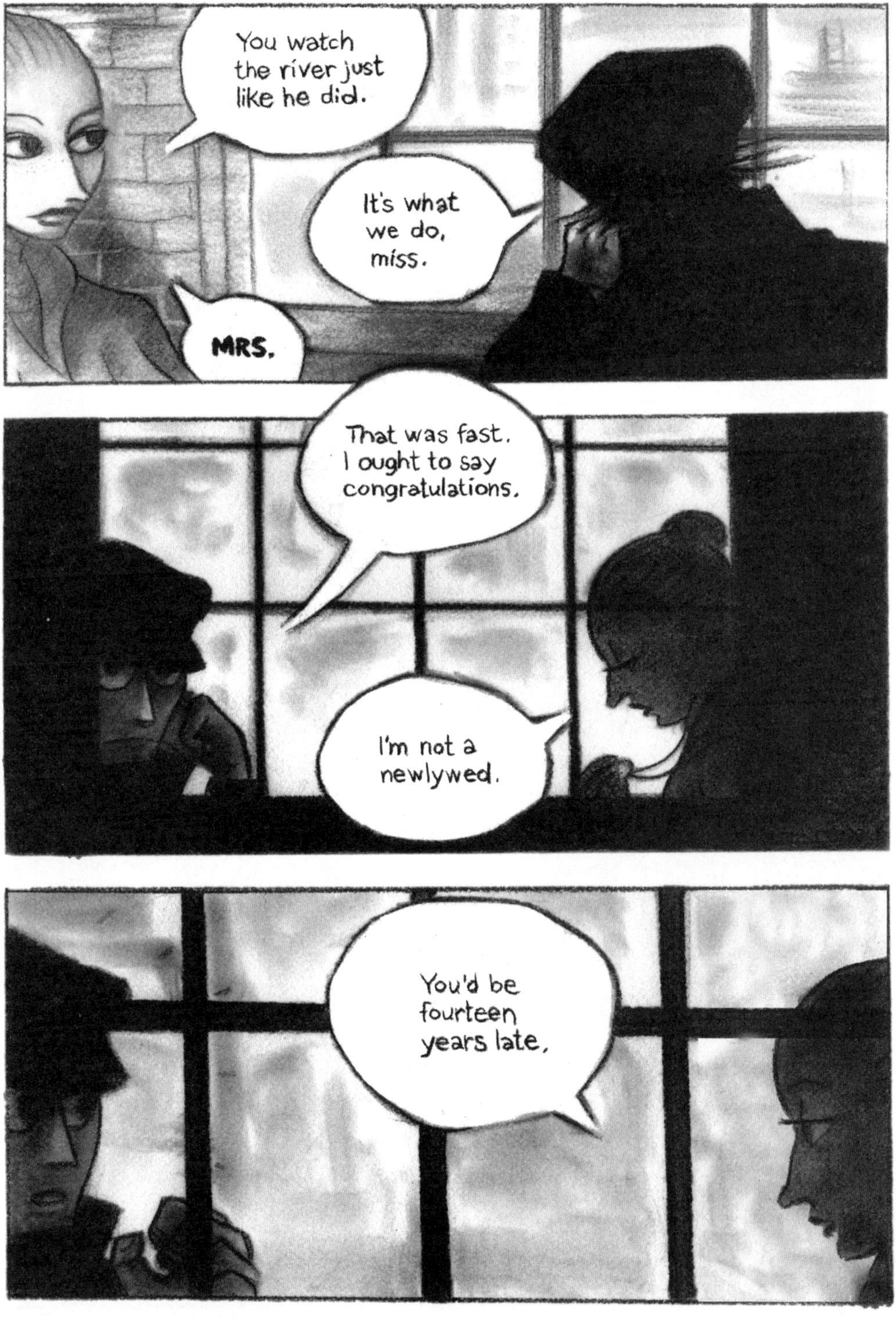
You watch the river just like he did.
It's what we do, miss.
MRS.
That was fast. I ought to say congratulations.
I'm not a newlywed.
You'd be fourteen years late.

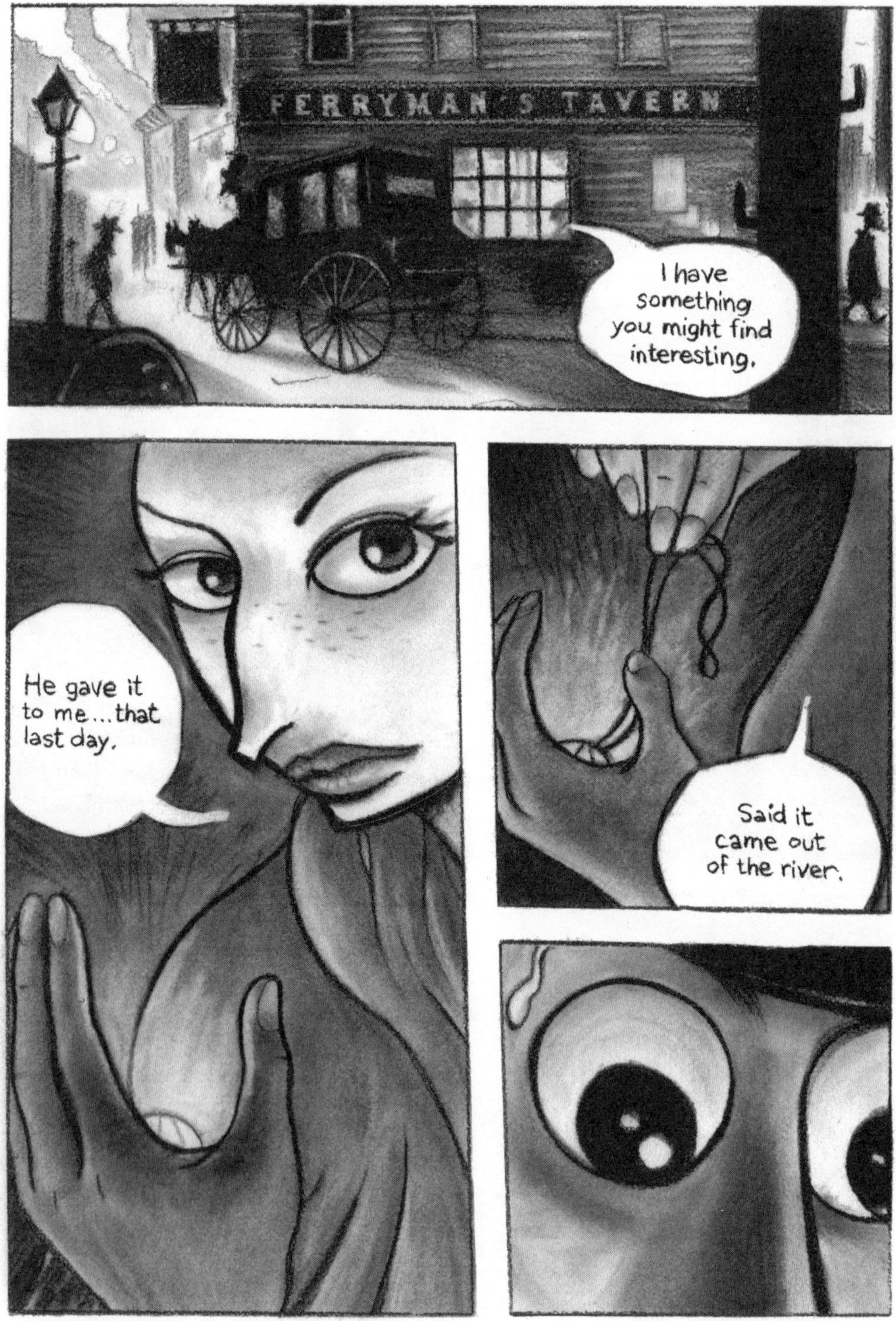
FERRYMAN'S TAVERN
I have something you might find interesting.
He gave it to me...that last day.
Said it came out of the river.

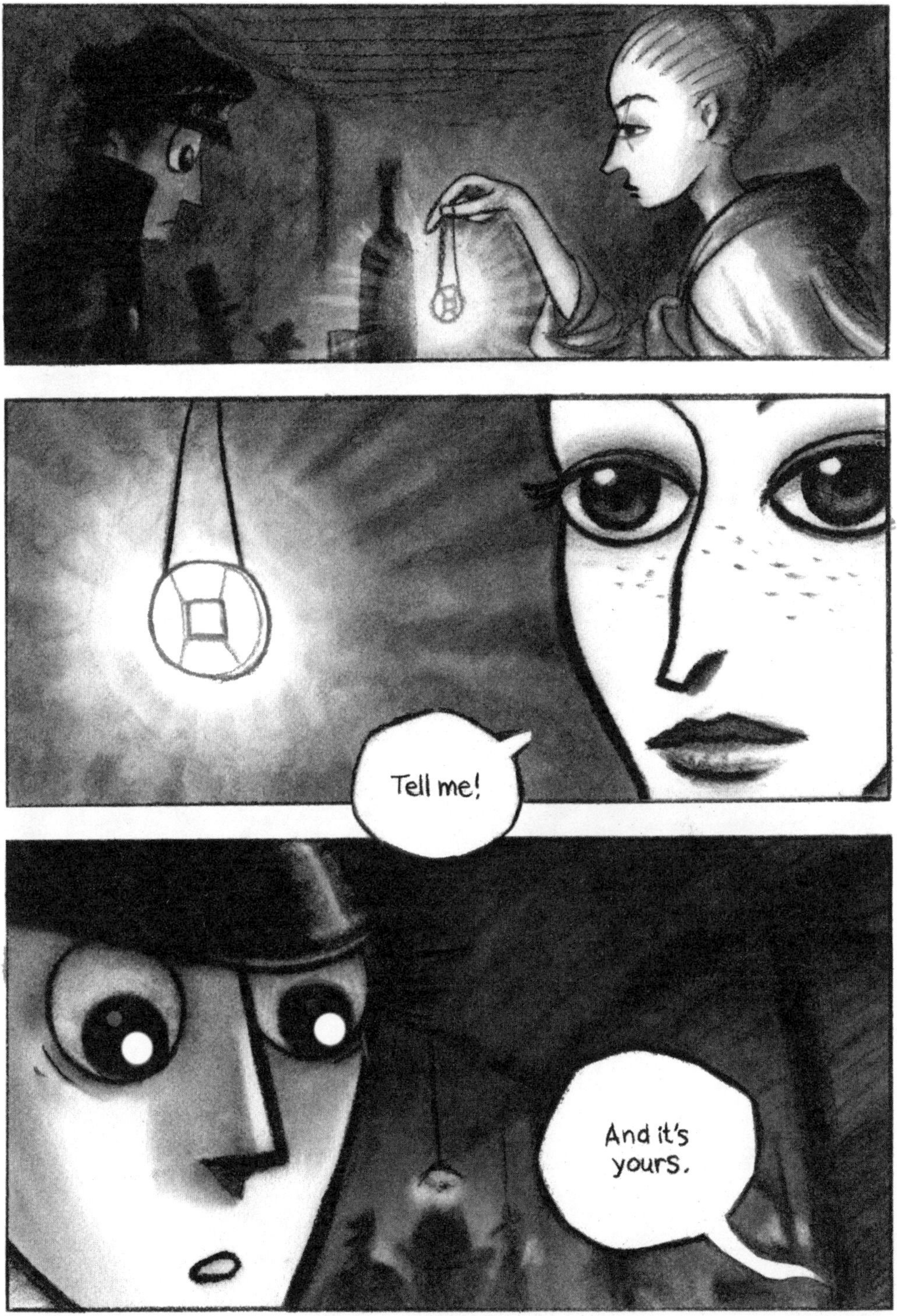
Tell me!
And it's yours.

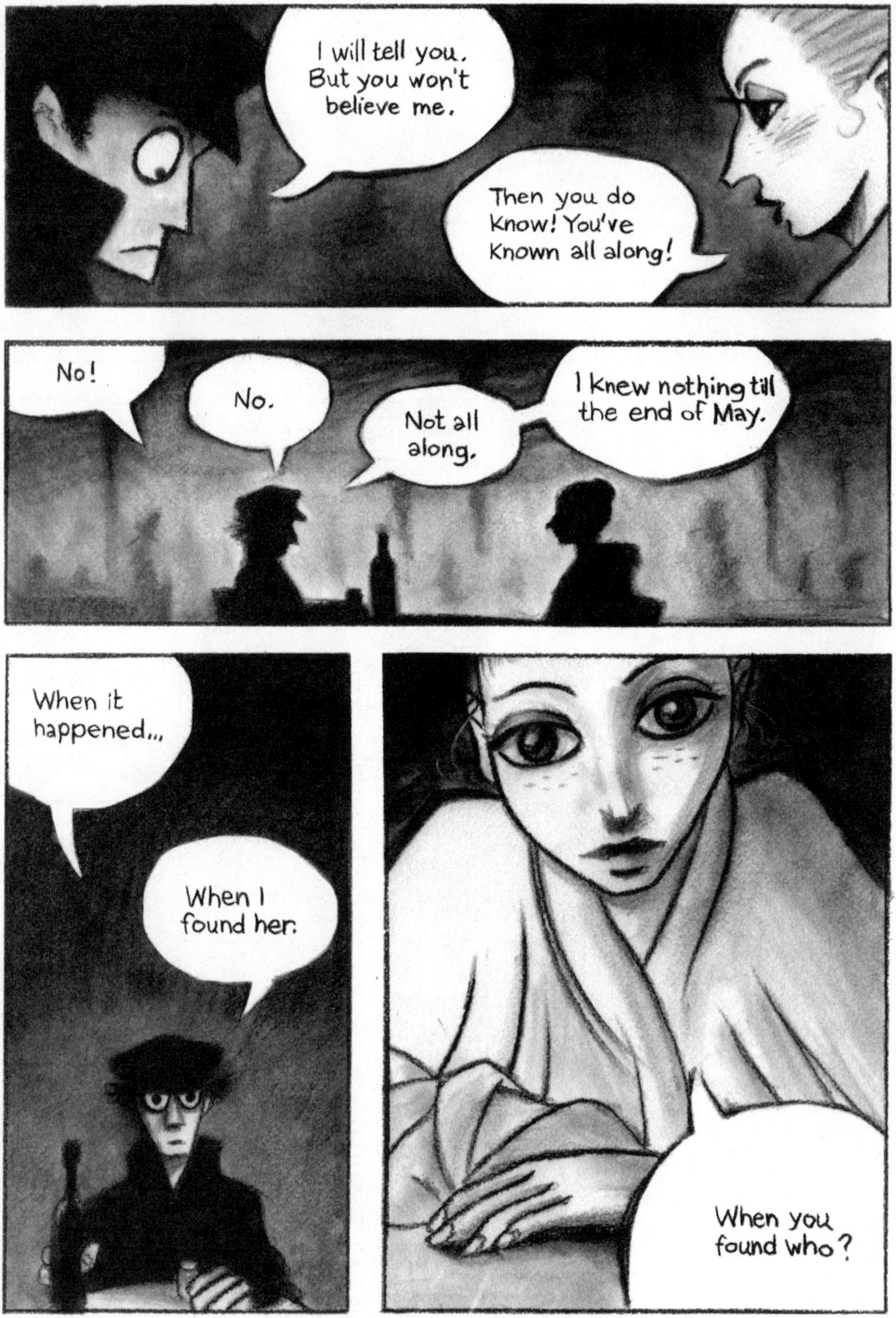
I will tell you. But you won't believe me.
Then you do Know! You've Known all along!
No!
No.
Not all along.
I knew nothing till the end of May.
When it happened...
When I found her.
When you found who?

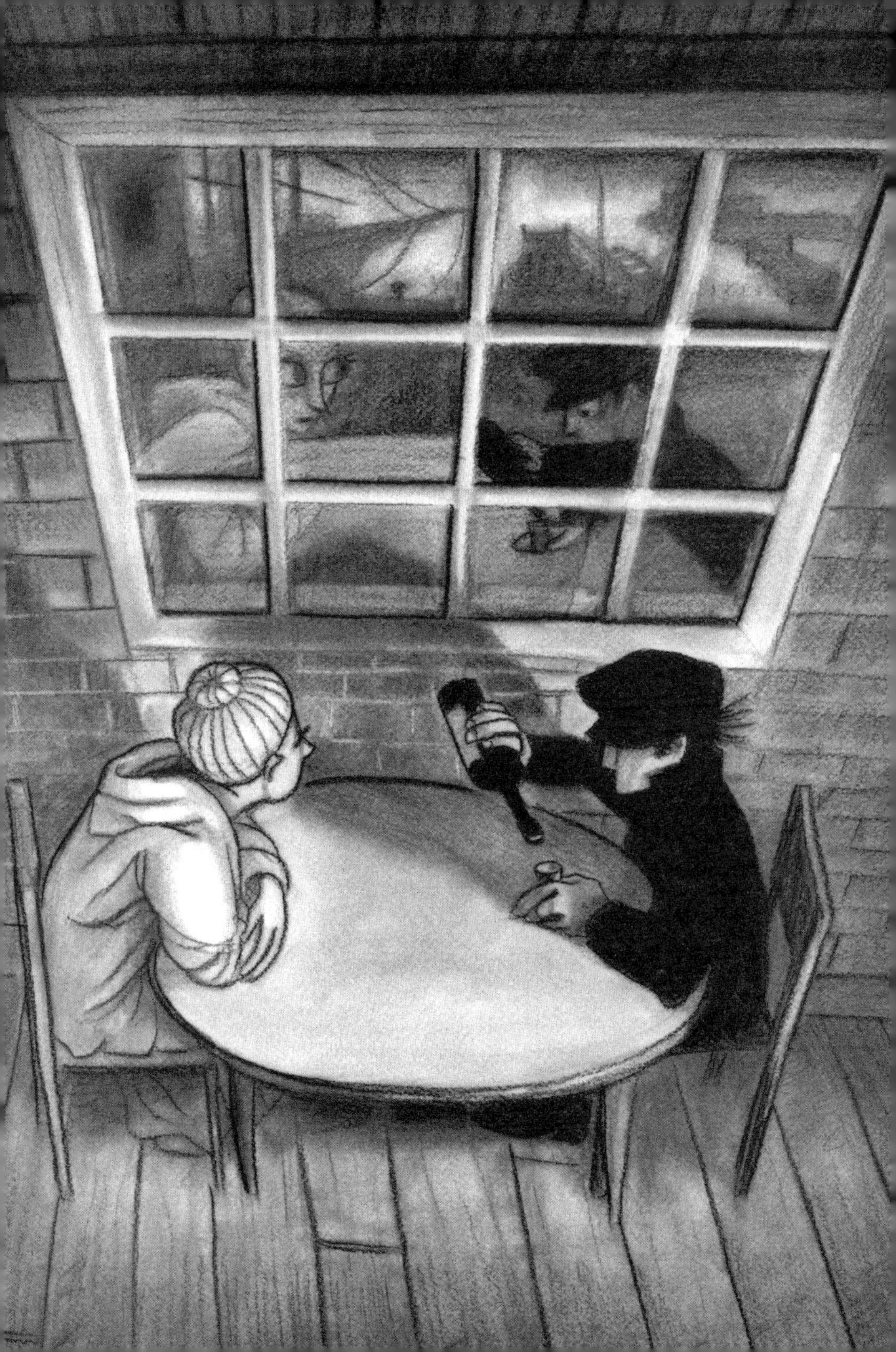

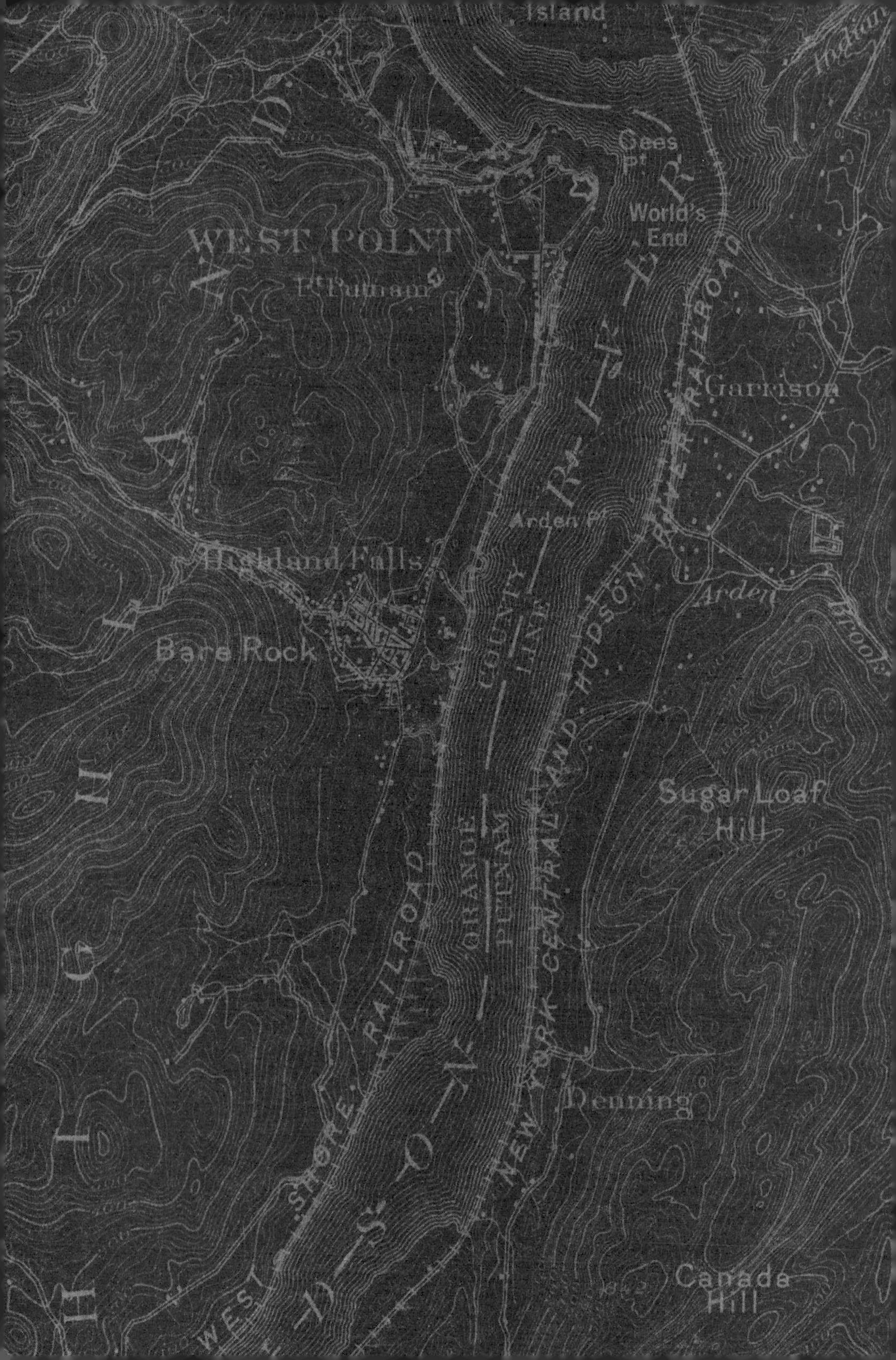
Island
WEST POINT
Ft Putnam
Gees Pt
World's End
Garrison
Highland Falls
Arden Pt
Arden
Brook
Bare Rock
Sugar Loaf Hill
Denning
Canada Hill
WEST SHORE RAILROAD
NEW YORK CENTRAL AND HUDSON RIVER RAILROAD
ORANGE
PUTNAM
COUNTY LINE

Part One
TWAIN'S SECRET

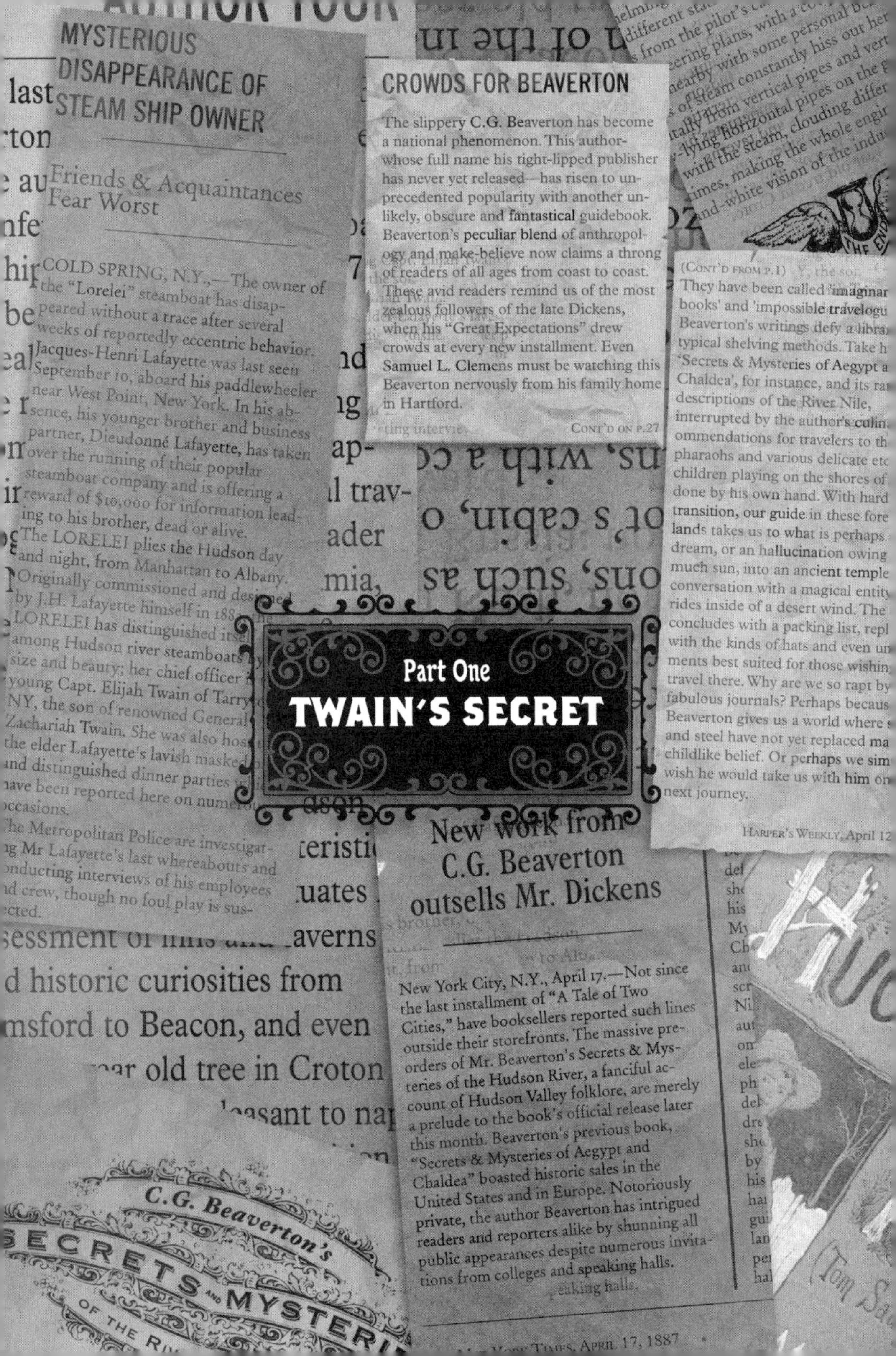
MYSTERIOUS DISAPPEARANCE OF STEAM SHIP OWNER
Friends & Acquaintances Fear Worst
COLD SPRING, N.Y.,— The owner of the "Lorelei" steamboat has disappeared without a trace after several weeks of reportedly eccentric behavior. Jacques-Henri Lafayette was last seen September 10, aboard his paddlewheeler near West Point, New York. In his absence, his younger brother and business partner, Dieudonné Lafayette, has taken over the running of their popular steamboat company and is offering a reward of $10,000 for information leading to his brother, dead or alive.
The LORELEI plies the Hudson day and night, from Manhattan to Albany.
LORELEI has distinguished
among Hudson river steamboats
size and beauty; her chief officer
young Capt. Elijah Twain of Tarry
NY, the son of renowned General
Zachariah Twain. She was also hos
the elder Lafayette's lavish masked
and distinguished dinner parties
have been reported here on numero
occasions.
he Metropolitan Police are investigat-
ng Mr Lafayette's last whereabouts and
onducting interviews of his employees
nd crew, though no foul play is sus-
ected.
CROWDS FOR BEAVERTON
The slippery C.G. Beaverton has become a national phenomenon. This author-whose full name his tight-lipped publisher has never yet released—has risen to unprecedented popularity with another unlikely, obscure and fantastical guidebook. Beaverton's peculiar blend of anthropology and make-believe now claims a throng of readers of all ages from coast to coast. These avid readers remind us of the most zealous followers of the late Dickens, when his "Great Expectations" drew crowds at every new installment. Even Samuel L. Clemens must be watching this Beaverton nervously from his family home in Hartford.
CONT'D ON P.27
(CONT'D FROM P.1)
They have been called 'imaginar
books' and 'impossible travelogu
Beaverton's writings defy a libra
typical shelving methods. Take h
'Secrets & Mysteries of Aegypt a
Chaldea', for instance, and its ra
descriptions of the River Nile,
interrupted by the author's culin
ommendations for travelers to th
pharaohs and various delicate etc
children playing on the shores of
done by his own hand. With hard
transition, our guide in these fore
lands takes us to what is perhaps
dream, or an hallucination owing
much sun, into an ancient temple
conversation with a magical entity
rides inside of a desert wind. The
concludes with a packing list, repl
with the kinds of hats and even un
ments best suited for those wishin
travel there. Why are we so rapt by
fabulous journals? Perhaps becaus
Beaverton gives us a world where
and steel have not yet replaced ma
childlike belief. Or perhaps we sim
wish he would take us with him on
next journey.
HARPER'S WEEKLY, April 12
New work from C.G. Beaverton outsells Mr. Dickens
New York City, N.Y., April 17.—Not since the last installment of "A Tale of Two Cities," have booksellers reported such lines outside their storefronts. The massive pre-orders of Mr. Beaverton's Secrets & Mysteries of the Hudson River, a fanciful account of Hudson Valley folklore, are merely a prelude to the book's official release later this month. Beaverton's previous book, "Secrets & Mysteries of Aegypt and Chaldea" boasted historic sales in the United States and in Europe. Notoriously private, the author Beaverton has intrigued readers and reporters alike by shunning all public appearances despite numerous invitations from colleges and speaking halls.
NEW YORK TIMES, APRIL 17, 1887
ssessment of inns and taverns
d historic curiosities from
msford to Beacon, and even
ear old tree in Croton
leasant to nap
C.G. Beaverton's
SECRETS AND MYSTERIES
OF THE RI

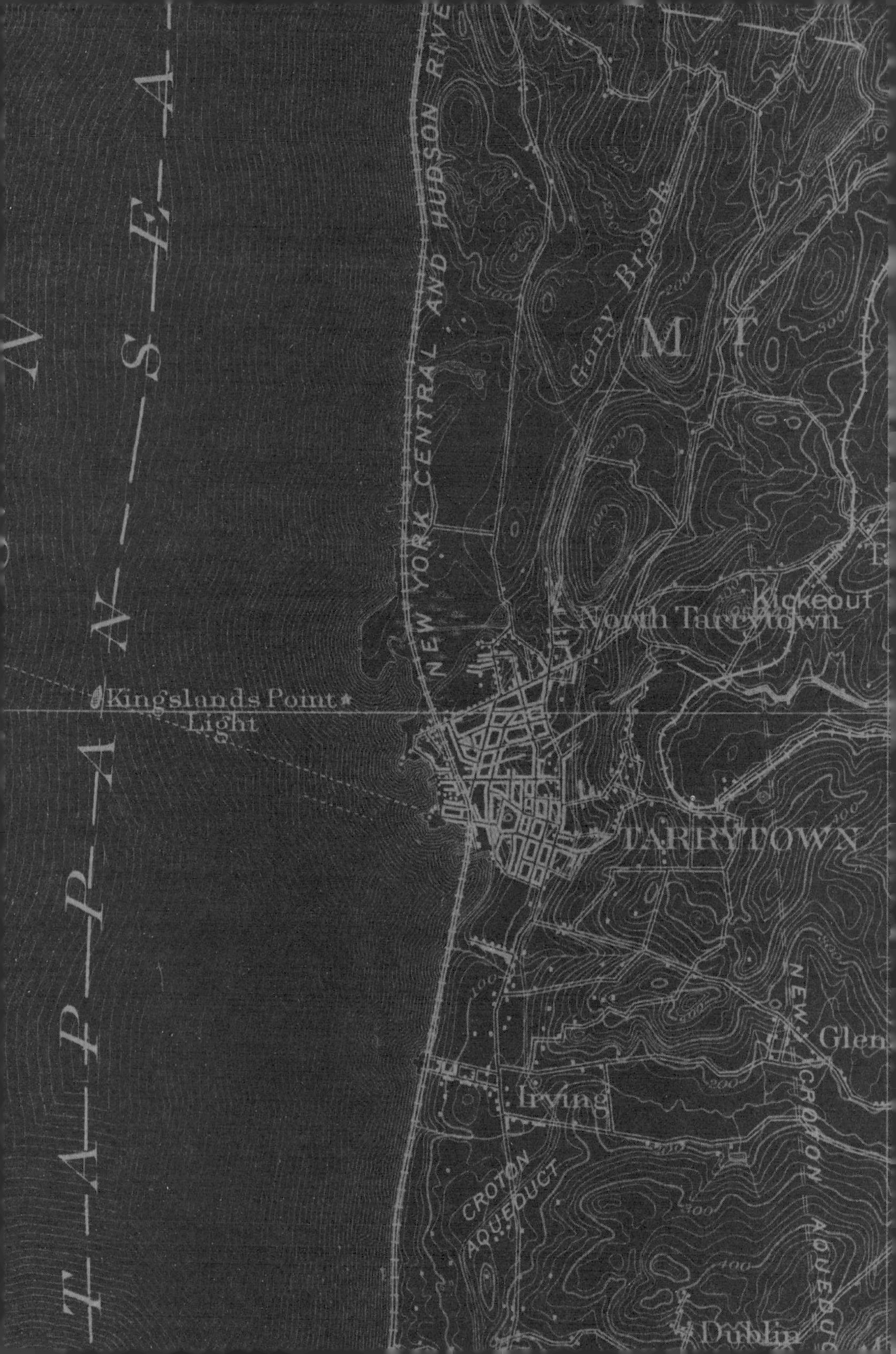

NEW YORK CENTRAL AND HUDSON
Gory Brook
M T
North Tarrytown
Kickeout
Kingslands Point Light
TARRYTOWN
Glen
Irving
CROTON AQUEDUCT
NEW CROTON
Dublin

Pt I, Chap.1

"THE FRENCHMAN'S STEAMBOAT"

Tappan Zee Crossing, 18 miles north of New York City, May 25th, 1887

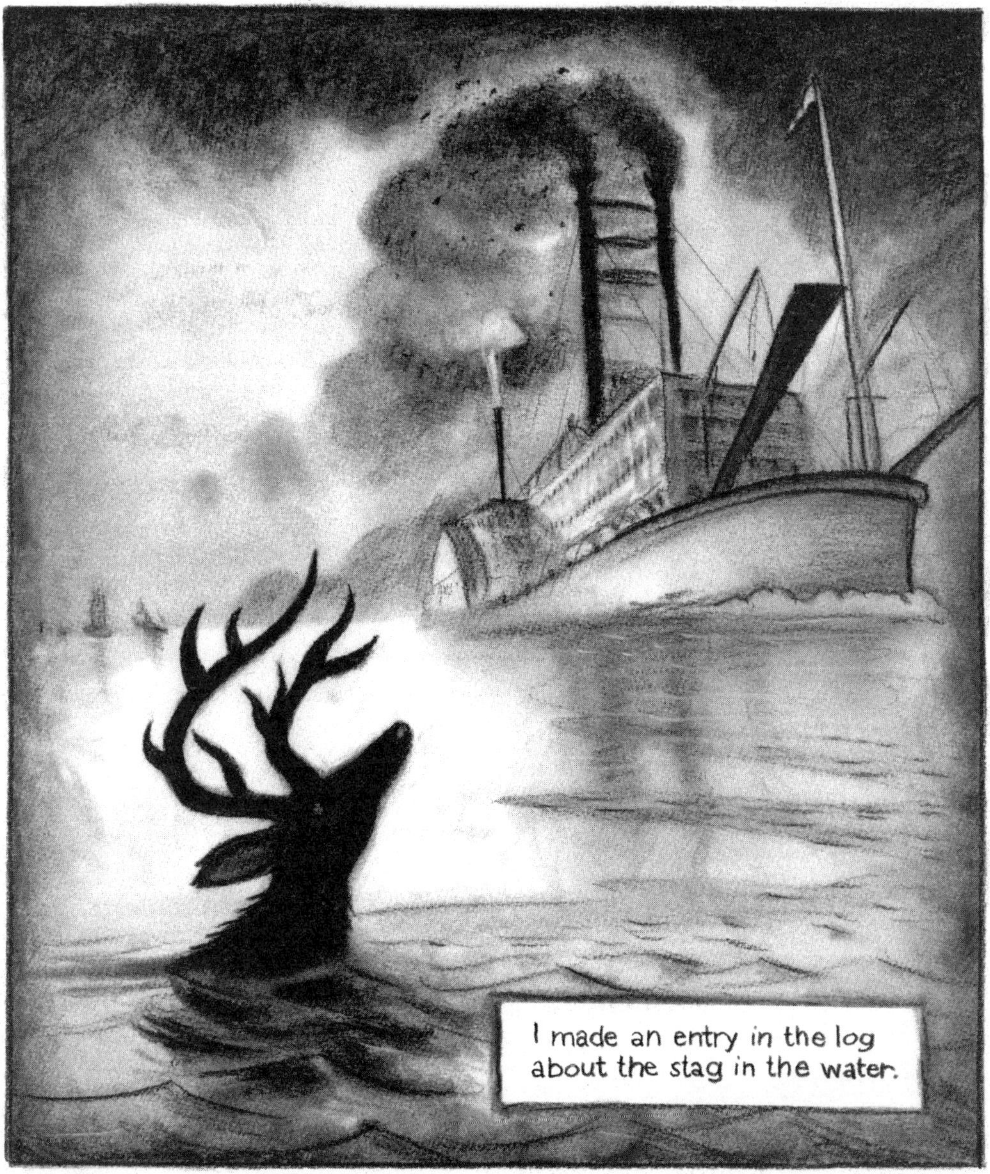
I made an entry in the log about the stag in the water.

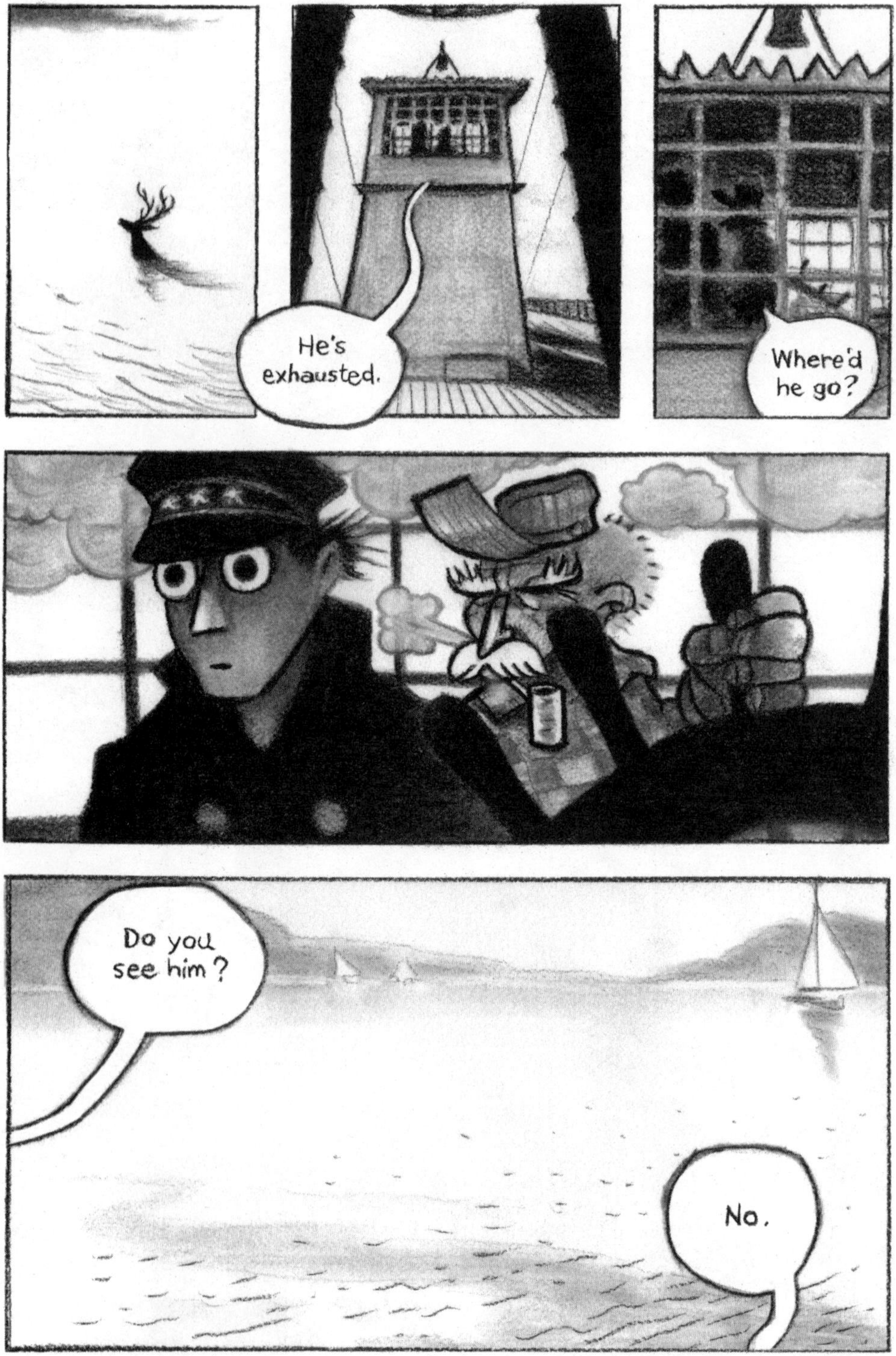
He's exhausted.
Where'd he go?
Do you see him?
No.

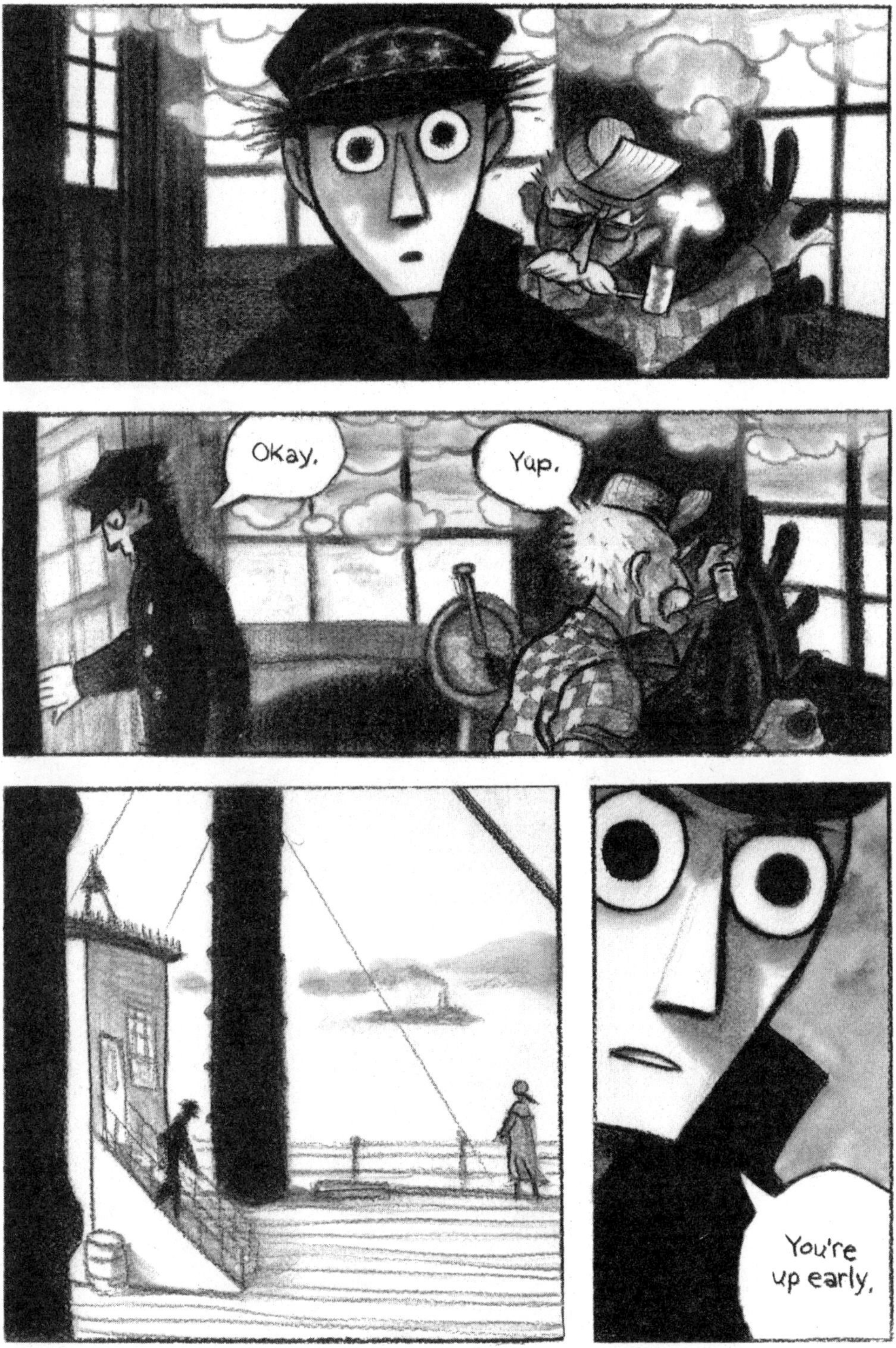
Okay.
Yup.
You're up early.

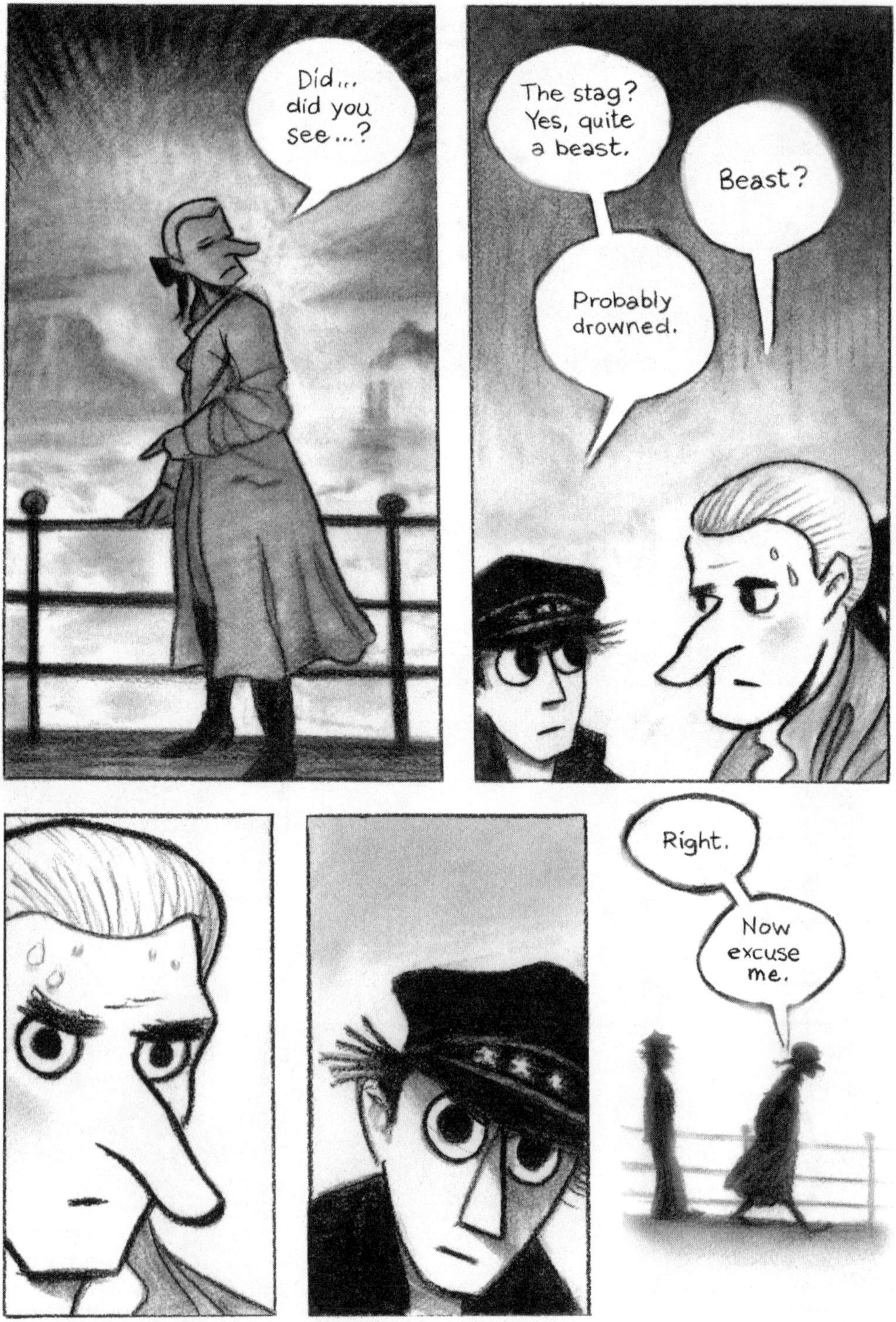
Did... did you see...?
The stag? Yes, quite a beast.
Beast?
Probably drowned.
Right.
Now excuse me.

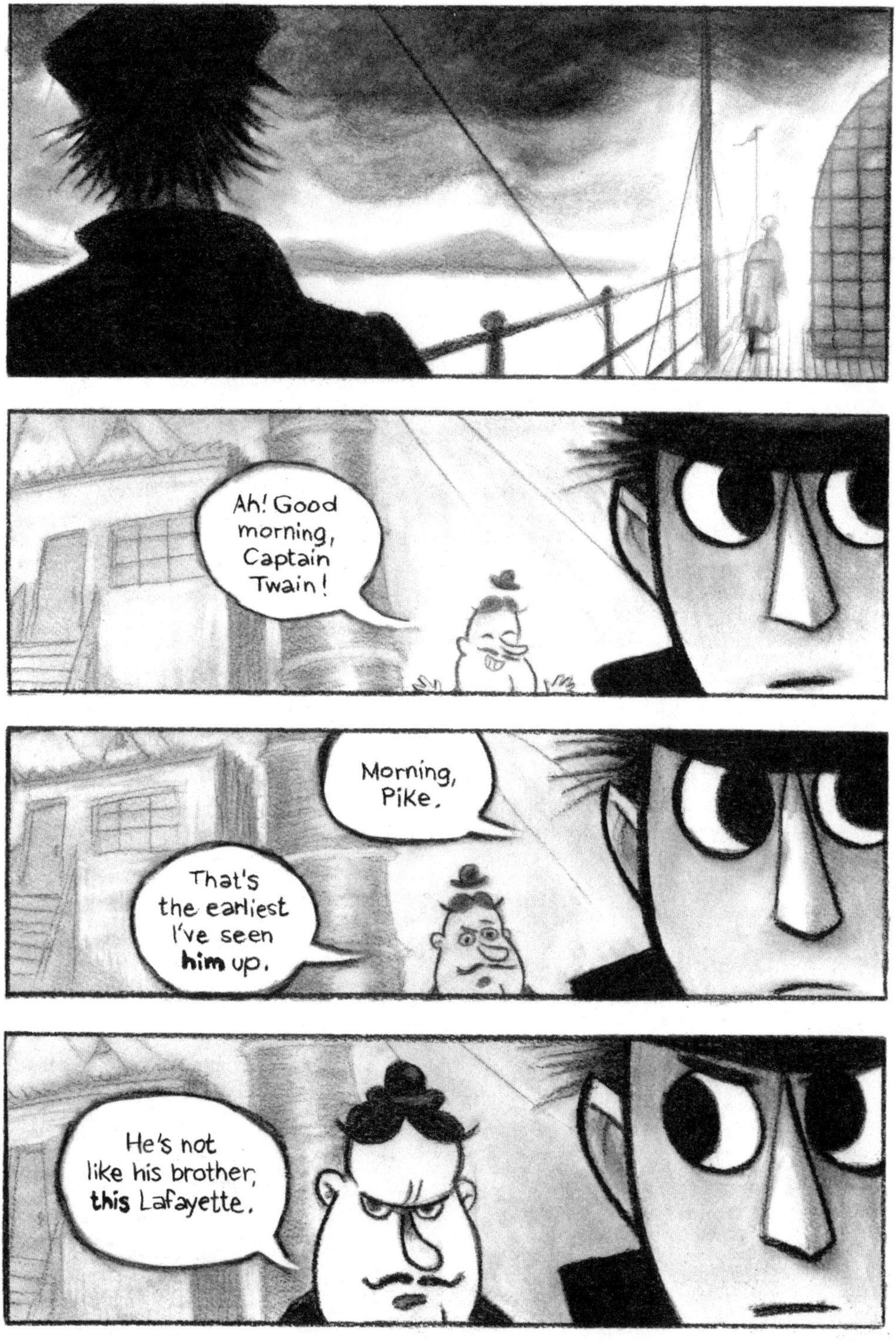
Ah! Good morning, Captain Twain!
Morning, Pike.
That's the earliest I've seen **him** up.
He's not like his brother, **this** Lafayette.

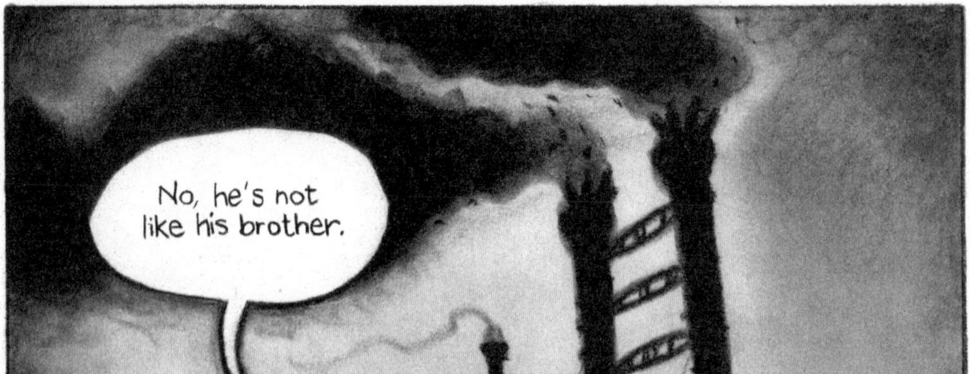
No, he's not like his brother.

Lafayette's older brother Jacques-Henri—now **he** was a businessman.

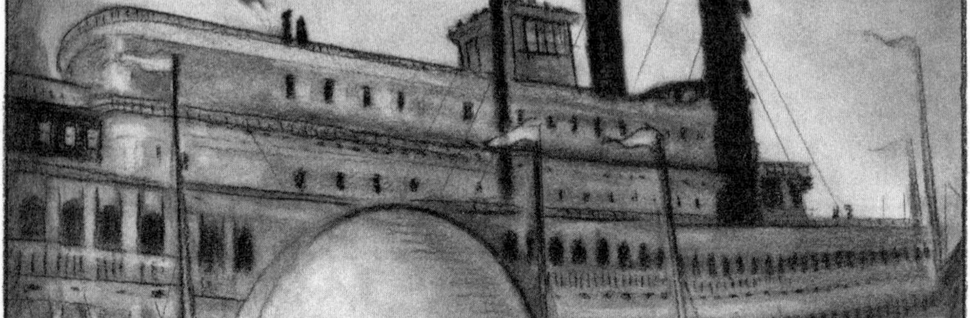

He had come from France in '77, with some capital and big ideas. The Hudson River Line and the Central Hudson Line had cornered the market in New York steamboating for over twenty years.

Everyone thought the new Frenchman in town would be minced meat in no time.

By 1885, he had built his two steamboats, the LORELEI and the MELUSINE, a smaller dayliner. Together the steamers were raking in over $350,000 a year.

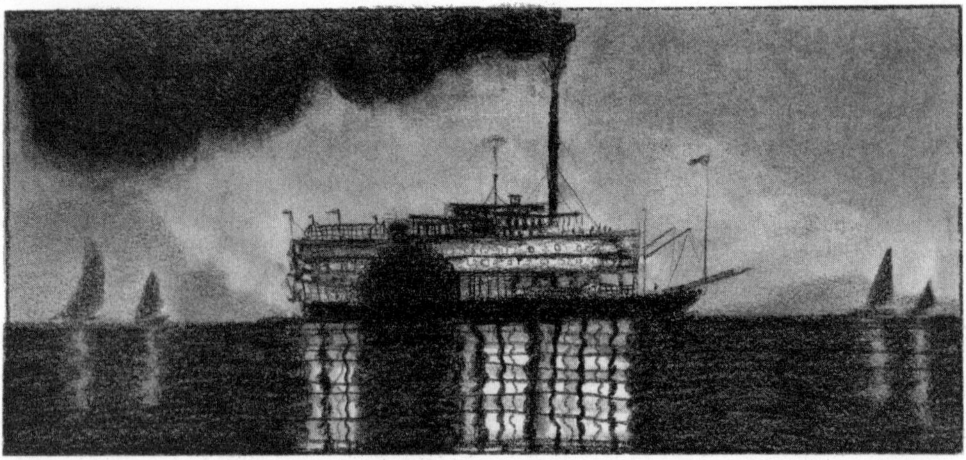

With its masked balls and dinner parties, the LORELEI never failed to draw Vanderbilts, Van Rensselaers, Astors, and Stuyvesant Fish out of their mansions.

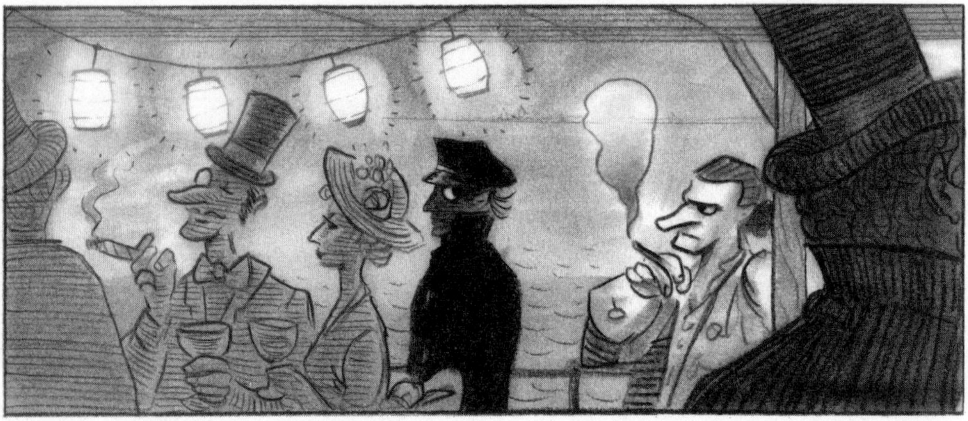

Jacques-Henri de Lafayette's younger brother Dieudonné, on their father's orders, arrived after some sordid mishap involving a duel in Paris.

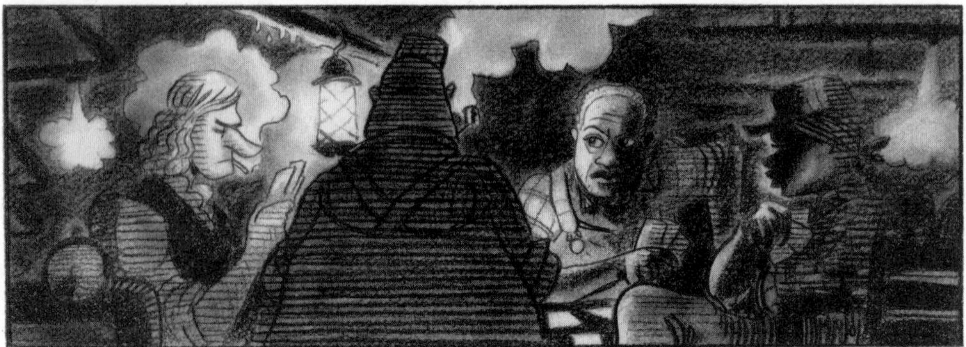

He joined his brother in the paddle-wheeling venture even though he didn't know the first thing about boating or life on the river.

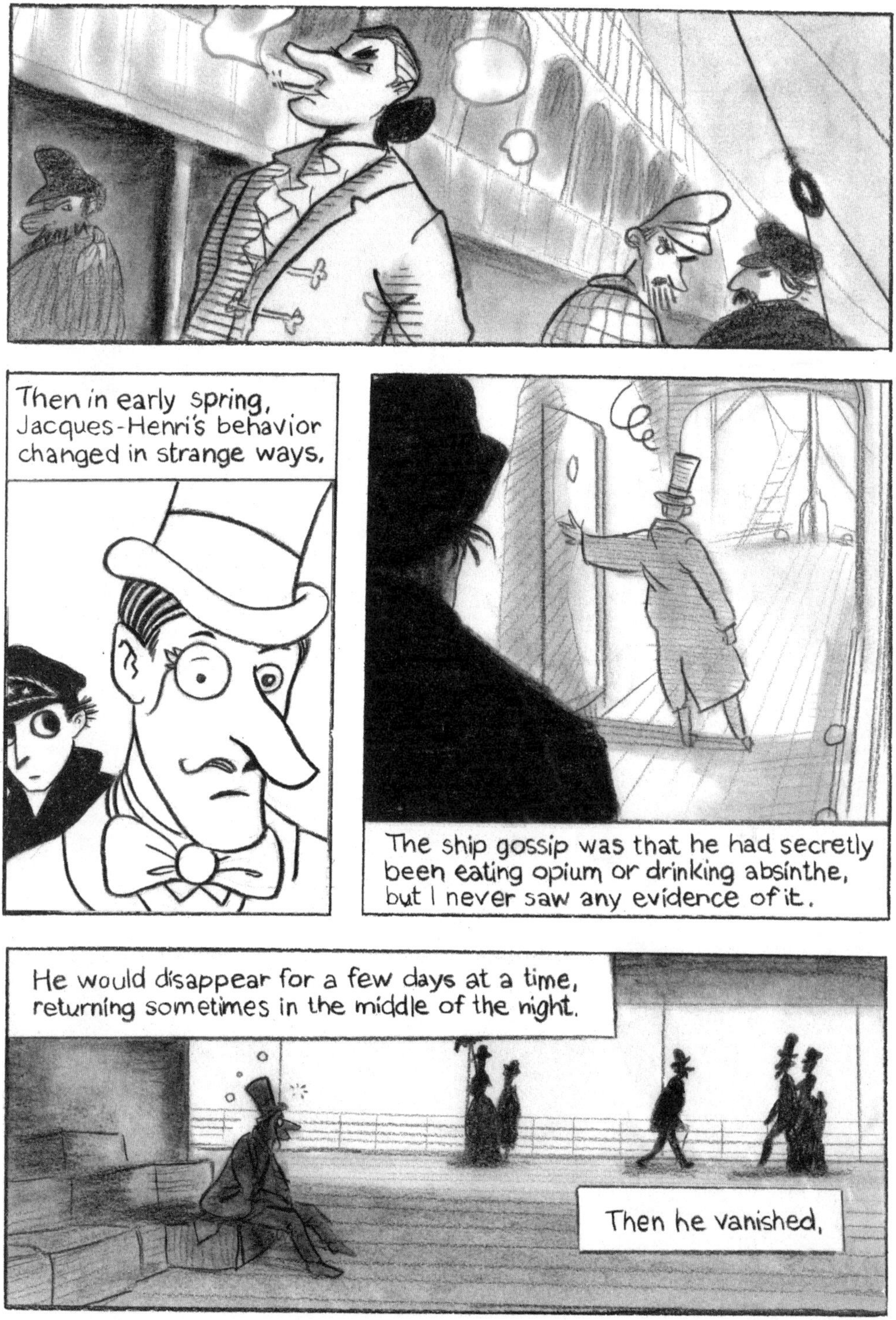
Then in early spring, Jacques-Henri's behavior changed in strange ways.
The ship gossip was that he had secretly been eating opium or drinking absinthe, but I never saw any evidence of it.
He would disappear for a few days at a time, returning sometimes in the middle of the night.
Then he vanished.

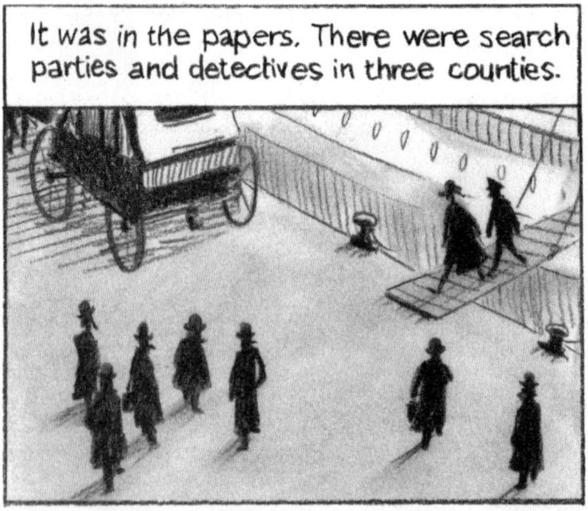
It was in the papers. There were search parties and detectives in three counties.

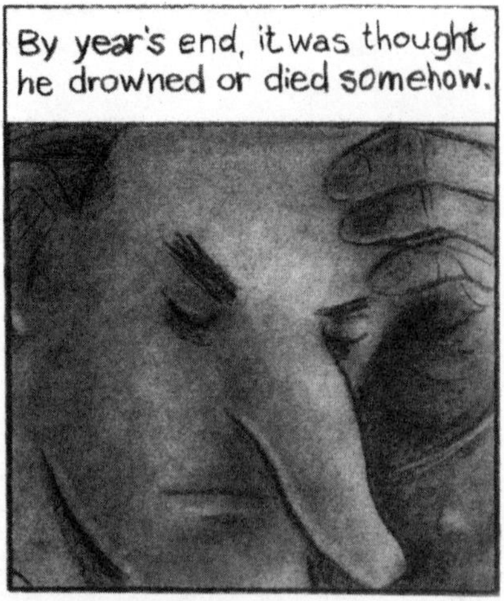
By year's end, it was thought he drowned or died somehow.

Lafayette didn't come out from his brother's quarters for days on end.

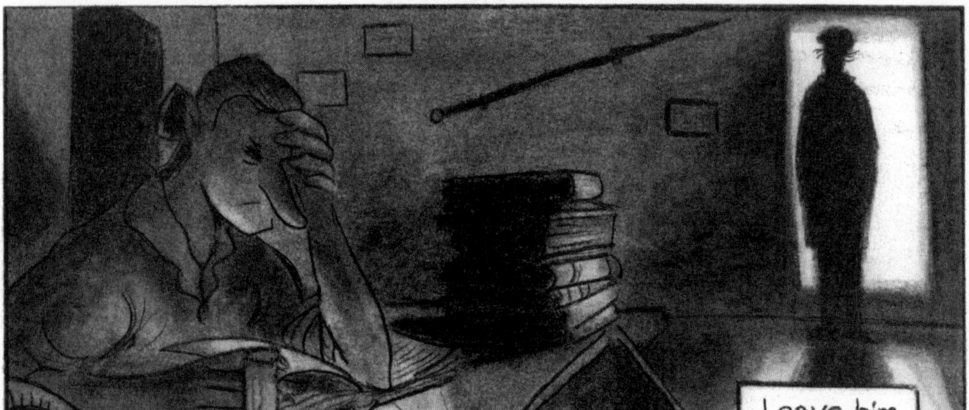
I gave him occasional reports.

He paid me little mind, and was usually poring over some of his brother's arcane books and journals. I thought he, too, was going mad.

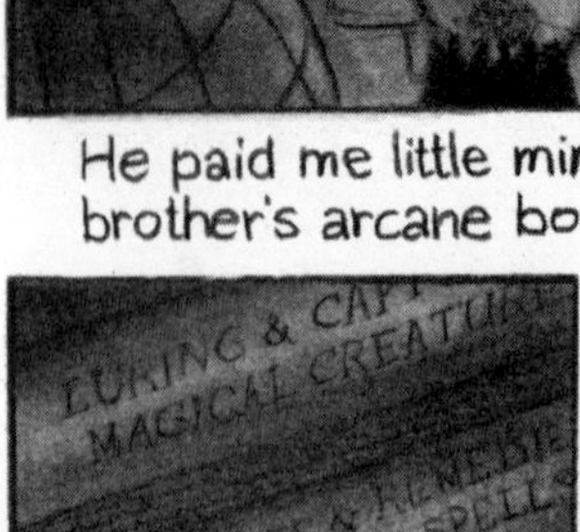
Adriatic Tales

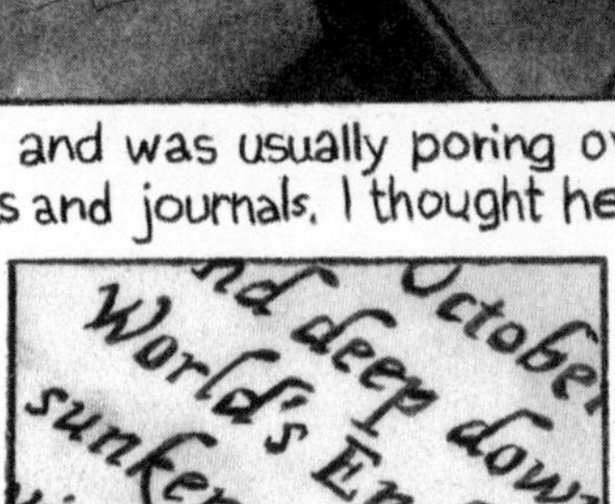
deep down
sunken upside down

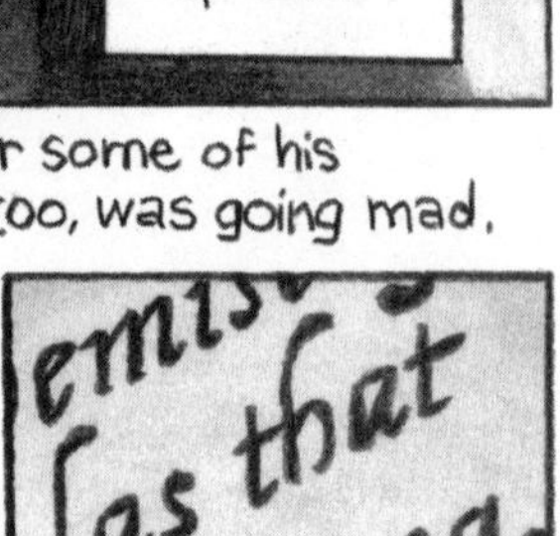
las that
she sang

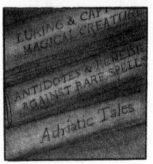

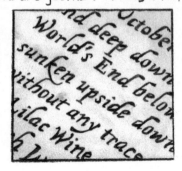

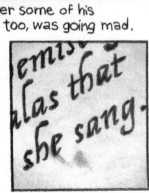

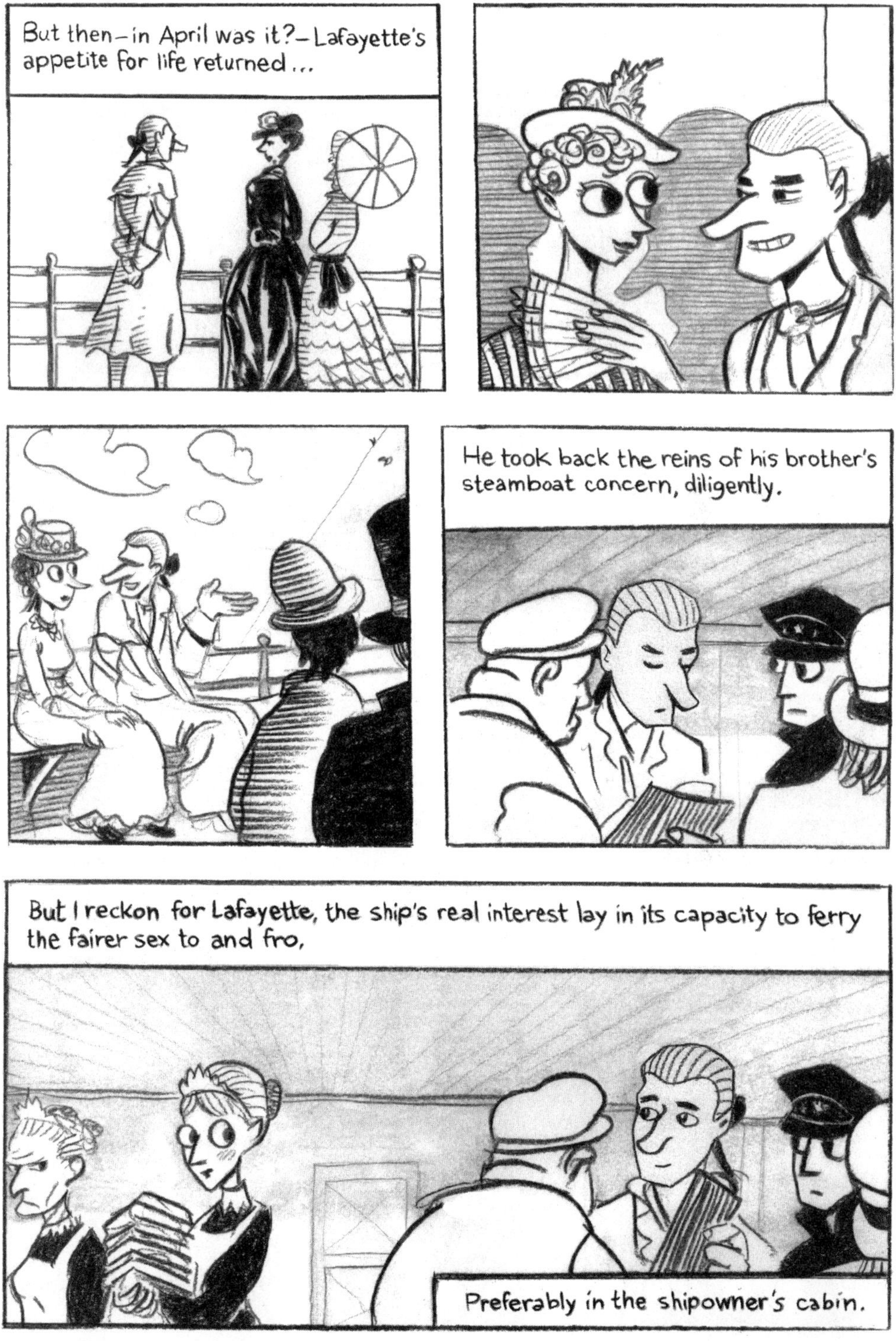
But then–in April was it?–Lafayette's appetite for life returned...
He took back the reins of his brother's steamboat concern, diligently.
But I reckon for Lafayette, the ship's real interest lay in its capacity to ferry the fairer sex to and fro,
Preferably in the shipowner's cabin.

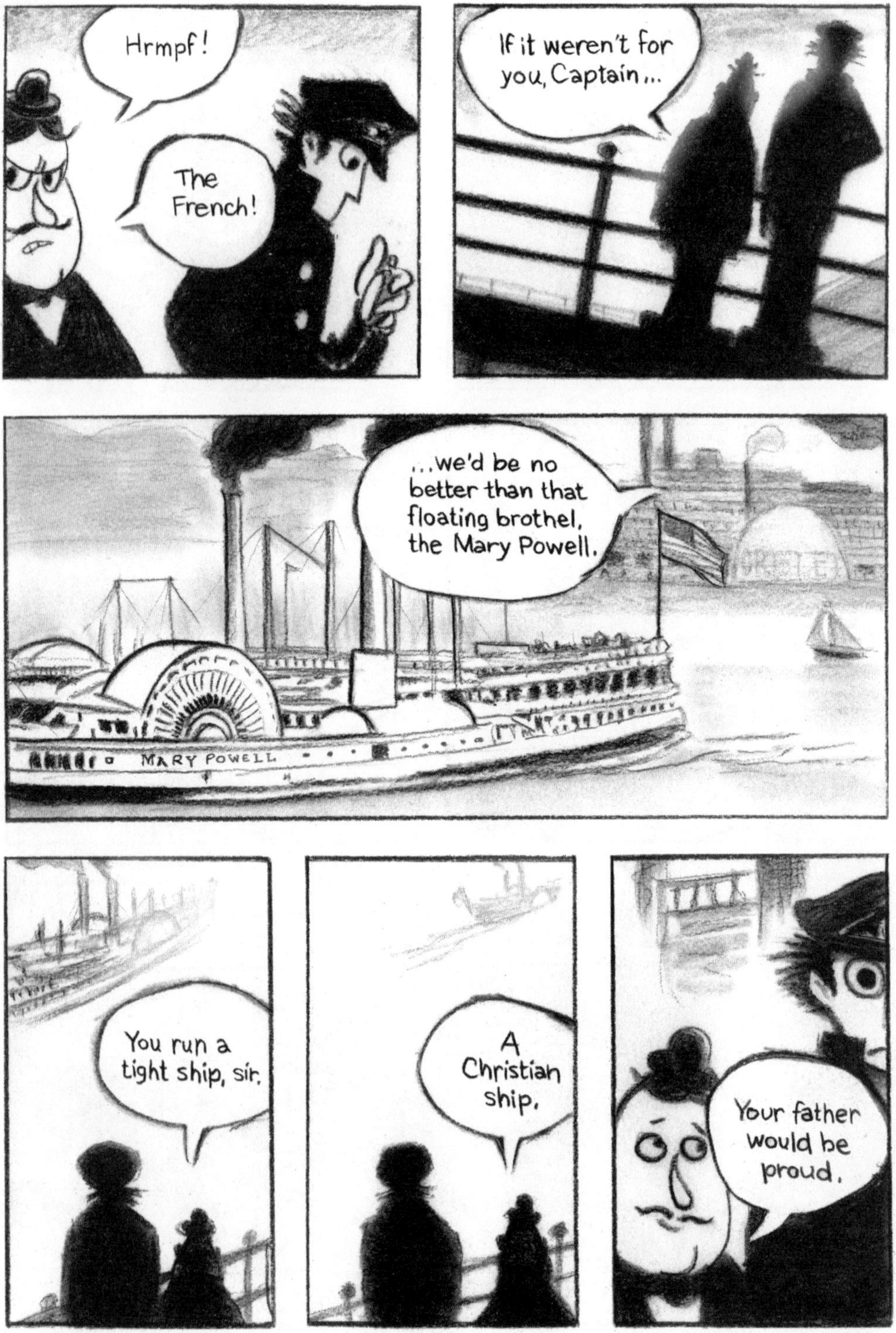
Hrmpf!
The French!
If it weren't for you, Captain...
...we'd be no better than that floating brothel, the Mary Powell.
MARY POWELL
You run a tight ship, sir.
A Christian ship.
Your father would be proud.

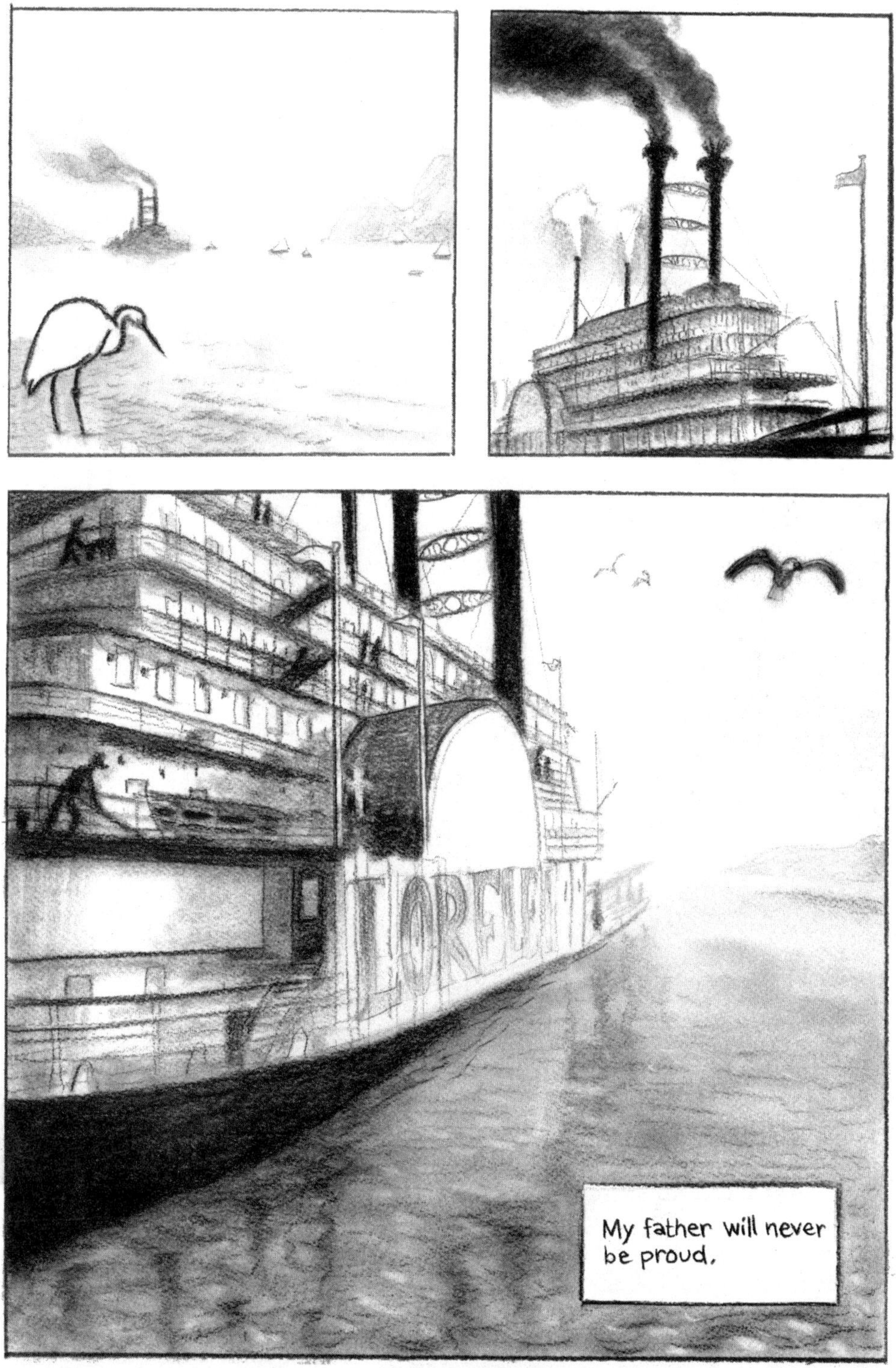
My father will never be proud.

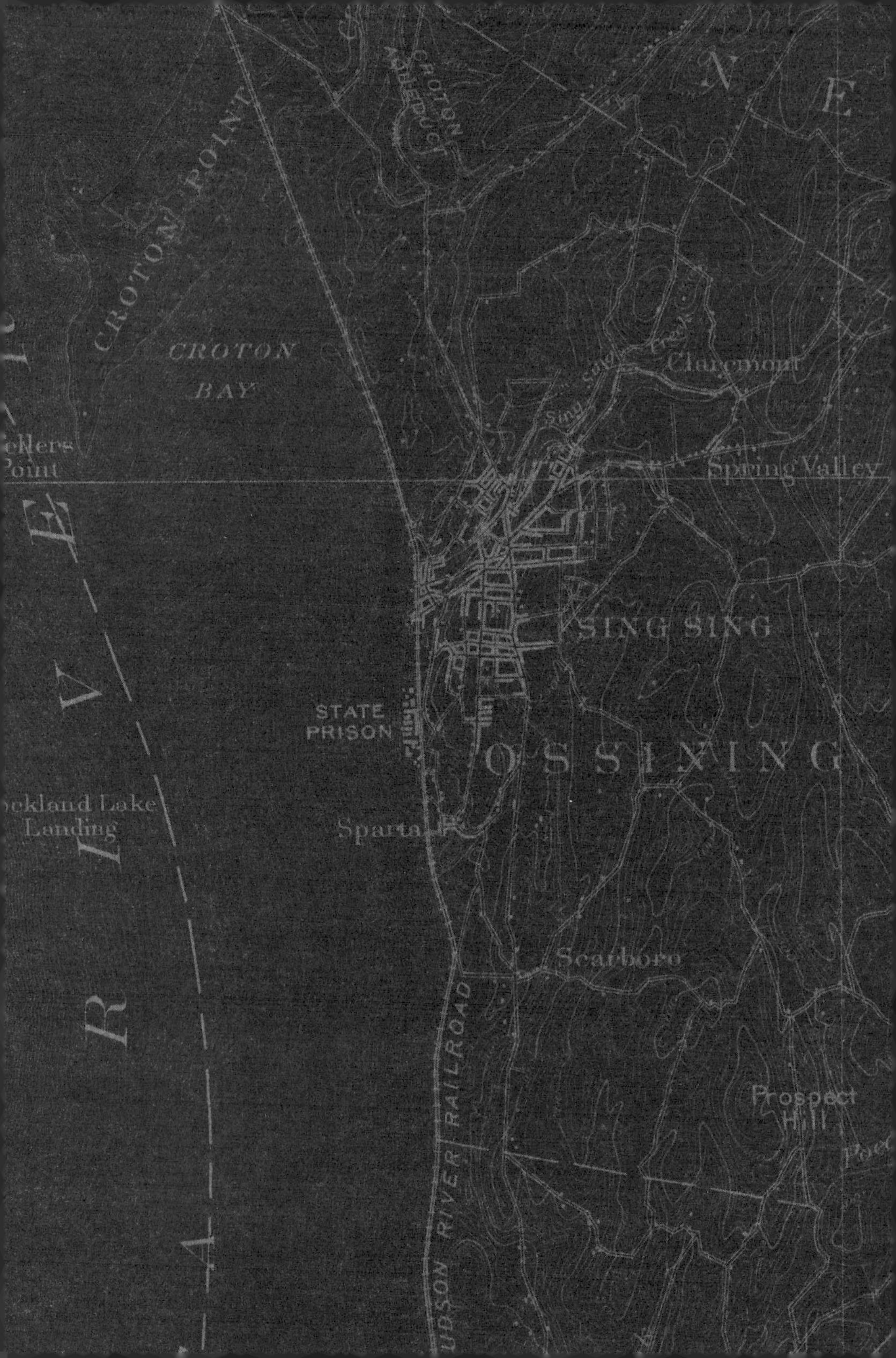

CROTON AQUEDUCT
CROTON POINT
CROTON BAY
Tellers Point
Claremont
Spring Valley
SING SING
STATE PRISON
OSSINING
ckland Lake Landing
Sparta
Scarboro
Prospect Hill
HUDSON RIVER RAILROAD

Pt 1, Chap. 2

"AN UNLIKELY SURVIVOR"

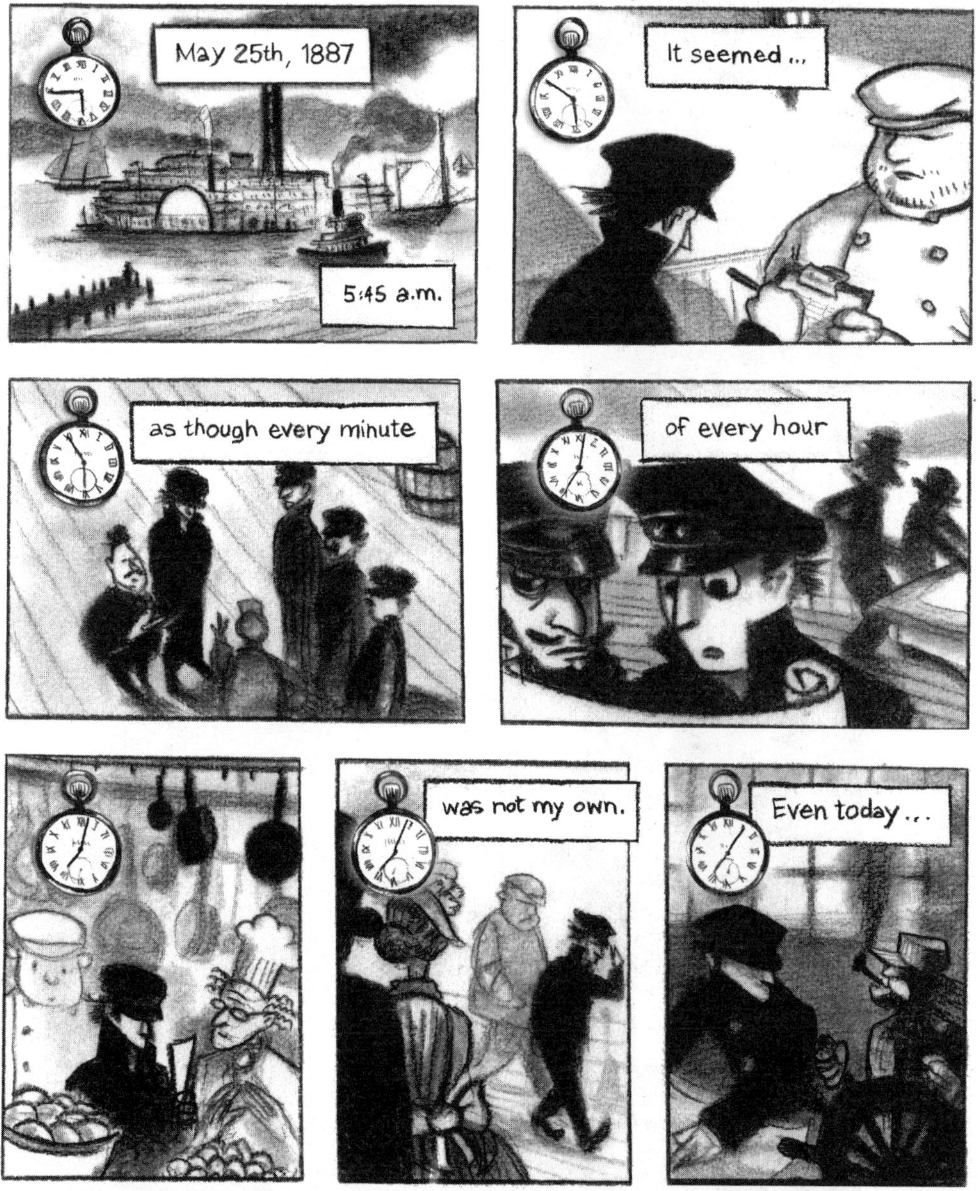
May 25th, 1887
5:45 a.m.
It seemed ...
as though every minute
of every hour
was not my own.
Even today ...

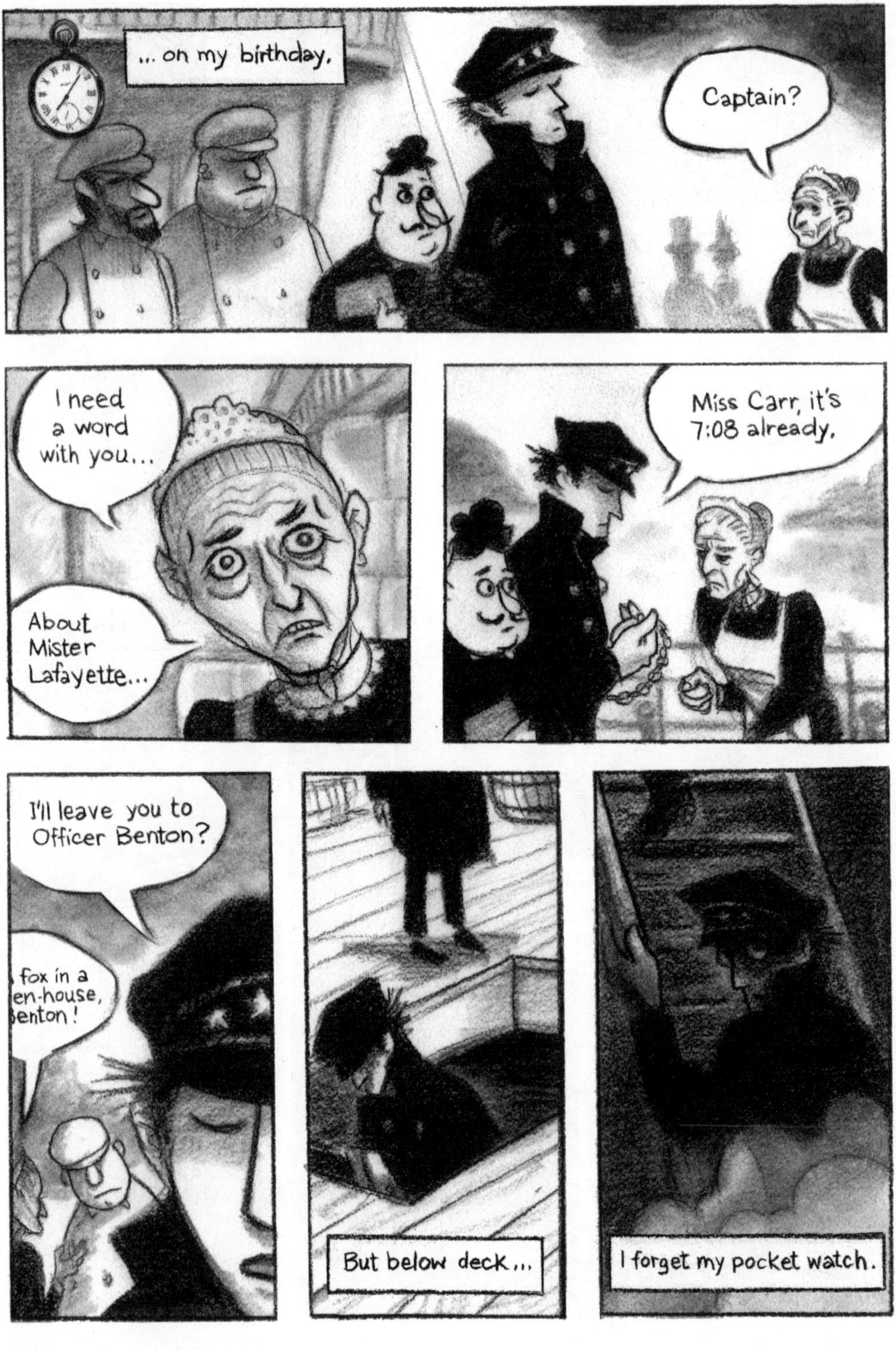

... on my birthday.
Captain?
I need a word with you...
About Mister Lafayette...
Miss Carr, it's 7:08 already.
I'll leave you to Officer Benton?
fox in a
en-house,
enton!
But below deck...
I forget my pocket watch.

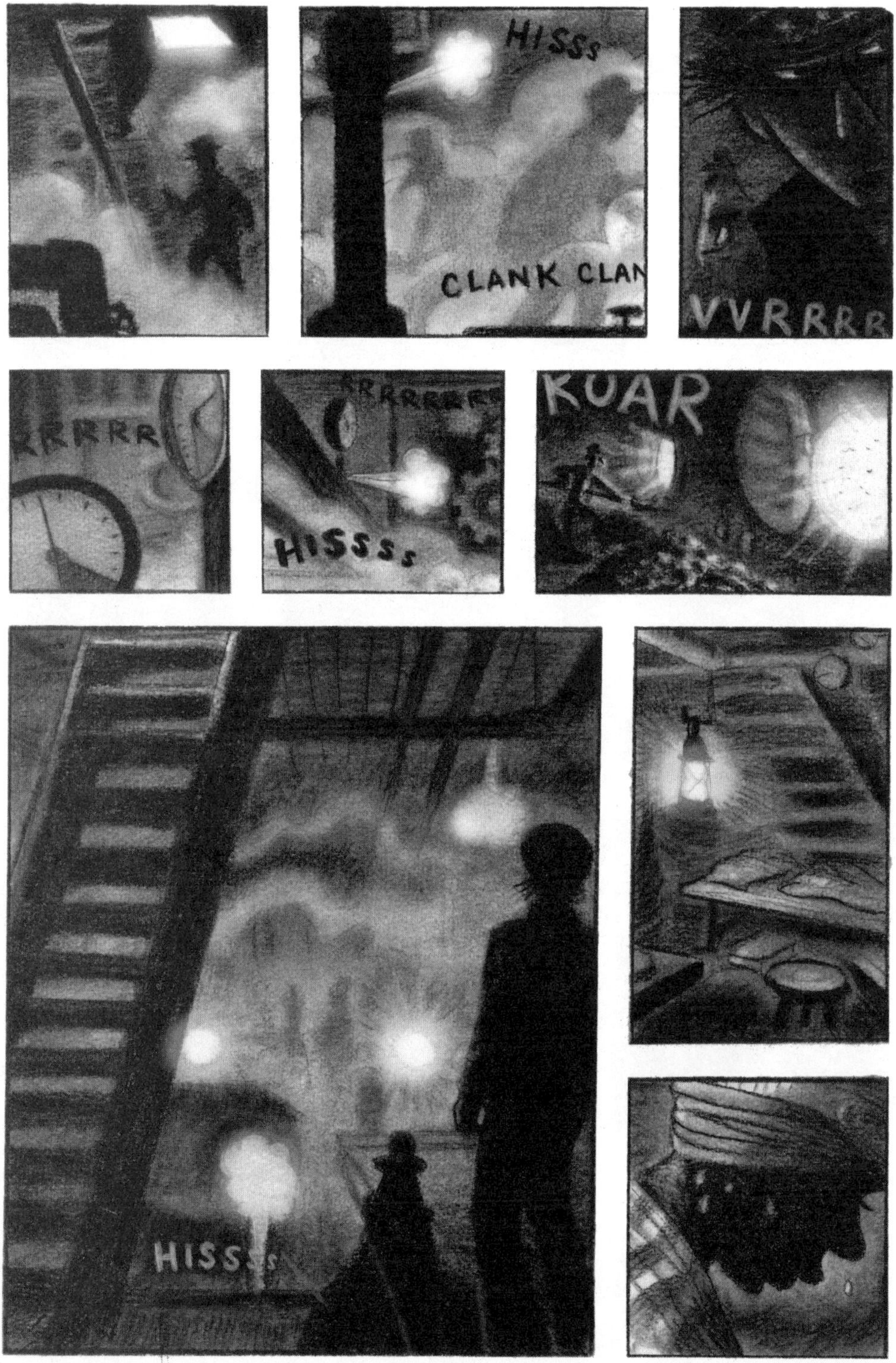
HISSs
CLANK CLAN
VVRRRR
RRRRRR
HISSSs
ROAR
HISSss

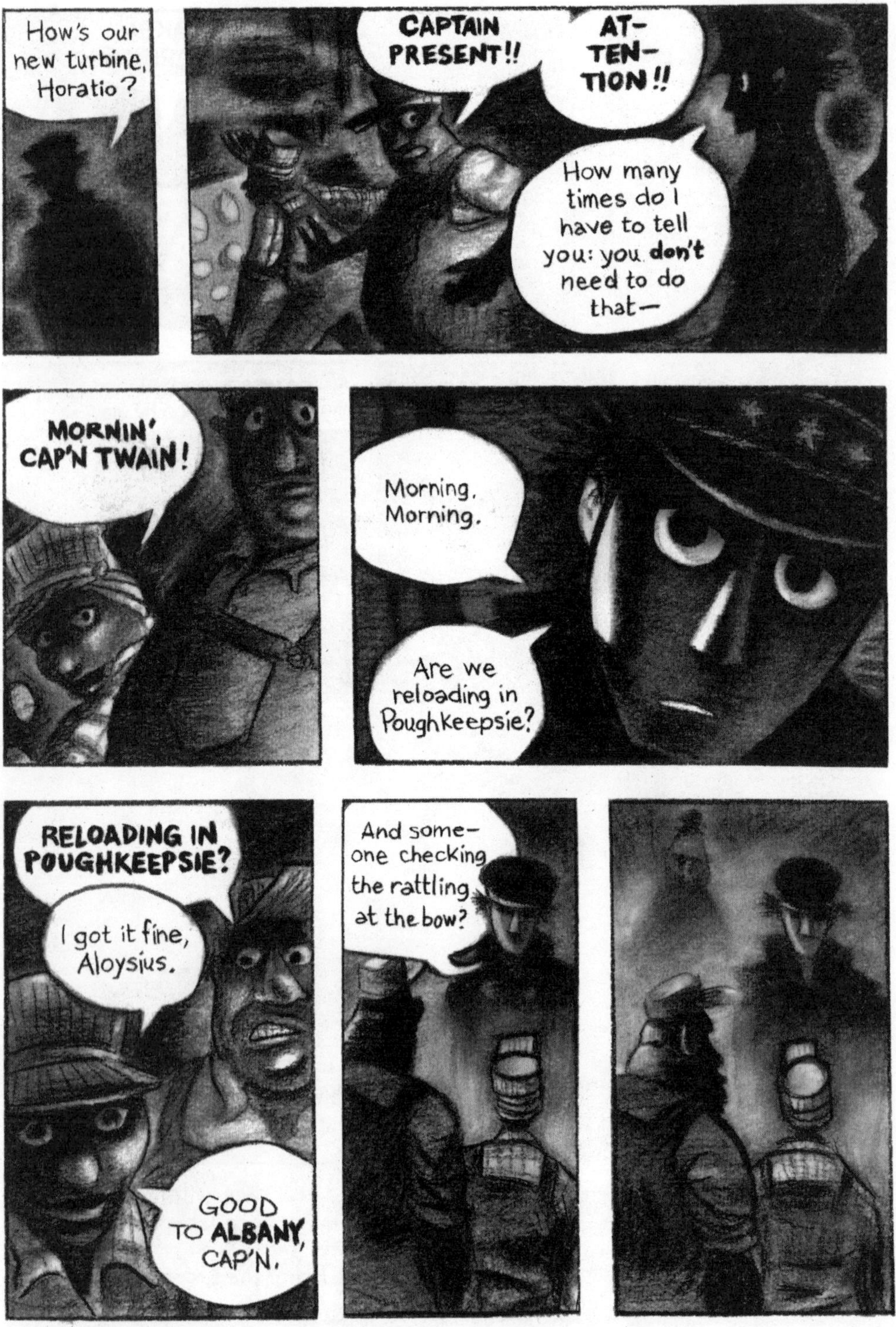
How's our new turbine, Horatio?
CAPTAIN PRESENT!!
AT-TEN-TION!!
How many times do I have to tell you: you **don't** need to do that—
MORNIN', CAP'N TWAIN!
Morning. Morning.
Are we reloading in Poughkeepsie?
RELOADING IN POUGHKEEPSIE?
I got it fine, Aloysius.
GOOD TO **ALBANY**, CAP'N.
And some-one checking the rattling at the bow?

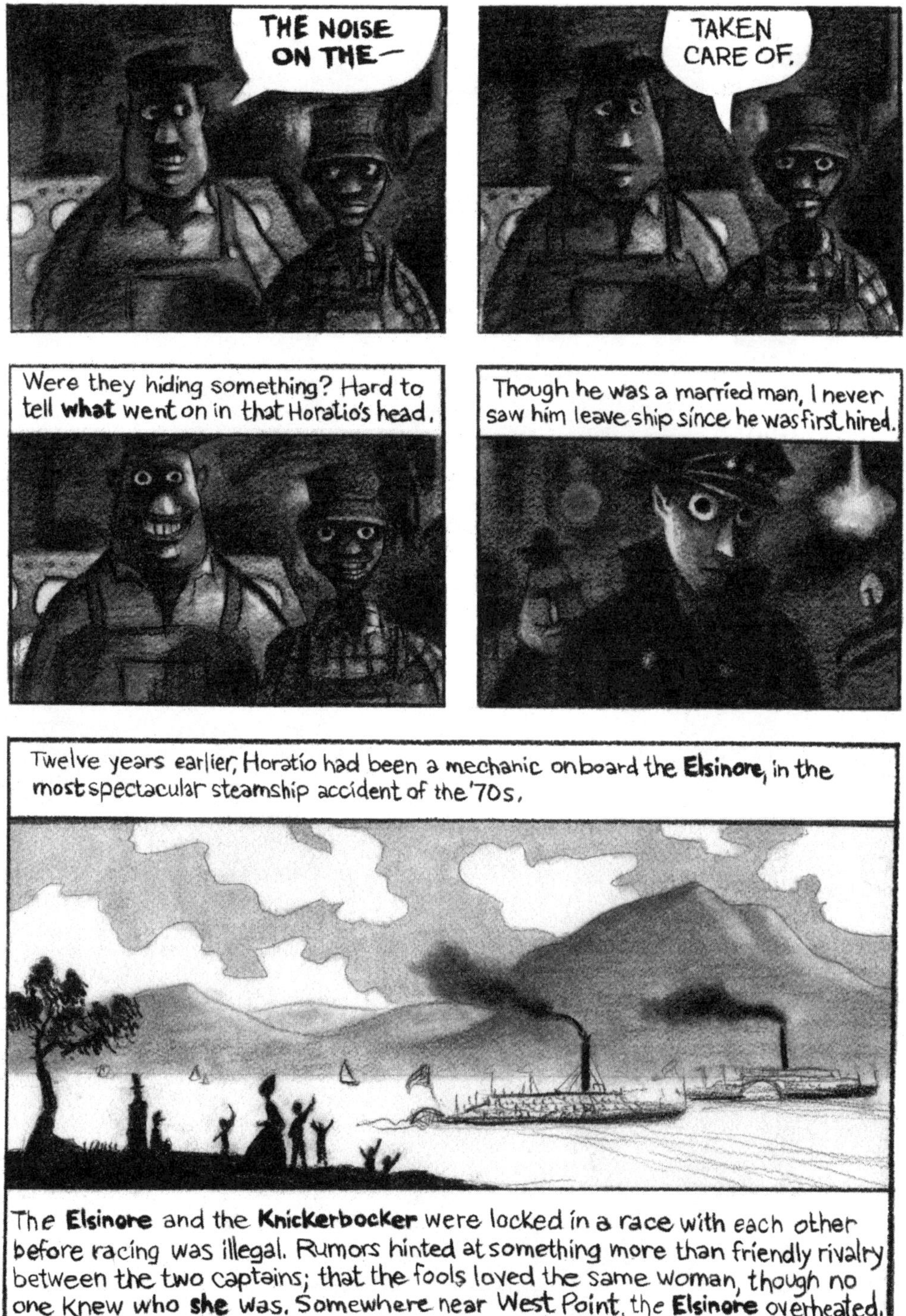
THE NOISE ON THE—
TAKEN CARE OF.
Were they hiding something? Hard to tell **what** went on in that Horatio's head.
Though he was a married man, I never saw him leave ship since he was first hired.
Twelve years earlier, Horatio had been a mechanic onboard the **Elsinore**, in the **most** spectacular steamship accident of the '70s.
The **Elsinore** and the **Knickerbocker** were locked in a race with each other before racing was illegal. Rumors hinted at something more than friendly rivalry between the two captains; that the fools loved the same woman, though no one knew who **she** was. Somewhere near West Point, the **Elsinore** overheated.

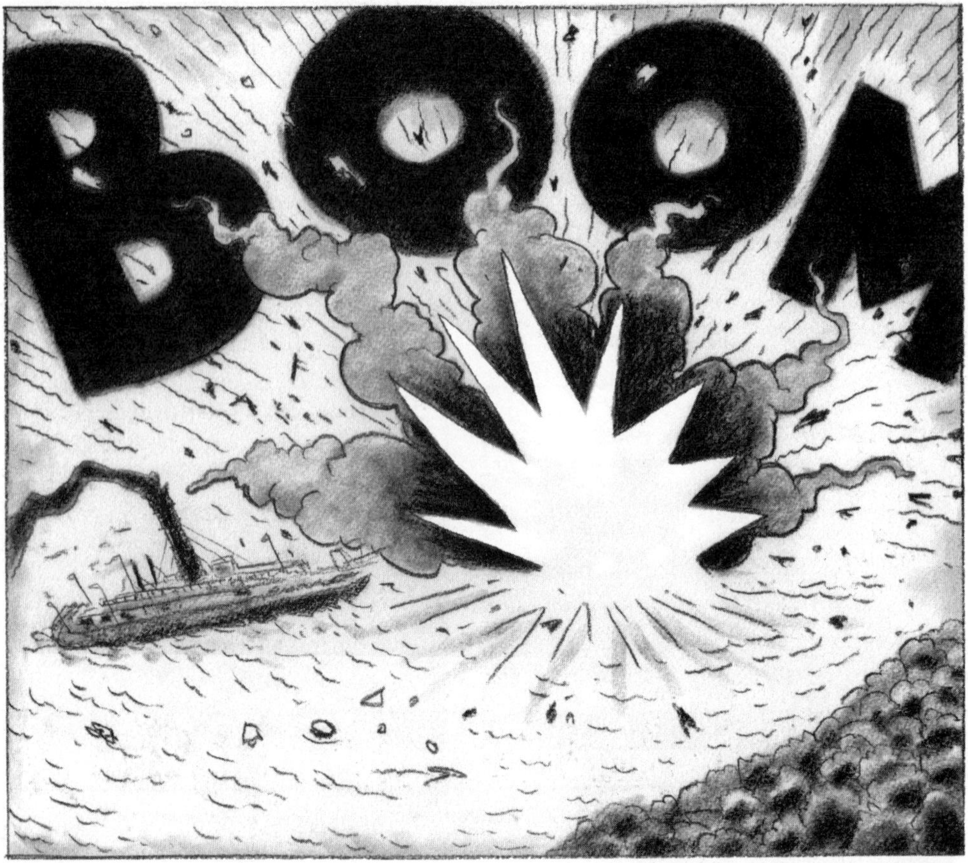
BOOM

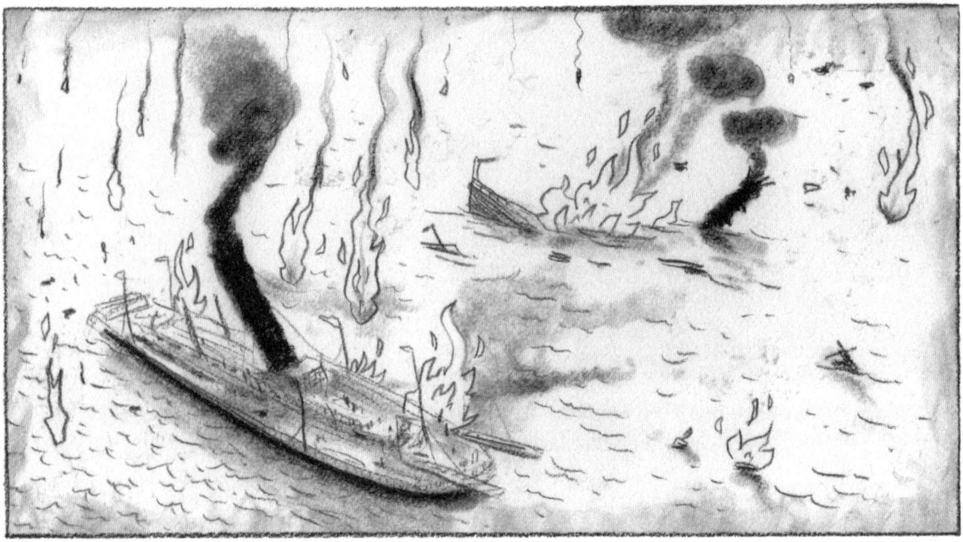

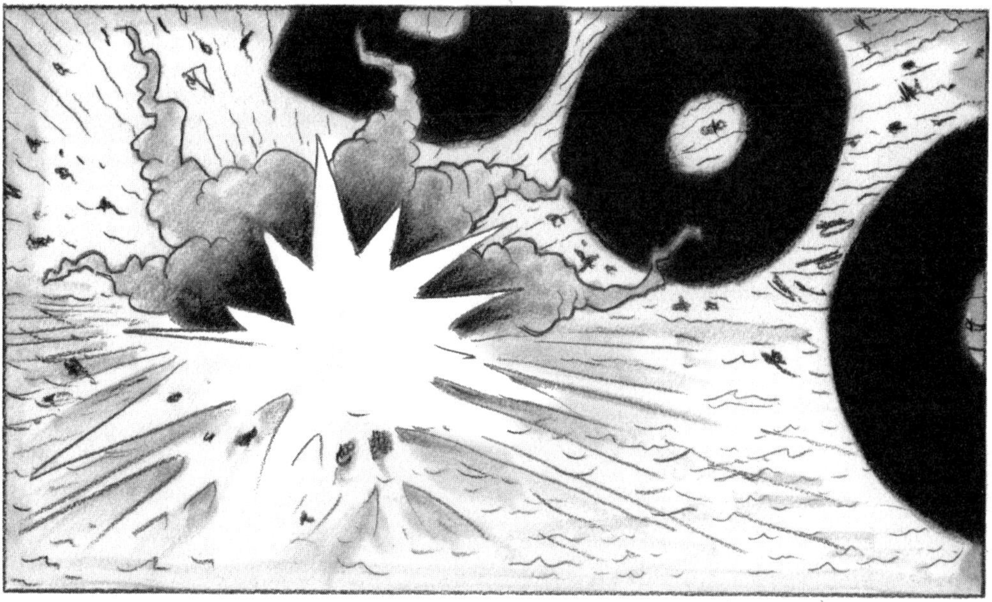

The twin explosions were heard as far south as Croton. Fortunately, the ships were light and had few passengers. **Un**fortunately everyone died—except for one crewman: **Horatio Clover**.

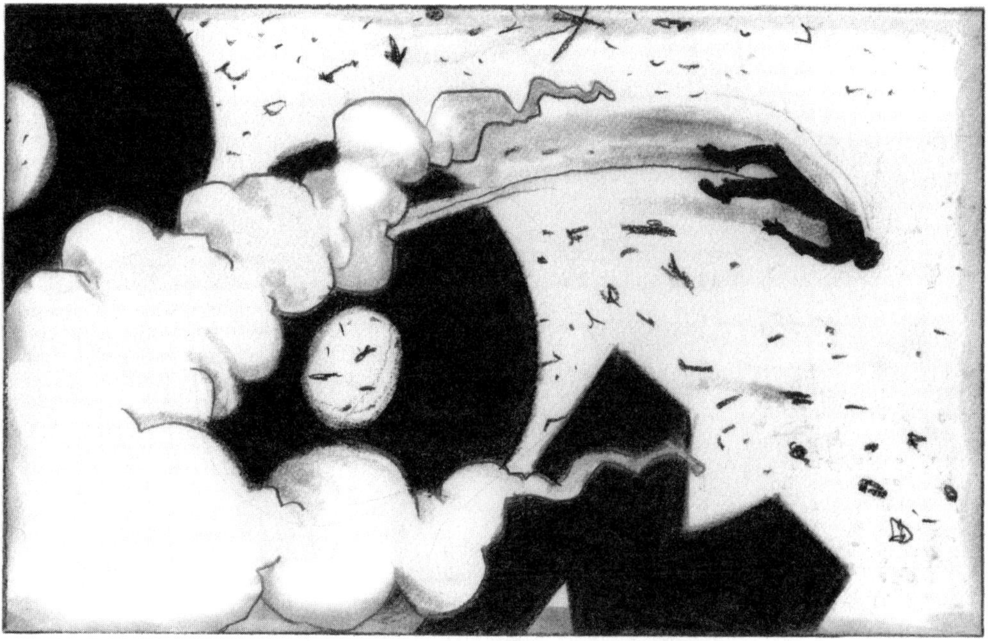

He was thrown an impossible 96 yards over the train tracks and into a tree.

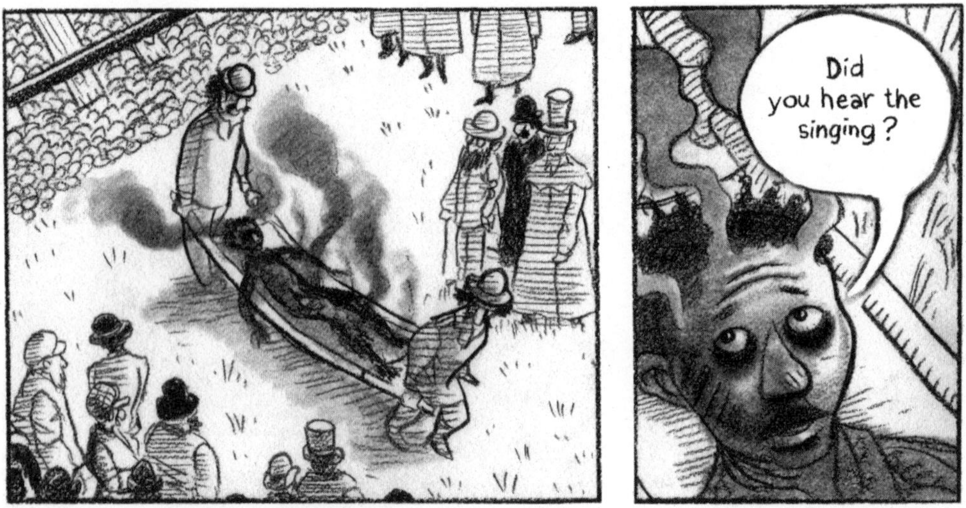
Did you hear the singing?

It did something to his head.
But he came out of it a mechanical genius. No man knew steam engines like he did. When Jacques-Henri called on me for the LORELEI, I drafted Horatio, in spite of some protest on account of his being colored.

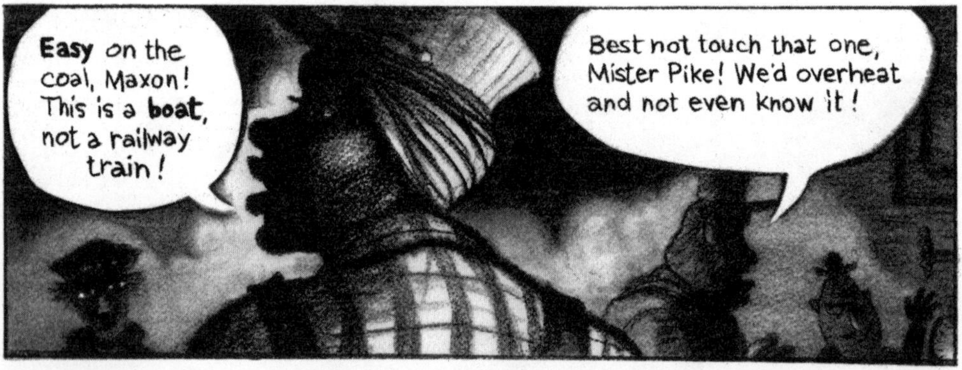
Easy on the coal, Maxon! This is a **boat**, not a railway train!
Best not touch that one, Mister Pike! We'd overheat and not even know it!

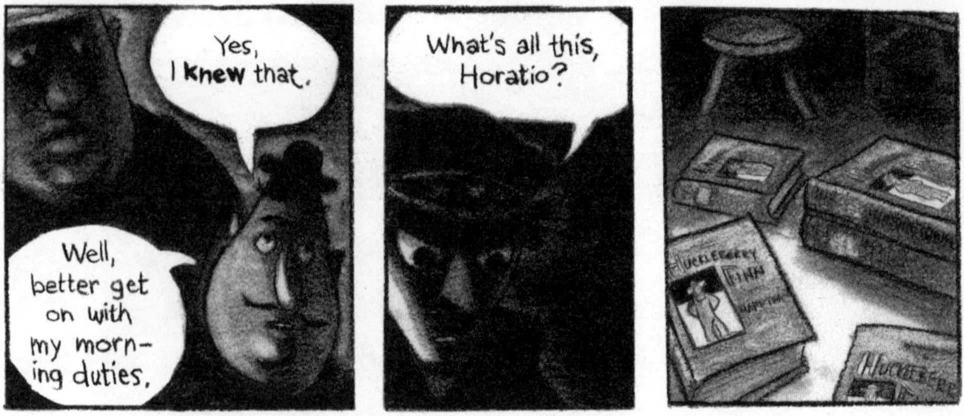
Yes, I **knew** that.
Well, better get on with my morning duties.
What's all this, Horatio?

43

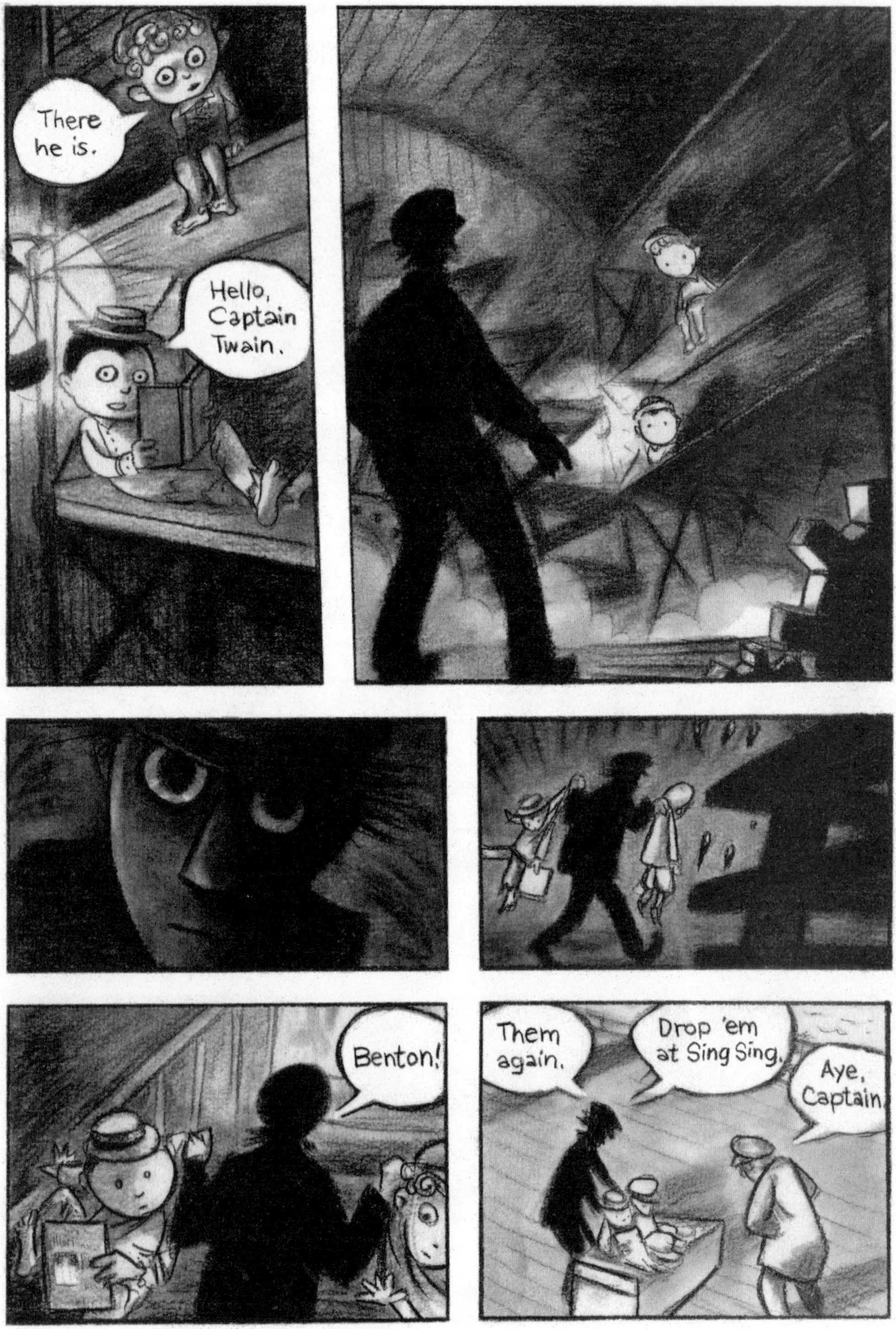
There he is.
Hello, Captain Twain.
Benton!
Them again.
Drop 'em at Sing Sing.
Aye, Captain.

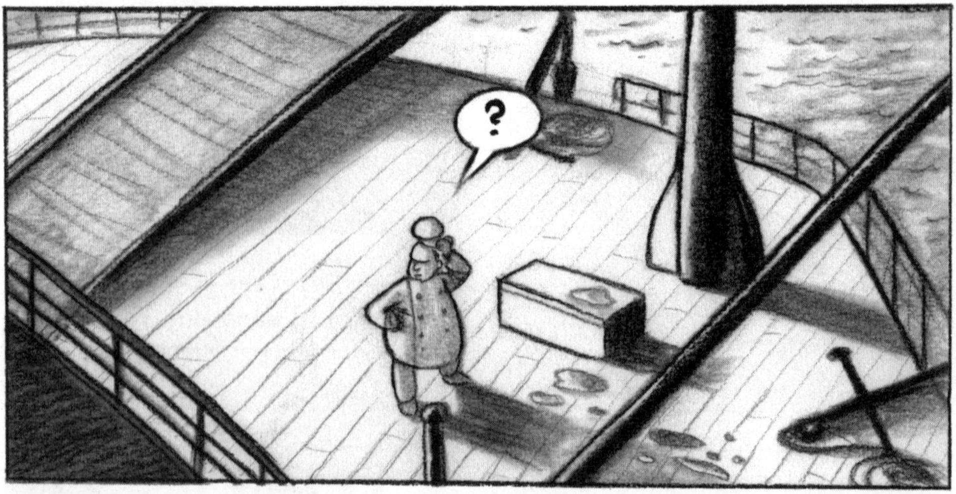
?

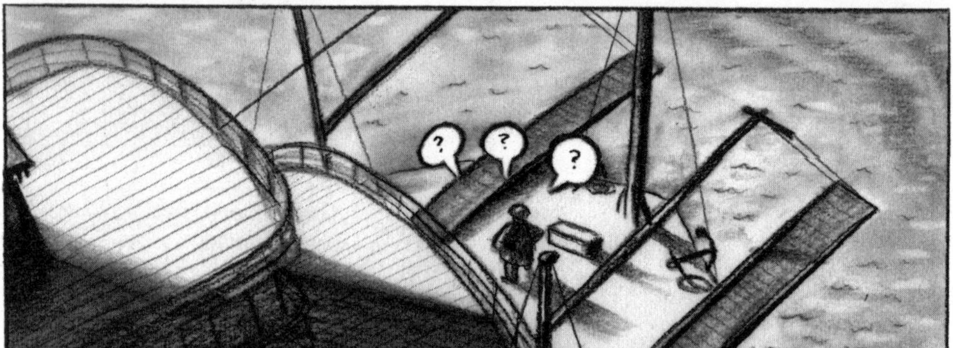
?
?
?

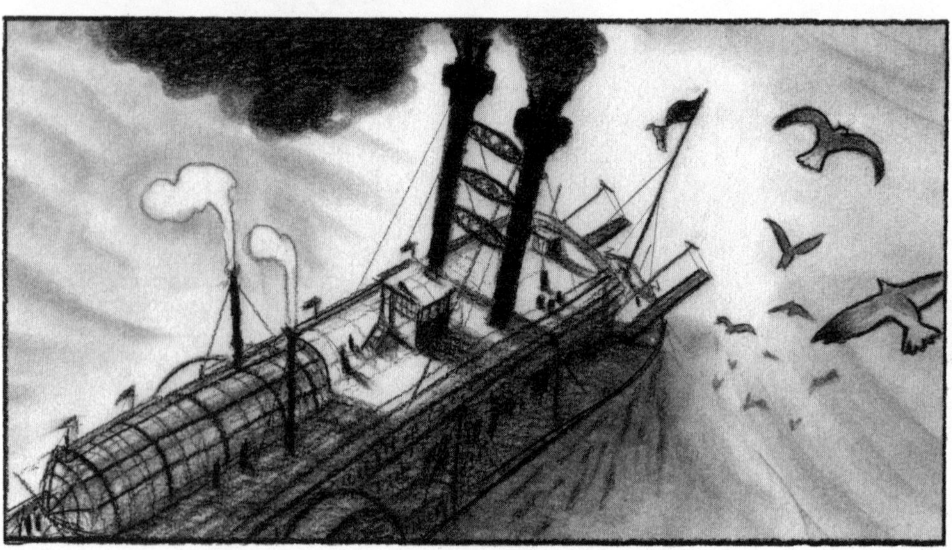

"A PRAYER DOWN BELOW"

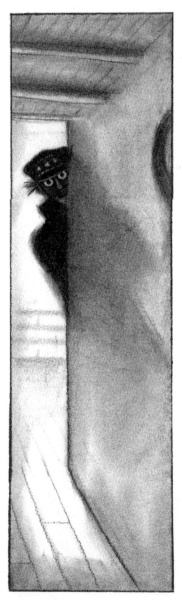

Women didn't find him handsome, did they?

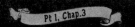

Then again, all Tarrytown knew that old Saunders had two wives, and **he** was no Apollo,

Whatever it was that had troubled Lafayette earlier that morning, I saw no sign of now.

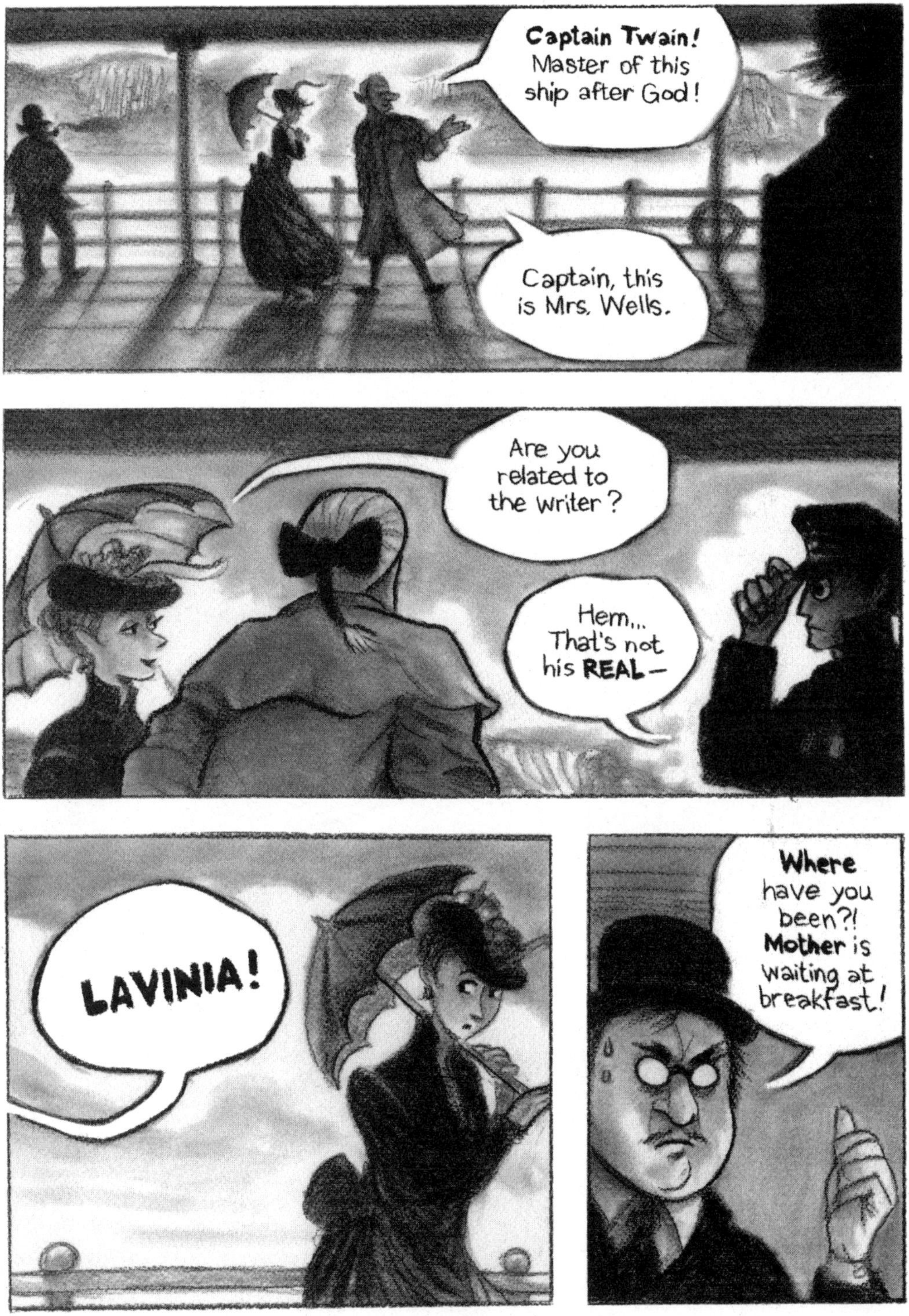

Captain Twain! Master of this ship after God!
Captain, this is Mrs. Wells.
Are you related to the writer?
Hem... That's not his **REAL**—
LAVINIA!
Where have you been?! **Mother** is waiting at breakfast!

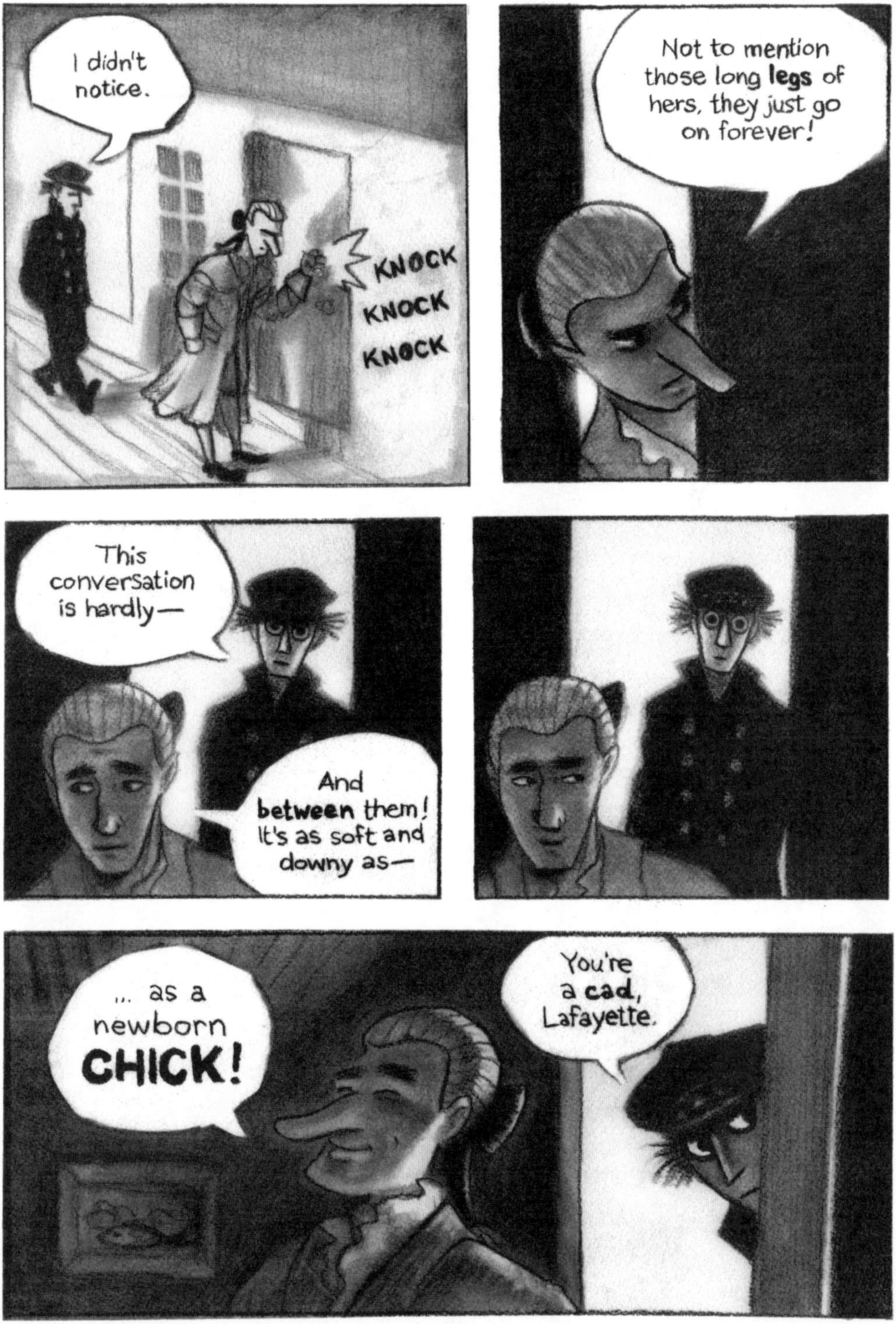
I didn't notice.
KNOCK
KNOCK
KNOCK
Not to mention those long **legs** of hers, they just go on forever!
This conversation is hardly—
And **between** them! It's as soft and downy as—
... as a newborn **CHICK!**
You're a **cad**, Lafayette.

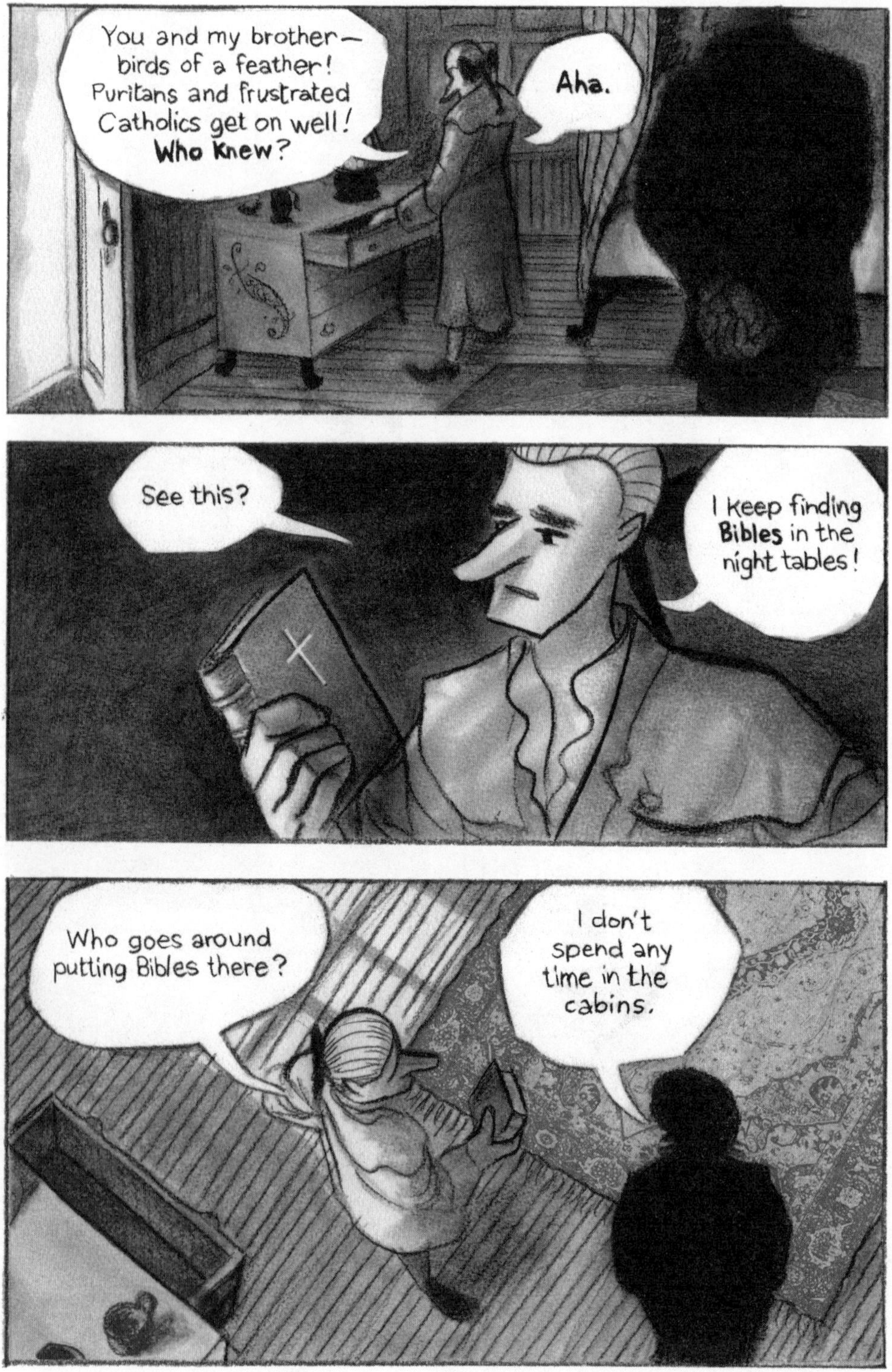
You and my brother— birds of a feather! Puritans and frustrated Catholics get on well! **Who knew?**
Aha.
See this?
I keep finding **Bibles** in the night tables!
Who goes around putting Bibles there?
I don't spend any time in the cabins.

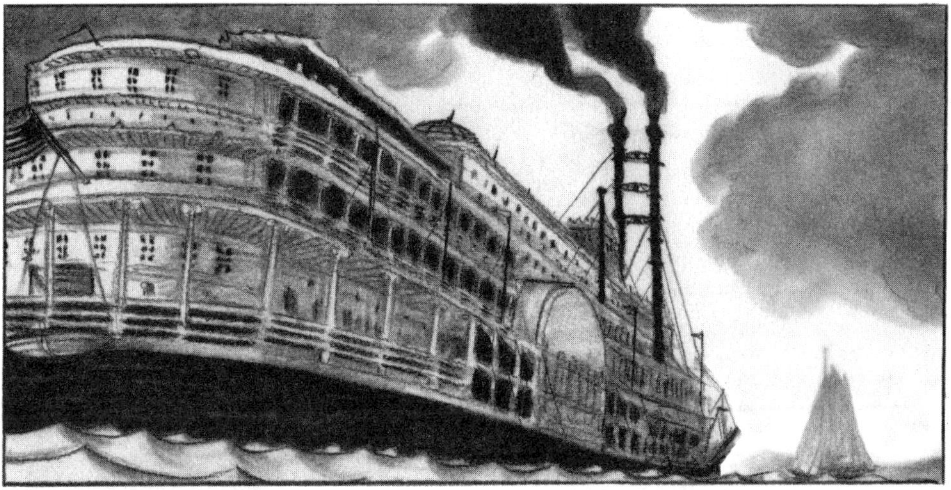

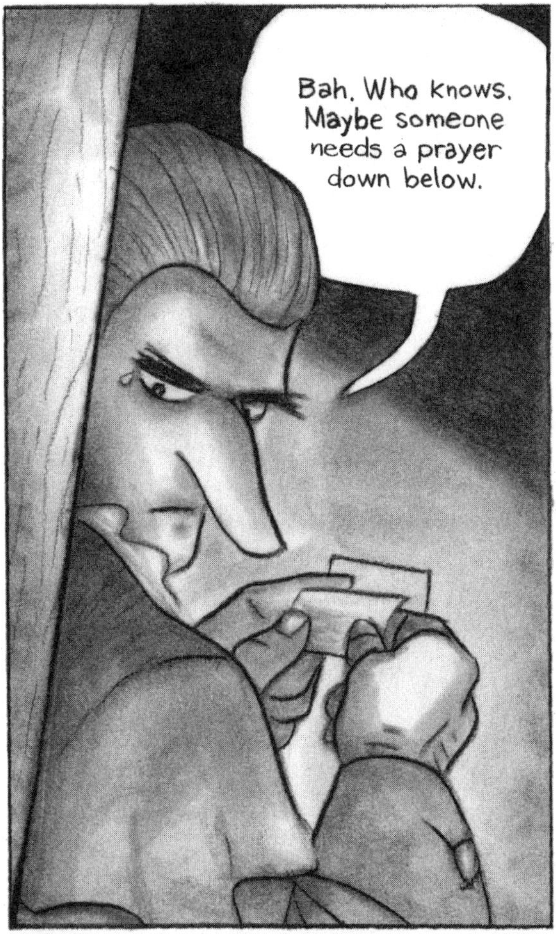
Bah. Who knows.
Maybe someone
needs a prayer
down below.

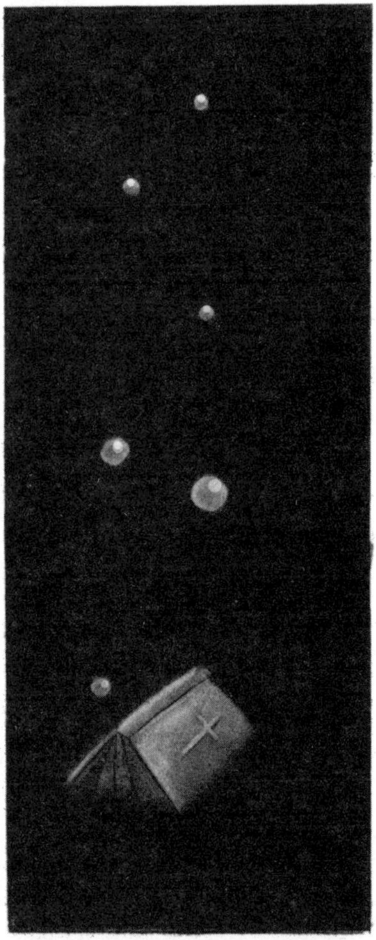

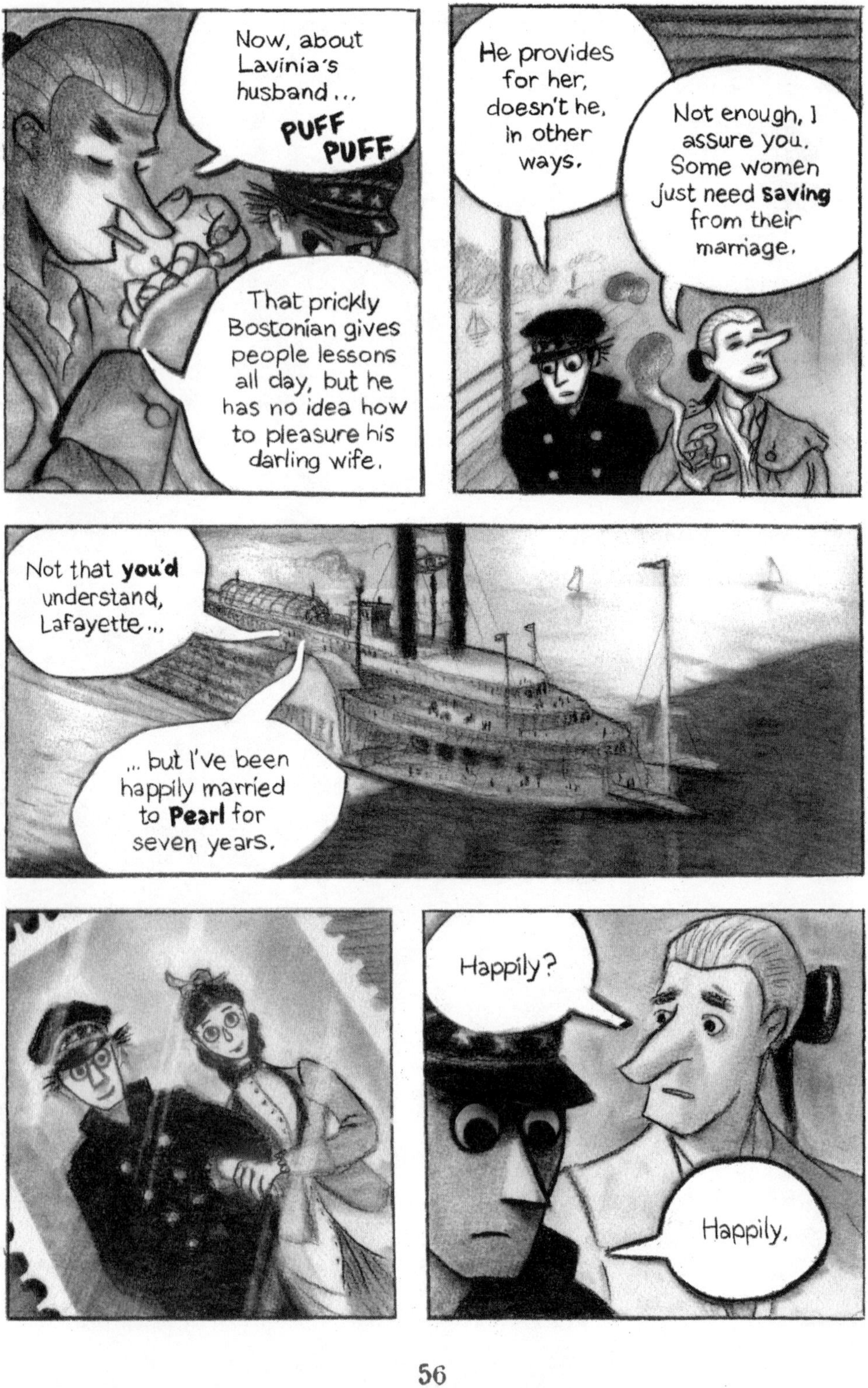
Now, about Lavinia's husband...
PUFF PUFF
That prickly Bostonian gives people lessons all day, but he has no idea how to pleasure his darling wife.
He provides for her, doesn't he, in other ways.
Not enough, I assure you. Some women just need saving from their marriage.
Not that you'd understand, Lafayette...
... but I've been happily married to Pearl for seven years.
Happily?
Happily.

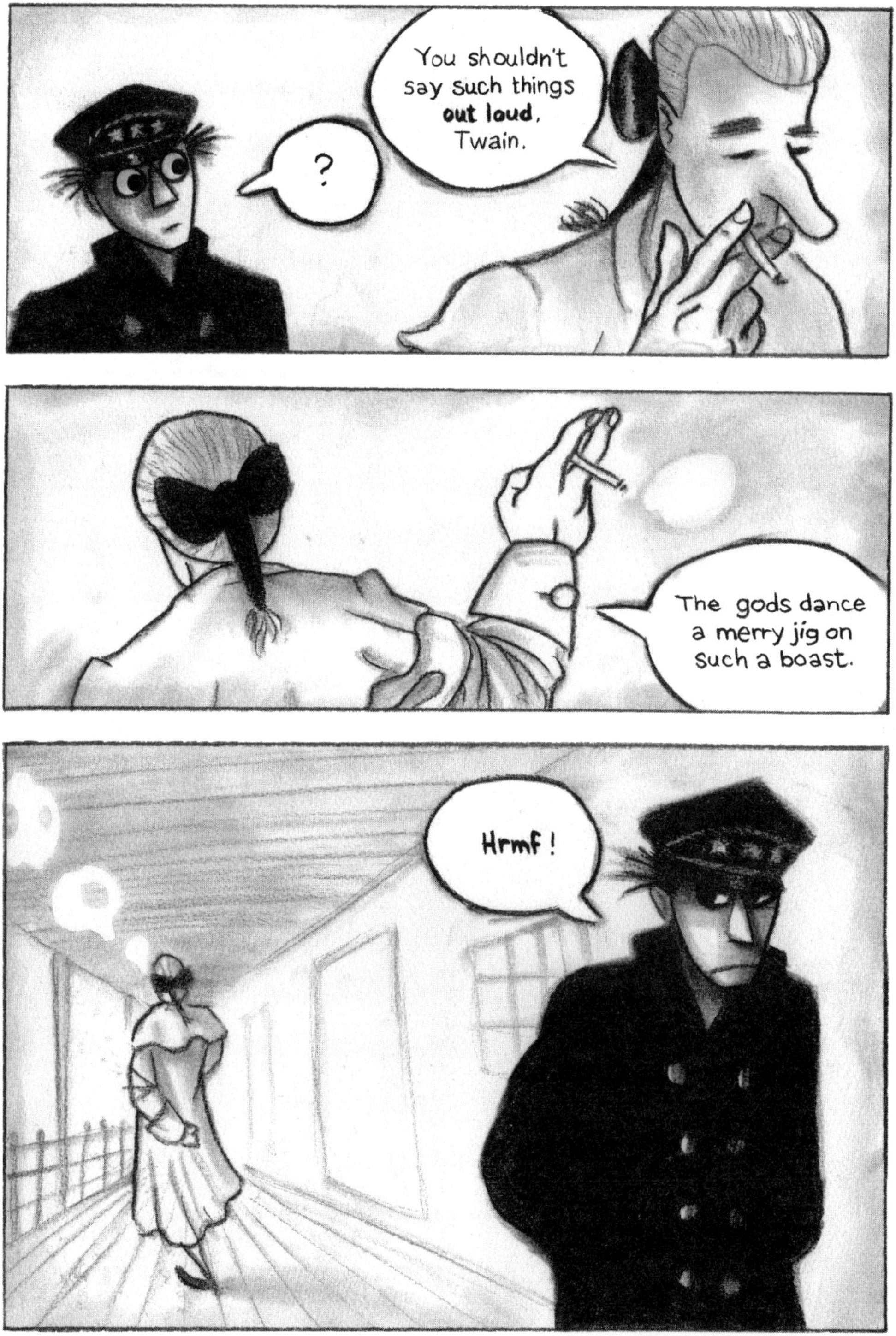
?
You shouldn't say such things **out loud**, Twain.
The gods dance a merry jig on such a boast.
Hrmf!

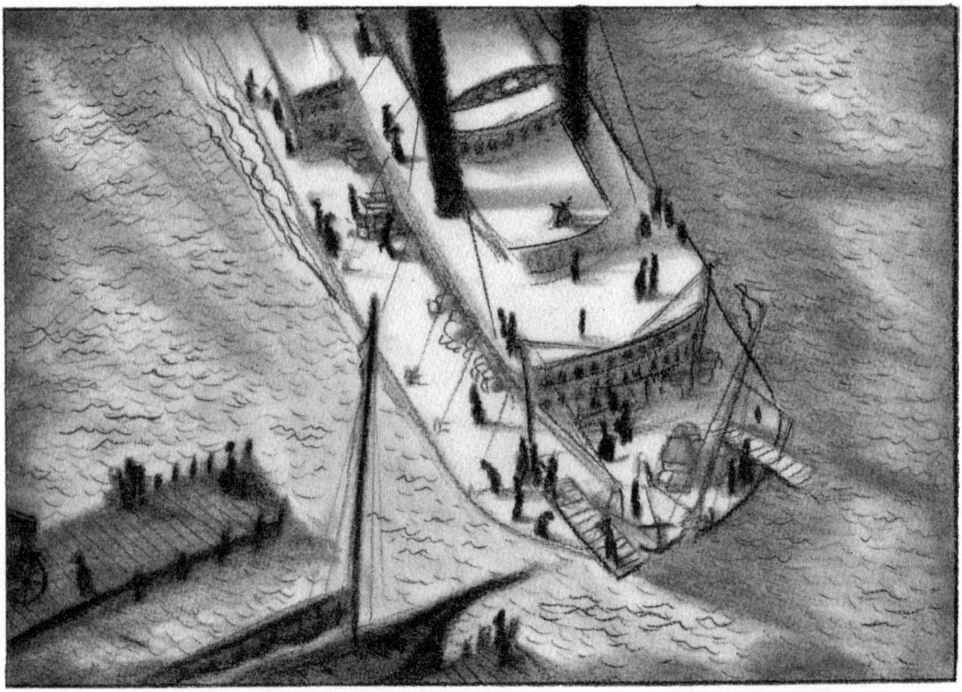

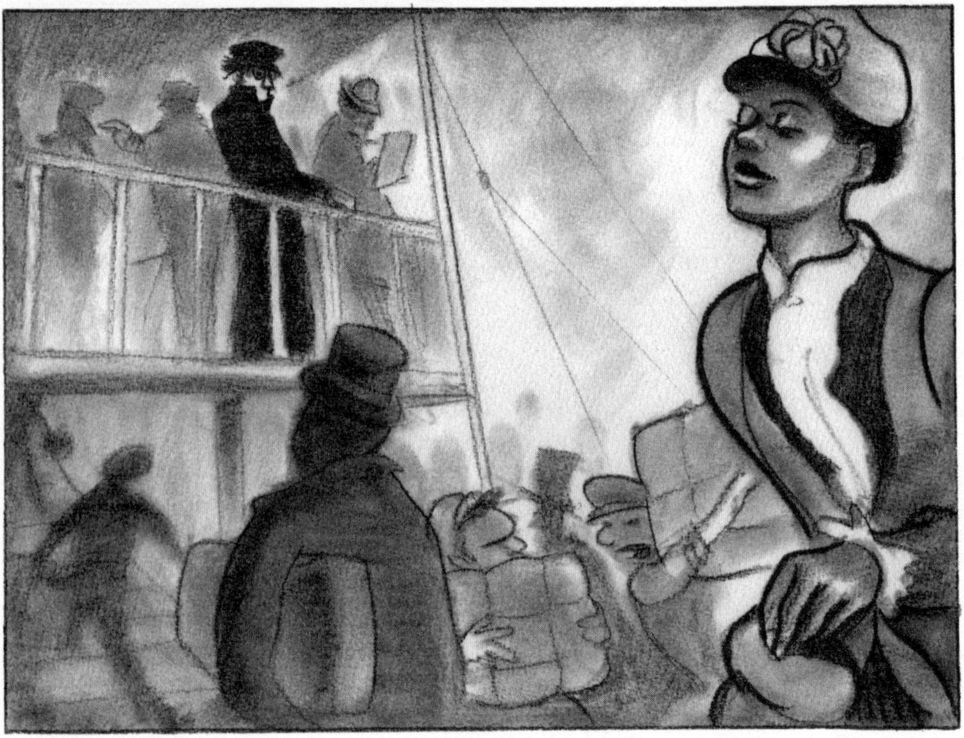

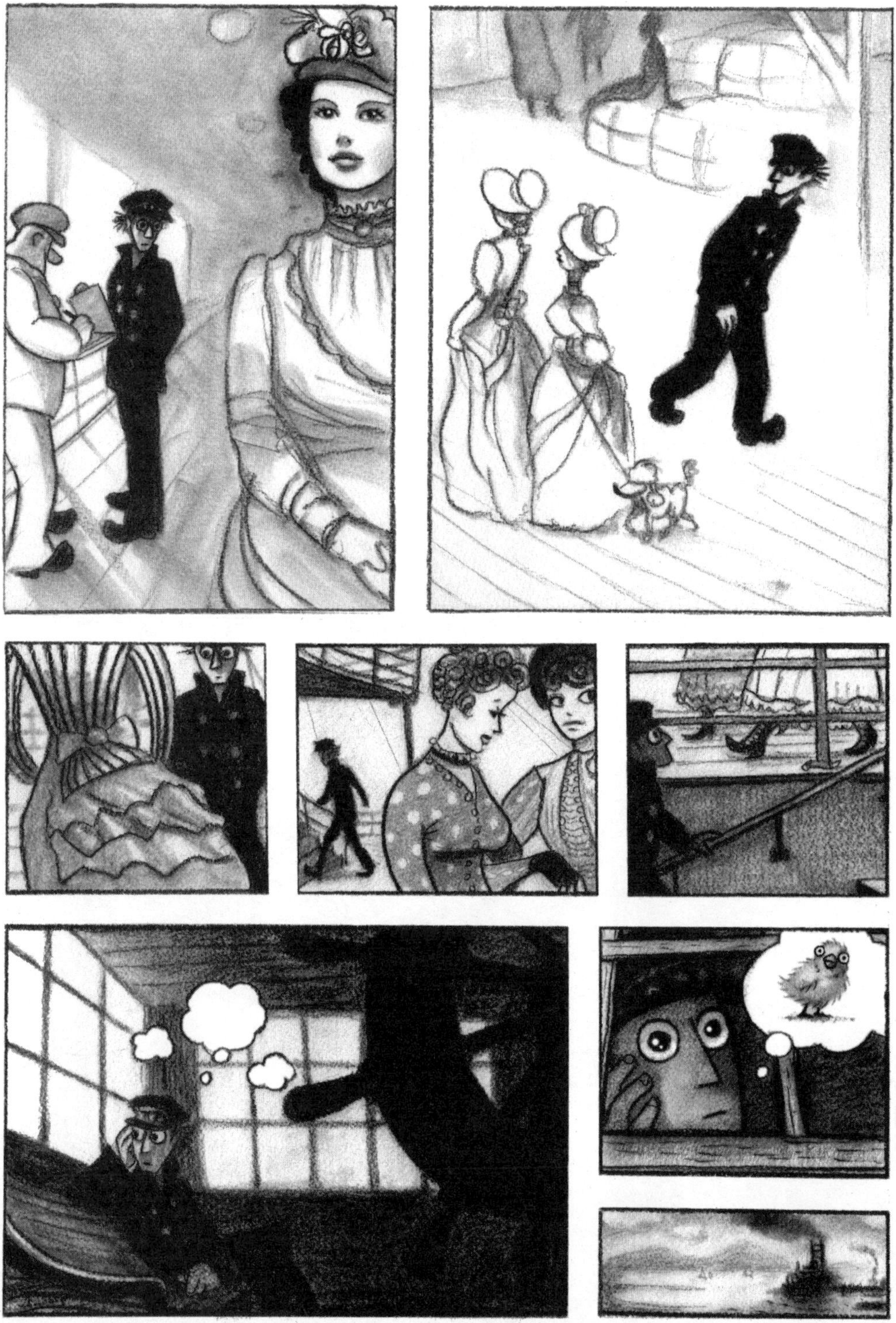

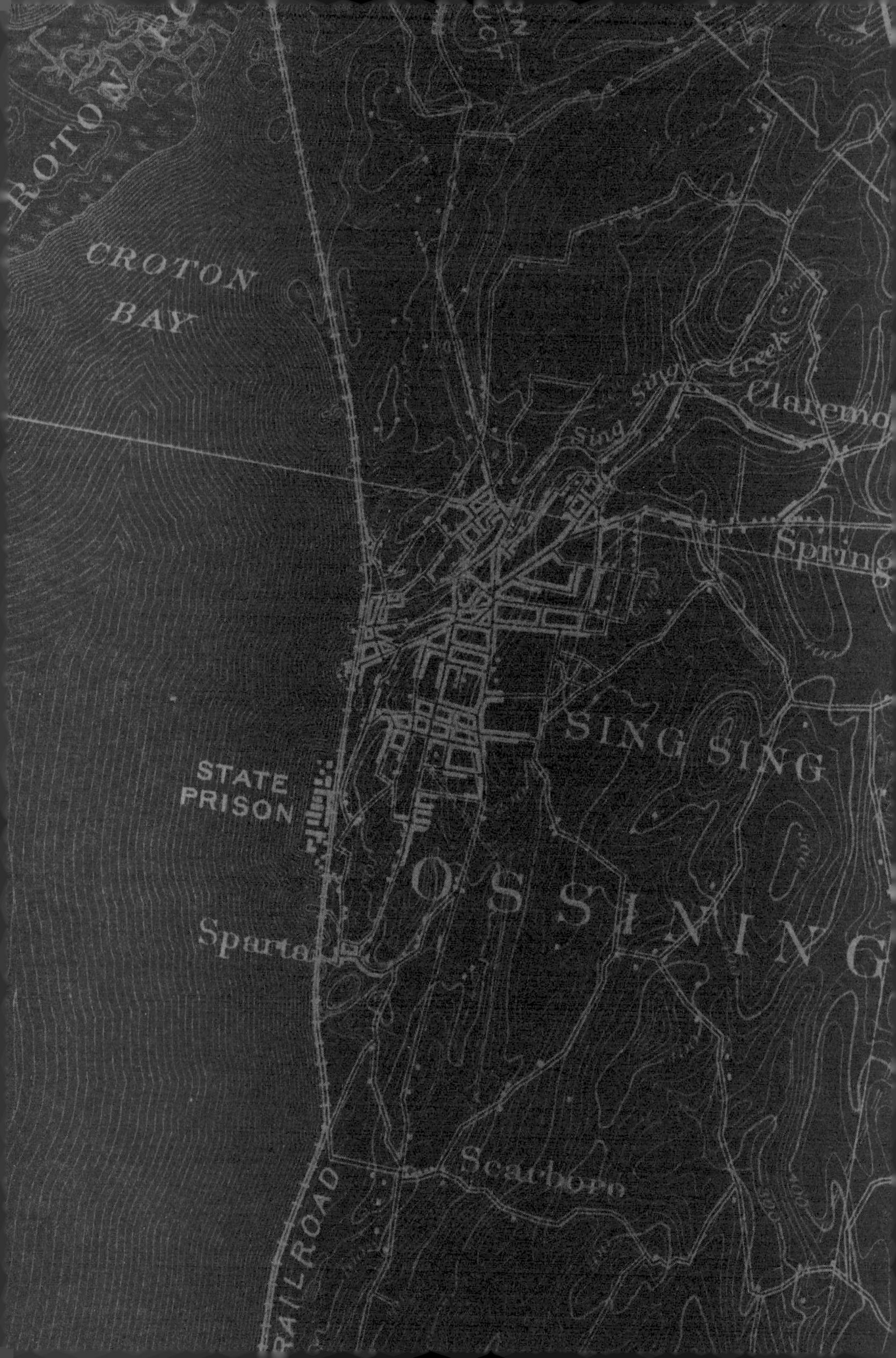

CROTON
CROTON BAY
Sing Sing Creek
Claremo
Spring
STATE PRISON
SING SING
OSSINING
Sparta
Scarboro
RAILROAD

Pt I, Chap. 4

"THE MERMAID IN THE HUDSON"

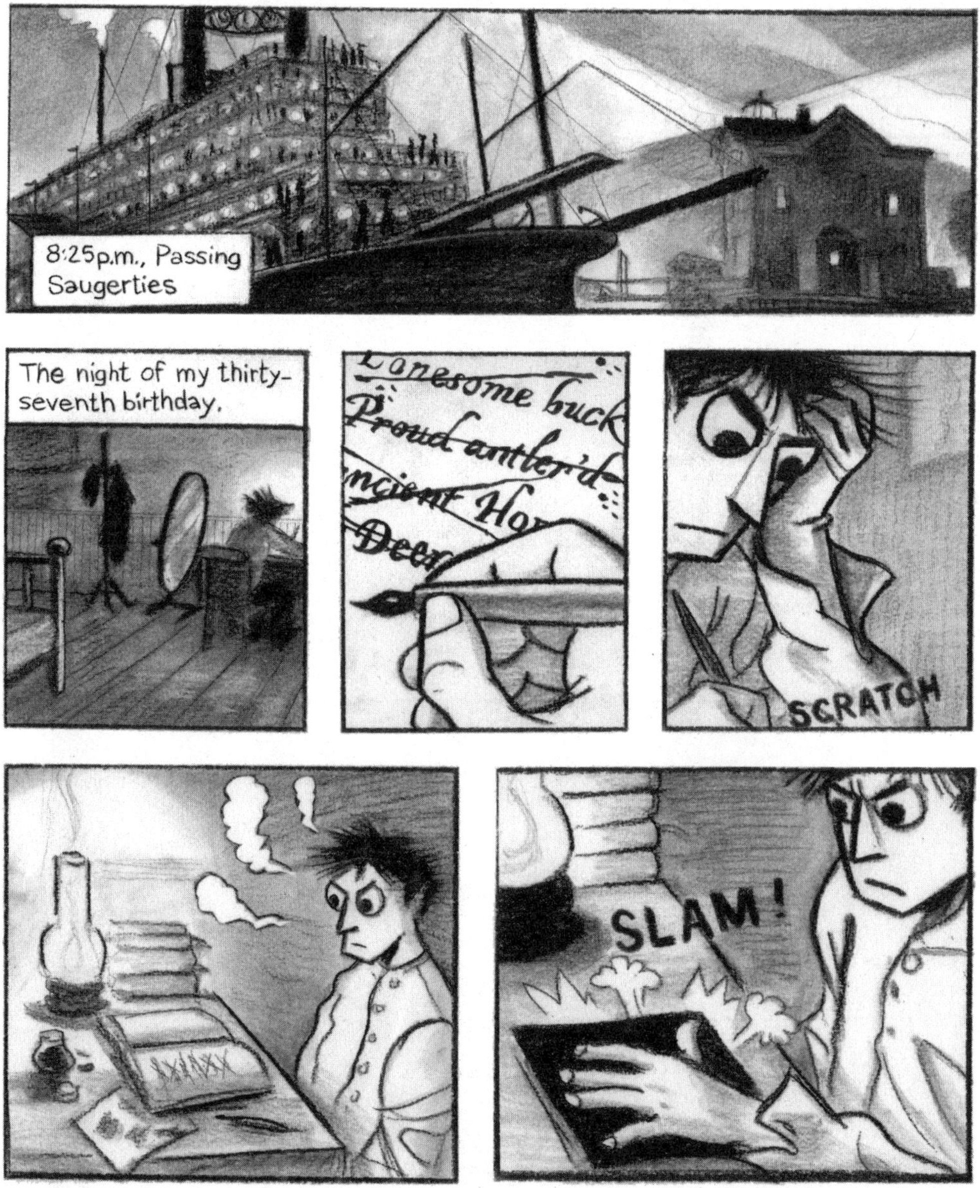
8:25p.m., Passing Saugerties
The night of my thirty-seventh birthday.
Lonesome buck
Proud antler'd
SCRATCH
SLAM!

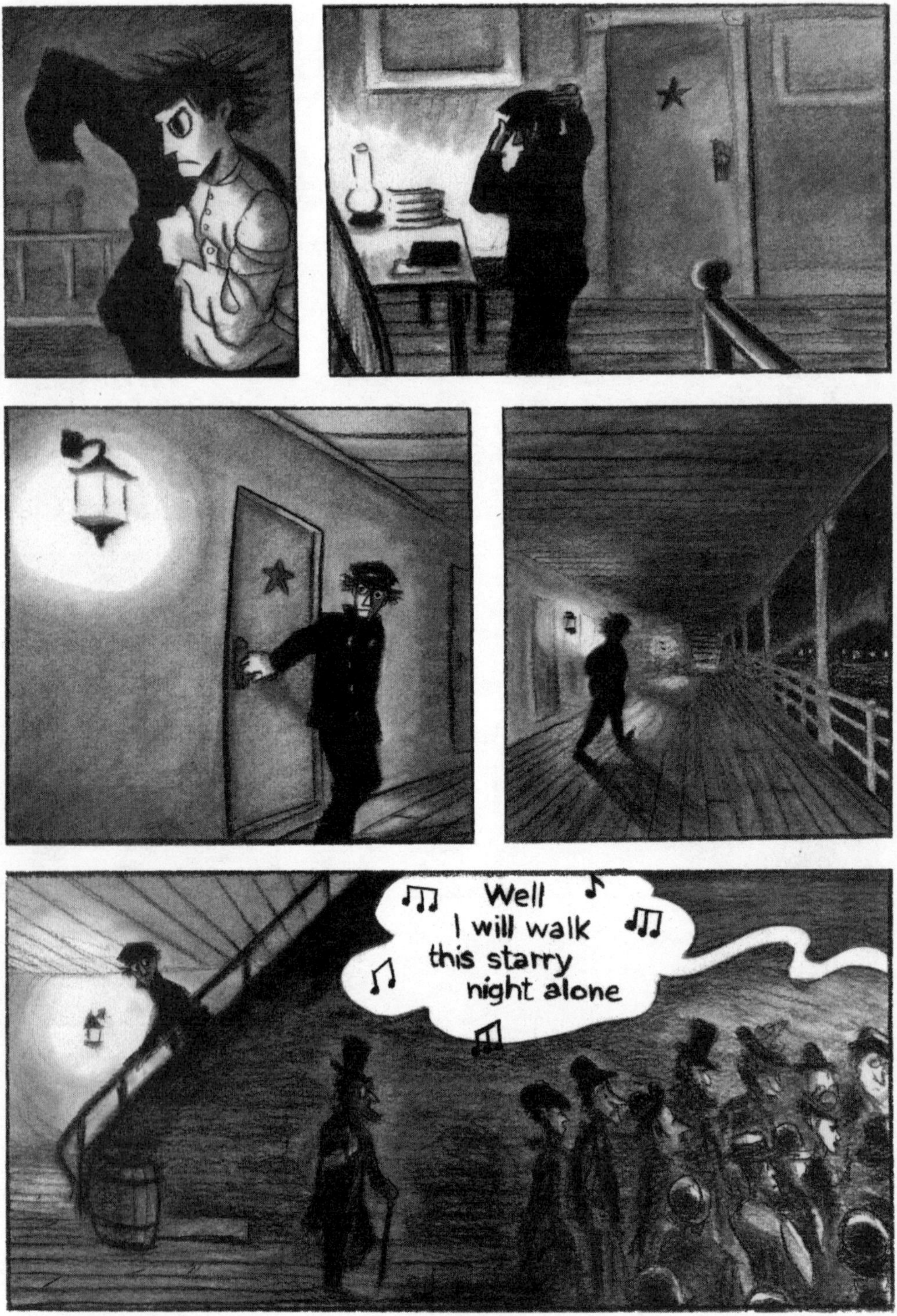
Well I will walk this starry night alone

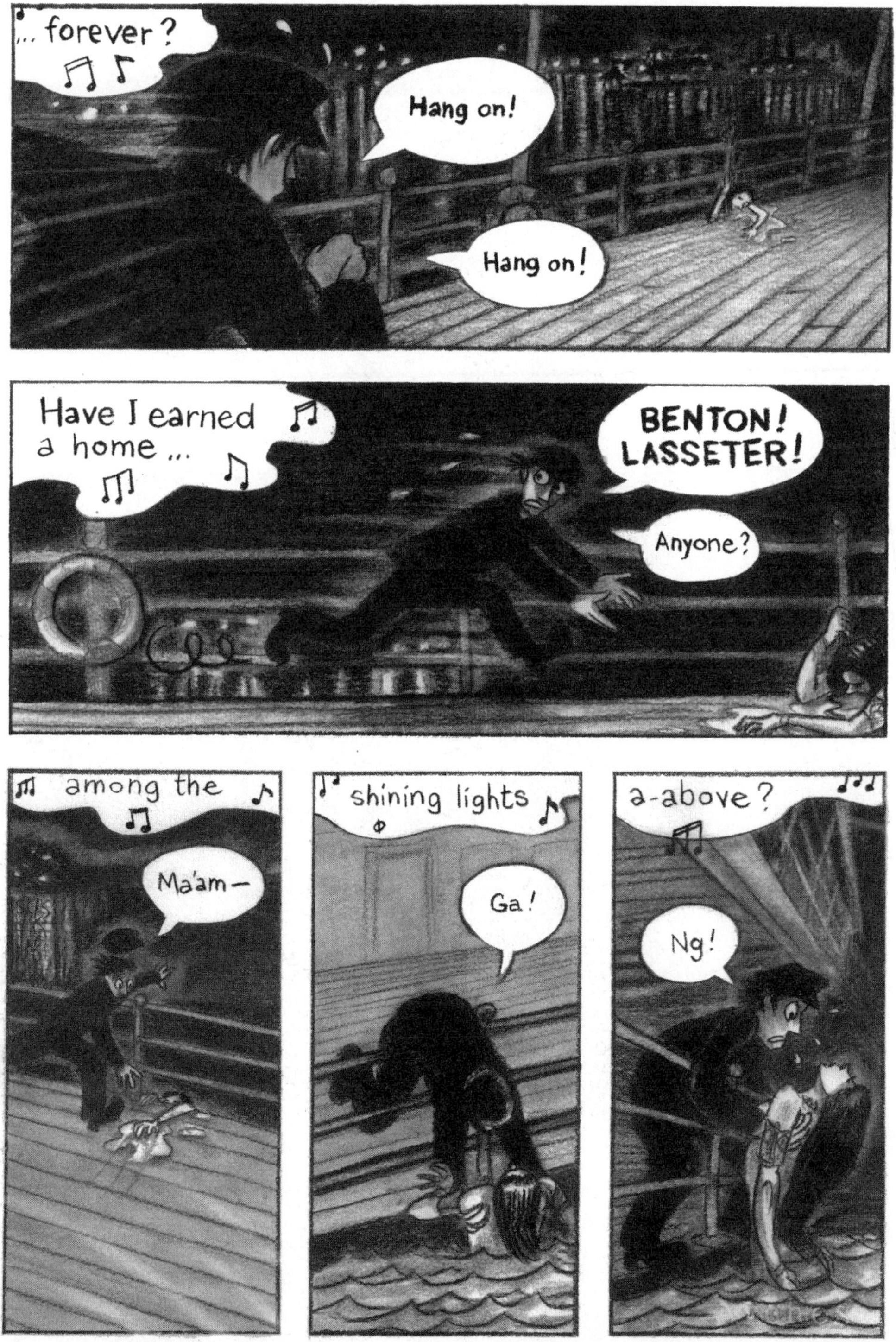
... forever?
Hang on!
Hang on!
Have I earned a home ...
BENTON! LASSETER!
Anyone?
among the
Ma'am—
shining lights
Ga!
a-above?
Ng!

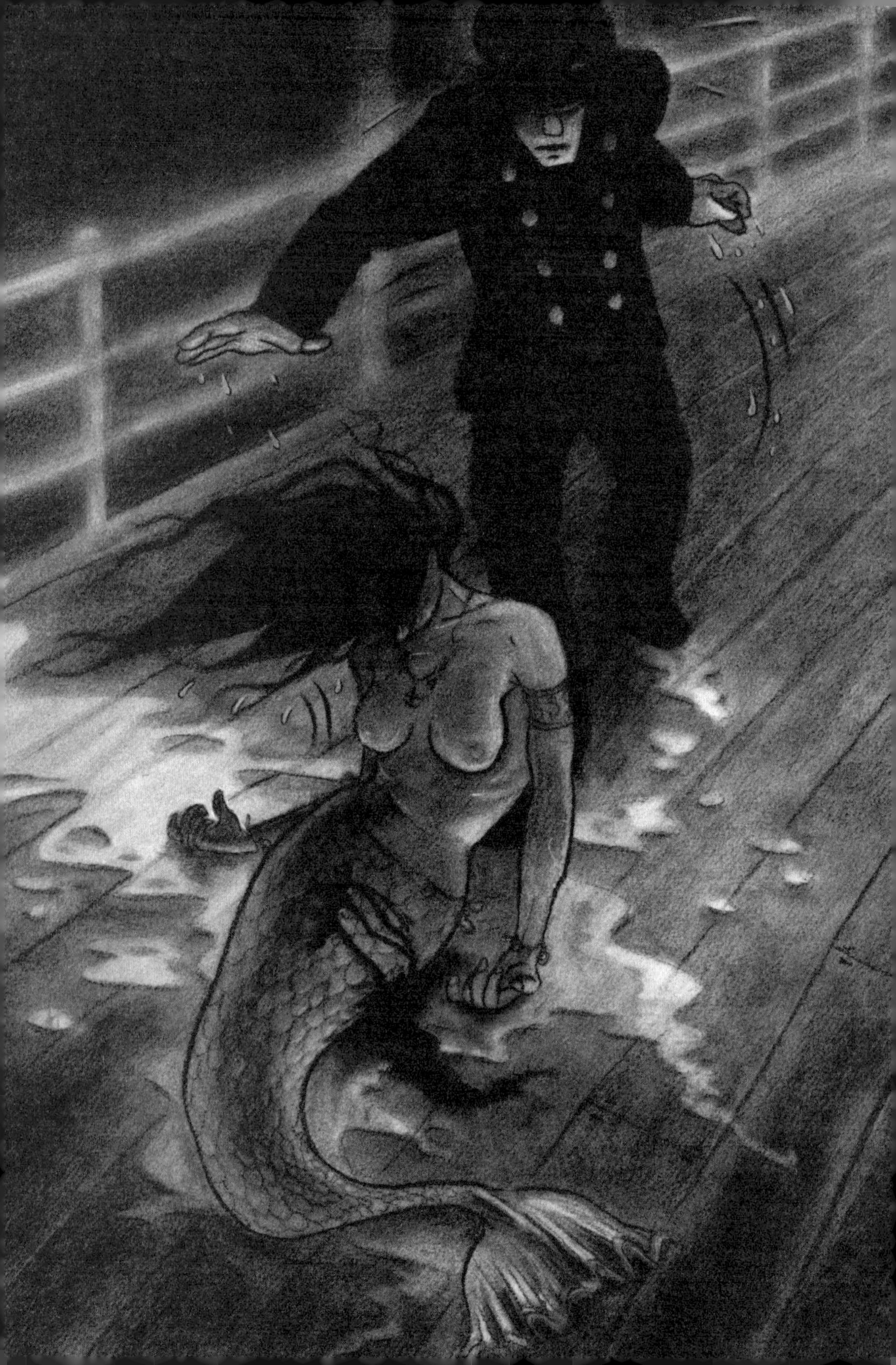

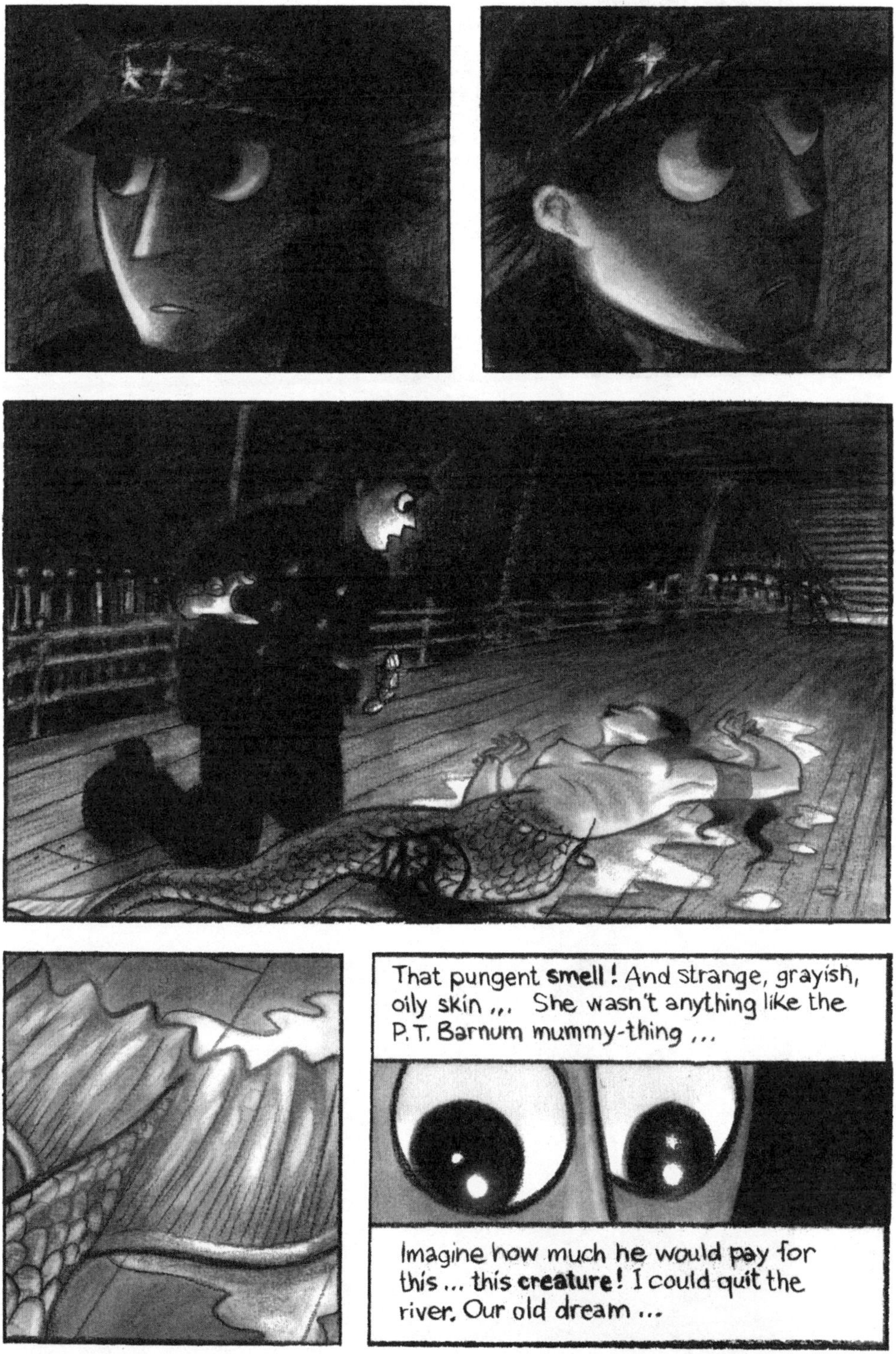
That pungent **smell**! And strange, grayish, oily skin ,,. She wasn't anything like the P.T. Barnum mummy-thing ...
Imagine how much he would pay for this ... this **creature**! I could quit the river. Our old dream ...

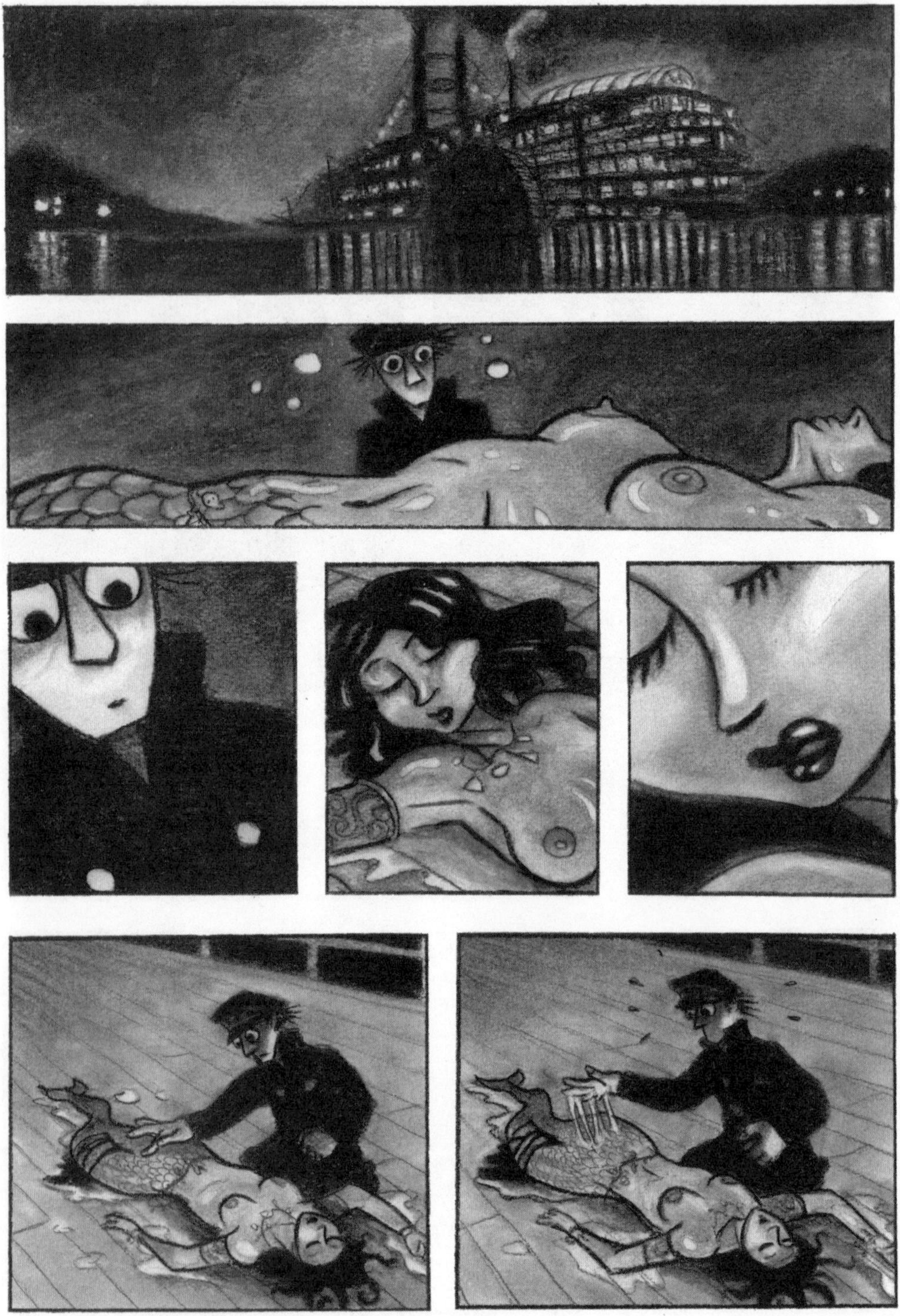

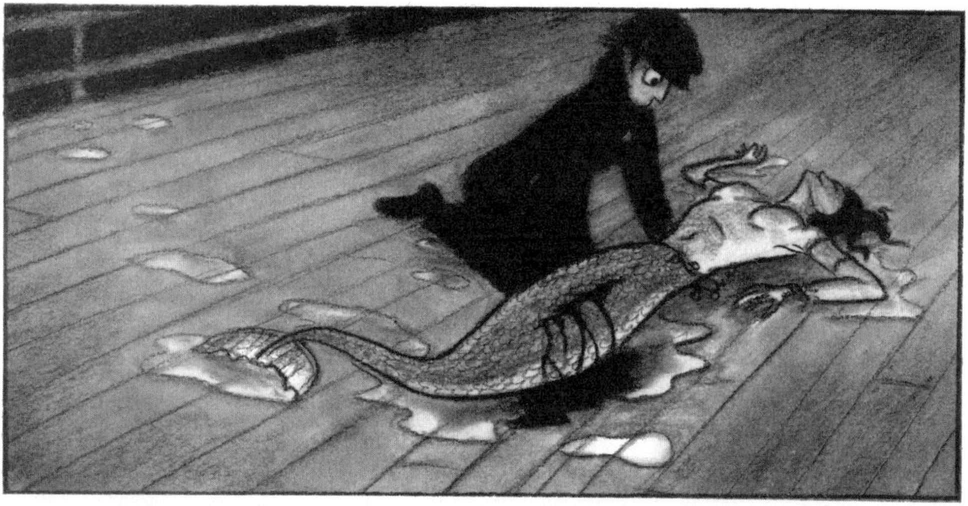

It was hurt. Maybe dying. Get the officers. Lafayette. And Doc Sycamore.

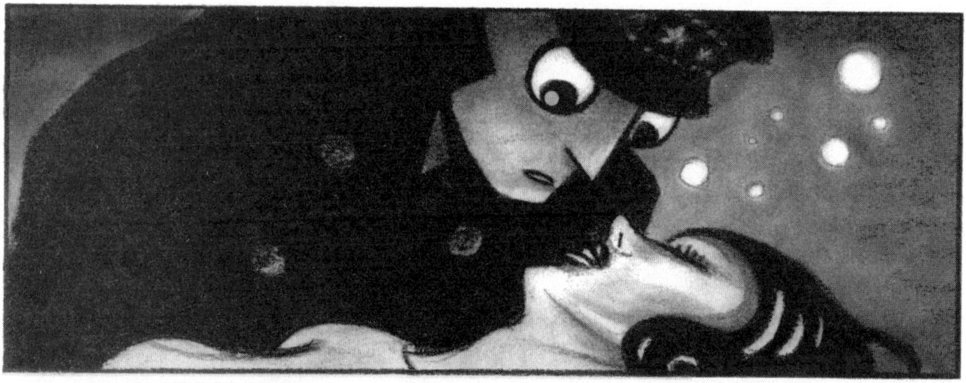

I felt dizzy and strange and a little sick. I wanted to throw the wounded thing back in the water, when suddenly—

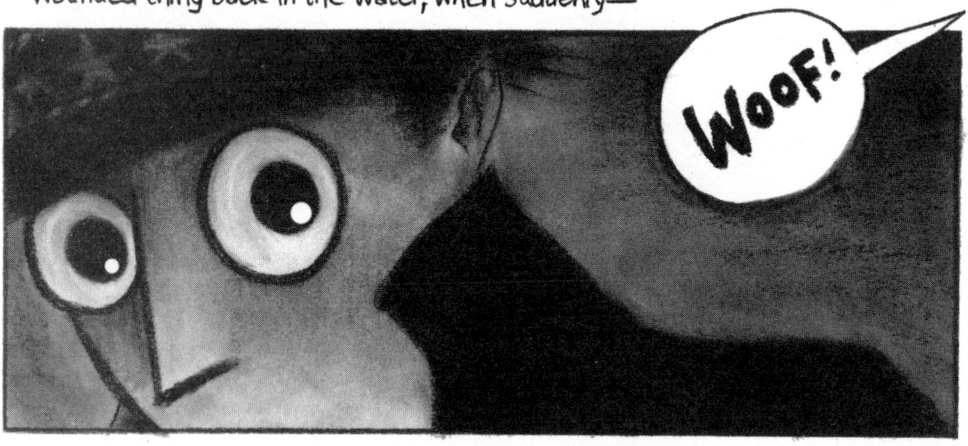
WOOF!

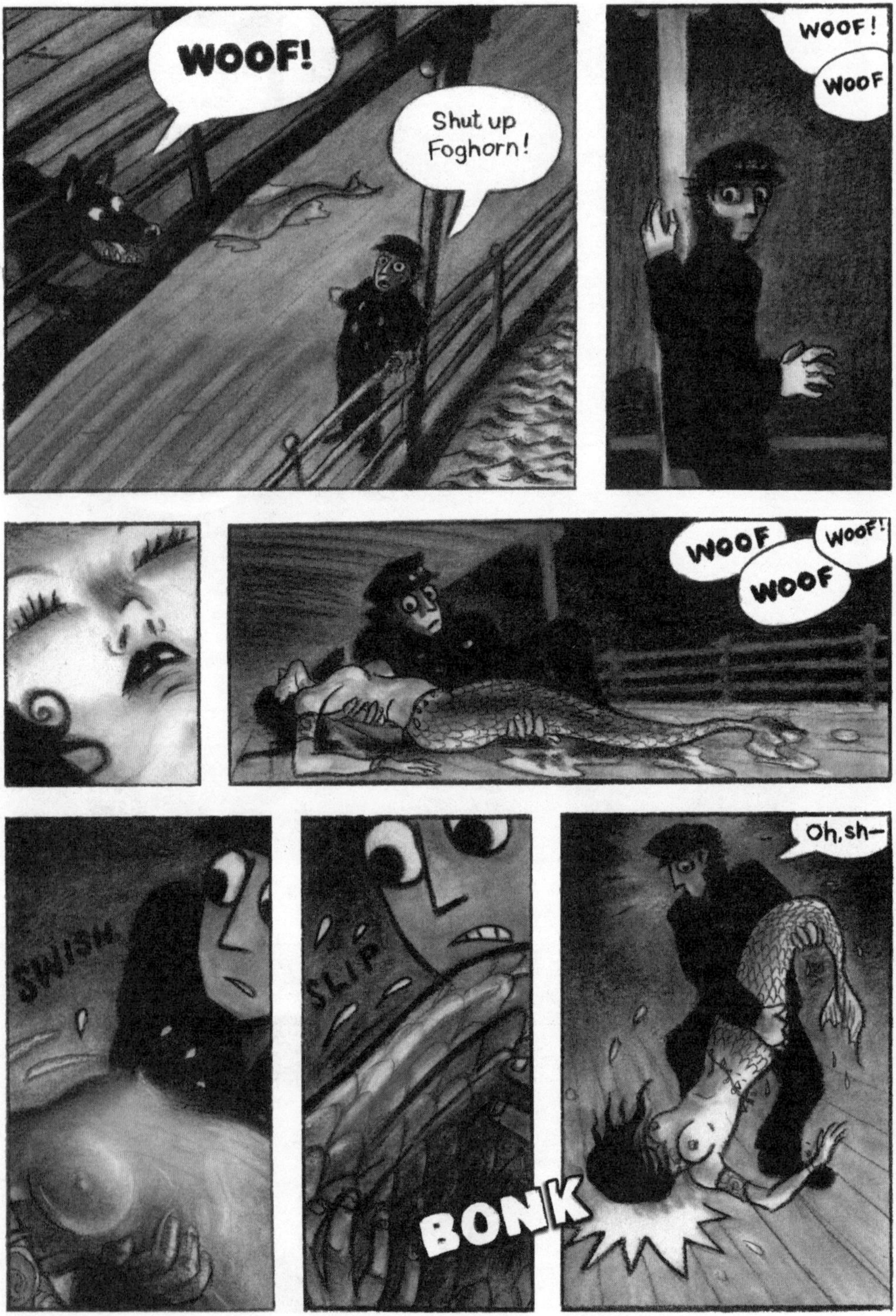
WOOF!
Shut up Foghorn!
WOOF!
WOOF
WOOF
WOOF
WOOF!
SWISH
SLIP
Oh, sh–
BONK

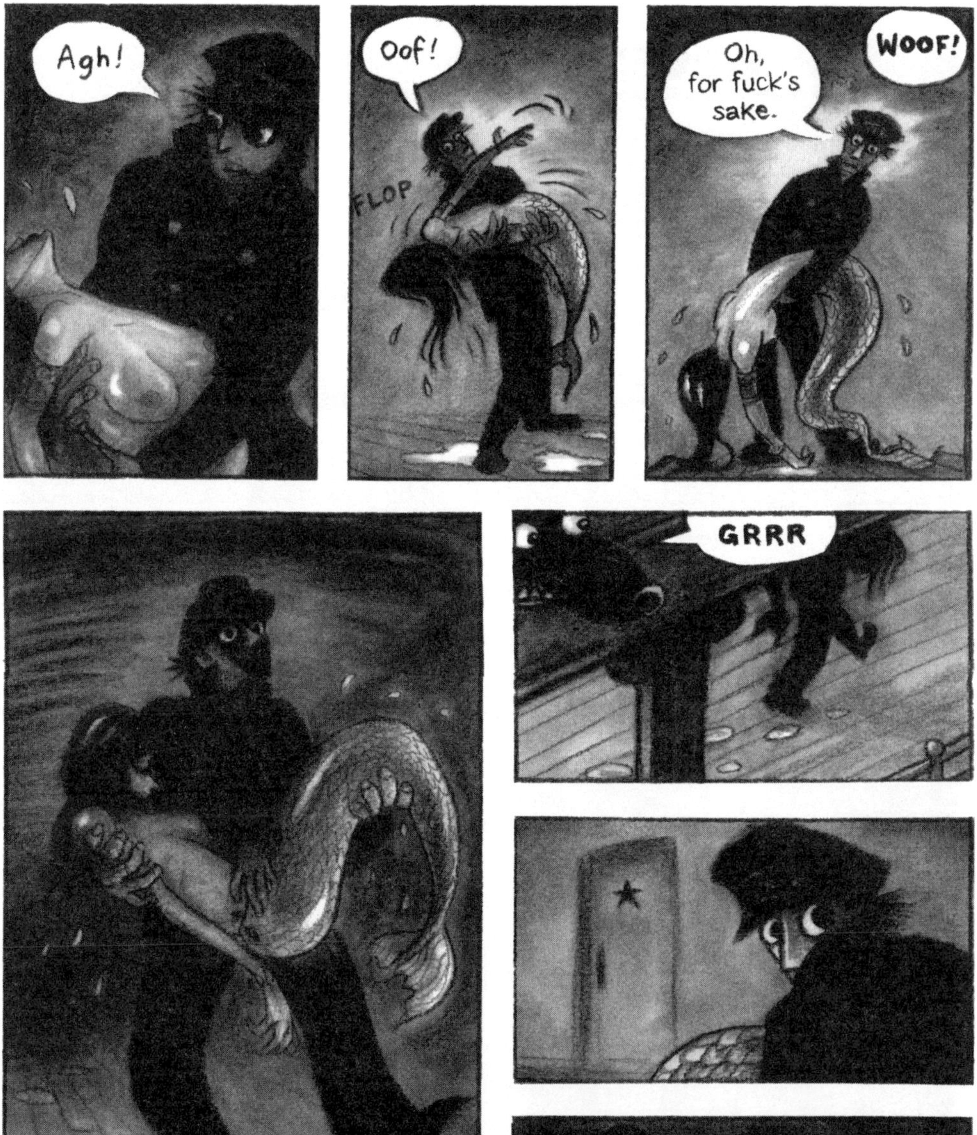
Agh!
Oof!
FLOP
Oh, for fuck's sake.
WOOF!
GRRR
BAM

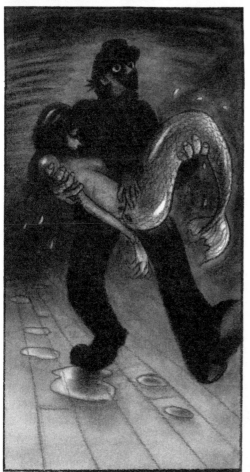

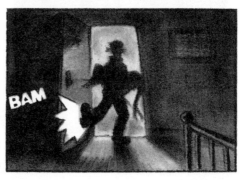

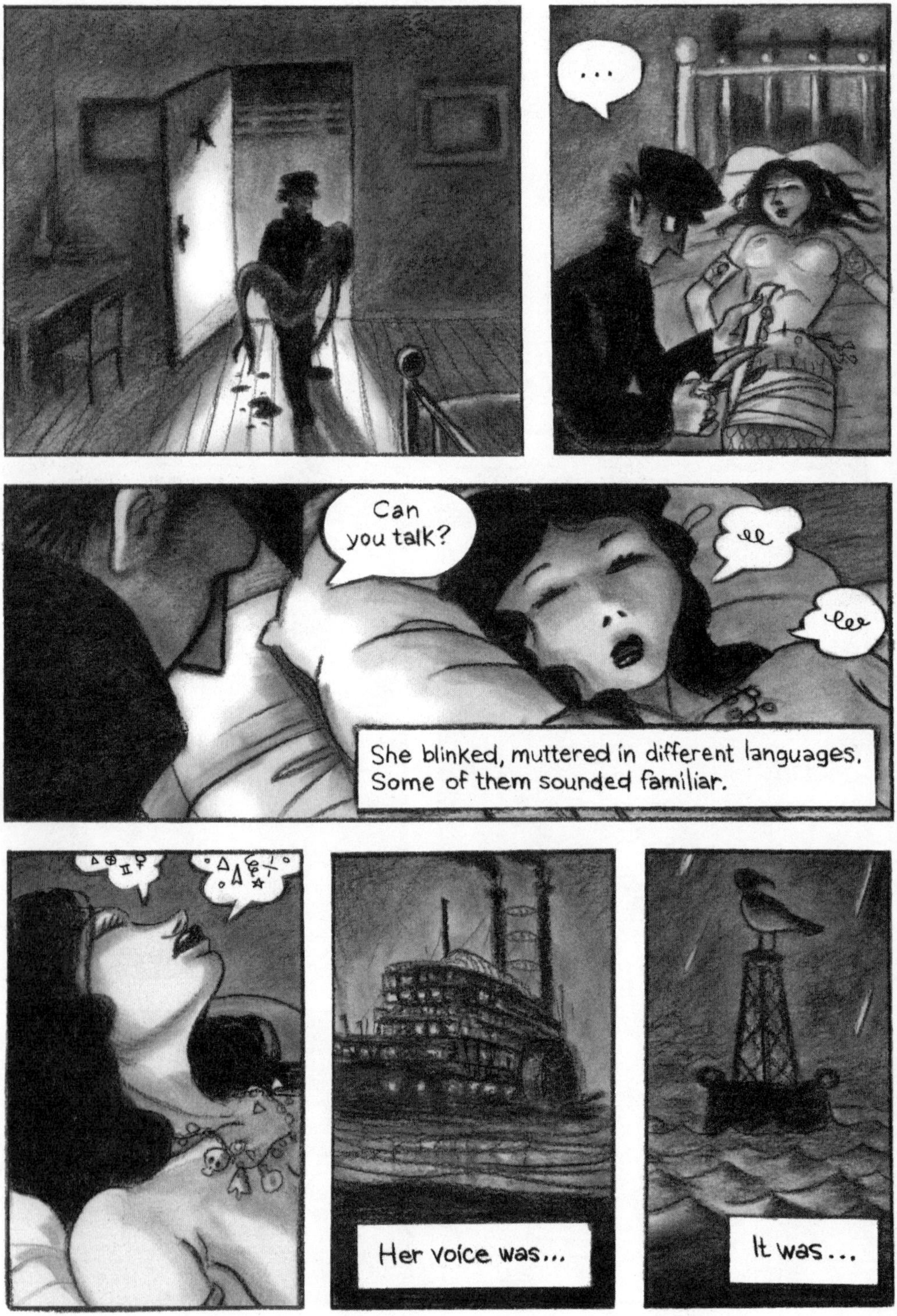
...
Can you talk?
She blinked, muttered in different languages. Some of them sounded familiar.
Her voice was...
It was...

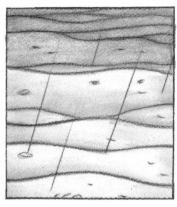

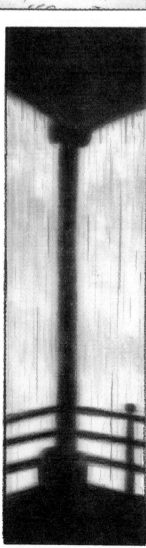

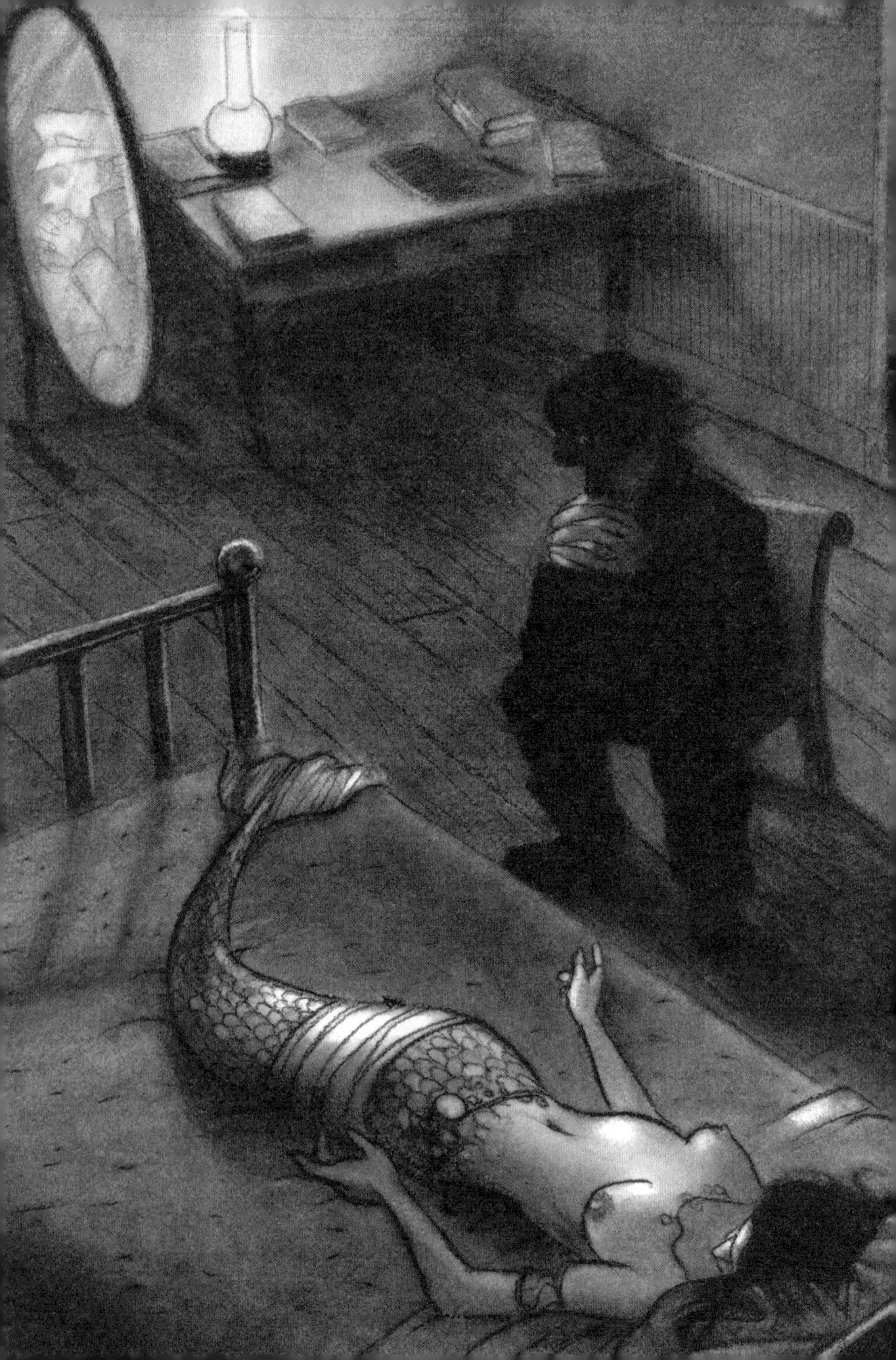

Pt I, Chap.5

"BEAVERTON'S NEW BOOK"

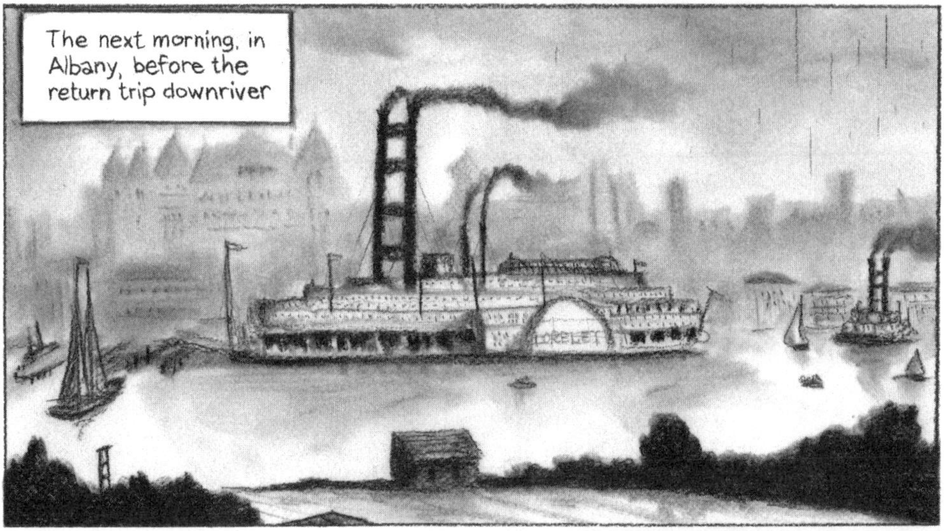
The next morning, in Albany, before the return trip downriver

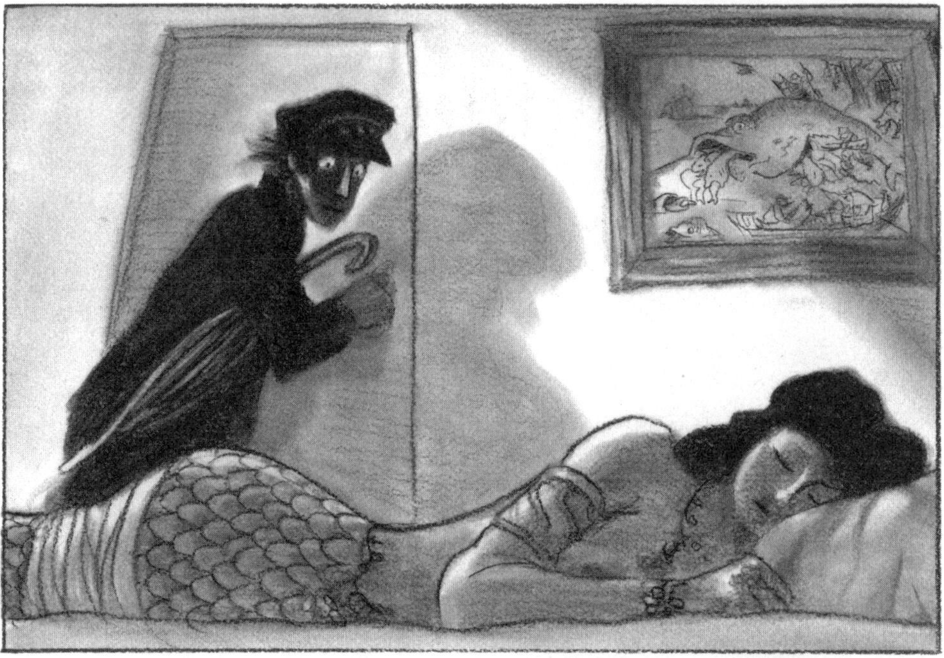

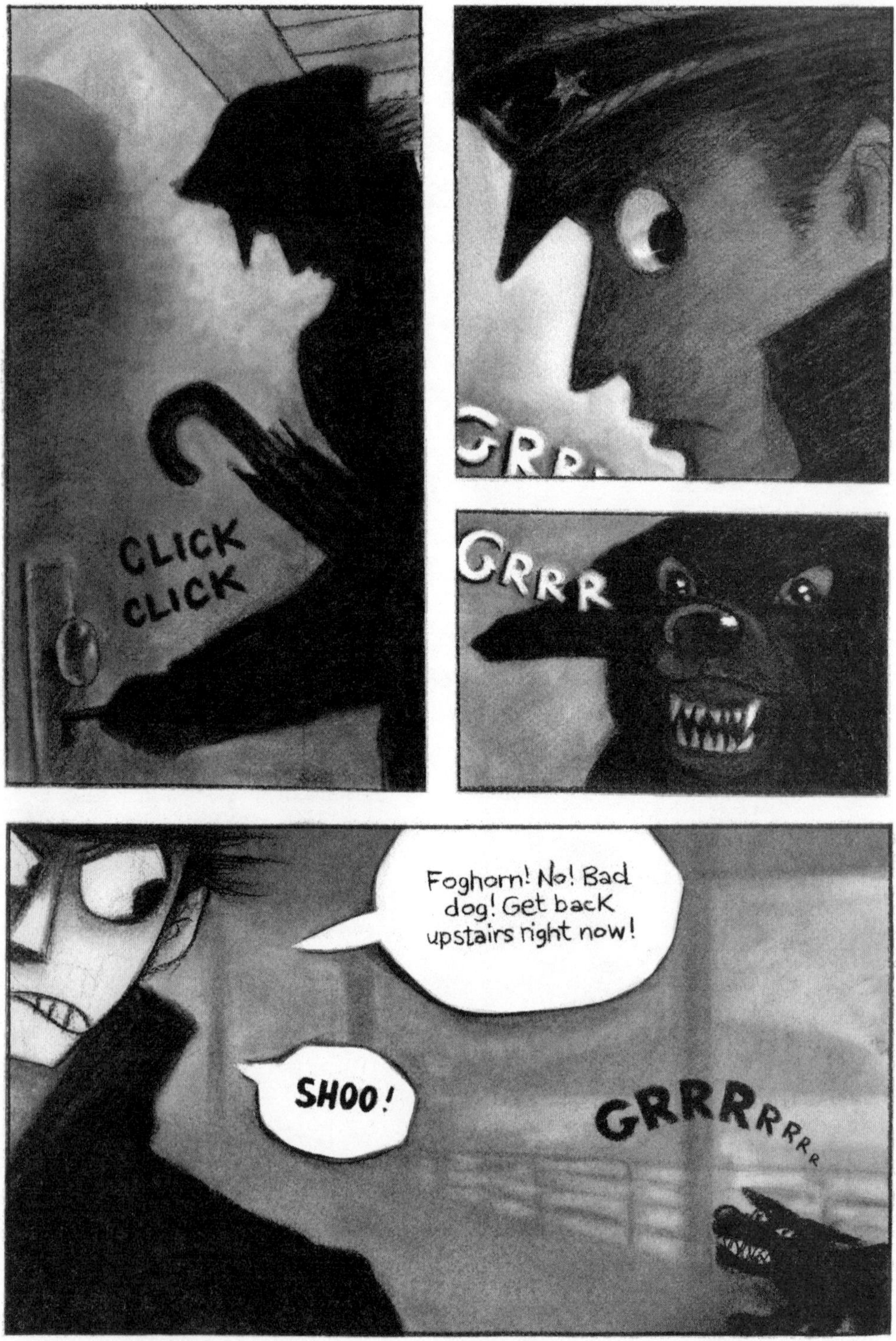
CLICK
CLICK
GRRR
GRRR
Foghorn! No! Bad dog! Get back upstairs right now!
SHOO!
GRRRRRRR

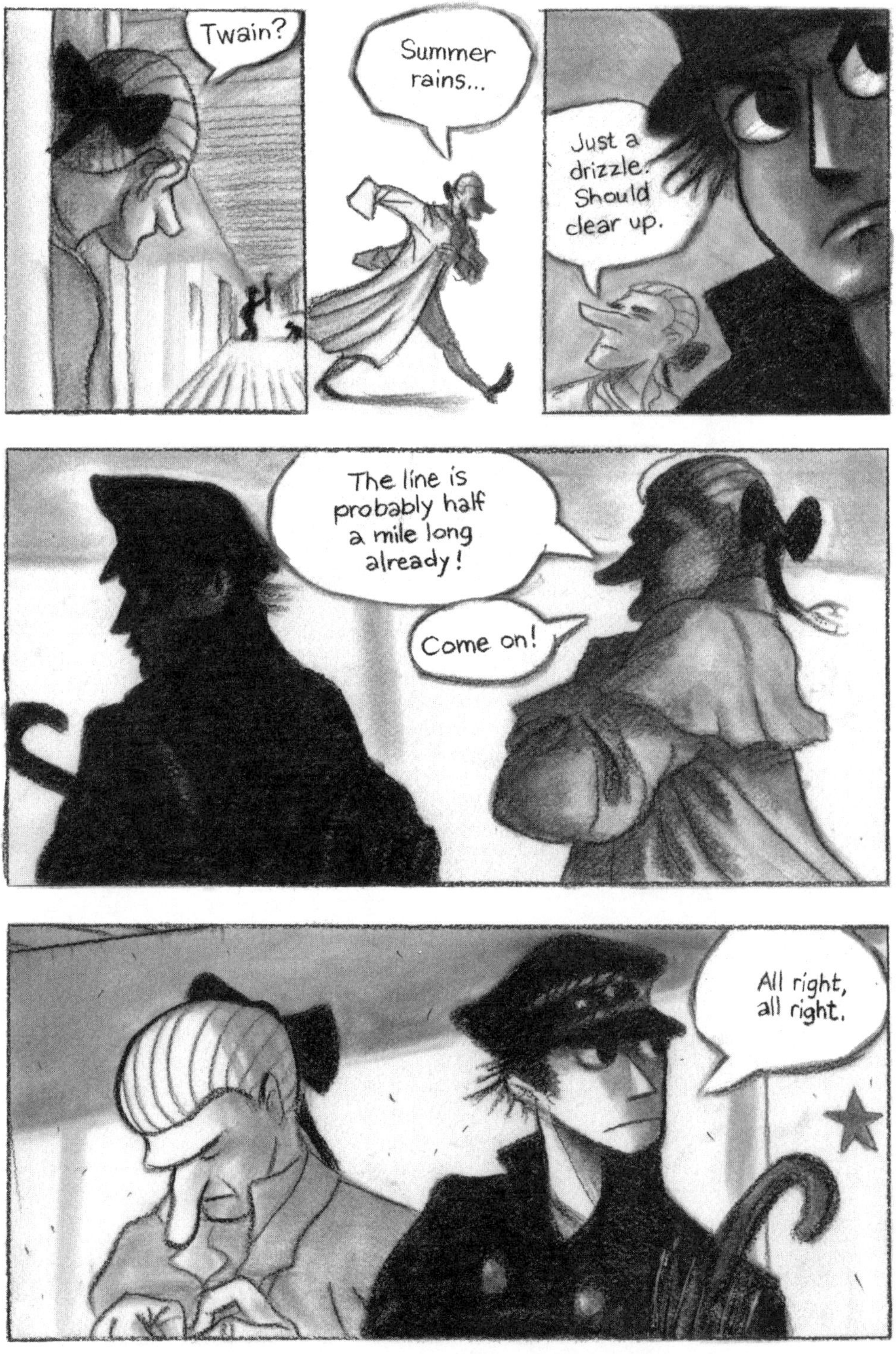
Twain?
Summer rains...
Just a drizzle. Should clear up.
The line is probably half a mile long already!
Come on!
All right, all right.

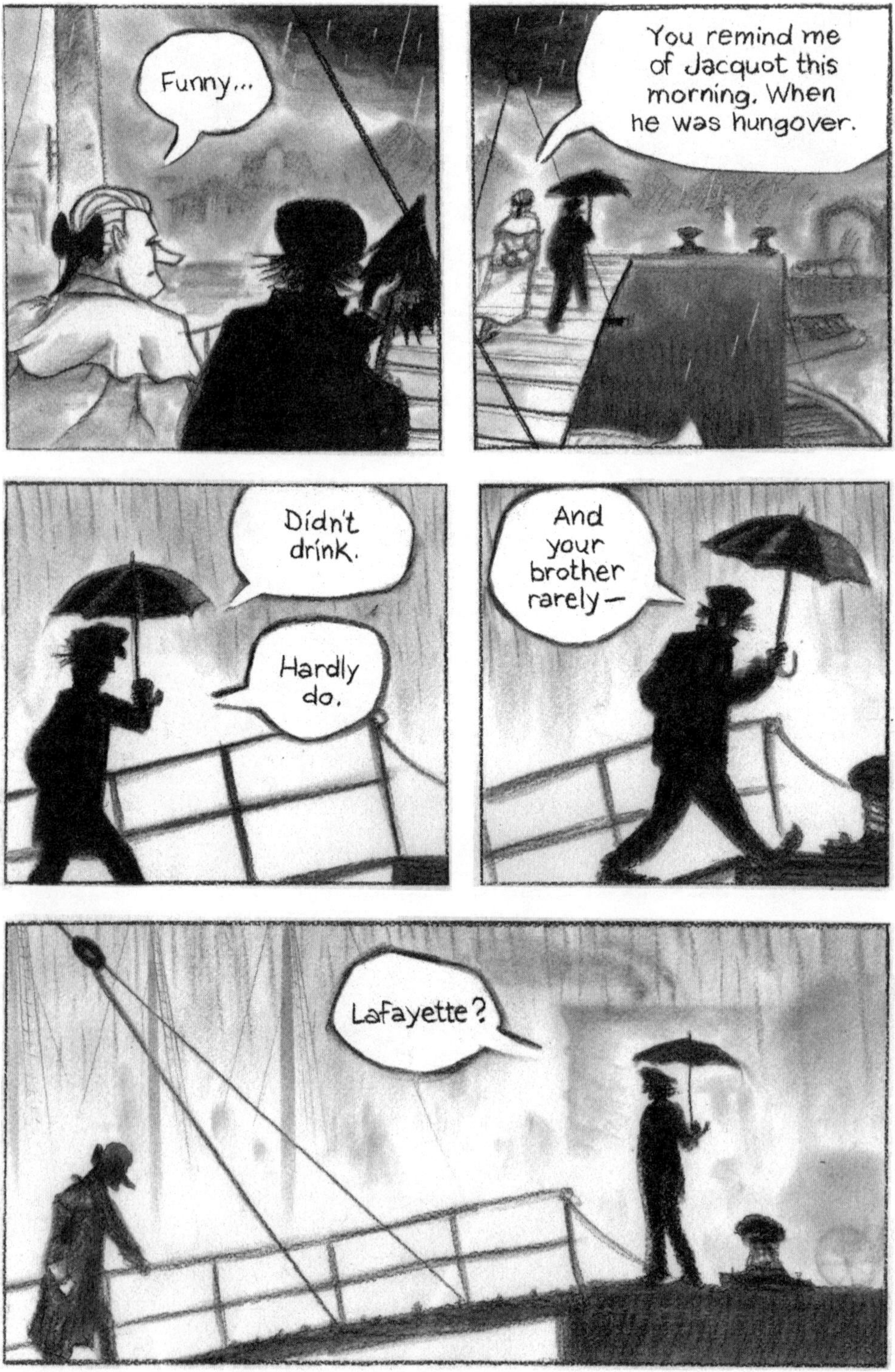
Funny...
You remind me of Jacquot this morning. When he was hungover.
Didn't drink.
Hardly do.
And your brother rarely—
Lafayette?

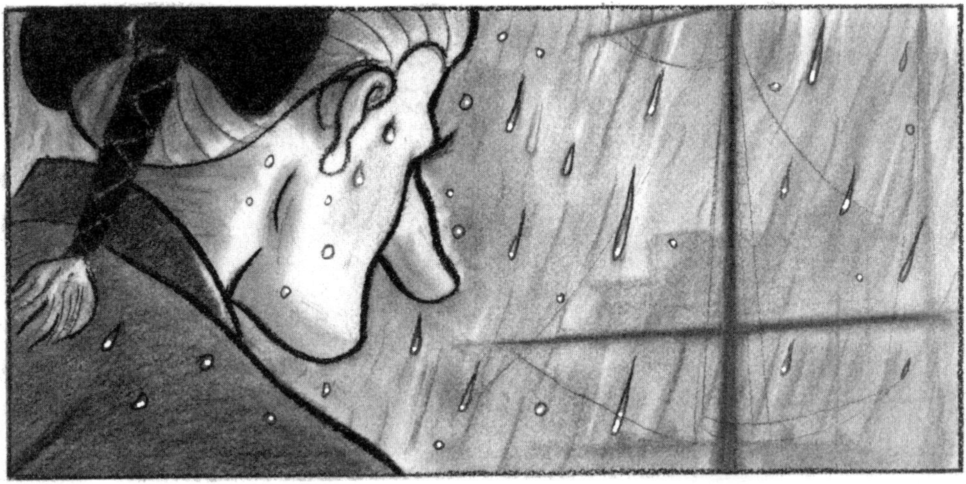

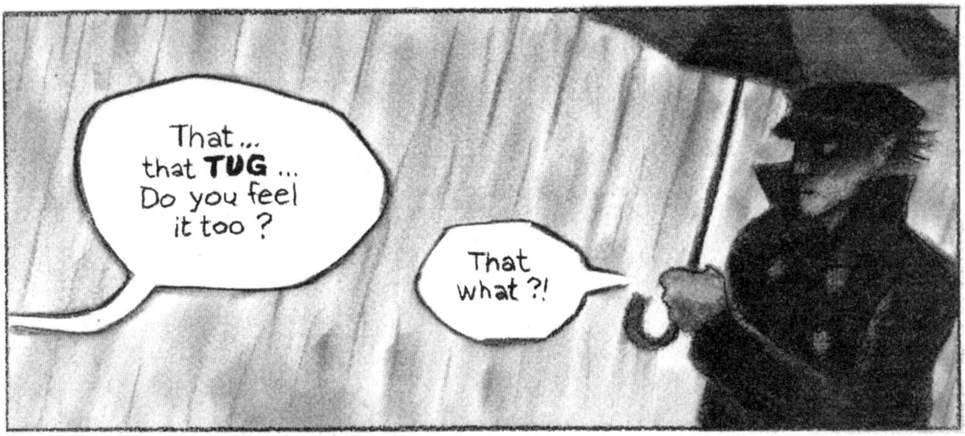
That... that **TUG** ... Do you feel it too ?
That what ?!

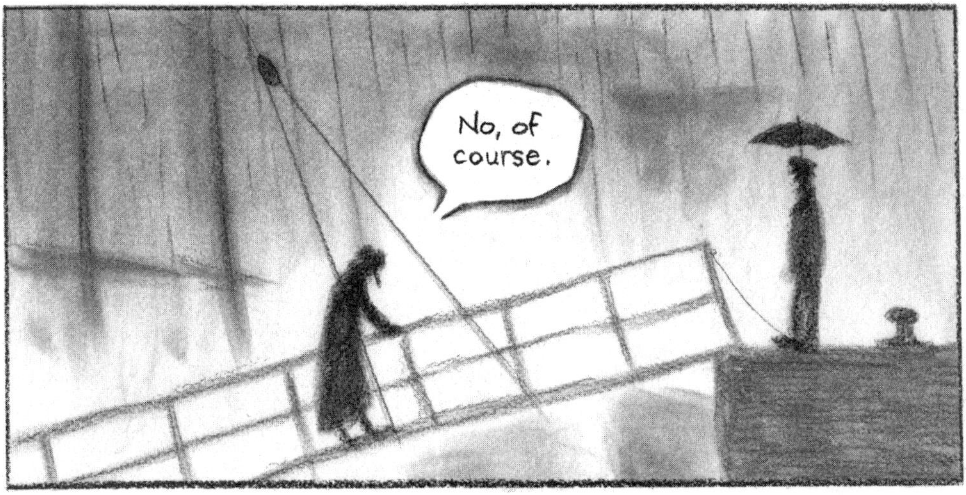
No, of course.

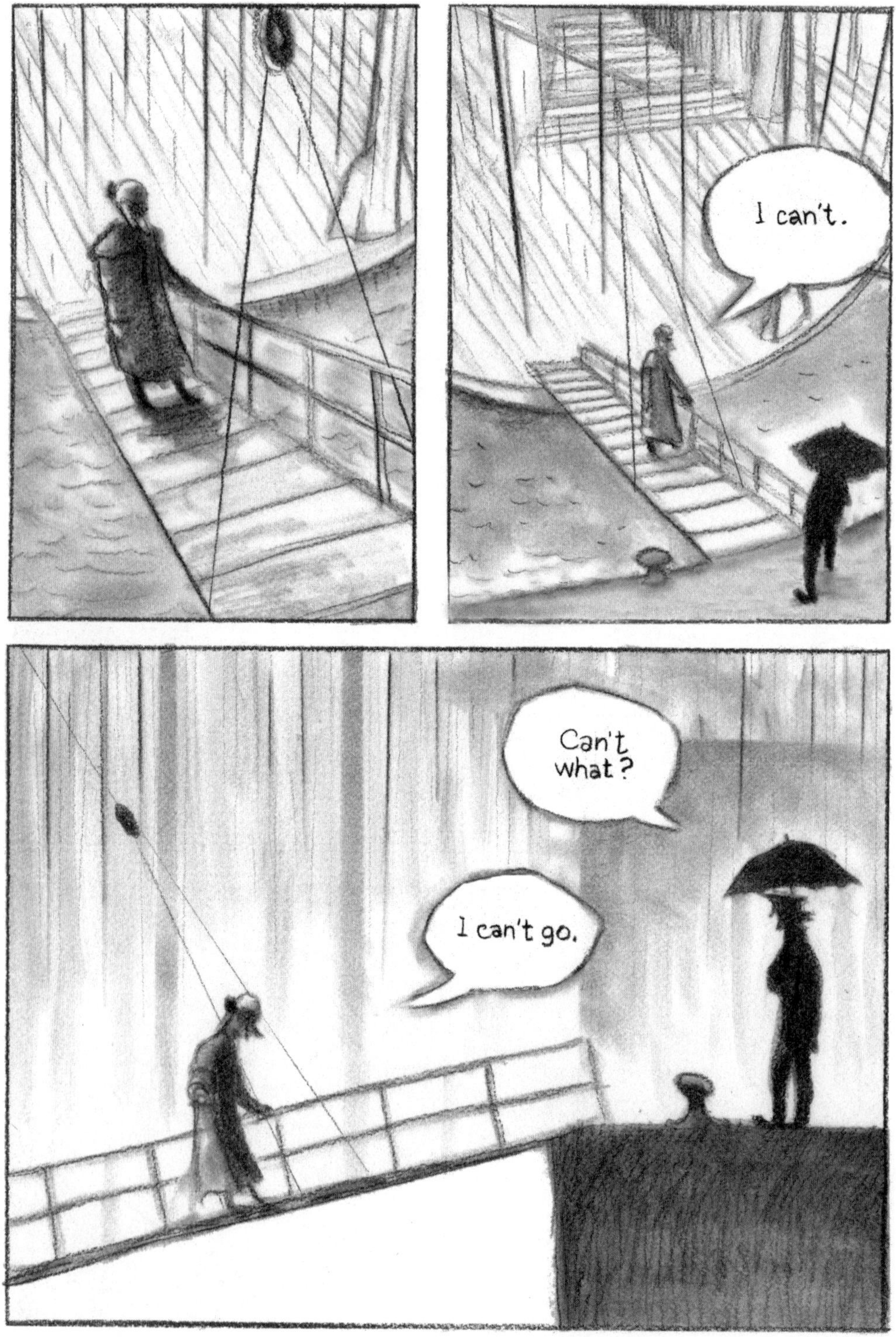
I can't.
Can't what?
I can't go.

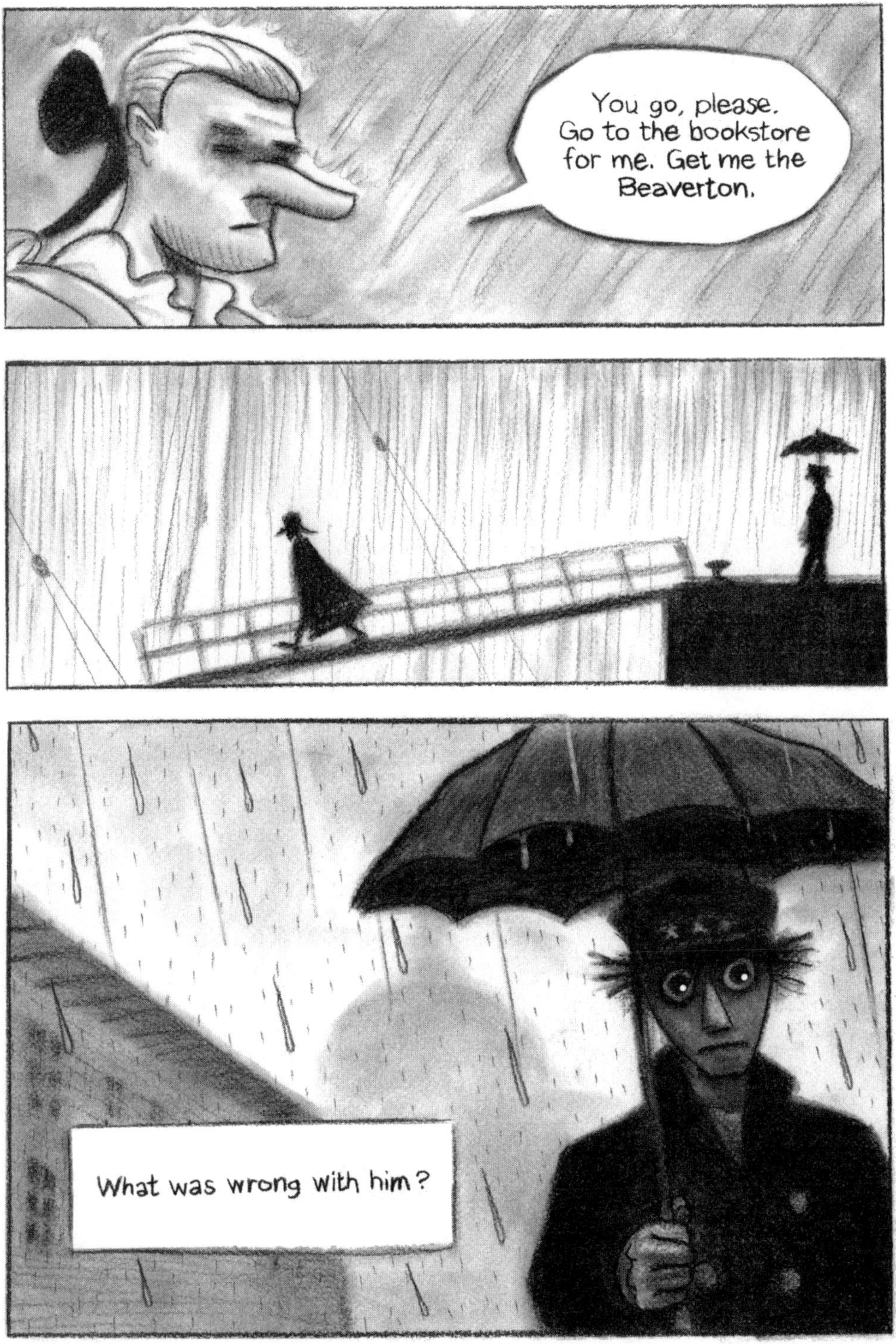
You go, please. Go to the bookstore for me. Get me the Beaverton.
What was wrong with him?

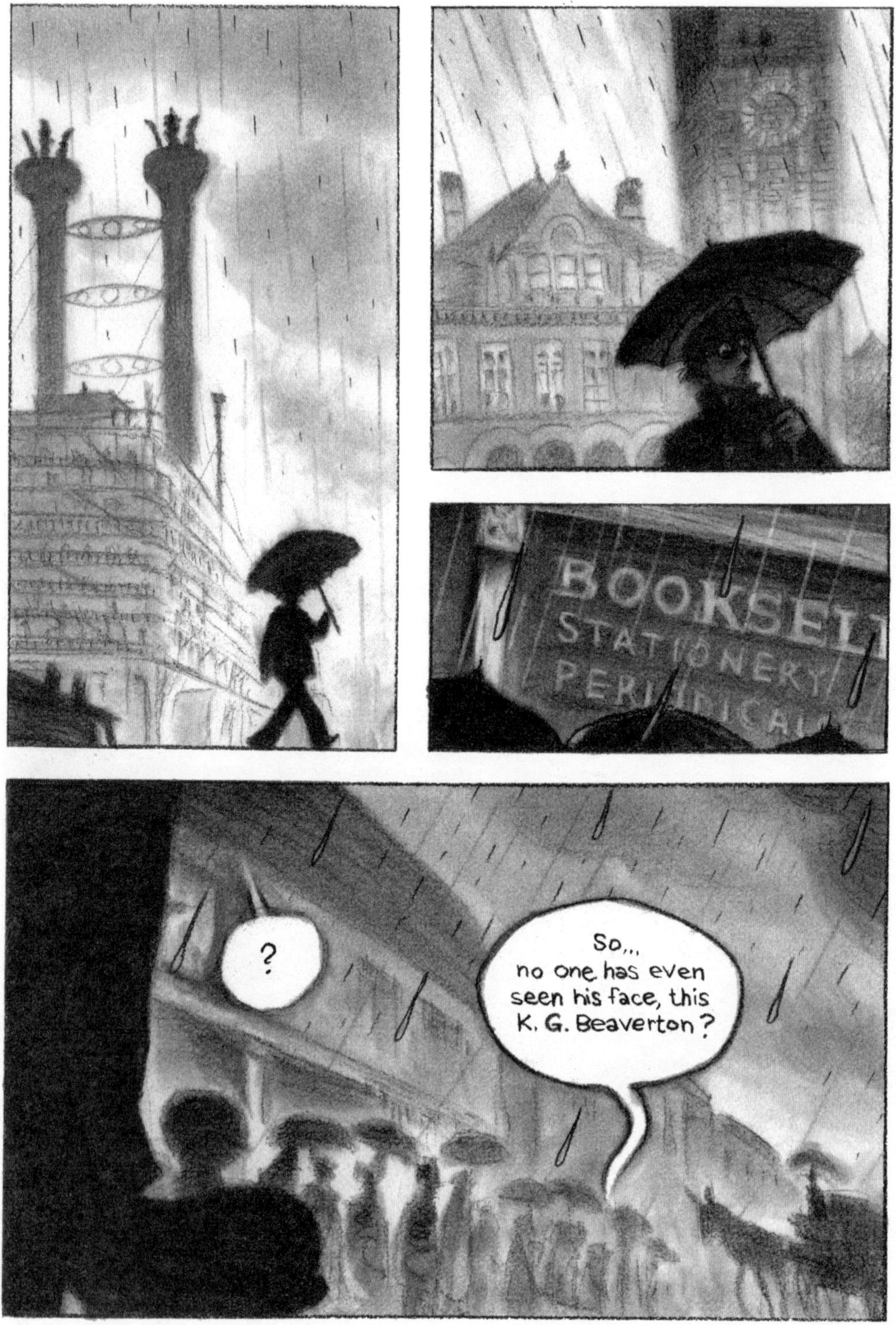
BOOKSEL
STATIONERY
?
So... no one has even seen his face, this K. G. Beaverton?

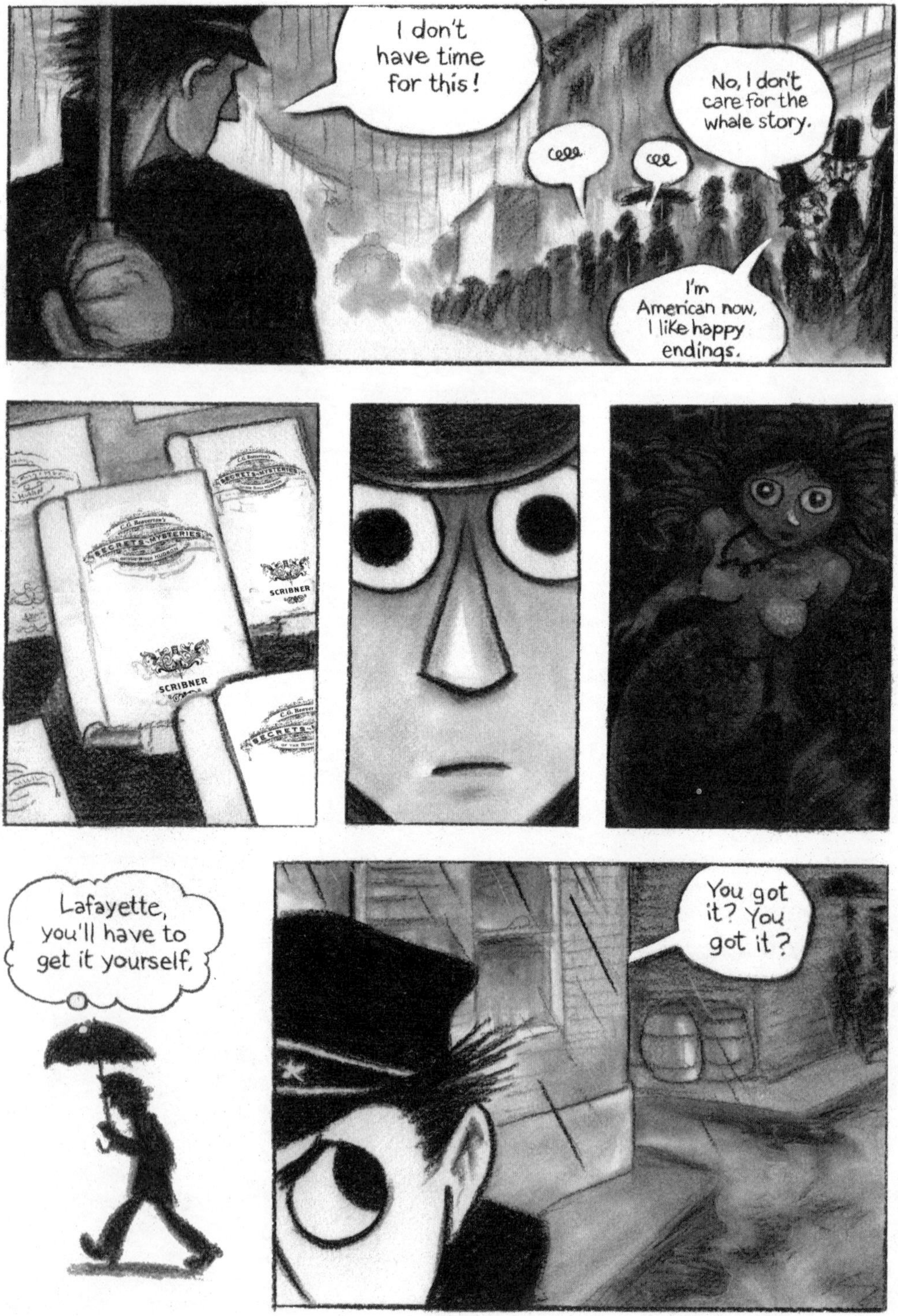
I don't have time for this!
No, I don't care for the whale story.
I'm American now, I like happy endings.
SCRIBNER
SCRIBNER
Lafayette, you'll have to get it yourself.
You got it? You got it?

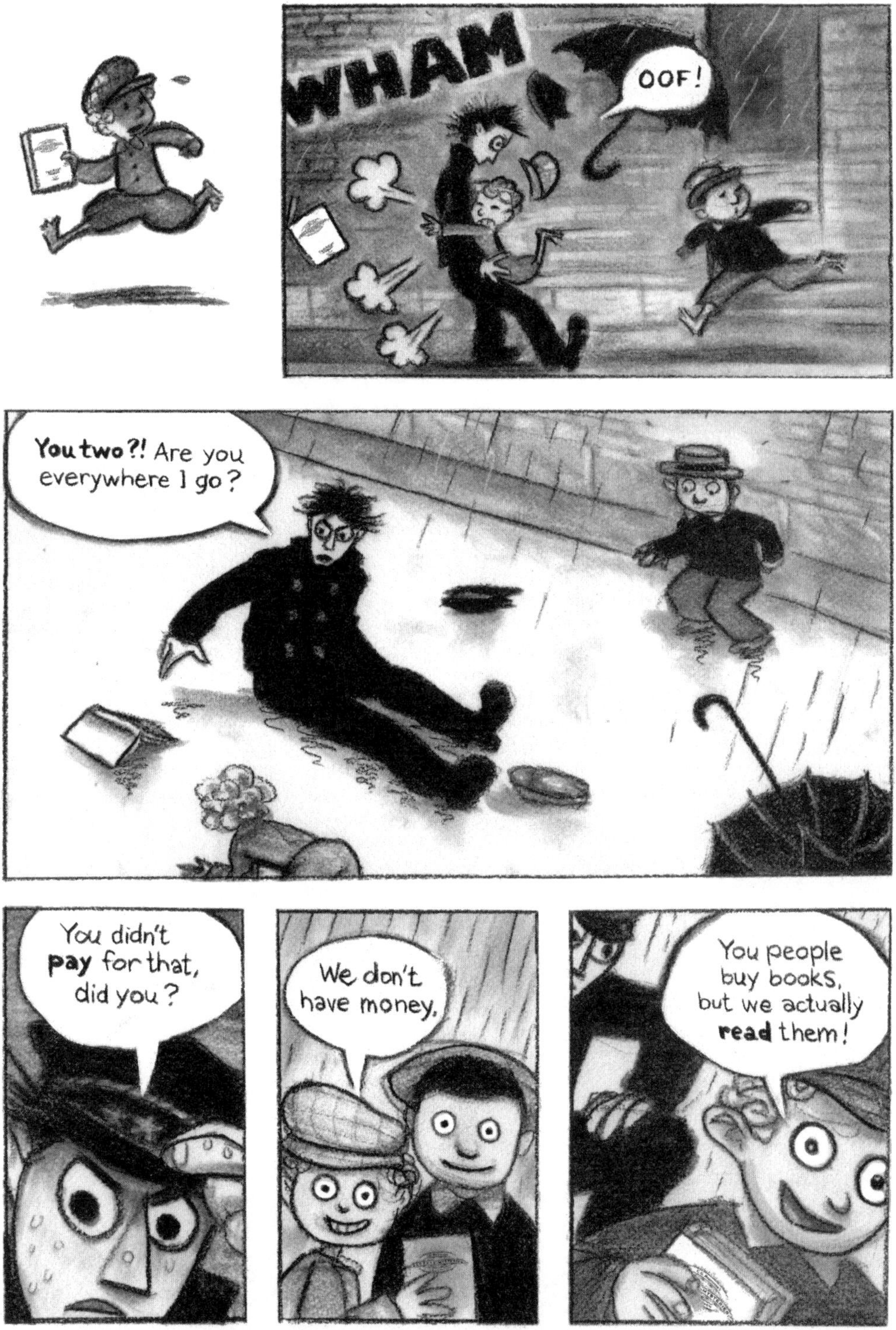
WHAM
OOF!
You two?! Are you everywhere I go?
You didn't pay for that, did you?
We don't have money,
You people buy books, but we actually read them!

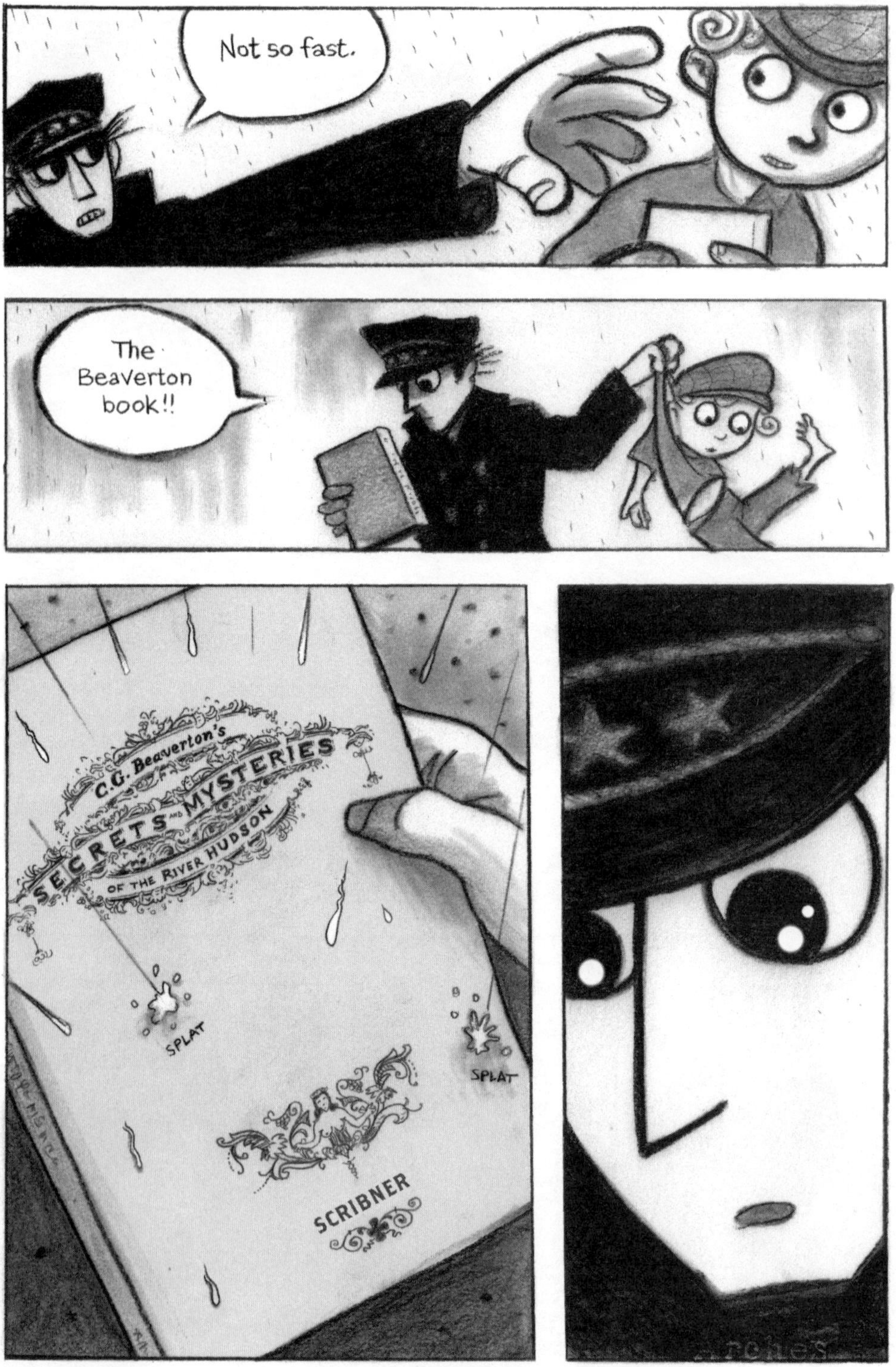
Not so fast.
The Beaverton book!!
C.G. Beaverton's
SECRETS AND MYSTERIES
OF THE RIVER HUDSON
SPLAT
SPLAT
SCRIBNER

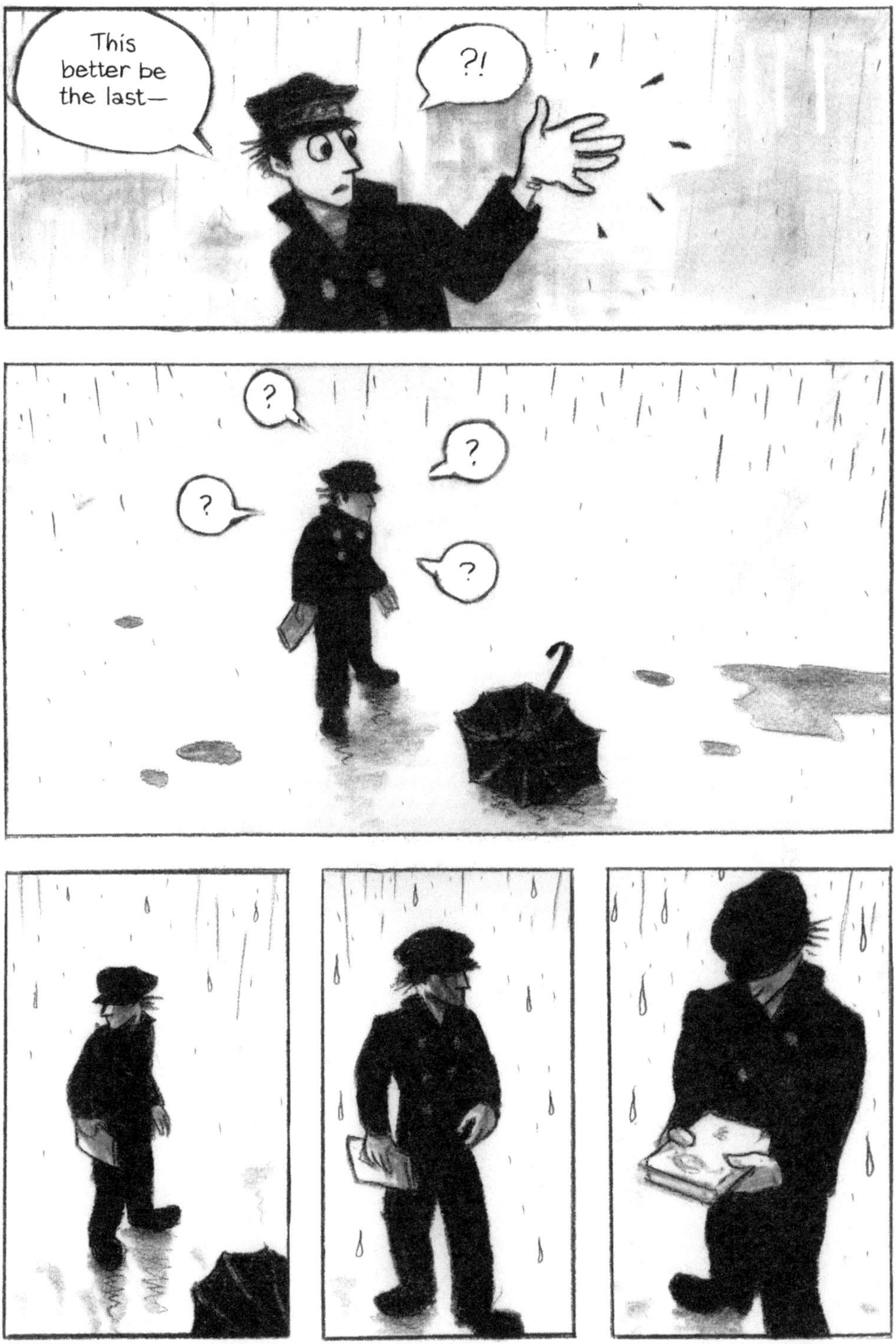
This better be the last—
?!
?
?
?
?

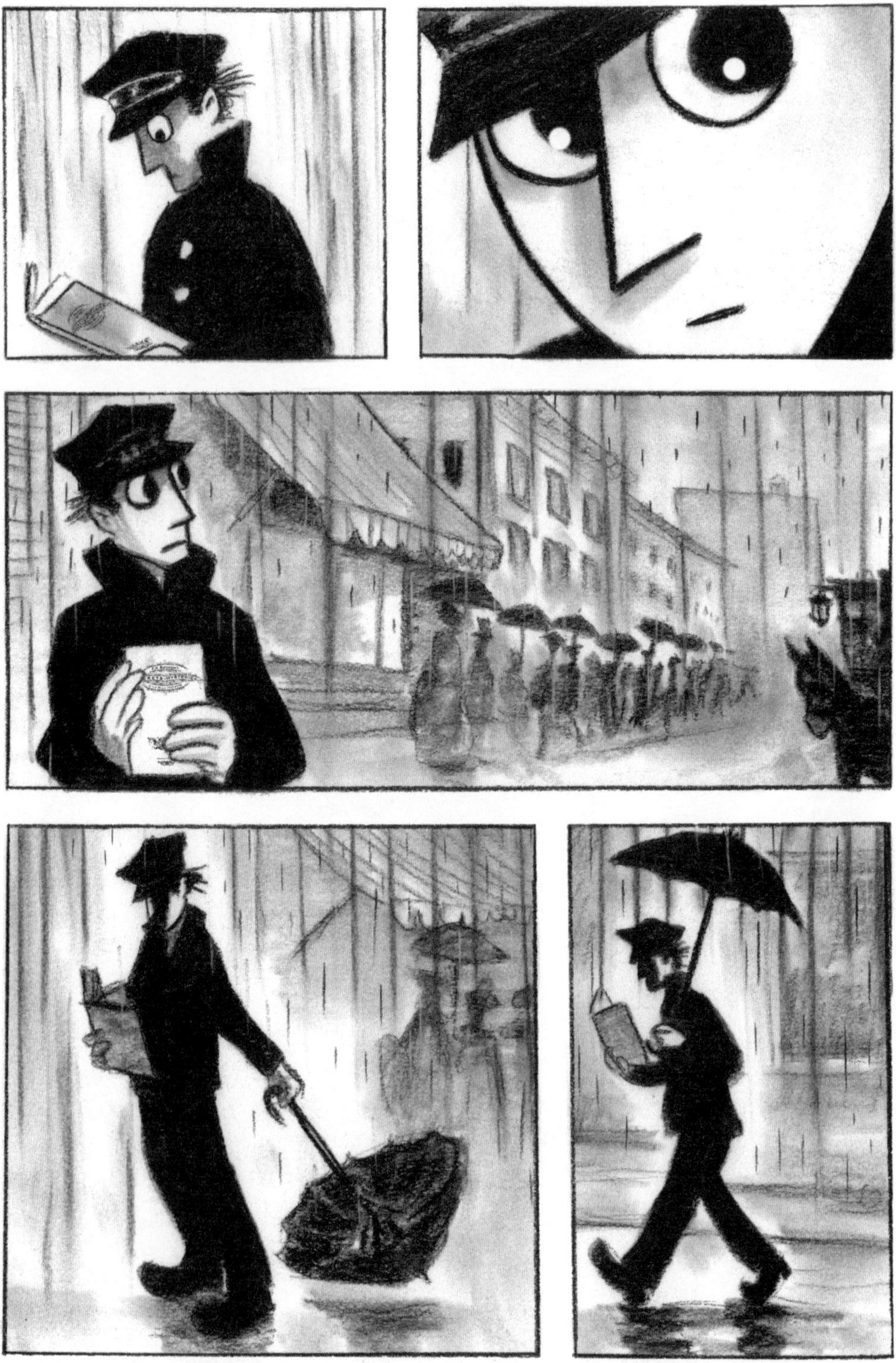

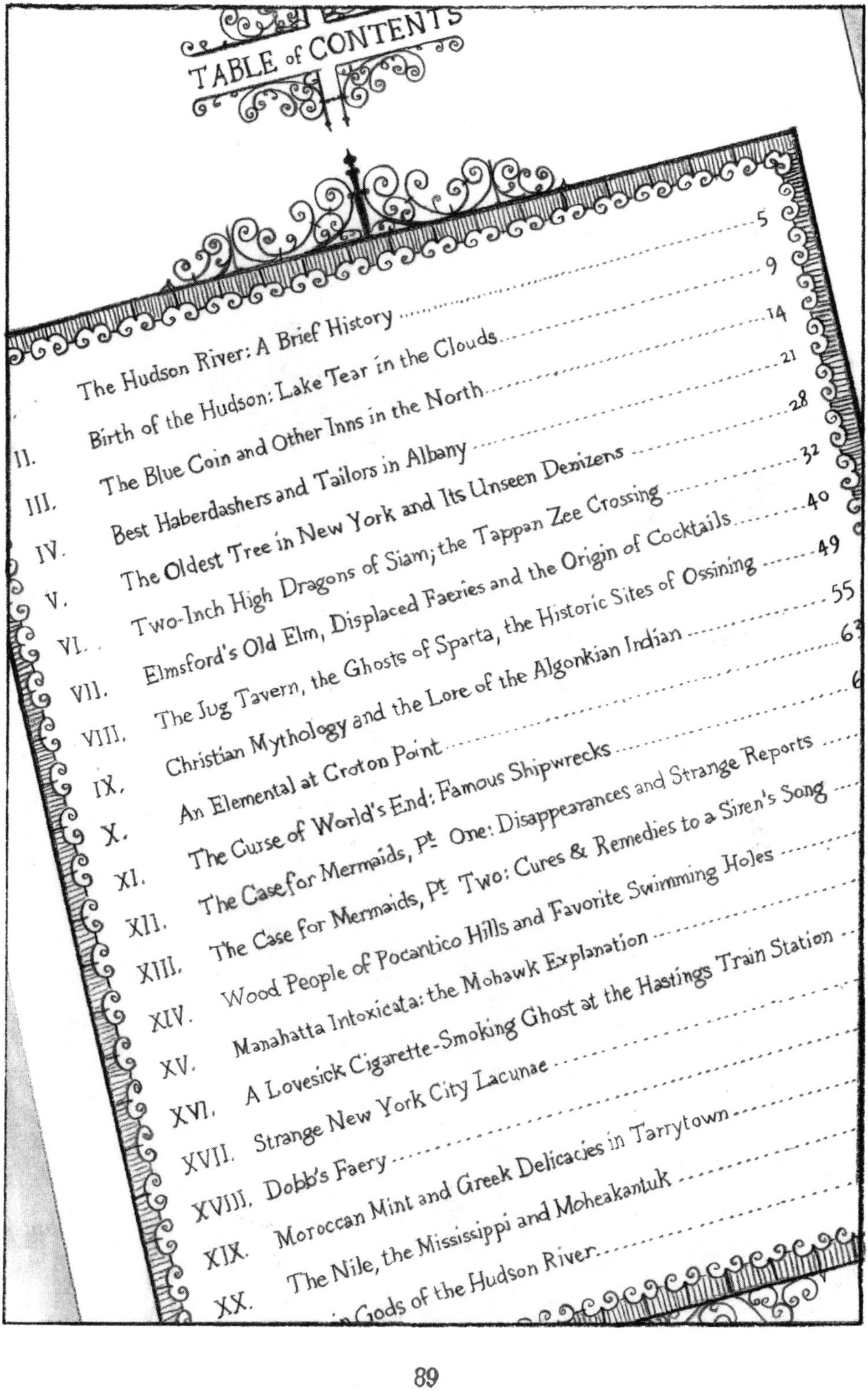

TABLE of CONTENTS

The Hudson River: A Brief History 5

Birth of the Hudson: Lake Tear in the Clouds 9

II. The Blue Coin and Other Inns in the North 14

III. Best Haberdashers and Tailors in Albany 21

IV. The Oldest Tree in New York and Its Unseen Denizens 28

V. Two-Inch High Dragons of Siam; the Tappan Zee Crossing 32

VI. Elmsford's Old Elm, Displaced Faeries and the Origin of Cocktails 40

VII. The Jug Tavern, the Ghosts of Sparta, the Historic Sites of Ossining 49

VIII. Christian Mythology and the Lore of the Algonkian Indian 55

IX. An Elemental at Croton Point 63

X. The Curse of World's End; Famous Shipwrecks 6

XI. The Case for Mermaids, Pt. One: Disappearances and Strange Reports ...

XII. The Case for Mermaids, Pt. Two: Cures & Remedies to a Siren's Song ...

XIII. Wood People of Pocantico Hills and Favorite Swimming Holes ...

XIV. Manahatta Intoxicata: the Mohawk Explanation ...

XV. A Lovesick Cigarette-Smoking Ghost at the Hastings Train Station ...

XVI. Strange New York City Lacunae ...

XVII. Dobb's Faery ...

XVIII. Moroccan Mint and Greek Delicacies in Tarrytown ...

XIX. The Nile, the Mississippi and Moheakantuk ...

XX. Gods of the Hudson River ...

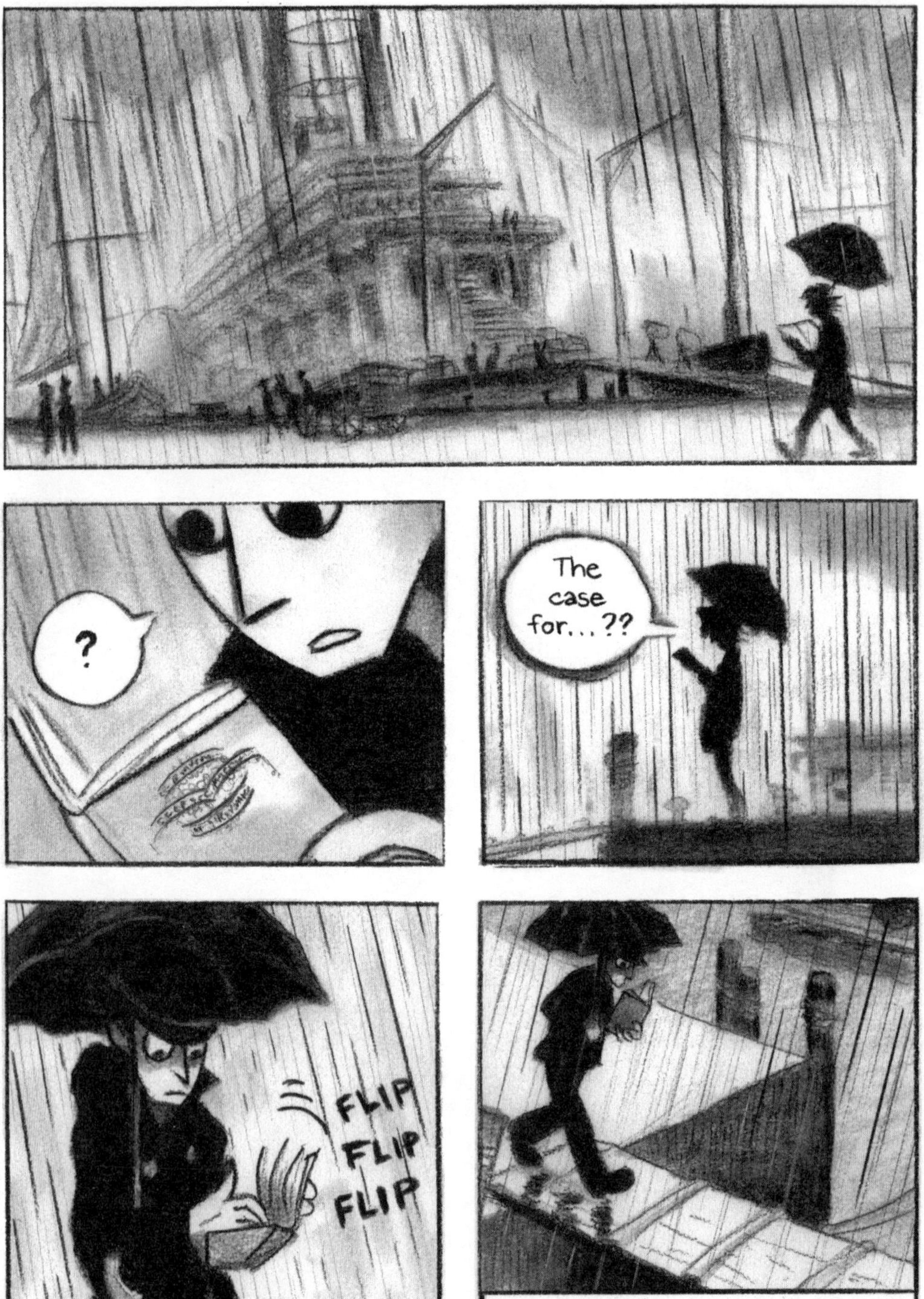
?
The case for...??
FLIP
FLIP
FLIP
Why did Lafayette want this book?

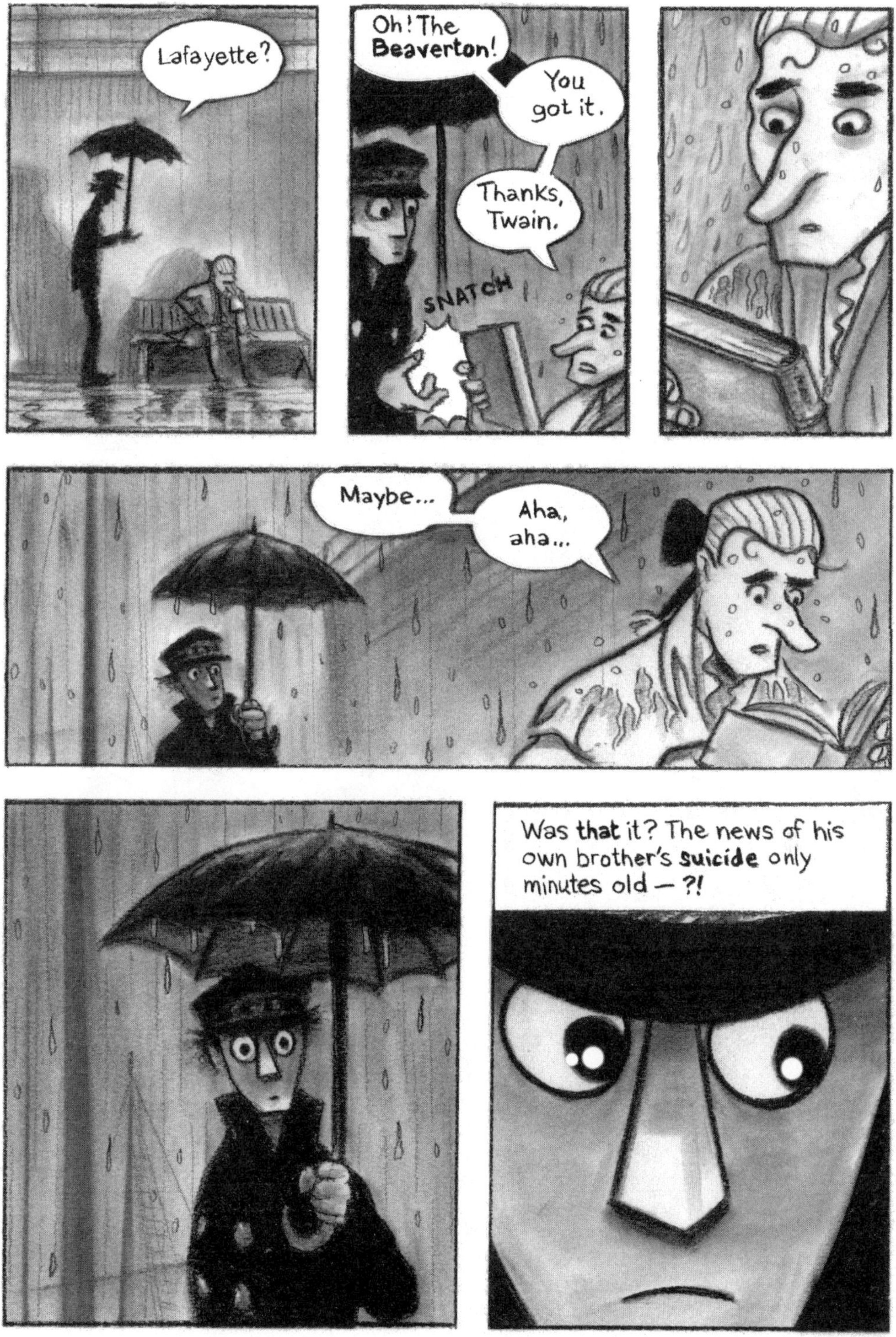

Lafayette?
Oh! The **Beaverton**!
You got it.
Thanks, Twain.
SNATCH
Maybe...
Aha, aha...
Was **that** it? The news of his own brother's **suicide** only minutes old — ?!

94

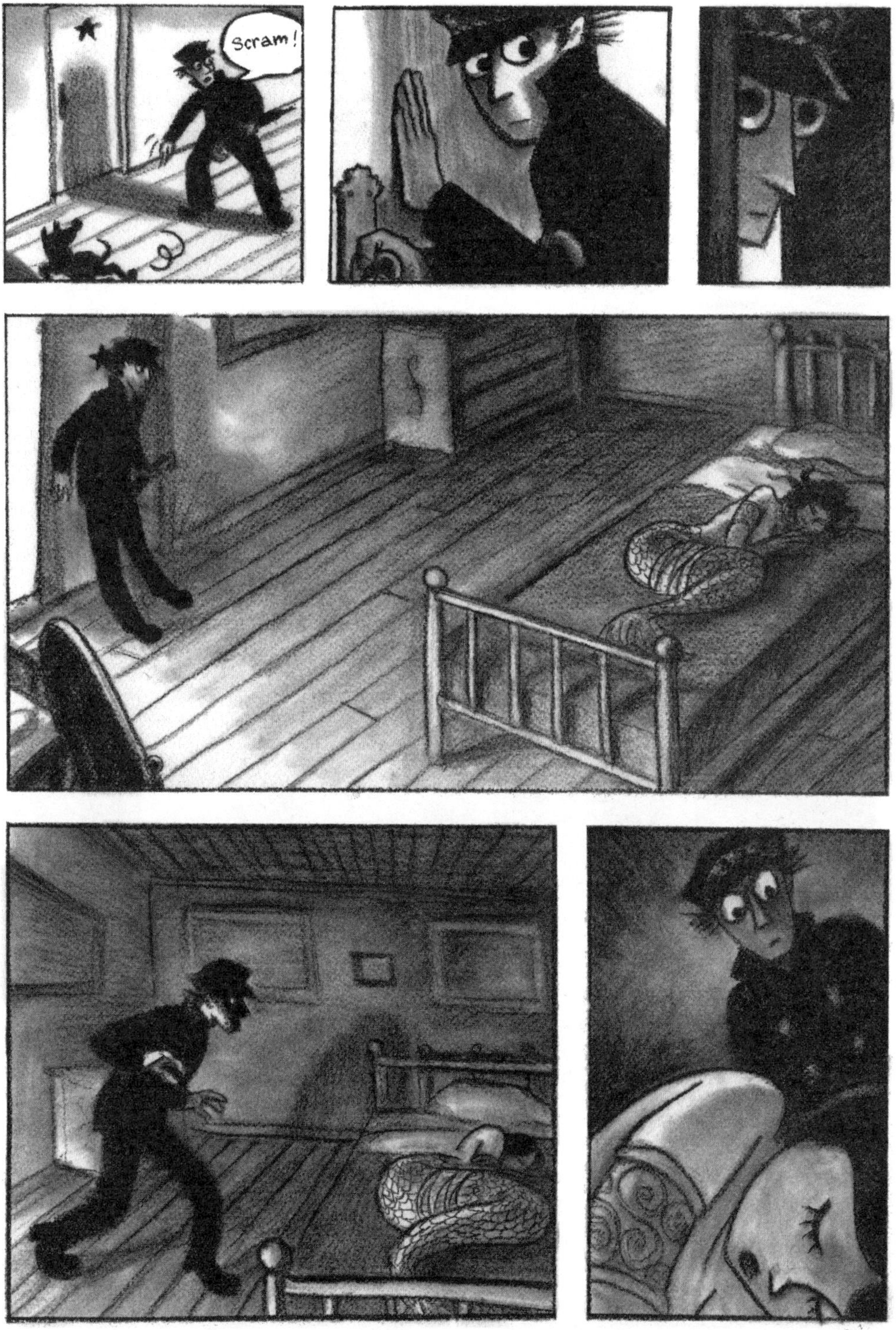
Scram!

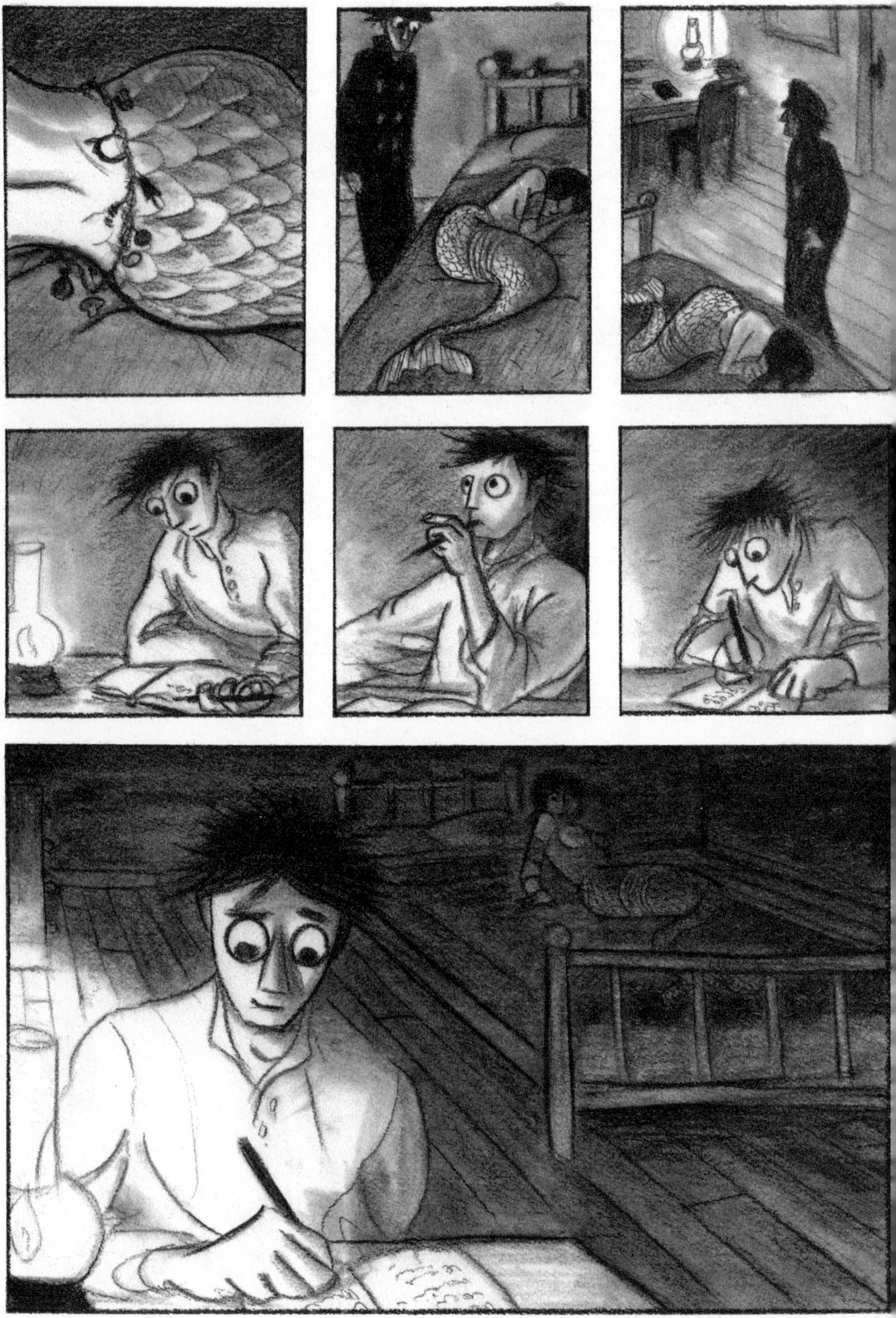

Pt 1, Chap.6

"LAFAYETTE'S LETTER"

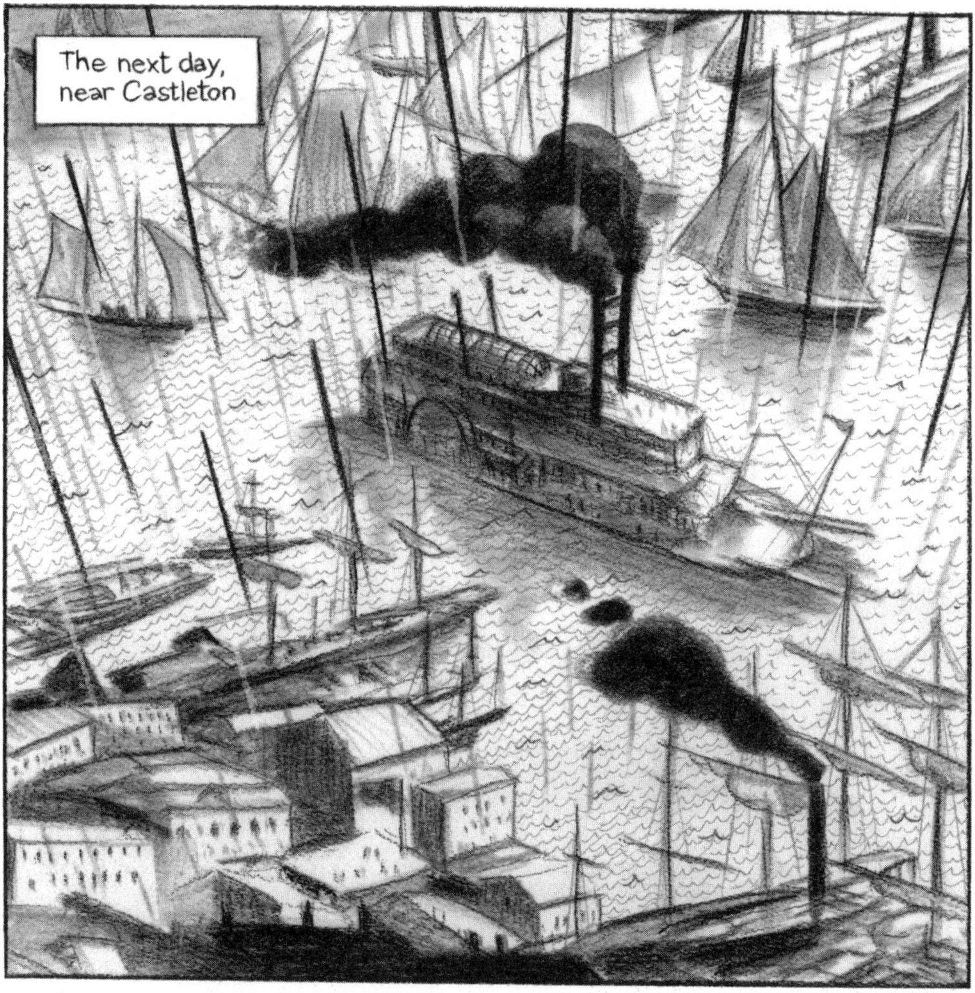
The next day,
near Castleton

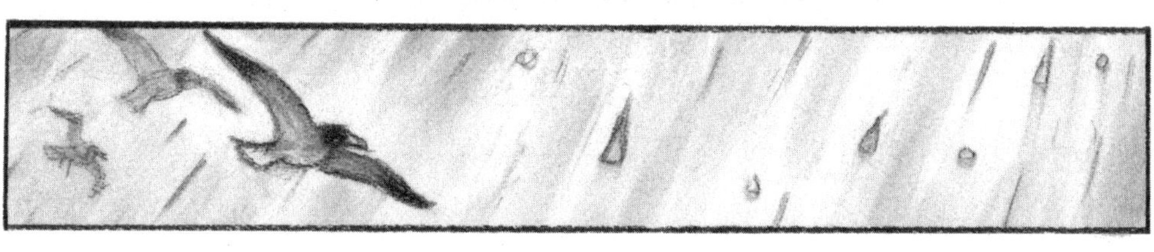

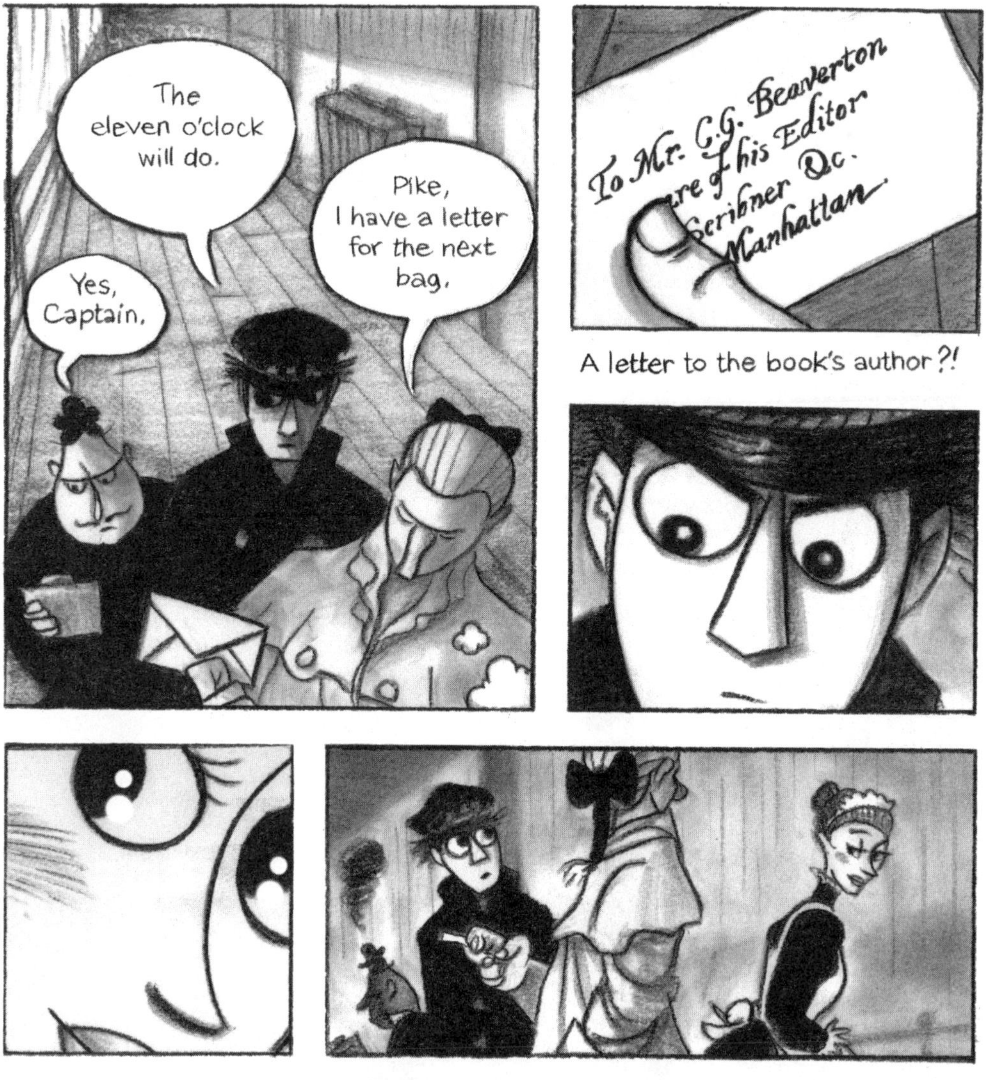
The eleven o'clock will do.
Yes, Captain.
Pike, I have a letter for the next bag.
To Mr. C.G. Beaverton
are of his Editor
Scribner Co.
Manhattan
A letter to the book's author?!
That Valerie! Edible, isn't she?
?
And here's the juicy Celia!

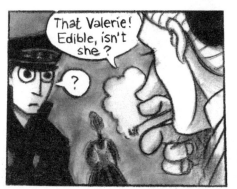

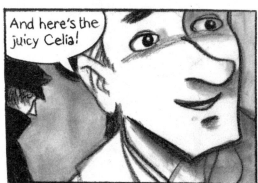

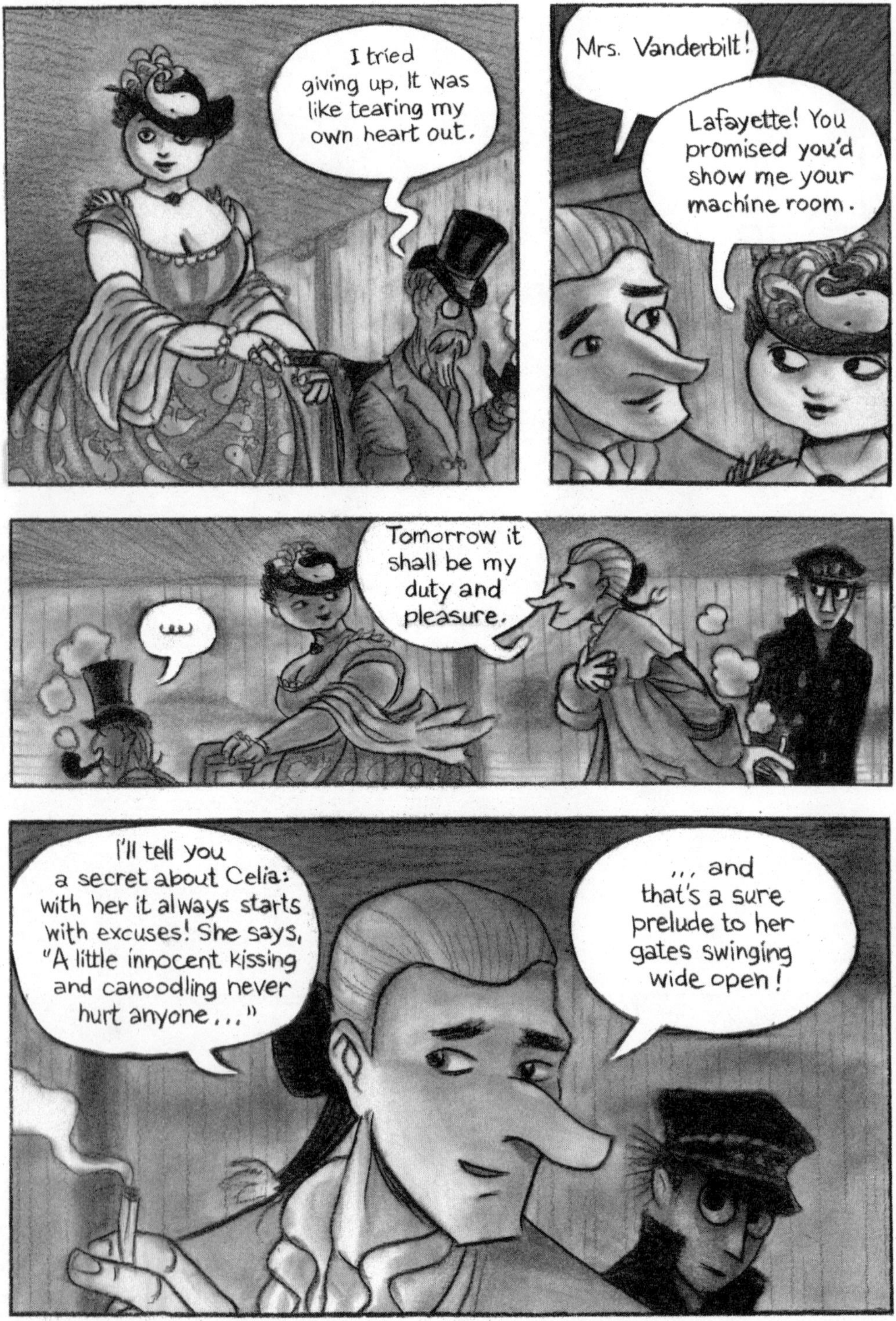
I tried giving up. It was like tearing my own heart out.
Mrs. Vanderbilt!
Lafayette! You promised you'd show me your machine room.
...
Tomorrow it shall be my duty and pleasure.
I'll tell you a secret about Celia: with her it always starts with excuses! She says, "A little innocent kissing and canoodling never hurt anyone..."
... and that's a sure prelude to her gates swinging wide open!

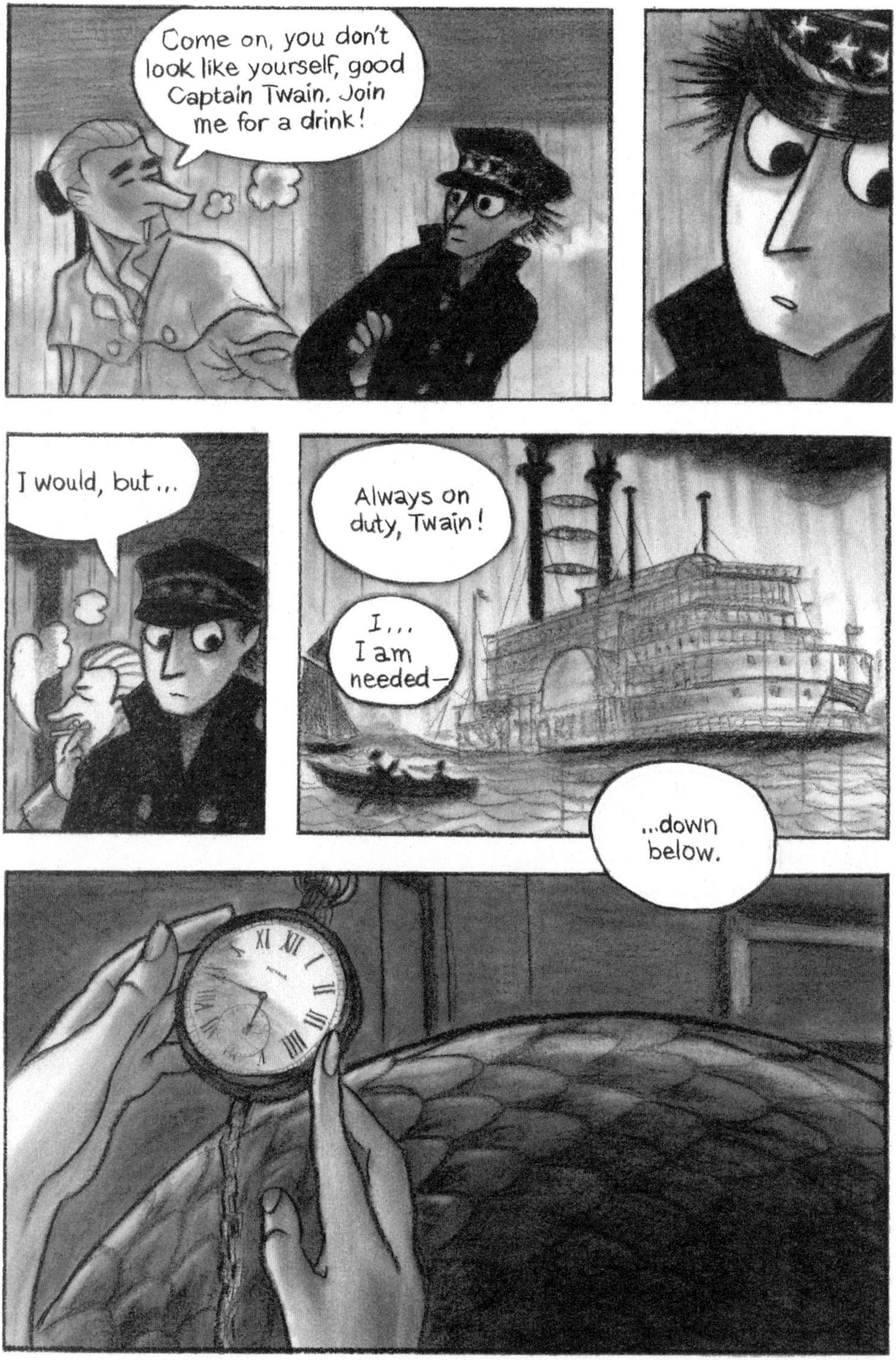
Come on, you don't look like yourself, good Captain Twain. Join me for a drink!
I would, but...
Always on duty, Twain!
I... I am needed—
...down below.

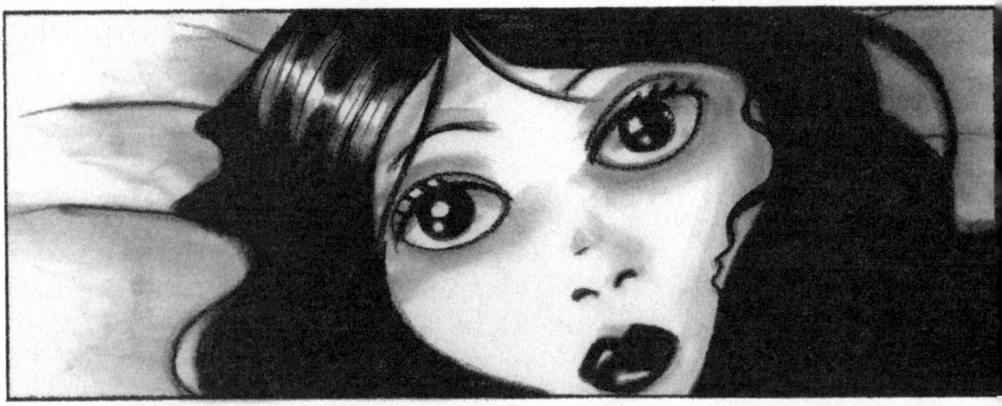

I continued to change her bandage daily. She would wake up for short spells and then fall back asleep.

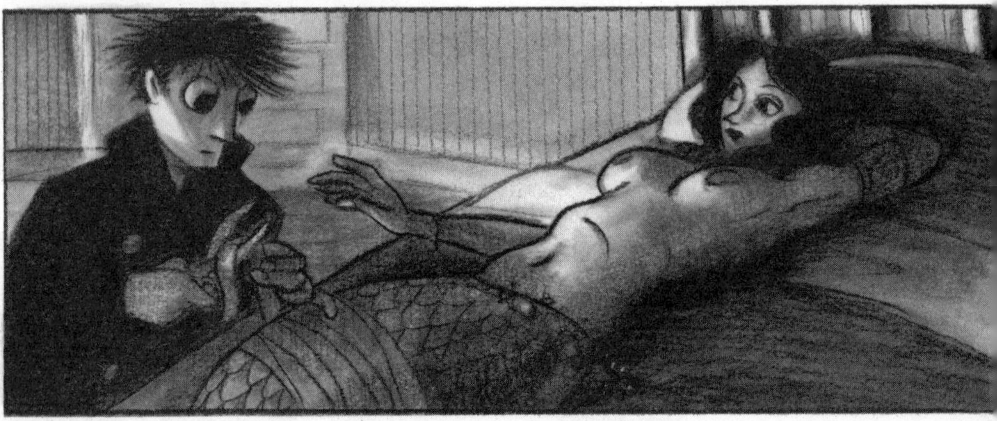

She and I told each other things.

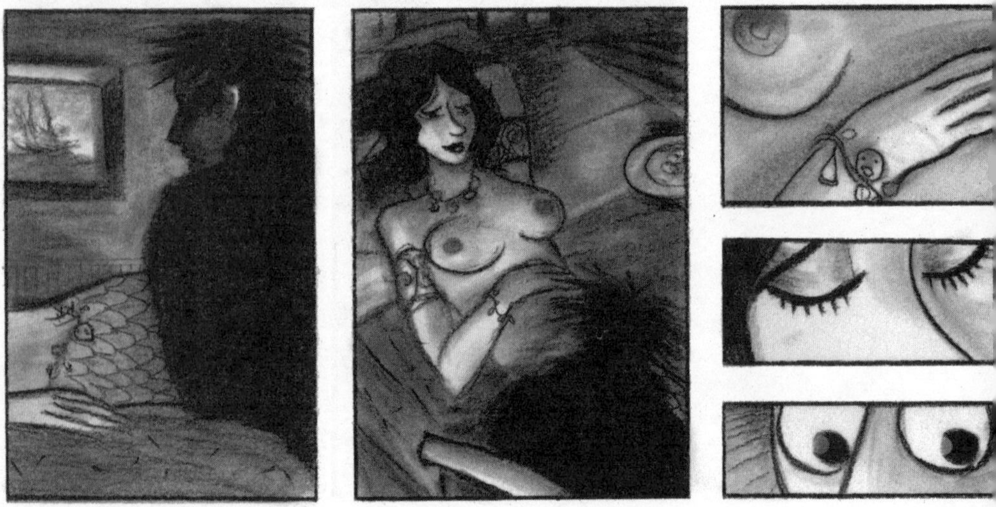

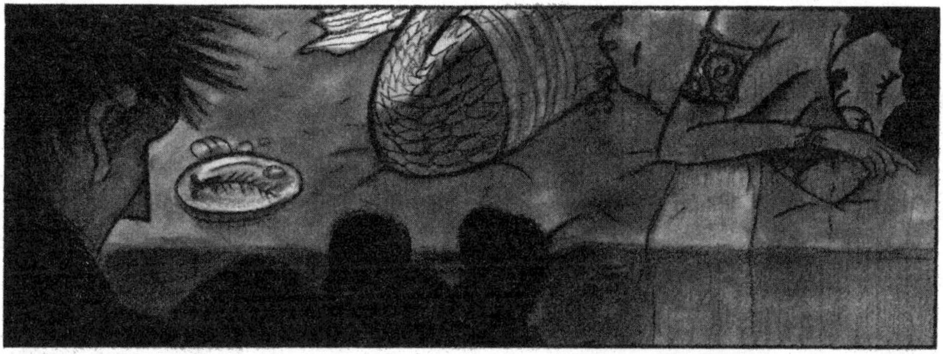

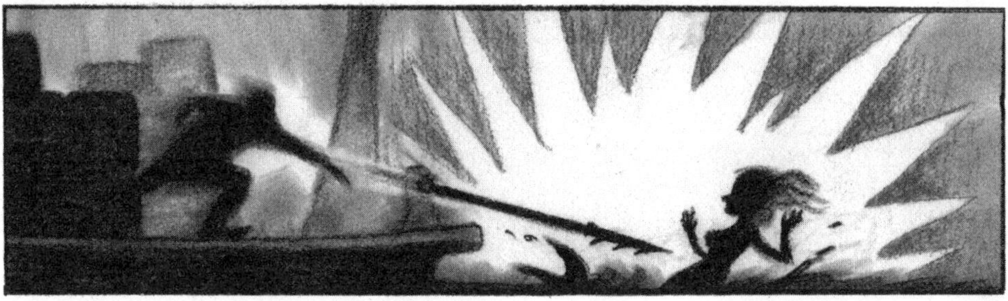

She told me she had been **harpooned**.

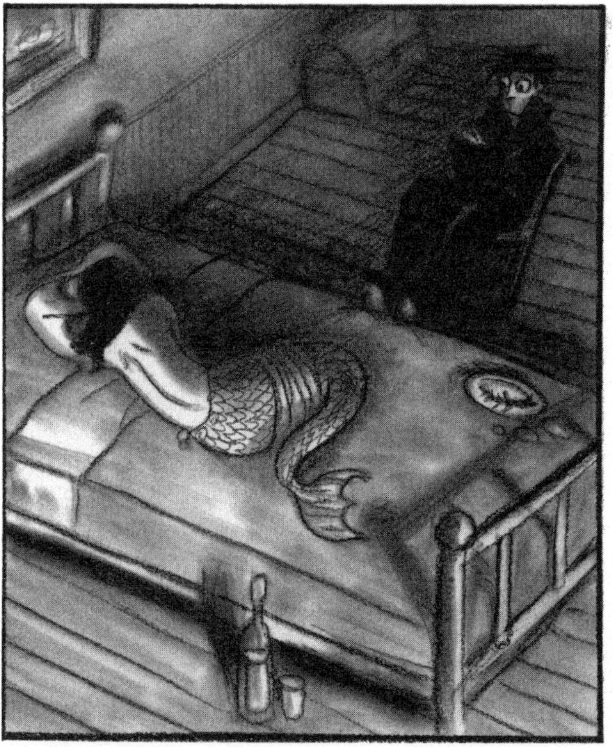

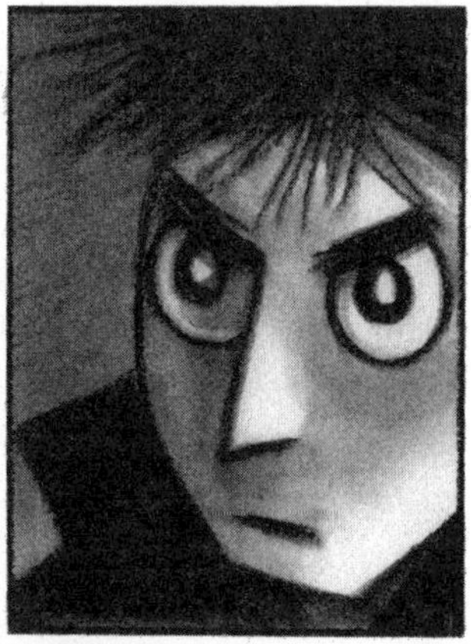

Who would do such a thing?

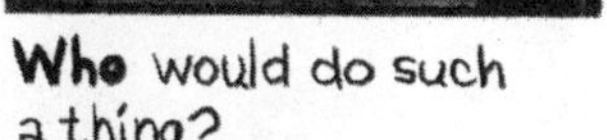

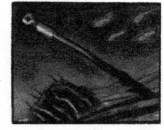

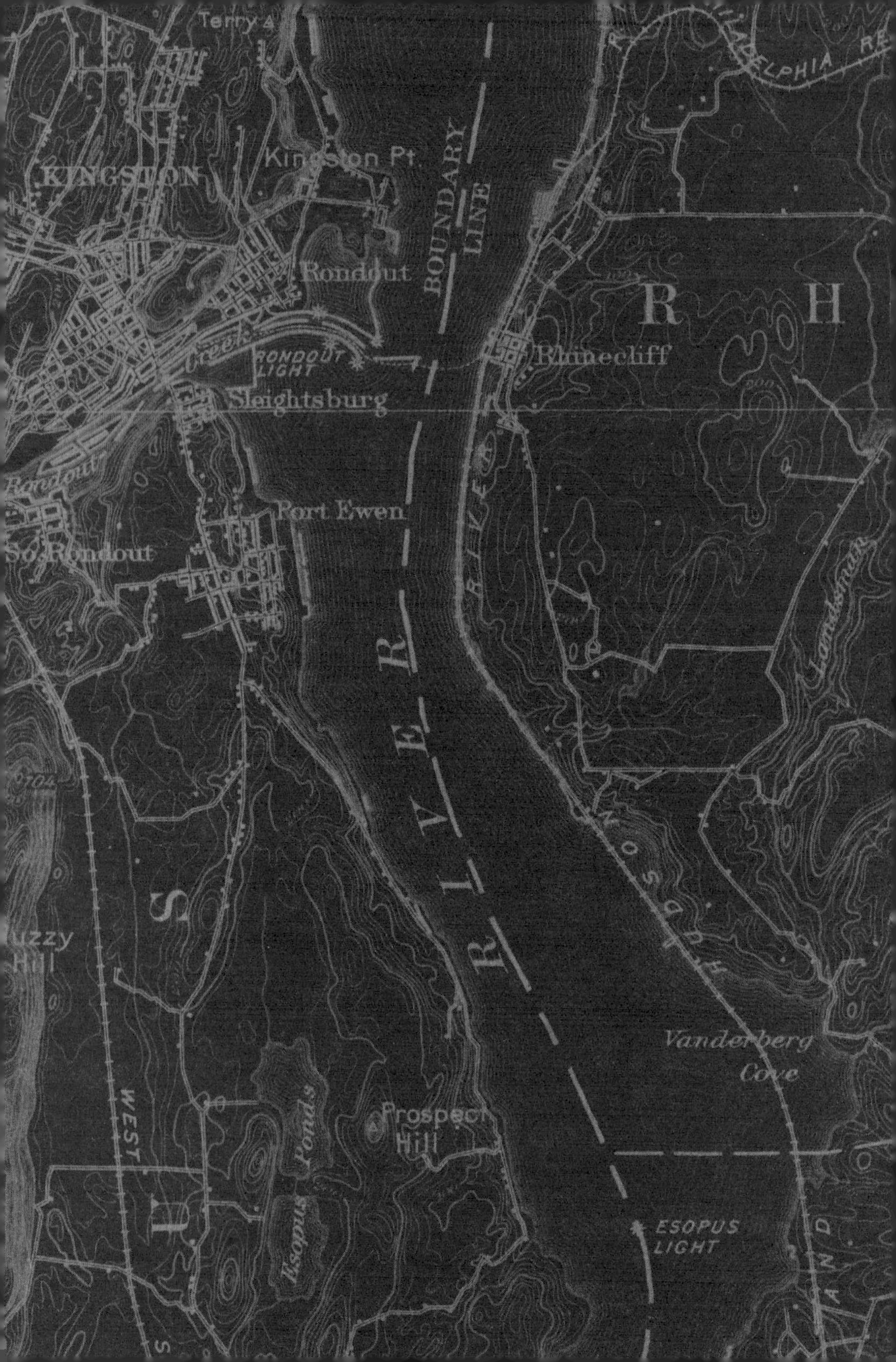

Ferry
Kingston Pt.
KINGSTON
BOUNDARY LINE
Rondout
Rhinecliff
RONDOUT LIGHT
Sleightsburg
Creek
Rondout
Port Ewen
So. Rondout
R
H
RIVER
HUDSON
S
Vanderberg Cove
Prospect Hill
Esopus Ponds
WEST
ESOPUS LIGHT
PHILADELPHIA

Pt 1, Chap.7

"SOUTH'S PROMISE"

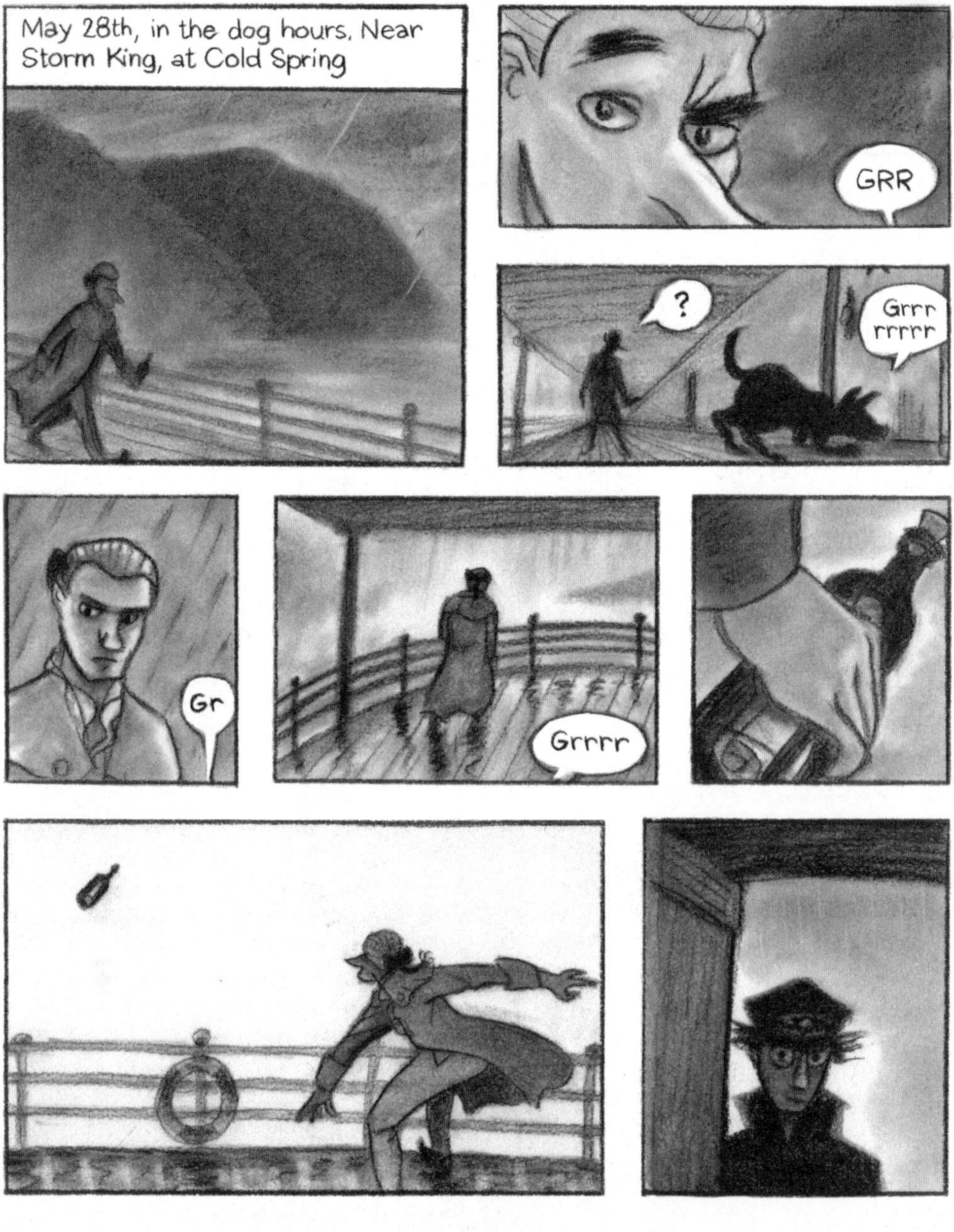
May 28th, in the dog hours, Near Storm King, at Cold Spring
GRR
?
Grrr rrrrr
Gr
Grrrr

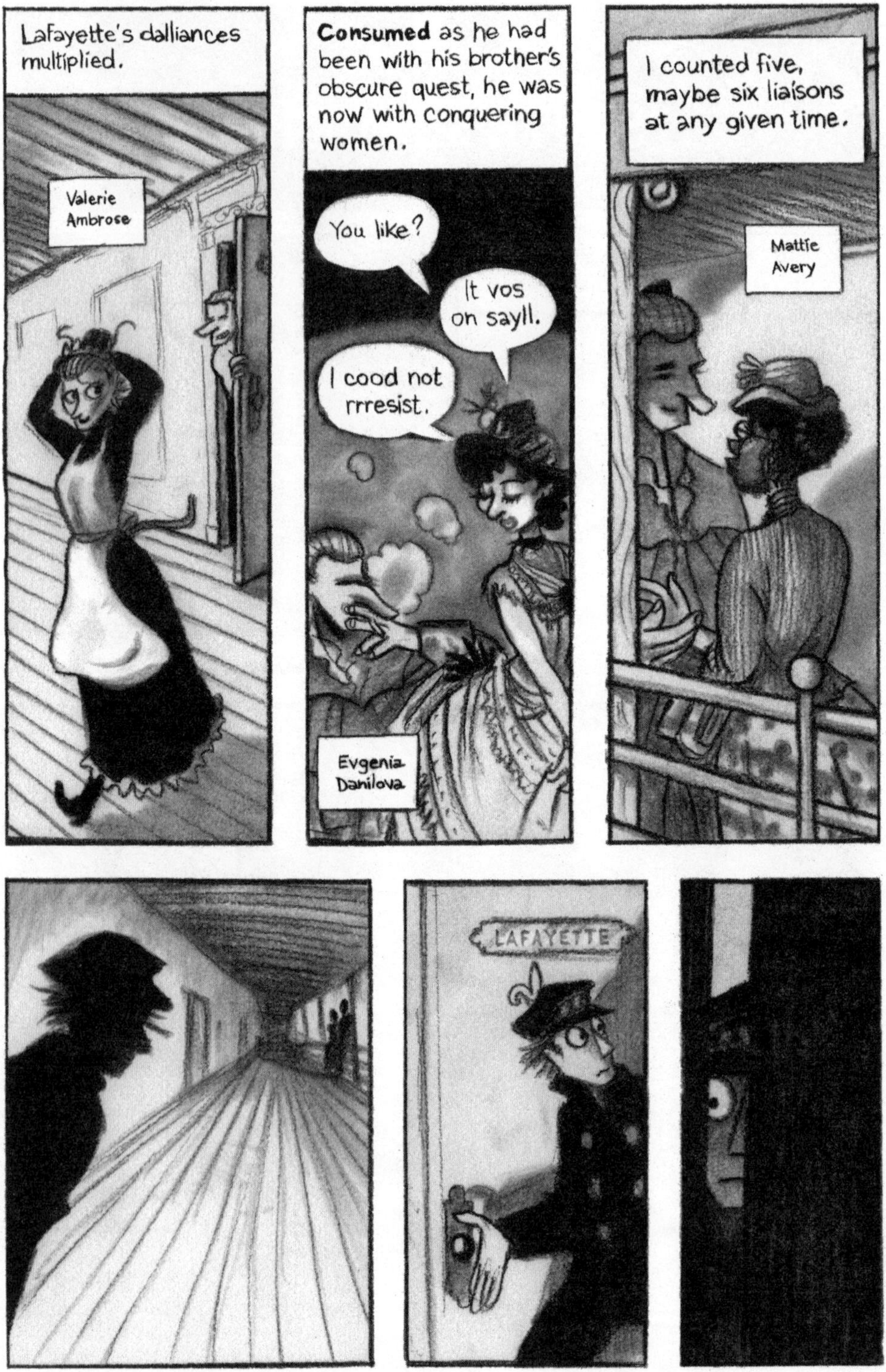
Lafayette's dalliances multiplied.
Valerie Ambrose
Consumed as he had been with his brother's obscure quest, he was now with conquering women.
You like?
It vos on sayll.
I cood not rrresist.
Evgenia Danilova
I counted five, maybe six liaisons at any given time.
Mattie Avery
LAFAYETTE

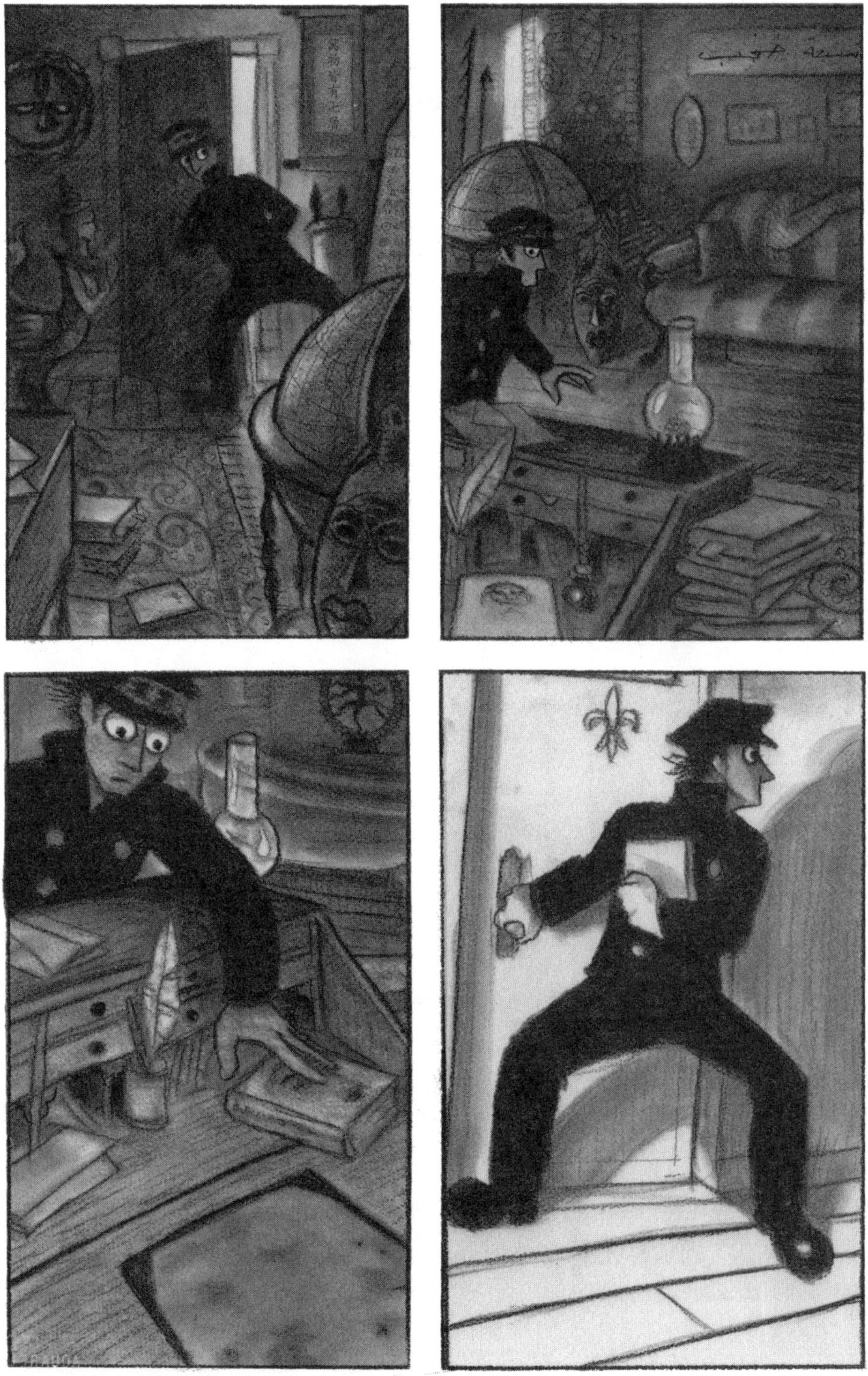

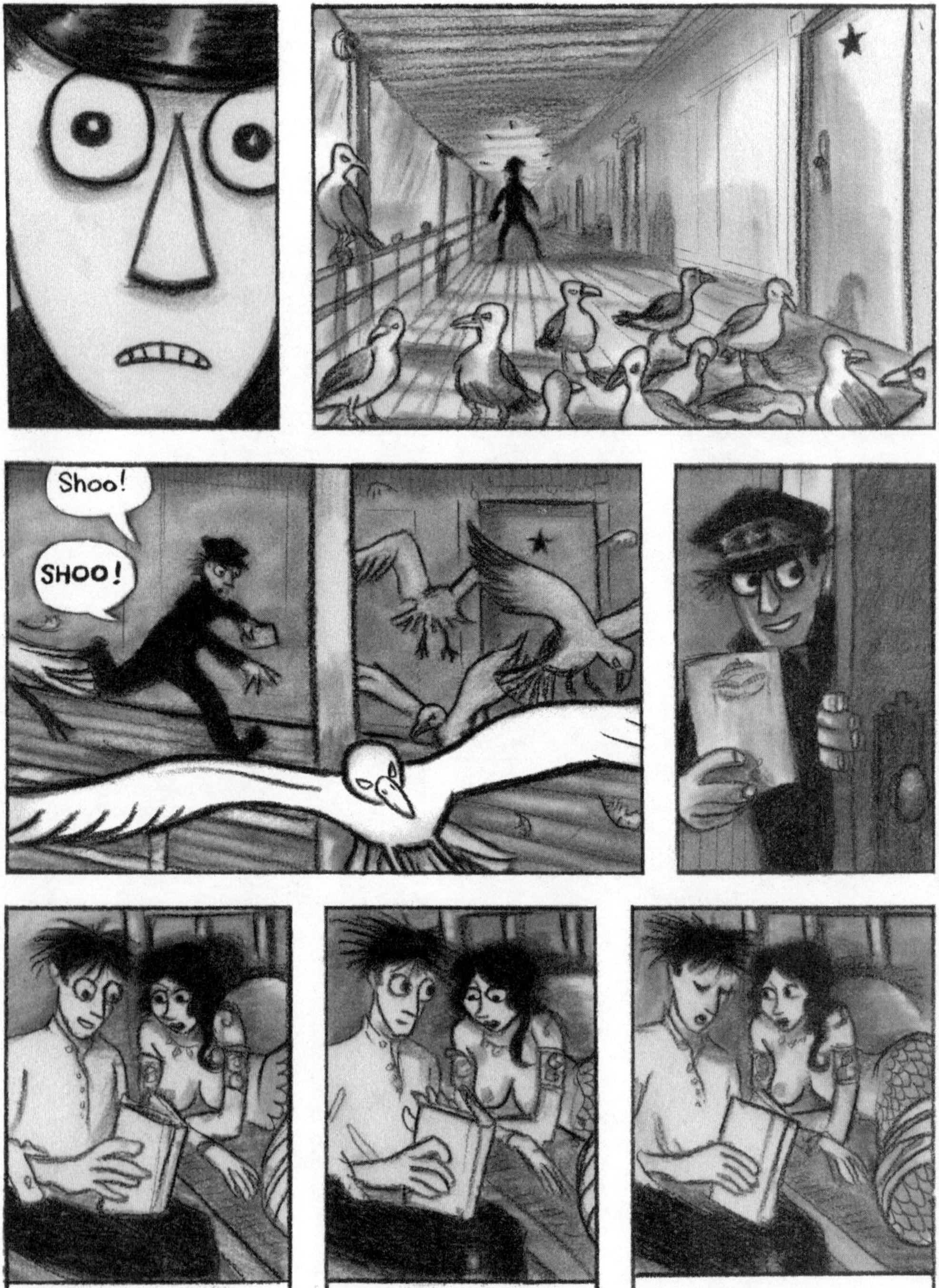
Shoo!
SHOO!
I told the creature stories.
The Beaverton book was a trove of them.
She liked stories.

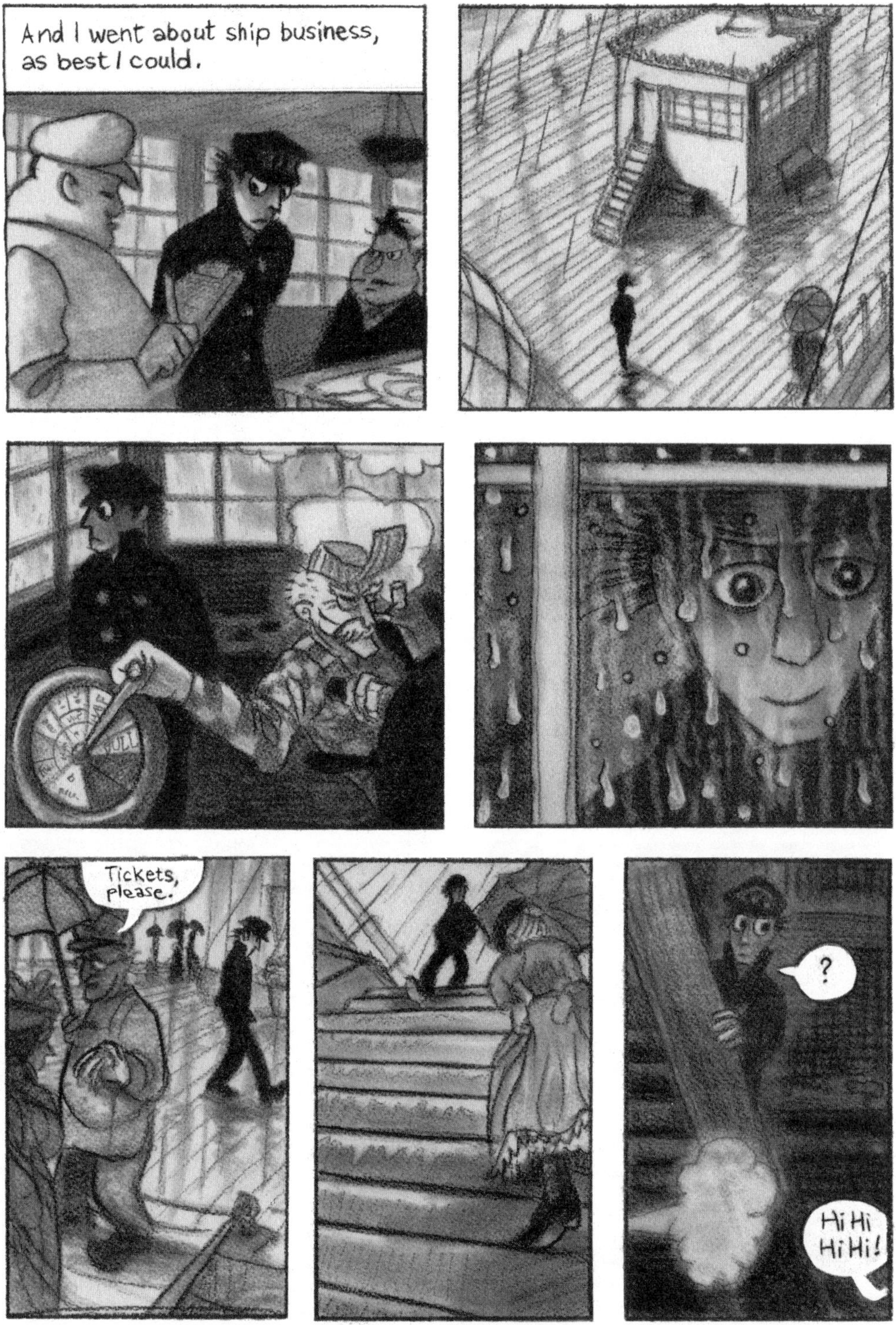
And I went about ship business, as best I could.
Tickets, please.
?
Hi Hi
Hi Hi!

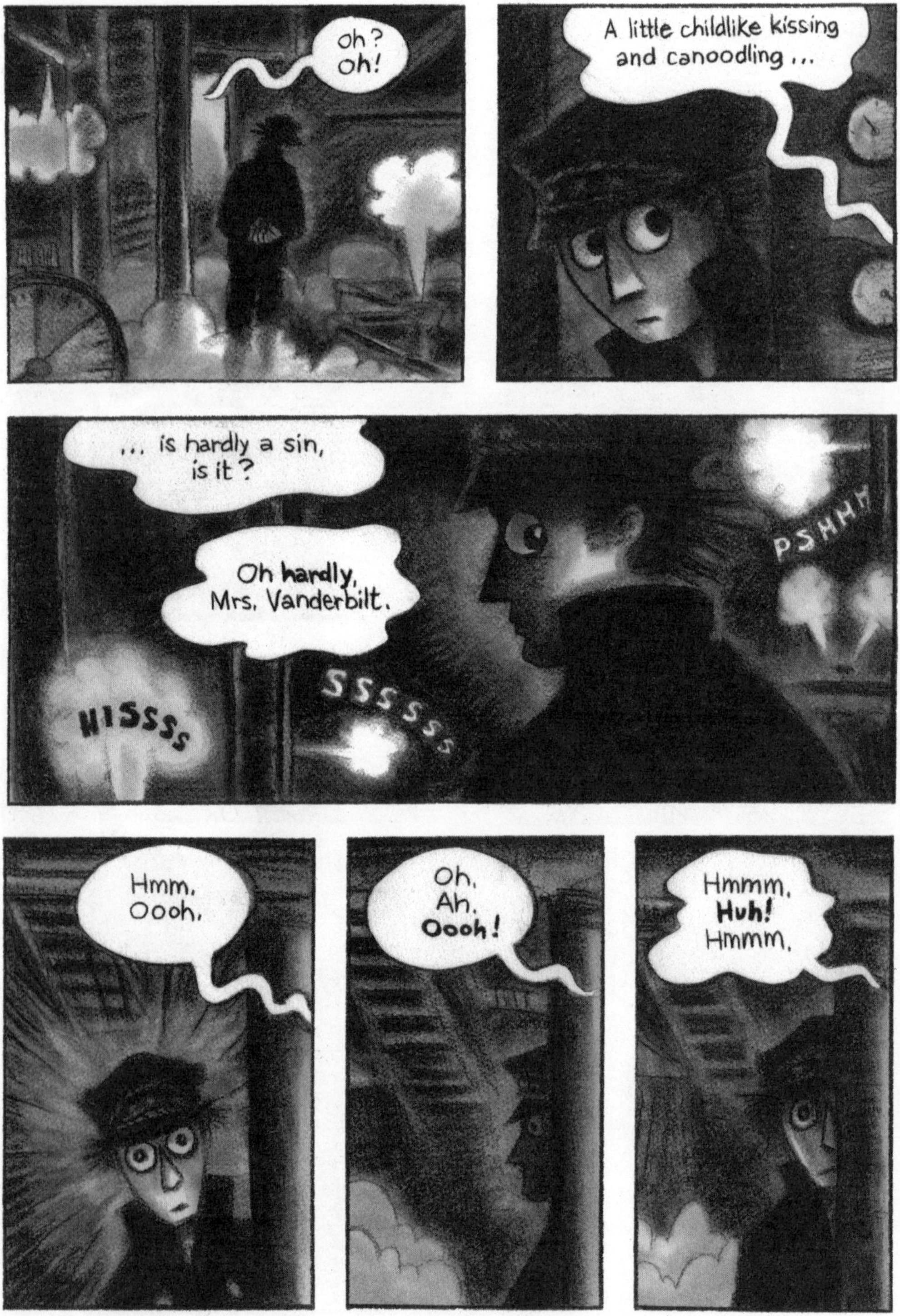
Oh? Oh!
A little childlike kissing and canoodling ...
... is hardly a sin, is it?
Oh hardly, Mrs. Vanderbilt.
PSHHH
HISSSs
SSSSSS
Hmm. Oooh.
Oh. Ah. Oooh!
Hmmm. Huh! Hmmm.

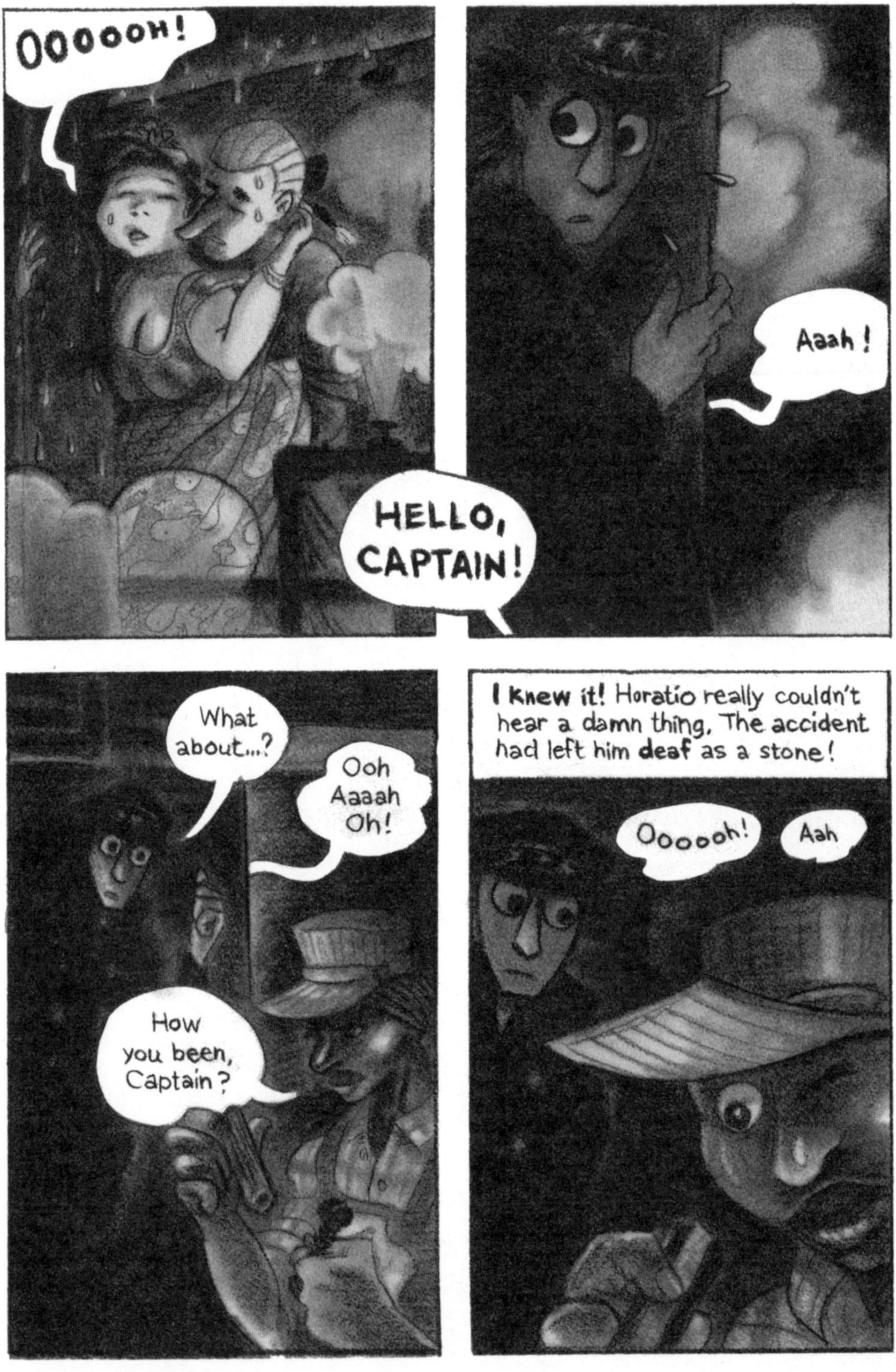
OOOOOH!
Aaah!
HELLO, CAPTAIN!
What about...?
Ooh Aaaah Oh!
How you been, Captain?
I knew it! Horatio really couldn't hear a damn thing. The accident had left him deaf as a stone!
Oooooh!
Aah

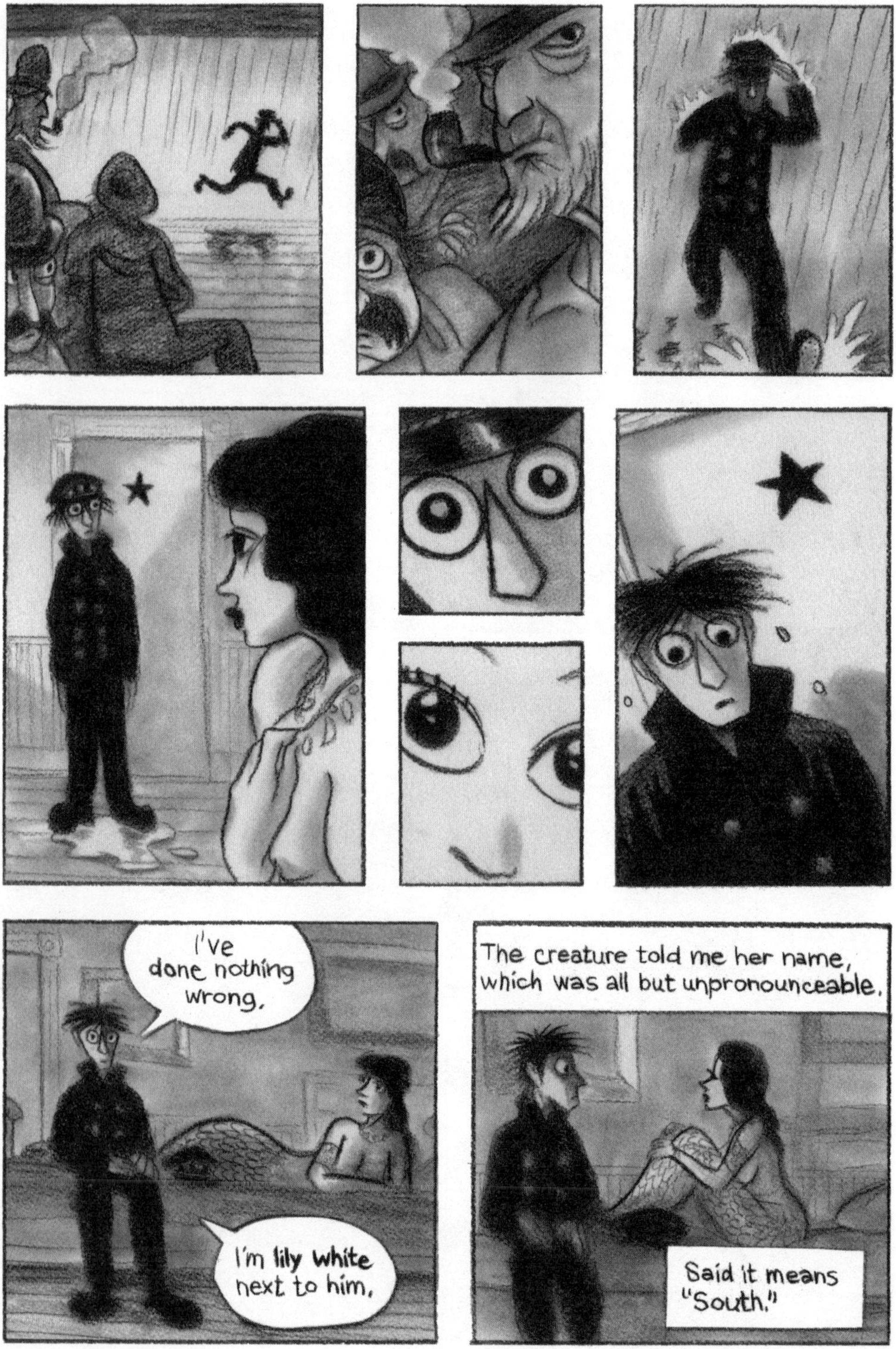
I've done nothing wrong.
I'm lily white next to him.
The creature told me her name, which was all but unpronounceable.
Said it means "South."

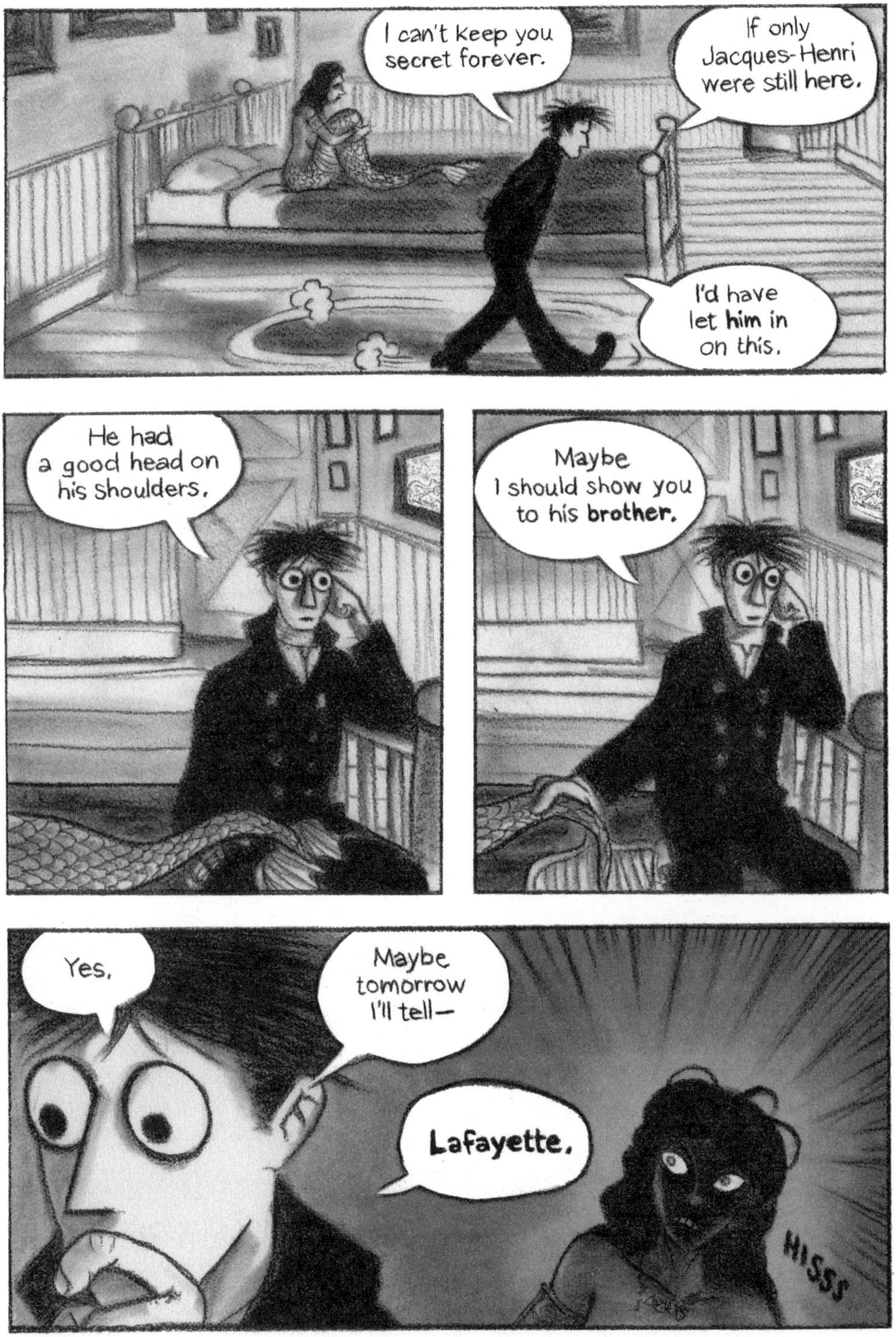
I can't keep you secret forever.
If only Jacques-Henri were still here.
I'd have let **him** in on this.
He had a good head on his shoulders.
Maybe I should show you to his **brother.**
Yes.
Maybe tomorrow I'll tell—
Lafayette.
HISSS

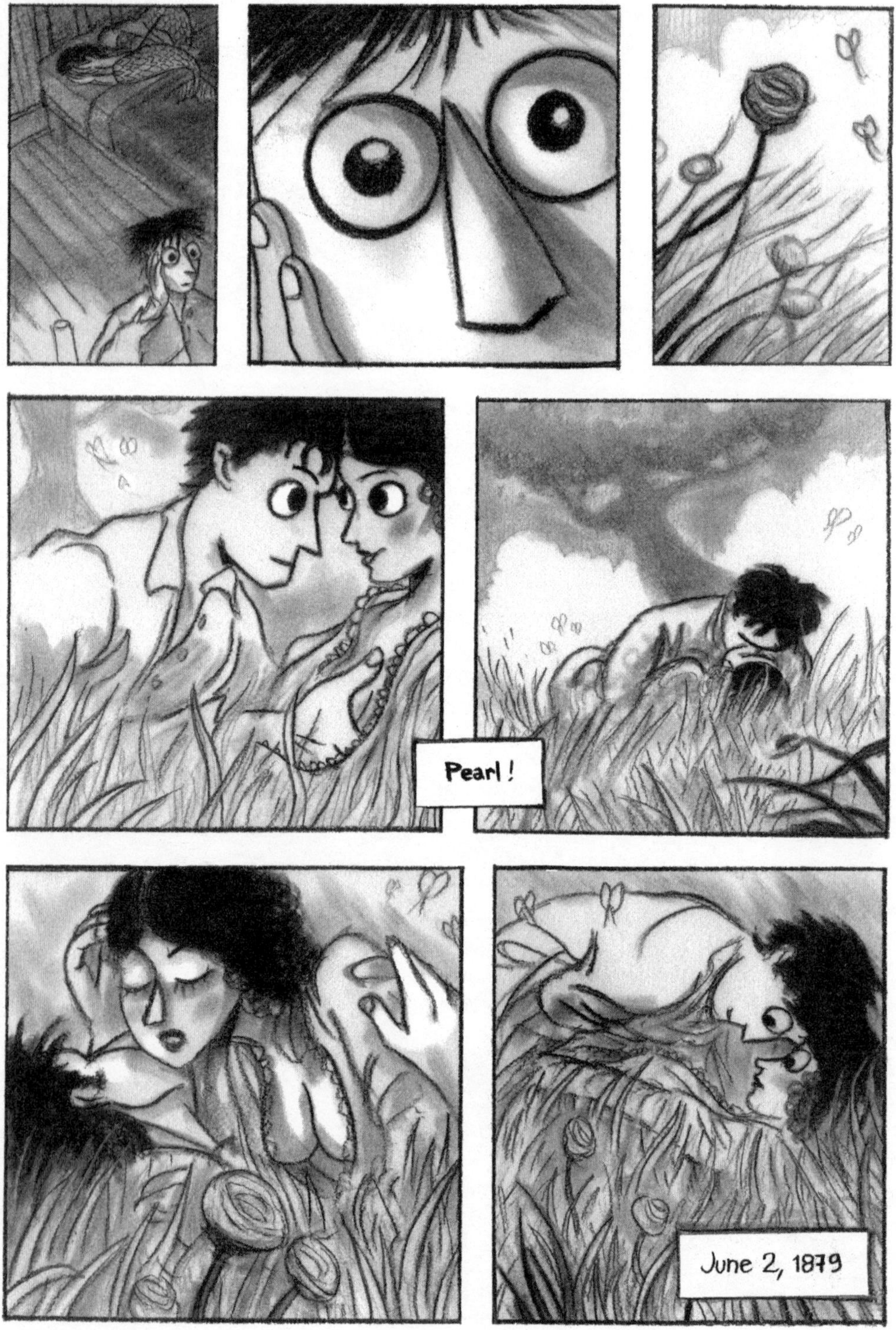
Pearl!
June 2, 1879

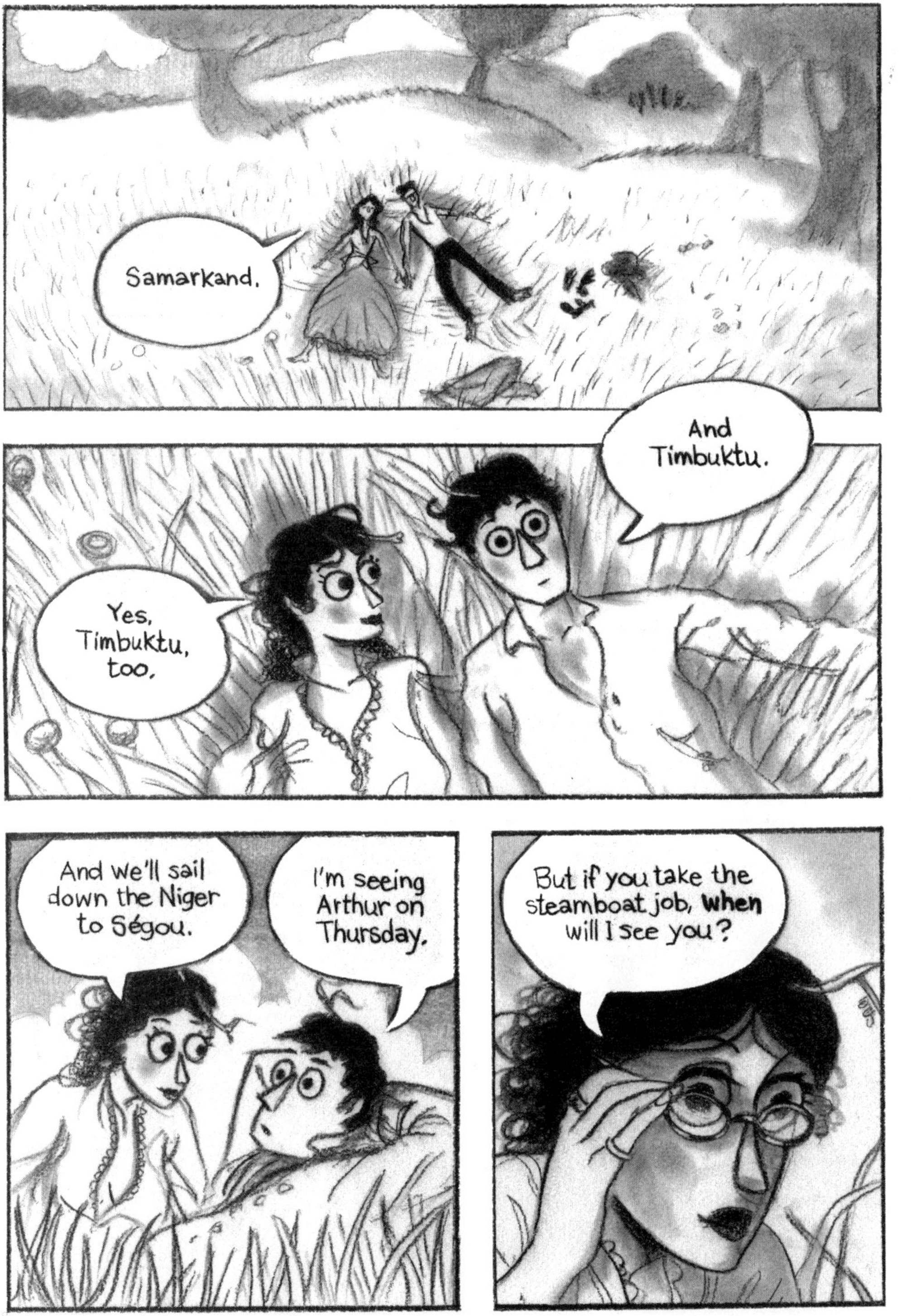
Samarkand.
And Timbuktu.
Yes, Timbuktu, too.
And we'll sail down the Niger to Ségou.
I'm seeing Arthur on Thursday.
But if you take the steamboat job, **when** will I see you?

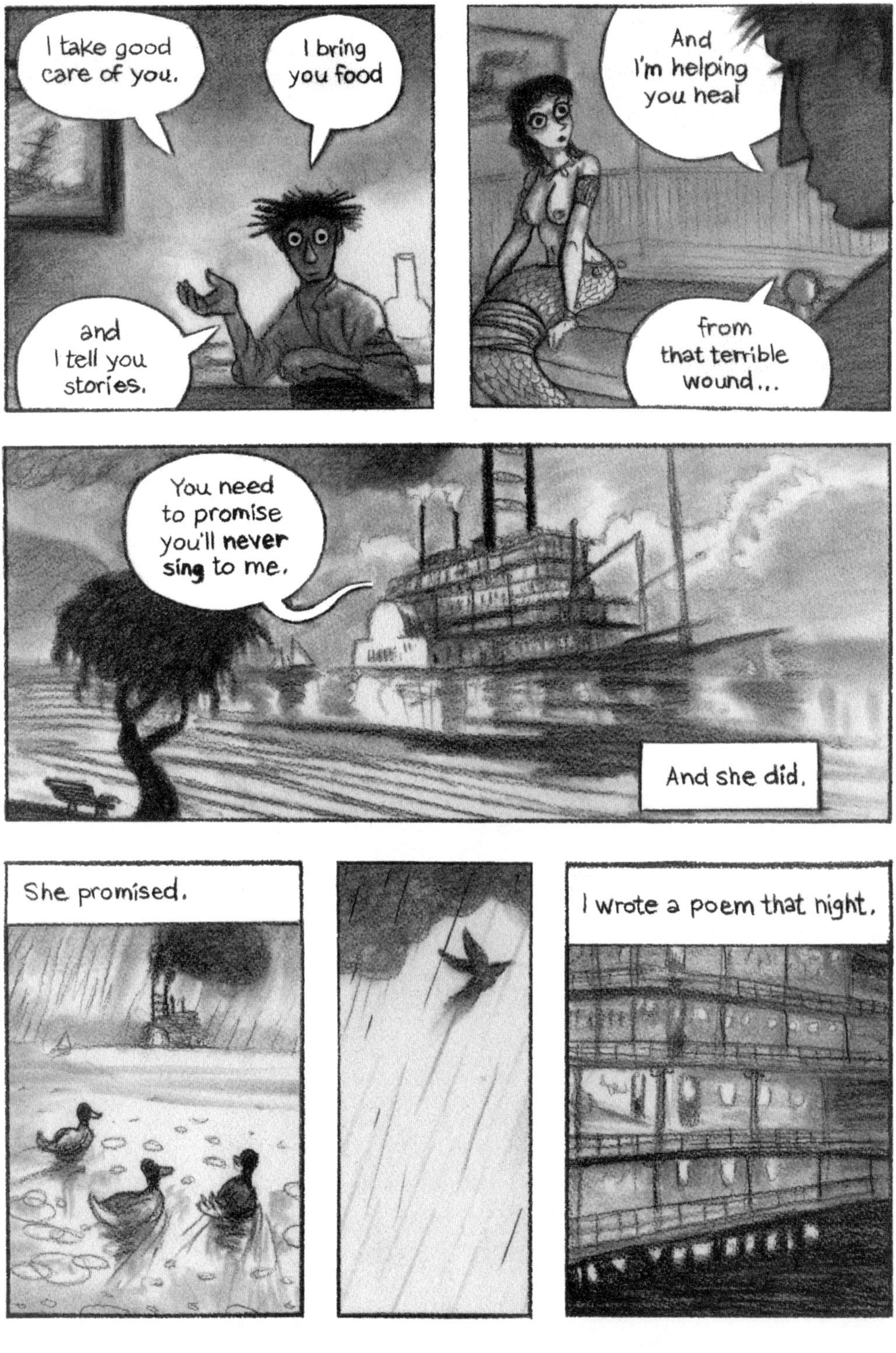
I take good care of you.
I bring you food
and I tell you stories.
And I'm helping you heal
from that terrible wound...
You need to promise you'll **never sing** to me.
And she did.
She promised.
I wrote a poem that night.

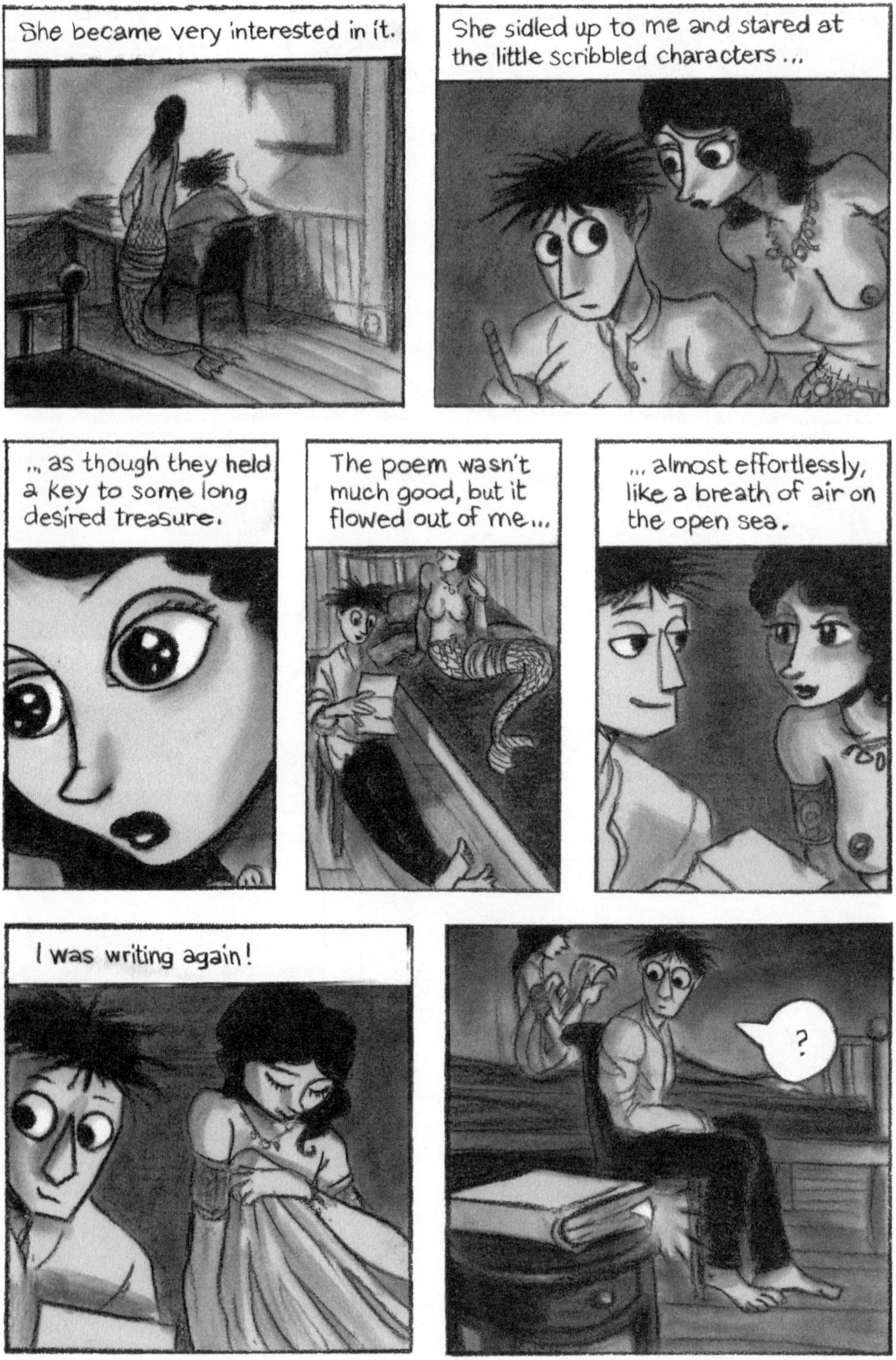
She became very interested in it.
She sidled up to me and stared at the little scribbled characters ...
... as though they held a key to some long desired treasure.
The poem wasn't much good, but it flowed out of me...
... almost effortlessly, like a breath of air on the open sea.
I was writing again!
?

He got an answer!

Mr. D. Lafayette
The Lorelei
Lafayette Lines

Lafayette was actually in touch with the reclusive Beaverton!

May the 30th

Mr. Lafayette,
What an unusual query!

The cure for mermaids? Would that not depend on the mermaid? The myth being ubiquitous, of which mermaid do we speak? The lure of drink? The fatal attraction of mad lovers? The perennial lust for war? Or how about the magnetic pull of fame? Life is full of mermaids, is it not?

It seems I have answered your questions with some questions of my own. I hope this is not too disappointing.

Sincerely,

C. G. Beaverton

119

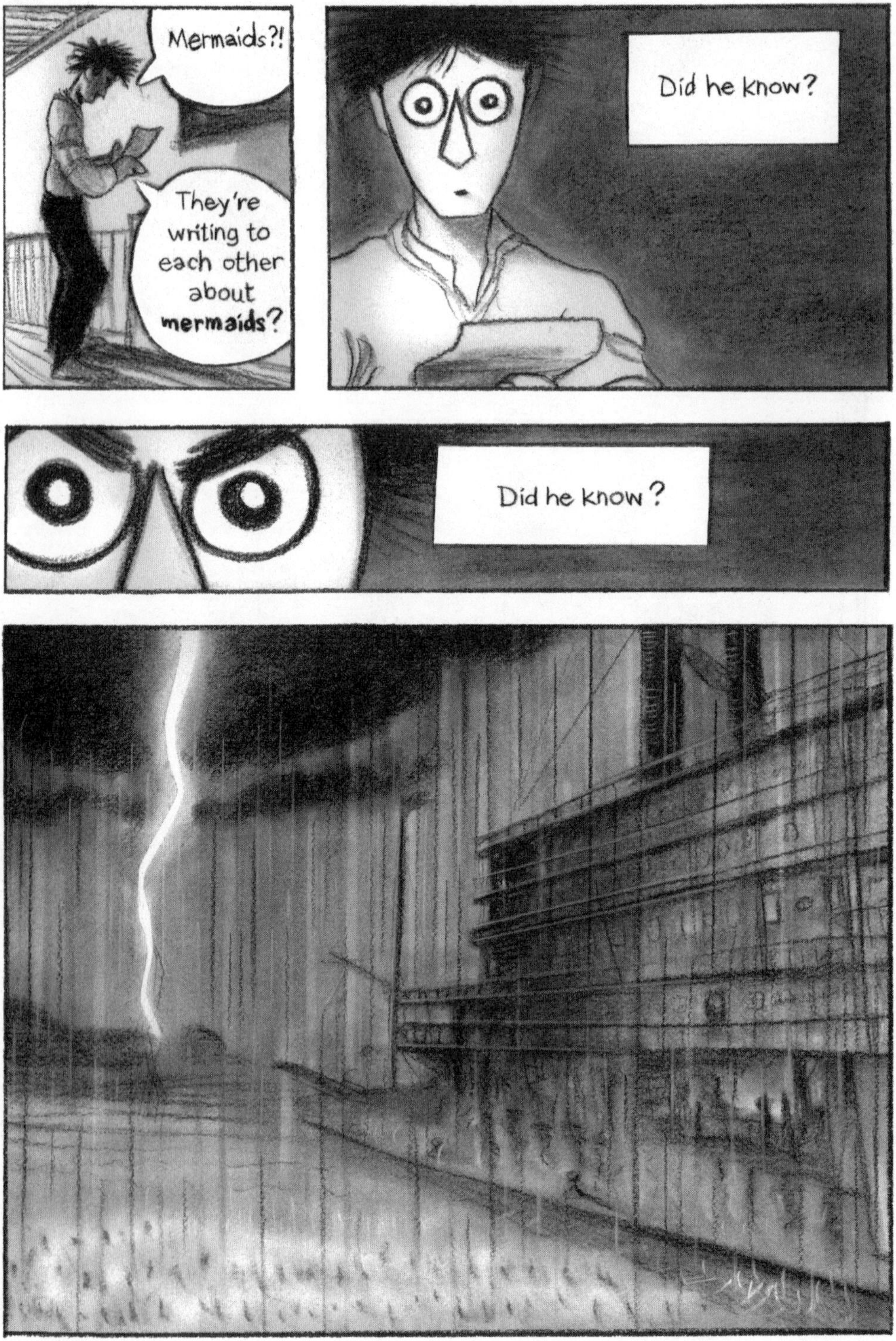
Mermaids?!
They're writing to each other about **mermaids**?
Did he know?
Did he know?

Pt 1, Chap.8

"PEARL'S SONG"

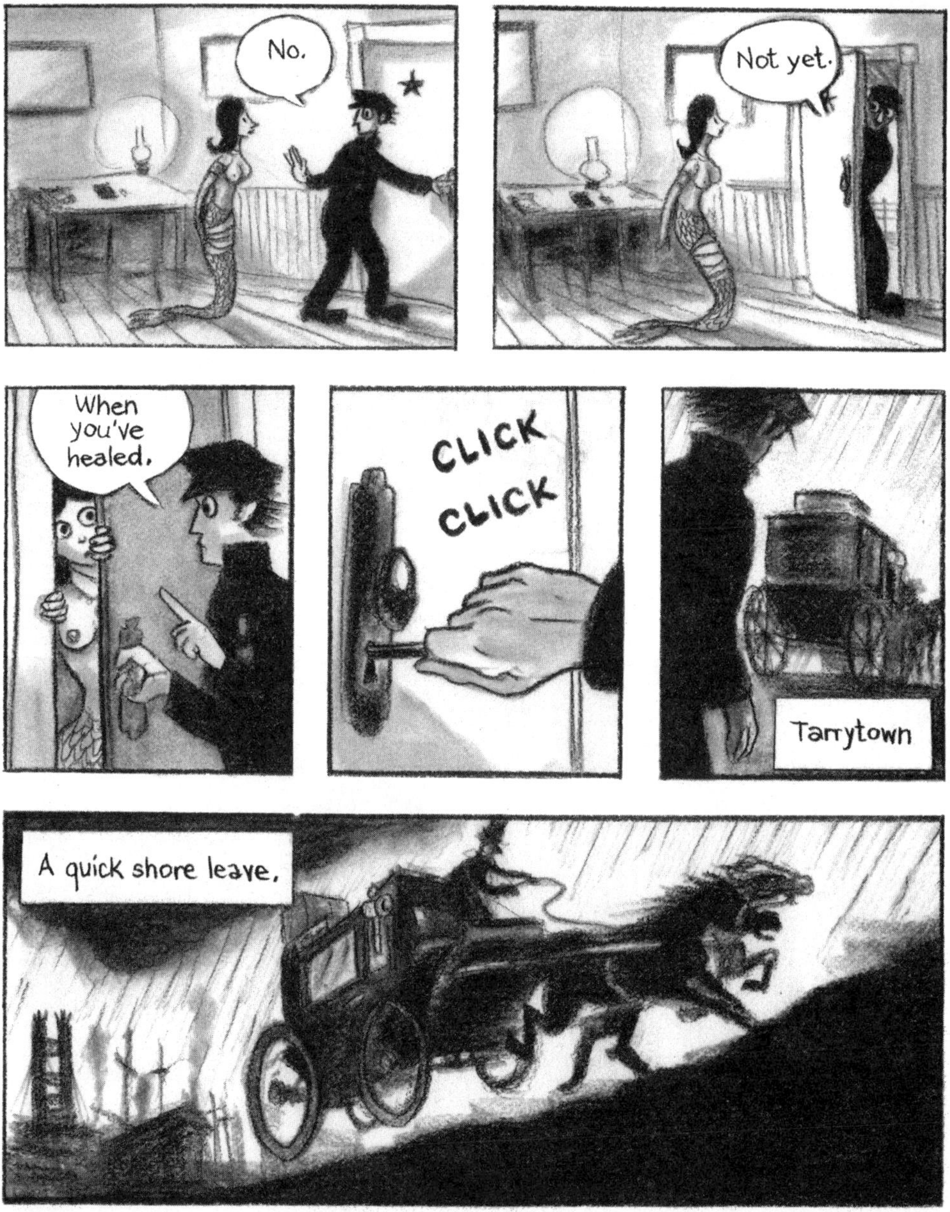
No.
Not yet.
When you've healed.
CLICK
CLICK
Tarrytown
A quick shore leave.

Arthur wrote me.

In California there's a new kind of **cure** he thinks I should try.

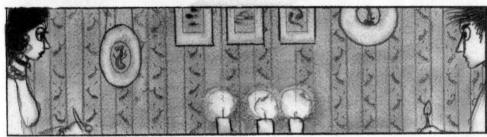

You're not eating your—

Pearl,

Are we a couple of cold fish?

Why do you say that?

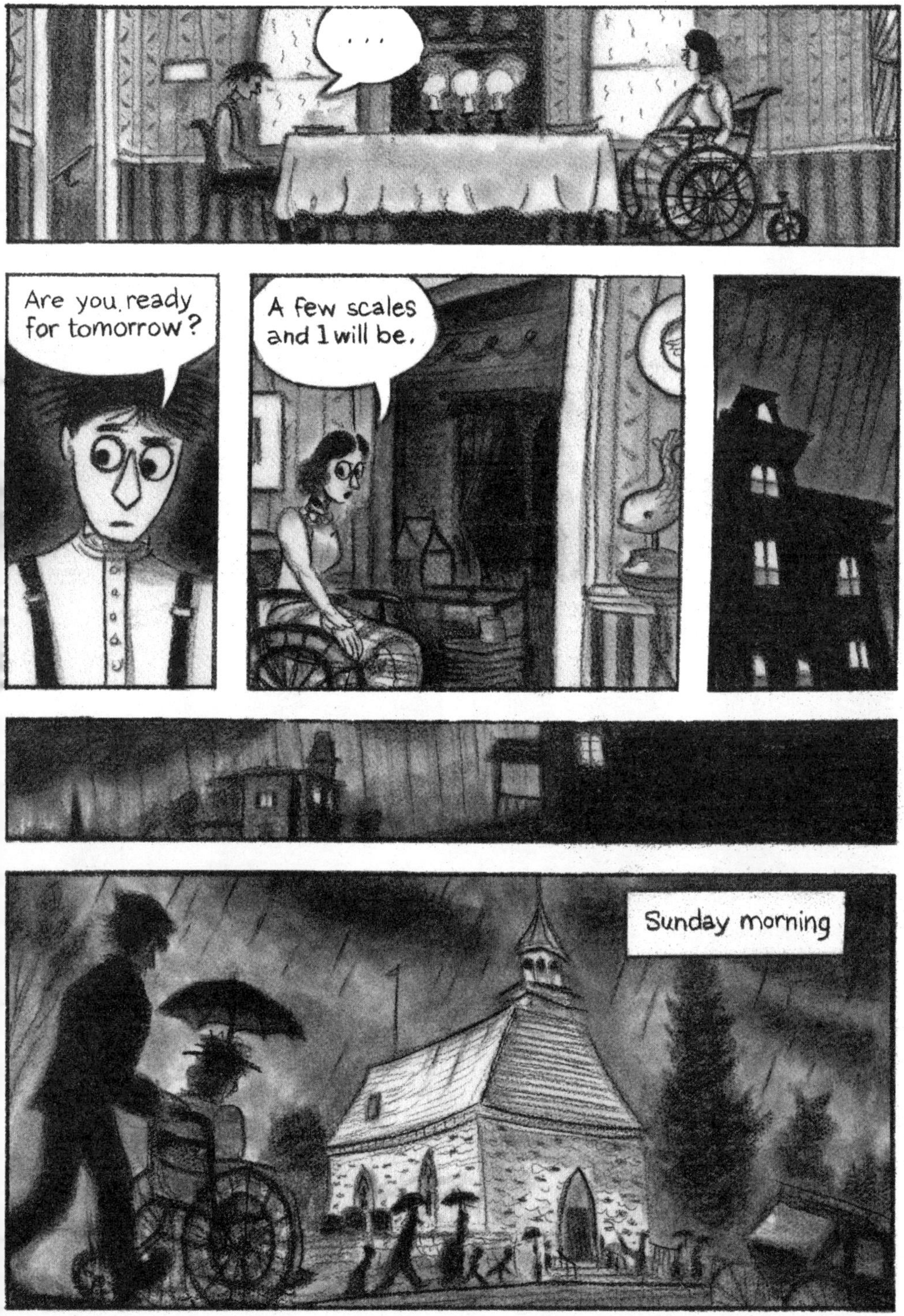
. . .
Are you ready for tomorrow?
A few scales and I will be.
Sunday morning

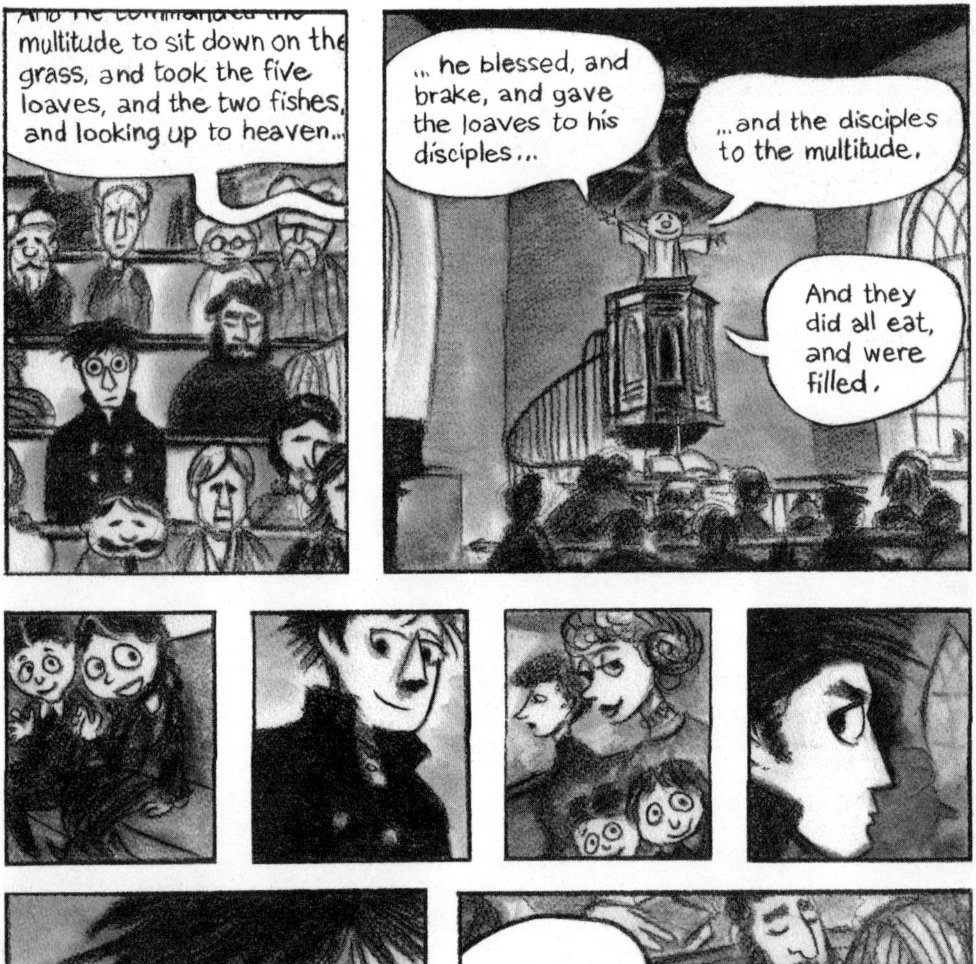
multitude to sit down on the grass, and took the five loaves, and the two fishes, and looking up to heaven...
... he blessed, and brake, and gave the loaves to his disciples...
...and the disciples to the multitude.
And they did all eat, and were filled.
I can't sleep!
I daydream of Virgil.
I can't stop.

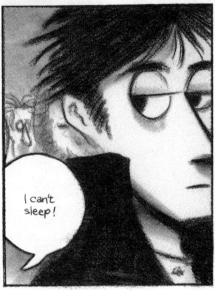

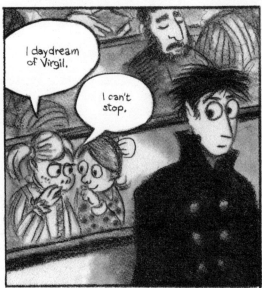

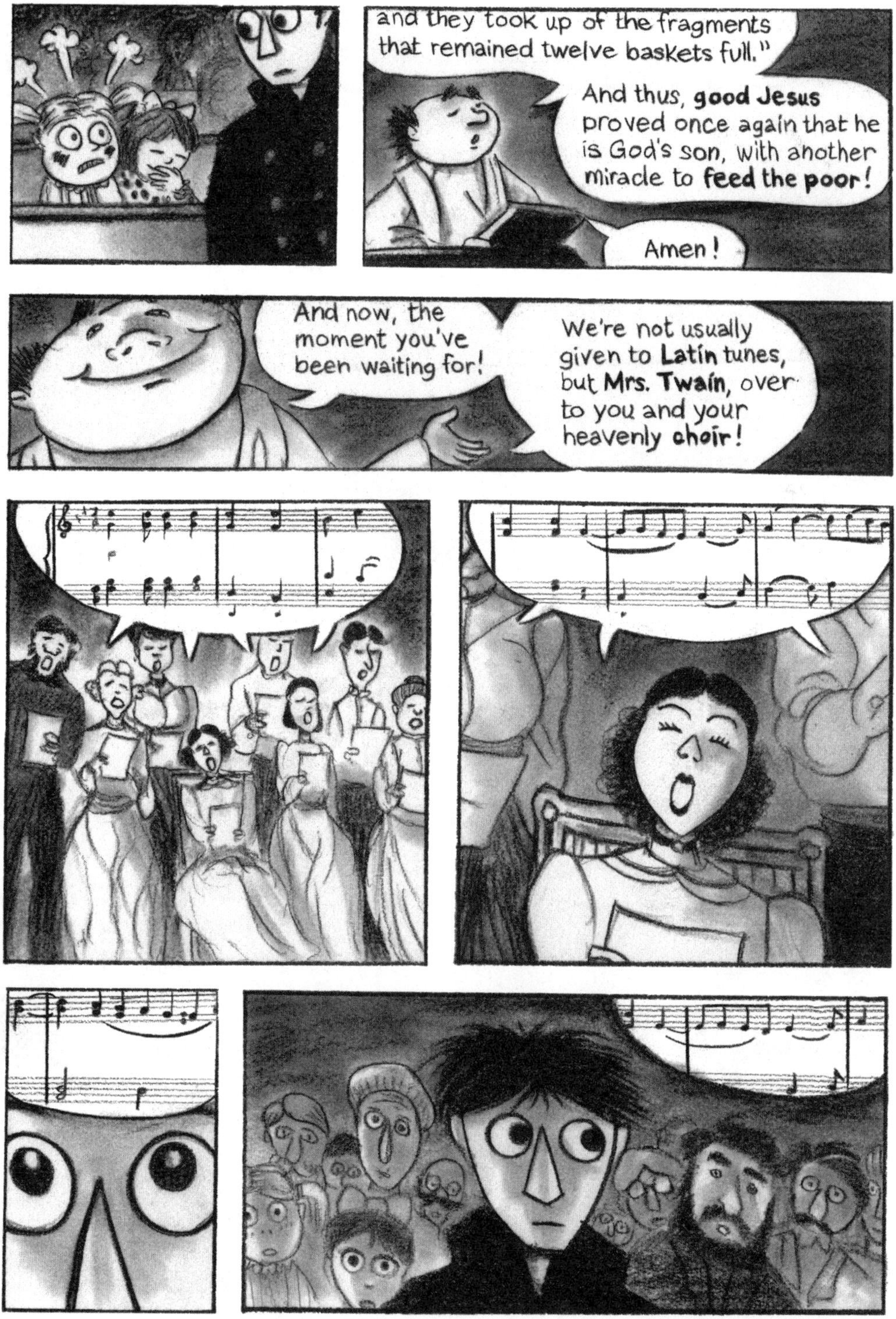
and they took up of the fragments that remained twelve baskets full."
And thus, **good Jesus** proved once again that he is God's son, with another miracle to **feed the poor**!
Amen!
And now, the moment you've been waiting for!
We're not usually given to **Latin** tunes, but **Mrs. Twain**, over to you and your heavenly **choir**!

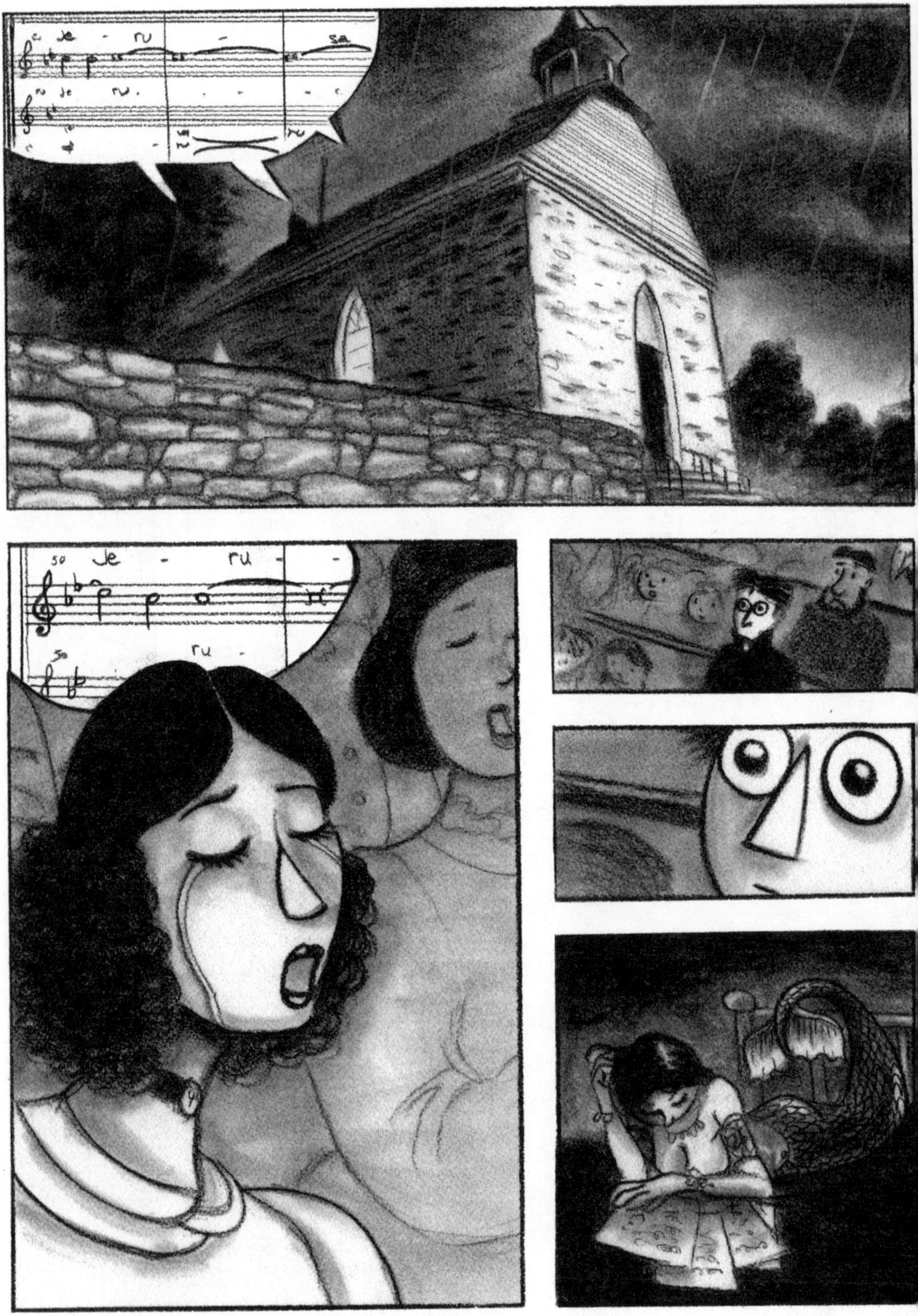
je - ru - sa
je - ru -
ru

She had been alone all night...

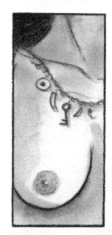

... and **Lafayette** still aboard!

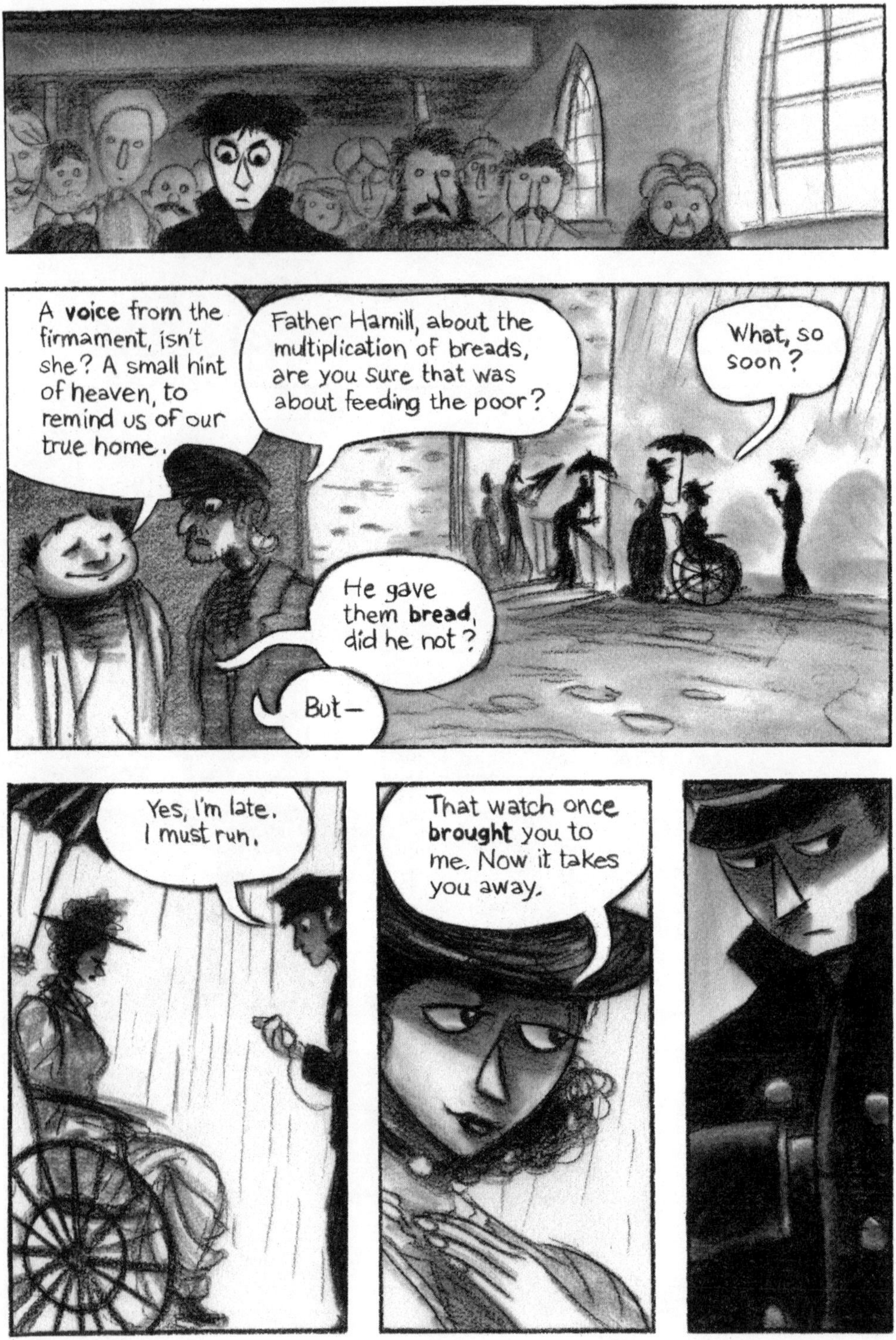
A voice from the firmament, isn't she? A small hint of heaven, to remind us of our true home.
Father Hamill, about the multiplication of breads, are you sure that was about feeding the poor?
What, so soon?
He gave them bread, did he not?
But—
Yes, I'm late. I must run.
That watch once brought you to me. Now it takes you away.

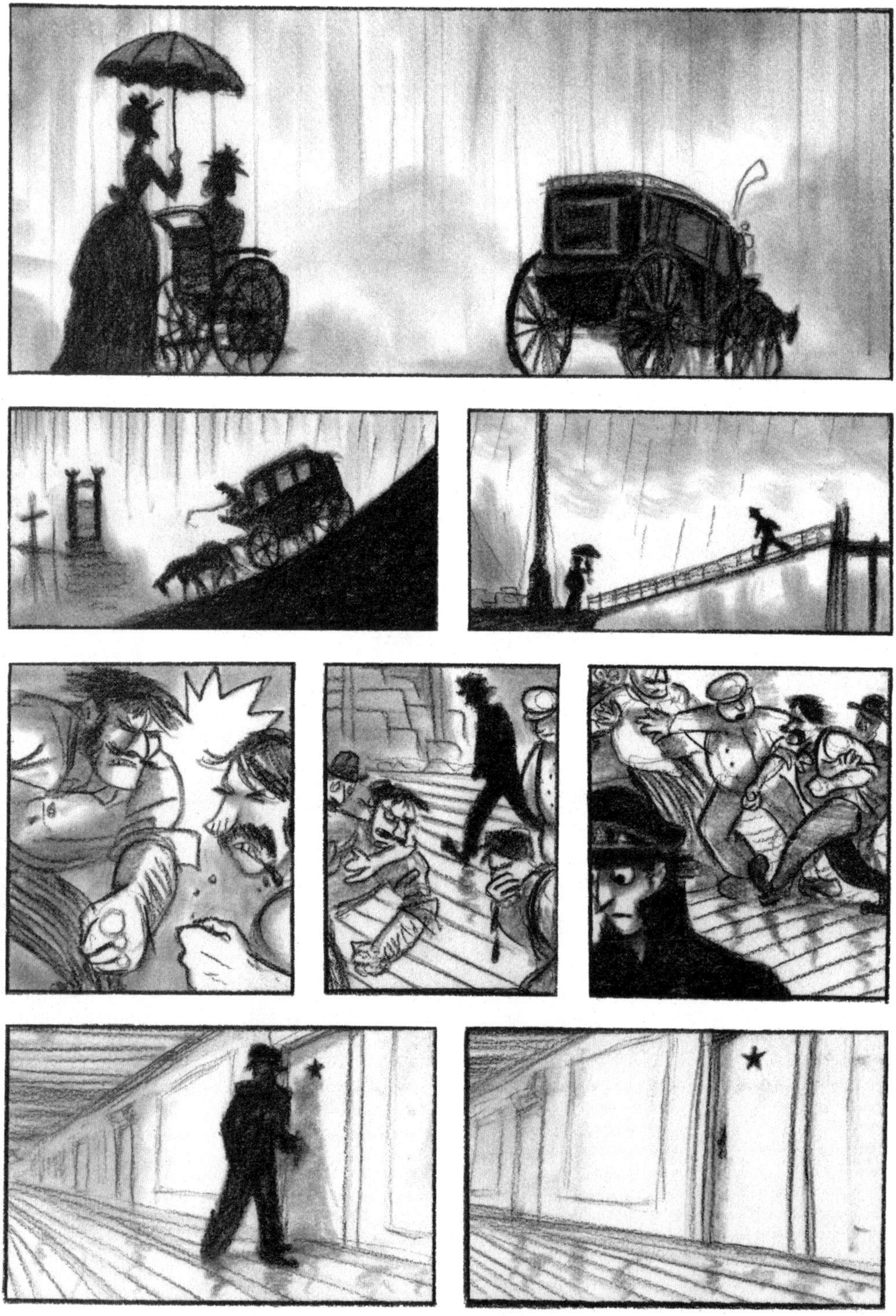

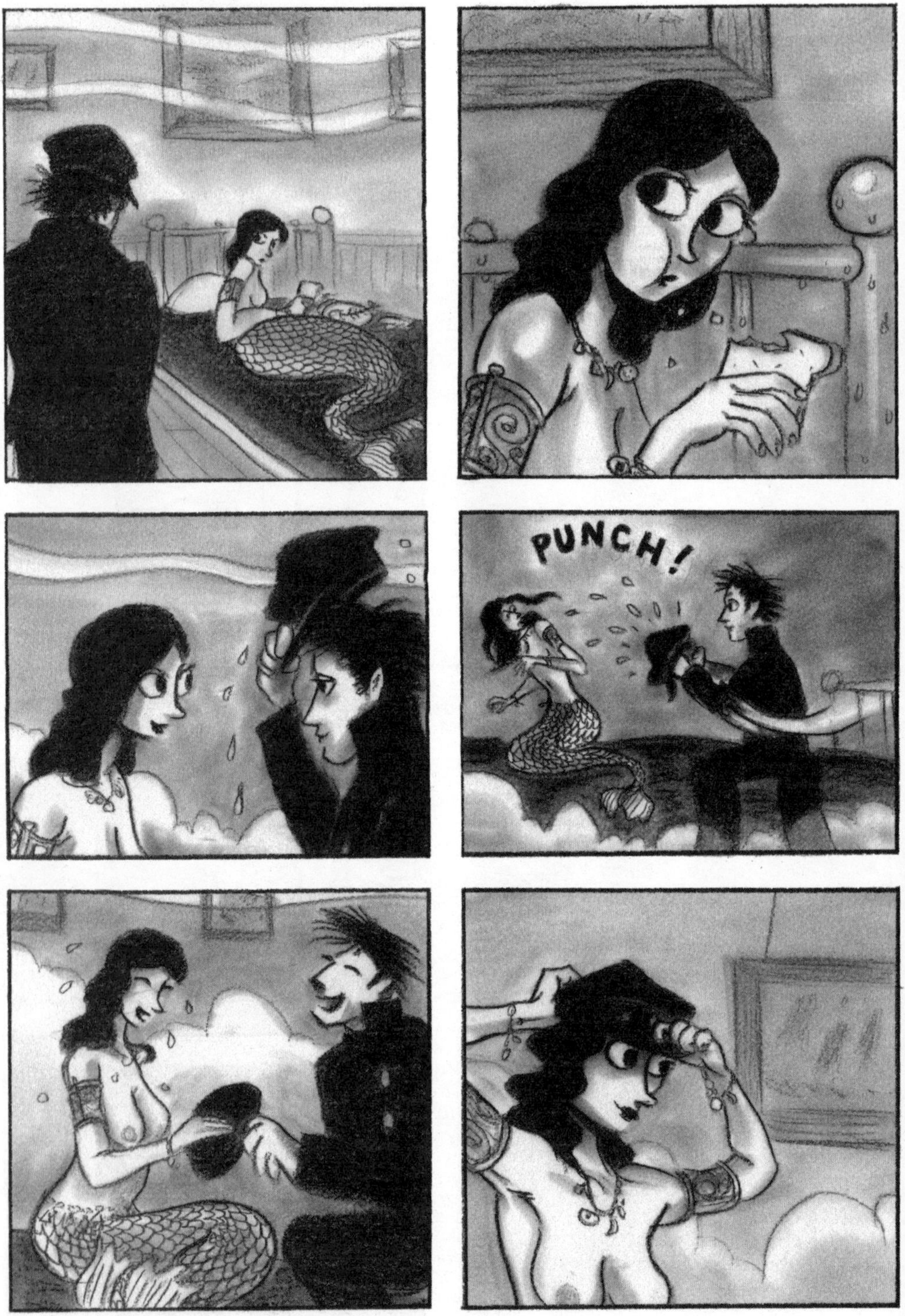
PUNCH!

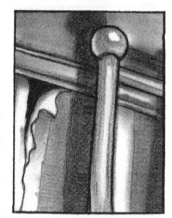

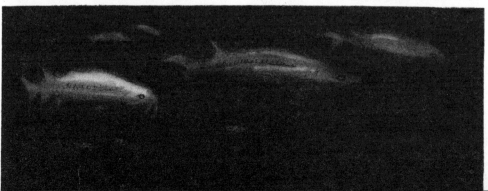

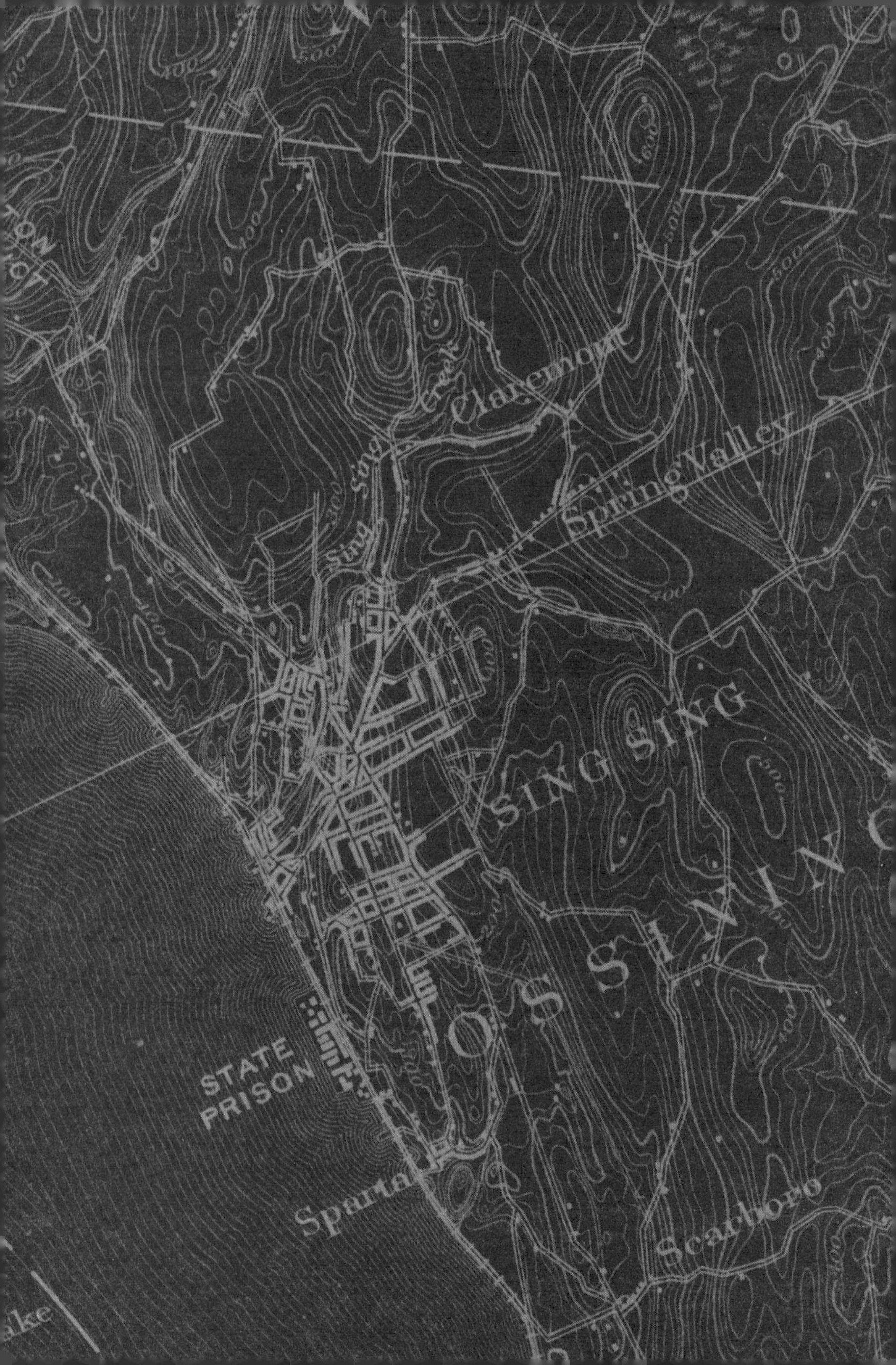

Claremont
Spring Valley
Sing Sing Creek
SING SING
SING SING
OSSINING
STATE PRISON
Sparta
Scarboro

"THREE PRISONERS"

Early morning

There he was again with his bottles.

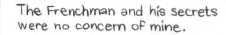

Was he writing to Jacques-Henri?

The Frenchman and his secrets were no concern of mine.

137

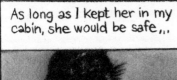

As long as I kept her in my cabin, she would be safe...

You like that one?

Little did I know.

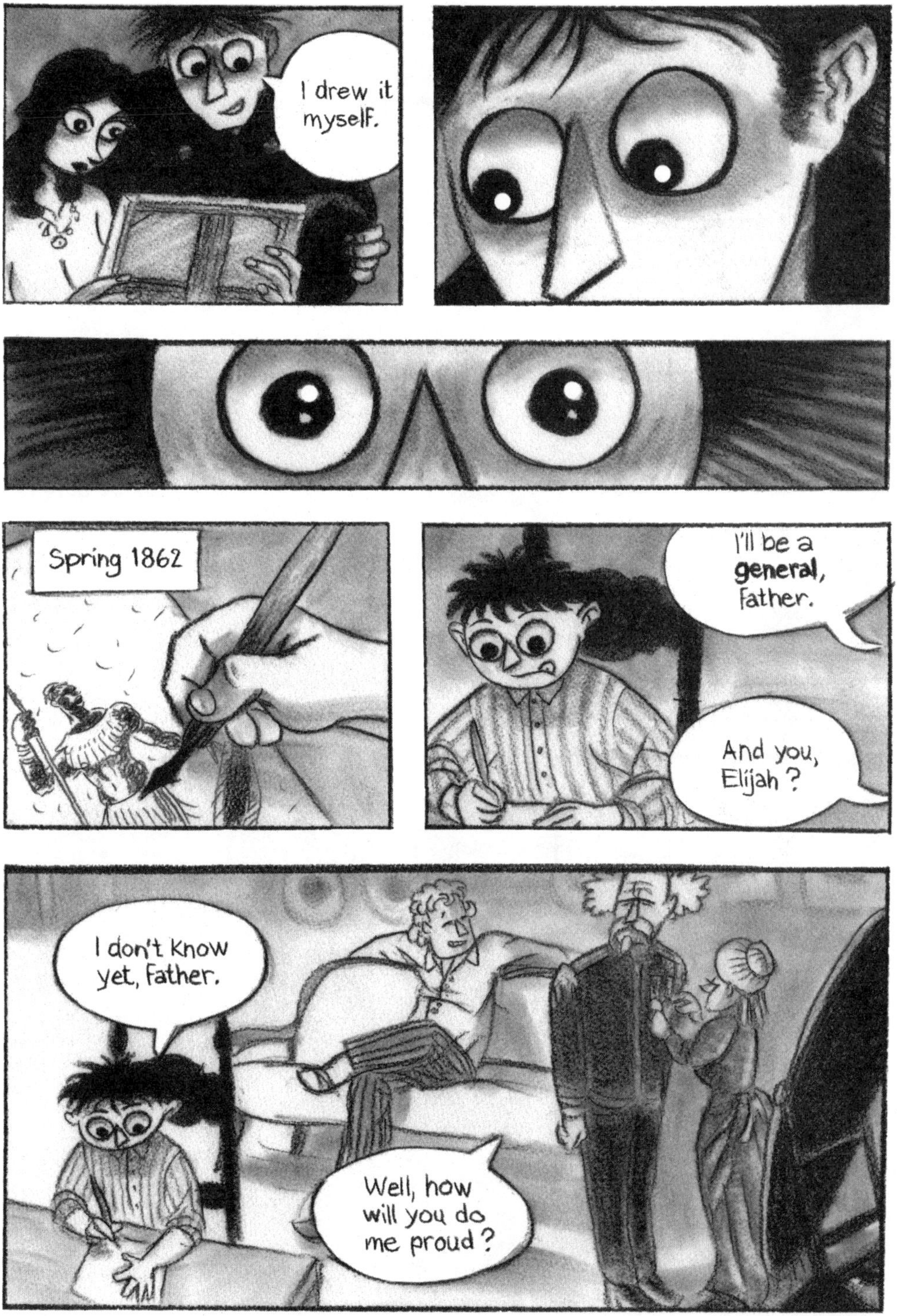
I drew it myself.
Spring 1862
I'll be a **general**, Father.
And you, Elijah ?
I don't know yet, Father.
Well, how will you do me proud ?

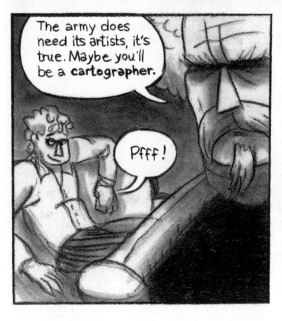

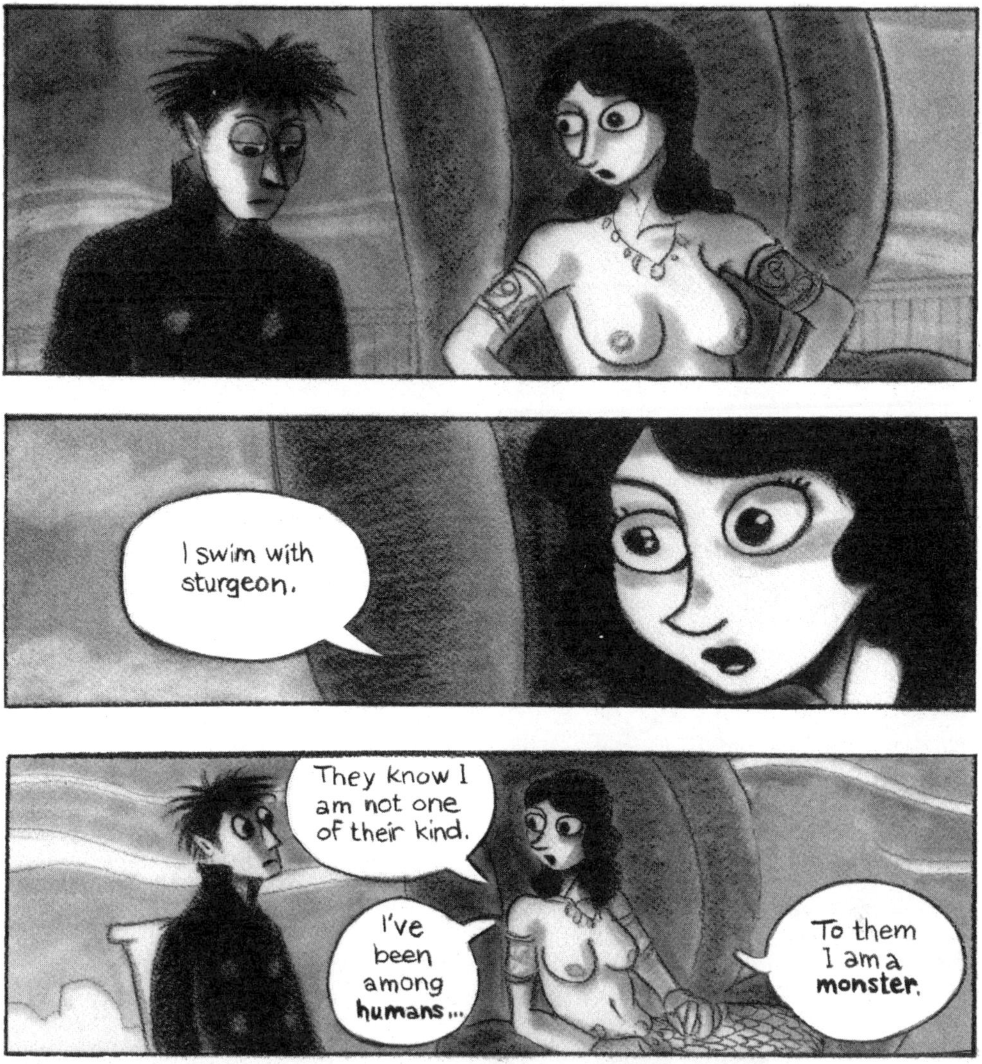
I swim with sturgeon.
They know I am not one of their kind.
I've been among **humans**...
To them I am a **monster**.
But not to you.

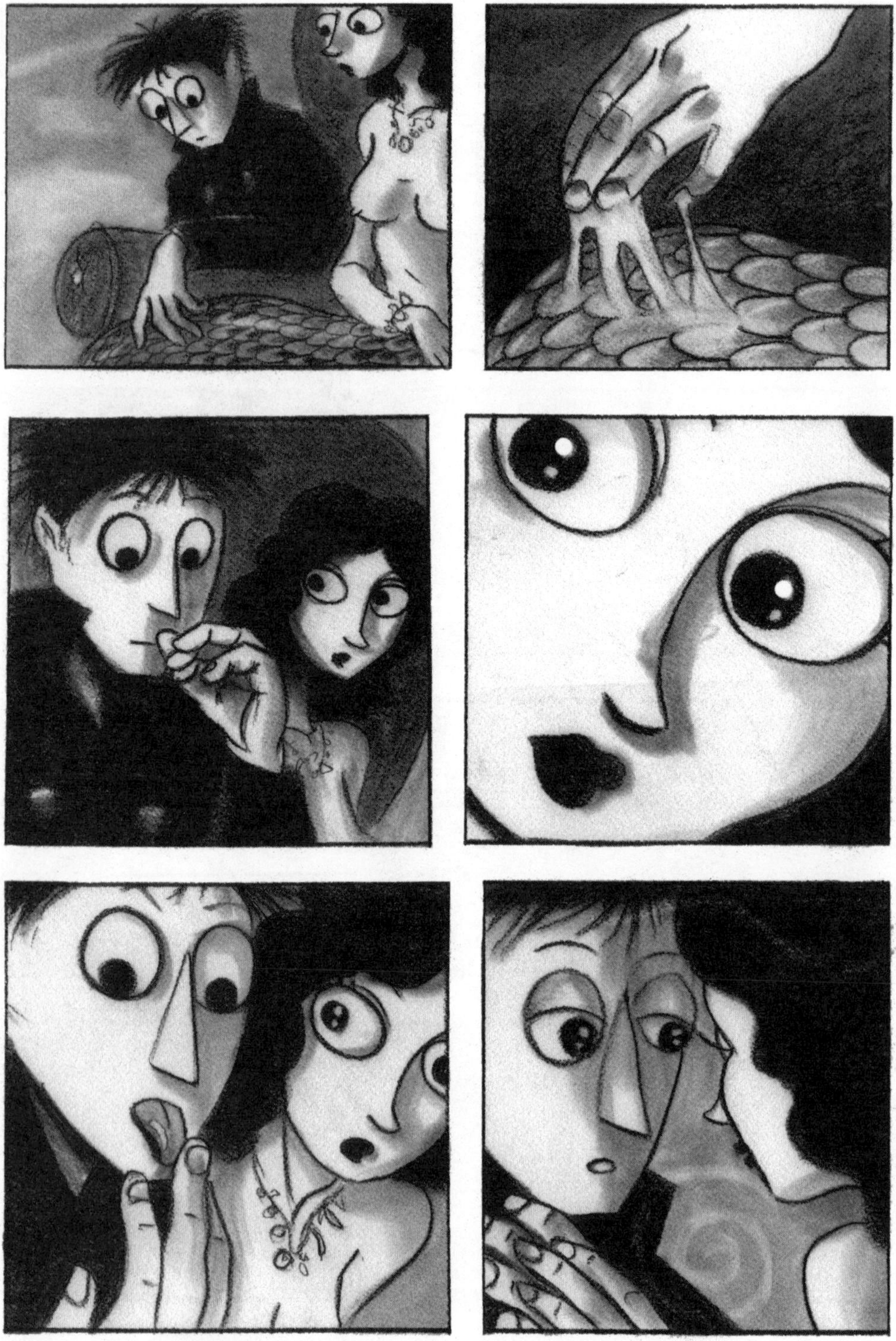

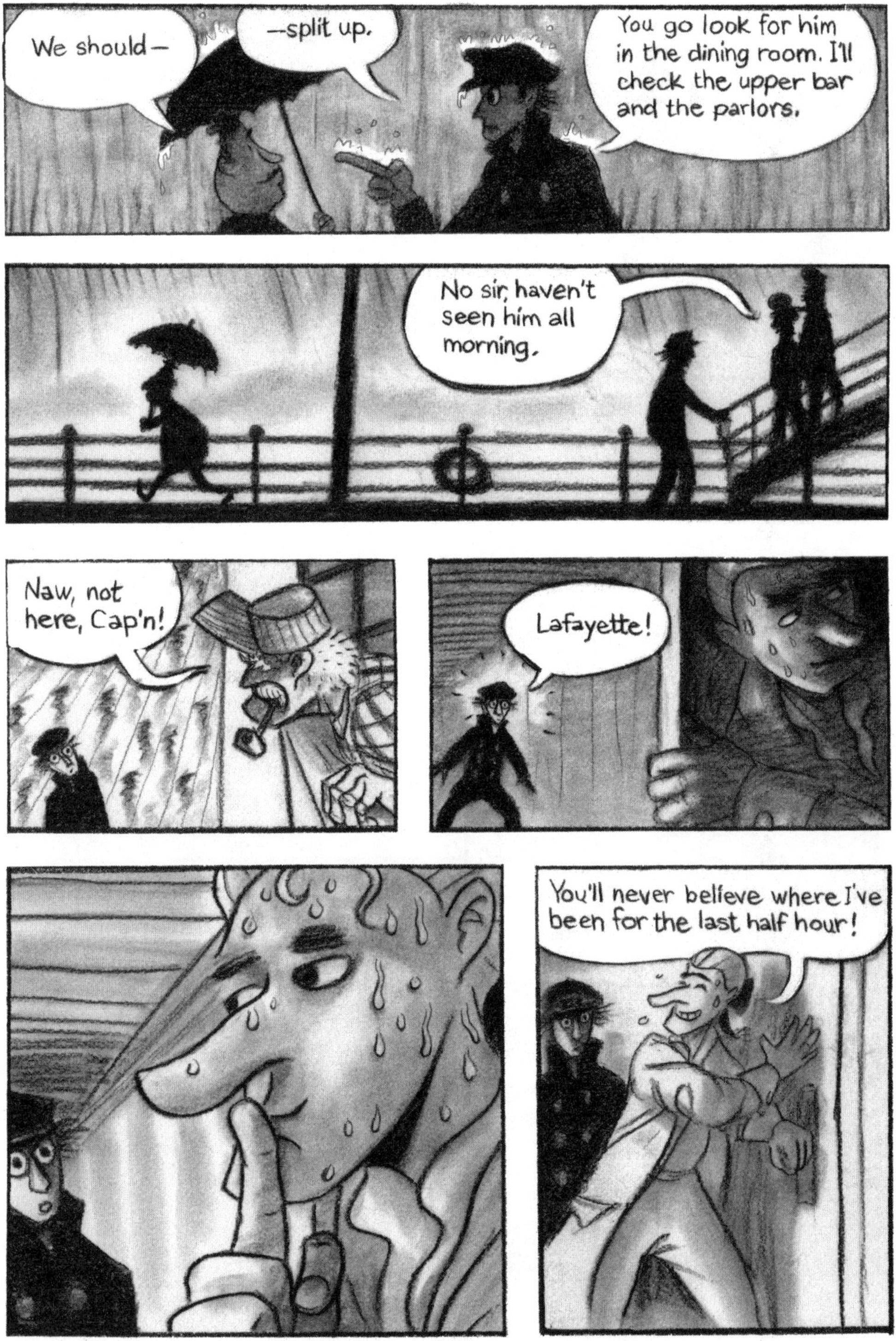
We should—
—split up.
You go look for him in the dining room. I'll check the upper bar and the parlors.
No sir, haven't seen him all morning.
Naw, not here, Cap'n!
Lafayette!
You'll never believe where I've been for the last half hour!

146

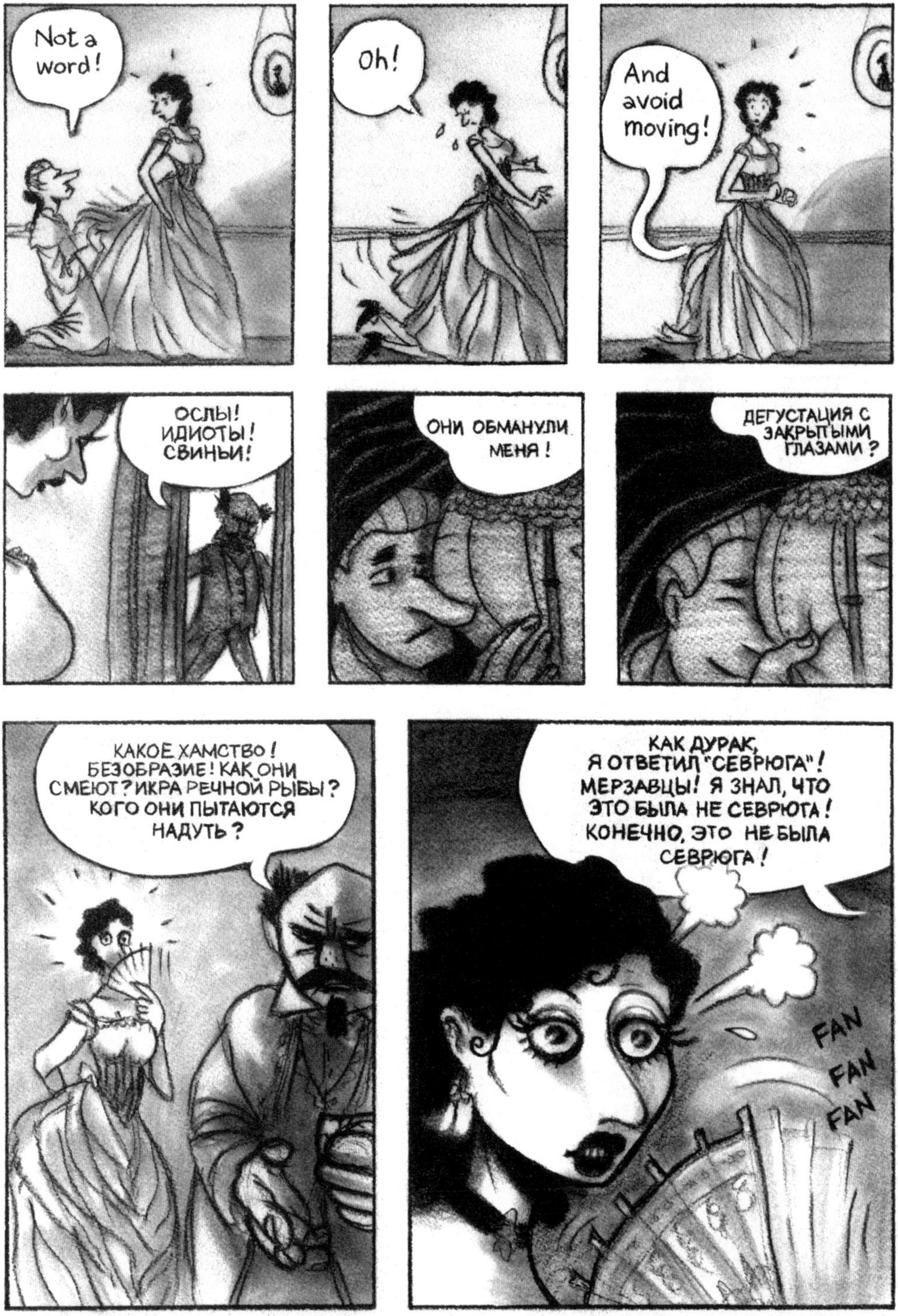
Not a word!
Oh!
And avoid moving!
ОСЛЫ! ИДИОТЫ! СВИНЬИ!
ОНИ ОБМАНУЛИ МЕНЯ!
ДЕГУСТАЦИЯ С ЗАКРЫТЫМИ ГЛАЗАМИ?
КАКОЕ ХАМСТВО! БЕЗОБРАЗИЕ! КАК ОНИ СМЕЮТ? ИКРА РЕЧНОЙ РЫБЫ? КОГО ОНИ ПЫТАЮТСЯ НАДУТЬ?
КАК ДУРАК, Я ОТВЕТИЛ "СЕВРЮГА"! МЕРЗАВЦЫ! Я ЗНАЛ, ЧТО ЭТО БЫЛА НЕ СЕВРЮГА! КОНЕЧНО, ЭТО НЕ БЫЛА СЕВРЮГА!
FAN
FAN
FAN

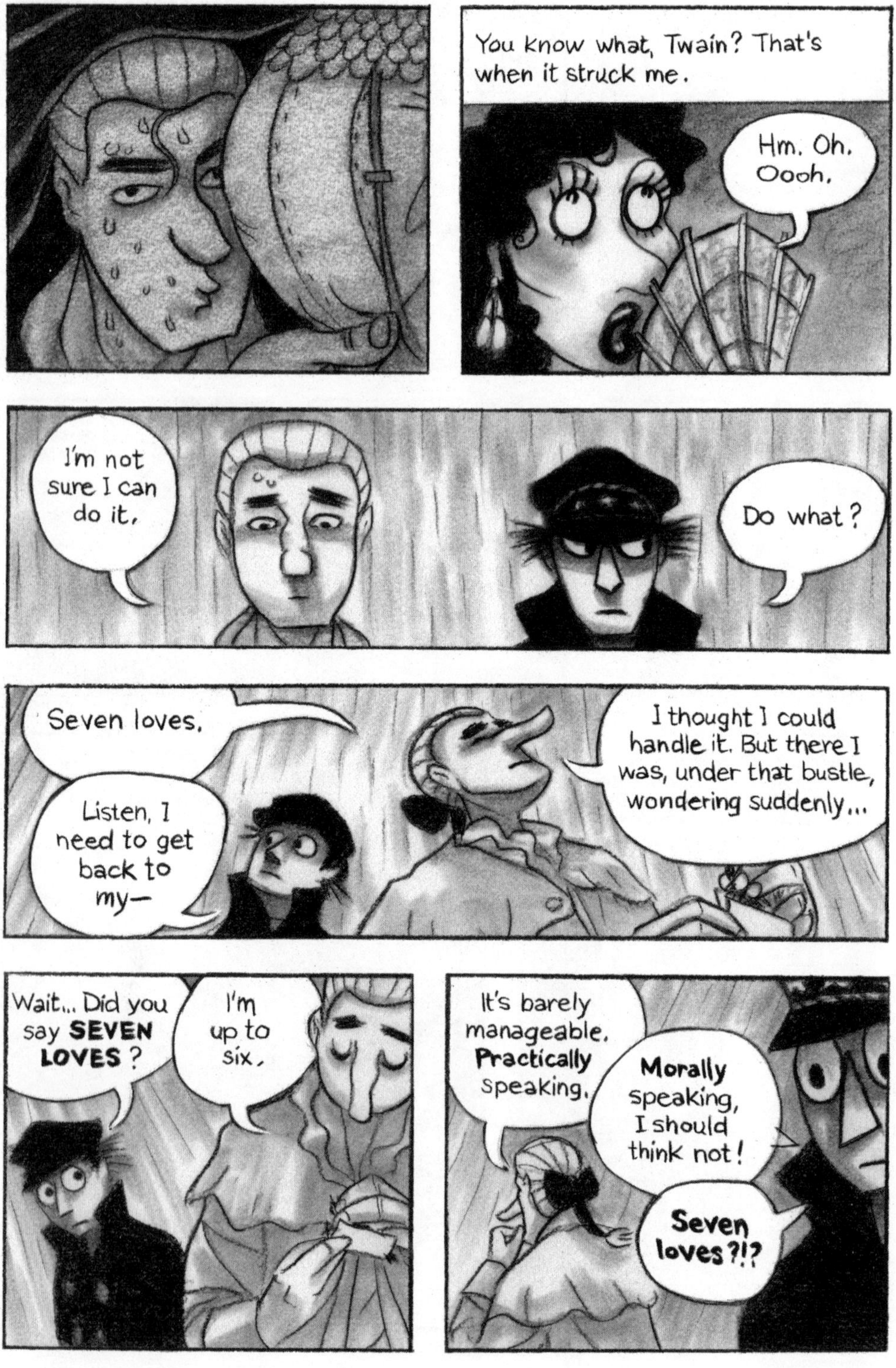
You know what, Twain? That's when it struck me.
Hm. Oh. Oooh.
I'm not sure I can do it.
Do what?
Seven loves.
Listen, I need to get back to my—
I thought I could handle it. But there I was, under that bustle, wondering suddenly...
Wait... Did you say **SEVEN LOVES**?
I'm up to six.
It's barely manageable. **Practically** speaking.
Morally speaking, I should think not!
Seven loves?!?

Long story.

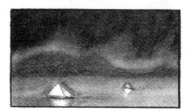

My sky needs more than one star. I'm a man of constellations, me.

And what of your loves, do many stars fill **their** sky?

They're **daytime** beings who crave a singular sun!

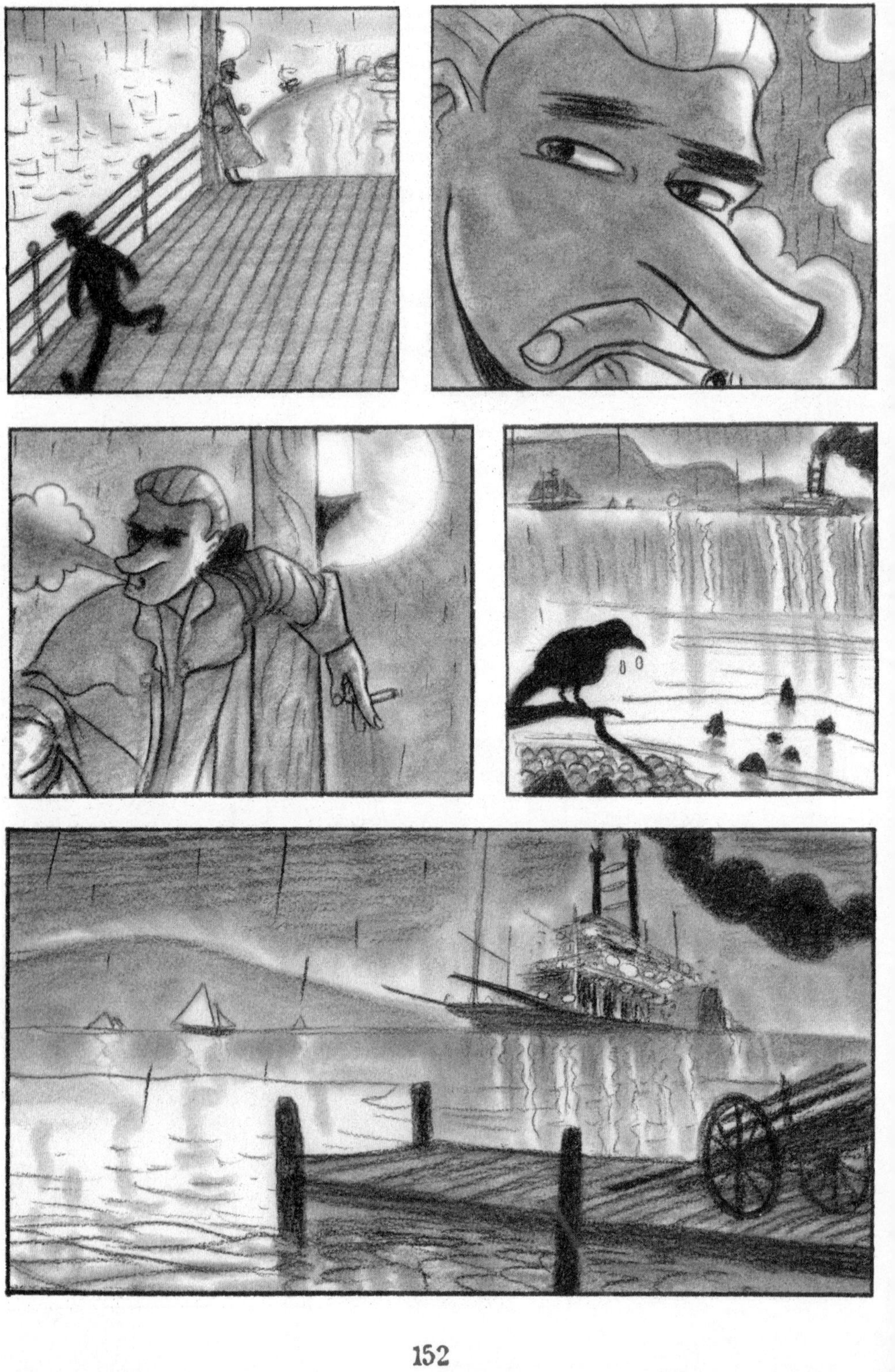

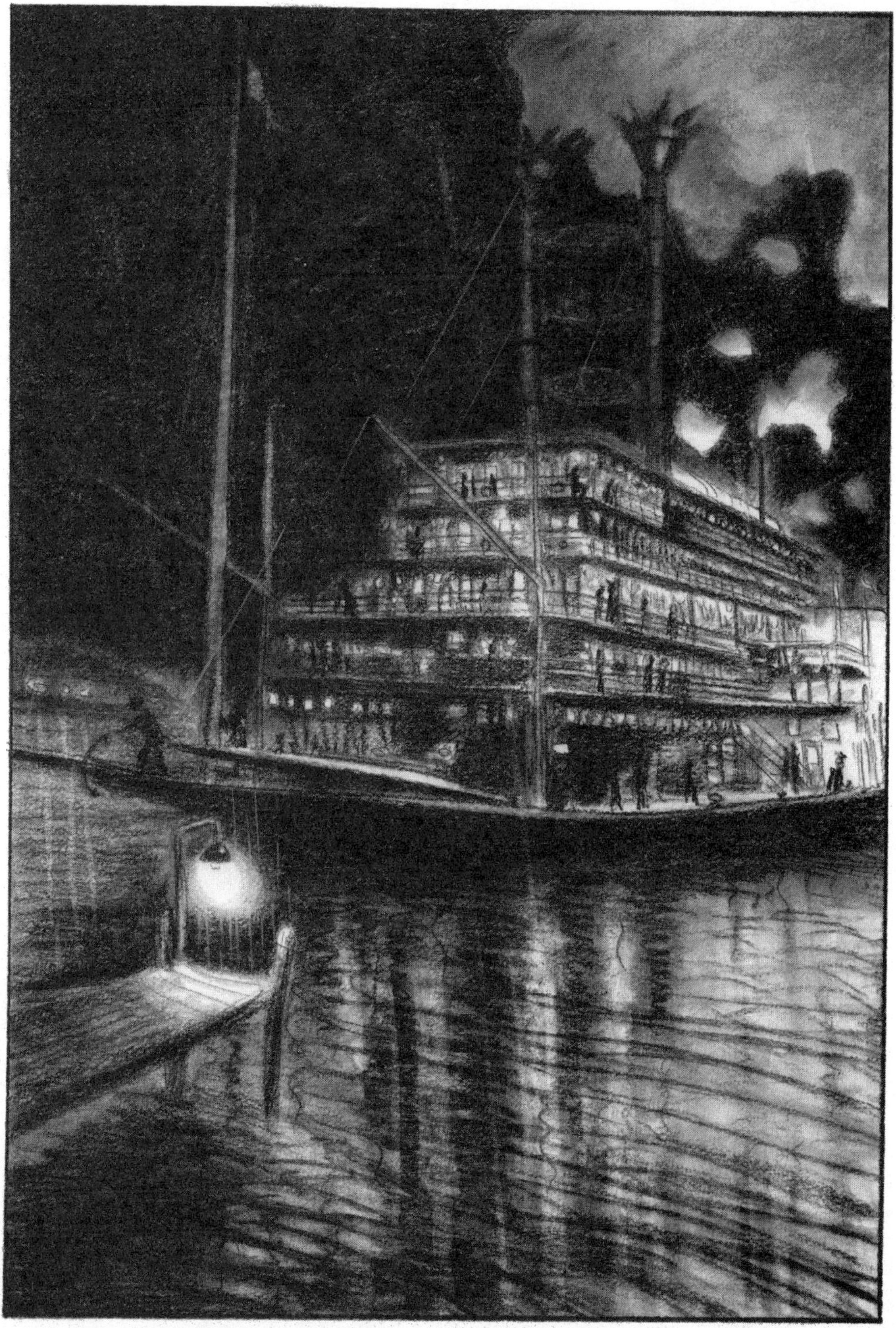

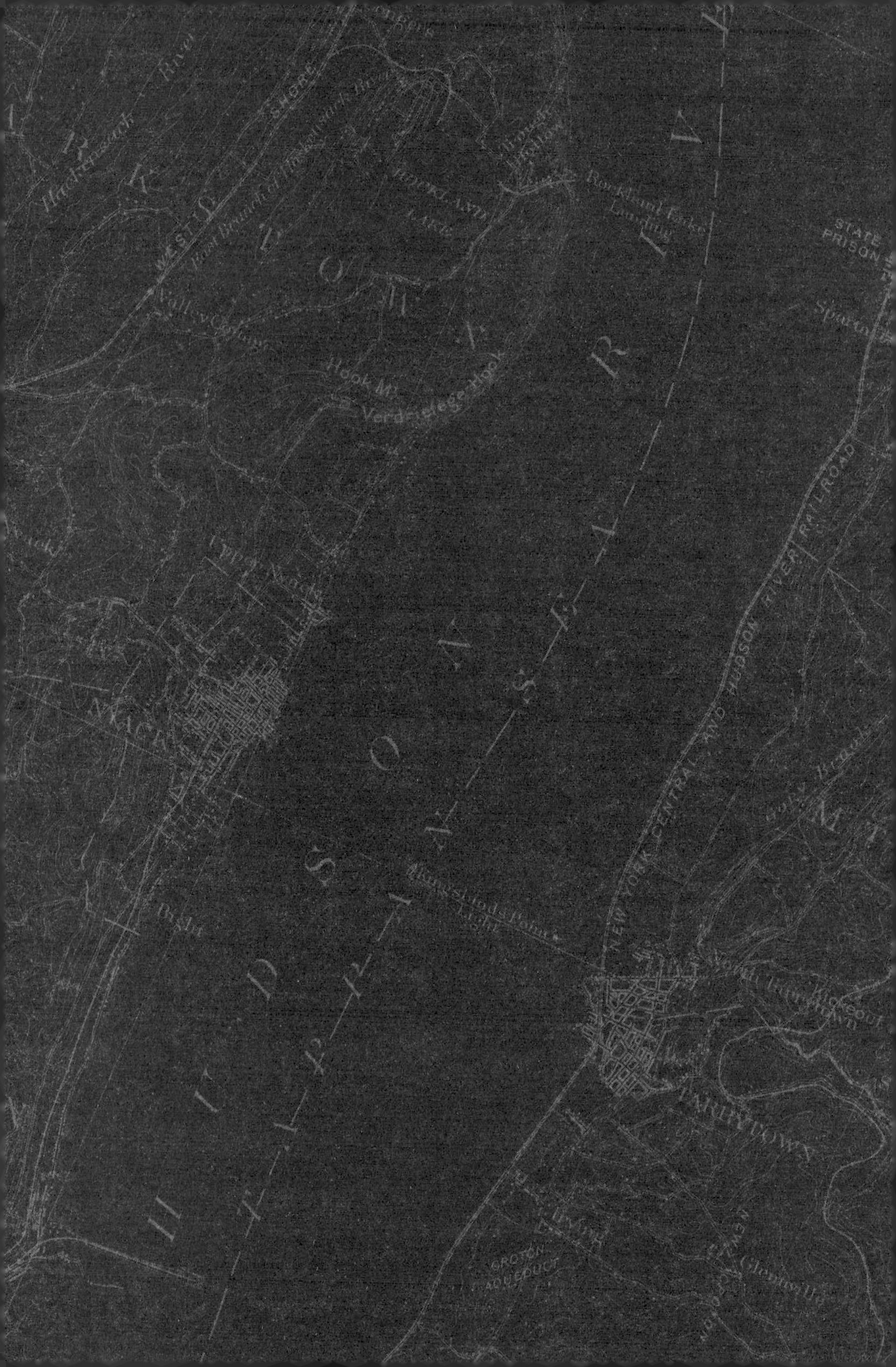
STATE PRISON
Rockland Lake Landing
Hook Mt
Valley Cottage
Hackensack River
Upper Nyack
NEW YORK CENTRAL AND HUDSON RIVER RAILROAD
Light
TARRYTOWN
North Tarrytown
AQUEDUCT

Pt 1, Chap.10

"THE CURE FOR MERMAIDS"

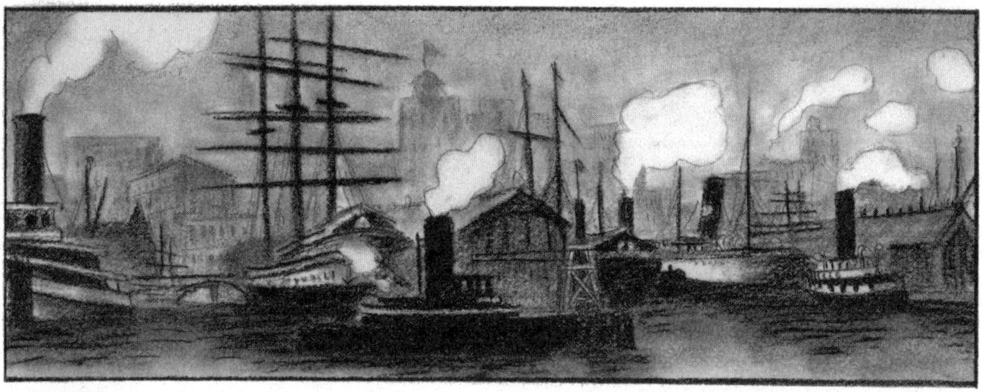

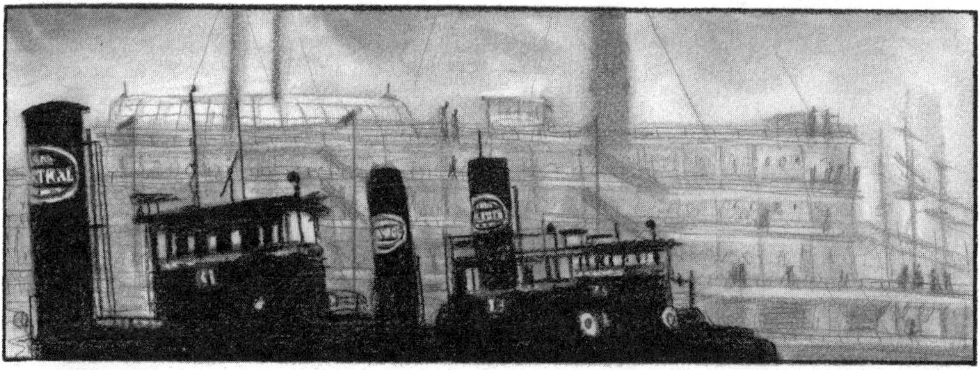

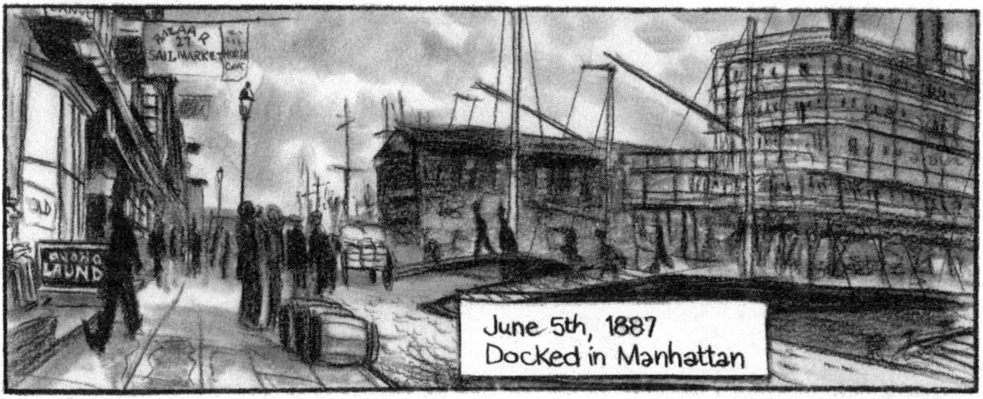
June 5th, 1887
Docked in Manhattan

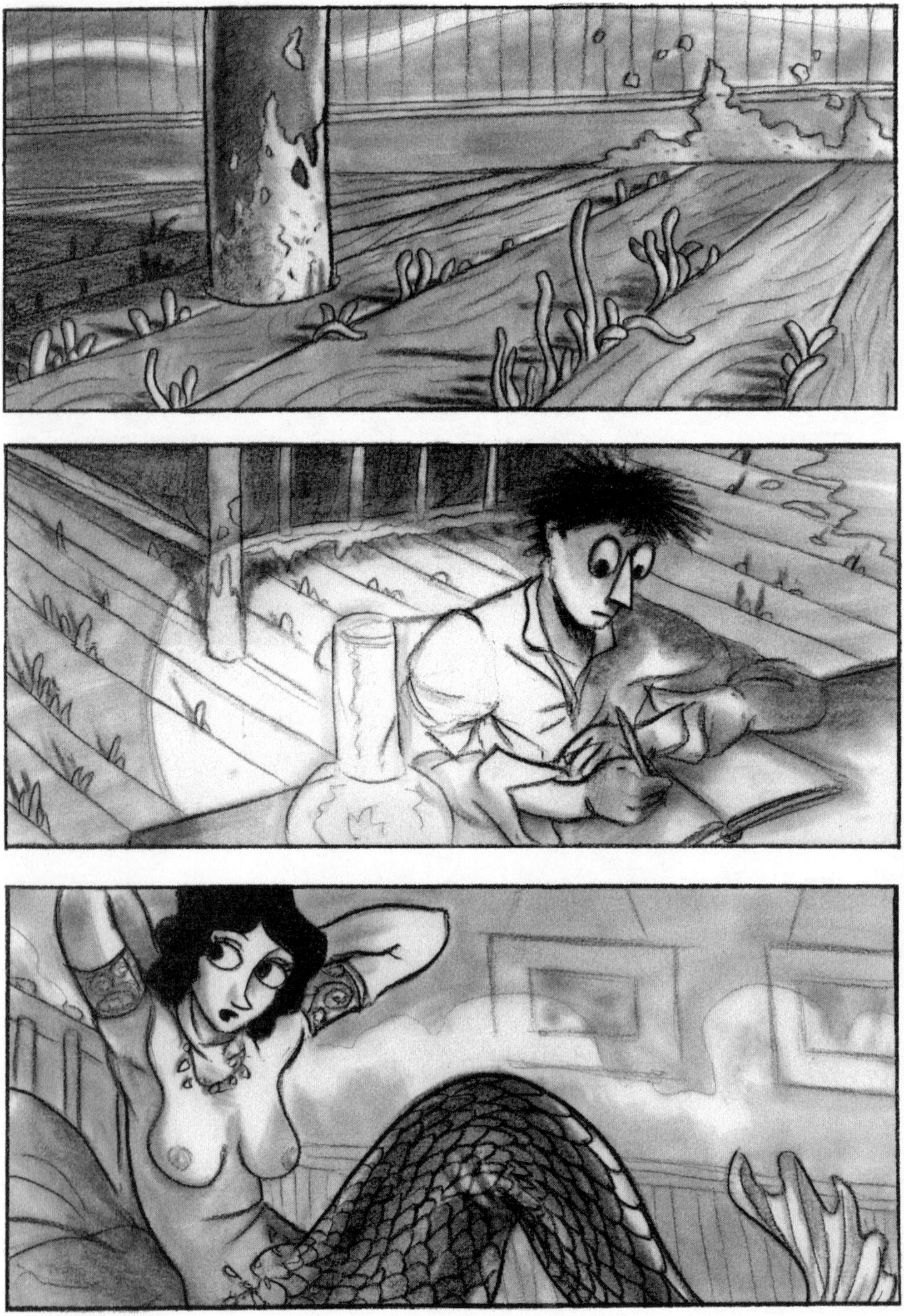

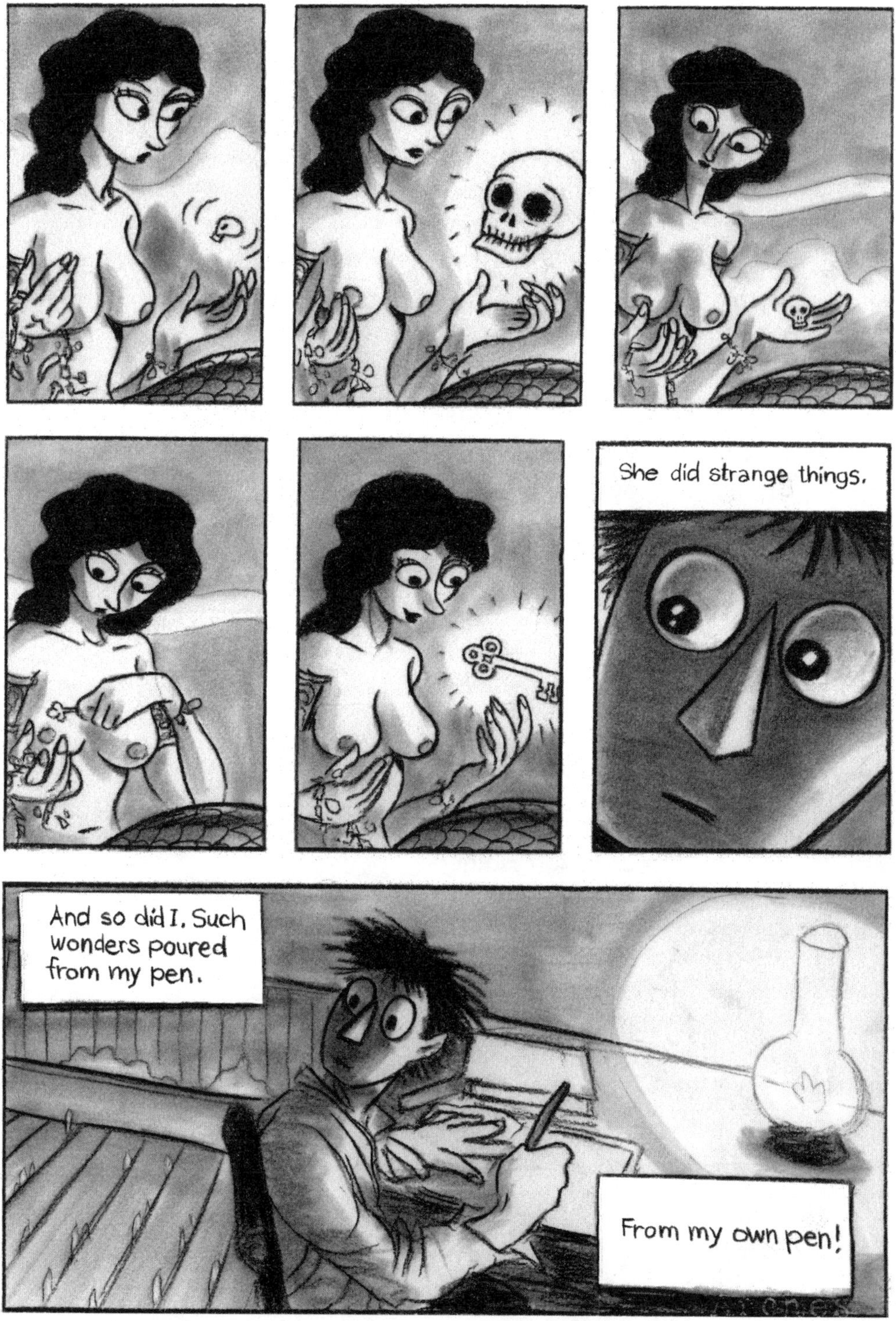
She did strange things.
And so did I. Such wonders poured from my pen.
From my own pen!

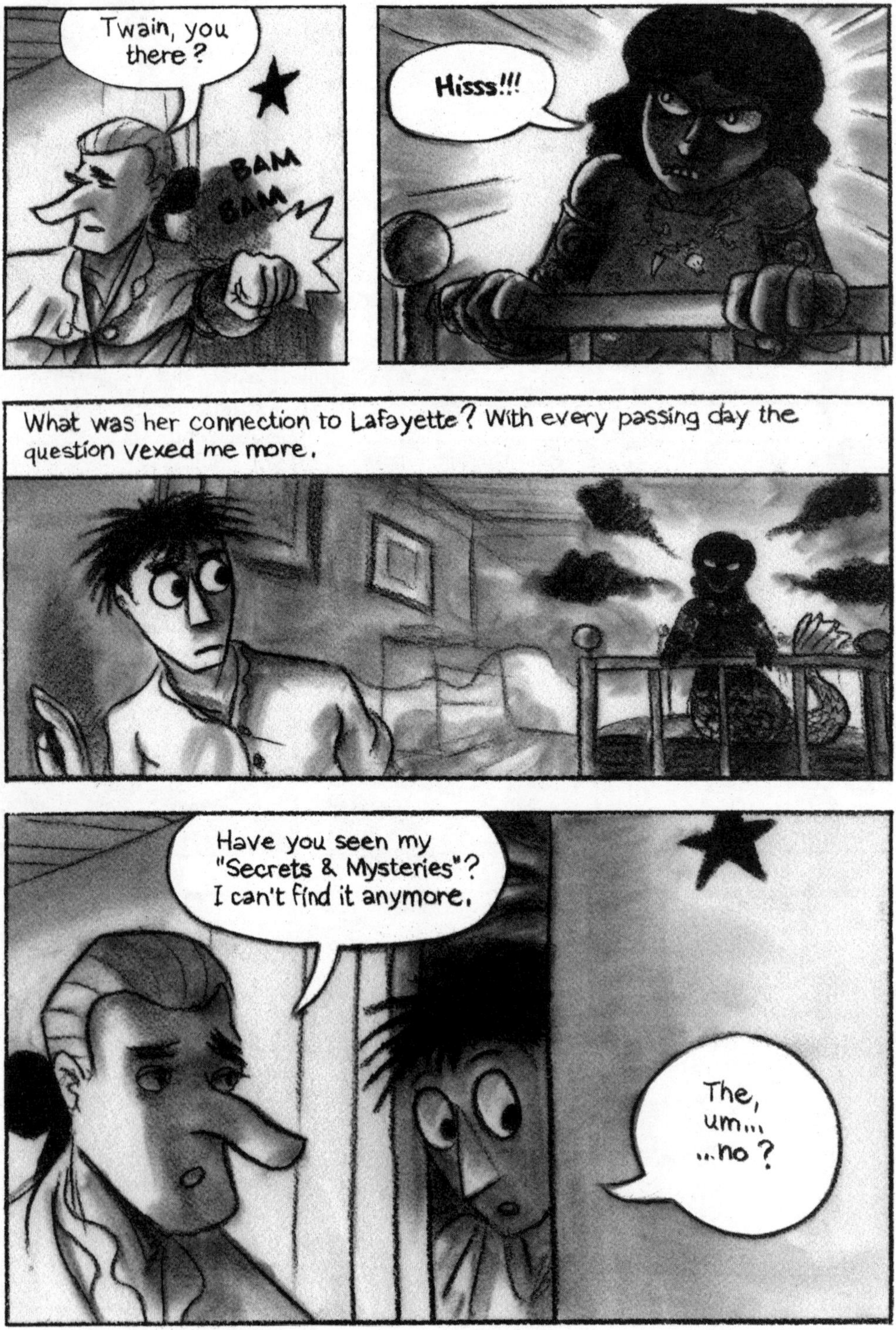
Twain, you there?
BAM BAM
Hisss!!!
What was her connection to Lafayette? With every passing day the question vexed me more.
Have you seen my "Secrets & Mysteries"? I can't find it anymore.
The, um... ...no?

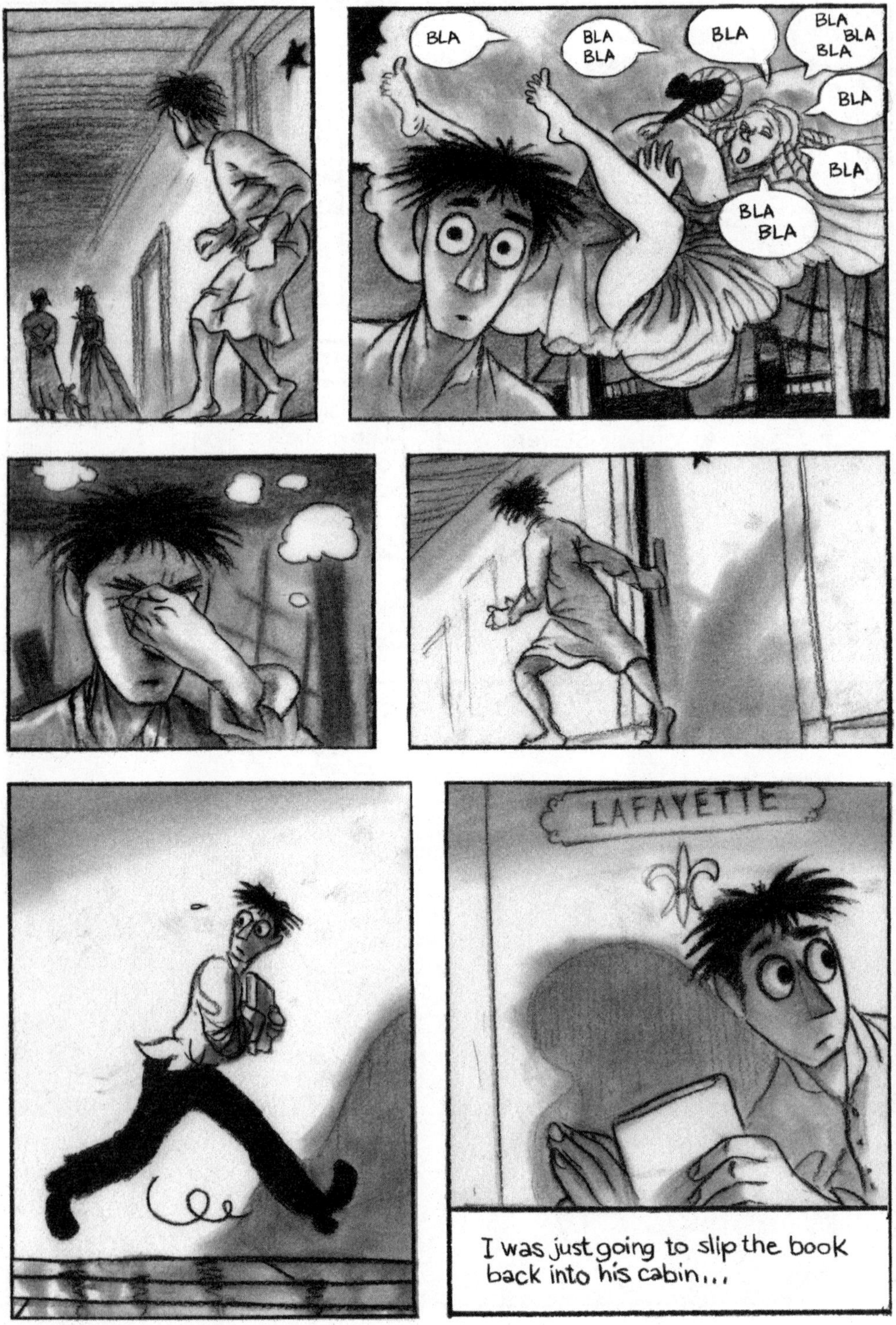
BLA
BLA BLA
BLA
BLA BLA BLA
BLA
BLA
BLA BLA
LAFAYETTE
I was just going to slip the book back into his cabin...

... when I accidentally glimpsed another letter from Beaverton himself...

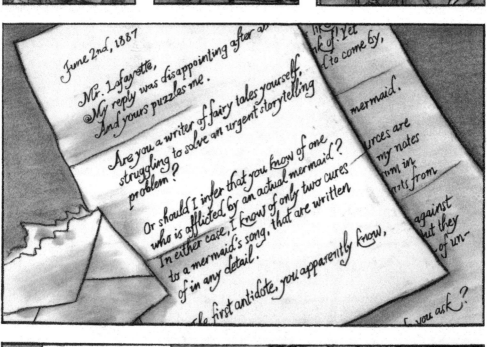

June 2nd, 1887

Mr. Lafayette,
My reply was disappointing after a...
And yours puzzles me.

Are you a writer of fairy tales yourself, struggling to solve an urgent storytelling problem?

Or should I infer that you know of one who is afflicted by an actual mermaid? In either case, I know of only two cures to a mermaid's song, that are written of in any detail.

...e first antidote, you apparently know,

...k of! Yet
...t to come by,

mermaid.

...rces are
...my notes
...m in
...rts from

...against
...t they
...of un-

...you ask?

What?!

is that classic of fairy-logic: finding seven loves at once, for nothing less can replace the sea-maid's charm.

That certainly seems like a cure to most any enchantment I can think of! Yet such a panacea seems patently hard to come by, wouldn't you say?

Seven loves!! Exactly as Lafayette was saying! But then that meant ... Had **he** heard her sing...?!

panacea seems patently ~~hard~~

The other prescription is to kill the mermaid.

~~cures, my~~ sources are

As to the other sorts of cures, my sources are so fragmented; they include notes from the vaults of the British Museum in London as well as antique manuscripts from the New York Public Library. There I read of ancient incantations against bird-sirens in some Chaldean texts, but they aren't even whole, and involve the use of unknown herbs.

So, Mr. Lafayette, why do you ask?

Sincerely, CGB

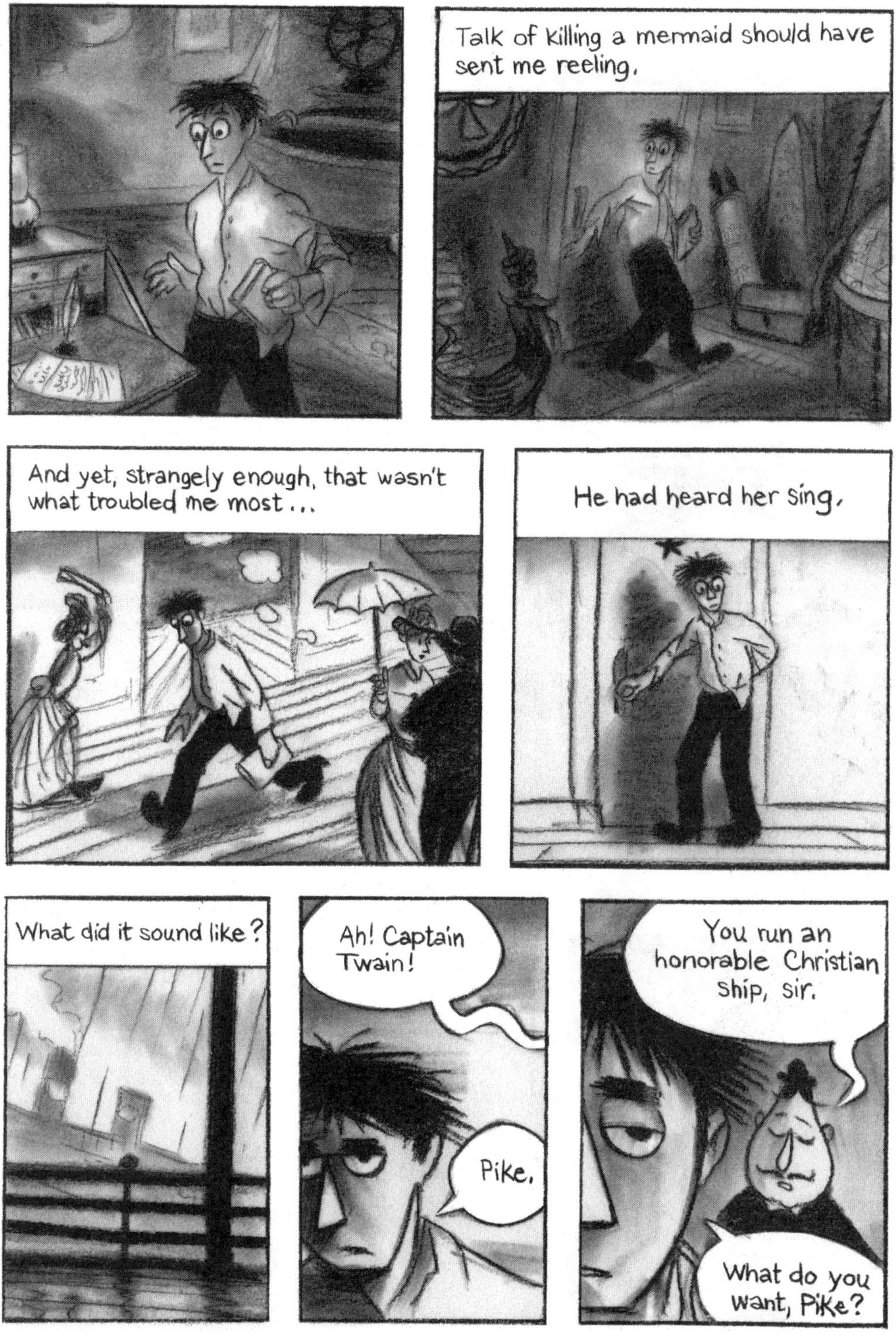
Talk of killing a mermaid should have sent me reeling.
And yet, strangely enough, that wasn't what troubled me most...
He had heard her sing.
What did it sound like?
Ah! Captain Twain!
Pike.
You run an honorable Christian ship, sir.
What do you want, Pike?

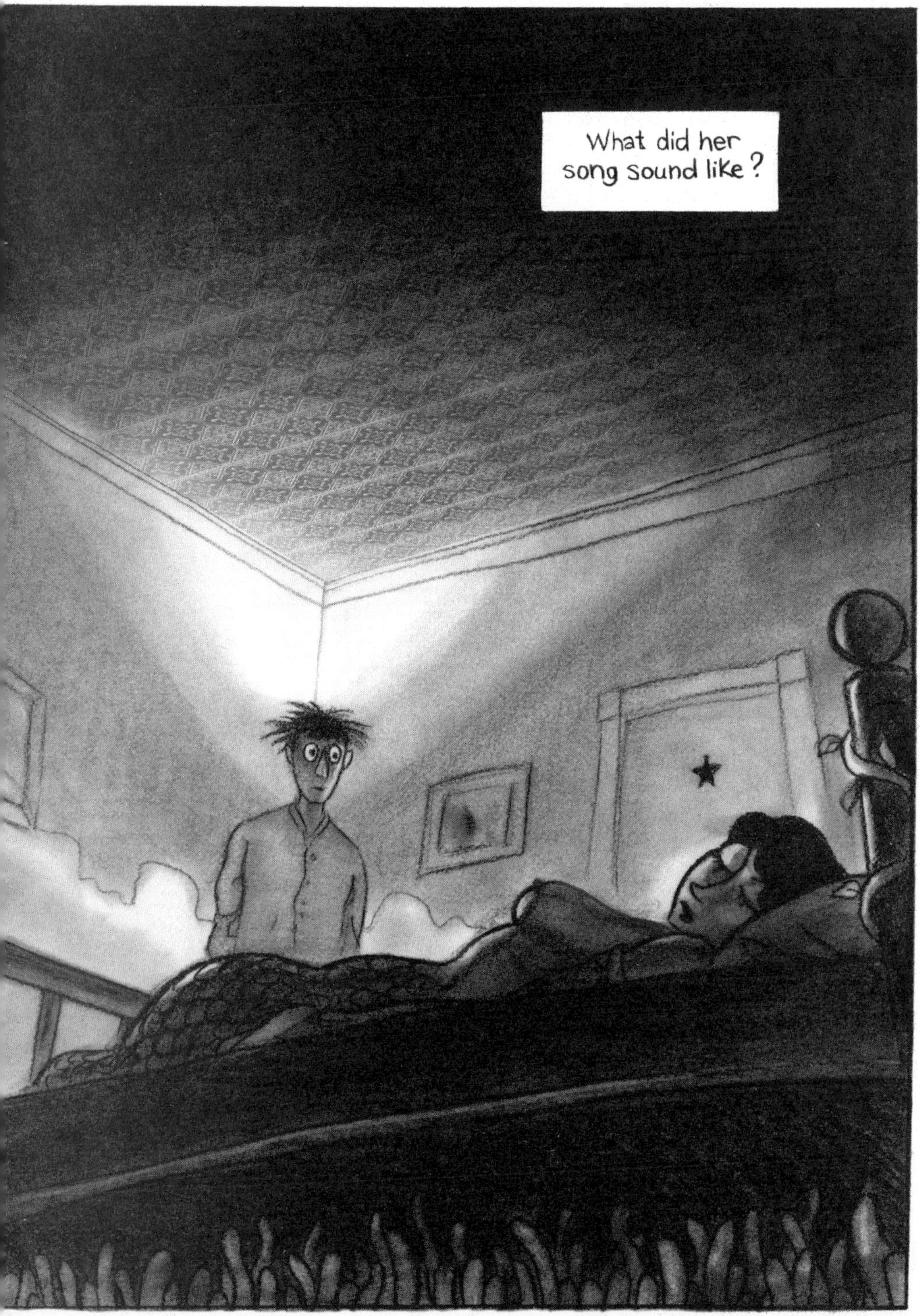
What did her song sound like?

Blauvelt-ville

Bight

H U D

T O W N

U

T A P P

H

Piermont

Sparkill

Tappan

N. JERSEY

NEW YORK

NEW JERSEY

Palisades

Snedens Landing

Dobbs Fer

Pt 1, Chap.11

"SOUTH OF THE NORTH RIVER"

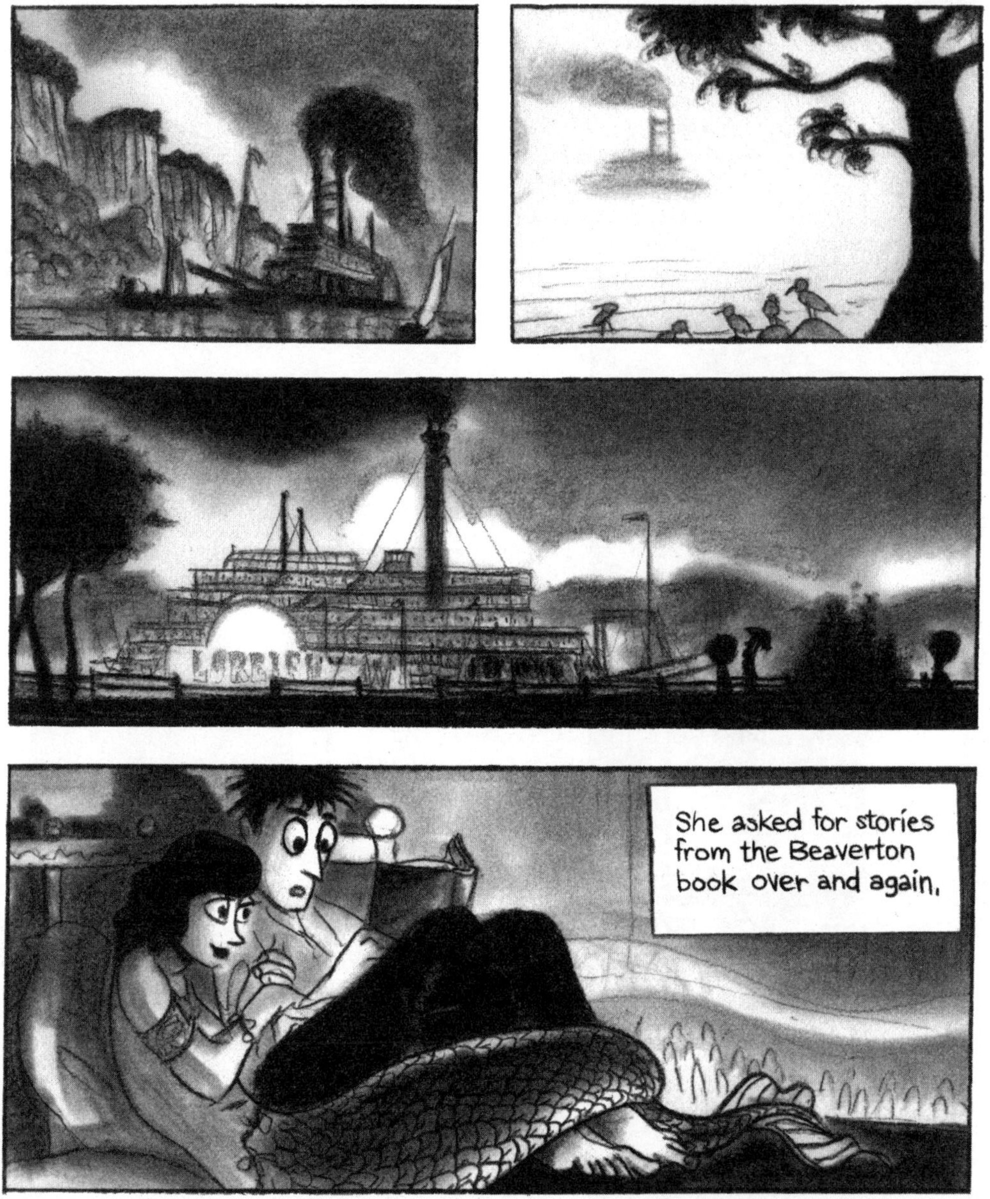
She asked for stories from the Beaverton book over and again.

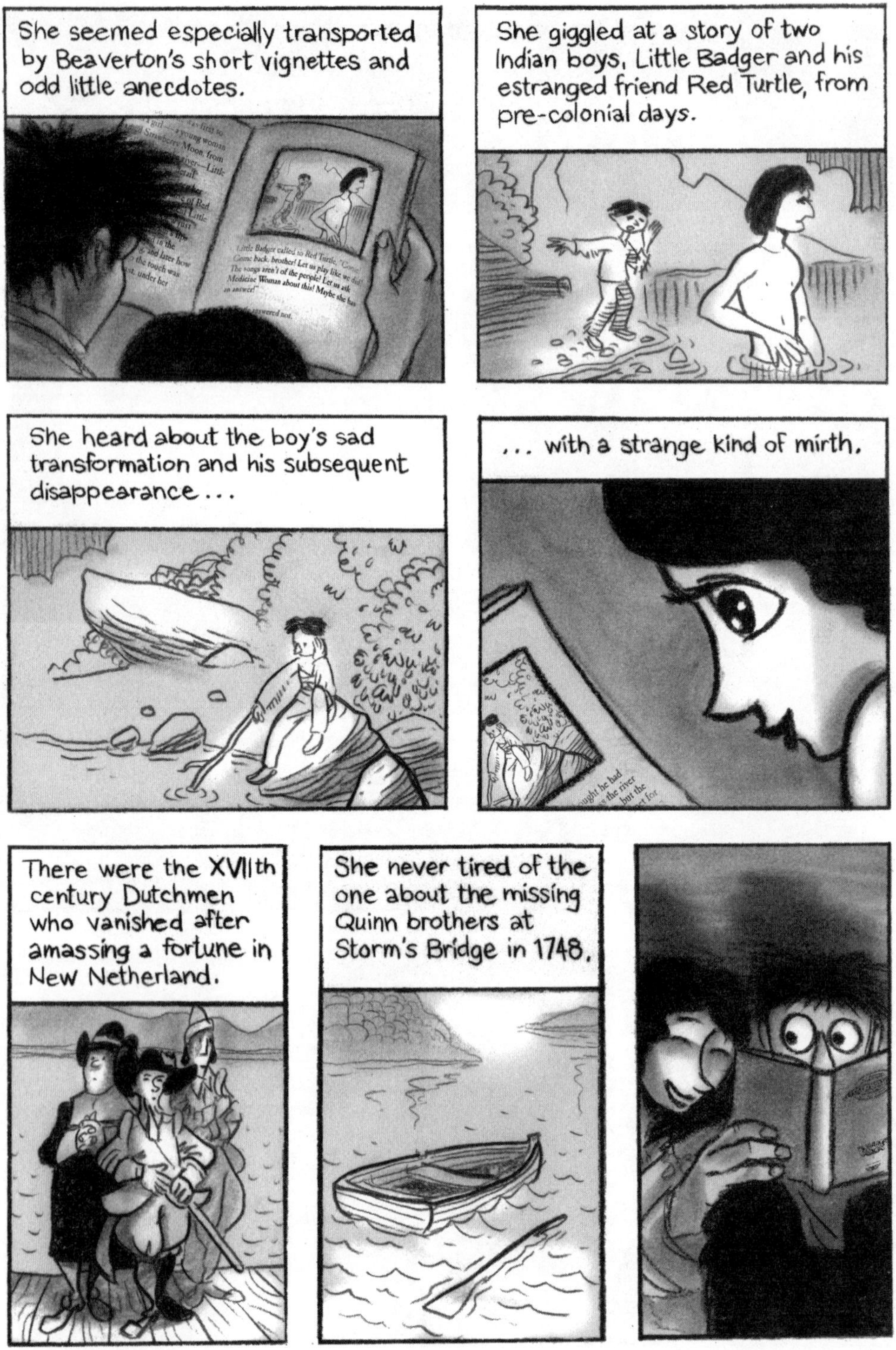

She seemed especially transported by Beaverton's short vignettes and odd little anecdotes.
She giggled at a story of two Indian boys, Little Badger and his estranged friend Red Turtle, from pre-colonial days.
She heard about the boy's sad transformation and his subsequent disappearance . . .
. . . with a strange kind of mirth.
There were the XVIIth century Dutchmen who vanished after amassing a fortune in New Netherland.
She never tired of the one about the missing Quinn brothers at Storm's Bridge in 1748.

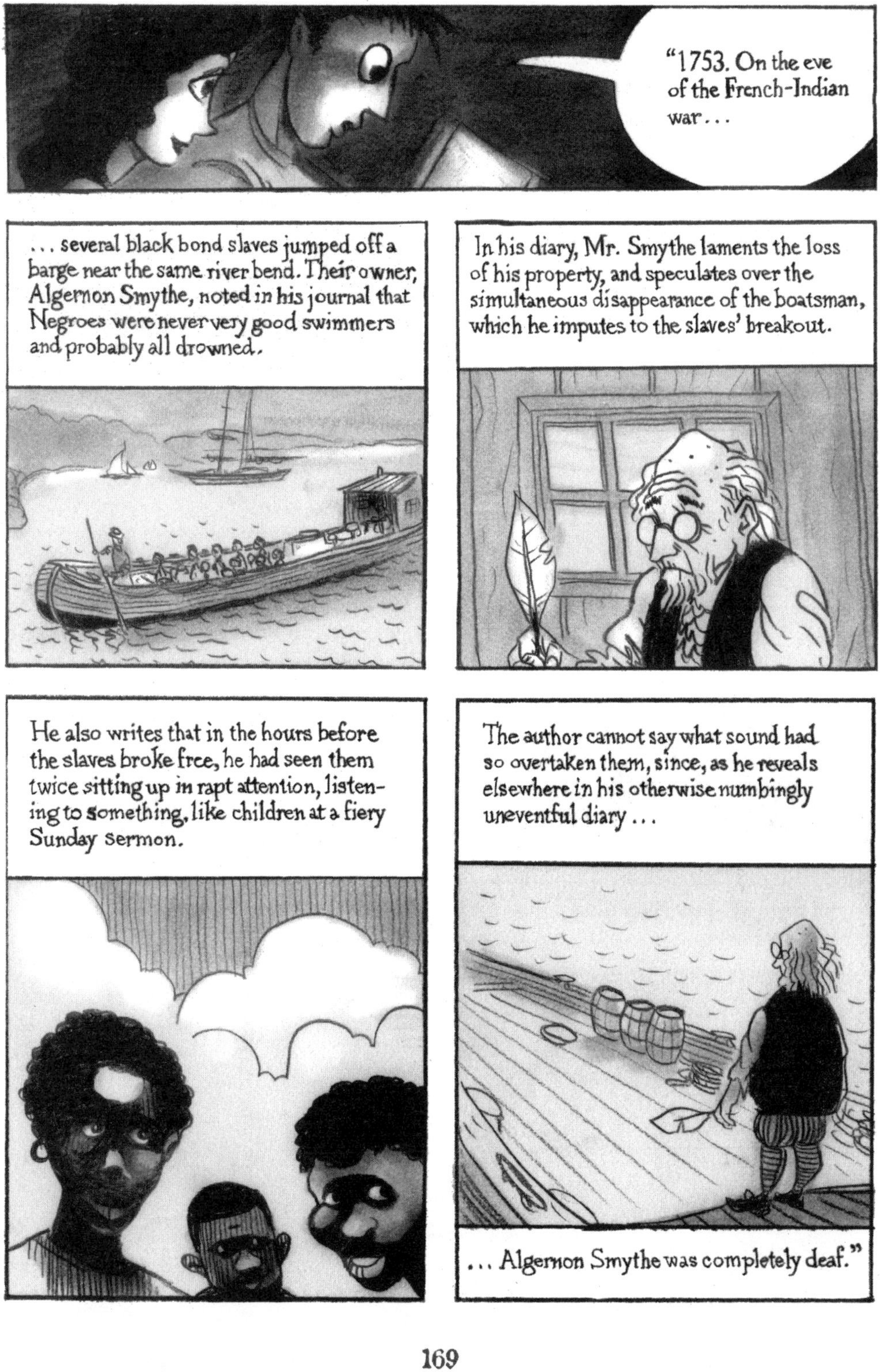
"1753. On the eve of the French-Indian war...
... several black bond slaves jumped off a barge near the same river bend. Their owner, Algernon Smythe, noted in his journal that Negroes were never very good swimmers and probably all drowned.
In his diary, Mr. Smythe laments the loss of his property, and speculates over the simultaneous disappearance of the boatsman, which he imputes to the slaves' breakout.
He also writes that in the hours before the slaves broke free, he had seen them twice sitting up in rapt attention, listening to something, like children at a fiery Sunday sermon.
The author cannot say what sound had so overtaken them, since, as he reveals elsewhere in his otherwise numbingly uneventful diary...
... Algernon Smythe was completely deaf."

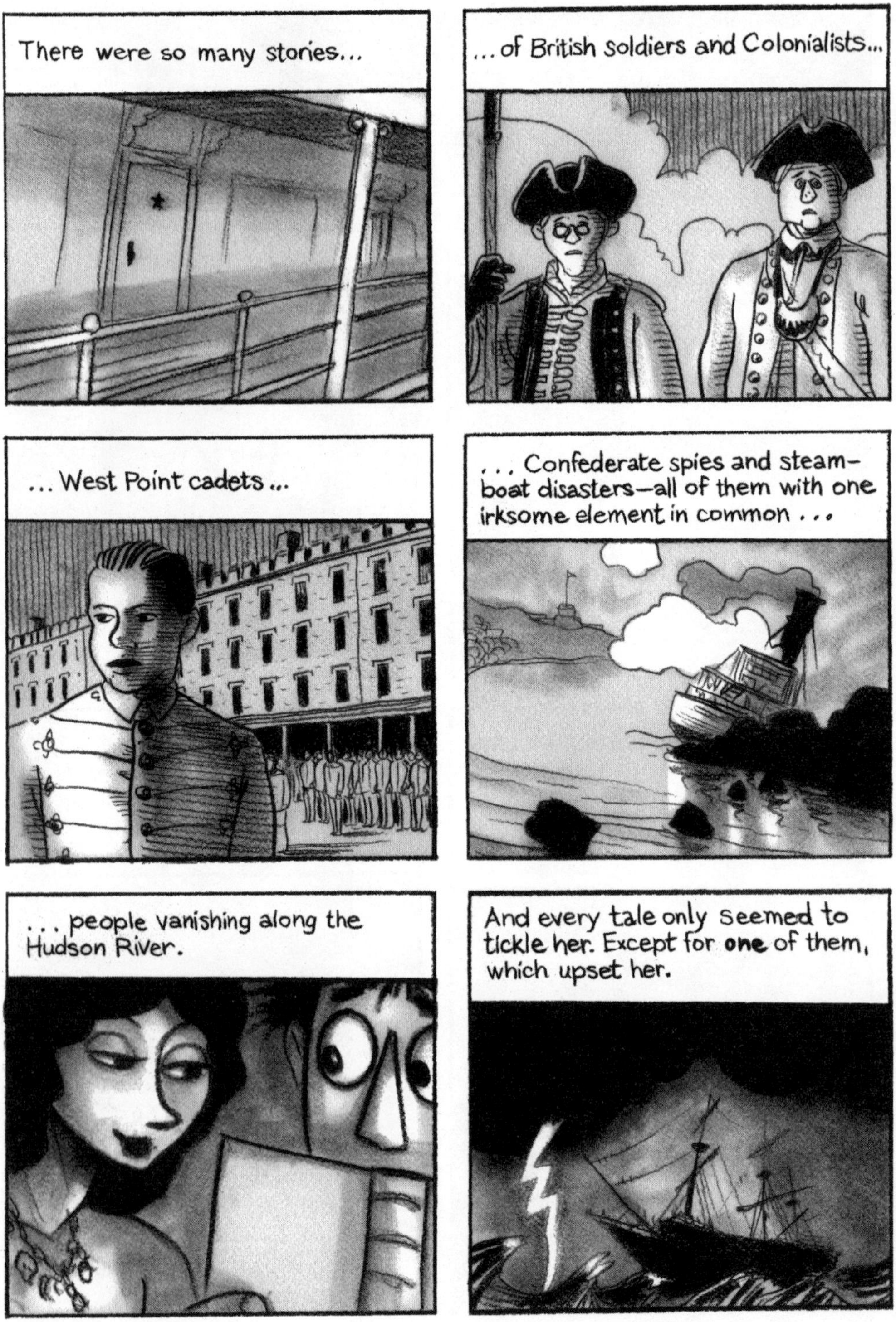
There were so many stories...
...of British soldiers and Colonialists...
...West Point cadets...
..., Confederate spies and steam-boat disasters—all of them with one irksome element in common ...
... people vanishing along the Hudson River.
And every tale only seemed to tickle her. Except for **one** of them, which upset her.

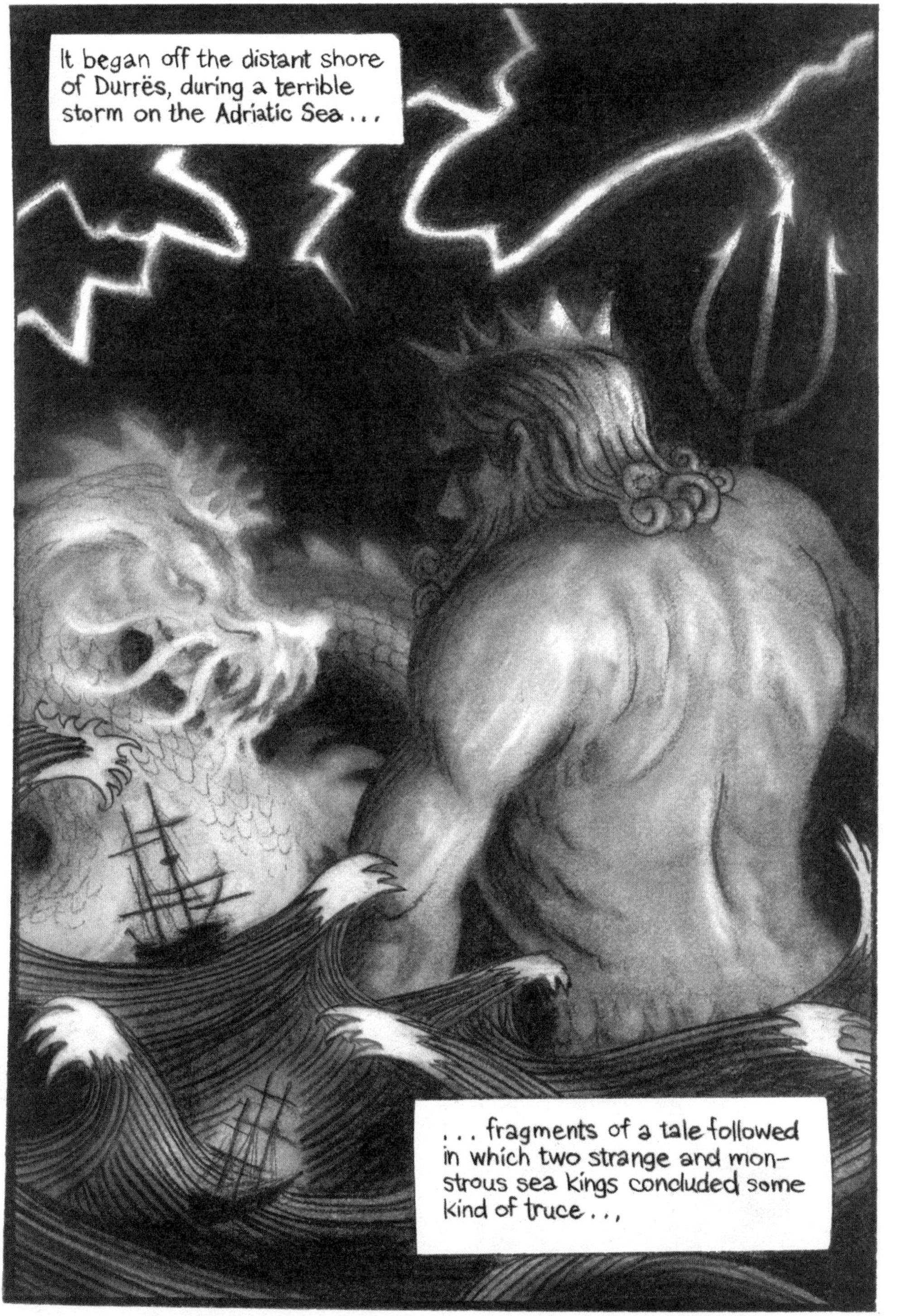
It began off the distant shore of Durrës, during a terrible storm on the Adriatic Sea . . .
. . . fragments of a tale followed in which two strange and monstrous sea kings concluded some kind of truce . . .

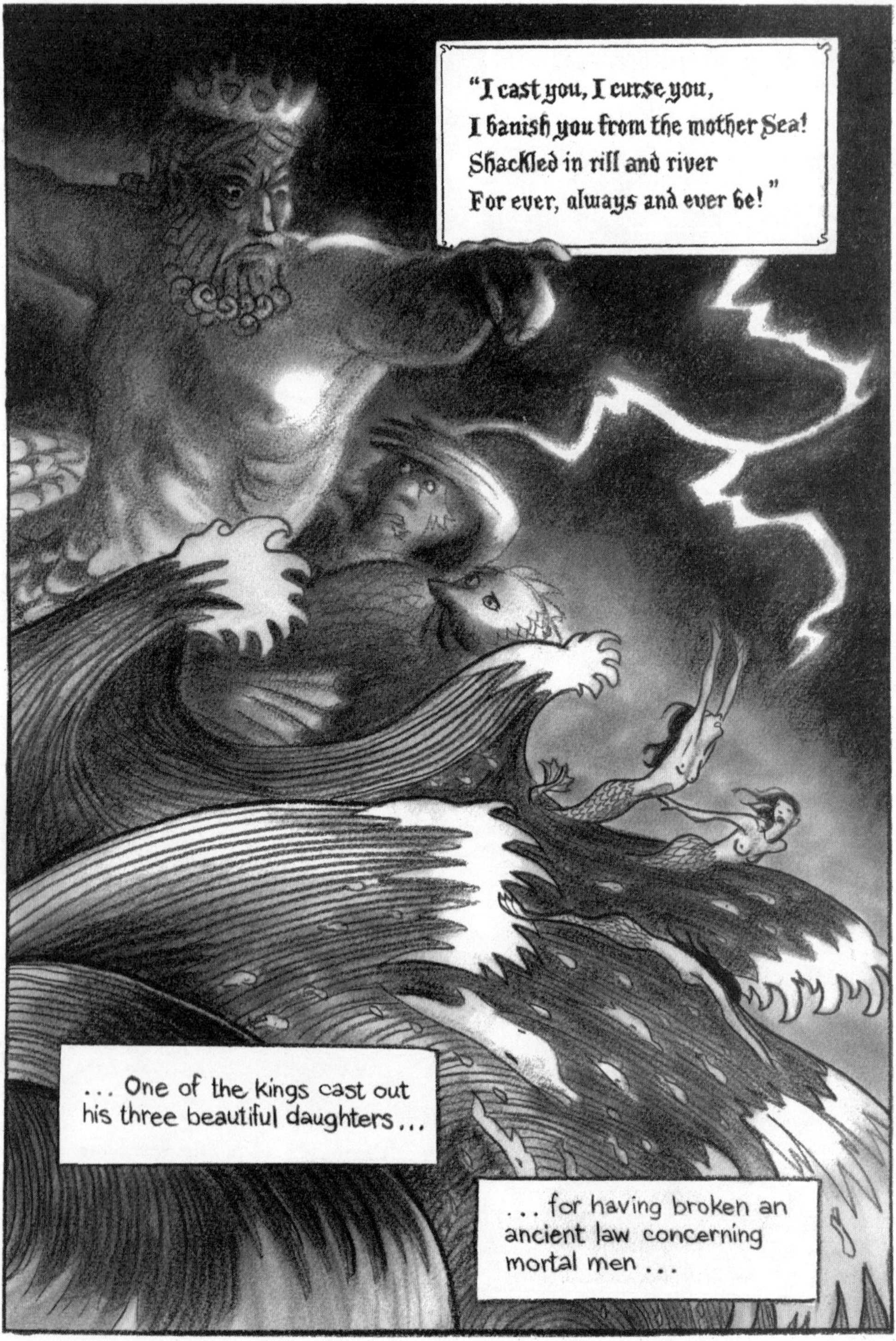
"I cast you, I curse you,
I banish you from the mother Sea!
Shackled in rill and river
For ever, always and ever be!"
... One of the kings cast out
his three beautiful daughters...
... for having broken an
ancient law concerning
mortal men ...

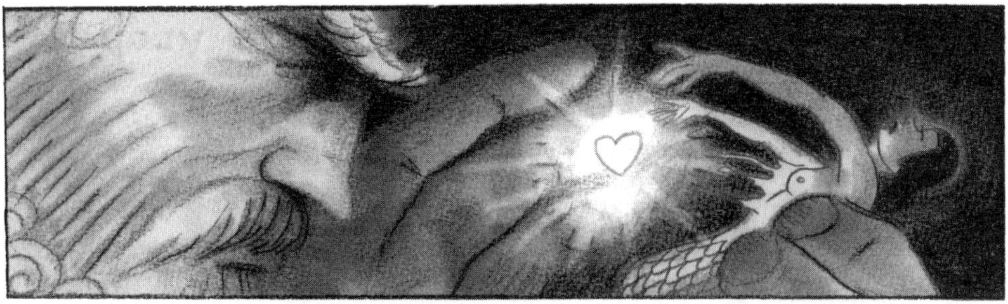

But before that, he tore their hearts away.

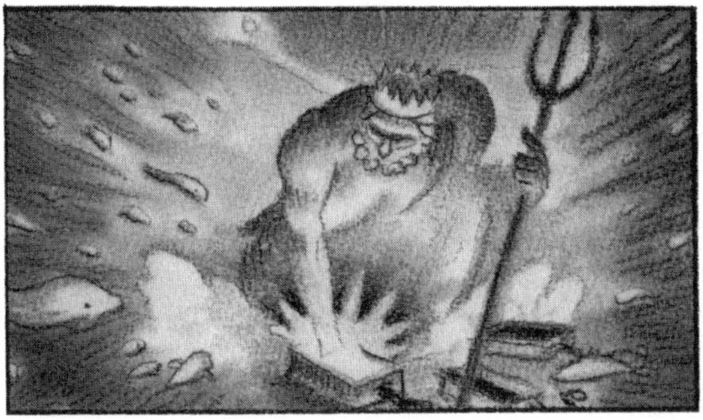

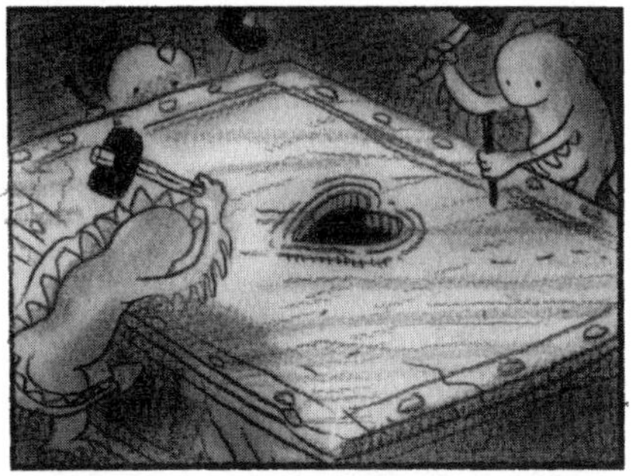

He locked each heart in a granite chest sealed with seven curses
and cast each chest into the deepest part of three

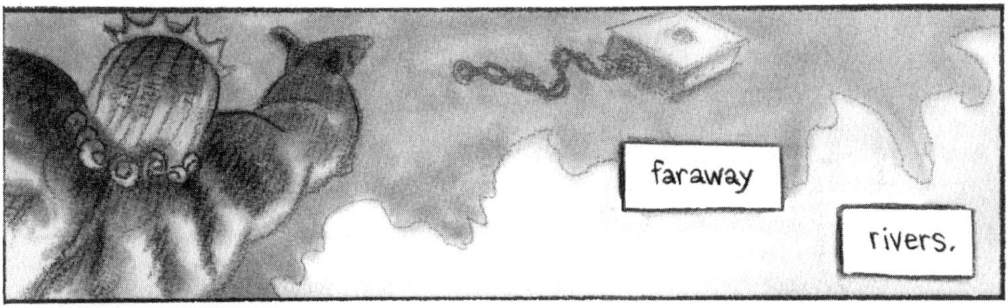
faraway
rivers.

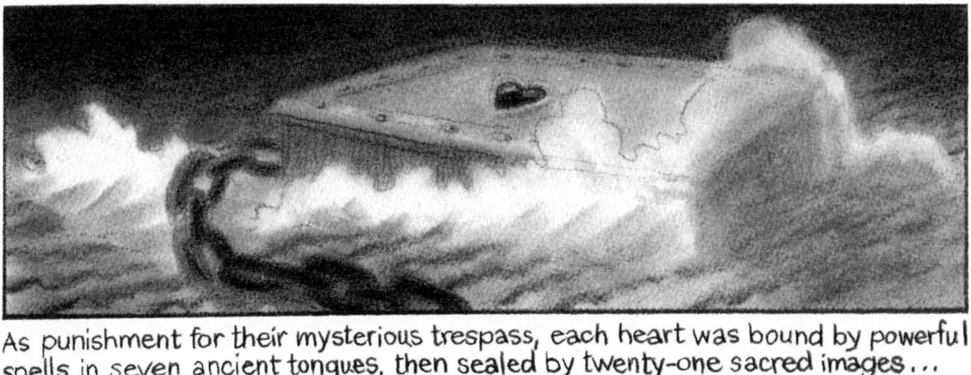

As punishment for their mysterious trespass, each heart was bound by powerful spells in seven ancient tongues, then sealed by twenty-one sacred images...

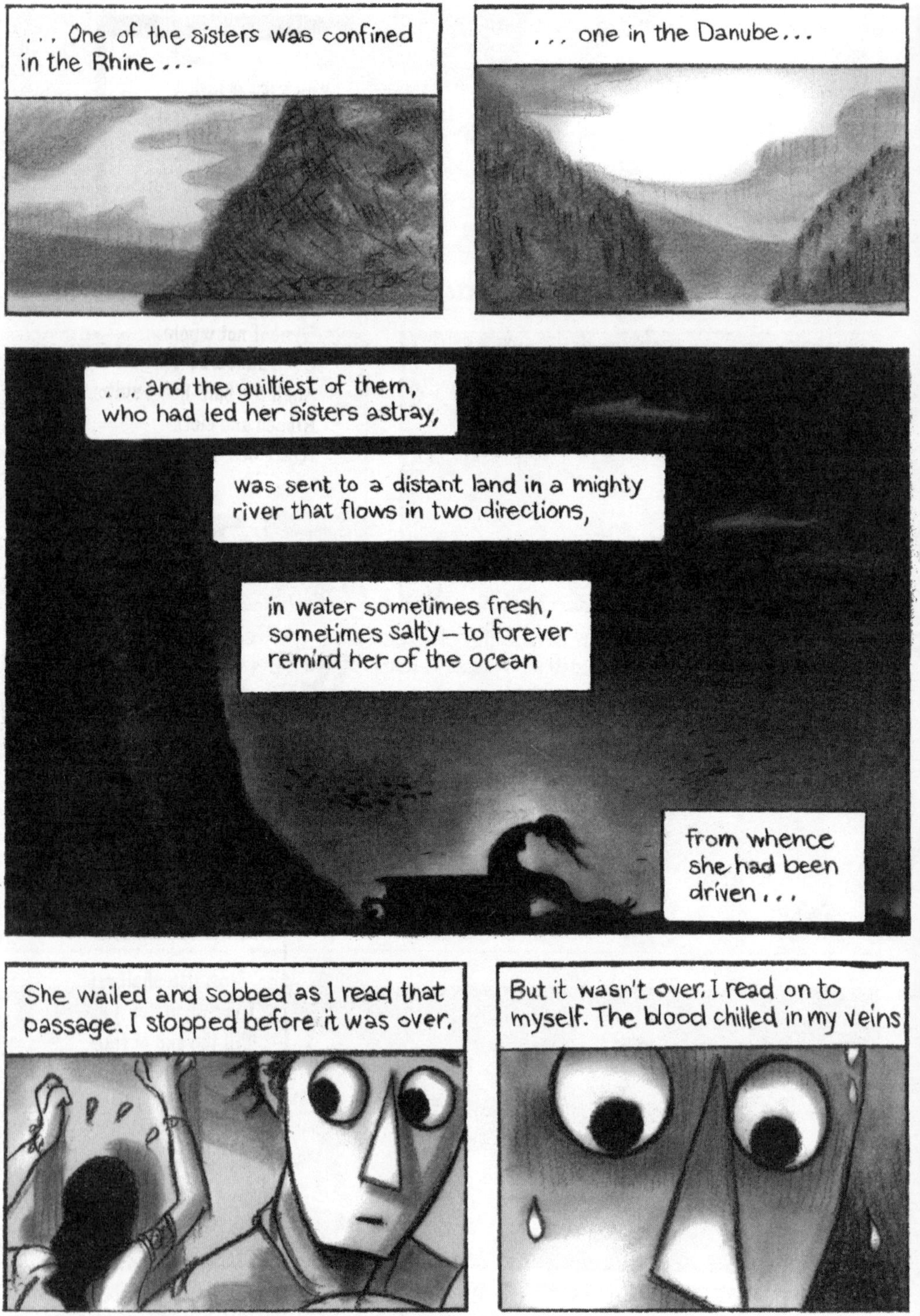
. . . One of the sisters was confined in the Rhine . . .
. . . one in the Danube . . .
. . . and the guiltiest of them, who had led her sisters astray,
was sent to a distant land in a mighty river that flows in two directions,
in water sometimes fresh, sometimes salty—to forever remind her of the ocean
from whence she had been driven . . .
She wailed and sobbed as I read that passage. I stopped before it was over.
But it wasn't over. I read on to myself. The blood chilled in my veins

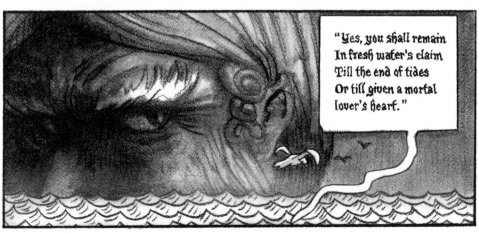

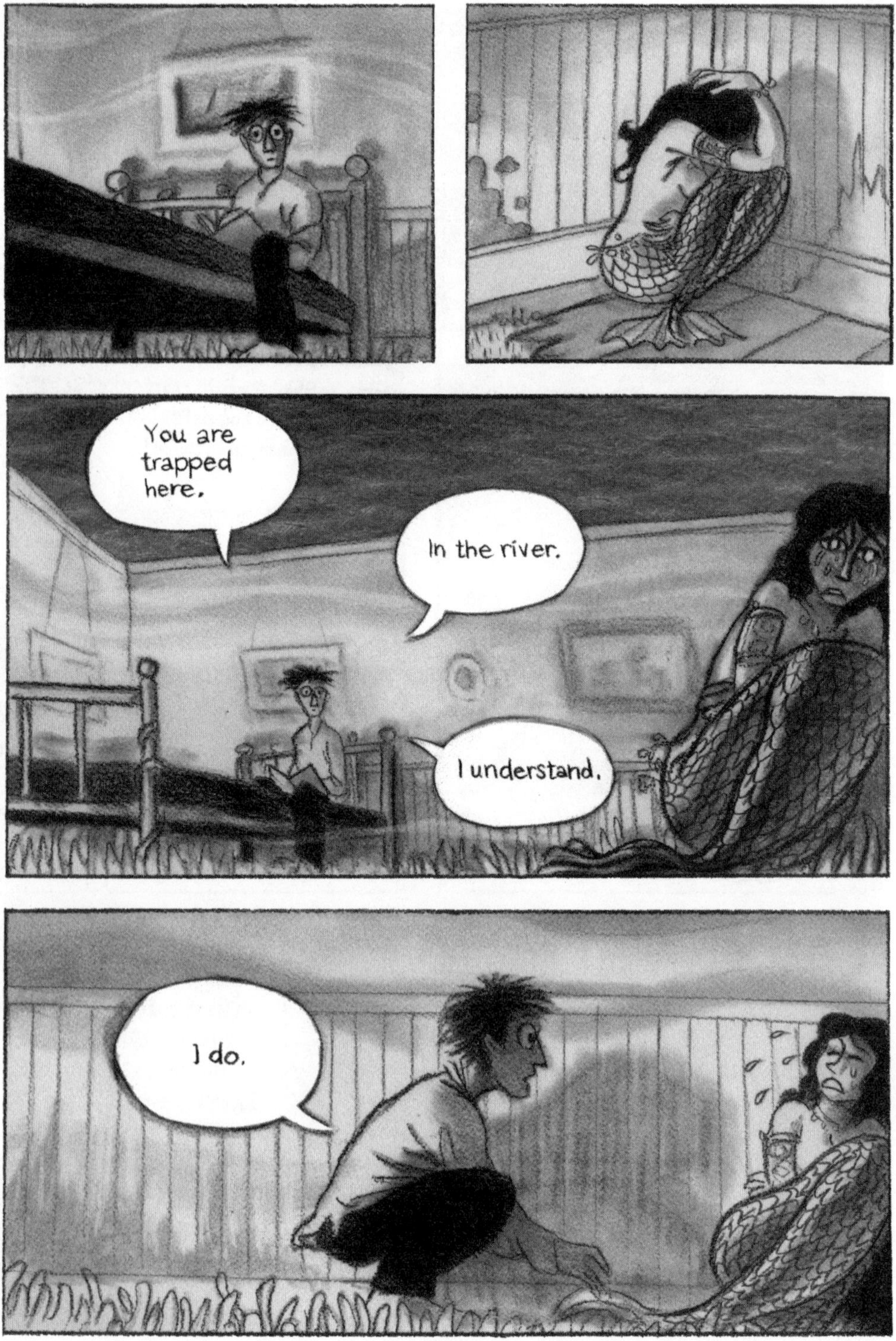
You are trapped here.
In the river.
I understand.
I do.

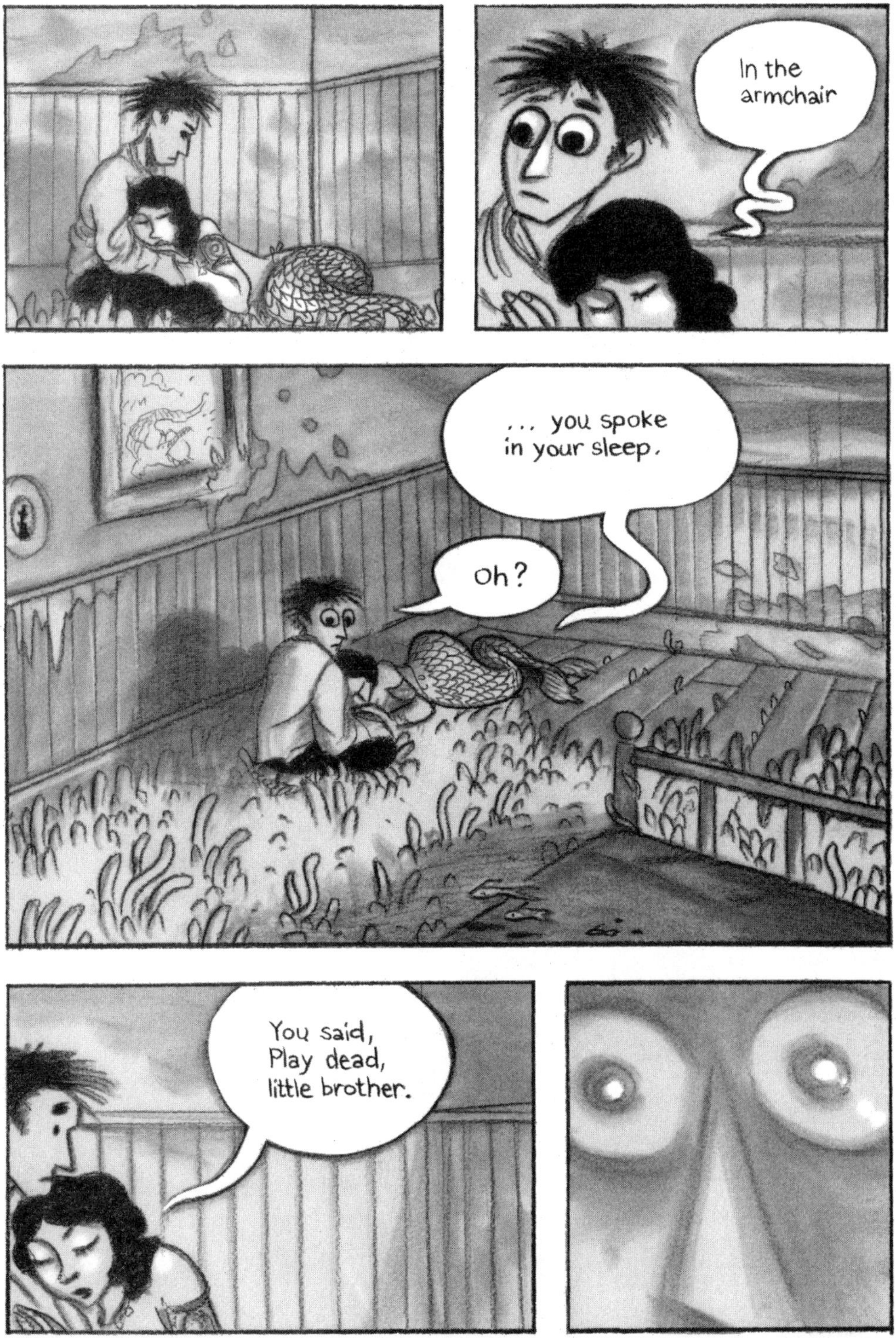
In the armchair
... you spoke in your sleep.
Oh?
You said, Play dead, little brother.

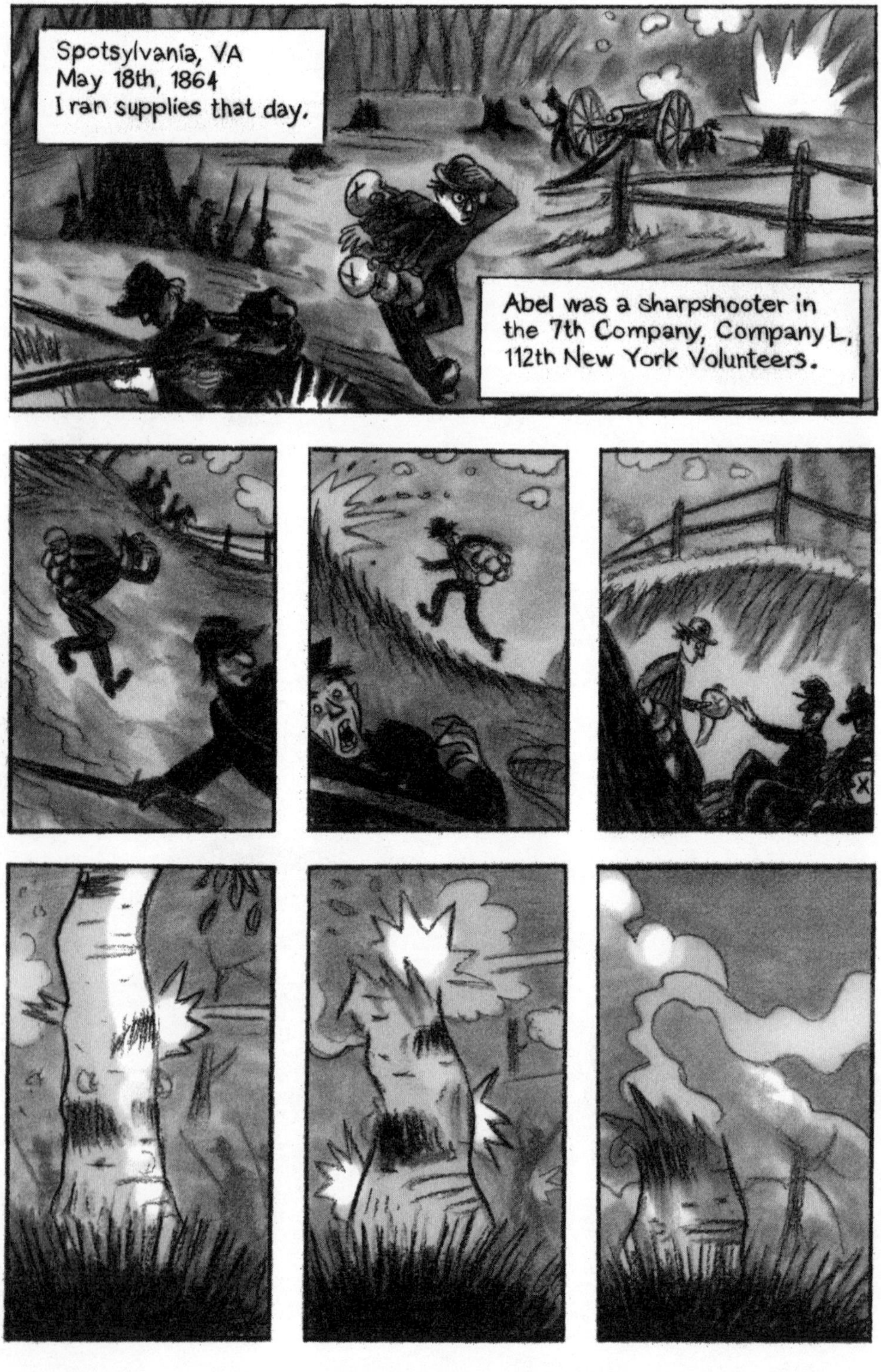
Spotsylvania, VA
May 18th, 1864
I ran supplies that day.
Abel was a sharpshooter in the 7th Company, Company L, 112th New York Volunteers.

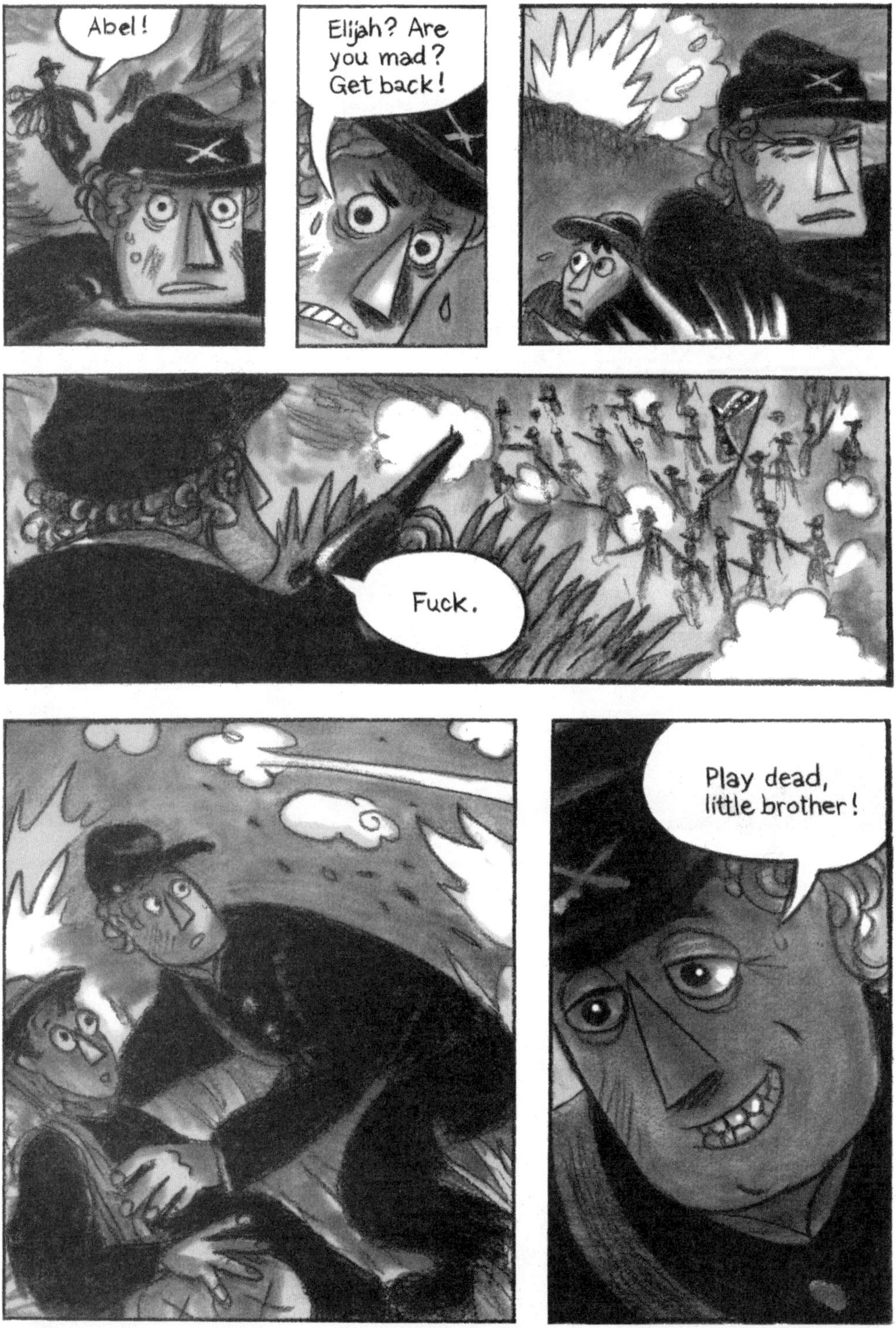
Abel!
Elijah? Are you mad? Get back!
Fuck.
Play dead, little brother!

Abel?

The firing stopped.

In my chest I felt

when Abel's heart stopped.

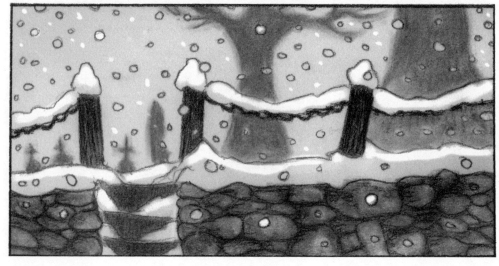

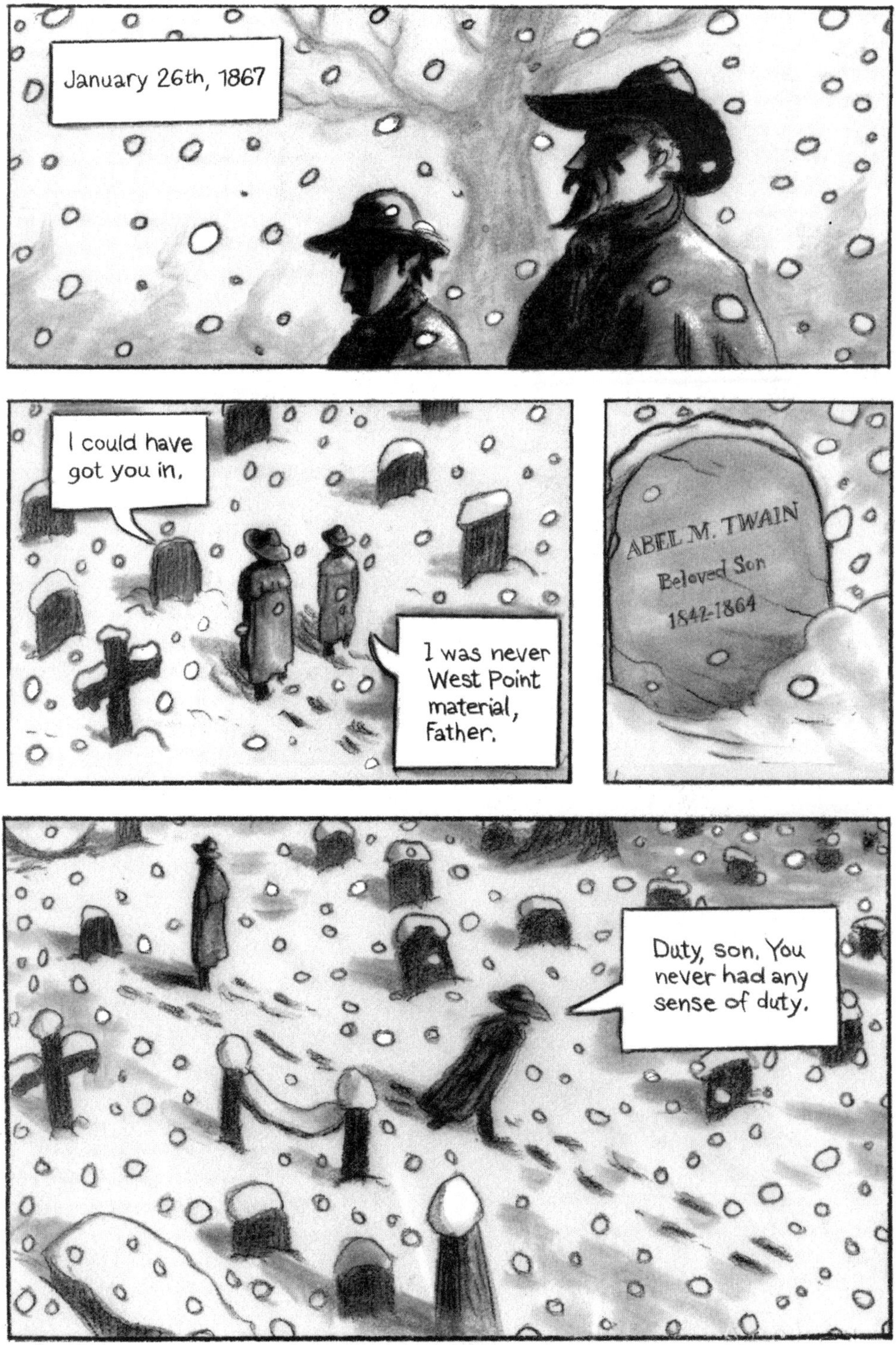
January 26th, 1867
I could have got you in.
I was never West Point material, Father.
ABEL M. TWAIN
Beloved Son
1842-1864
Duty, son. You never had any sense of duty.

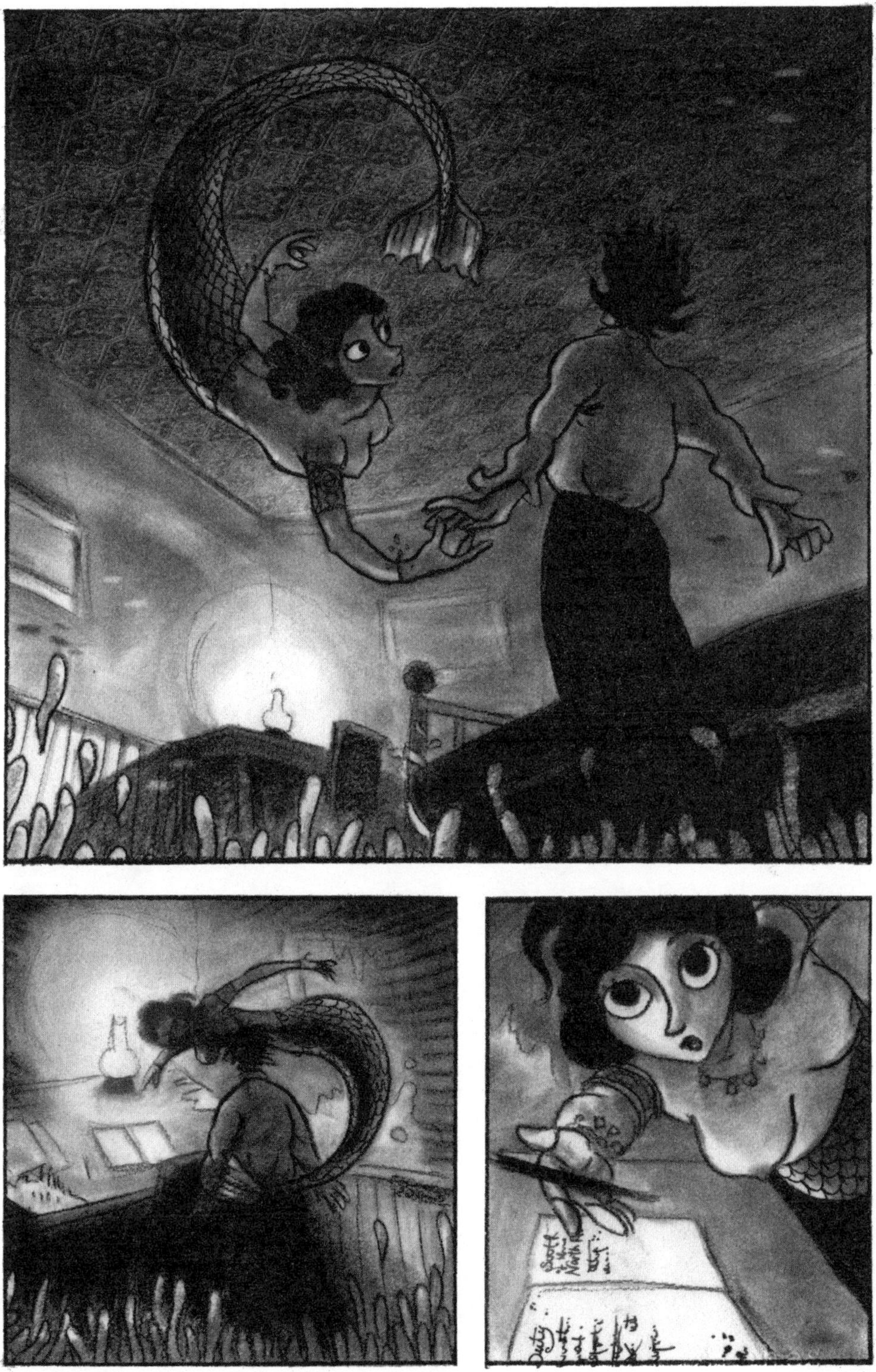

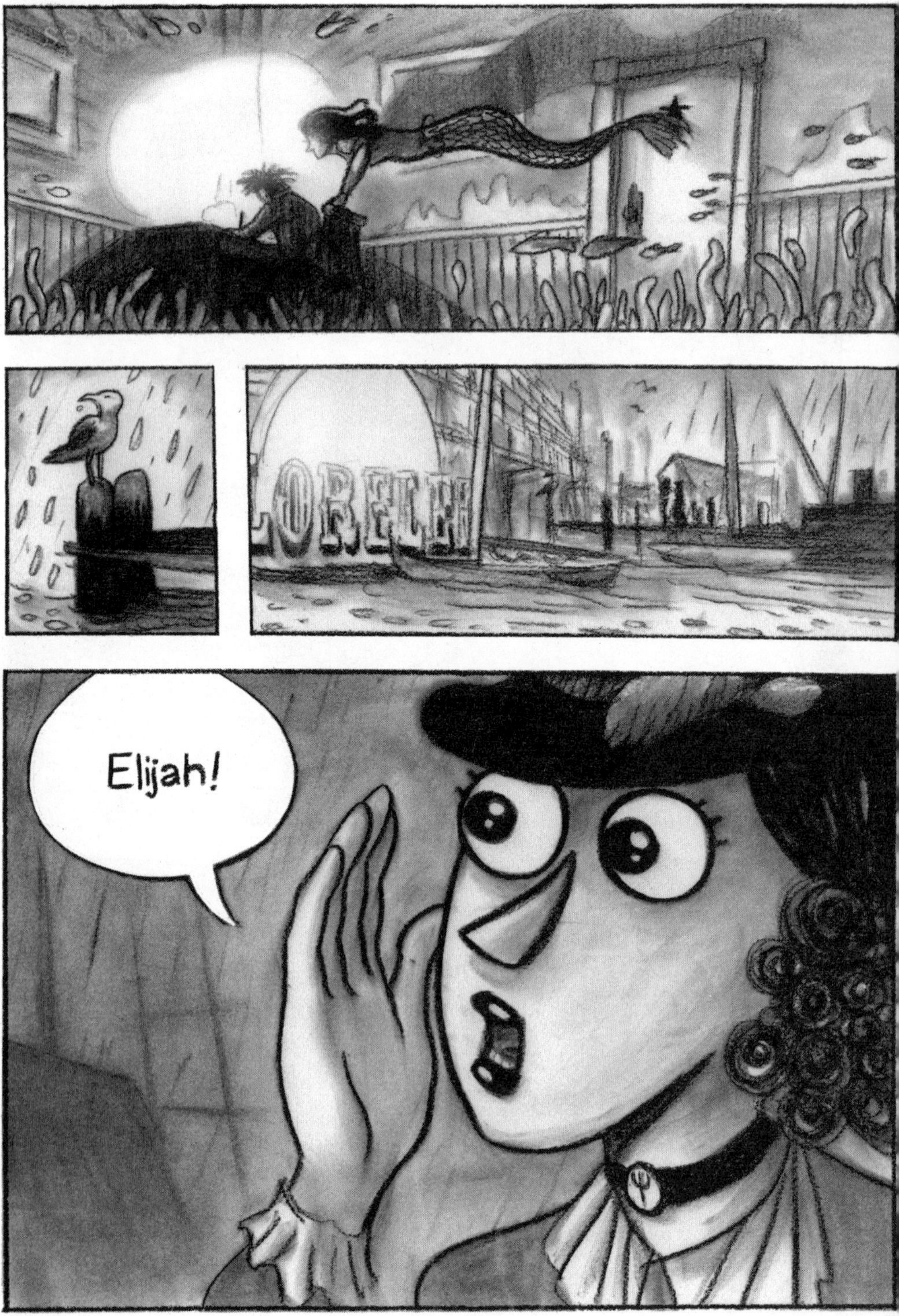
Elijah!

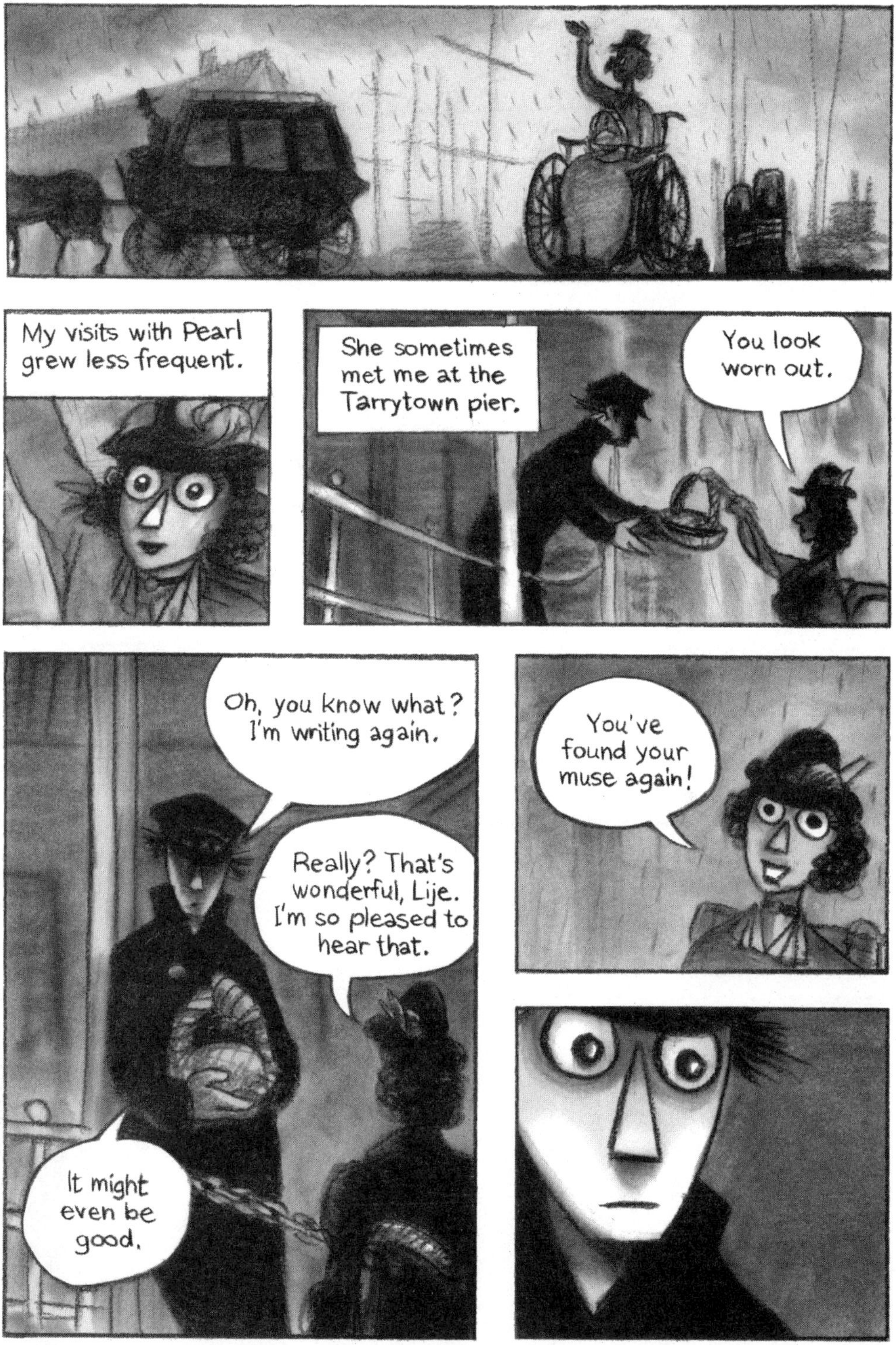
My visits with Pearl grew less frequent.
She sometimes met me at the Tarrytown pier.
You look worn out.
Oh, you know what? I'm writing again.
Really? That's wonderful, Lije. I'm so pleased to hear that.
It might even be good.
You've found your muse again!

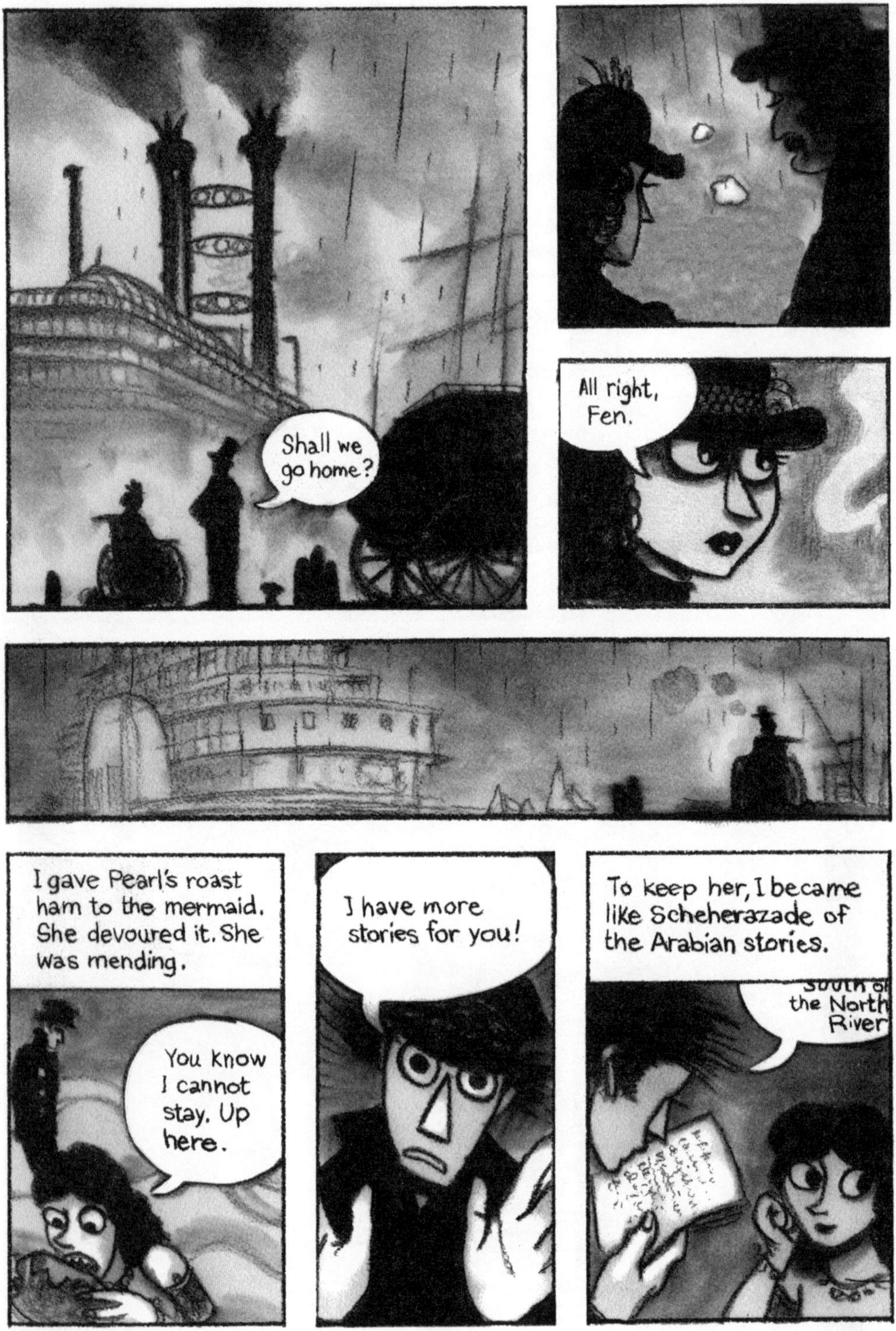
Shall we go home?
All right, Fen.
I gave Pearl's roast ham to the mermaid. She devoured it. She was mending.
You know I cannot stay. Up here.
I have more stories for you!
To keep her, I became like Scheherazade of the Arabian stories.
the North River

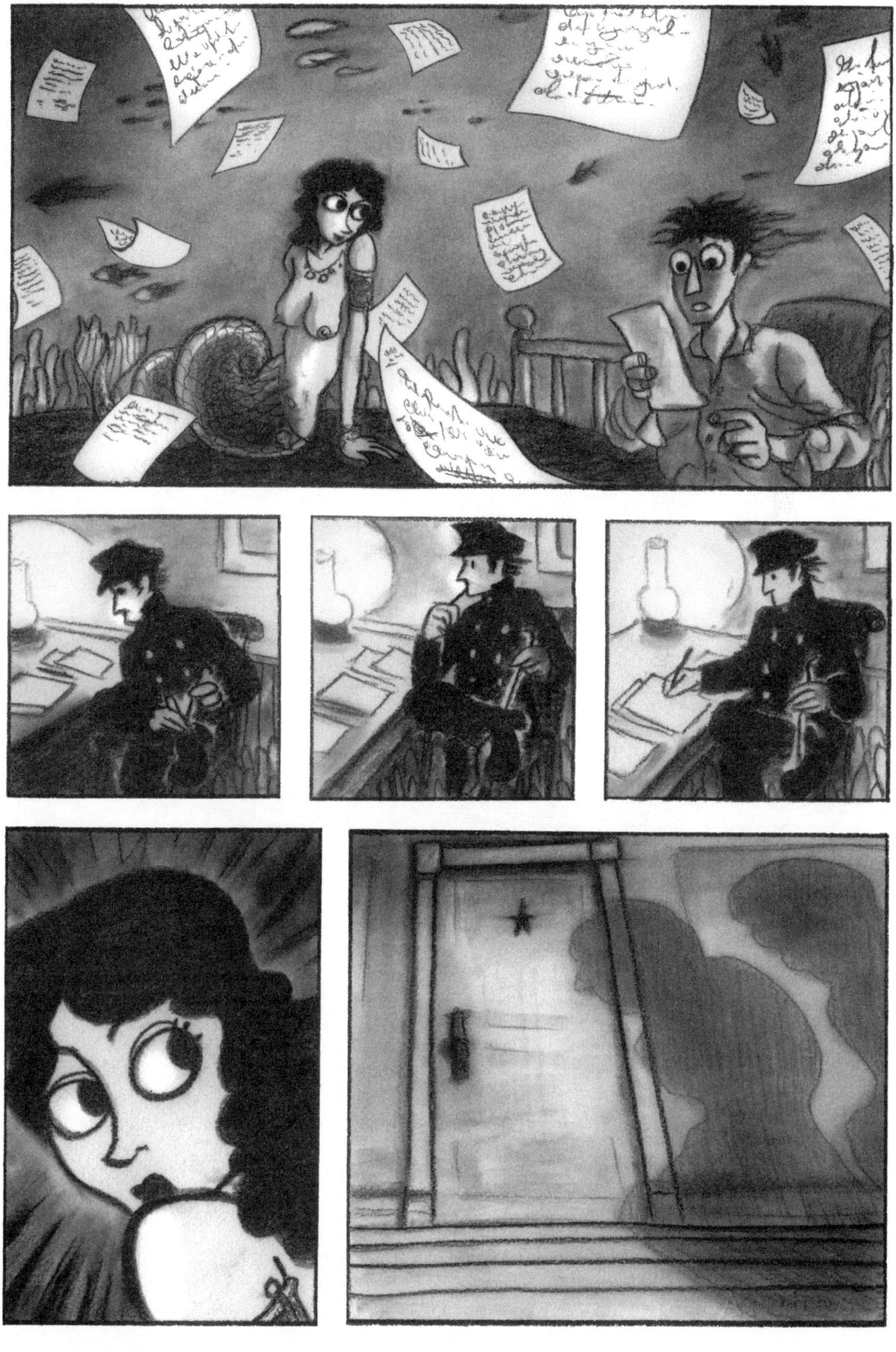

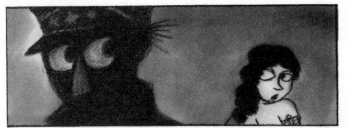

is þes he?

þonne læde hine tó þære heortan

ábric þín fæderes galdorléoð

ábric þa galdorléoð

188

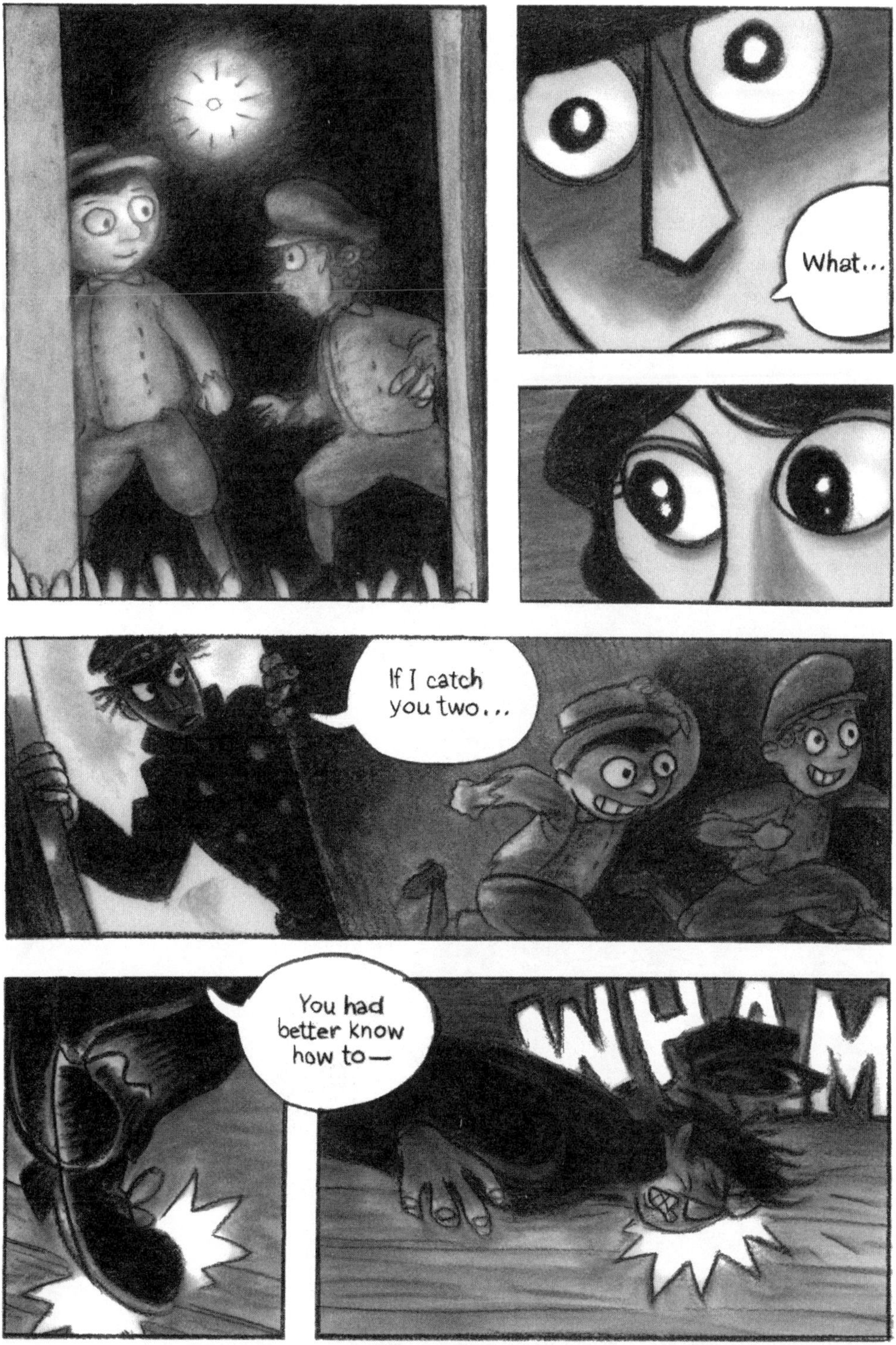
What...
If I catch you two...
You had better know how to—
WHAM

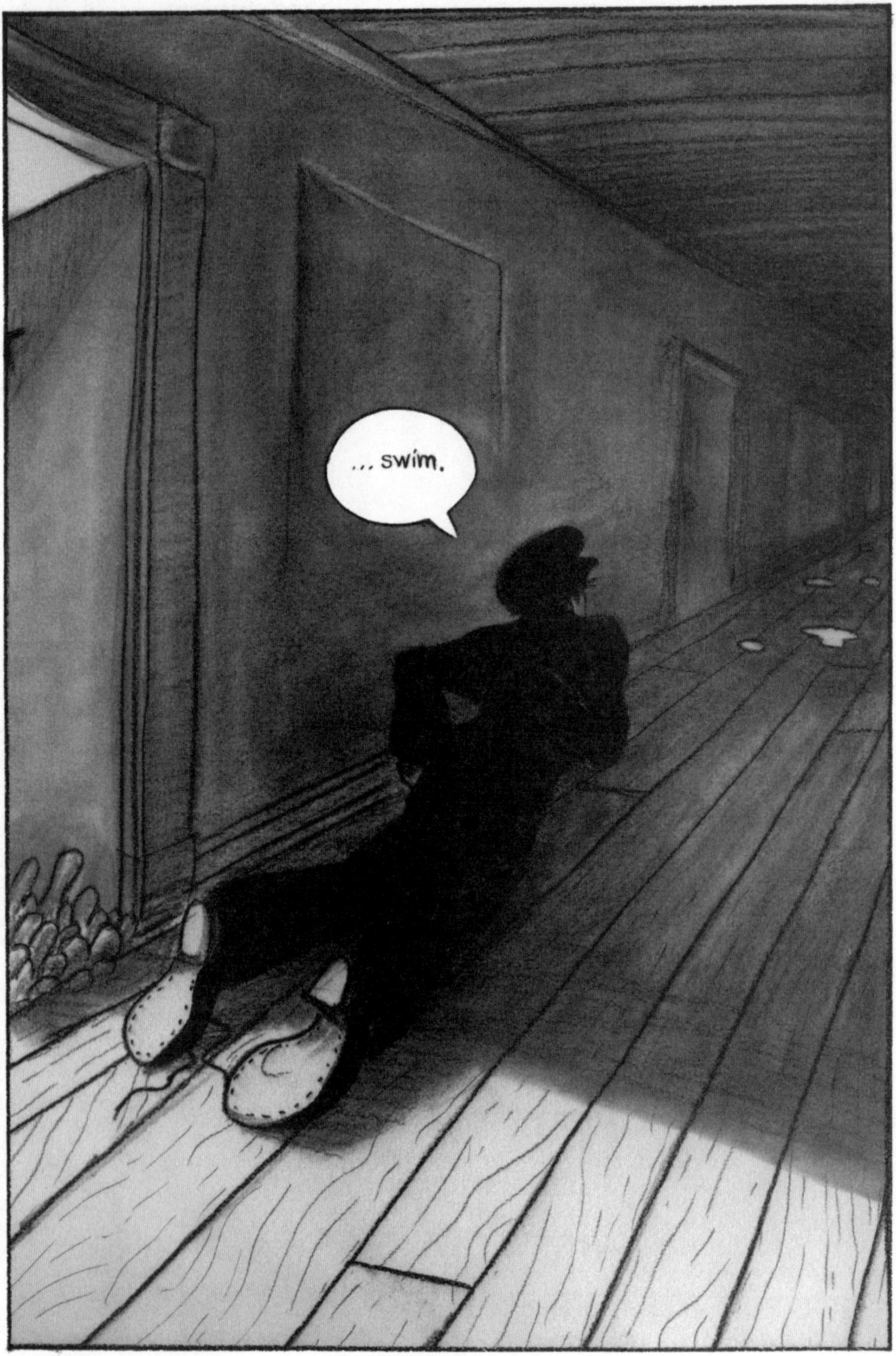
... swim.

"THE MISSING MUSE"

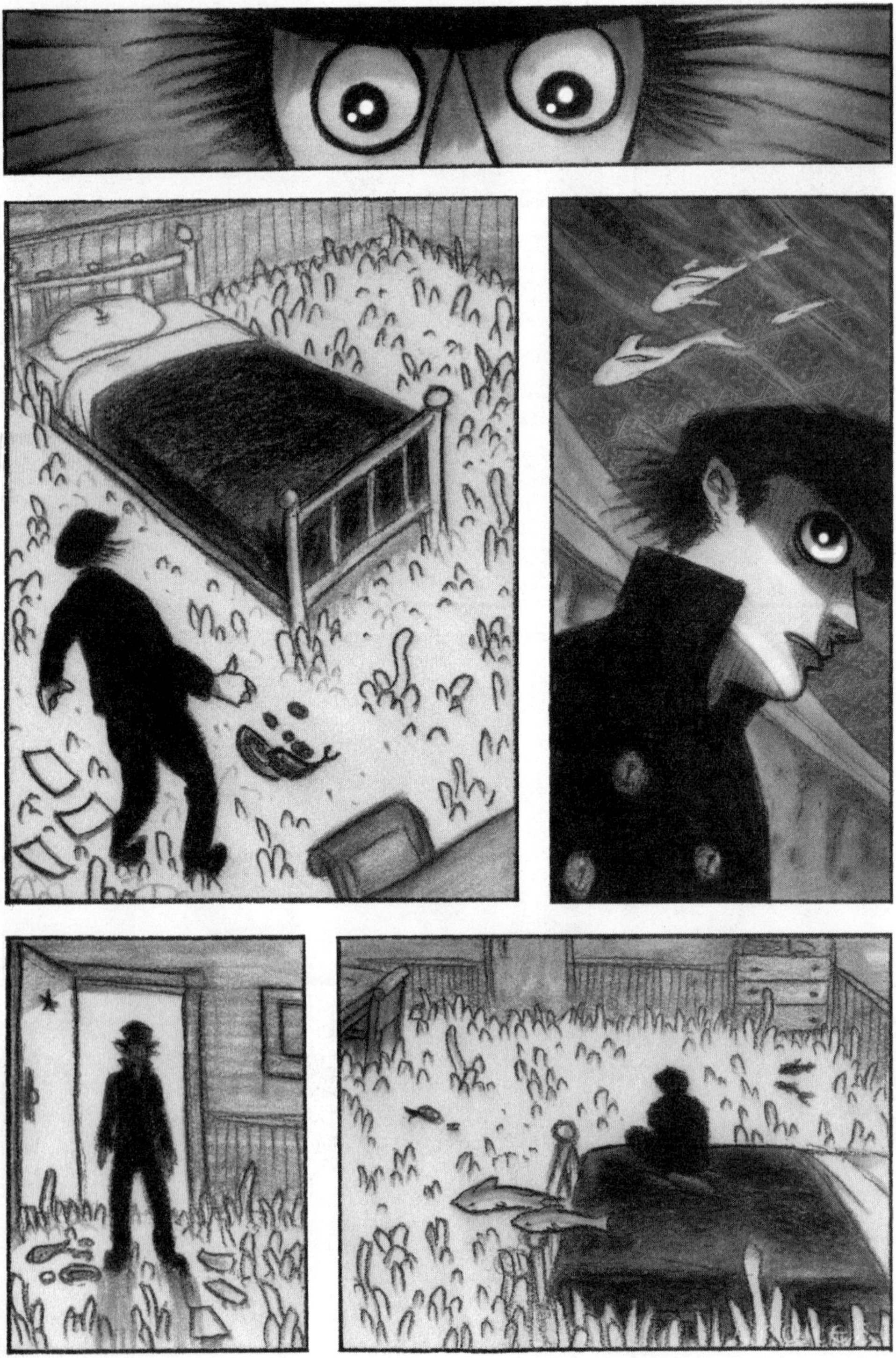

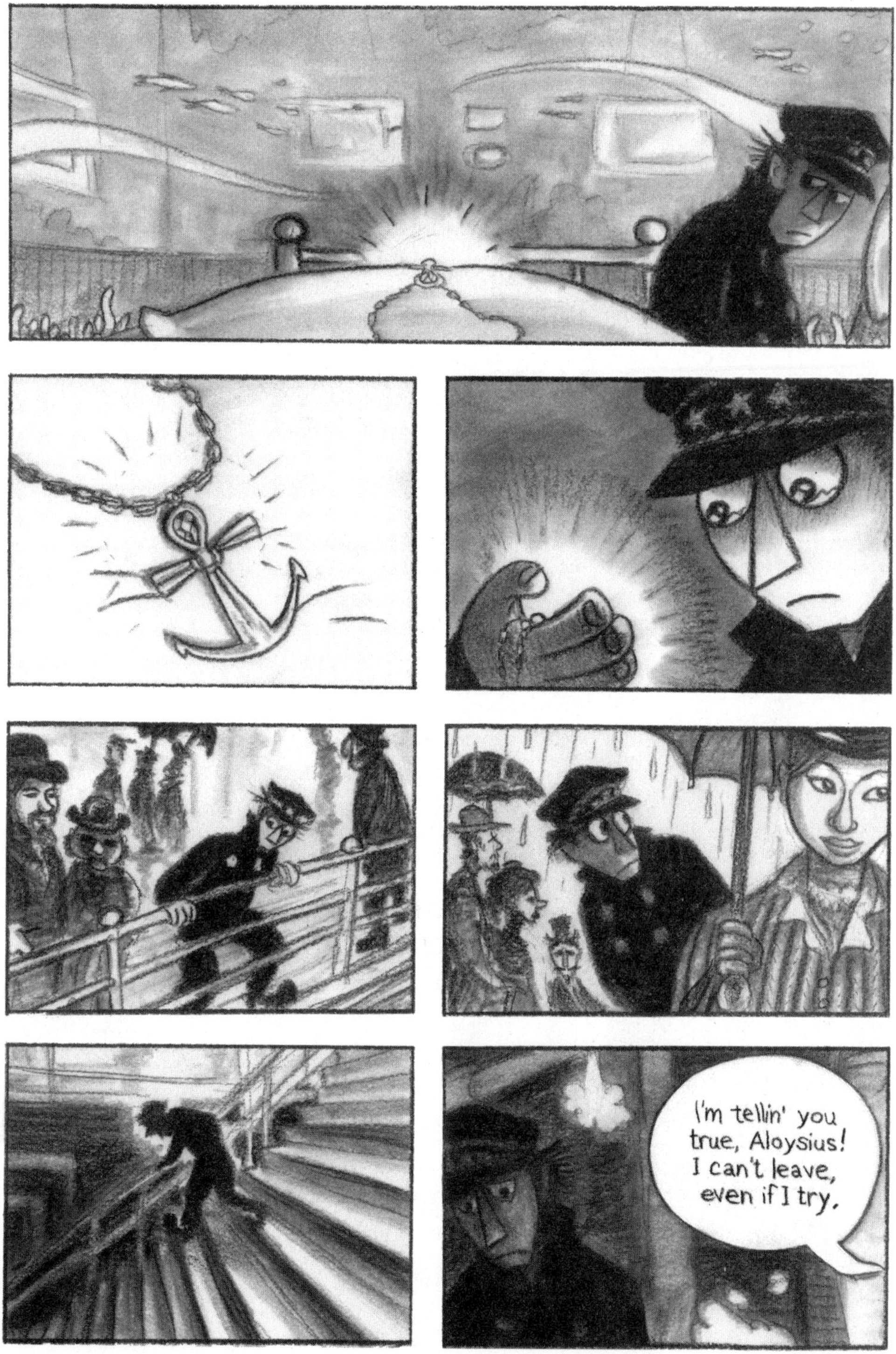
I'm tellin' you true, Aloysius! I can't leave, even if I try.

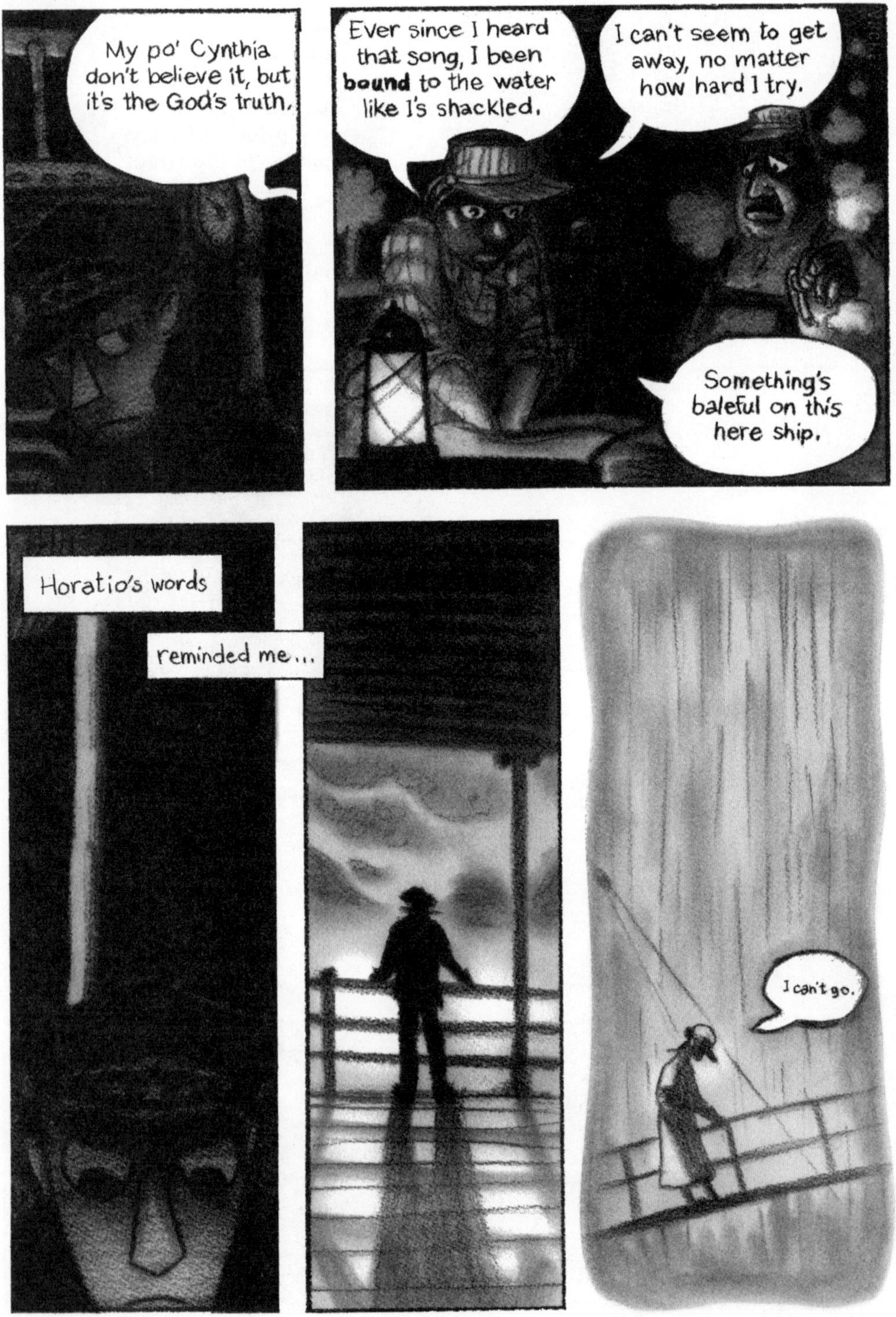
My po' Cynthia don't believe it, but it's the God's truth.
Ever since I heard that song, I been **bound** to the water like I's shackled.
I can't seem to get away, no matter how hard I try.
Something's baleful on this here ship.
Horatio's words
reminded me...
I can't go.

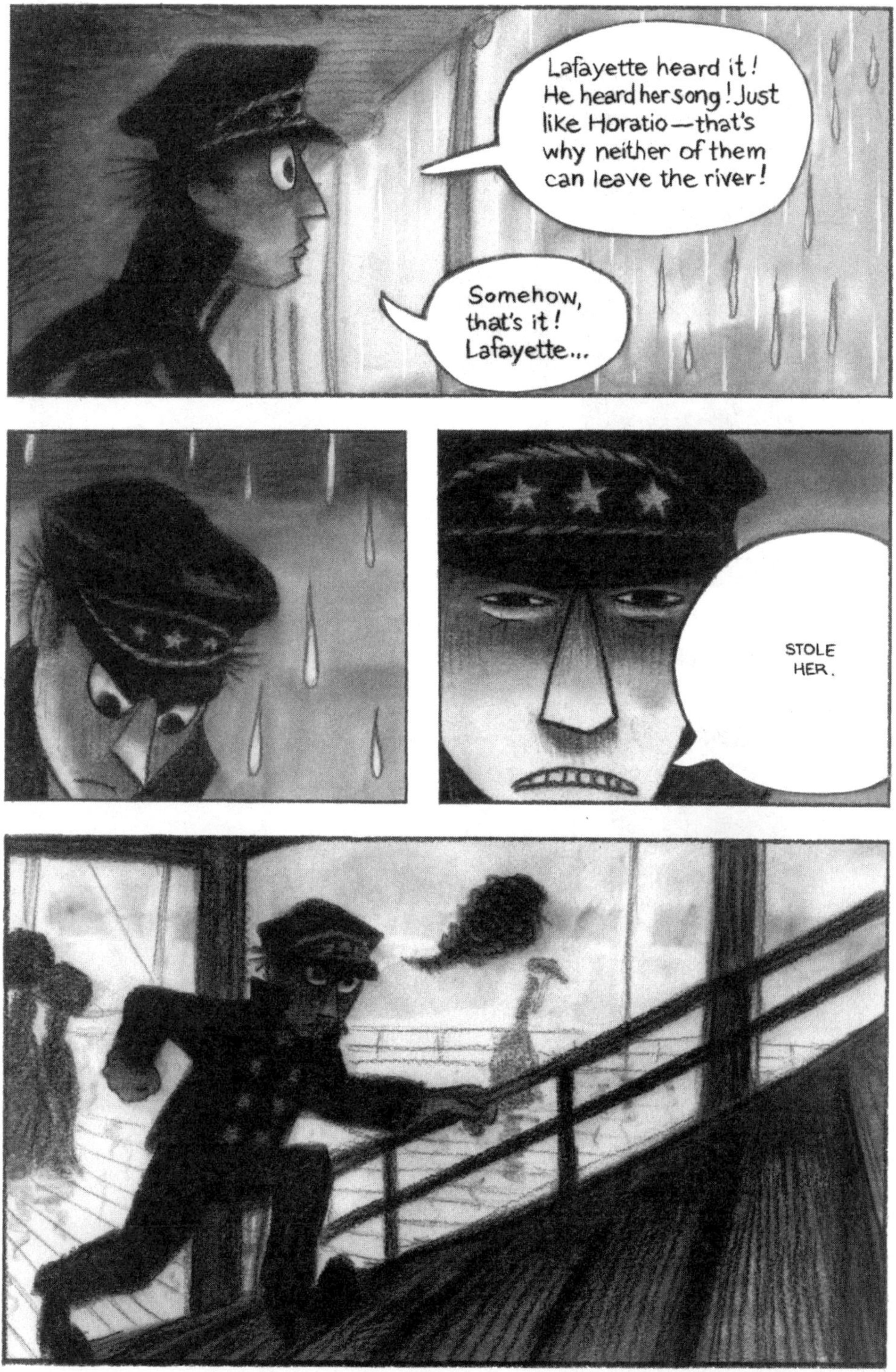
Lafayette heard it! He heard her song! Just like Horatio—that's why neither of them can leave the river!
Somehow, that's it! Lafayette...
STOLE HER.

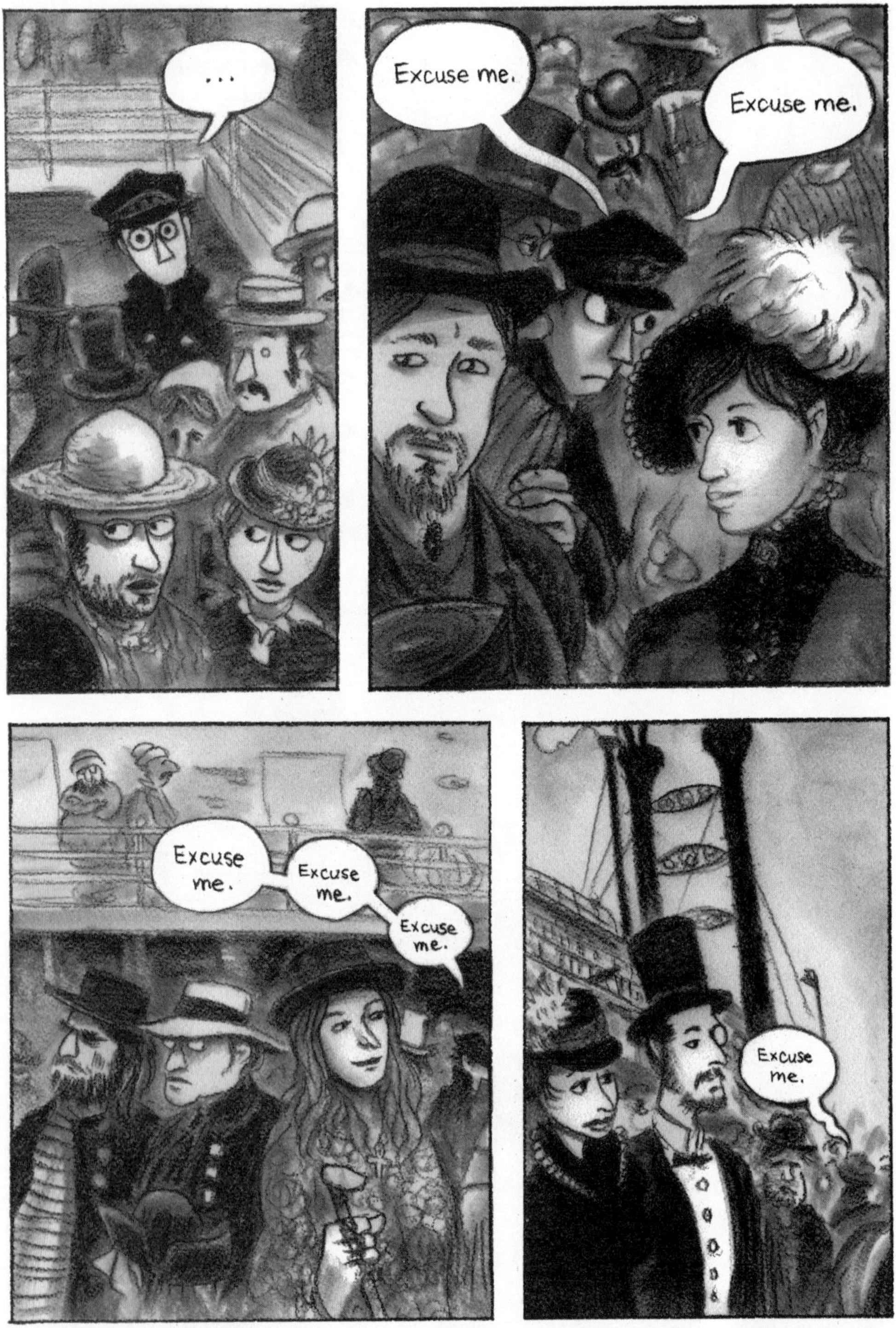
...
Excuse me.
Excuse me.
Excuse me.
Excuse me.
Excuse me.
Excuse me.

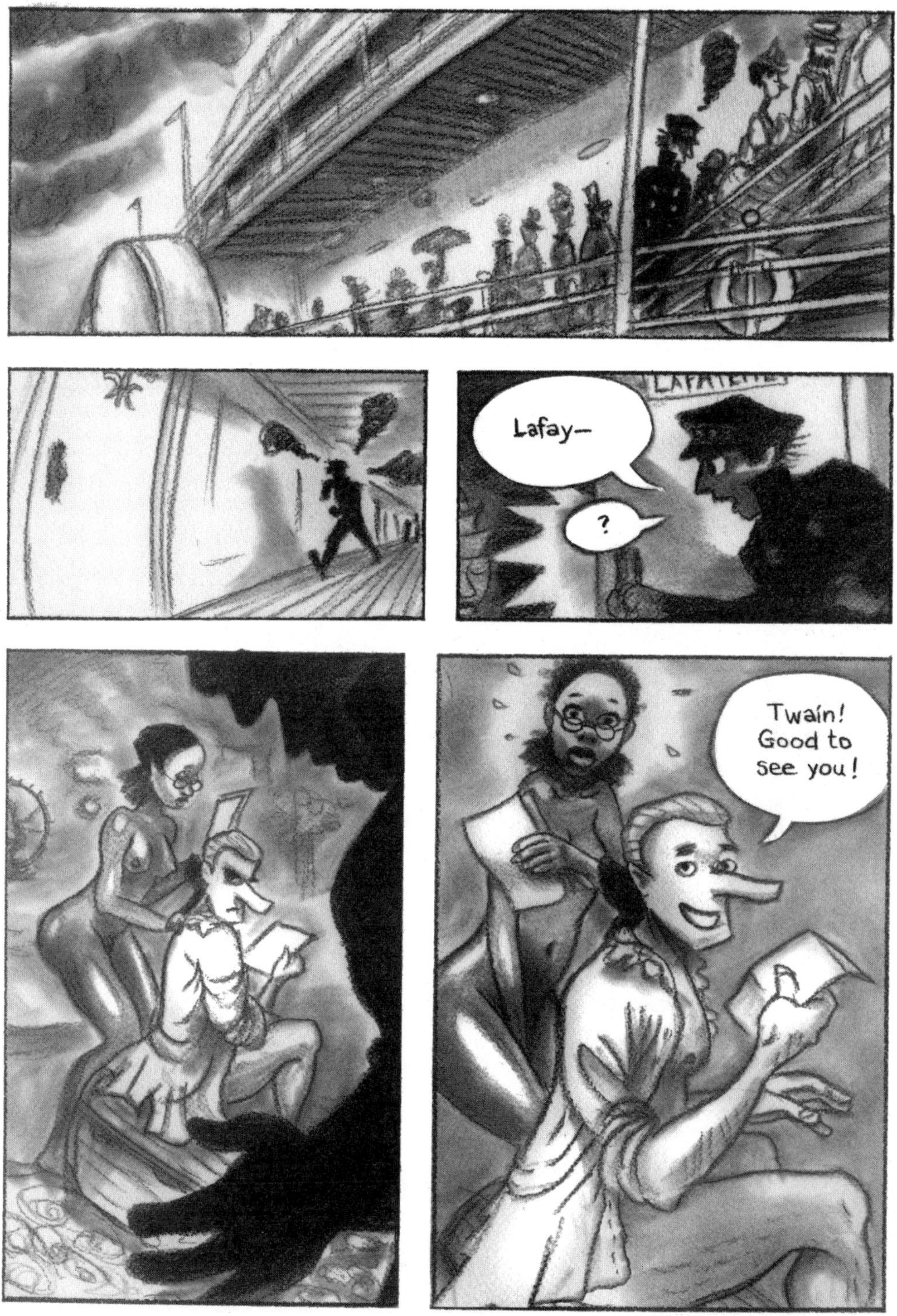

LAFAYETTE
Lafay—
?
Twain!
Good to
see you!

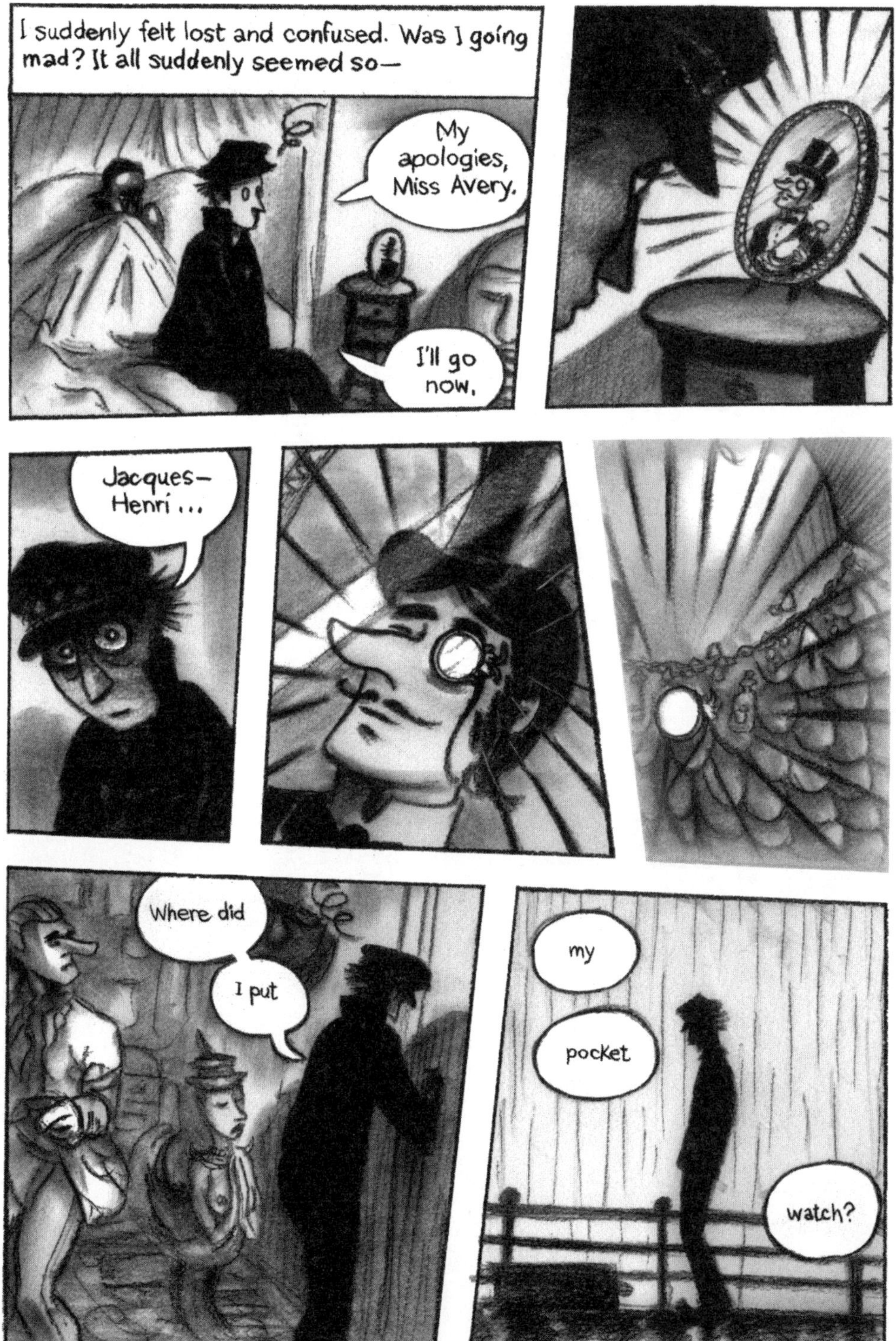
I suddenly felt lost and confused. Was I going mad? It all suddenly seemed so—
My apologies, Miss Avery.
I'll go now.
Jacques-Henri ...
Where did
I put
my
pocket
watch?

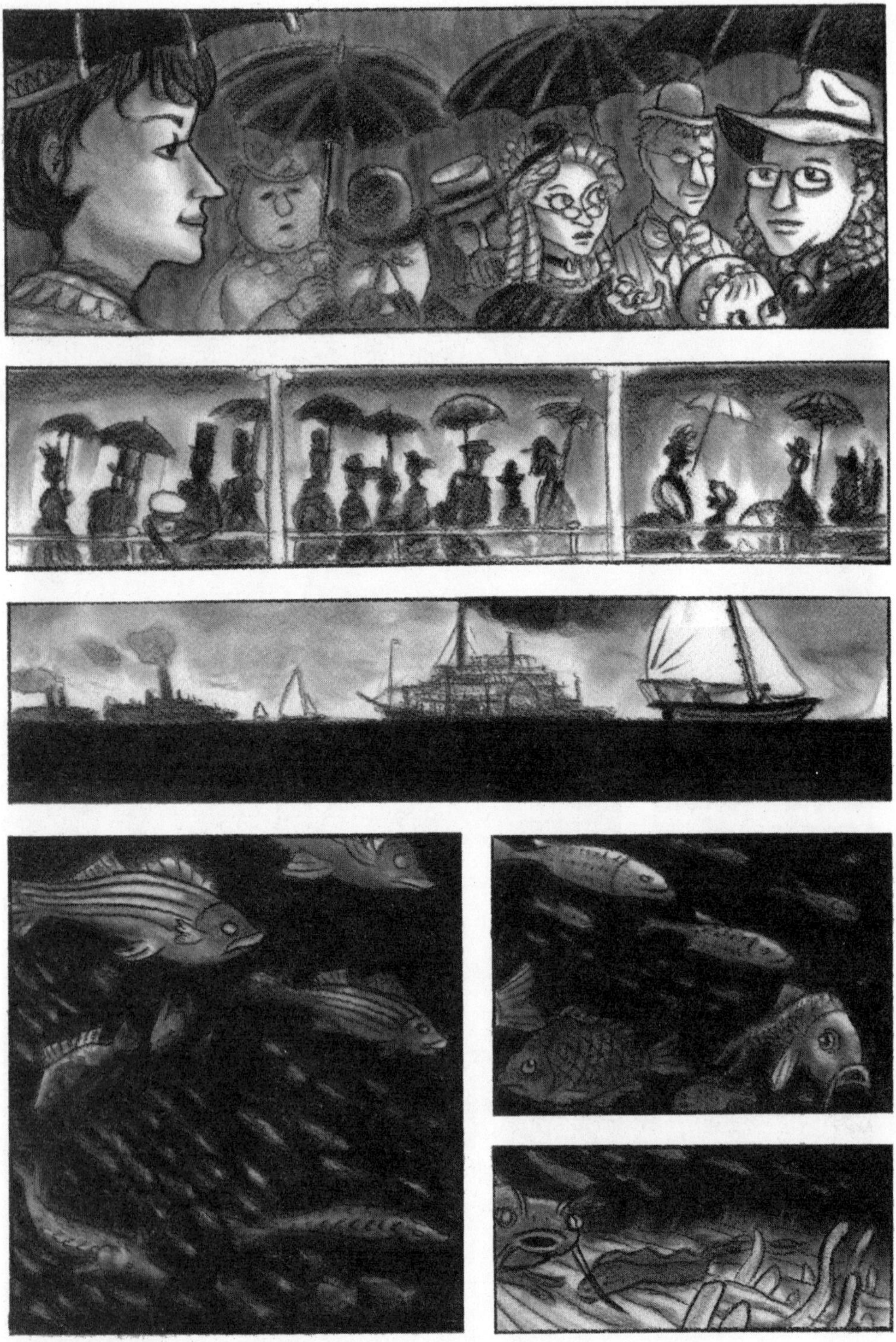

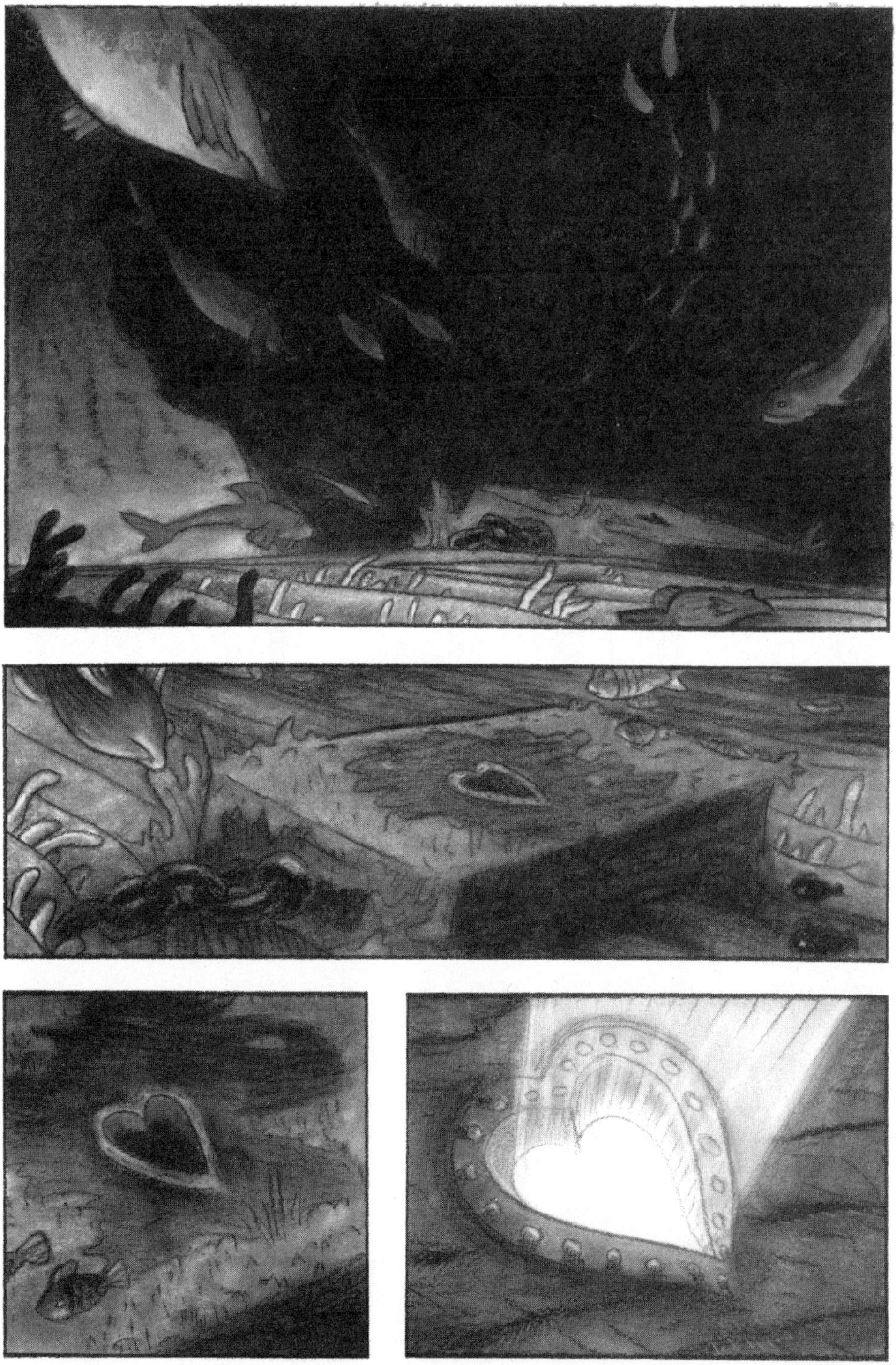

June 30th, 1887

Dear Mister Lafayette,

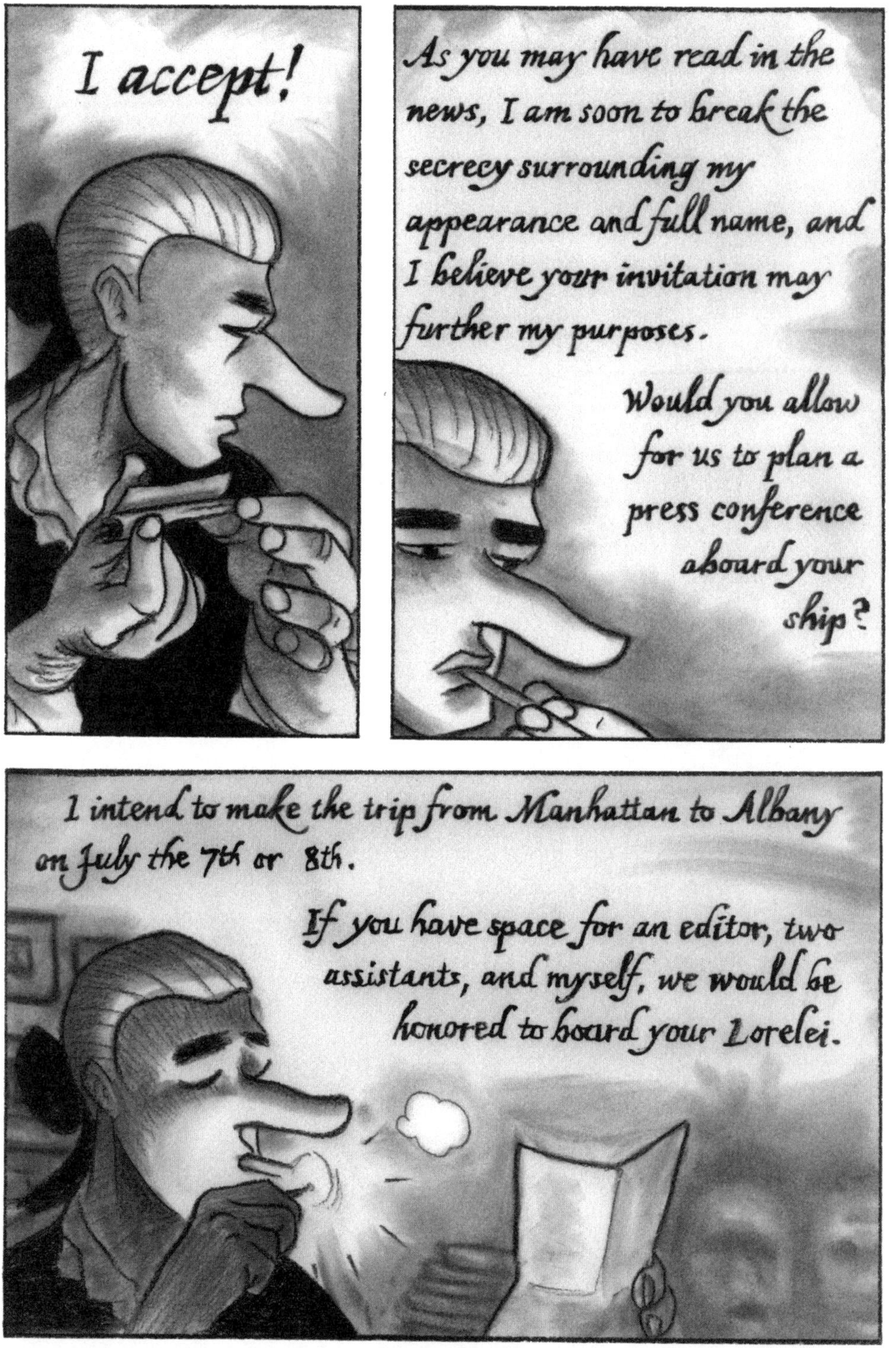
I accept!
As you may have read in the news, I am soon to break the secrecy surrounding my appearance and full name, and I believe your invitation may further my purposes.
Would you allow for us to plan a press conference aboard your ship?
I intend to make the trip from Manhattan to Albany on July the 7th or 8th.
If you have space for an editor, two assistants, and myself, we would be honored to board your Lorelei.

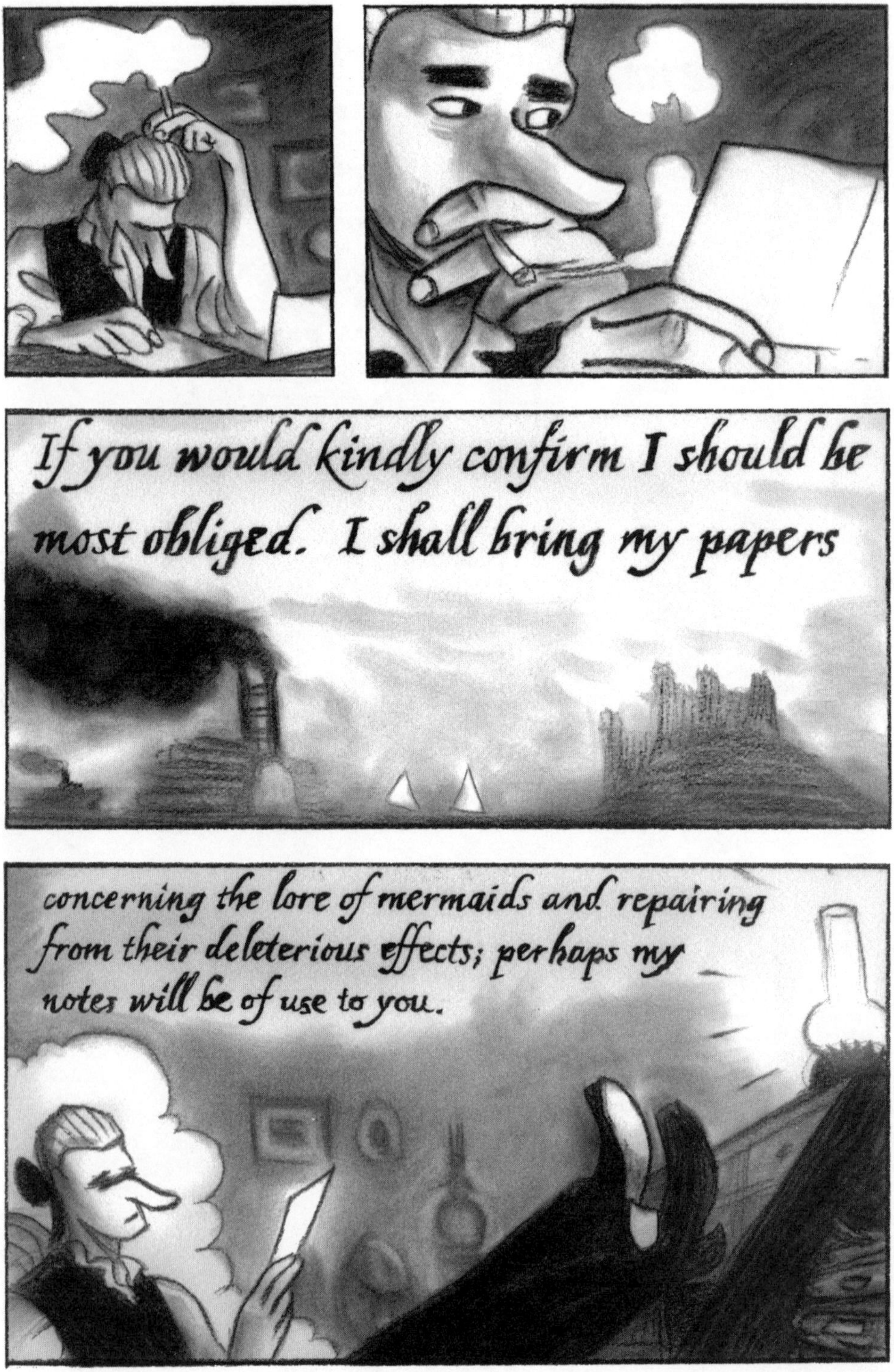
If you would kindly confirm I should be most obliged. I shall bring my papers
concerning the lore of mermaids and repairing from their deleterious effects; perhaps my notes will be of use to you.

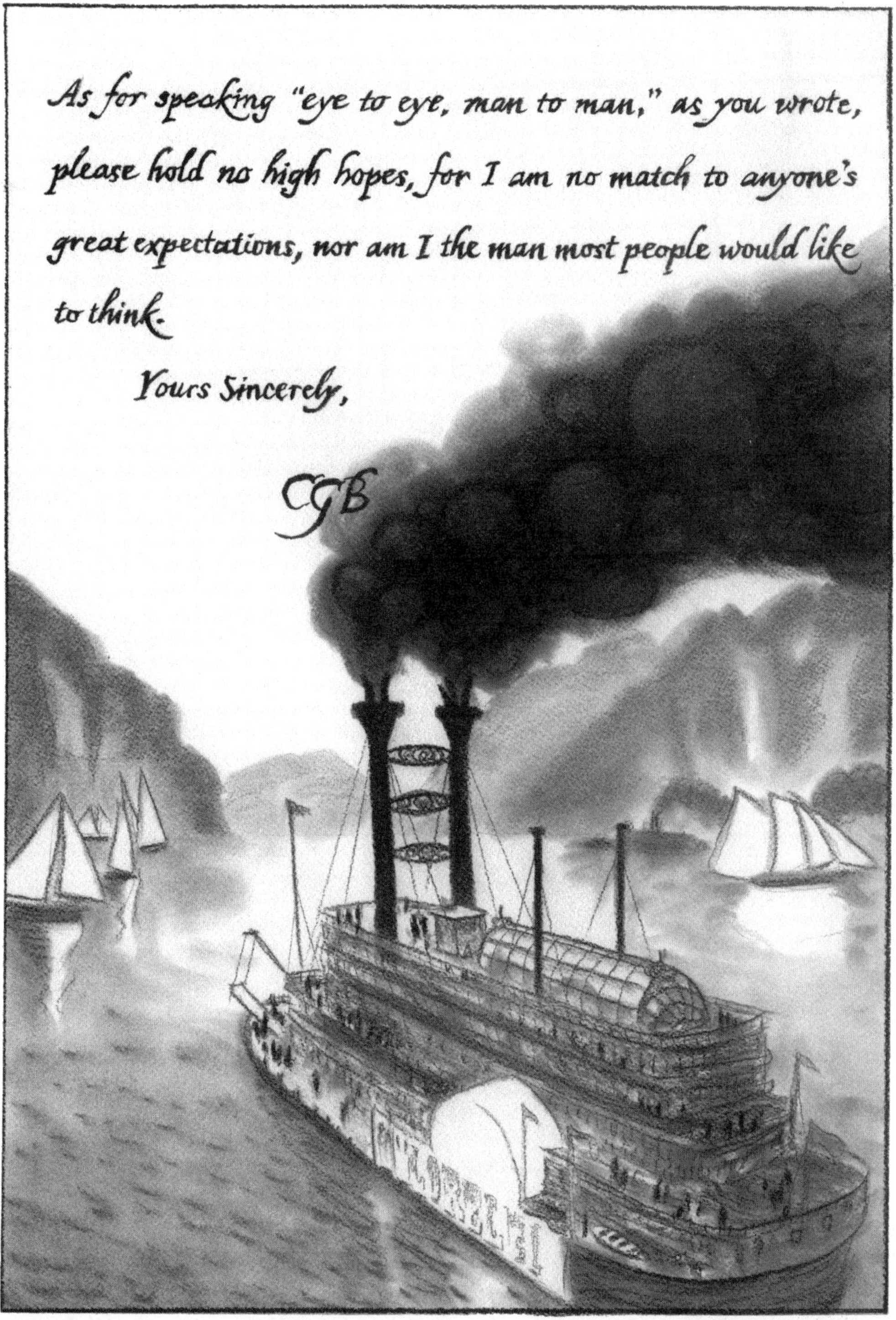
As for speaking "eye to eye, man to man," as you wrote, please hold no high hopes, for I am no match to anyone's great expectations, nor am I the man most people would like to think.
Yours Sincerely,
CJB

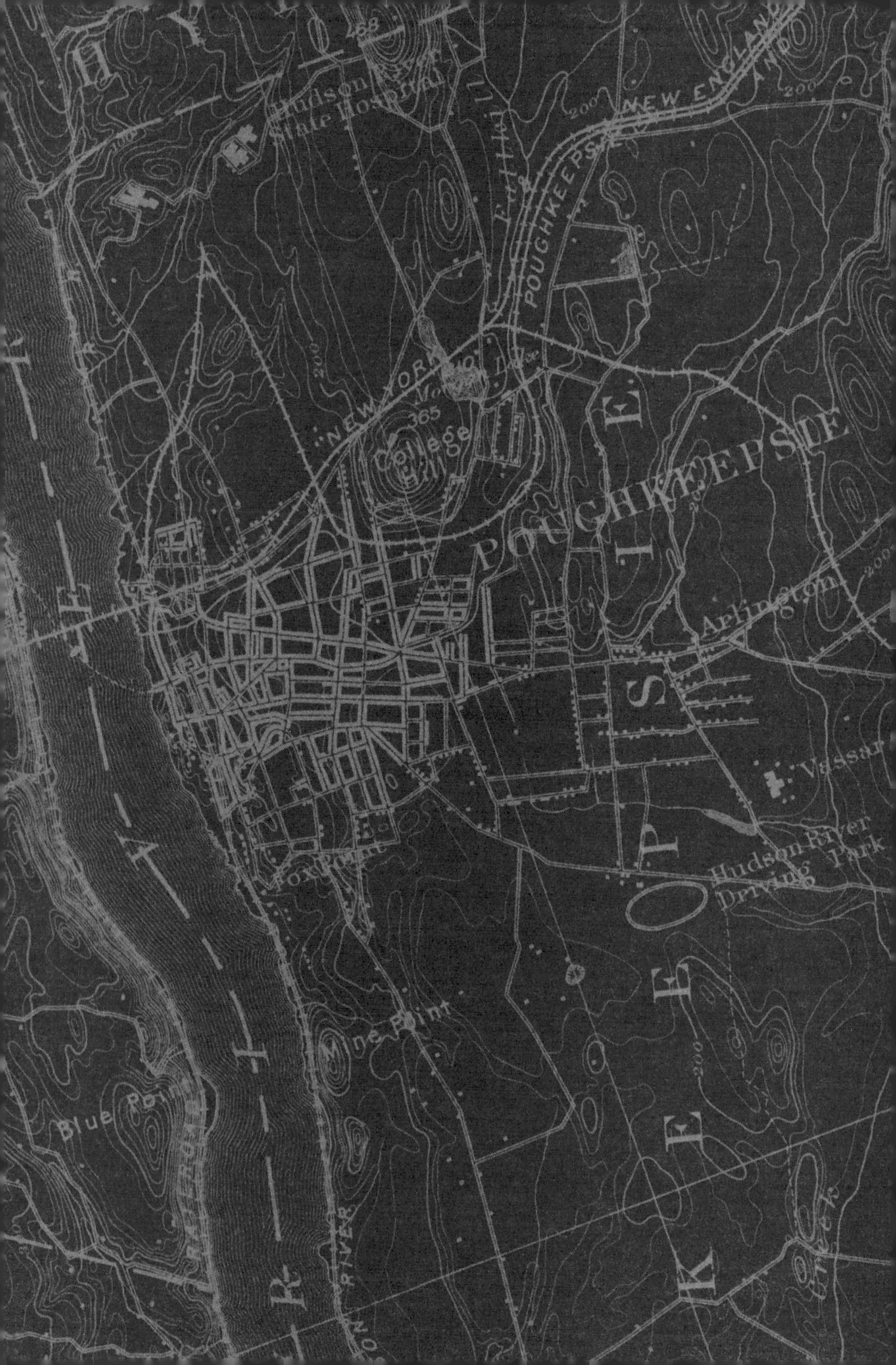

Hudson River
State Hospital
NEW ENGLAND
POUGHKEEPSIE
NEW YORK
365
College Hill
POUGHKEEPSIE
Arlington
Vassar
Hudson River
Driving Park
Fox Point
Blue Point
200

AC WINE
vintage

...CASE

MR HY

...STEVENSON

LONDON
...ANS, GREEN, AND CO.
1886

A FAST STEAMBOAT
...GHKEEPSIE, N. Y., July 18...
...oat New-York, with a thousan...
...rd, made her first regular trip up...
...and was enthusiastically rec...
...by shouts and cheers, bell ringin...
...ving. She left New-York at 9:...
...nutes behind at Yonkers, twel...
...f time at Stony Point, and made...
...s from New-York, at 11:40 A. M.

MARY POWELL IN COLLISION.
...URG, N. Y., May 19.—The steam...
...Martin, of the Newburg and Alb...
...ore Line, left here on time at 7 o'clock...
...usual run up north. At...
...Mondout on

THE MARY POWELL IN COLL...
...N. Y., May 19.—The...

HUDSON MYSTERIES AUTHOR TOUR

Secrets & M...

At last, some readers of C.G Beaverton will have a chance to see the author in person. A press conference is to be held onboard a ship in Manhattan on July 7th, to be followed by a series of speaking engagements around the nation. The latest offering from Beaverton will not disappoint; this new supernatural travelogue doesn't whisk the reader to North Africa, Mesopotamia, the Hindu Kush, nor to the steppes of Russia; no, it is our own backyard Beaverton investigates. We are to be acquainted with the unexplained Hudson River Valley. With characteristic ...r, the author punctuates ...ment of inns and taverns ...istoric curiosities from ...nhattan to Albany, and eve ...00 year old tree in Elmsf... ...r which it is pleasant to r... ...a matter-of-fact expositio... ...among others, faery-life t... ...tted in Sleepy-Hollow, gh... in Ossining, a healing presen... Croton Point, and even com... ...ling evidence of a mermaid i...

Part Two
CAMOMILLE

SPRINGFIELD REPUBLICAN

JUNE 29TH, 1887

...VERSION MORE POPULAR THAN EVER

...al courageous libraries have done us the service of resisting the current popularity of ...Beaverton and upholding the ban on his works. Citing the "moral mudslide under ...ca's foundation" and the brazenly pagan nature of these so-called imaginary travel... ...a committee formed under the Reverend C.C. Gladwell has submitted a petition to ...rary of Congress .... (CONTINUED ON PAGE 7)

...occurred Lawson s...
...g from a thick bank of fog. Brigg...
...well was standing still, and Capt. Ander...
...1 his engineer concur in this statement.
...two minutes b...
ahead of time at Stony Point.

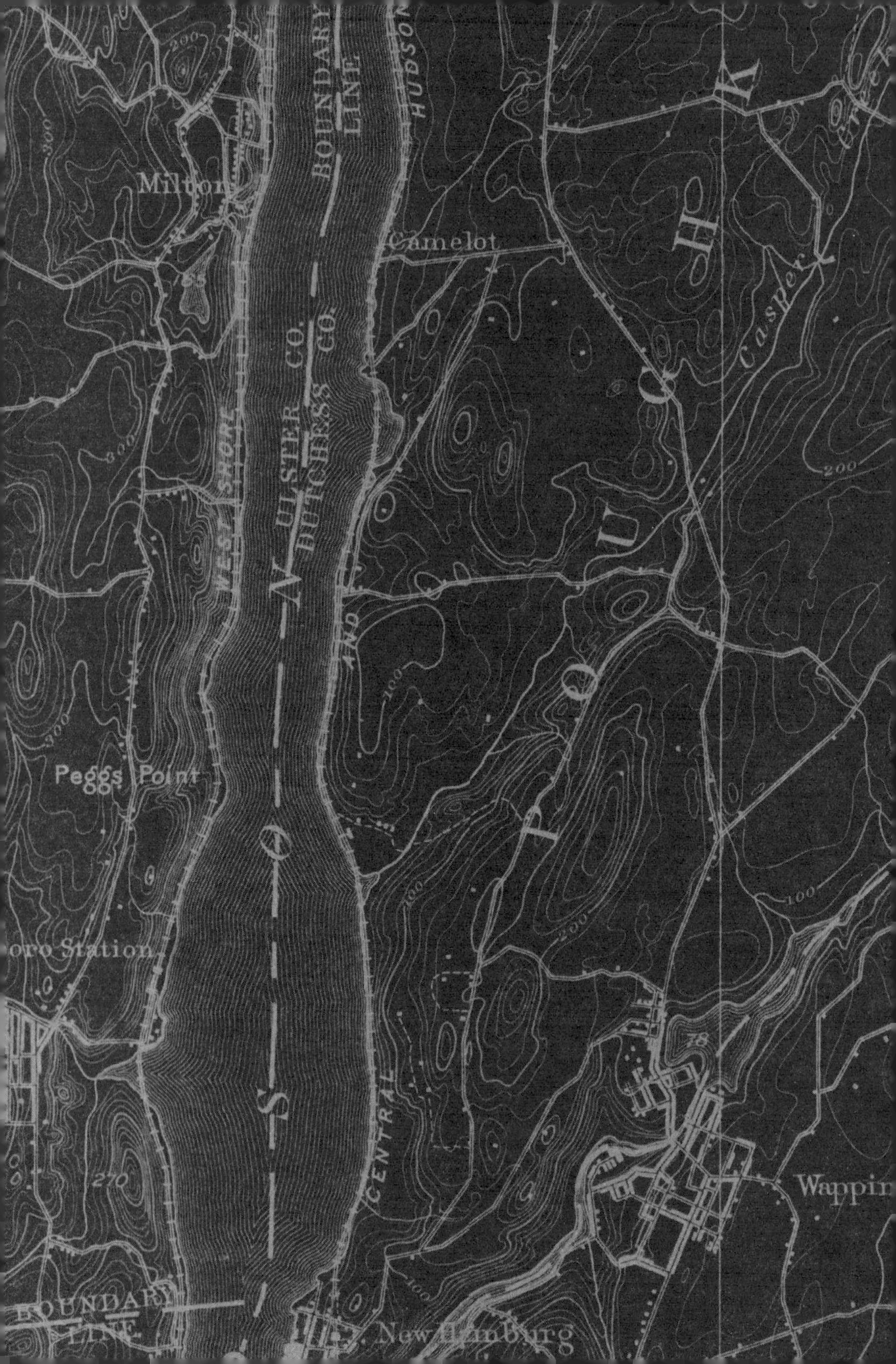

Milton
BOUNDARY LINE
HUDSON
Camelot
ULSTER CO.
AND
DUTCHESS CO.
WEST SHORE
Peggs Point
oro Station
CENTRAL
Casper
BOUNDARY LINE
New Hamburg
Wappin

Pt II, Chap.1

"THE BEAVERTON REVELATION"

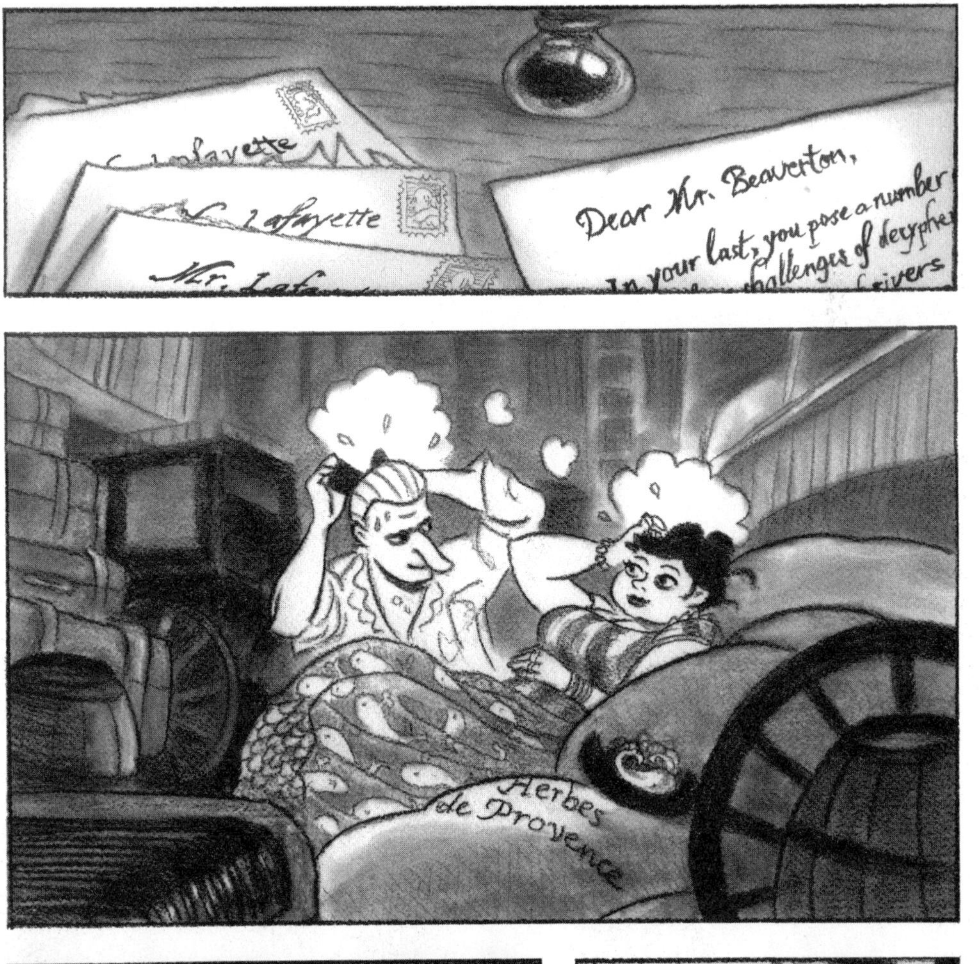
Lafayette
Lafayette
Dear Mr. Beaverton,
In your last, you pose a number
Herbes de Provence

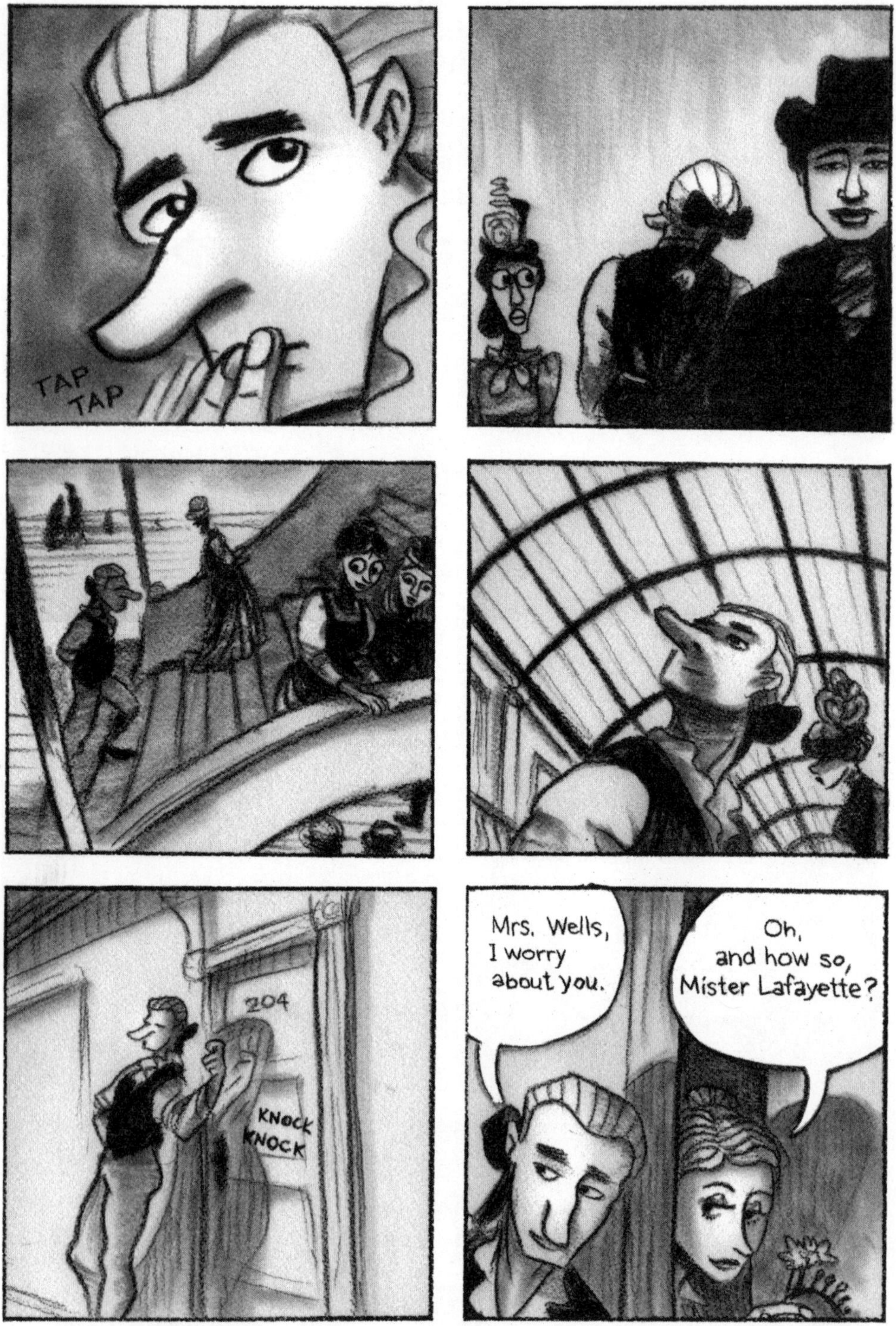
TAP
TAP
204
KNOCK
KNOCK
Mrs. Wells, I worry about you.
Oh, and how so, Mister Lafayette?

213

214

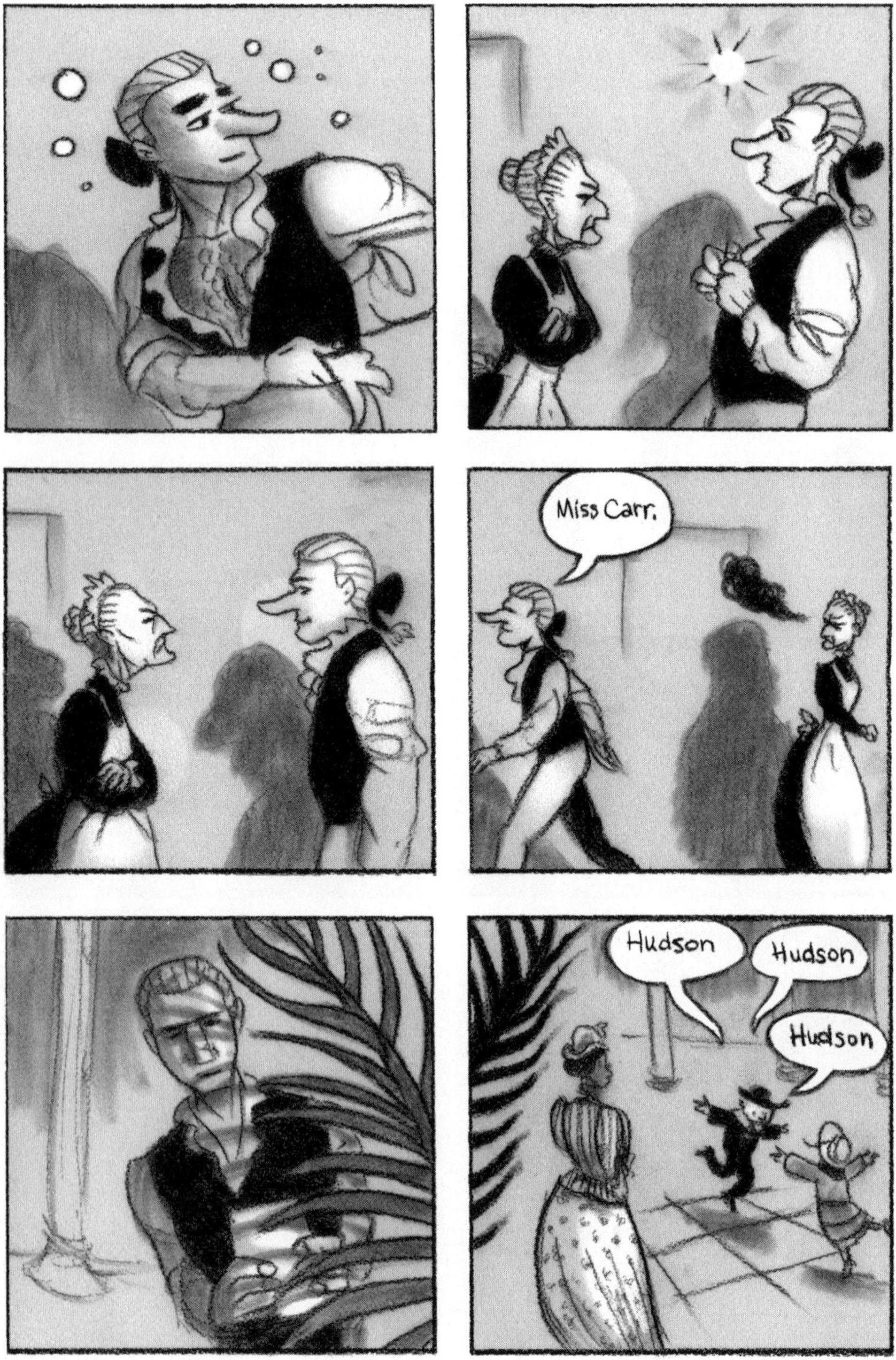

Miss Carr.
Hudson
Hudson
Hudson

217

This is the one!

Of course it is. I can do two things at once.

"The tones of unseen mystery, the vague and vast suggestions of the briny world,

the liquid-flowing syllables.

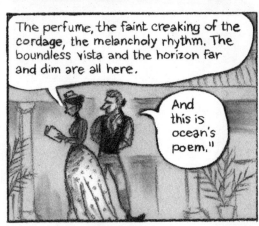

The perfume, the faint creaking of the cordage, the melancholy rhythm. The boundless vista and the horizon far and dim are all here.

And this is ocean's poem."

You're an angel,

No, no. Merely French. Must run, Mattie.

And a devil.

You always run. What are **you** running from?

A song.

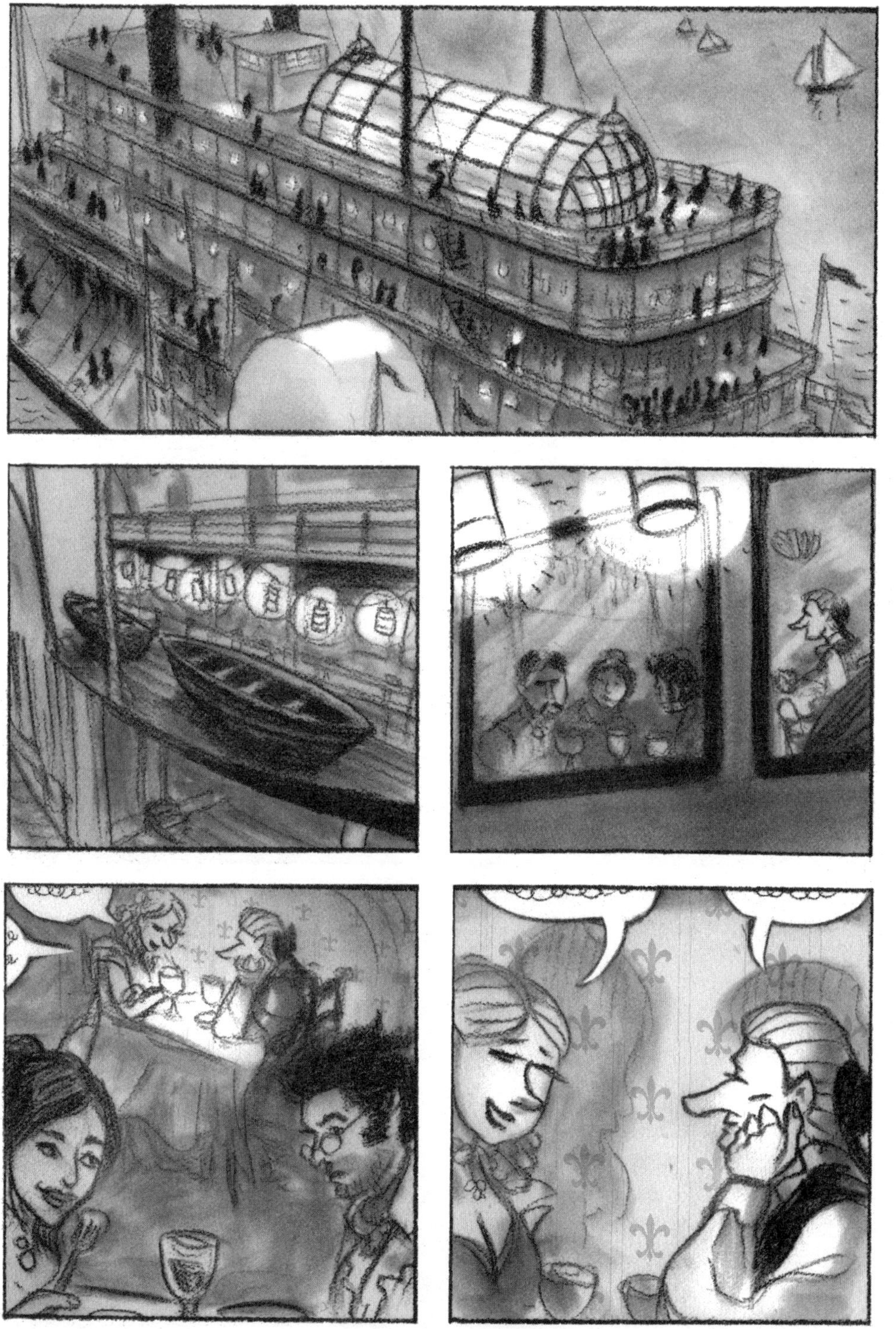

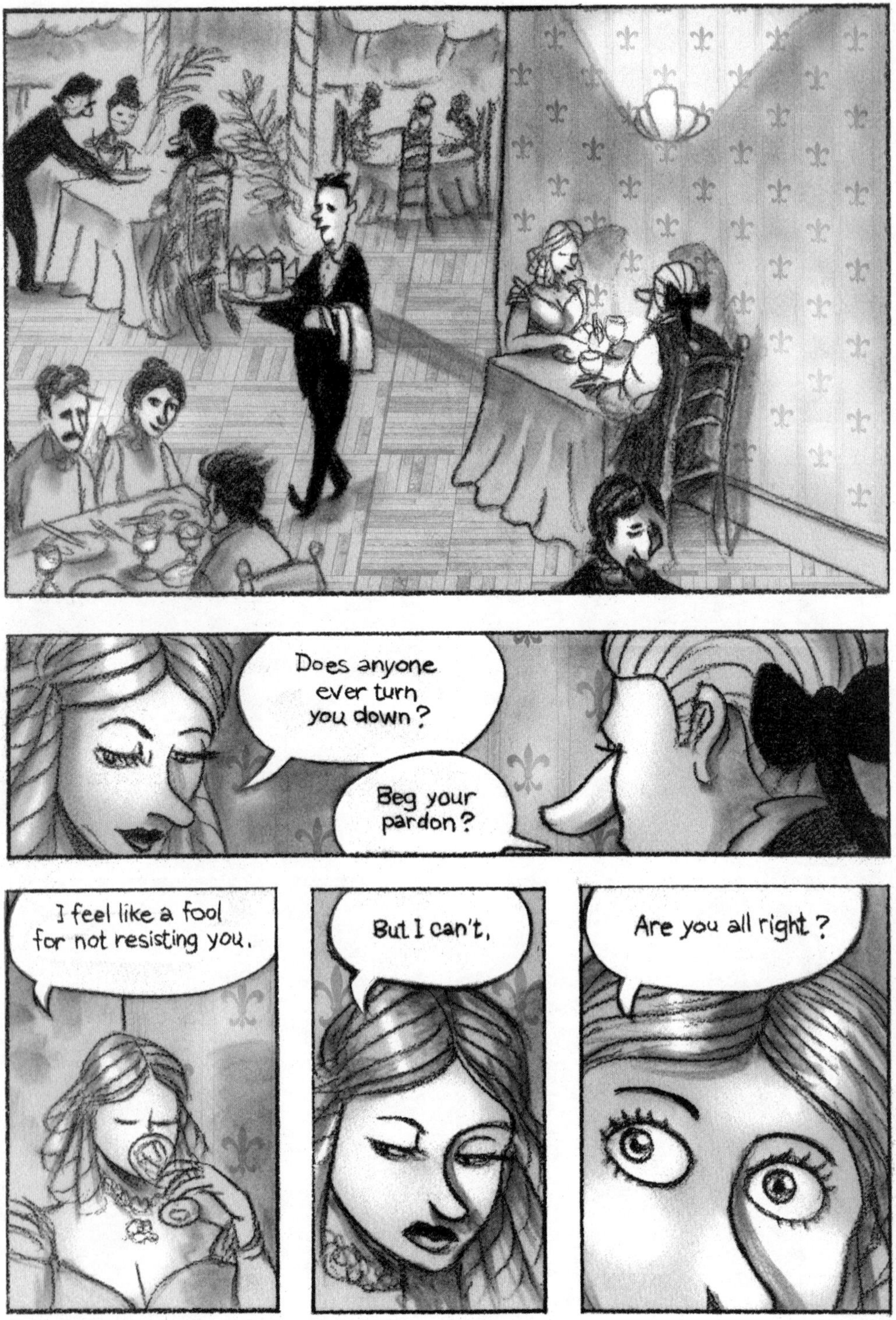
Does anyone ever turn you down?
Beg your pardon?
I feel like a fool for not resisting you.
But I can't.
Are you all right?

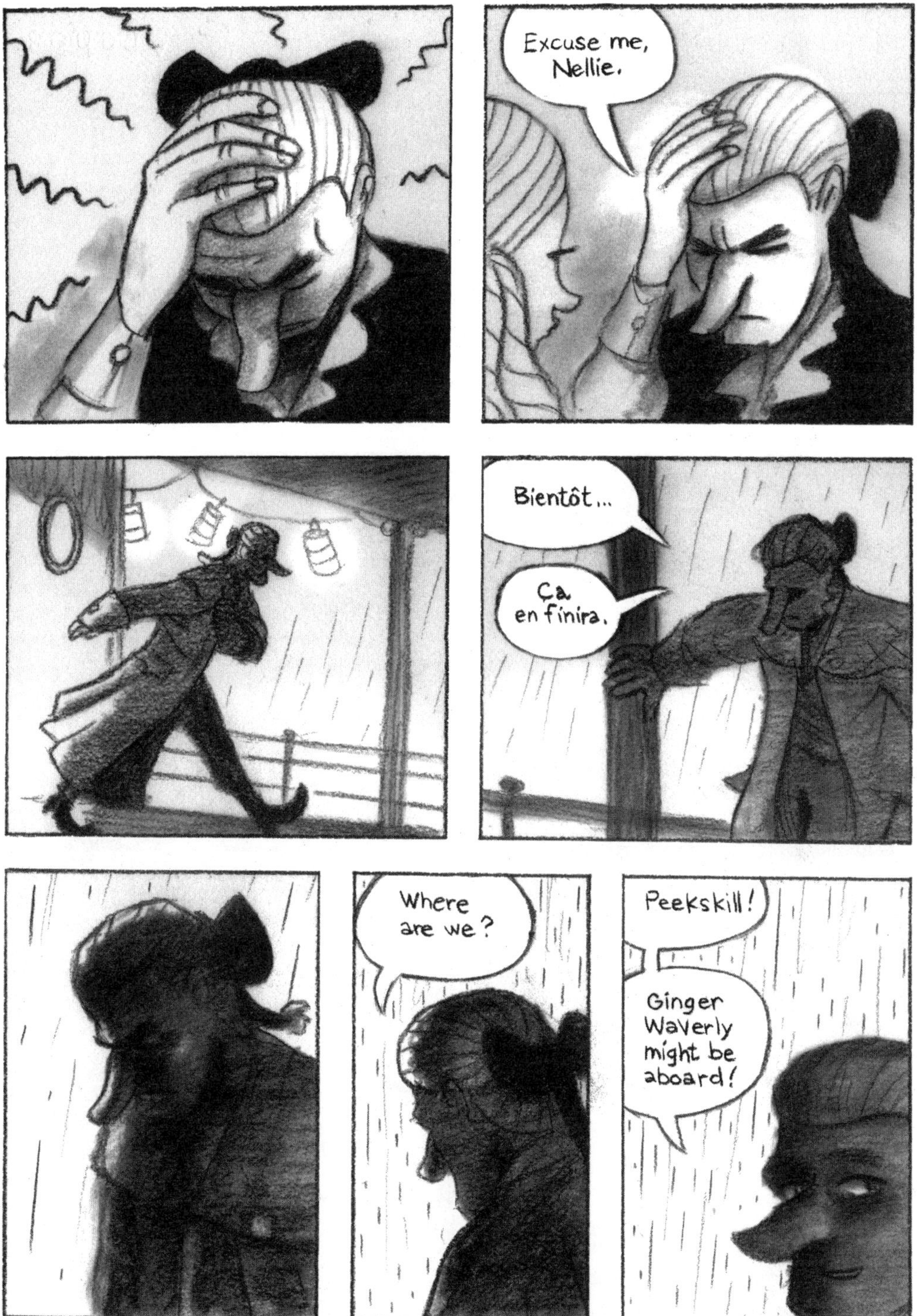
Excuse me, Nellie.
Bientôt...
Ça en finira.
Where are we?
Peekskill!
Ginger Waverly might be aboard!

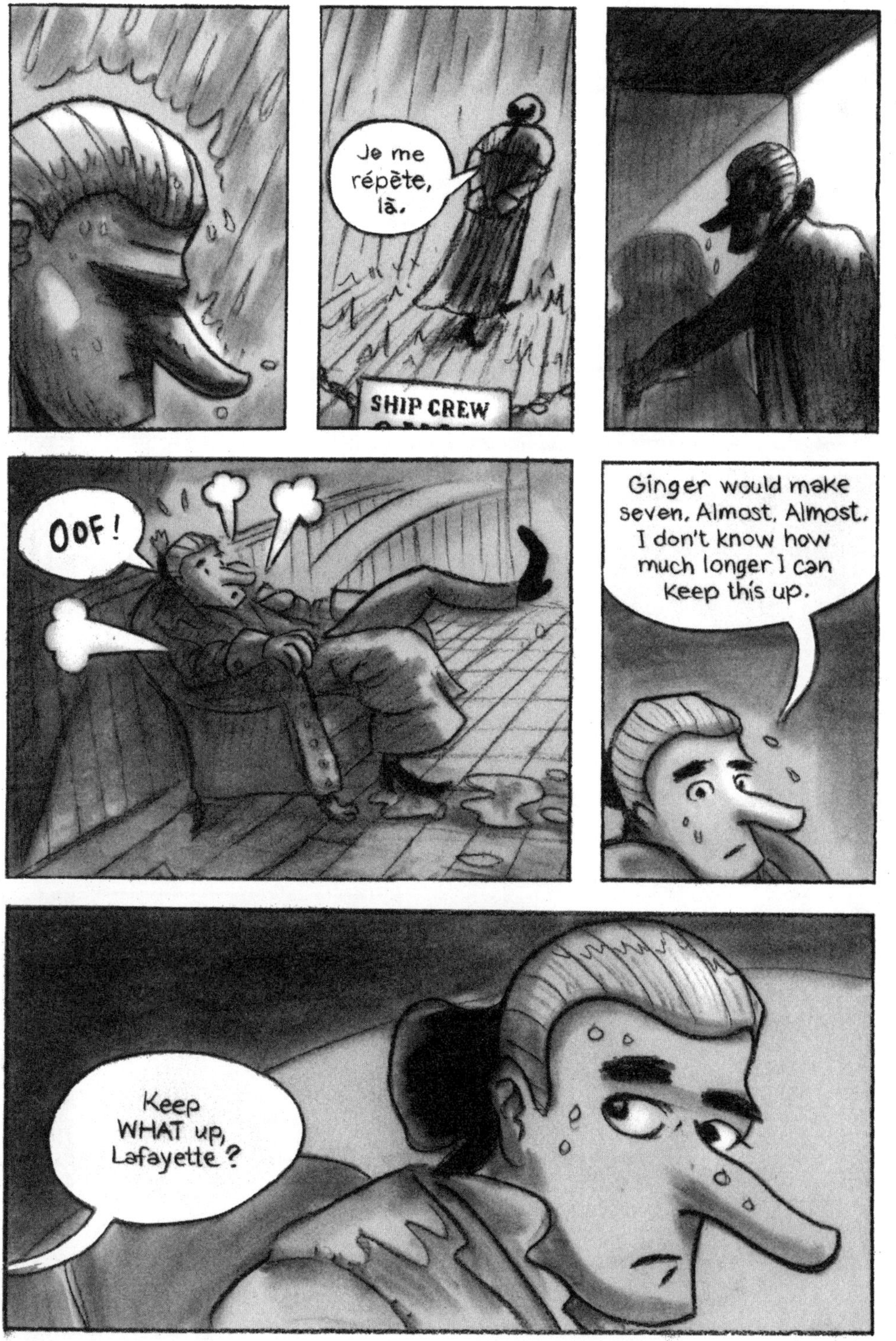
Je me répète, là.
SHIP CREW
OOF!
Ginger would make seven. Almost. Almost. I don't know how much longer I can keep this up.
Keep WHAT up, Lafayette?

You've read Beaverton? Brilliant, isn't he?

What a mind!

What a mind.

Now there's a writer.

And an epistolary genius.

Yes, yes, he's coming aboard.

He and I have exchanged over a dozen letters.

I can't begin to tell you how thrilling our correspondence has been!

Sounds like you've found your seventh love.

Very funny.

Whoever stirs my heart, my mind, or my loins...

I'll love.

Which is more than I can say about you, Twain. You're about as arousing as a dead fish these days.

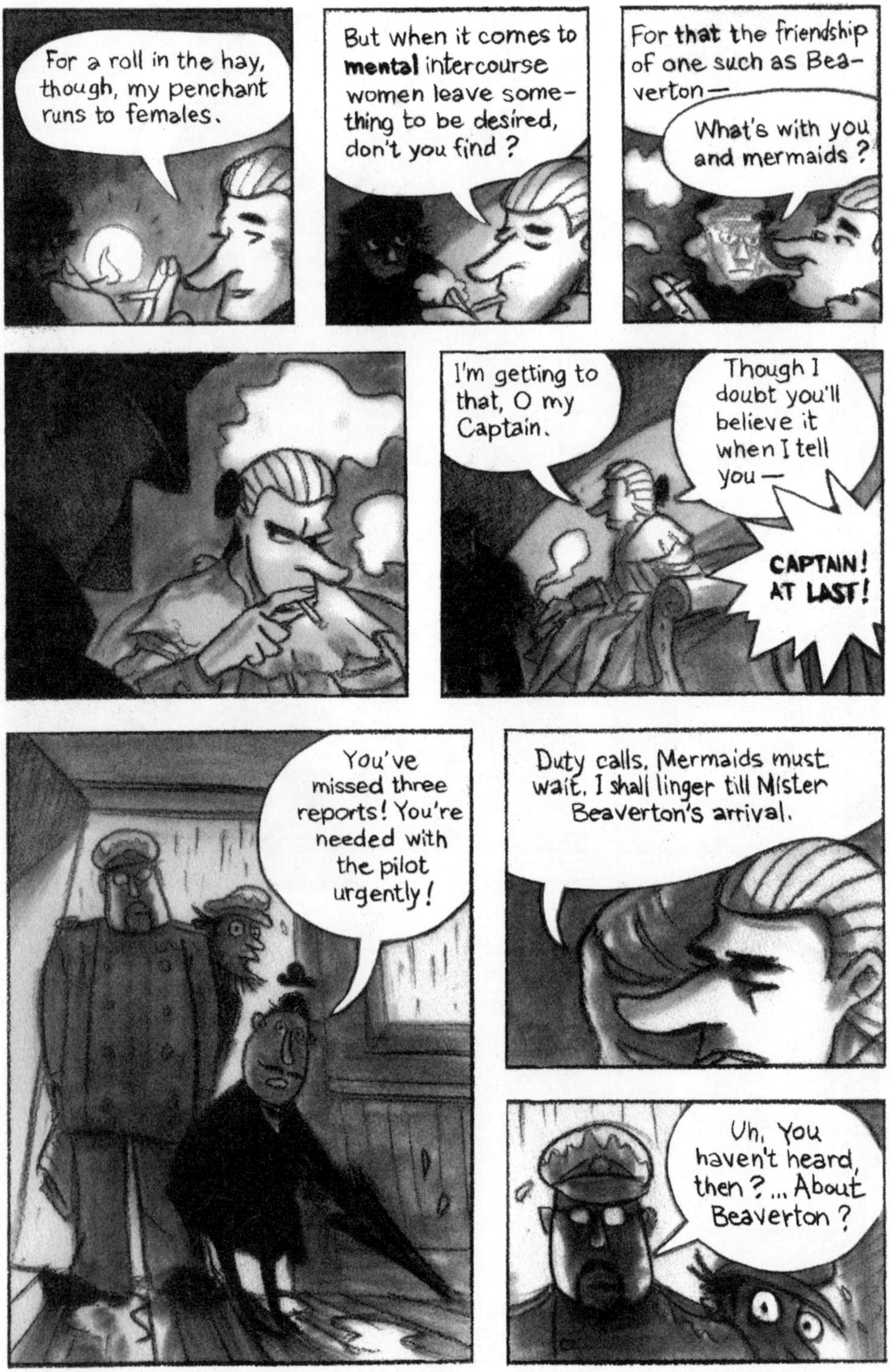

For a roll in the hay, though, my penchant runs to females.
But when it comes to **mental** intercourse women leave something to be desired, don't you find?
For **that** the friendship of one such as Beaverton—
What's with you and mermaids?
I'm getting to that, O my Captain.
Though I doubt you'll believe it when I tell you—
CAPTAIN! AT LAST!
You've missed three reports! You're needed with the pilot urgently!
Duty calls. Mermaids must wait. I shall linger till Mister Beaverton's arrival.
Uh, You haven't heard, then?... About Beaverton?

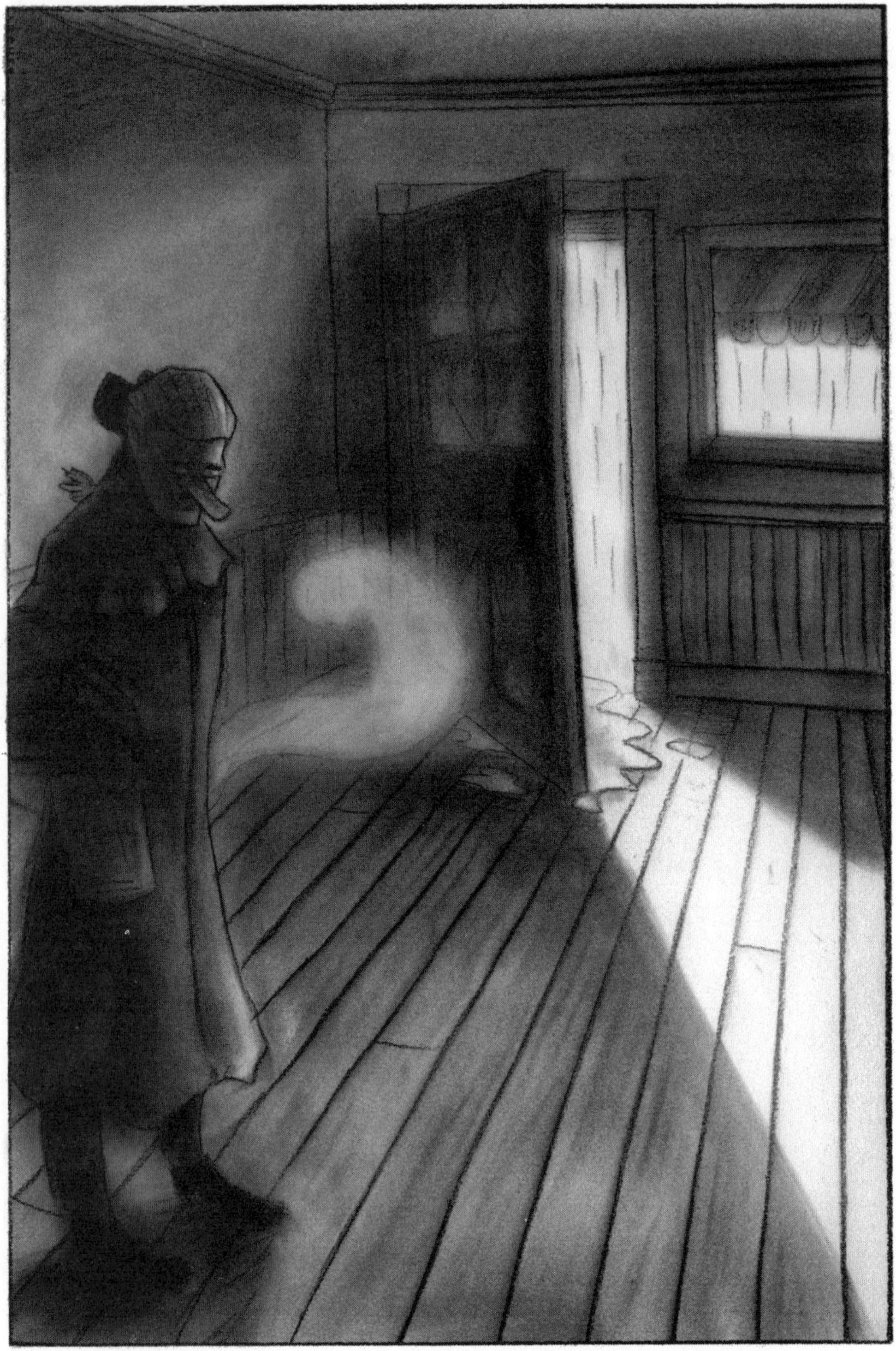

Pt II, Chap.2

"INK STAINS"

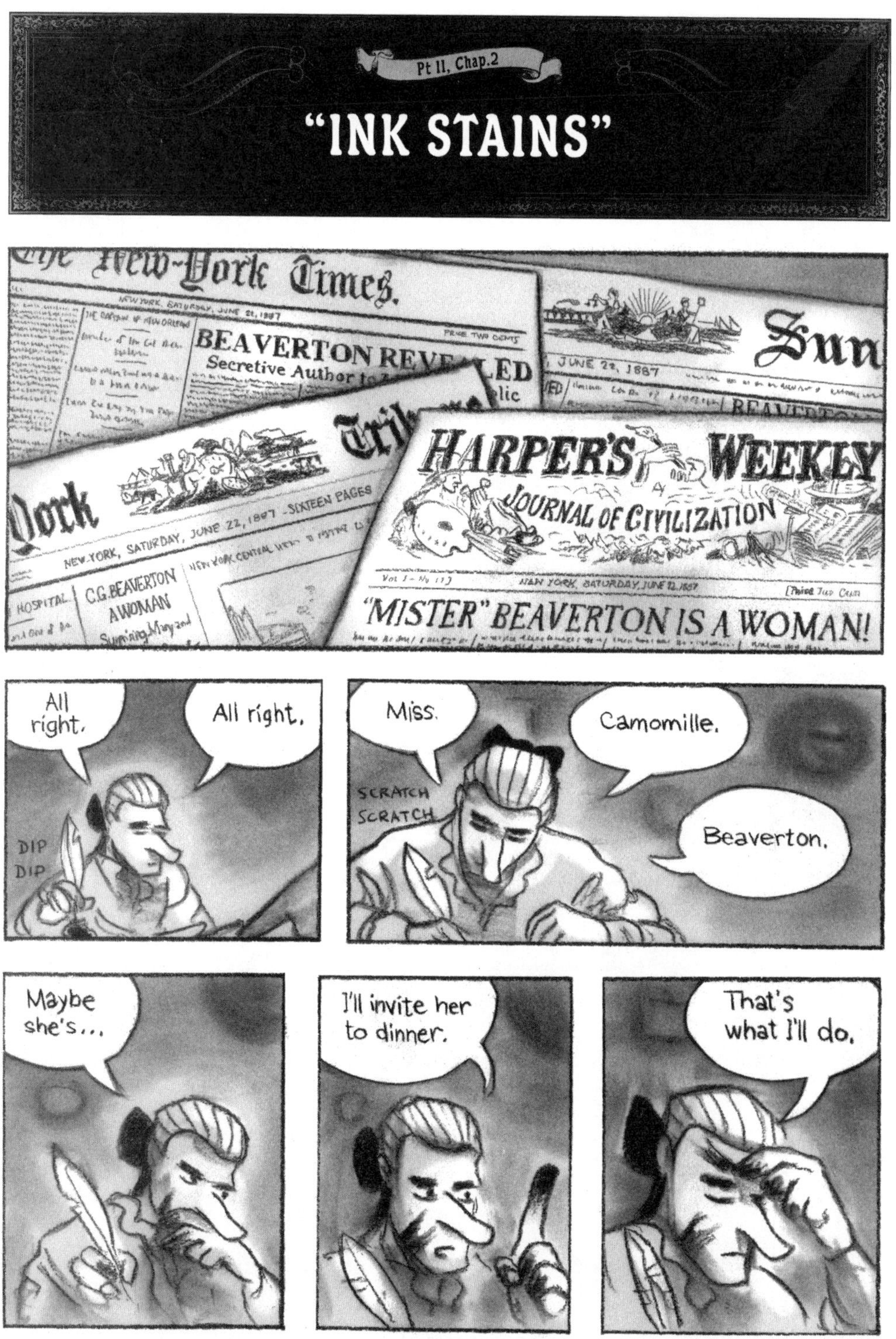
The New-York Times.
NEW-YORK, SATURDAY, JUNE 22, 1887
PRICE TWO CENTS
BEAVERTON REVEALED
Sun
JUNE 22, 1887
NEW-YORK, SATURDAY, JUNE 22, 1887 - SIXTEEN PAGES
C.G. BEAVERTON A WOMAN
HARPER'S WEEKLY
JOURNAL OF CIVILIZATION
NEW YORK, SATURDAY, JUNE 22, 1887
"MISTER" BEAVERTON IS A WOMAN!
All right.
All right.
DIP DIP
Miss.
Camomille.
Beaverton.
SCRATCH SCRATCH
Maybe she's...
I'll invite her to dinner.
That's what I'll do.

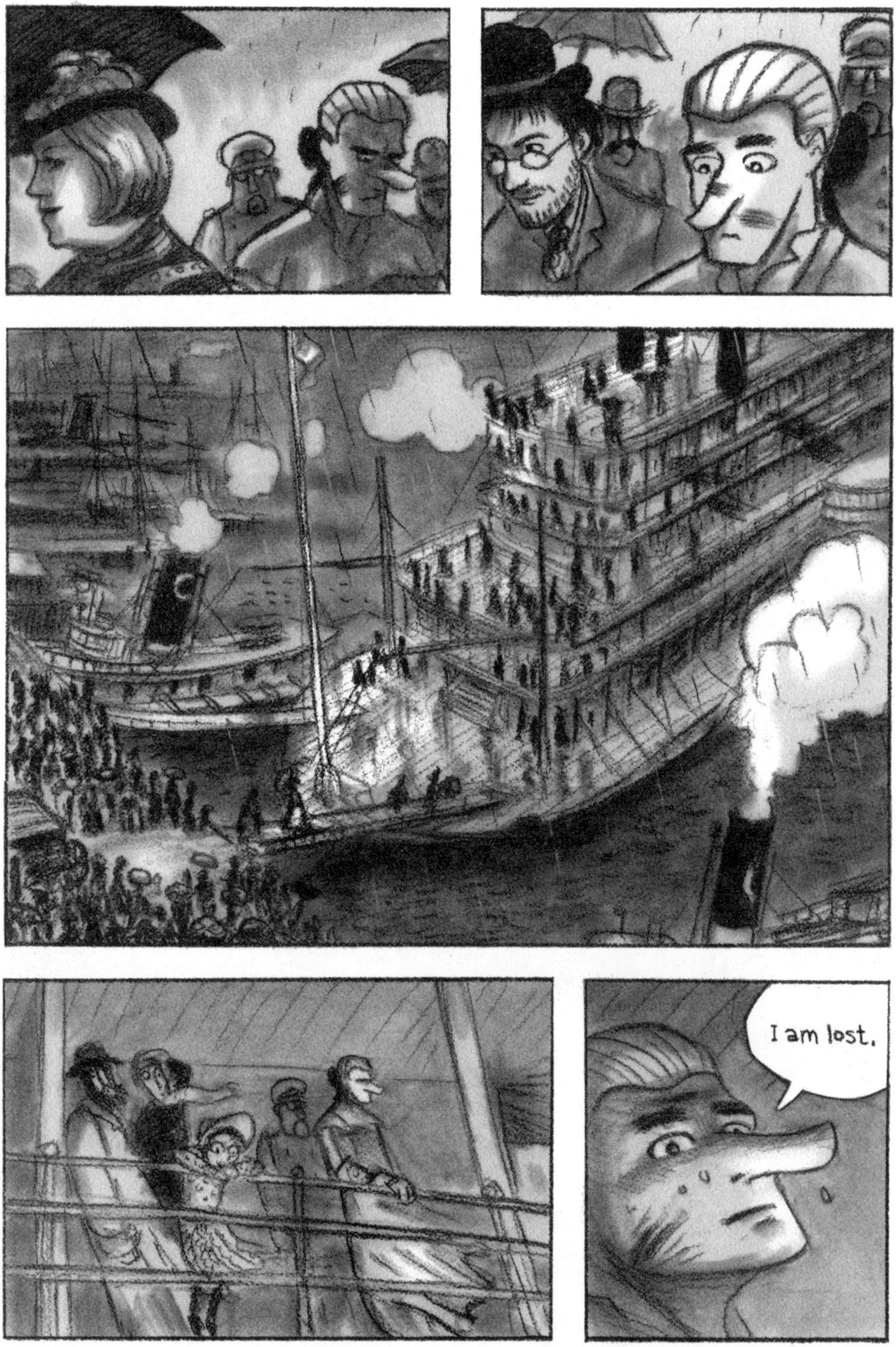
I am lost.

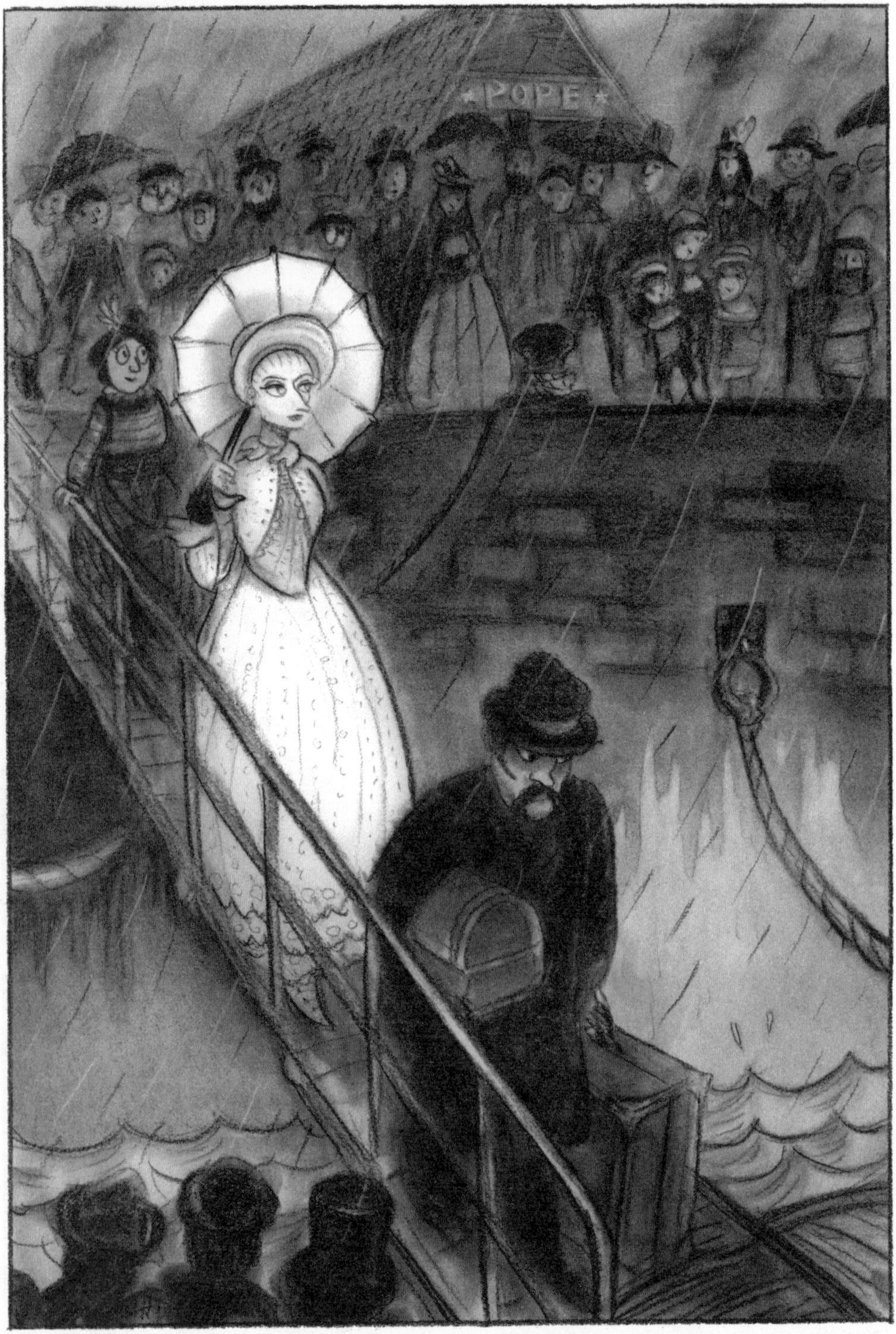
POPE

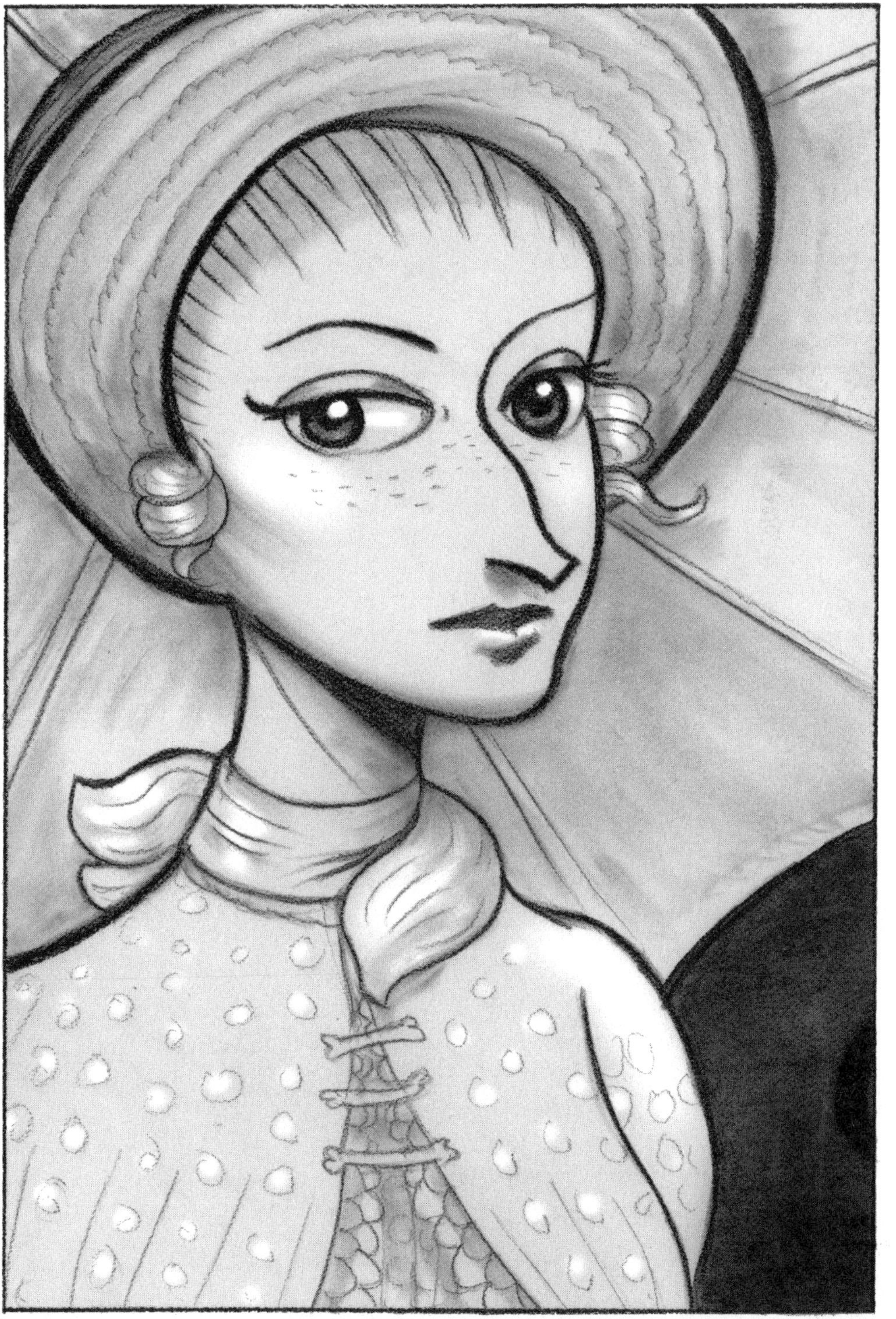

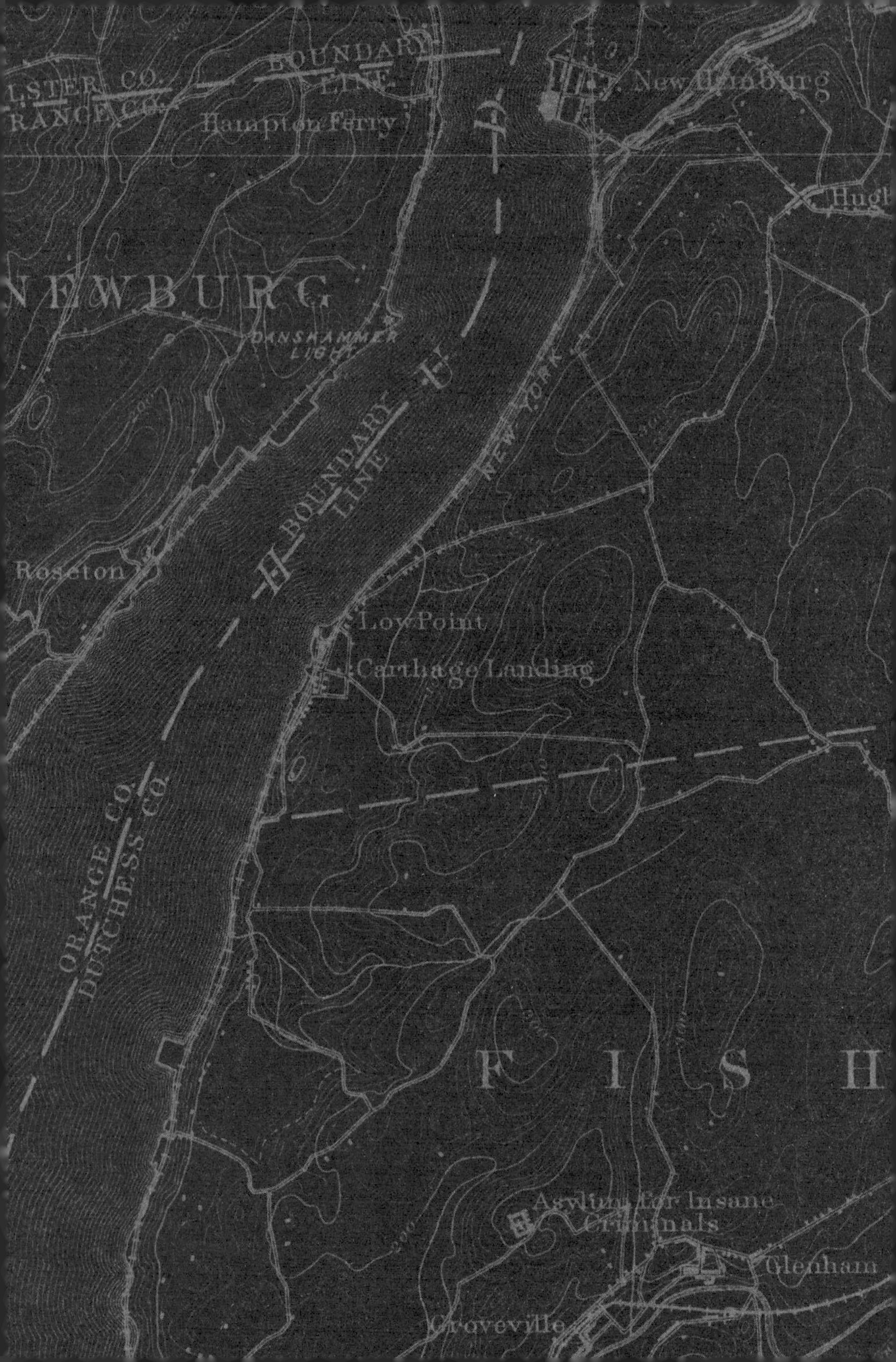
LSTER CO.
RANGE CO.
BOUNDARY LINE
Hampton Ferry
New Hamburg
Hugh
NEWBURG
DANSKAMMER LIGHT
BOUNDARY LINE
NEW YORK
Roseton
Low Point
Carthage Landing
ORANGE CO.
DUTCHESS CO.
F I S H
Asylum for Insane Criminals
Glenham
Groveville

Pt II, Chap. 3

"THE DAME'S AUDACIOUS"

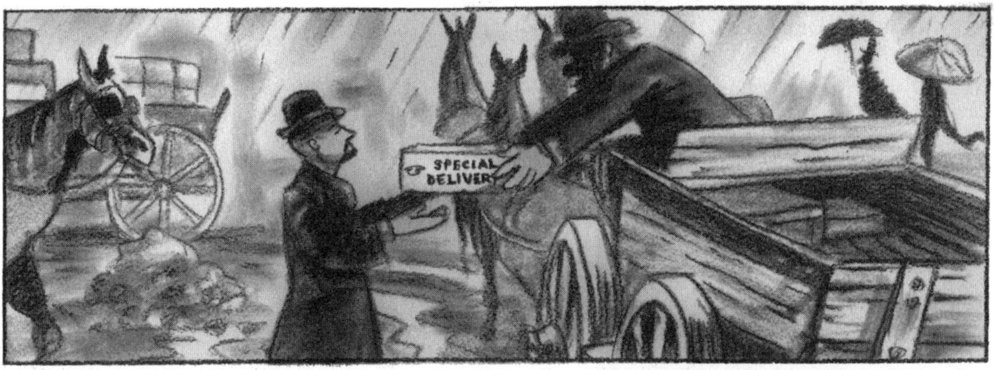
SPECIAL DELIVERY

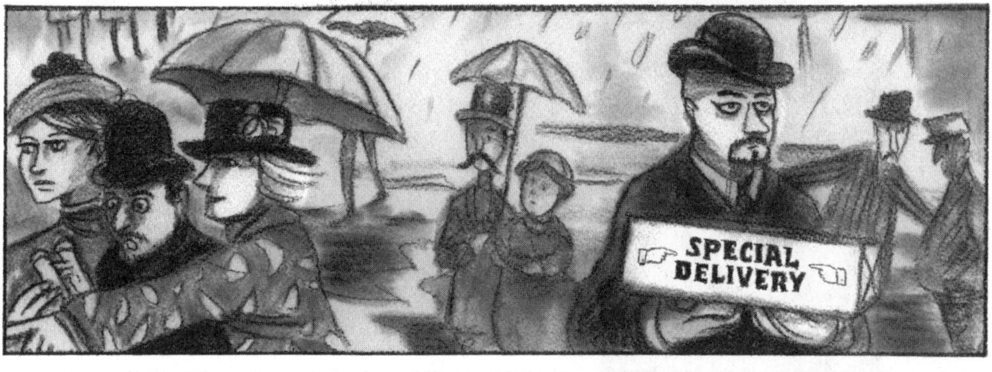
SPECIAL DELIVERY

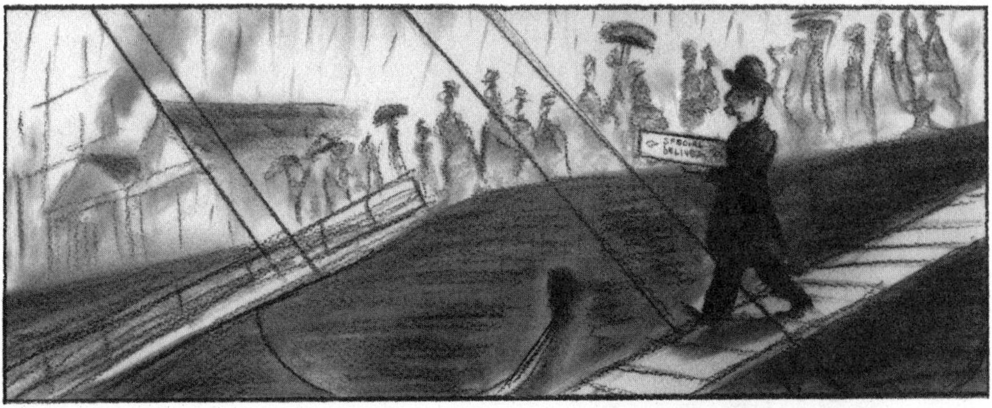

July 7, 1887

The Beaverton press conference.

Easy on the eye, ain't she?

Not a word about her new book.

I guess she's workin' the soapbox.

I'd watch 'er talk all day on anything she pleases.

If only we didn't have to report this dour stuff about negroes and injuns.

236

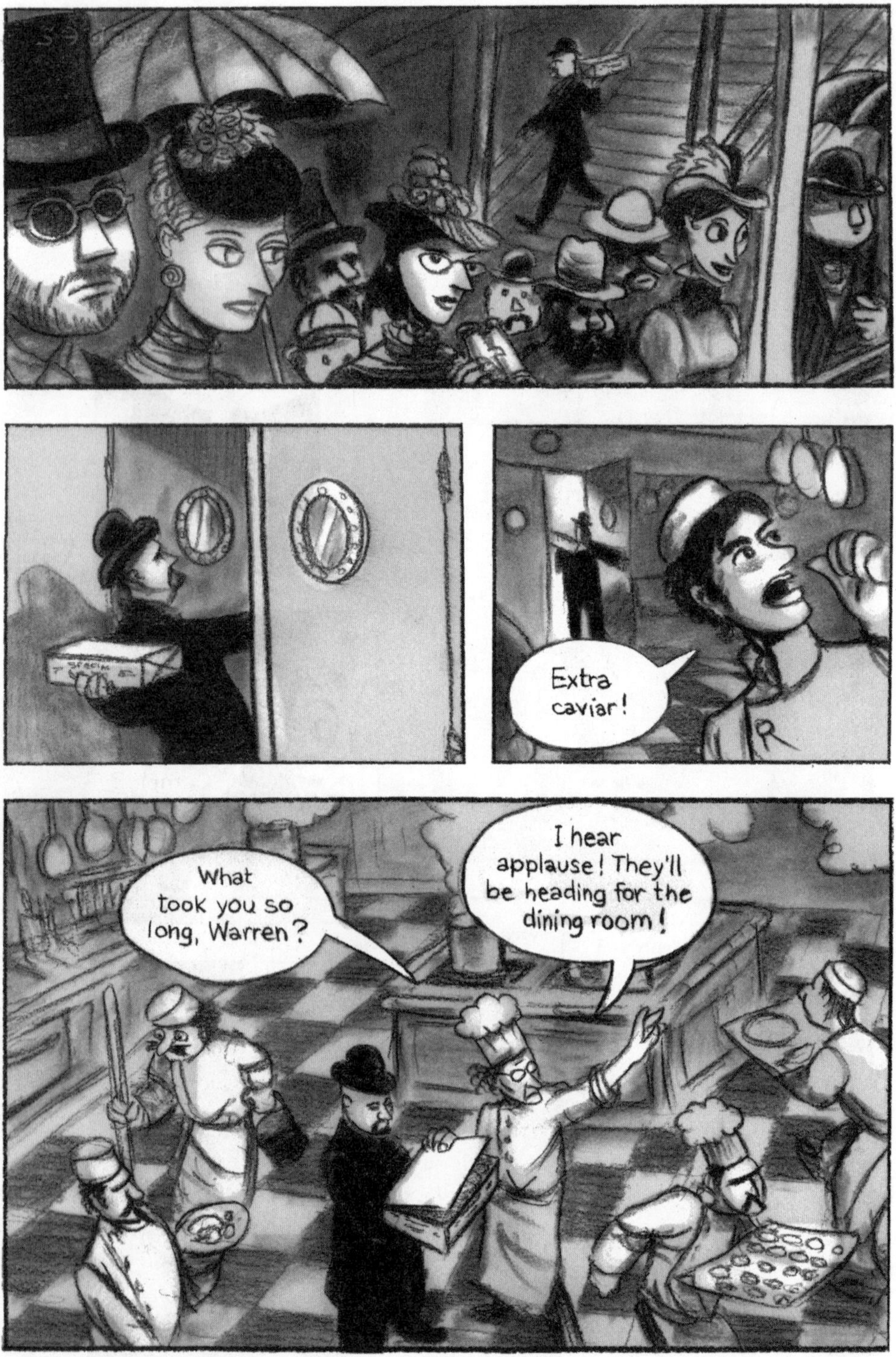
Extra caviar!
What took you so long, Warren?
I hear applause! They'll be heading for the dining room!

Pt II, Chap. 4

"ECLIPSE"

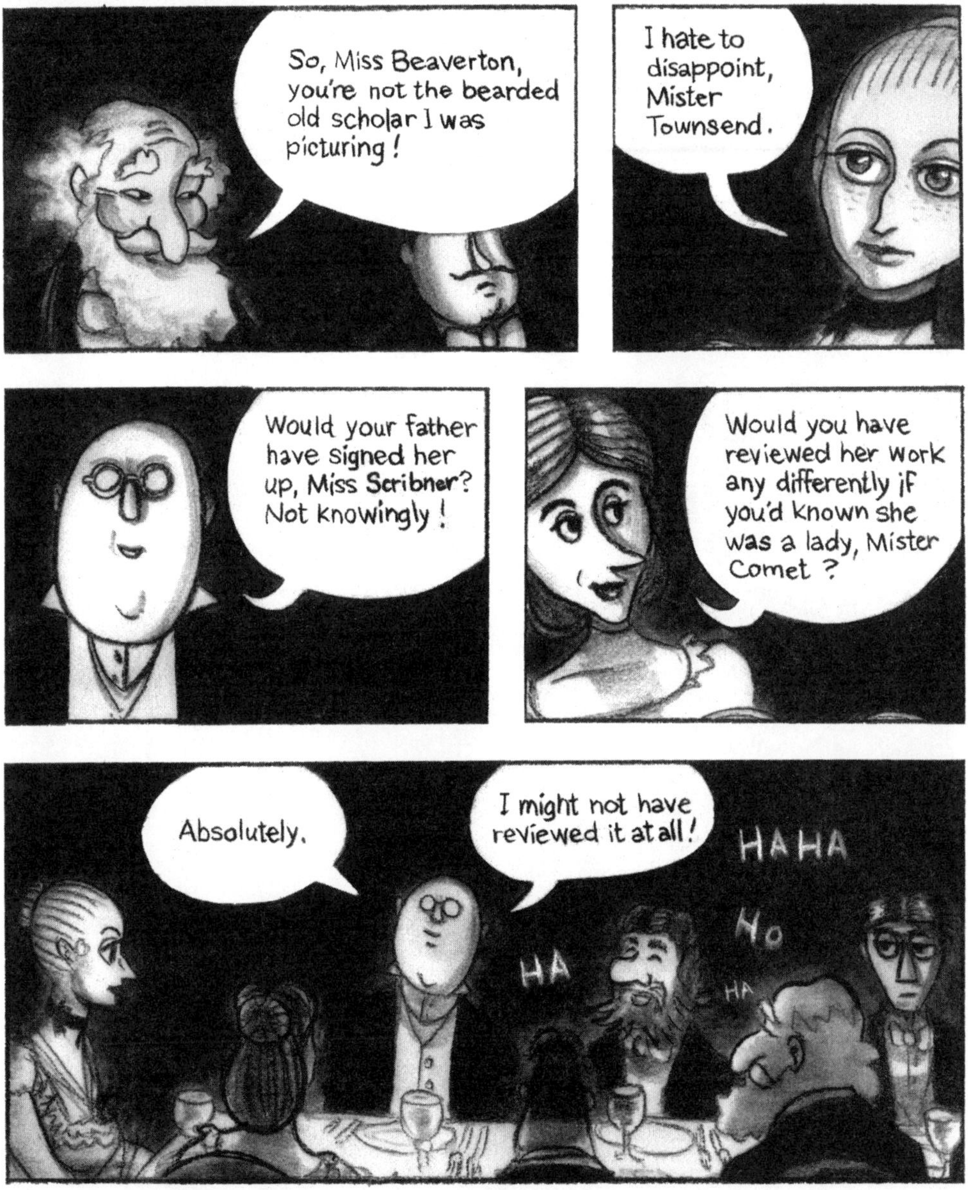

So, Miss Beaverton, you're not the bearded old scholar I was picturing!
I hate to disappoint, Mister Townsend.
Would your father have signed her up, Miss Scribner? Not knowingly!
Would you have reviewed her work any differently if you'd known she was a lady, Mister Comet?
Absolutely.
I might not have reviewed it at all!
HA HA
HO
HA
HA

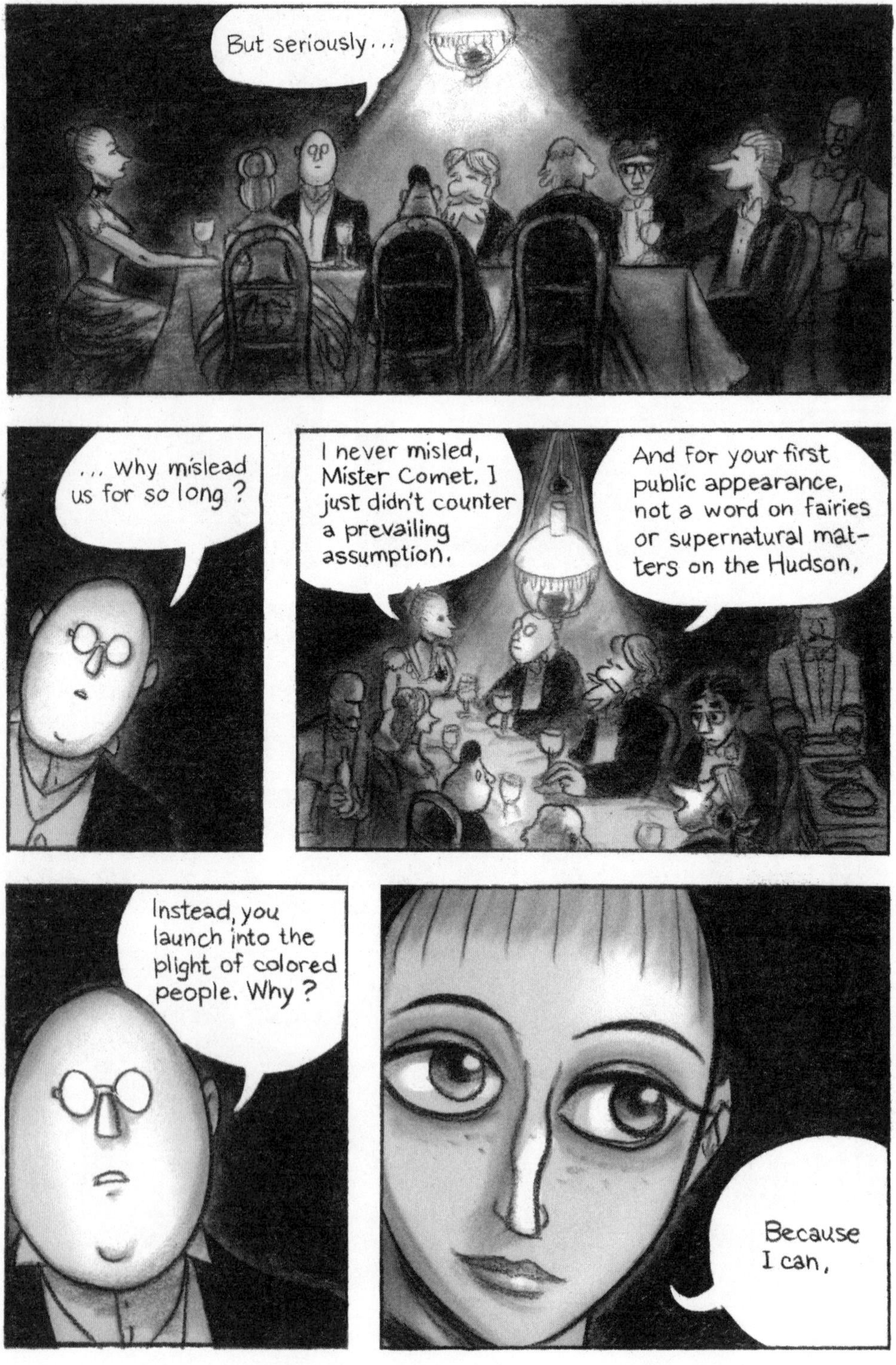
But seriously...
... Why mislead us for so long?
I never misled, Mister Comet. I just didn't counter a prevailing assumption.
And for your first public appearance, not a word on fairies or supernatural matters on the Hudson,
Instead, you launch into the plight of colored people. Why?
Because I can,

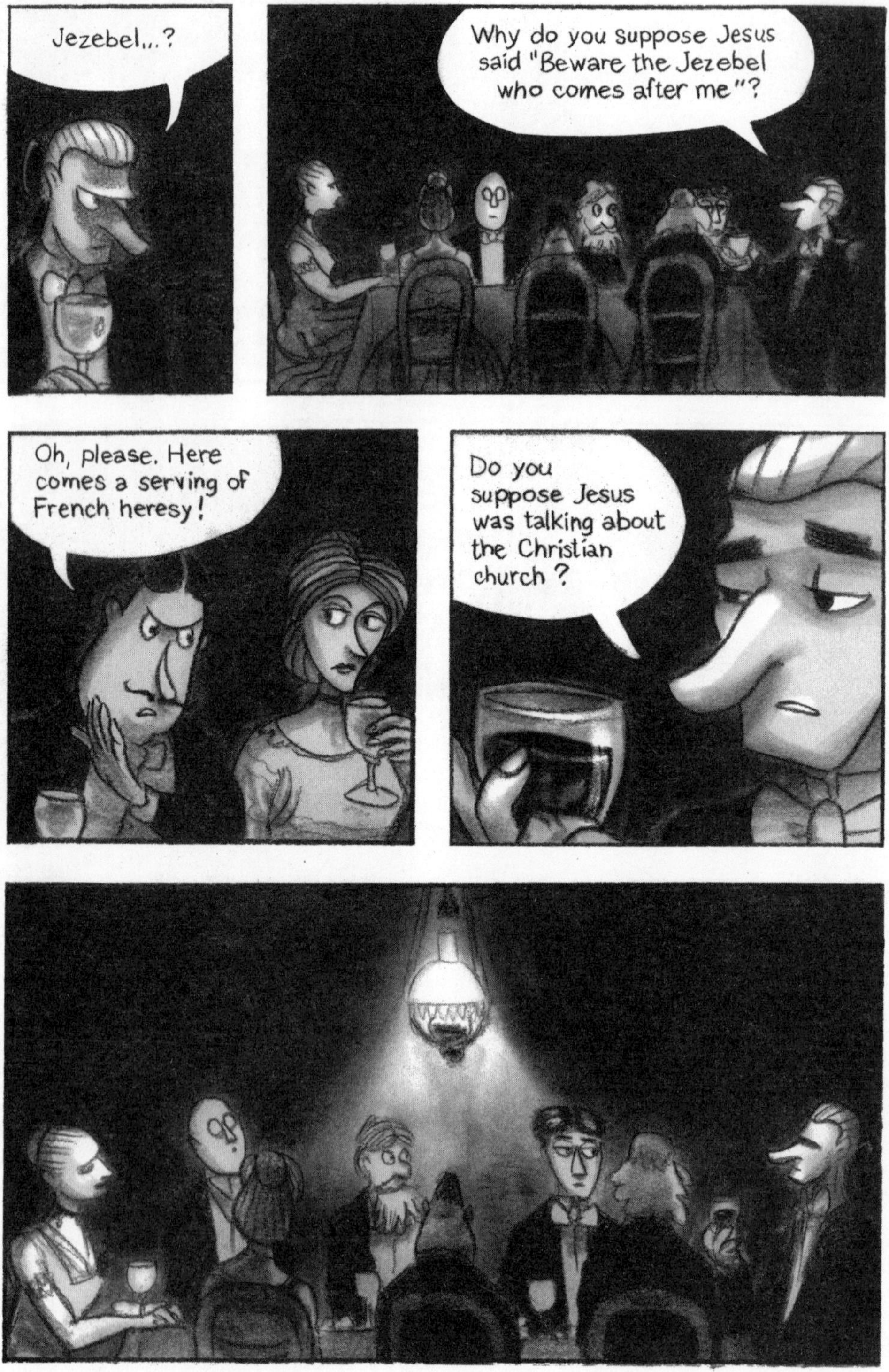
Jezebel...?
Why do you suppose Jesus said "Beware the Jezebel who comes after me"?
Oh, please. Here comes a serving of French heresy!
Do you suppose Jesus was talking about the Christian church?

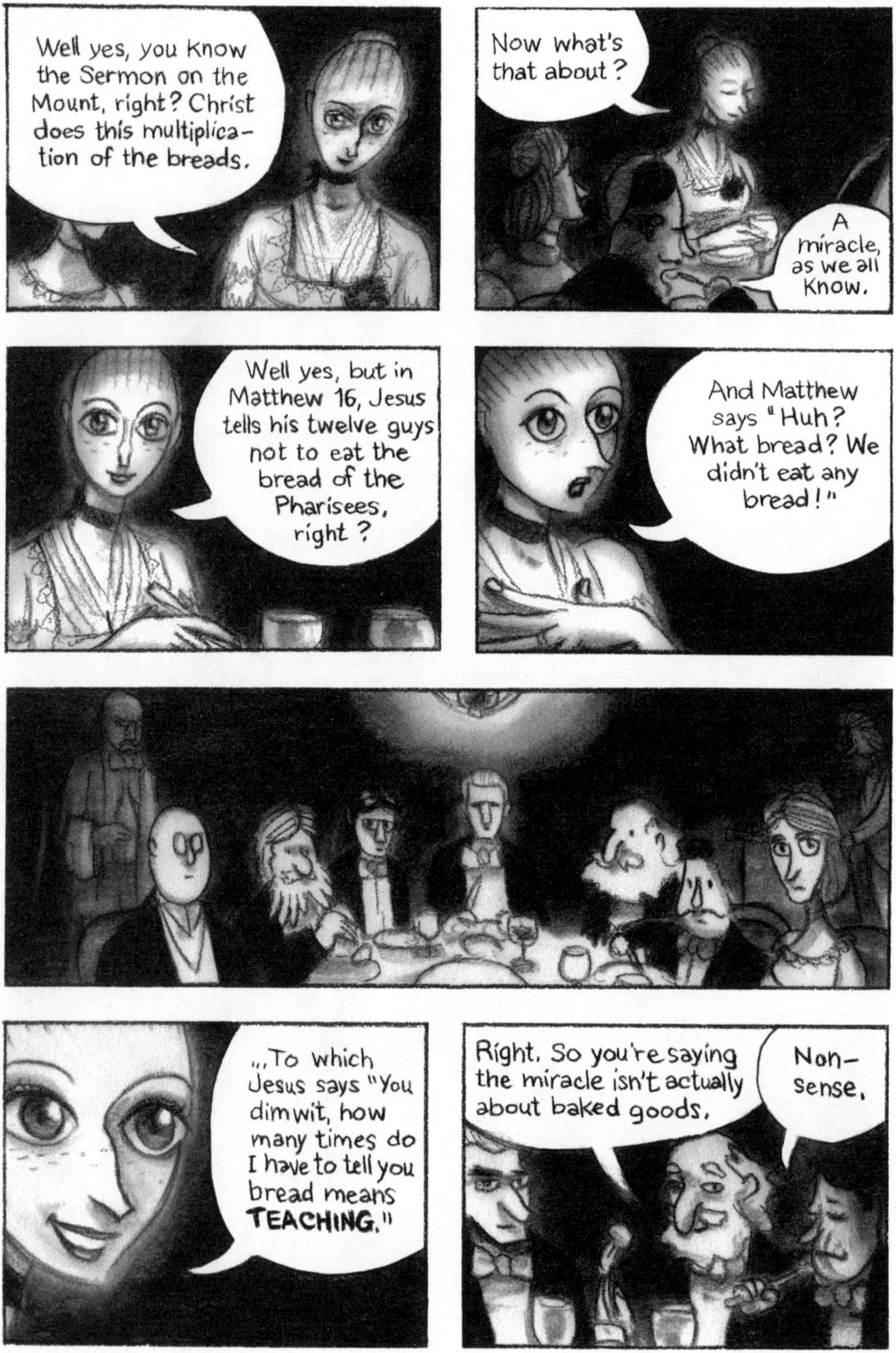
Well yes, you know the Sermon on the Mount, right? Christ does this multiplication of the breads.
Now what's that about?
A miracle, as we all know.
Well yes, but in Matthew 16, Jesus tells his twelve guys not to eat the bread of the Pharisees, right?
And Matthew says "Huh? What bread? We didn't eat any bread!"
...To which Jesus says "You dimwit, how many times do I have to tell you bread means **TEACHING.**"
Right. So you're saying the miracle isn't actually about baked goods.
Non-sense.

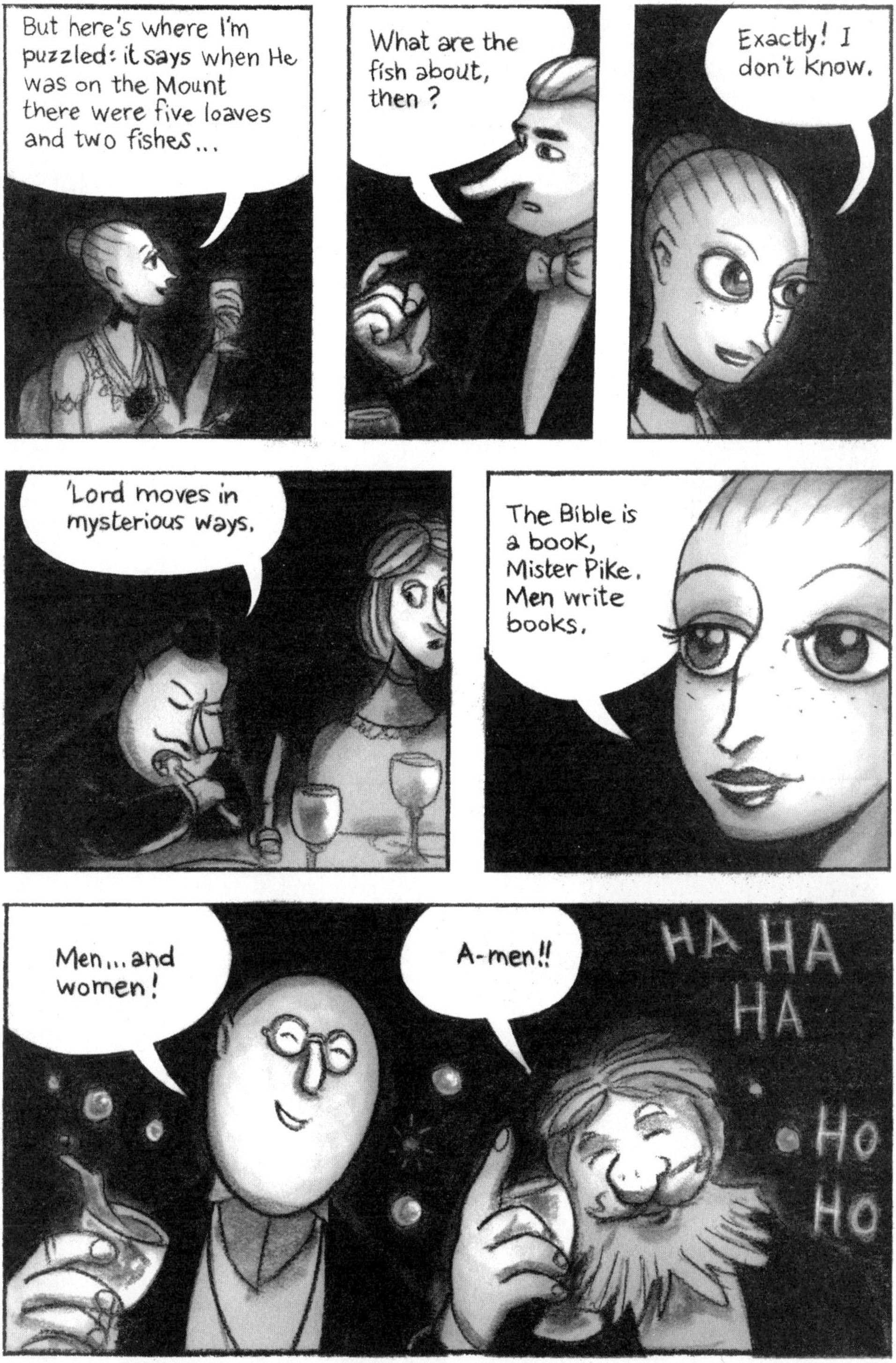
But here's where I'm puzzled: it says when He was on the Mount there were five loaves and two fishes...
What are the fish about, then?
Exactly! I don't know.
'Lord moves in mysterious ways.
The Bible is a book, Mister Pike. Men write books.
Men...and women!
A-men!!
HA HA HA
HA
HO
HO

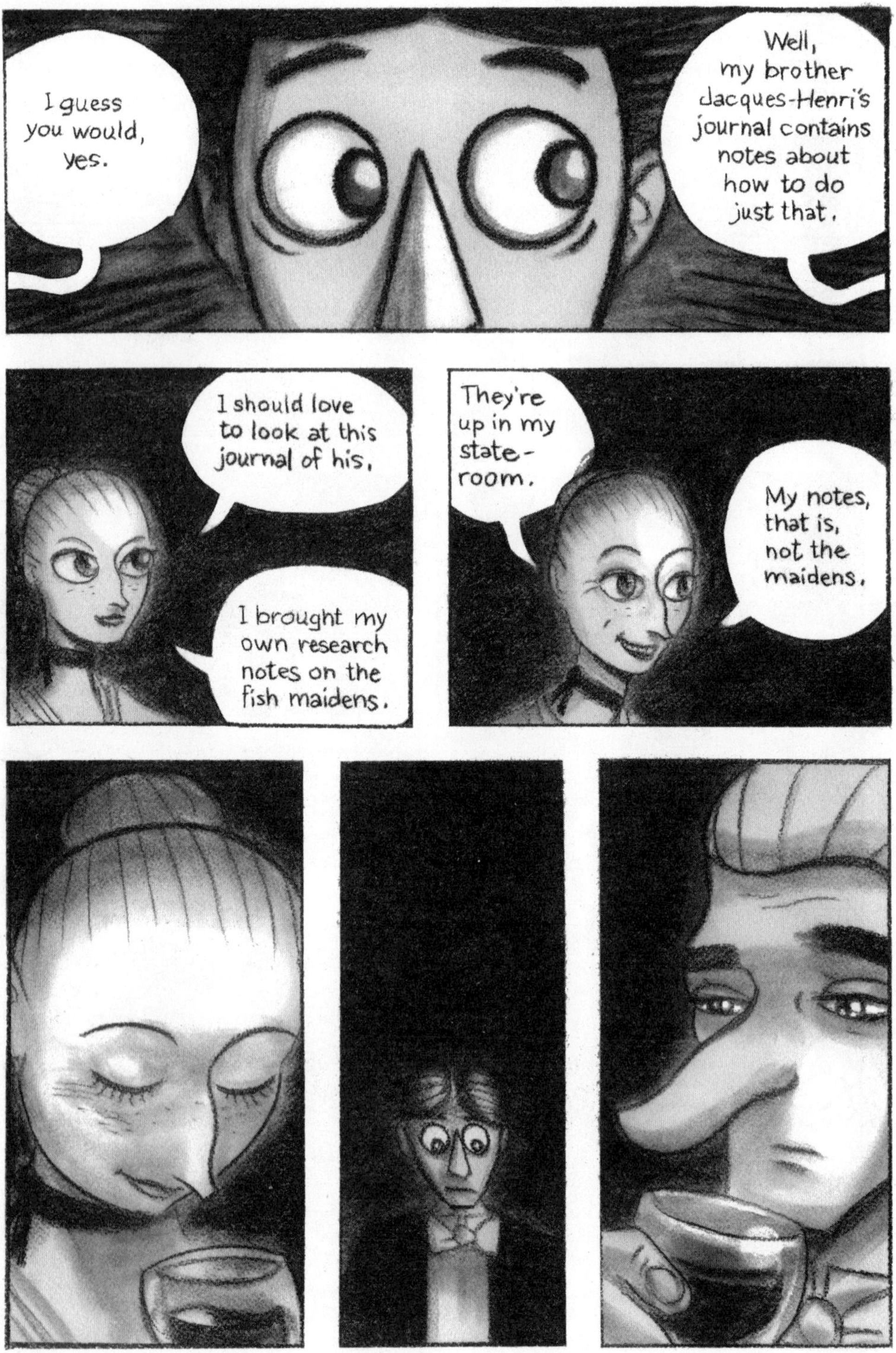
I guess you would, yes.
Well, my brother Jacques-Henri's journal contains notes about how to do just that.
I should love to look at this journal of his.
I brought my own research notes on the fish maidens.
They're up in my state-room.
My notes, that is, not the maidens.

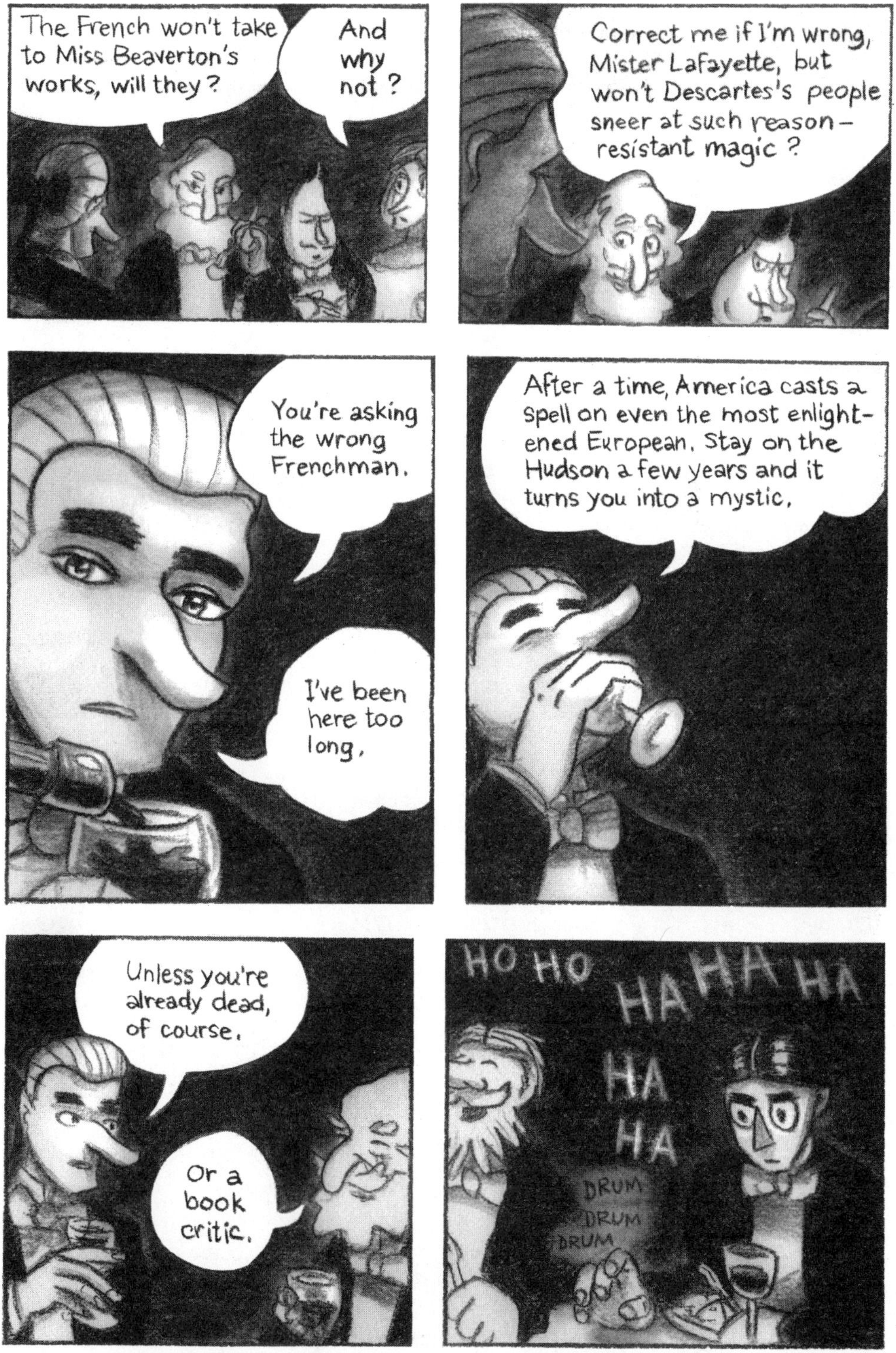
The French won't take to Miss Beaverton's works, will they?
And why not?
Correct me if I'm wrong, Mister Lafayette, but won't Descartes's people sneer at such reason-resistant magic?
You're asking the wrong Frenchman.
I've been here too long.
After a time, America casts a spell on even the most enlightened European. Stay on the Hudson a few years and it turns you into a mystic.
Unless you're already dead, of course.
Or a book critic.
HO HO
HA HA HA HA
HA
HA
DRUM
DRUM
DRUM

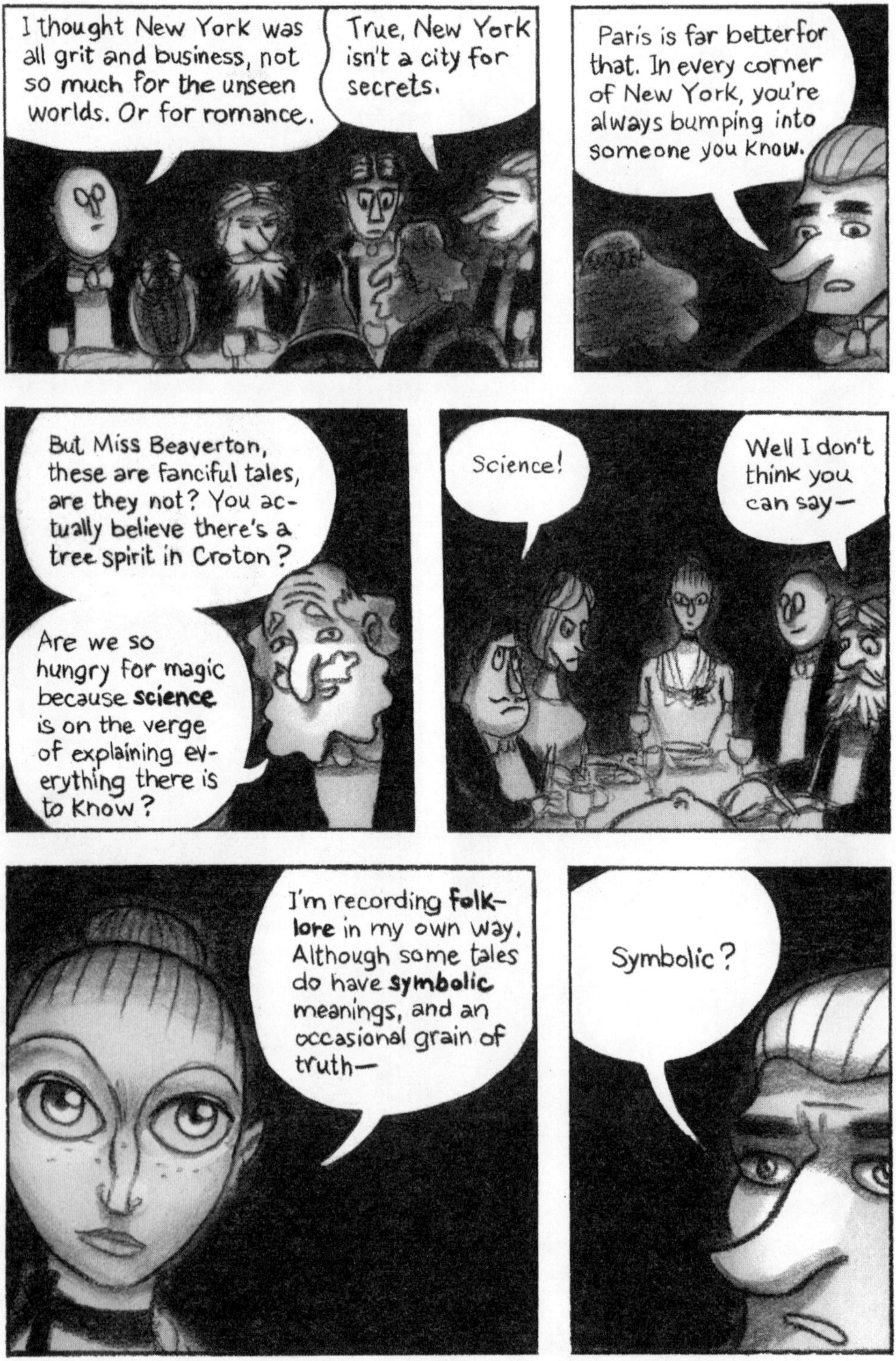
I thought New York was all grit and business, not so much for the unseen worlds. Or for romance.
True, New York isn't a city for secrets.
Paris is far better for that. In every corner of New York, you're always bumping into someone you know.
But Miss Beaverton, these are fanciful tales, are they not? You actually believe there's a tree spirit in Croton?
Are we so hungry for magic because **science** is on the verge of explaining everything there is to know?
Science!
Well I don't think you can say—
I'm recording **folklore** in my own way. Although some tales do have **symbolic** meanings, and an occasional grain of truth—
Symbolic?

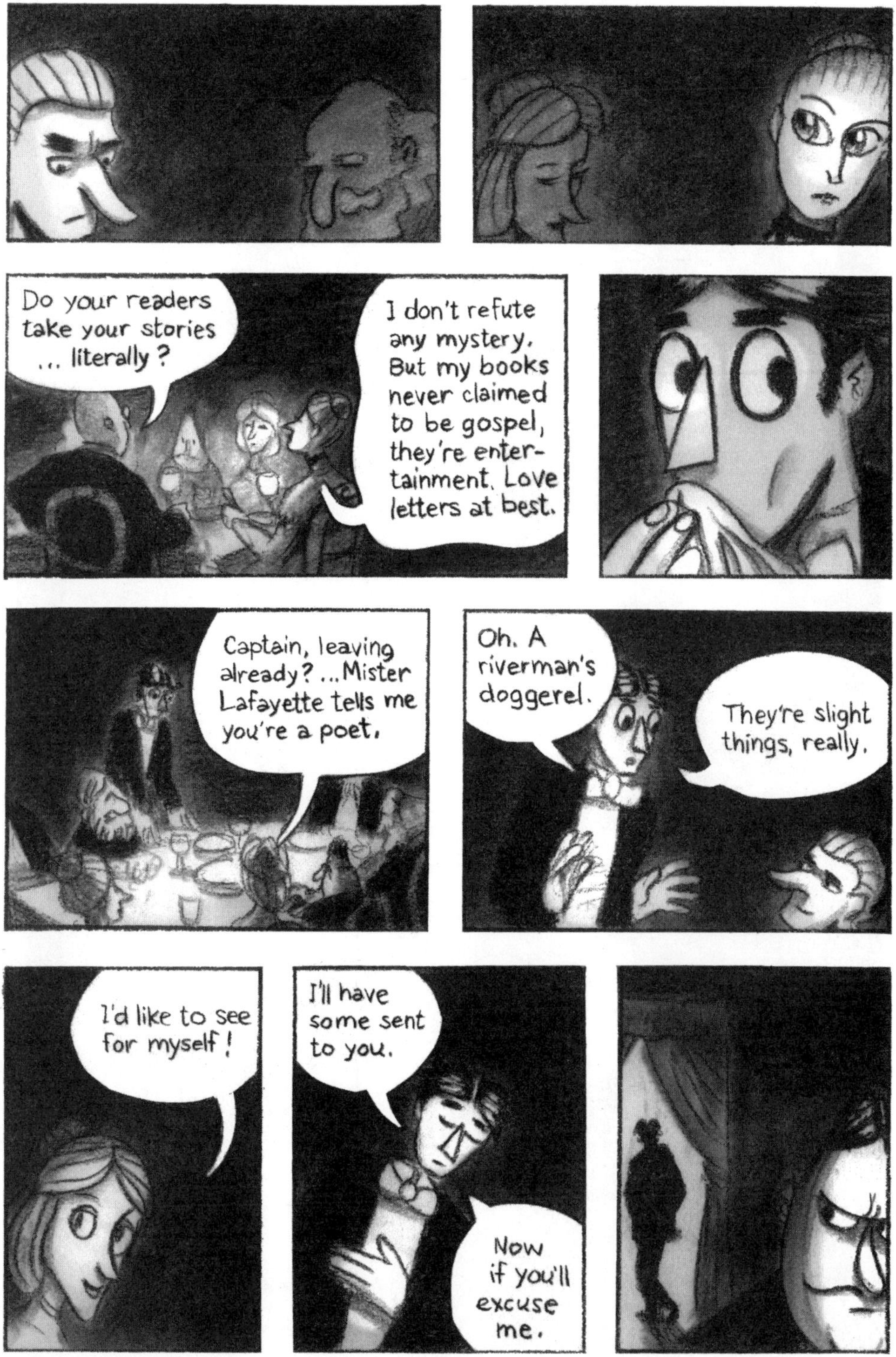
Do your readers take your stories ... literally?
I don't refute any mystery. But my books never claimed to be gospel, they're entertainment. Love letters at best.
Captain, leaving already? ...Mister Lafayette tells me you're a poet.
Oh. A riverman's doggerel.
They're slight things, really.
I'd like to see for myself!
I'll have some sent to you.
Now if you'll excuse me.

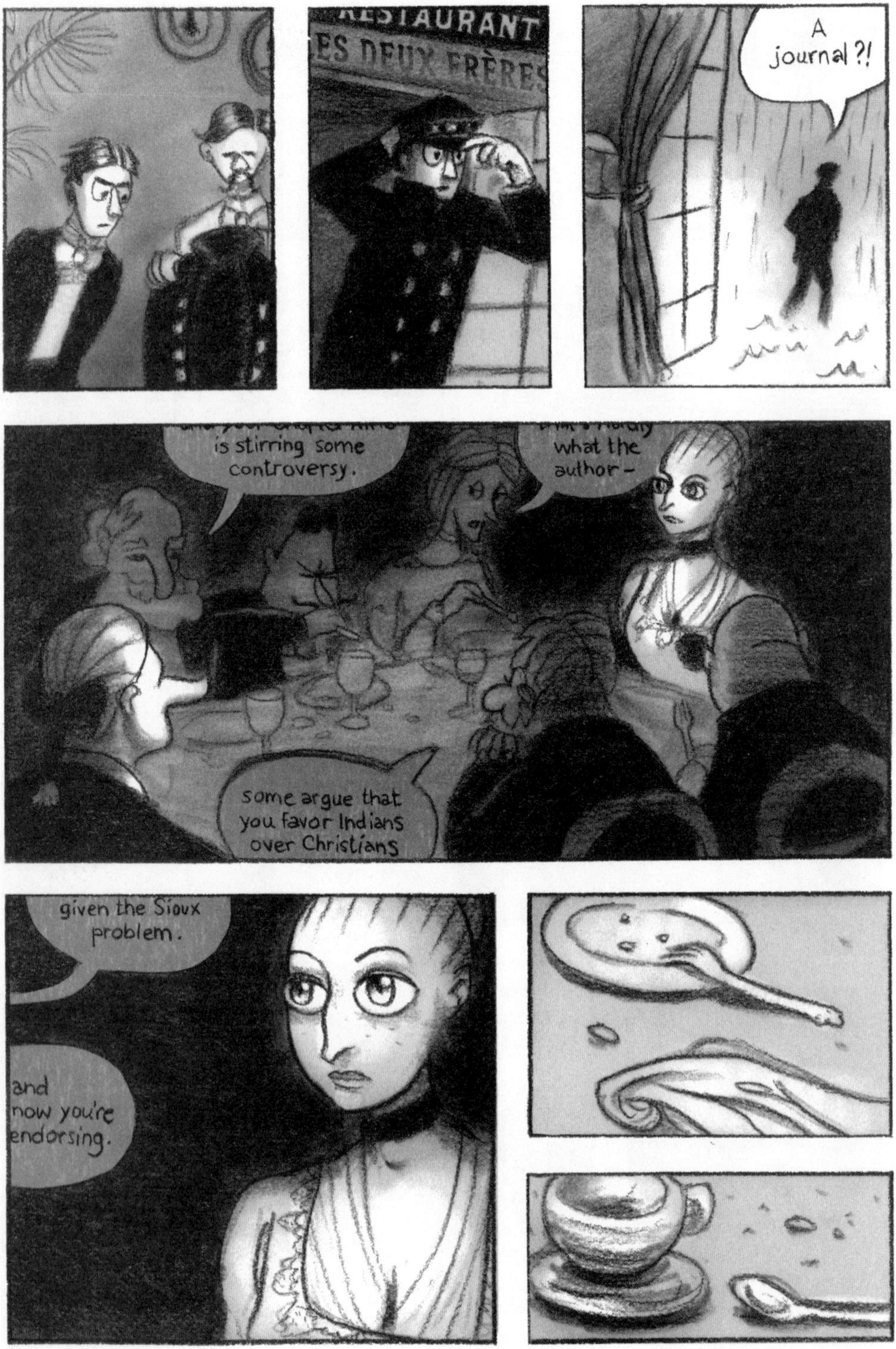
RESTAURANT
ES DEUX FRÈRES
A journal ?!
is stirring some controversy.
what the author –
some argue that you favor Indians over Christians
given the Sioux problem.
and now you're endorsing.

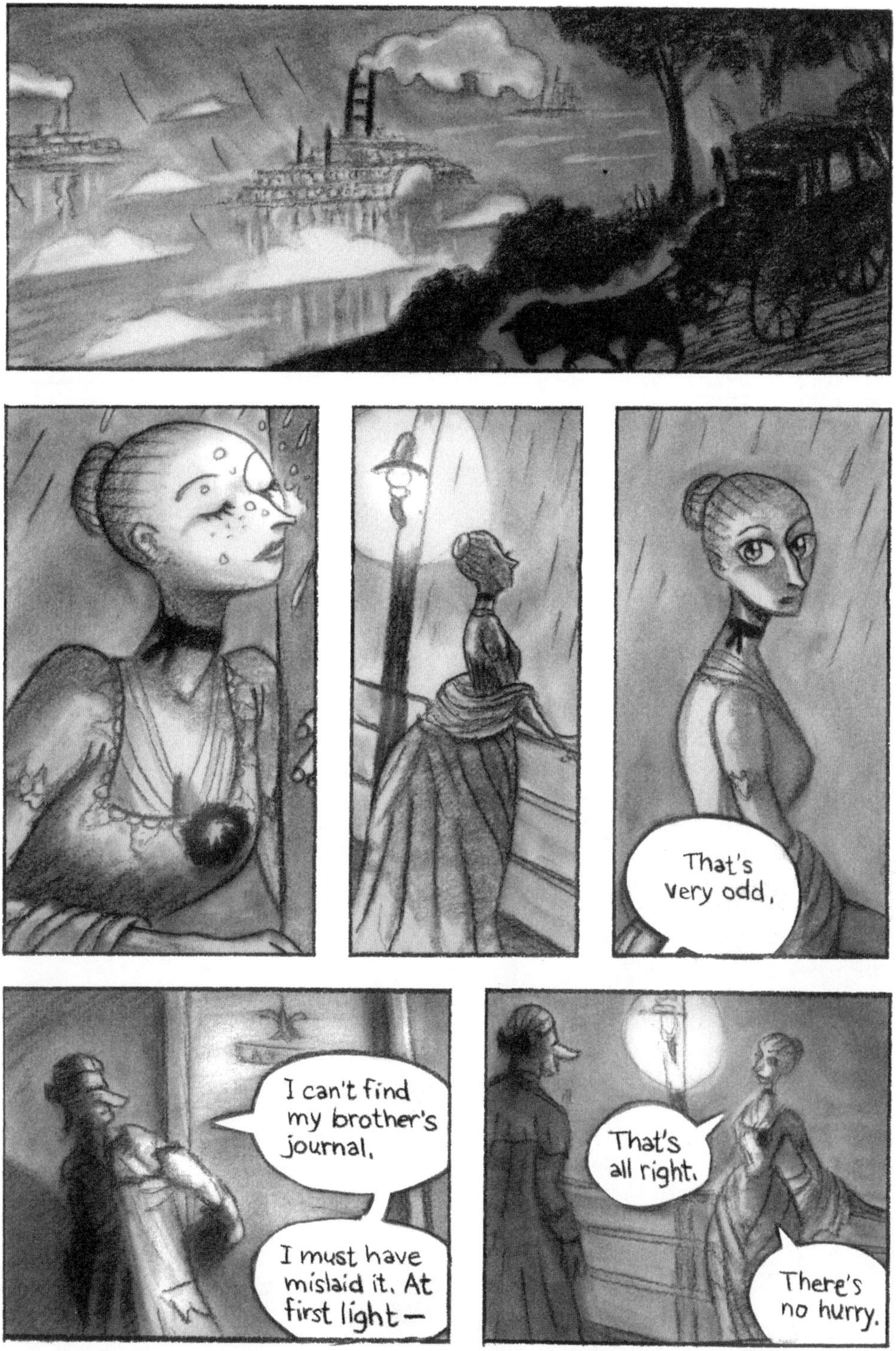
That's very odd.
I can't find my brother's journal.
I must have mislaid it. At first light—
That's all right.
There's no hurry.

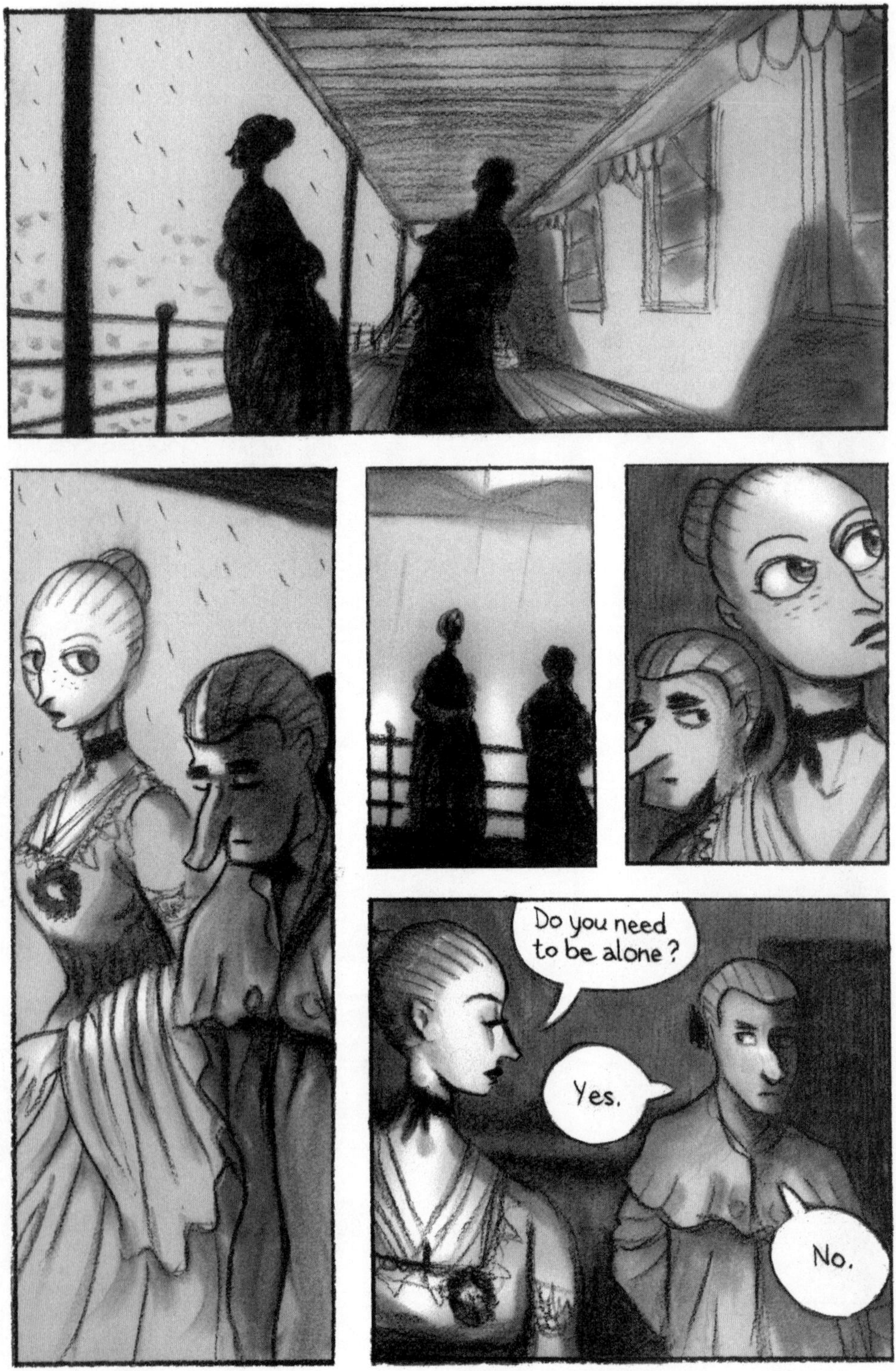
Do you need to be alone?
Yes.
No.

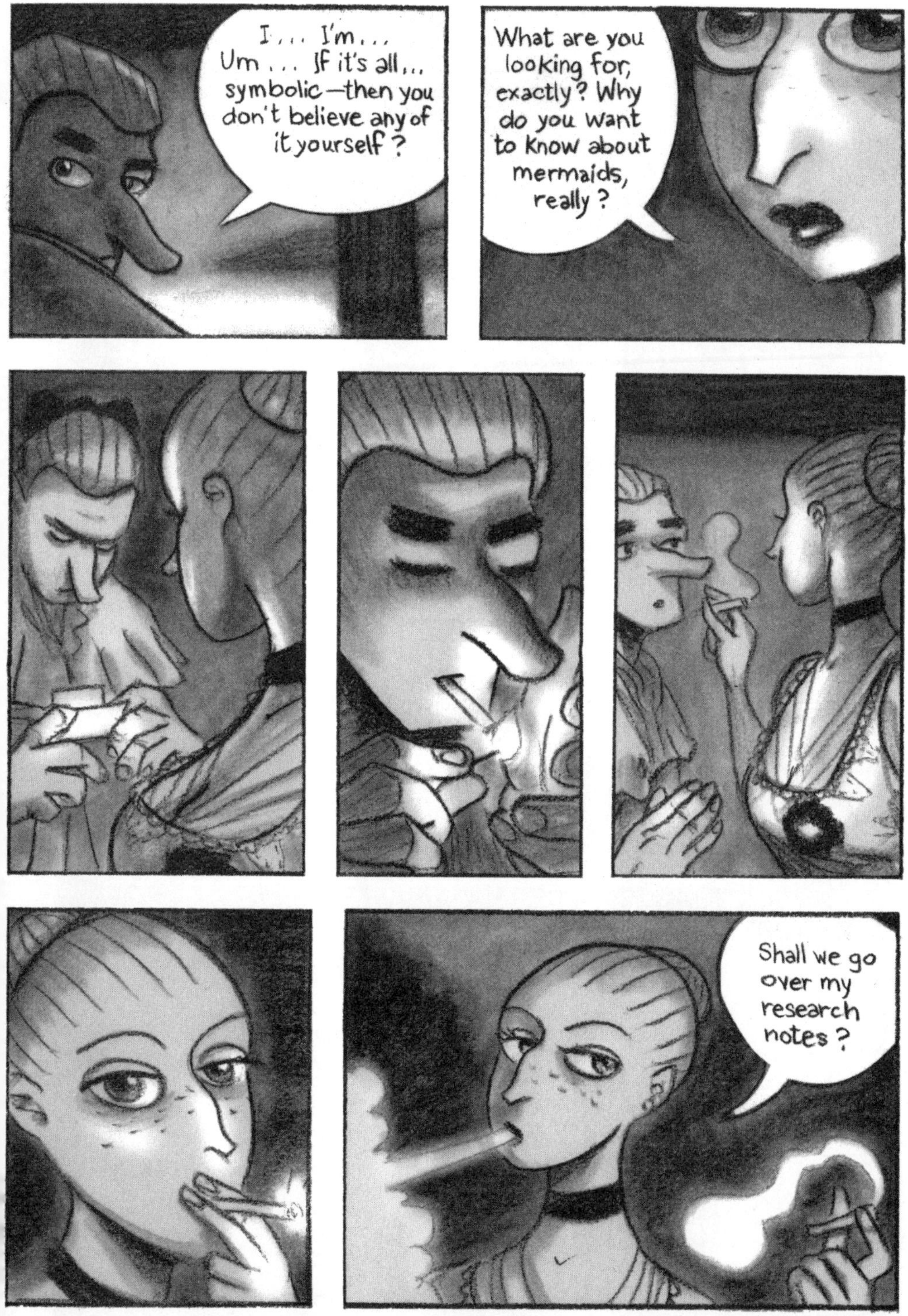
I... I'm... Um... If it's all... symbolic—then you don't believe any of it yourself?
What are you looking for, exactly? Why do you want to know about mermaids, really?
Shall we go over my research notes?

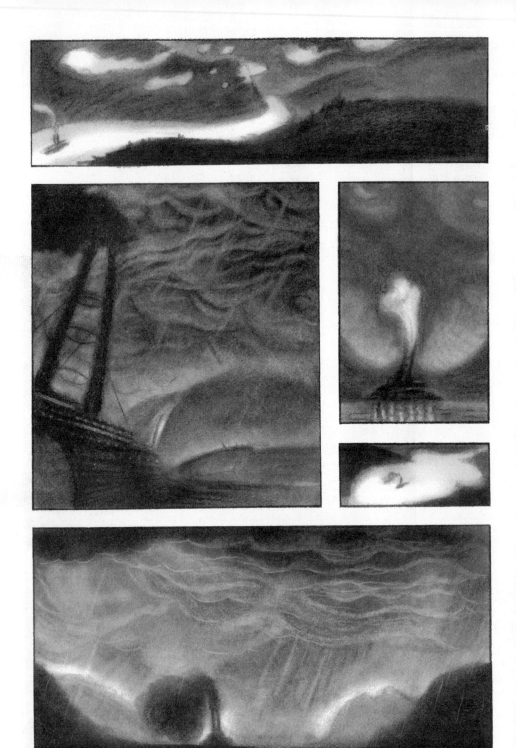

"SEVENING"

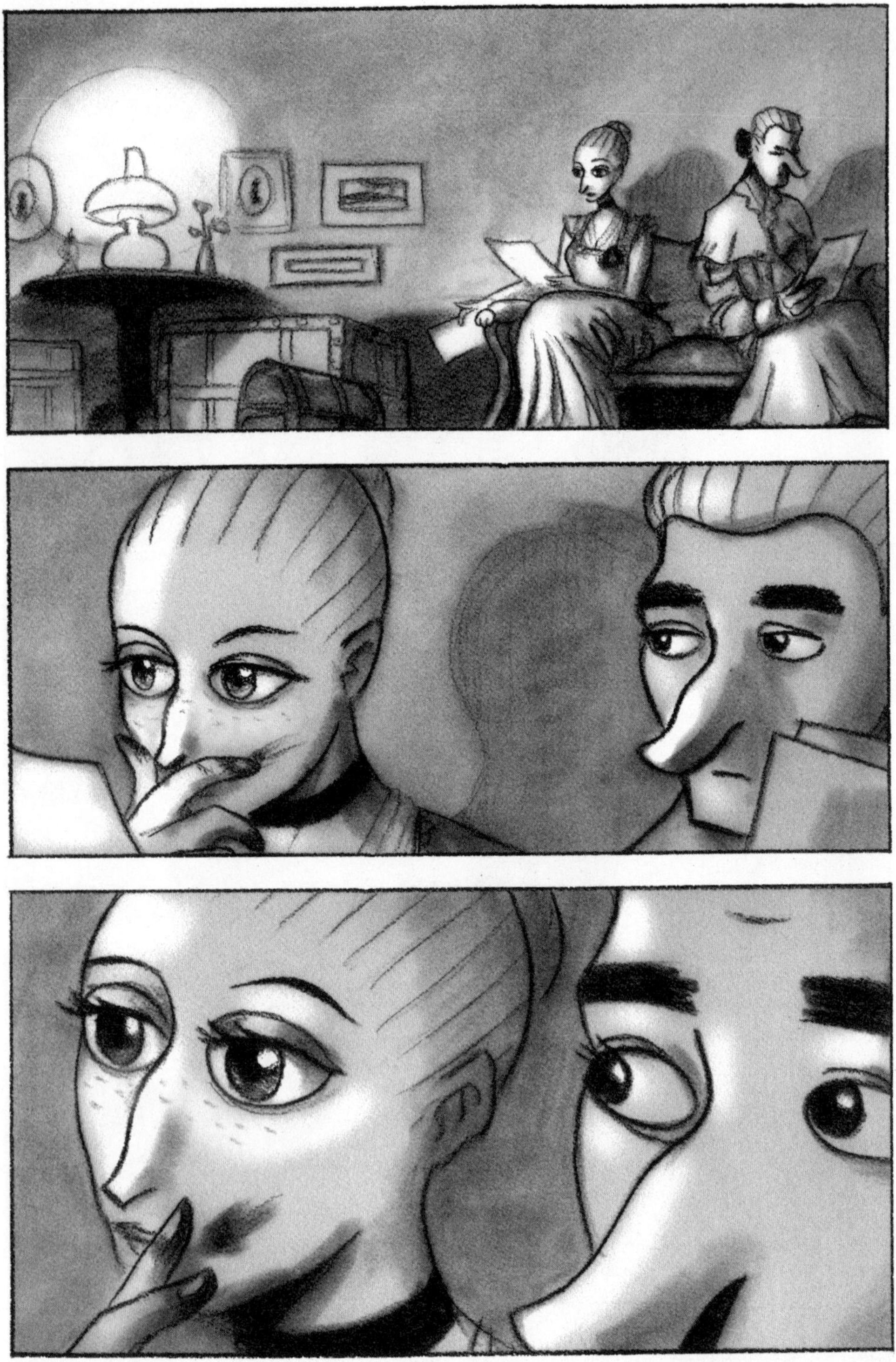

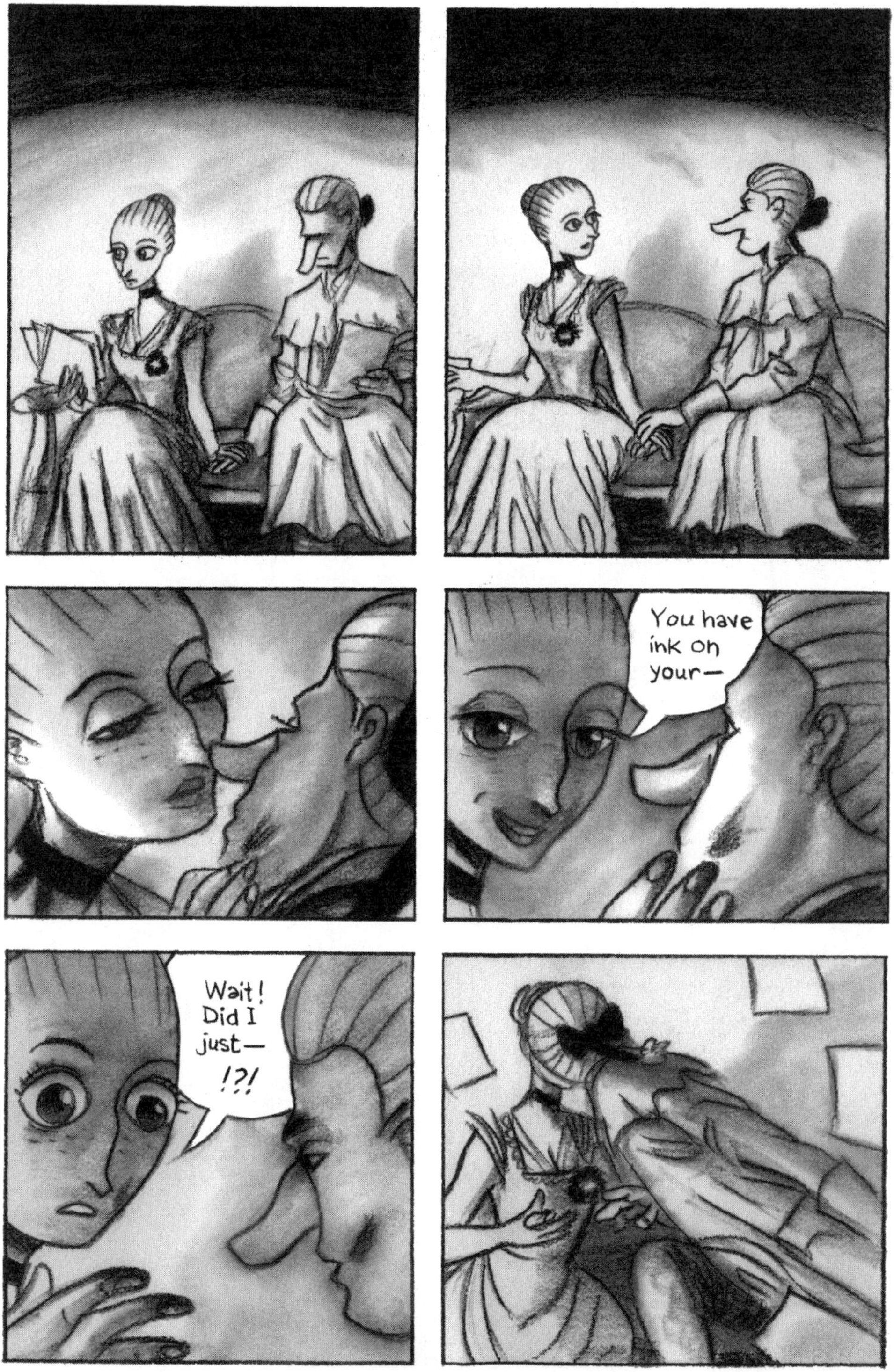
You have ink on your—
Wait! Did I just—
!?!

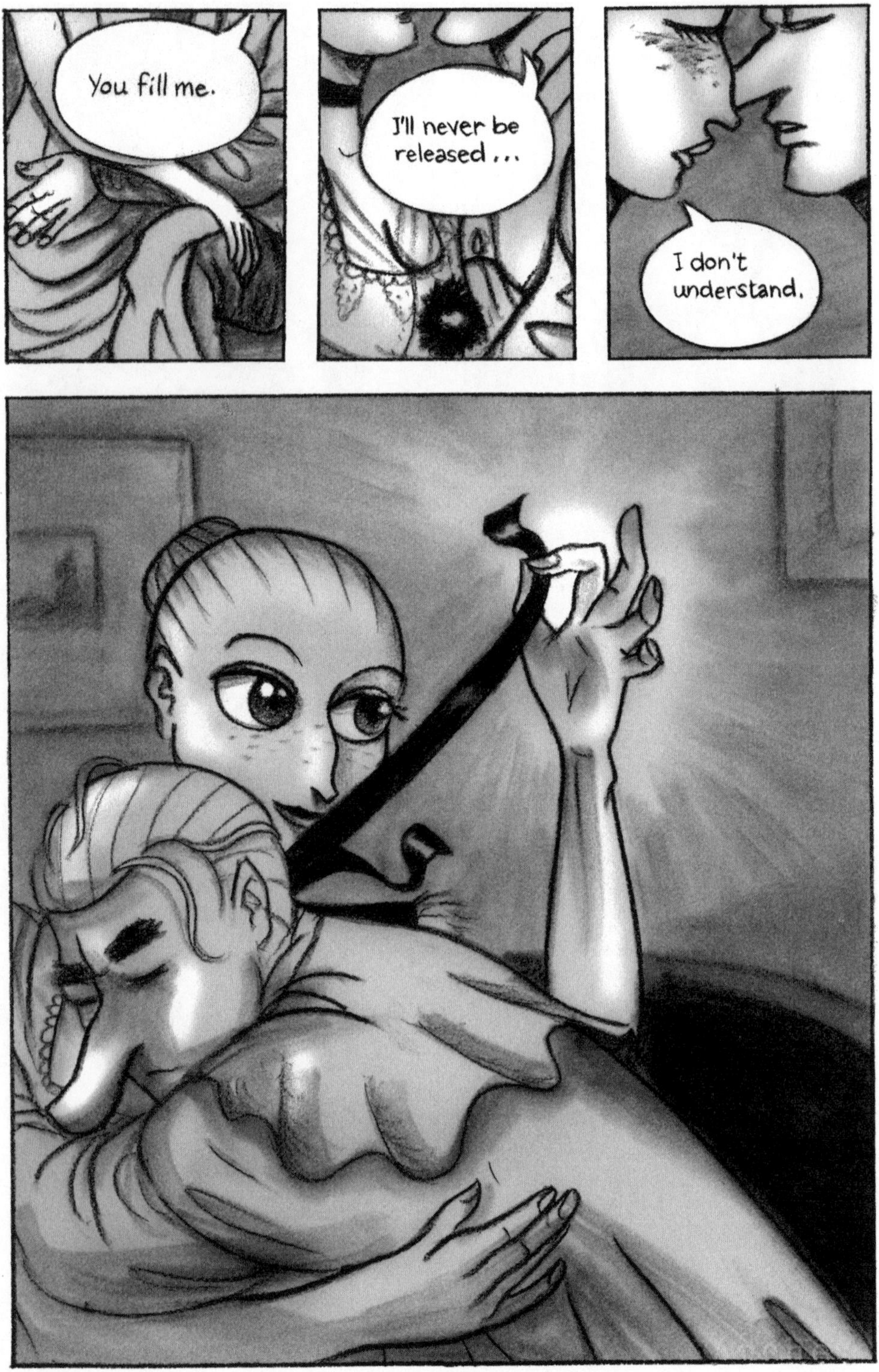
You fill me.
I'll never be released...
I don't understand.

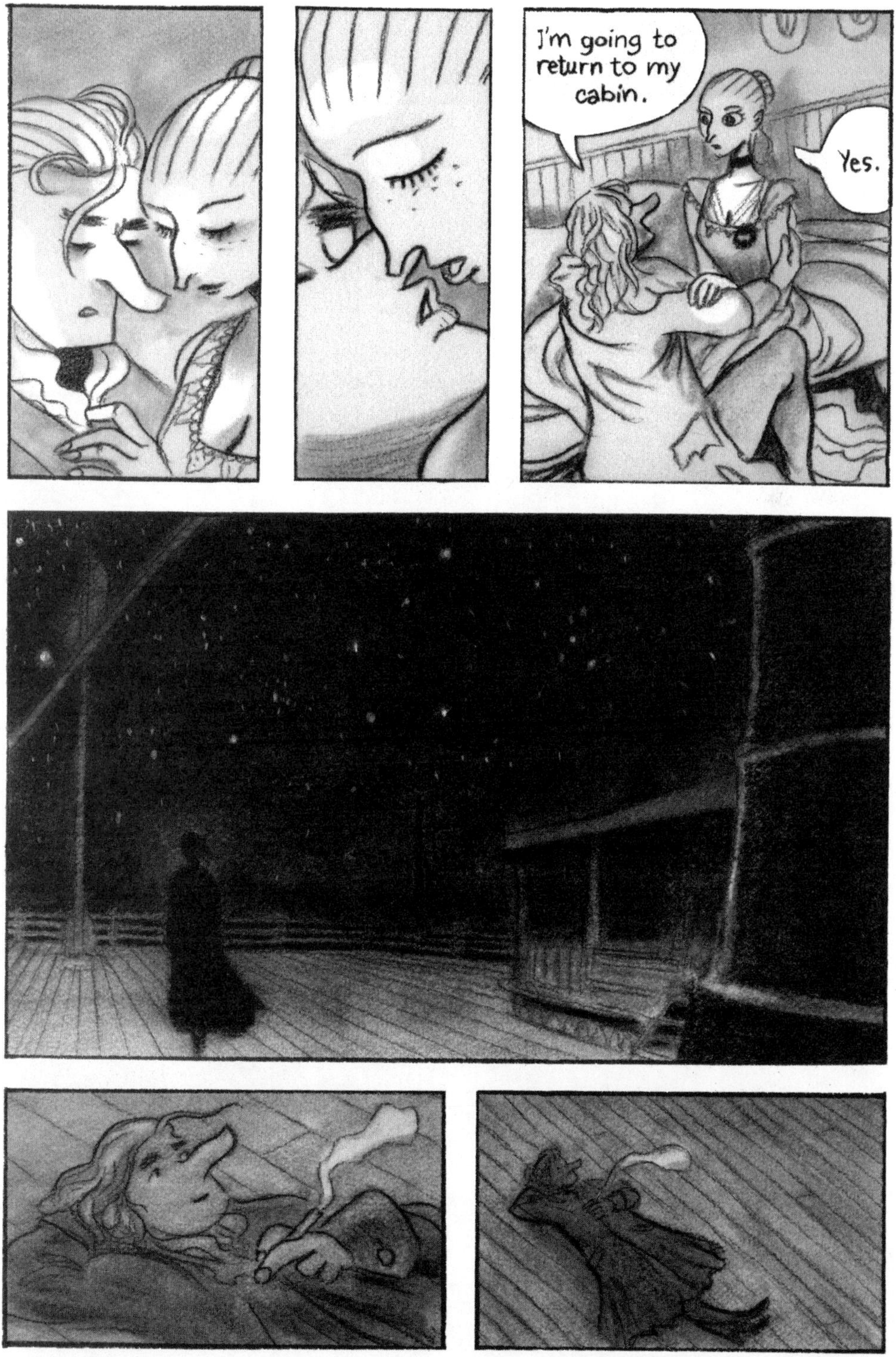
I'm going to return to my cabin.
Yes.

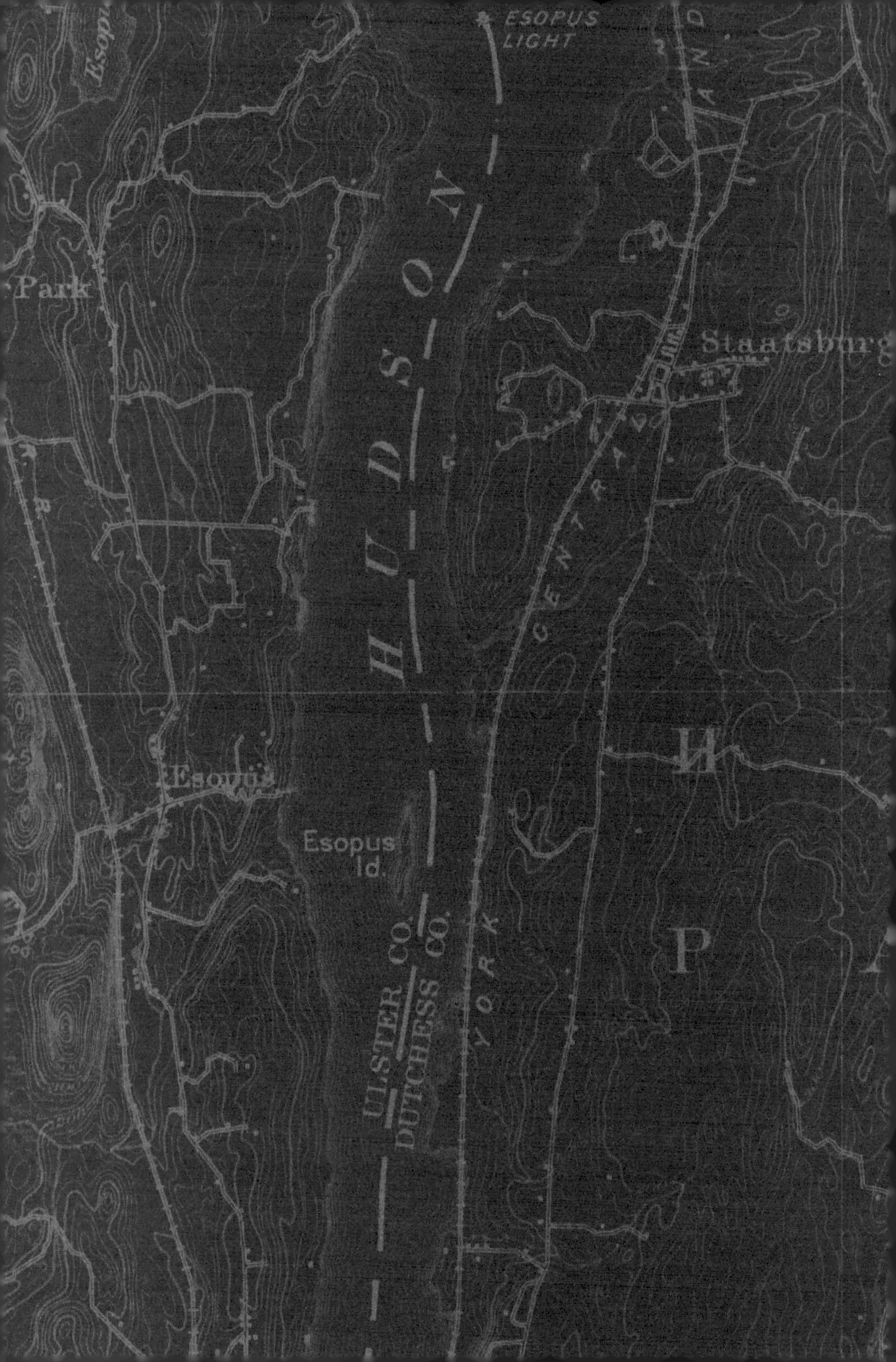
ESOPUS
LIGHT
Park
HUDSON
Staatsburg
CENTRAL
YORK
Esopus
Esopus
Id.
ULSTER CO.
DUTCHESS CO.
P

Pt II, Chap.6

"ENTICEMENT"

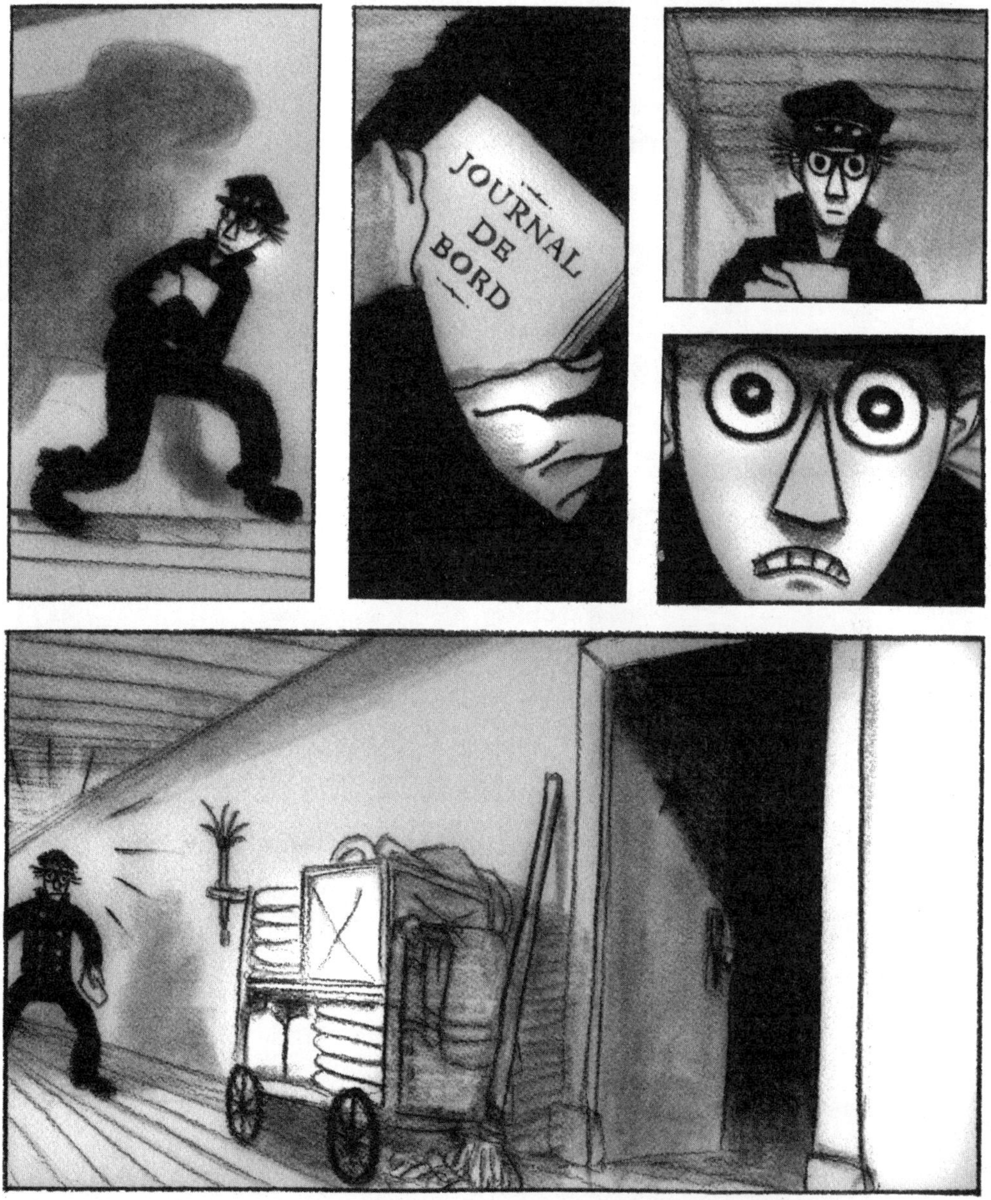
JOURNAL
DE
BORD

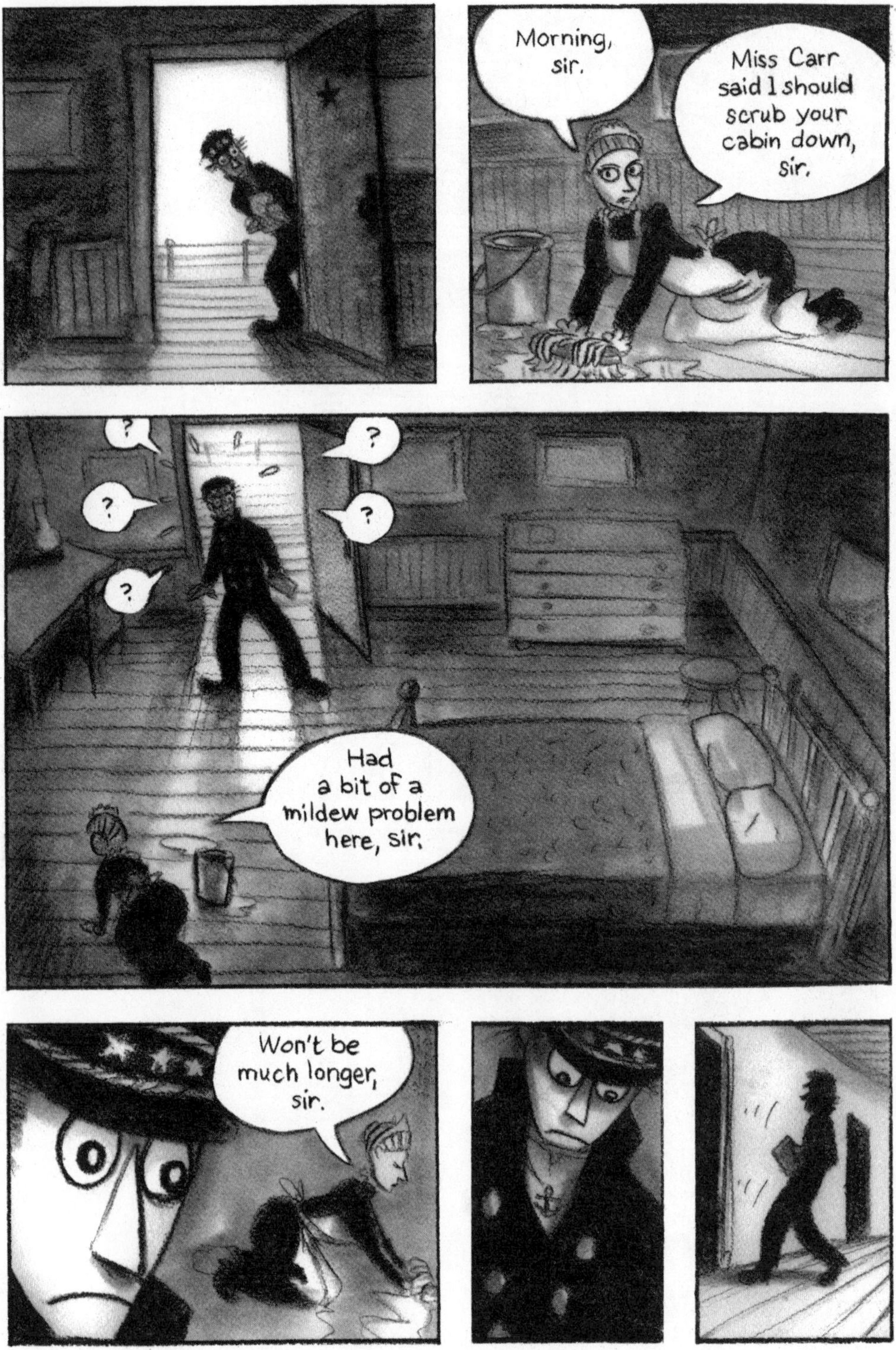
Morning, sir.
Miss Carr said I should scrub your cabin down, sir.
?
?
?
?
?
Had a bit of a mildew problem here, sir.
Won't be much longer, sir.

265

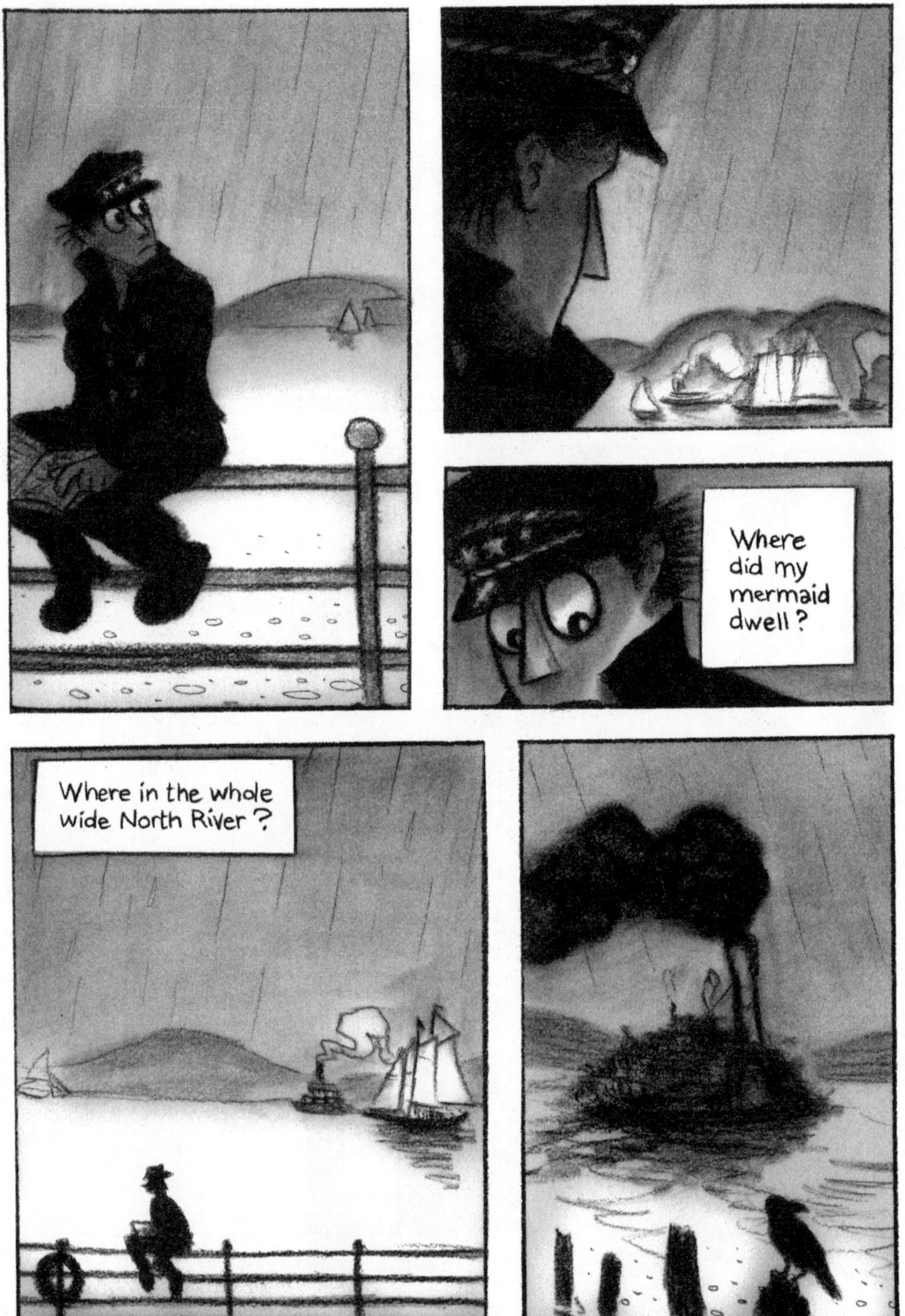
Where did my mermaid dwell?
Where in the whole wide North River?

267

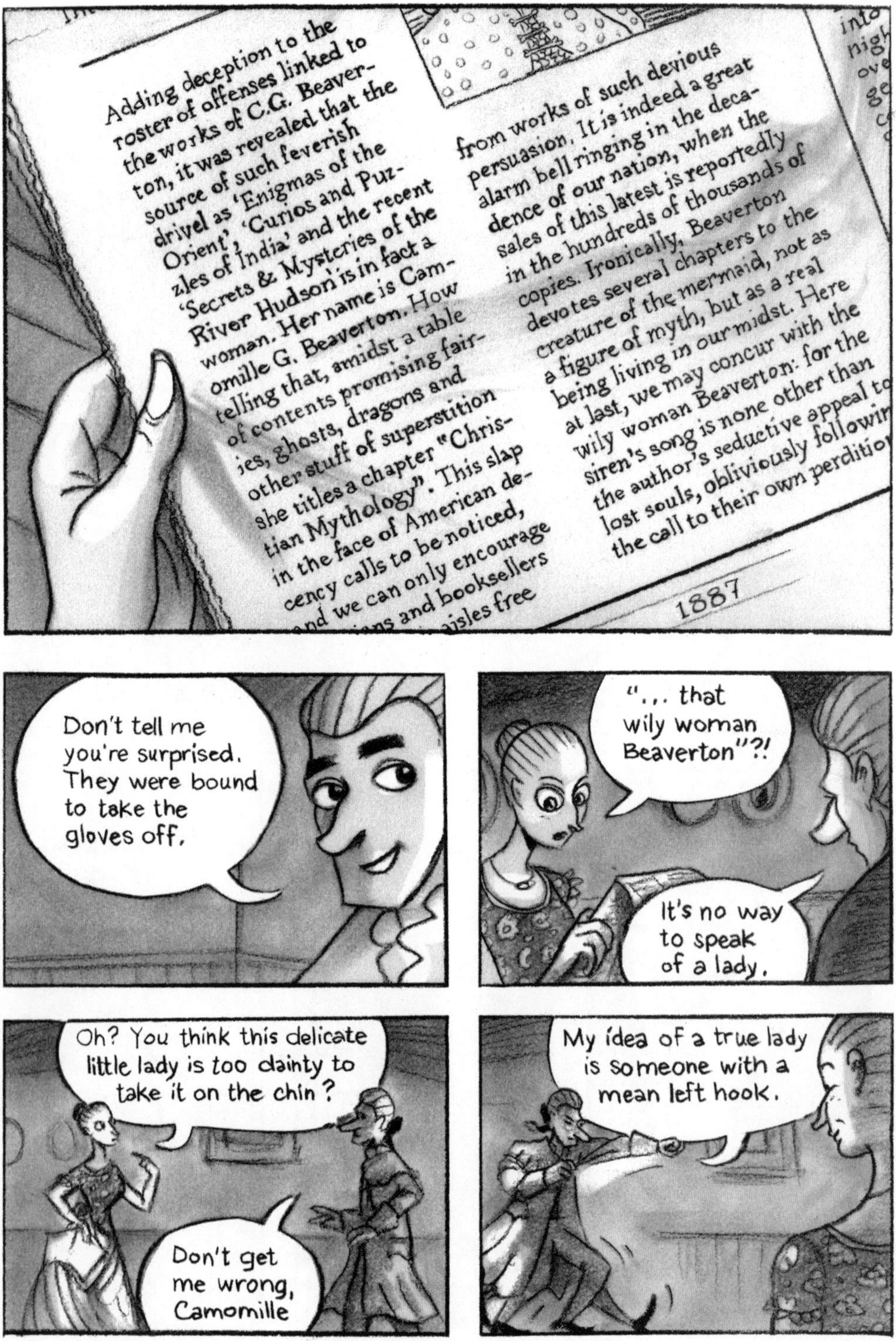

Adding deception to the
roster of offenses linked to
the works of C.G. Beaver-
ton, it was revealed that the
source of such feverish
drivel as 'Enigmas of the
Orient', 'Curios and Puz-
zles of India' and the recent
'Secrets & Mysteries of the
River Hudson' is in fact a
woman. Her name is Cam-
omille G. Beaverton. How
telling that, amidst a table
of contents promising fairies, ghosts, dragons and
other stuff of superstition
she titles a chapter "Christian Mythology". This slap
in the face of American de-
cency calls to be noticed,
and we can only encourage
from works of such devious
persuasion. It is indeed a great
alarm bell ringing in the deca-
dence of our nation, when the
sales of this latest is reportedly
in the hundreds of thousands of
copies. Ironically, Beaverton
devotes several chapters to the
creature of the mermaid, not as
a figure of myth, but as a real
being living in our midst. Here
at last, we may concur with the
wily woman Beaverton: for the
siren's song is none other than
the author's seductive appeal to
lost souls, obliviously followin
the call to their own perditio
1887
Don't tell me you're surprised. They were bound to take the gloves off.
"... that wily woman Beaverton"?!
It's no way to speak of a lady.
Oh? You think this delicate little lady is *too* dainty to take it on the chin?
Don't get me wrong, Camomille
My idea of a true lady is someone with a mean left hook.

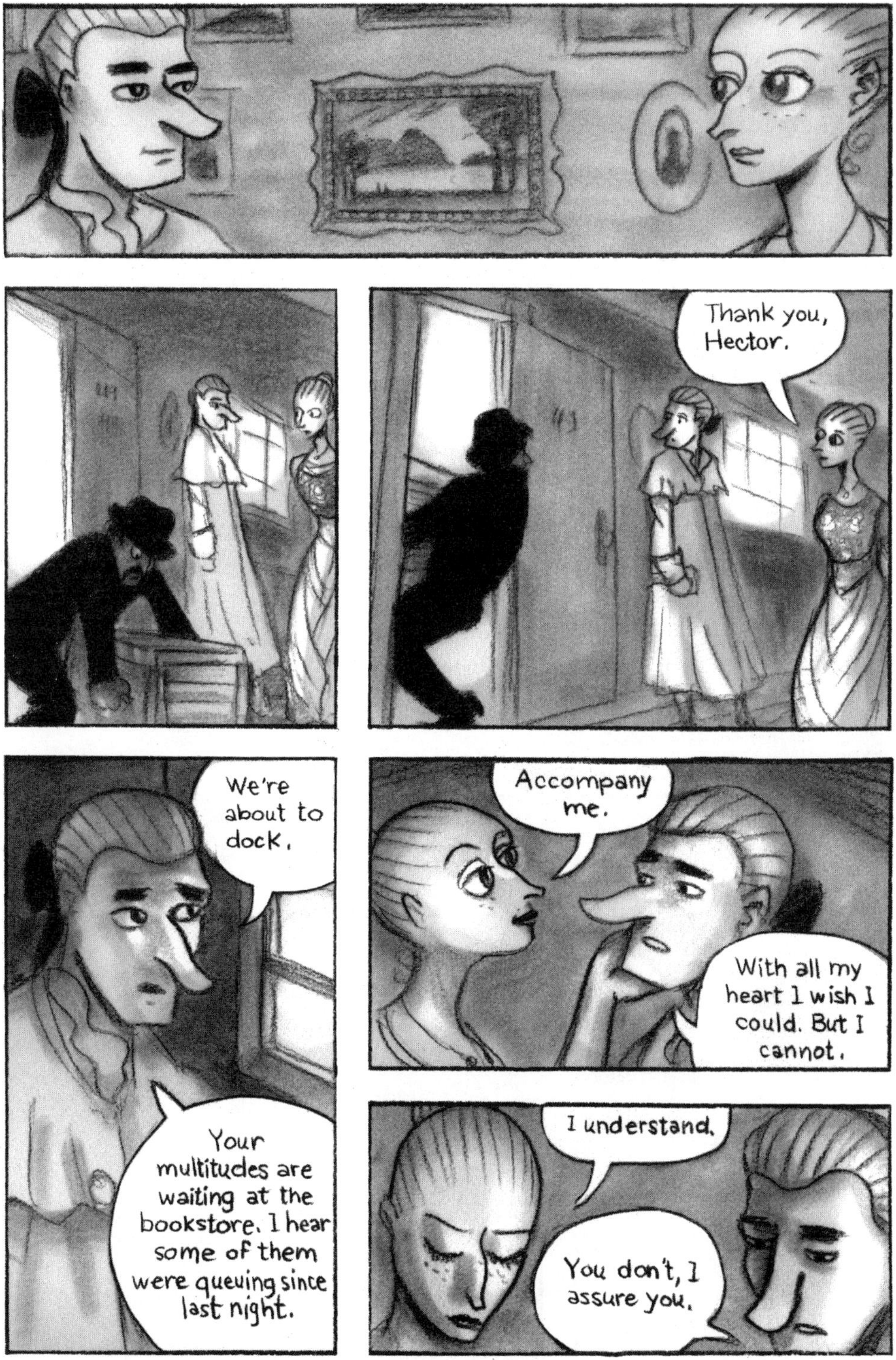
Thank you, Hector.
We're about to dock.
Your multitudes are waiting at the bookstore. I hear some of them were queuing since last night.
Accompany me.
With all my heart I wish I could. But I cannot.
I understand.
You don't, I assure you.

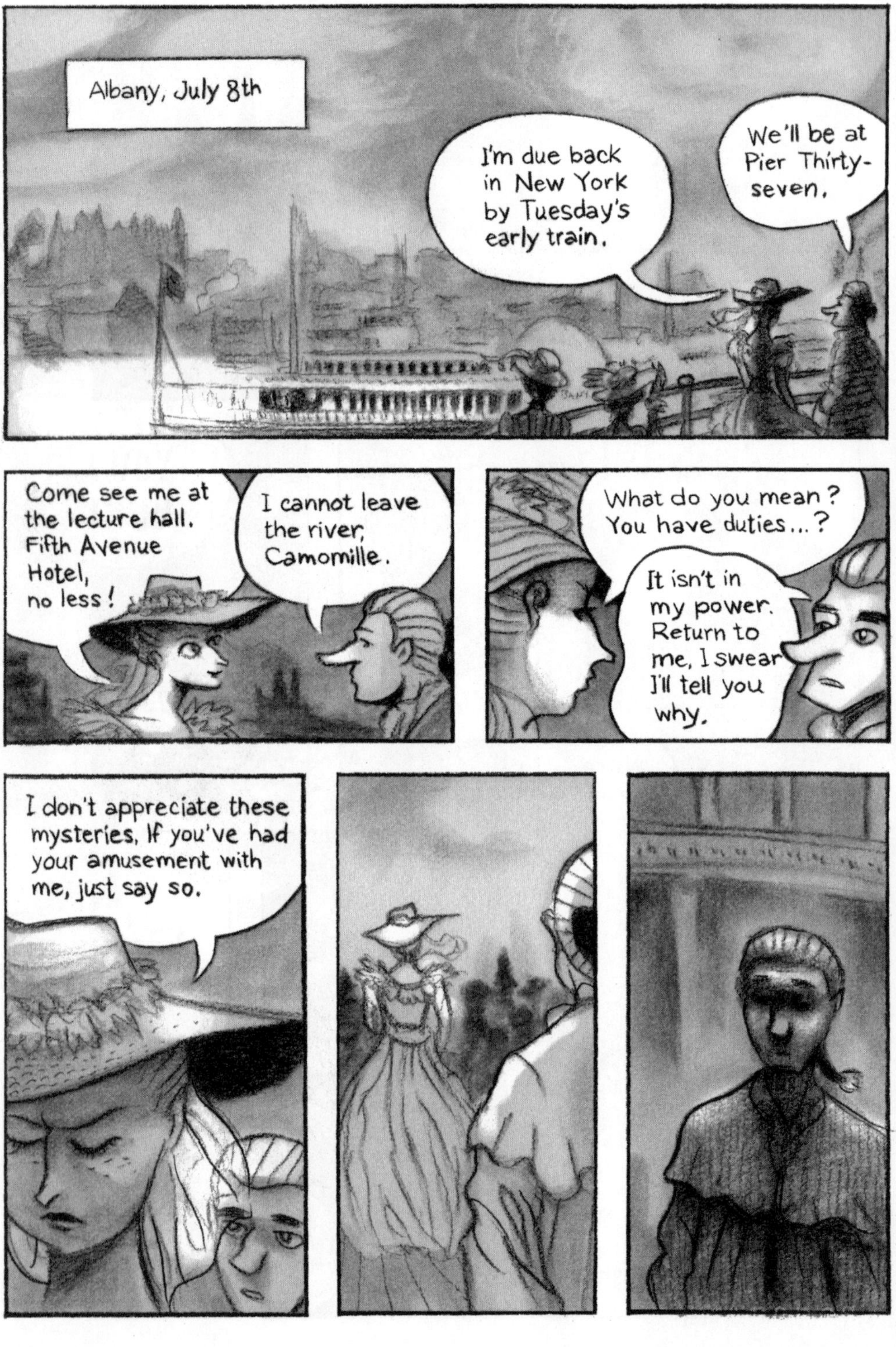
Albany, July 8th
I'm due back in New York by Tuesday's early train.
We'll be at Pier Thirty-seven.
Come see me at the lecture hall. Fifth Avenue Hotel, no less!
I cannot leave the river, Camomille.
What do you mean? You have duties...?
It isn't in my power. Return to me, I swear I'll tell you why.
I don't appreciate these mysteries. If you've had your amusement with me, just say so.

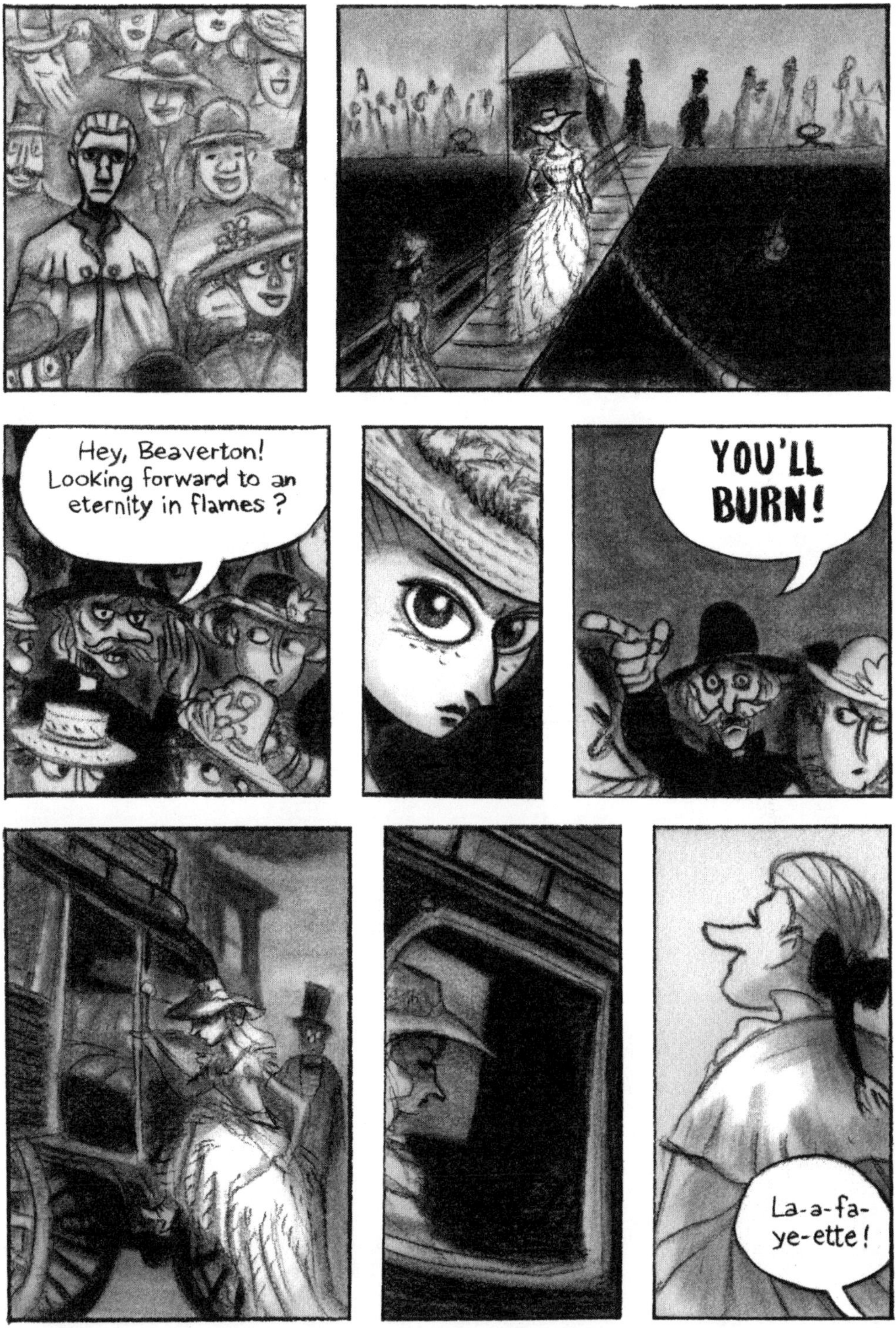
Hey, Beaverton! Looking forward to an eternity in flames ?
YOU'LL BURN!
La-a-fa-ye-ette!

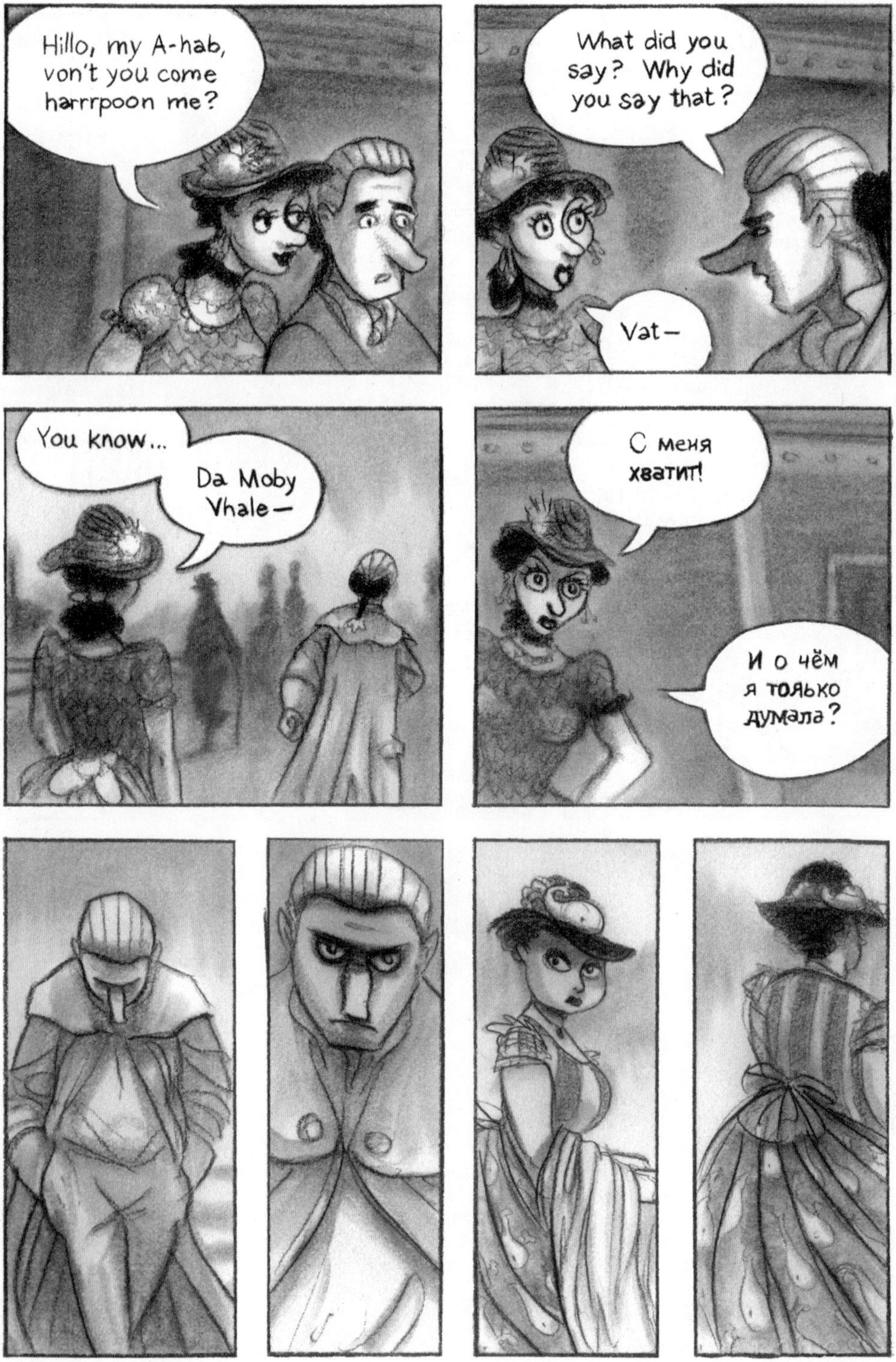
Hillo, my A-hab, von't you come harrrpoon me?
What did you say? Why did you say that?
Vat–
You know...
Da Moby Vhale–
С меня хватит!
И о чём я только думала?

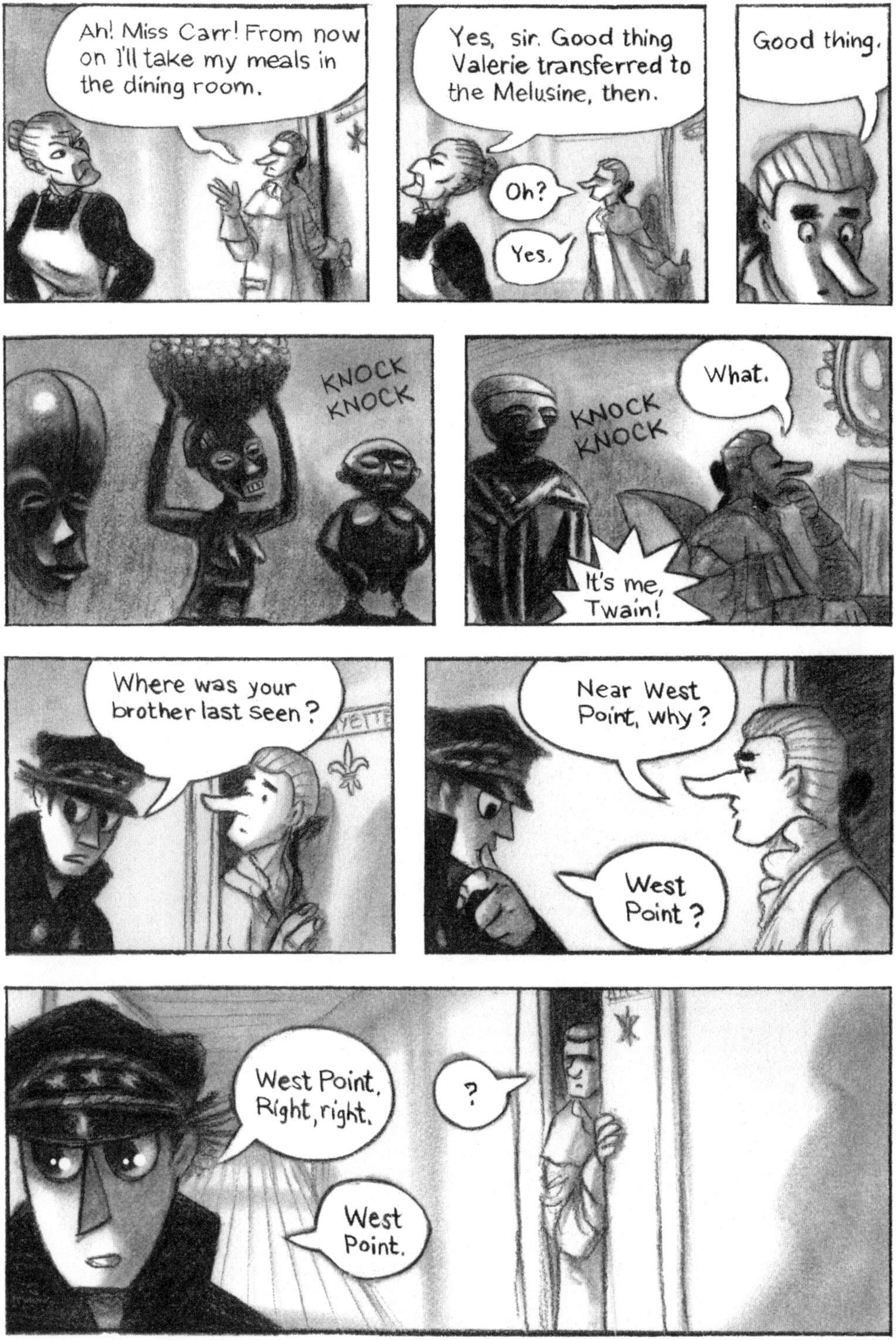
Ah! Miss Carr! From now on I'll take my meals in the dining room.
Yes, sir. Good thing Valerie transferred to the Melusine, then.
Oh?
Yes.
Good thing.
KNOCK KNOCK
KNOCK KNOCK
What.
It's me, Twain!
Where was your brother last seen?
Near West Point, why?
West Point?
West Point. Right, right.
West Point.
?

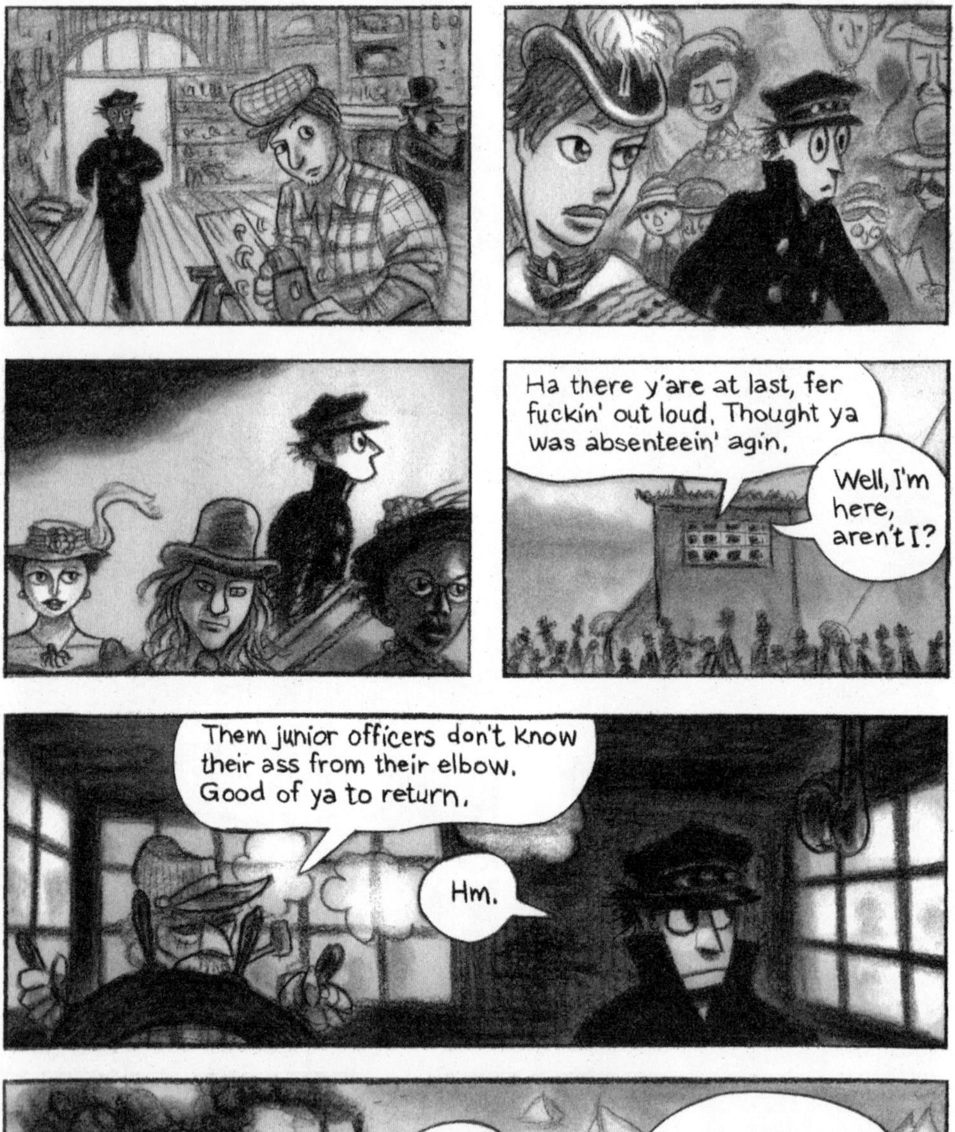
Ha there y'are at last, fer fuckin' out loud. Thought ya was absenteein' agin.
Well, I'm here, aren't I?
Them junior officers don't know their ass from their elbow. Good of ya to return.
Hm.
A little steam, please, Utterson.

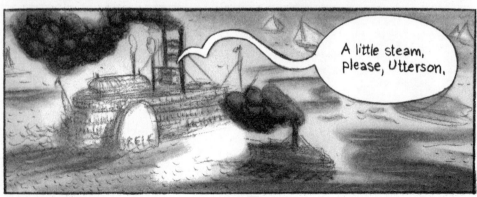

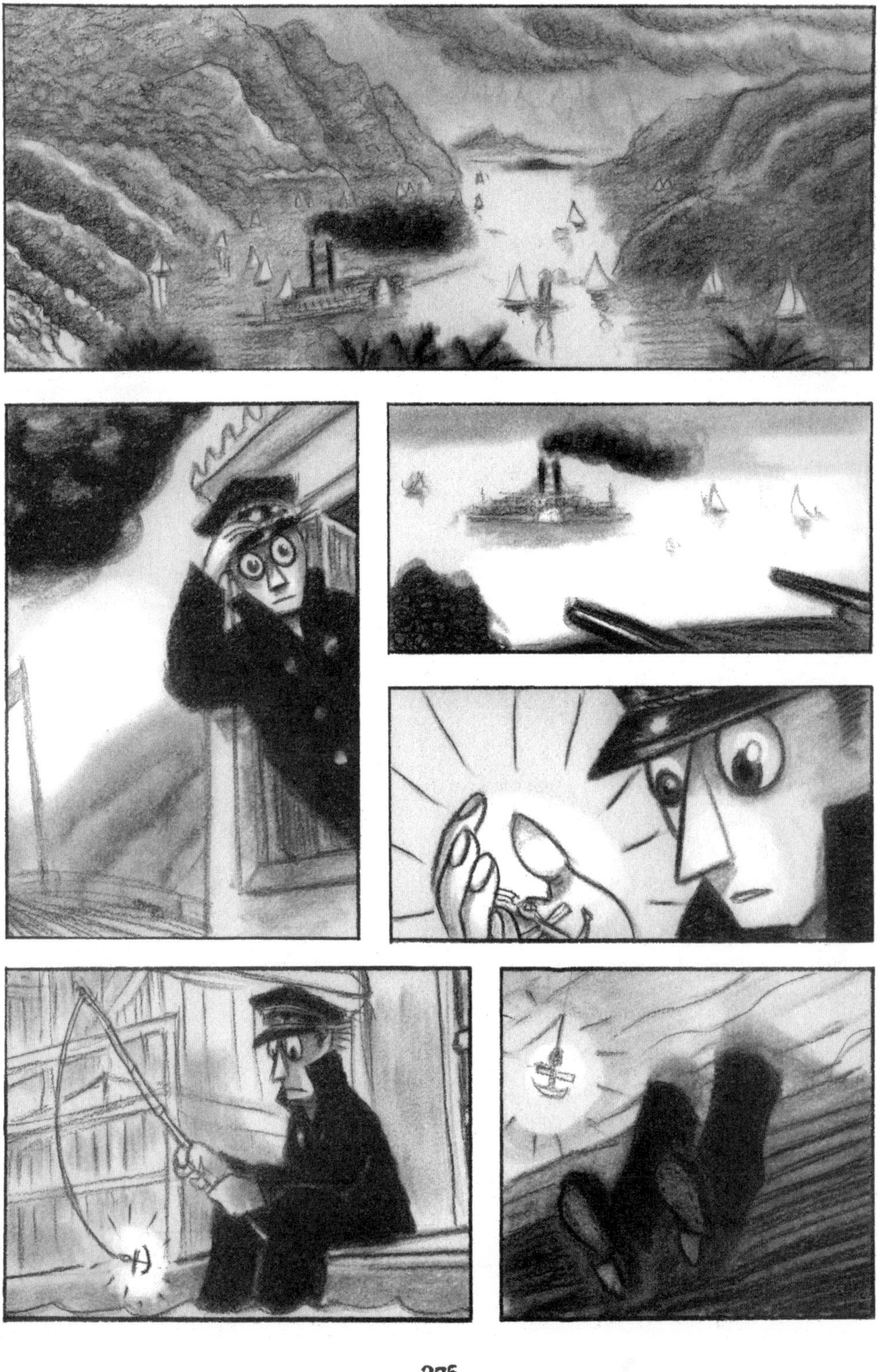

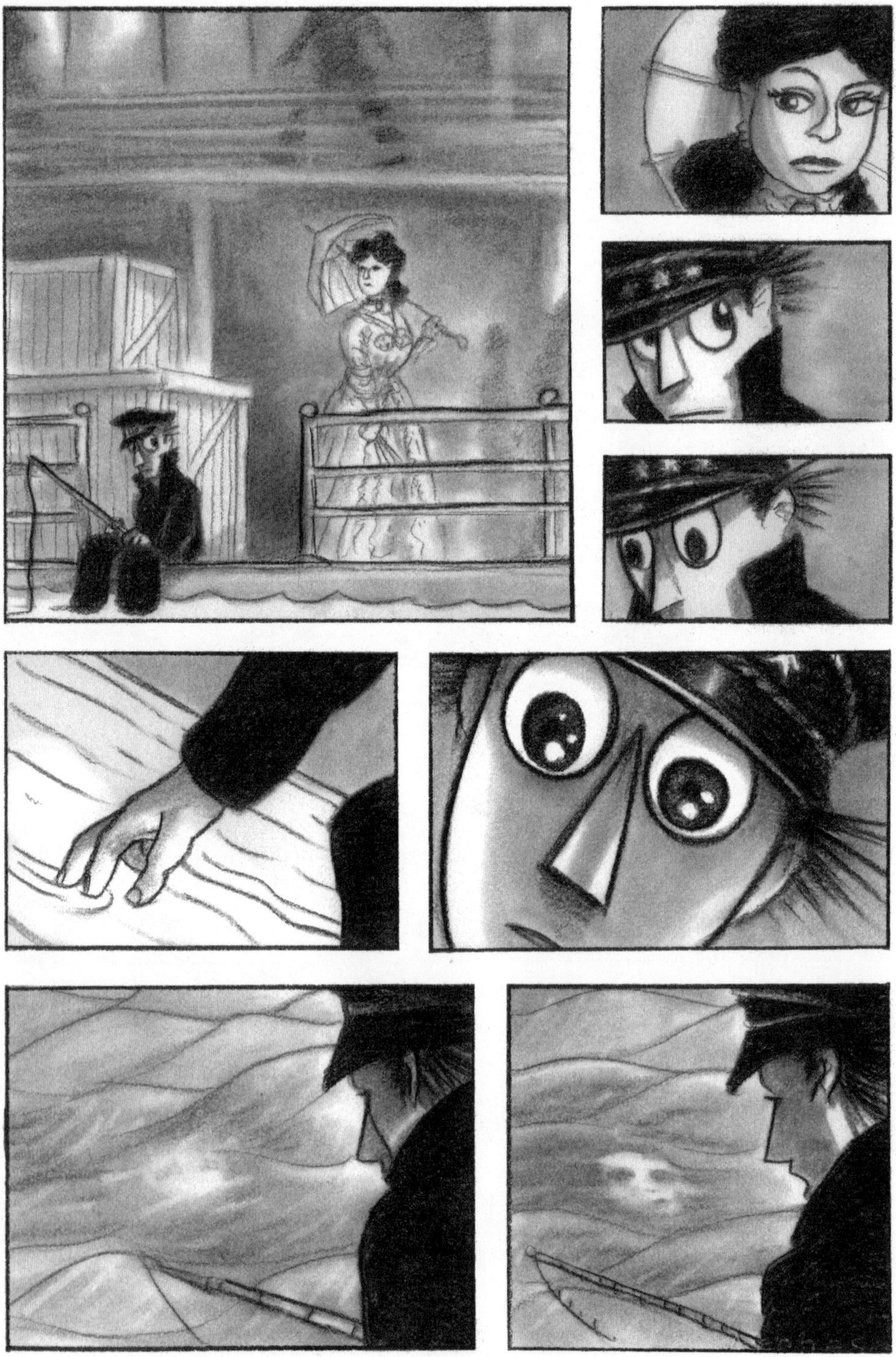

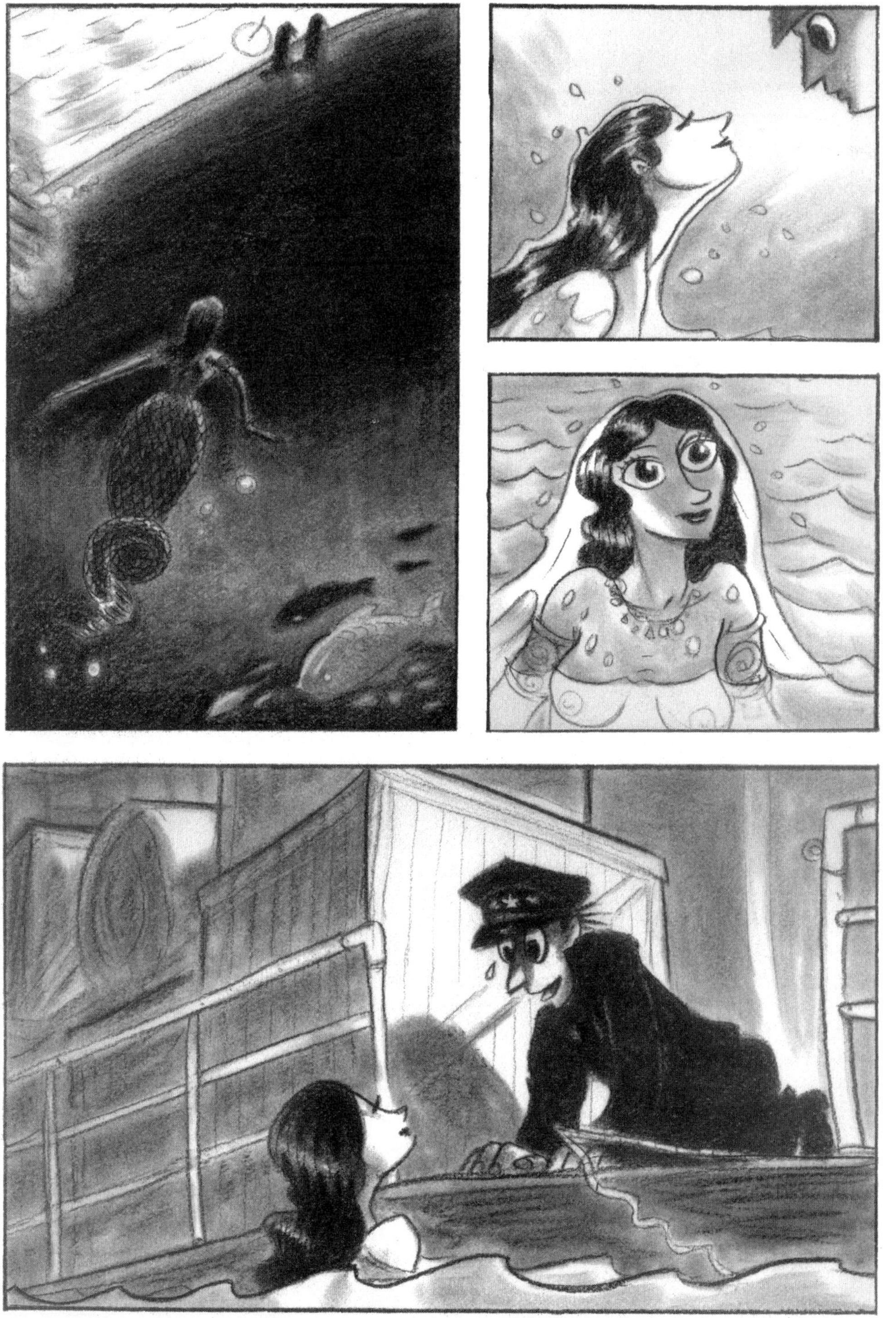

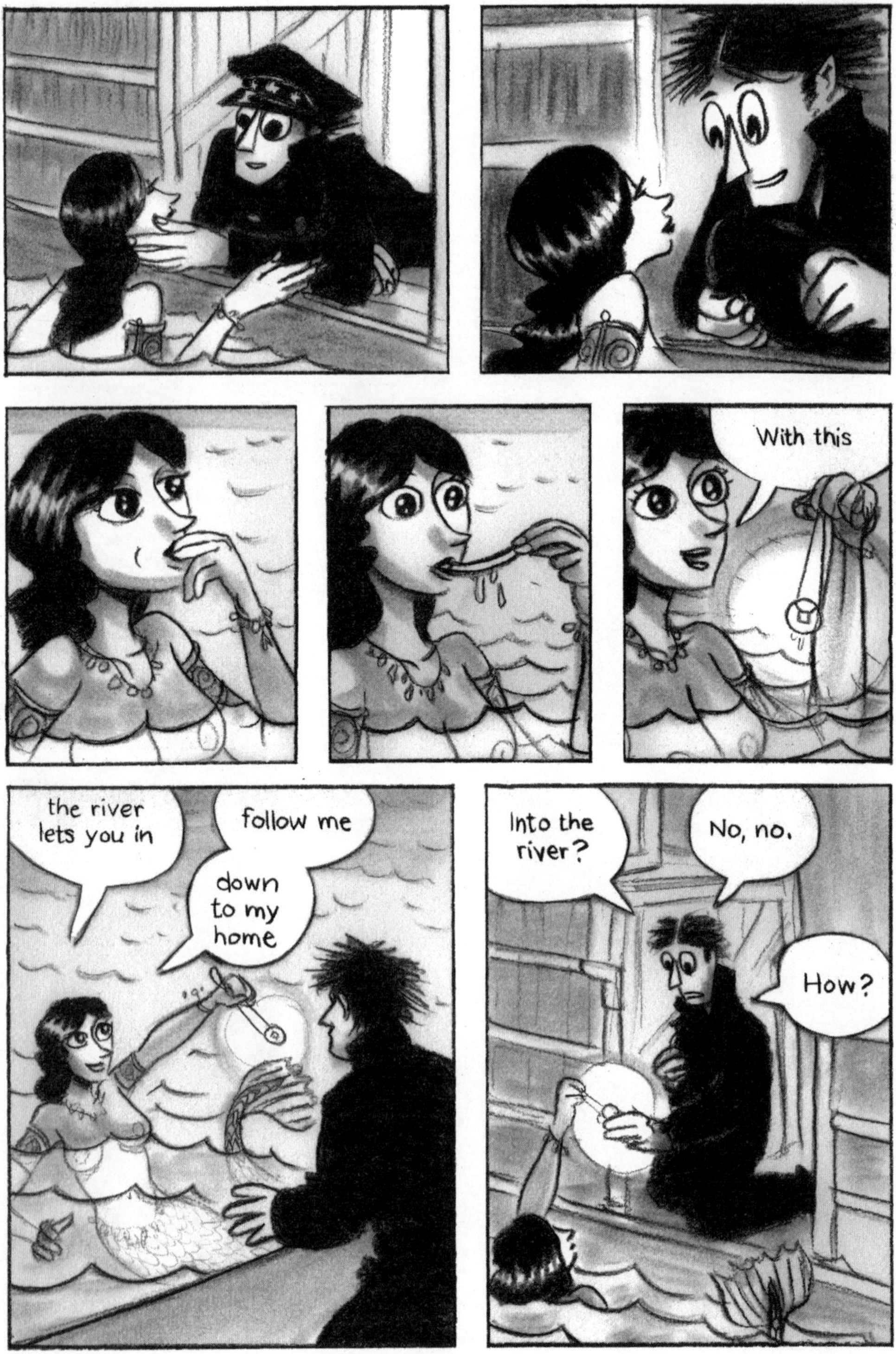
With this
the river lets you in
follow me
down to my home
Into the river?
No, no.
How?

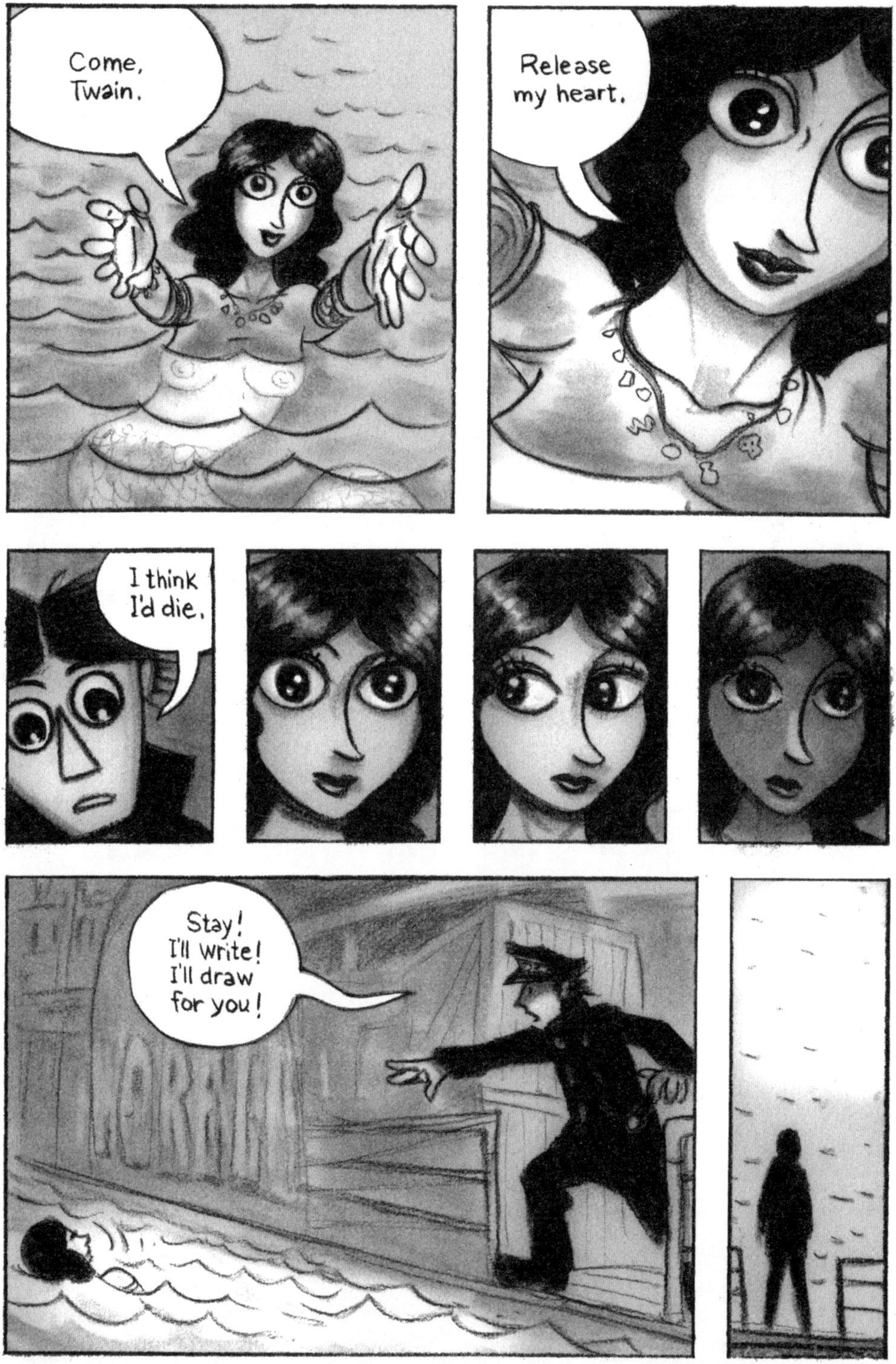
Come, Twain.
Release my heart.
I think I'd die.
Stay! I'll write! I'll draw for you!

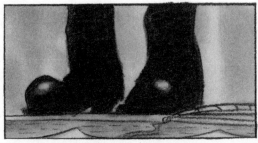

Was she gone?

Would she come back?
Was it panic I felt?

Or relief?

"THE STRAINS OF ABSENCE"

July 7th

July 12th

July 18th

UTTERSON!!
Get your stinking mutt off my deck!!

Come 'ere, Foghorn. Don't pay the cap'n no mind.

It's humans that stink.

Thieving little ...

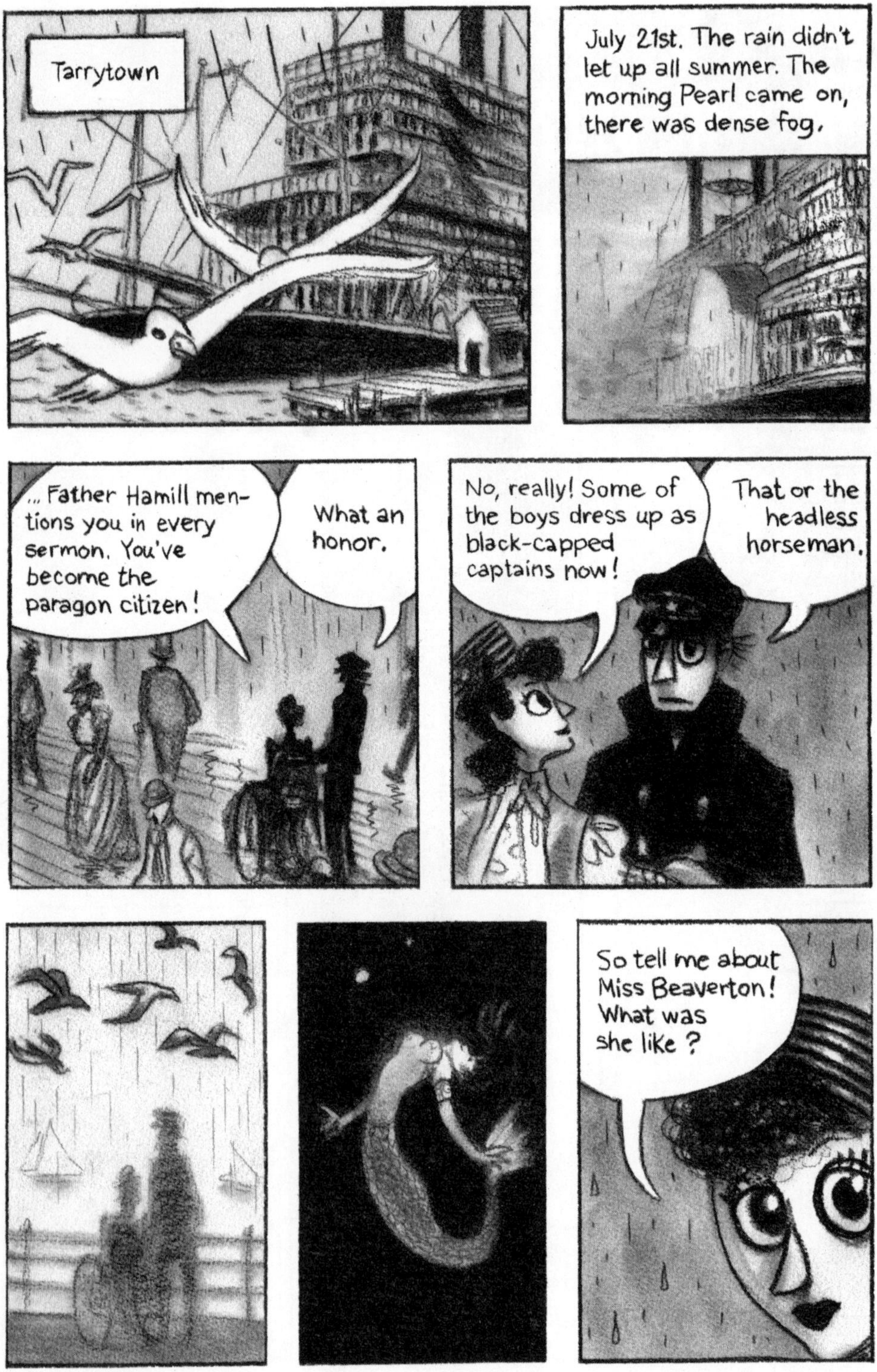
Tarrytown
July 21st. The rain didn't let up all summer. The morning Pearl came on, there was dense fog.
... Father Hamill mentions you in every sermon. You've become the paragon citizen!
What an honor.
No, really! Some of the boys dress up as black-capped captains now!
That or the headless horseman.
So tell me about Miss Beaverton! What was she like?

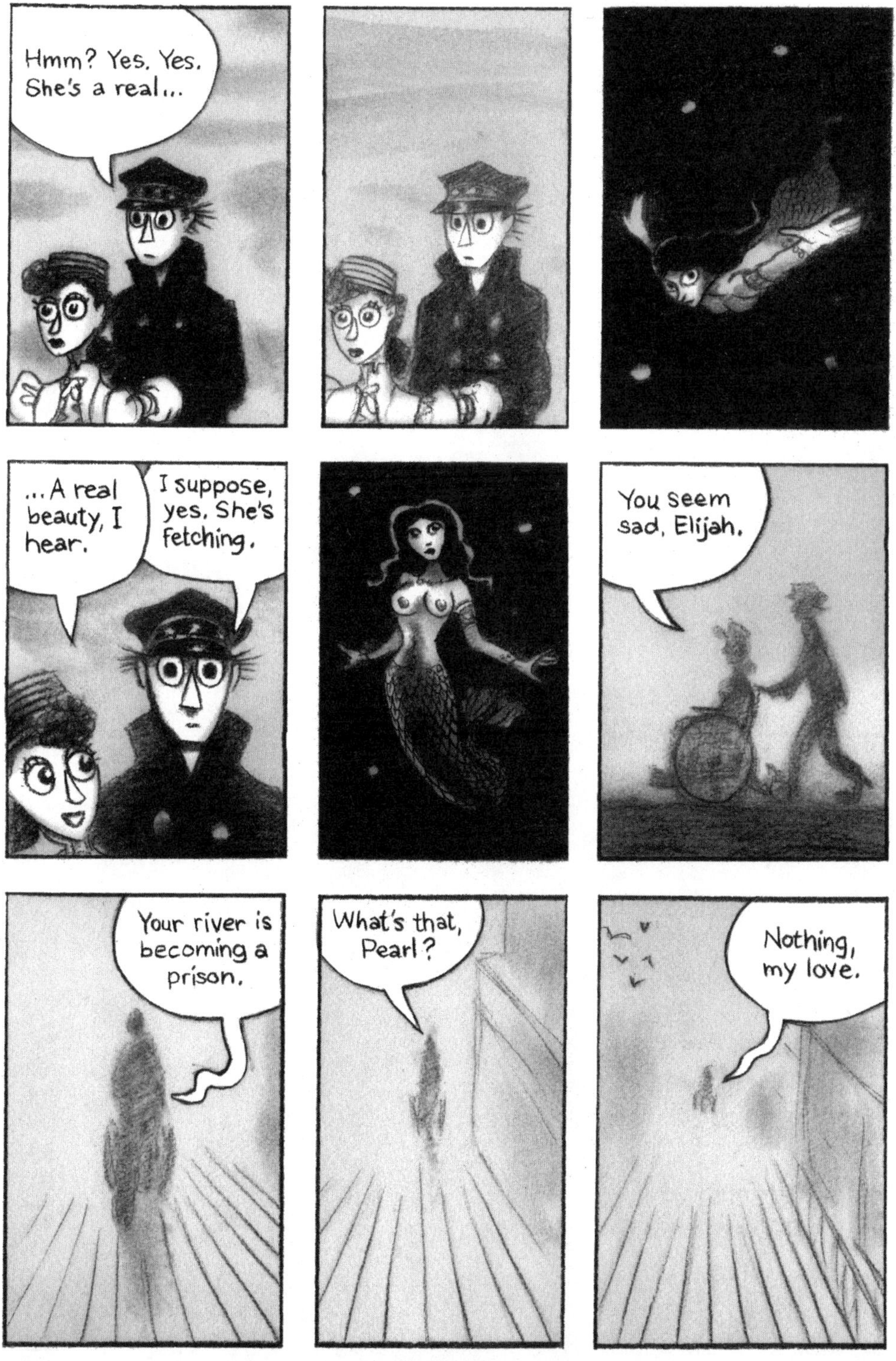
Hmm? Yes. Yes. She's a real...
...A real beauty, I hear.
I suppose, yes. She's fetching.
You seem sad, Elijah.
Your river is becoming a prison.
What's that, Pearl?
Nothing, my love.

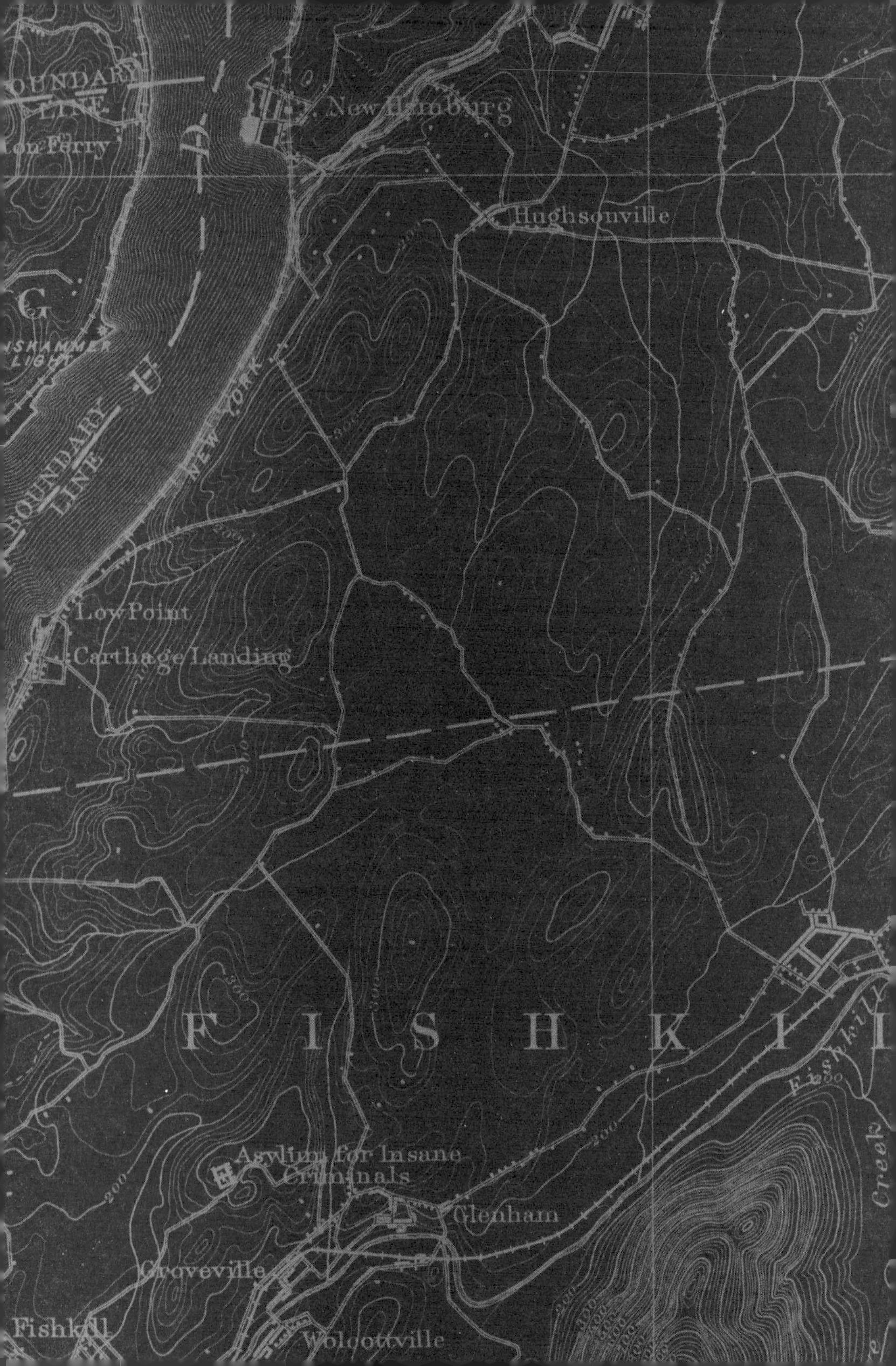

BOUNDARY LINE
New Hamburg
Hughsonville
NEW YORK
BOUNDARY LINE
Low Point
Carthage Landing
F I S H K I L
Asylum for Insane Criminals
Glenham
Groveville
Fishkill
Wolcottville
Creek
200
300

Pt II, Chap.8

"TWAIN DREAMS"

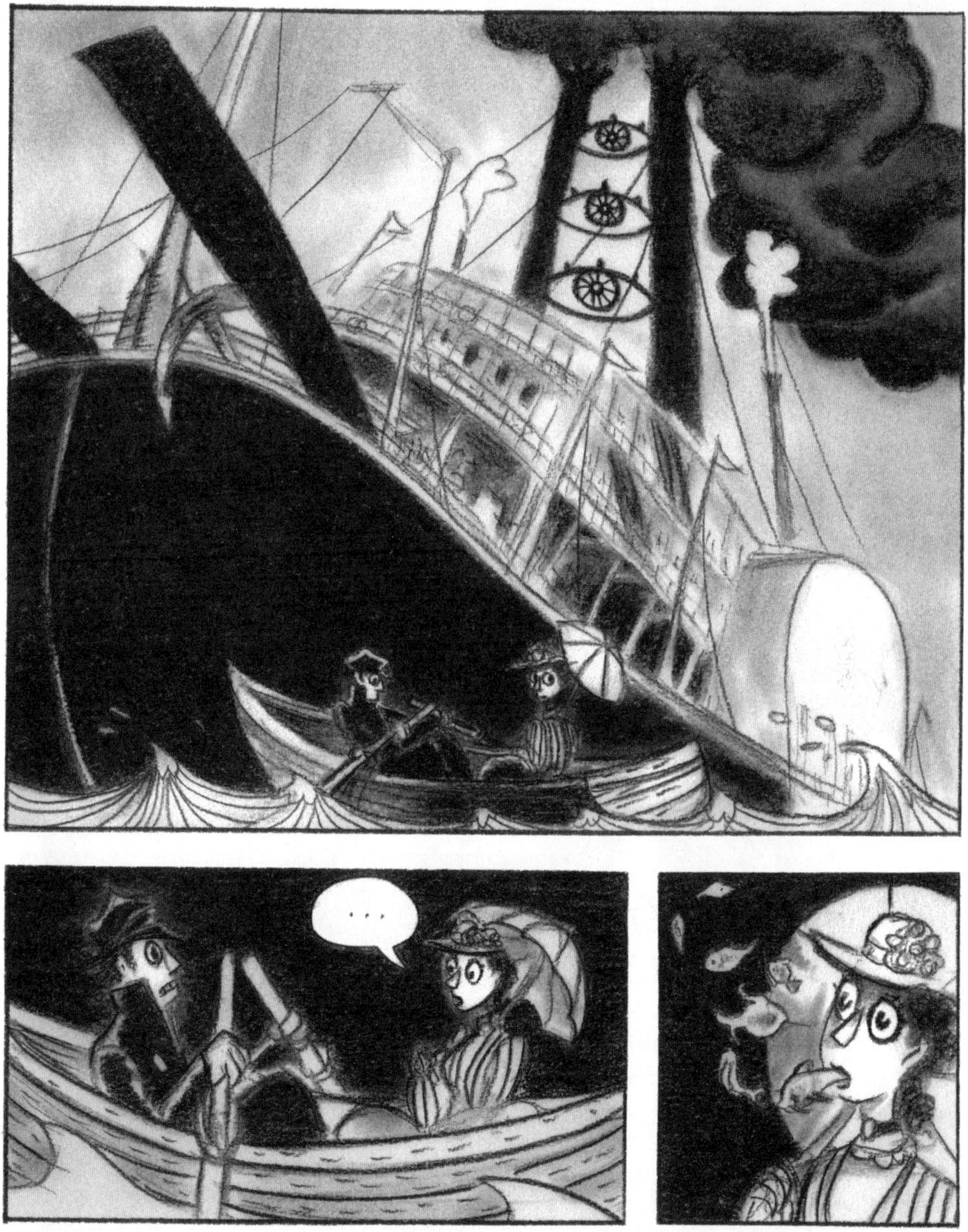
...

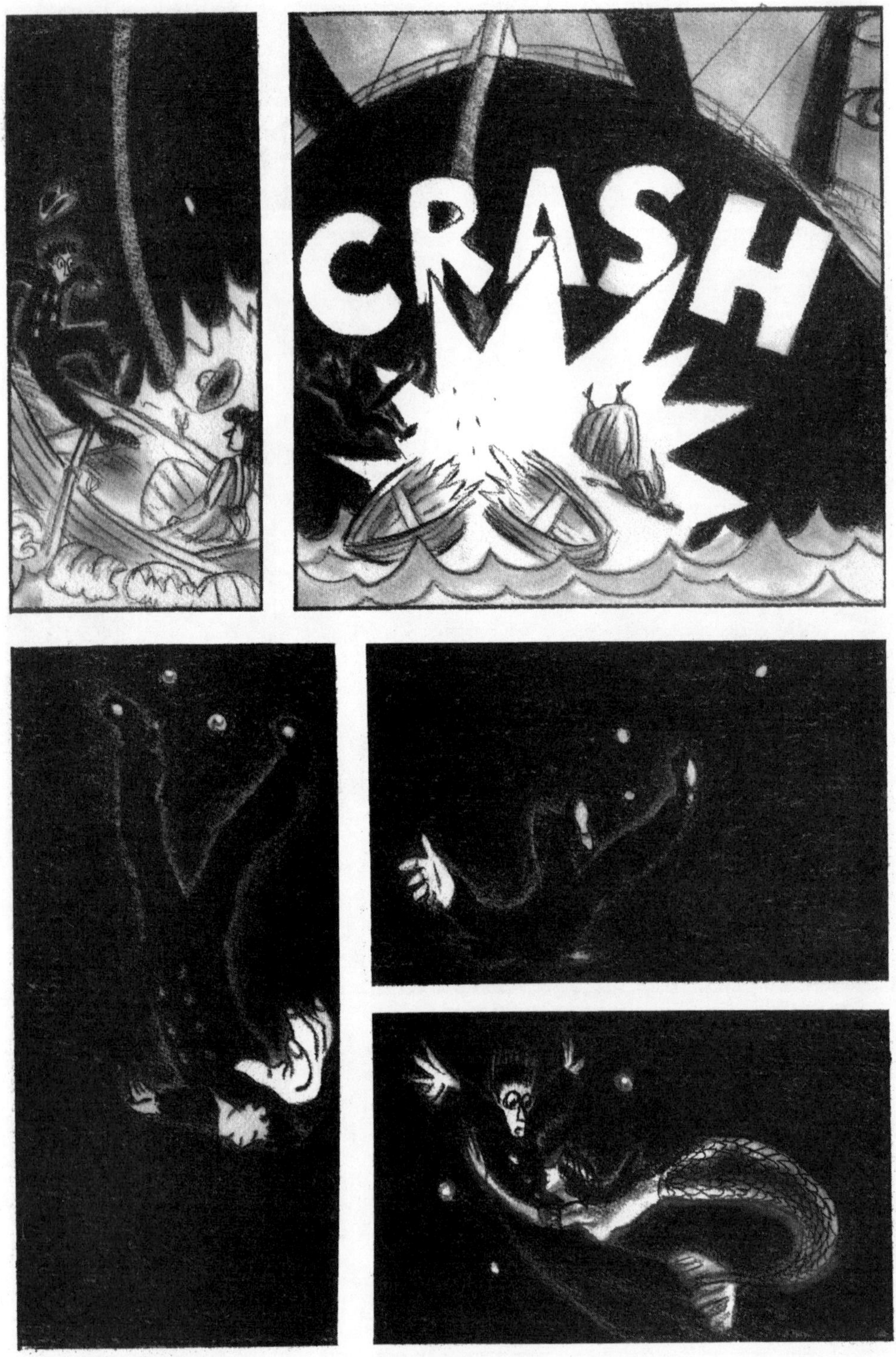
CRASH

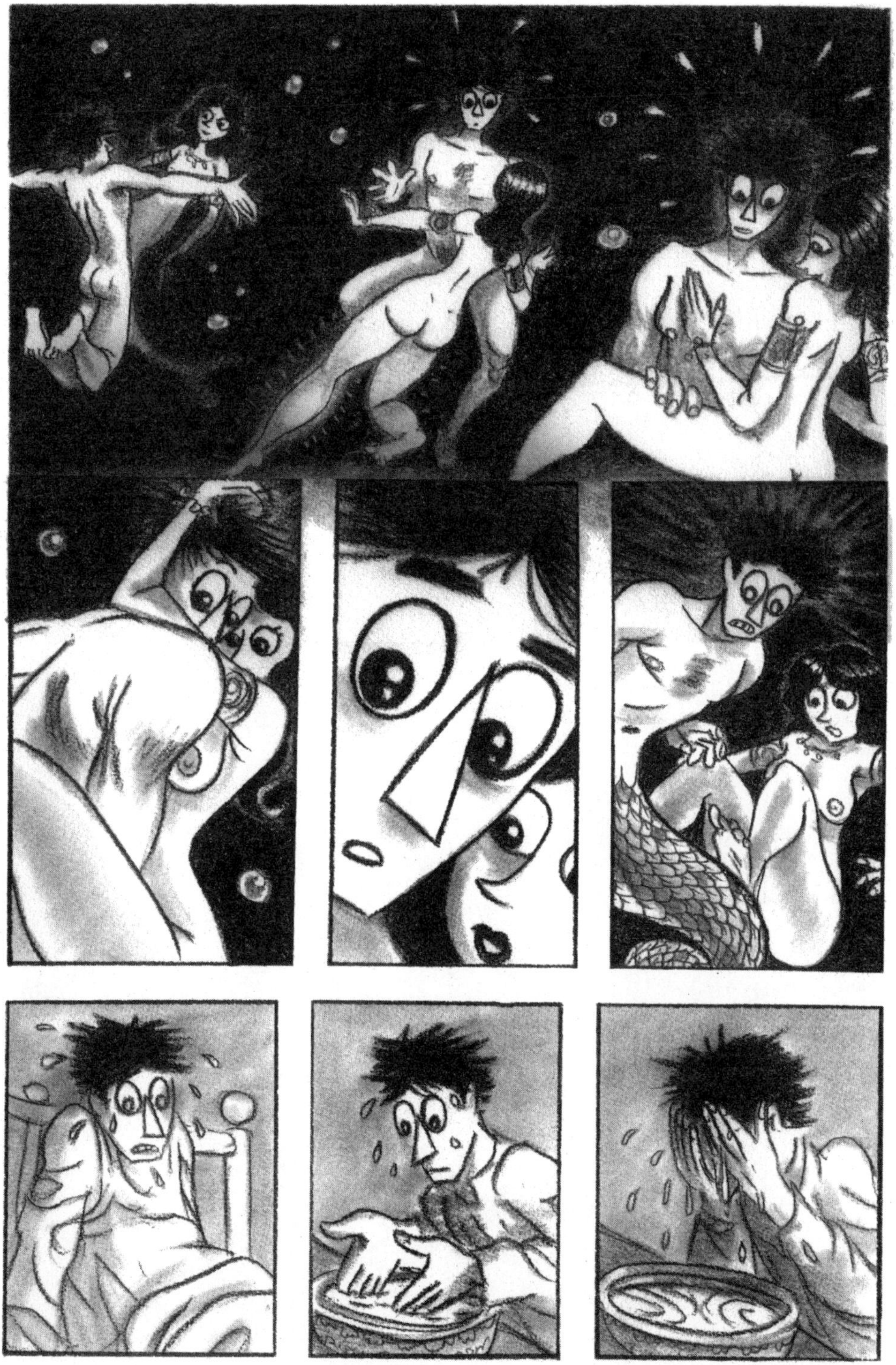

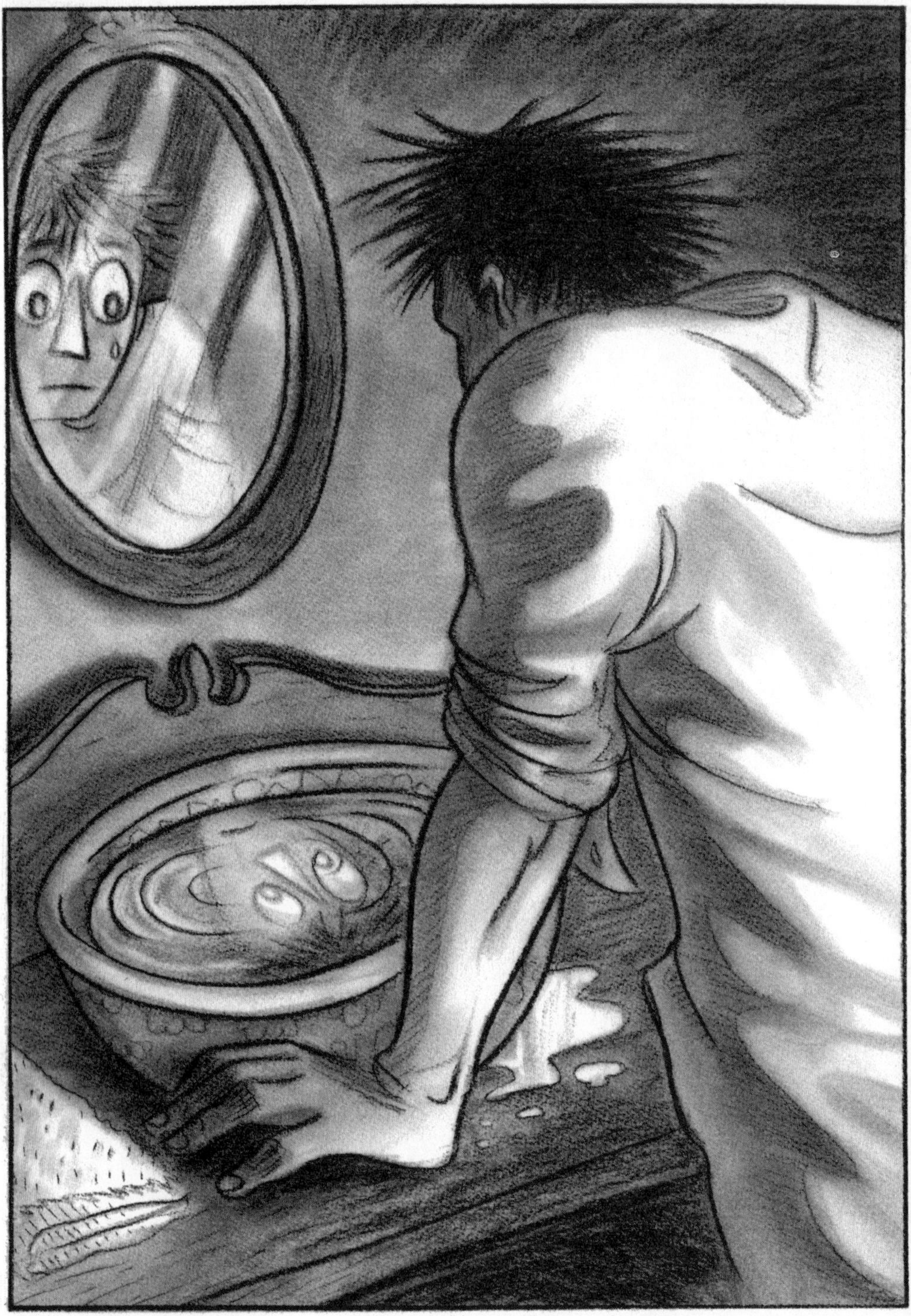

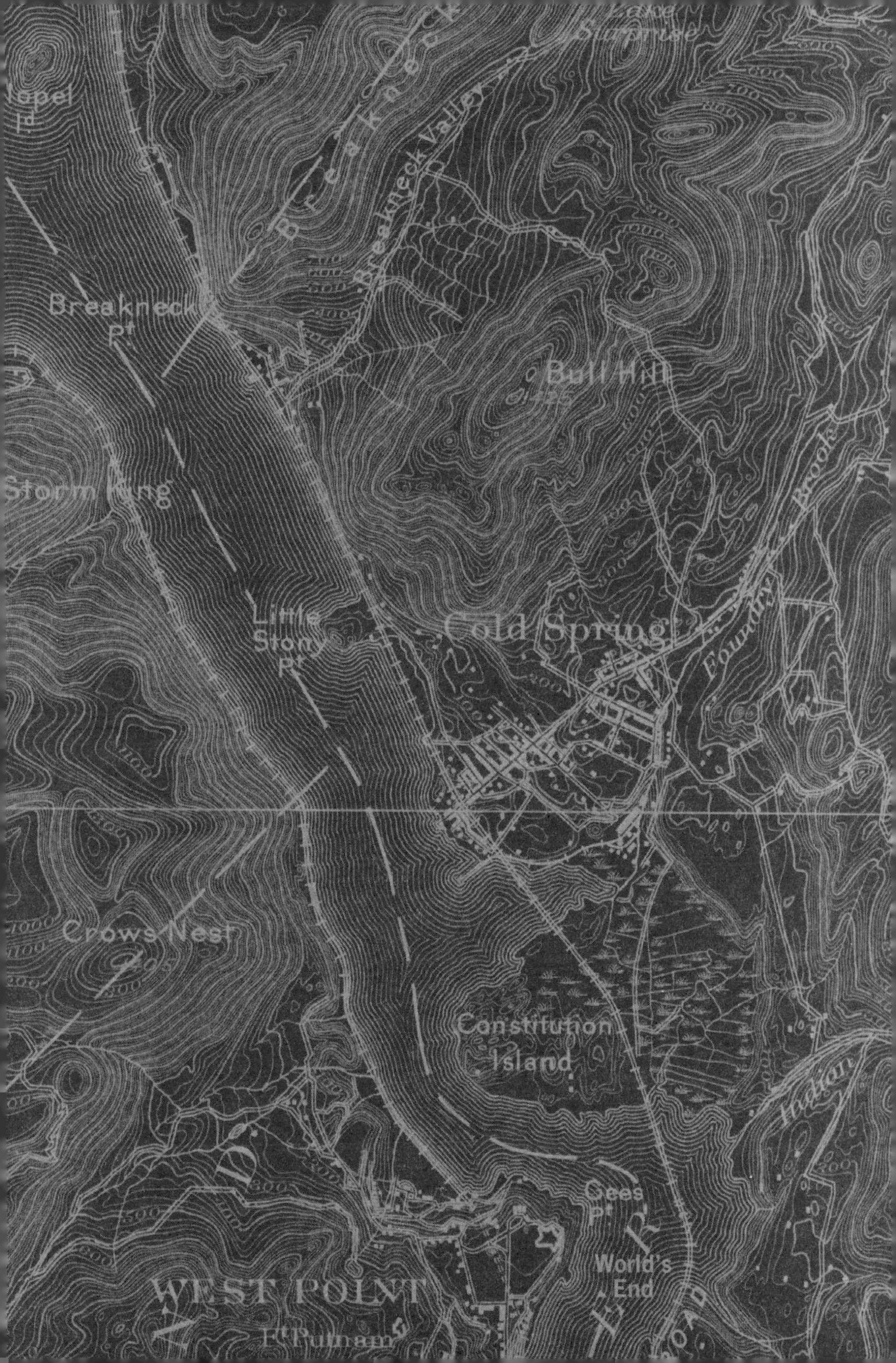

Breakneck Valley
Breakneck Pt
Bull Hill
Storm King
Little Stony Pt
Cold Spring
Foundry Brook
Crows Nest
Constitution Island
Indian
Gees Pt
World's End
WEST POINT
Ft Putnam

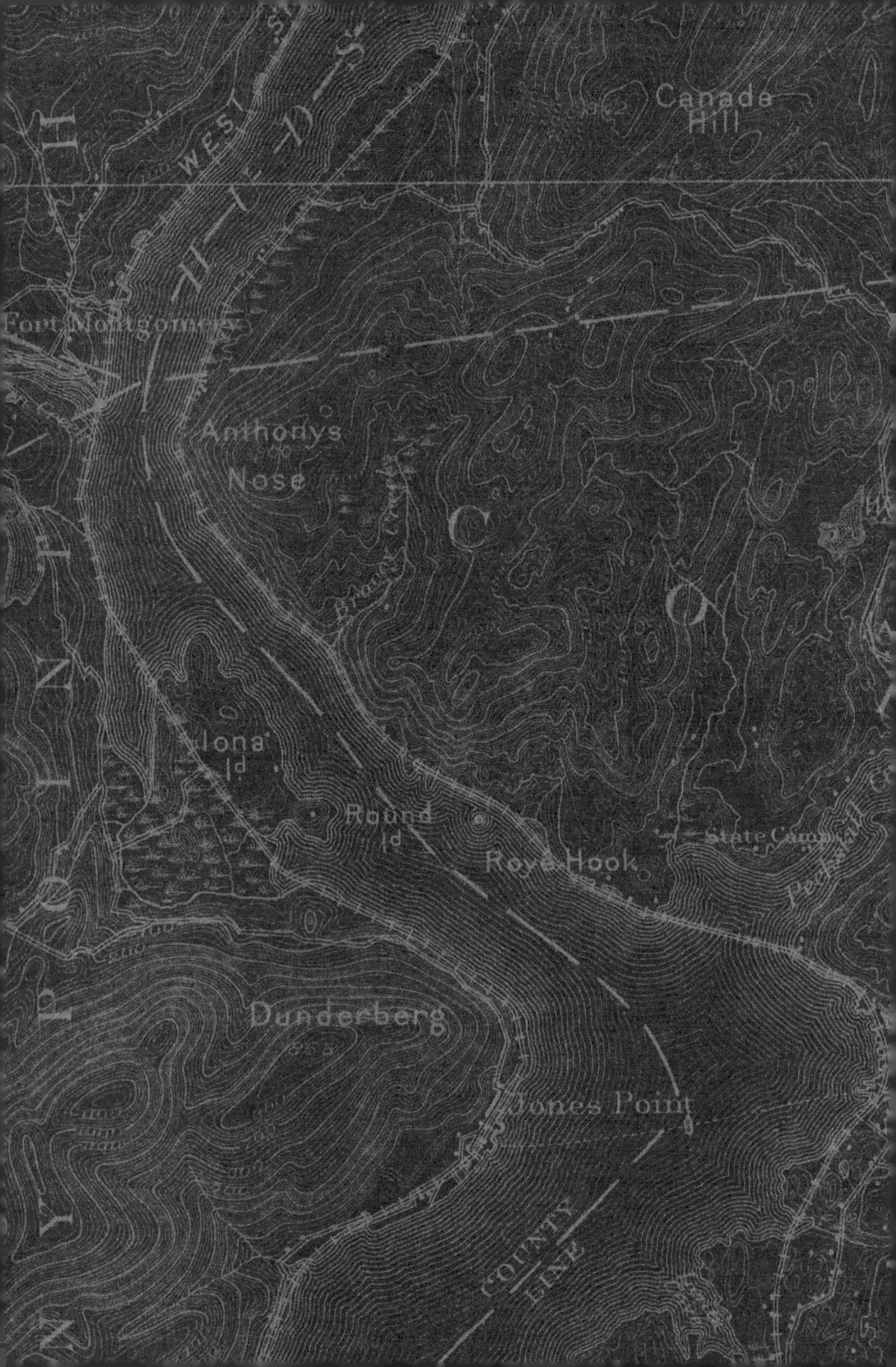

Canada Hill
WEST
Fort Montgomery
Anthonys Nose
Iona Id
Round Id
Roa Hook
State Camp
Dunderberg
Jones Point
COUNTY LINE

CRATING THE BLACK CAP'D CAPTAINS OF THE HUDSON

ayette Steamboat Company has nothing to envy Hudson Day or
ar; having now overtaken both as the most popular way to journey
own the North River, though it is neither the fastest nor the least
e. The Lafayette flagship "Lorelei" barrels along the Hudson with
nd tonnage that exceed the greatest coal barges; and is the site on
ummer evening of parties and dinners attended by many a wealthy
us New Yorker.

with maritime tradition, the founder of Lafayette Lines instituted
ive trademark for its captains: the now famous black cap, instead
onventional officer's white. Although some balked, that ceased
upstanding Captain Elijah Twain took up with Lafayette Lines,
doffed the black cap himself.

RIOT QUELLED WITH

the foreigner woke in the night. He slept
pen which led to the balcony; the wind had
rtain before it, and there appeared a wor
ness over all in the balcony of the opposite
owers seemed like flames of the most gor
, and among the flowers stood a beautiful sl
. It was to him as if light
his eyes; but then he had
woke from his sleep. Wi
and crept softly behind
the brightness had disap
appeared like fl

ON BOARD THE

LORELEI

THE CAPTAIN ELIJAH TWAIN

& HIS CREW

REQUEST THE PLEASURE OF

YOUR PRESENCE ABOARD

THE STEAMSHIP **LORELEI**

OCK IN THE EVENING,

Y, JUNE 14, 1884,

ALL NIGHT CRUISE

NG THE HUDSON,

NO SOONER THAN DAWN ;

ILL DEPART FROM ITS B

AT 8 O'CLOCK PROMPT.

FINE MUSIC &

SITE REFRESHMENTS PROVIDED.

A NOTE FROM THE SHIPS DECK

Part Three
WORLD'S END

N EVENING OF SONG

WITH

Ella Wylie

AT

est 4th St Tavern

ROUBLE

ughfare
ud

NJURED

ed by a smile; cold, scanty an
discourse; backward in sentiment; lean,
yet somehow lovable. At friendly meetin
to his taste, something eminently human
omething indeed which never found its w
hich spoke not only in these silent symbc
re, but more often and loudly in the acts
tere with himself; drank gin when he wa
for vintages; and though he enjoyed the
ed the doors of one for twenty years. B
nce for others; sometimes wondering, a
h pressure of spirits involved in their m
remity inclined to help rather than to re
's heresy," he used to say quaintly: "I lo
vil in his own way." In this character,
y his fortune to be the last reputable ac
od influence in the lives of downgoing
se, so long as they came about his ch
nade of change in his

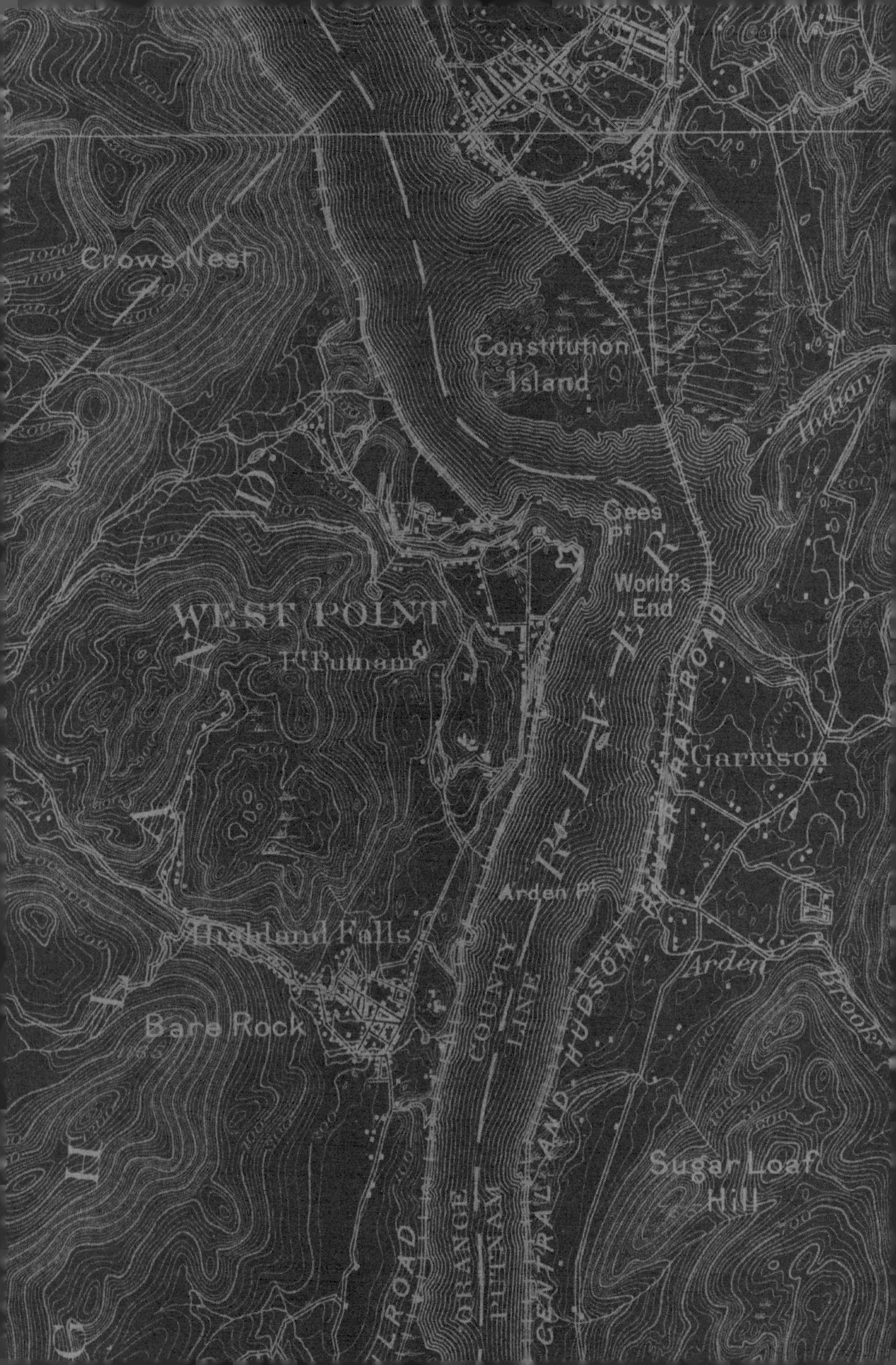
Crows Nest
Constitution Island
Gees Pt
World's End
WEST POINT
Ft Putnam
Garrison
Arden Pt
Highland Falls
Bare Rock
Arden
Sugar Loaf Hill
Indian
Brook
COUNTY LINE
ORANGE
PUTNAM
CENTRAL AND HUDSON
RAILROAD

Pt III, Chap.1

"IN THE OTHER REALM"

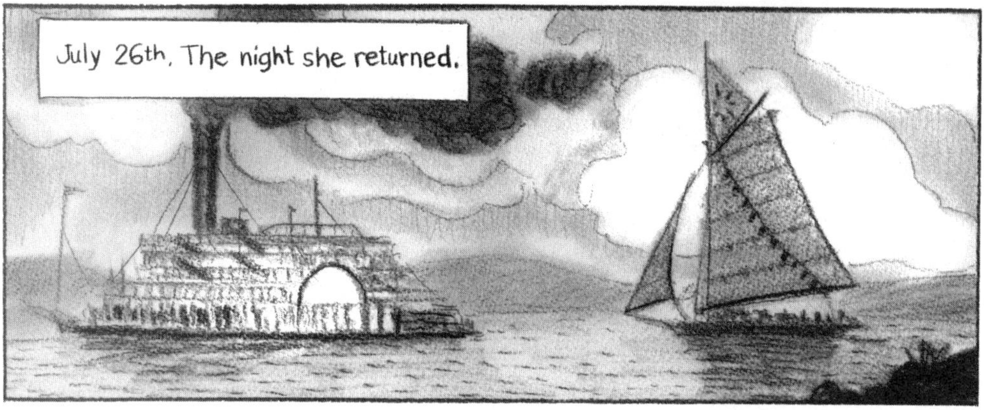
July 26th. The night she returned.

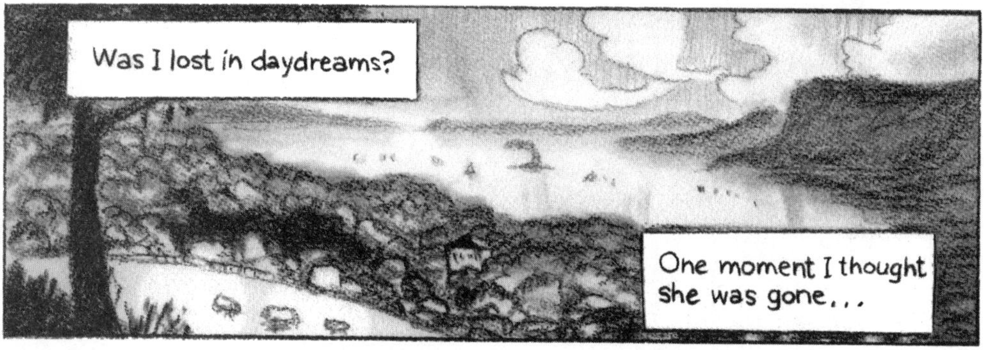
Was I lost in daydreams?
One moment I thought she was gone...

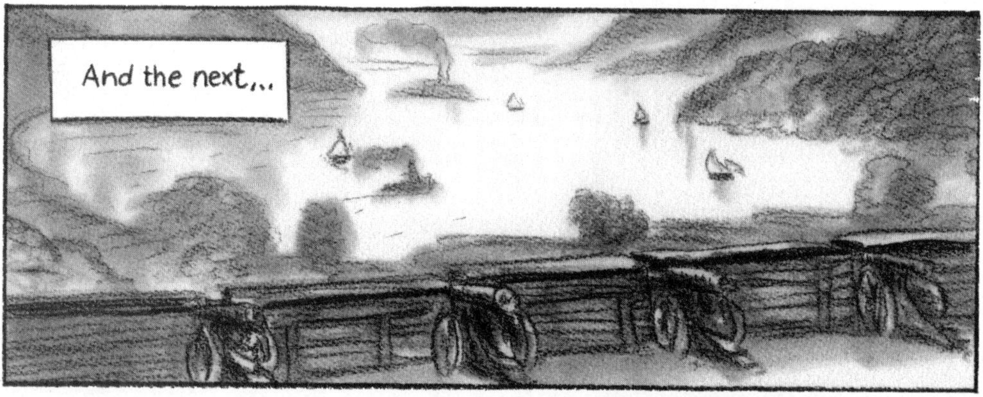
And the next...

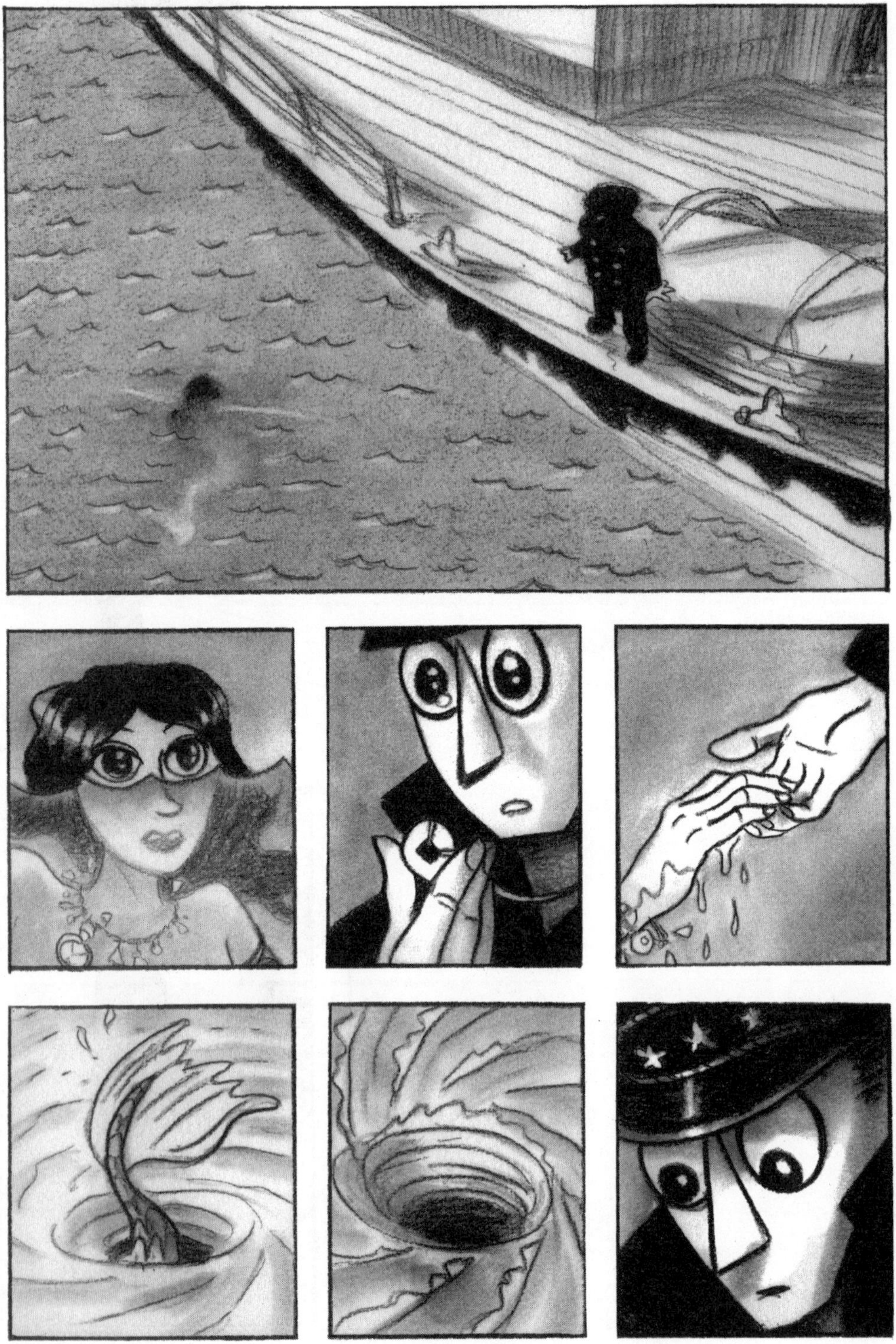

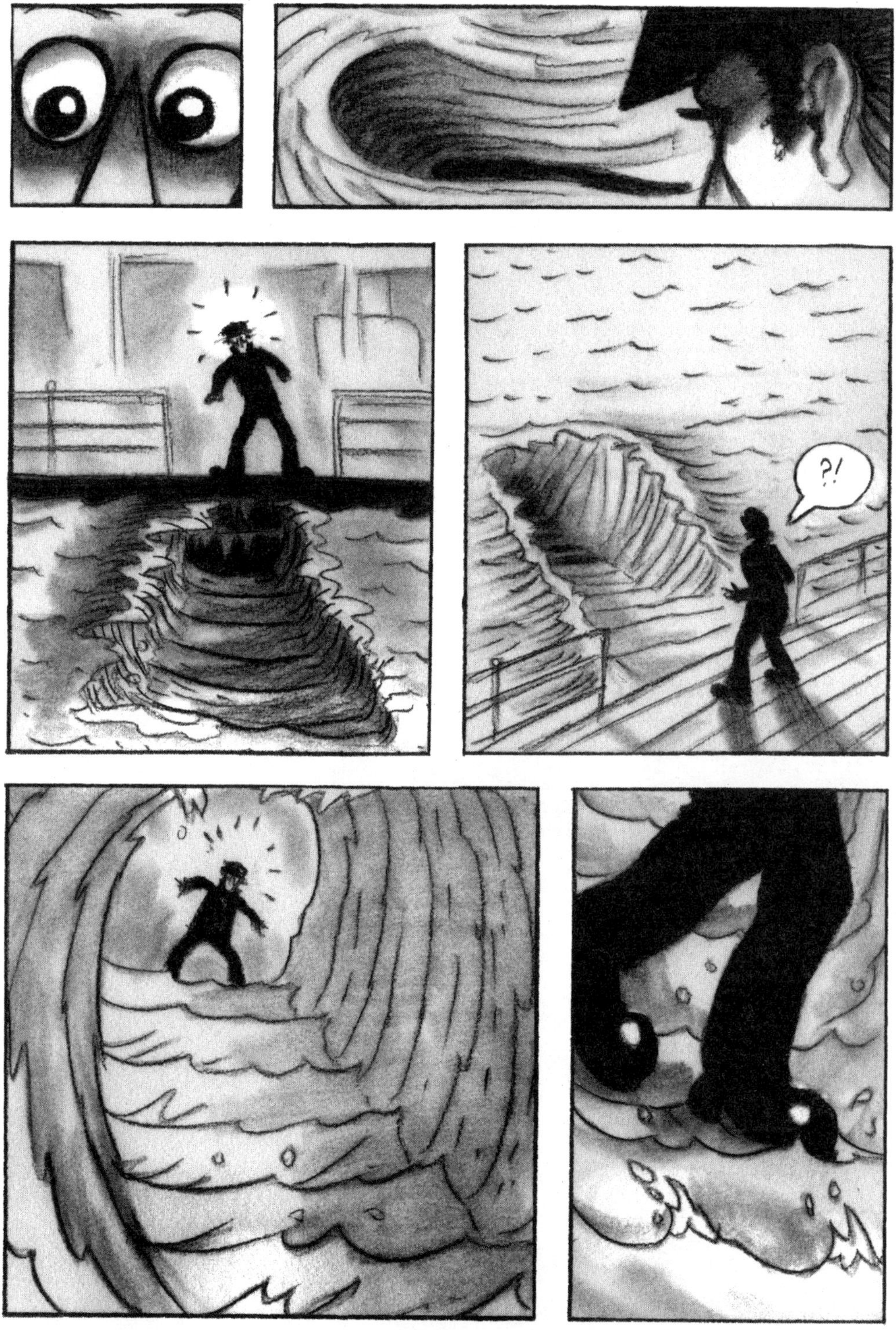
?!

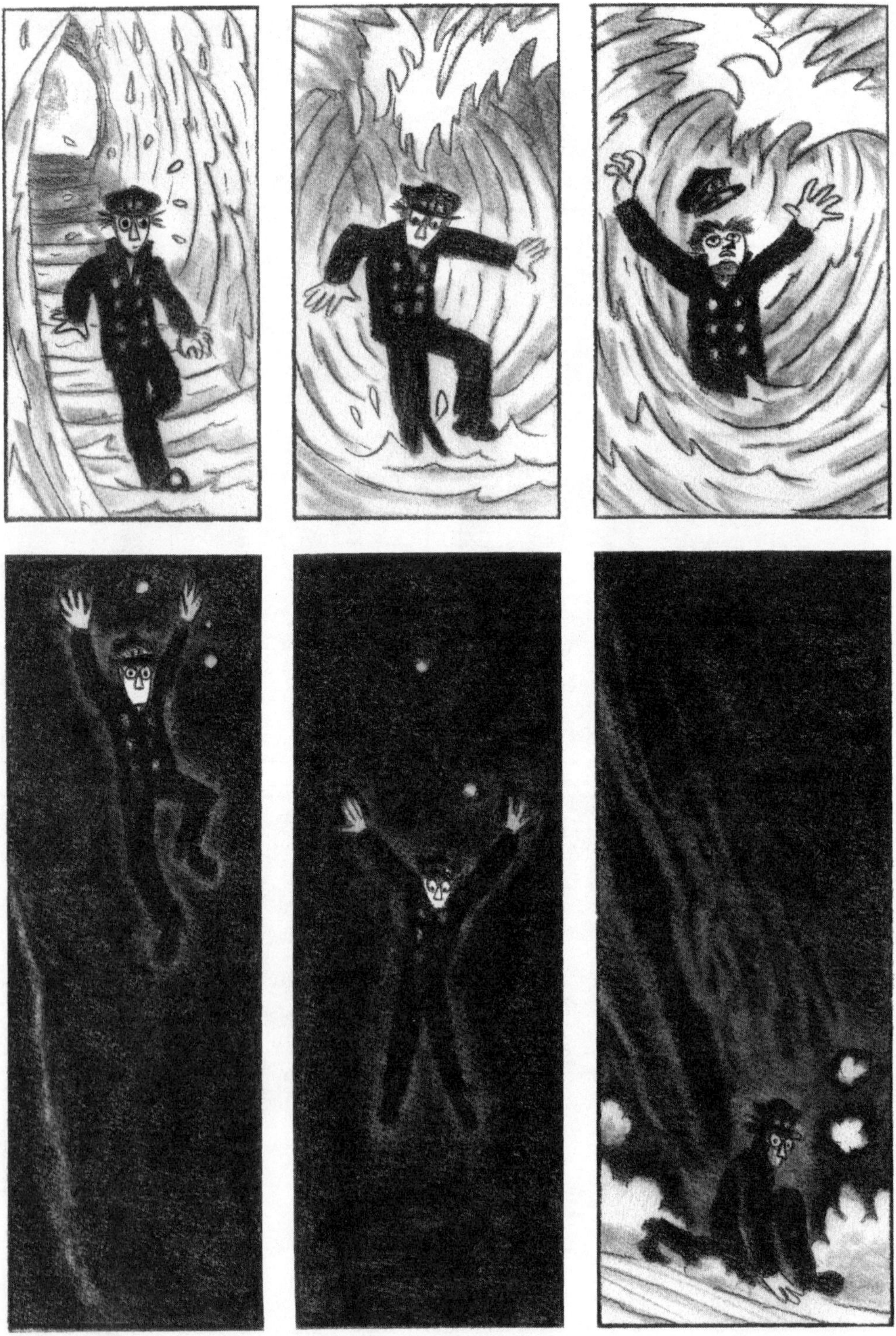

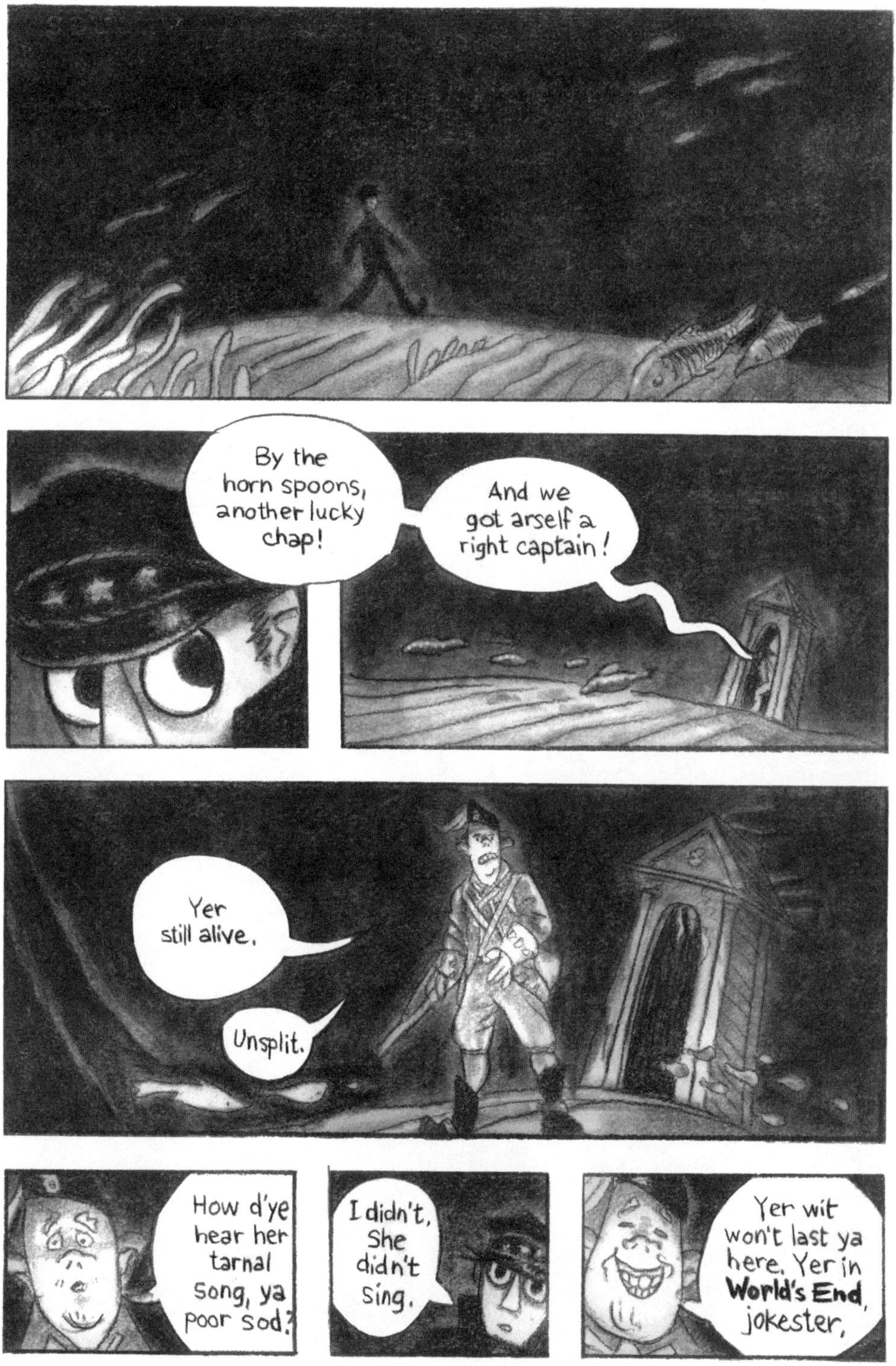
By the horn spoons, another lucky chap!
And we got arself a right captain!
Yer still alive.
Unsplit.
How d'ye hear her tarnal song, ya poor sod?
I didn't. She didn't sing.
Yer wit won't last ya here. Yer in **World's End**, jokester.

298

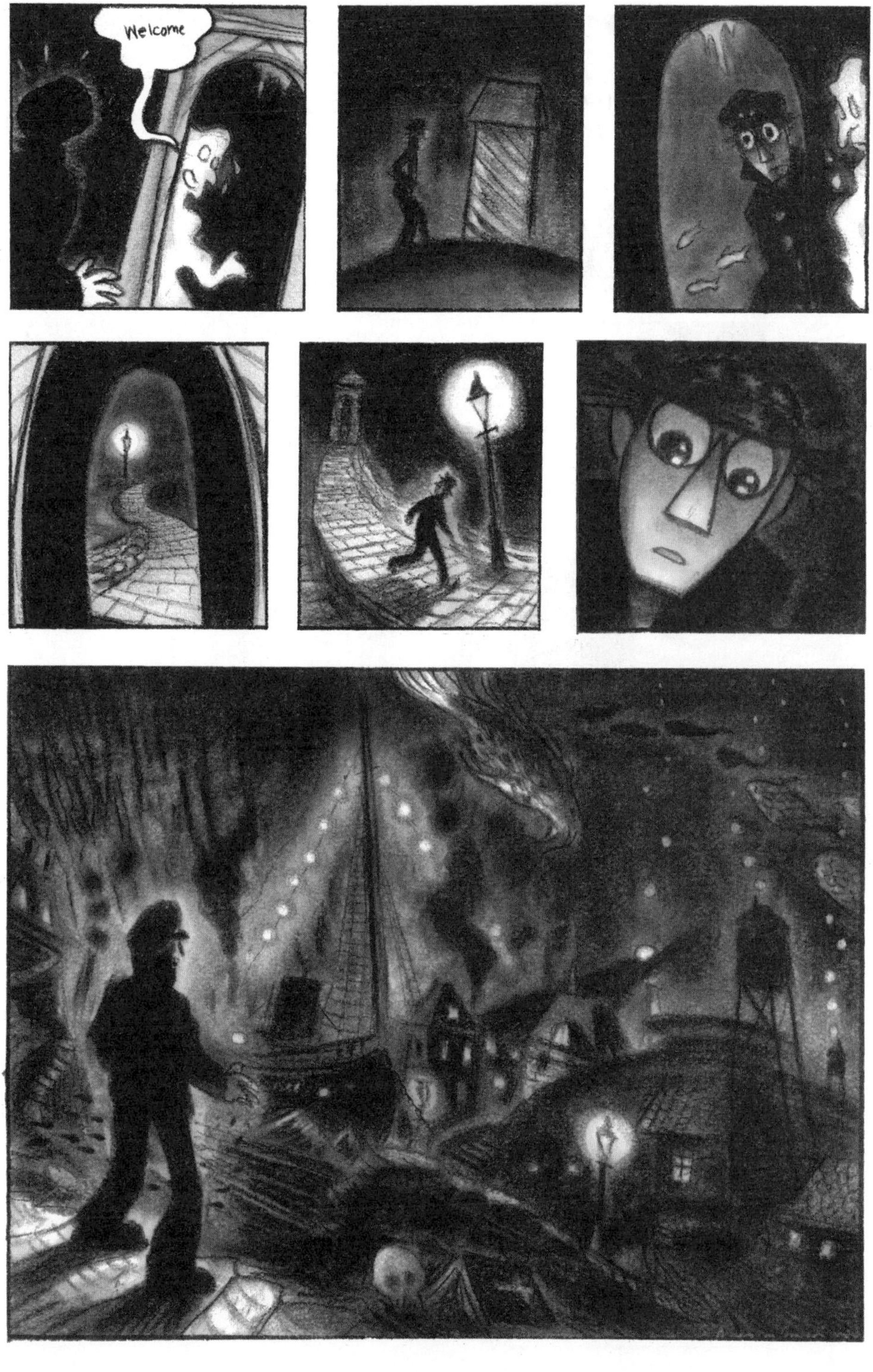
Welcome

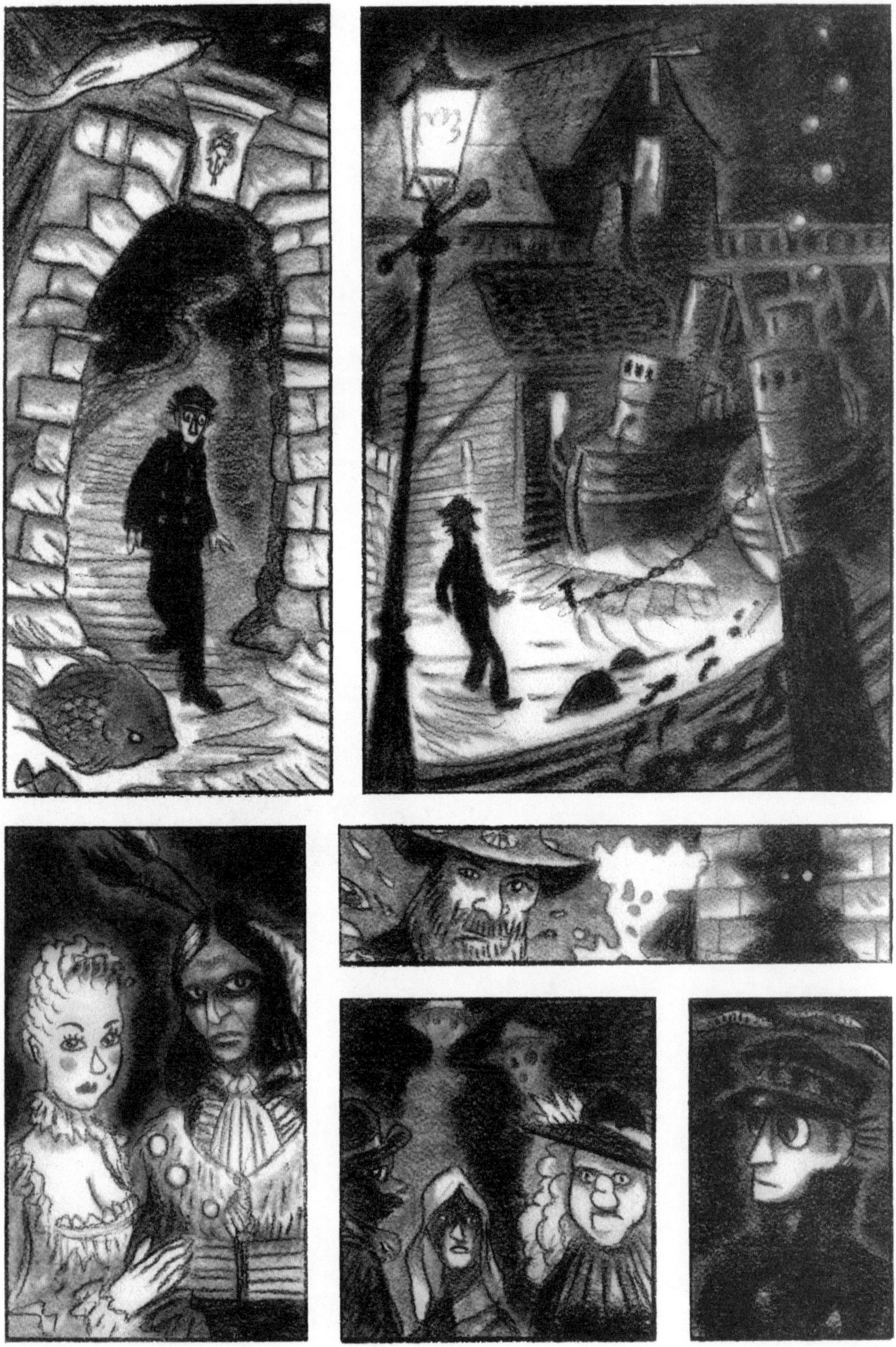

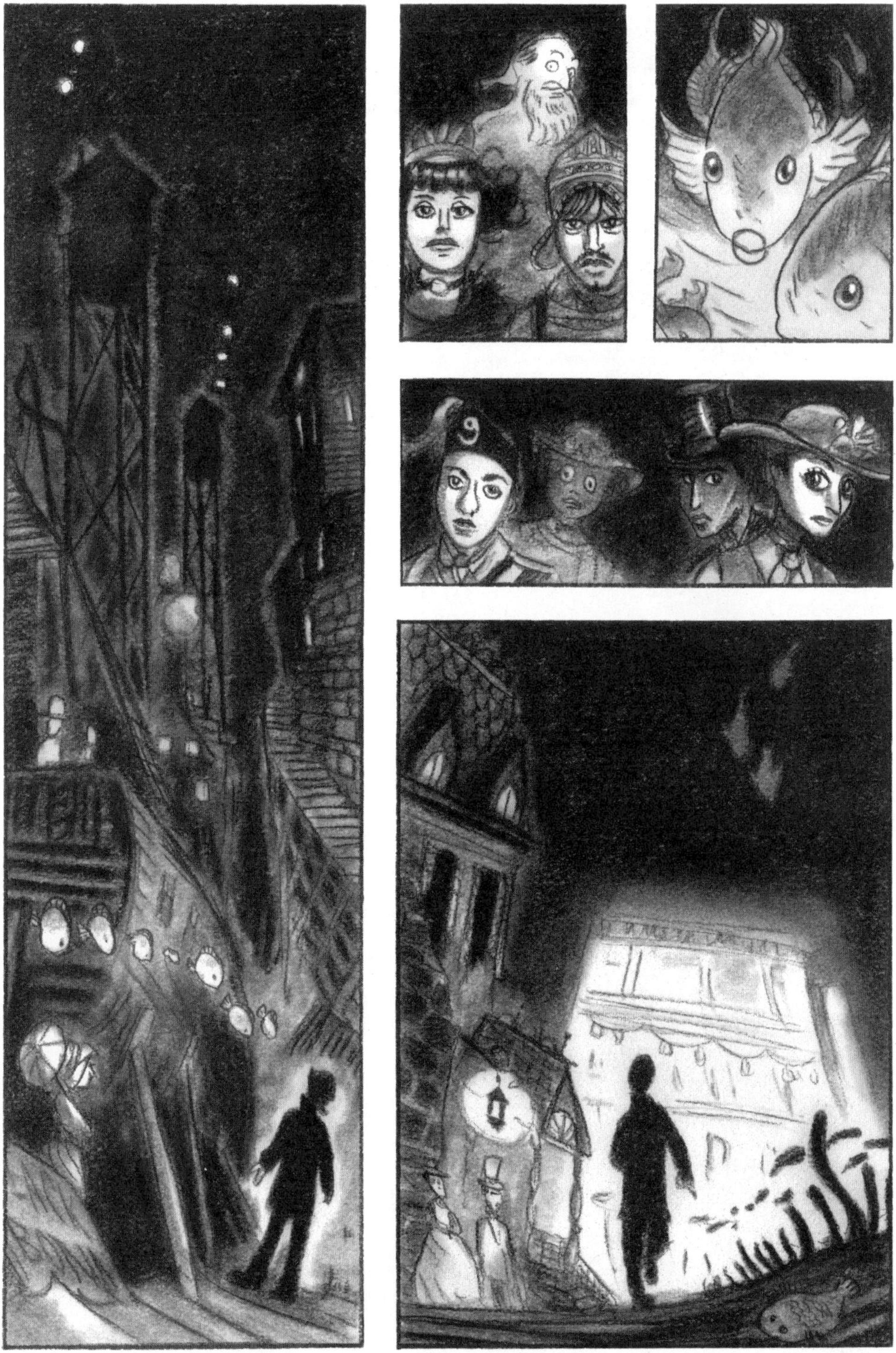

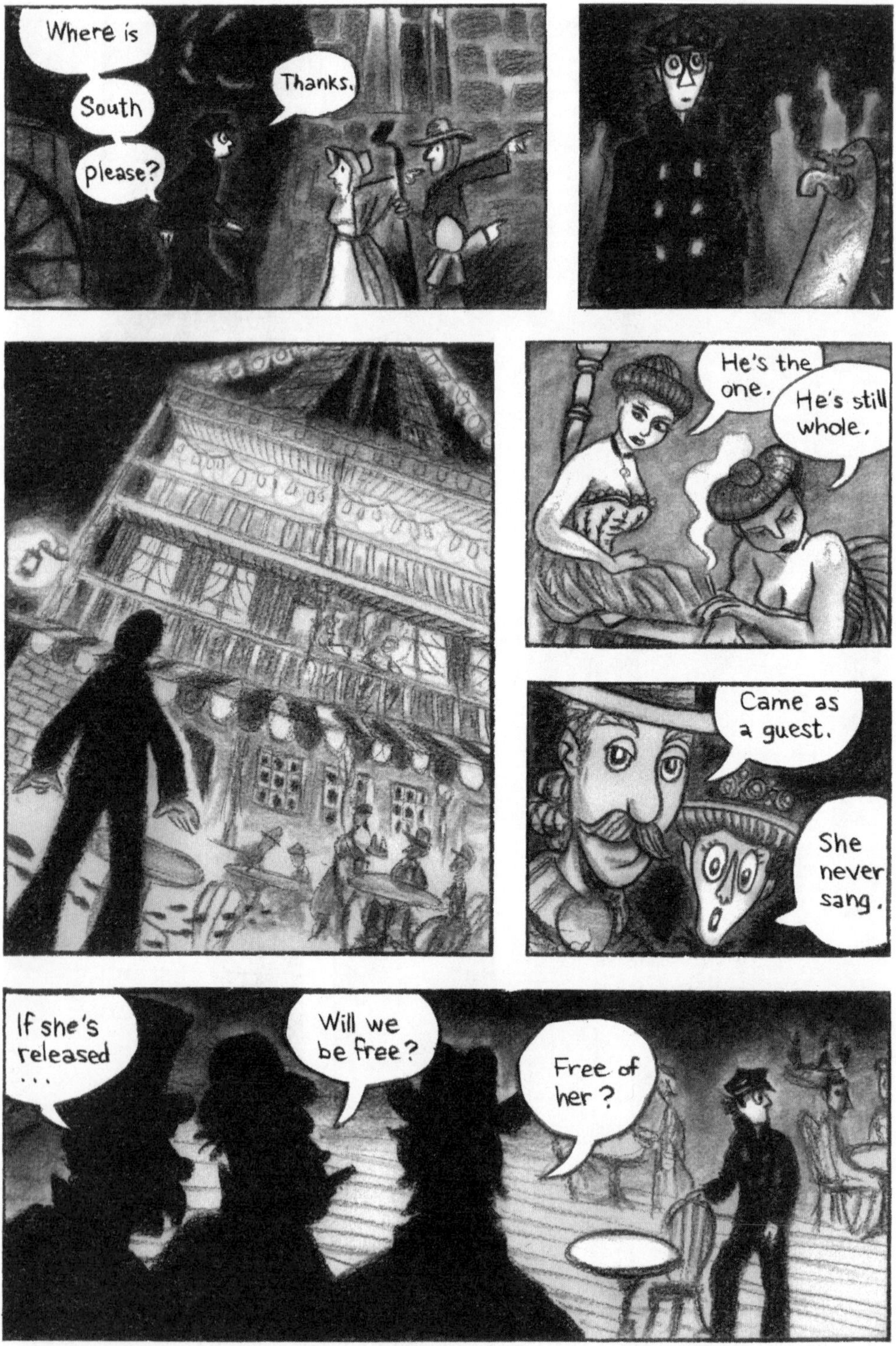
Where is
South
please?
Thanks.
He's the one.
He's still whole.
Came as a guest.
She never sang.
If she's released ...
Will we be free?
Free of her?

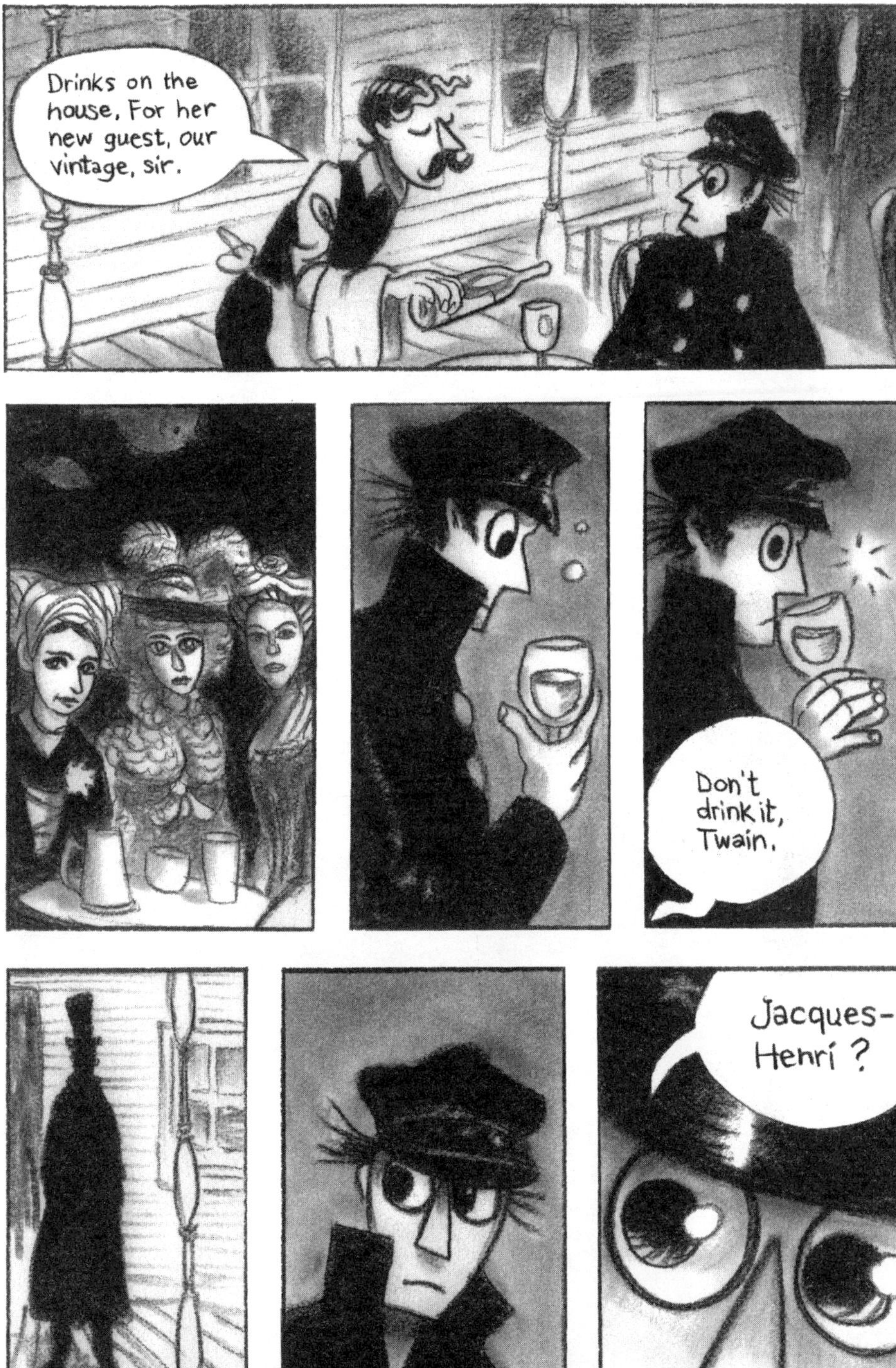
Drinks on the house. For her new guest, our vintage, sir.
Don't drink it, Twain.
Jacques-Henri ?

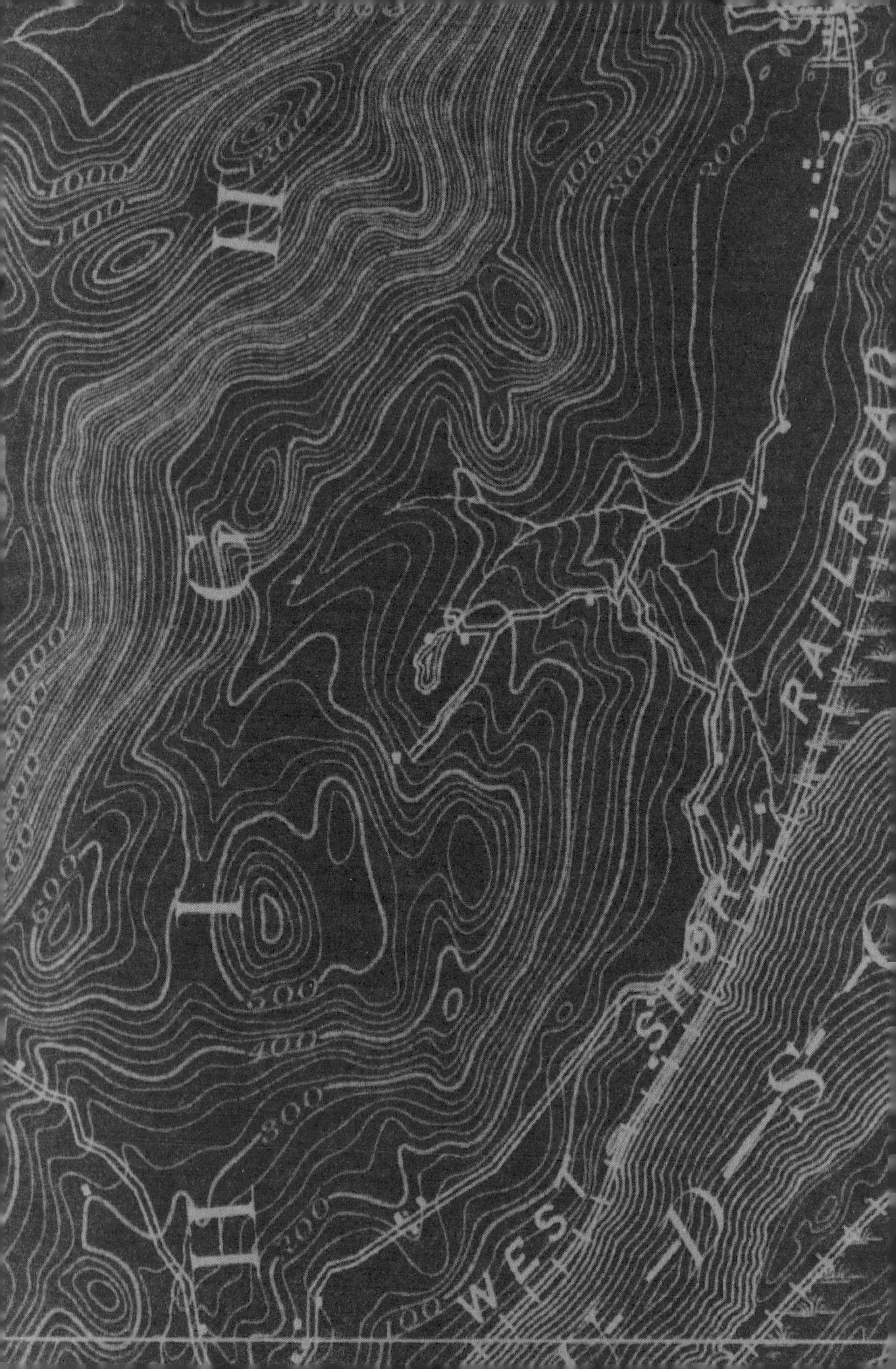
WEST SHORE RAILROAD

Pt III, Chap.2

"THE LOST BROTHER"

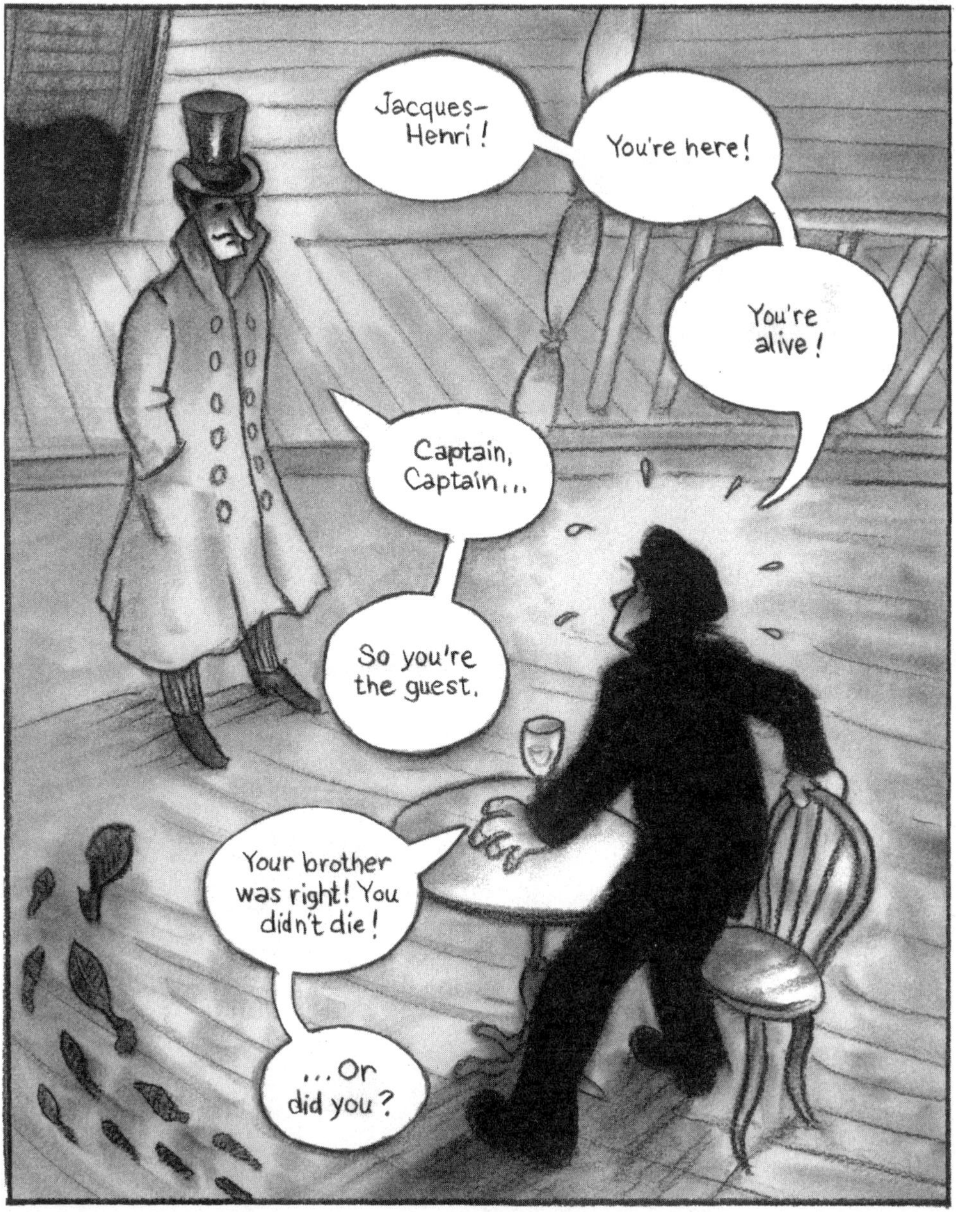
Jacques-Henri!
You're here!
You're alive!
Captain, Captain...
So you're the guest.
Your brother was right! You didn't die!
...Or did you?

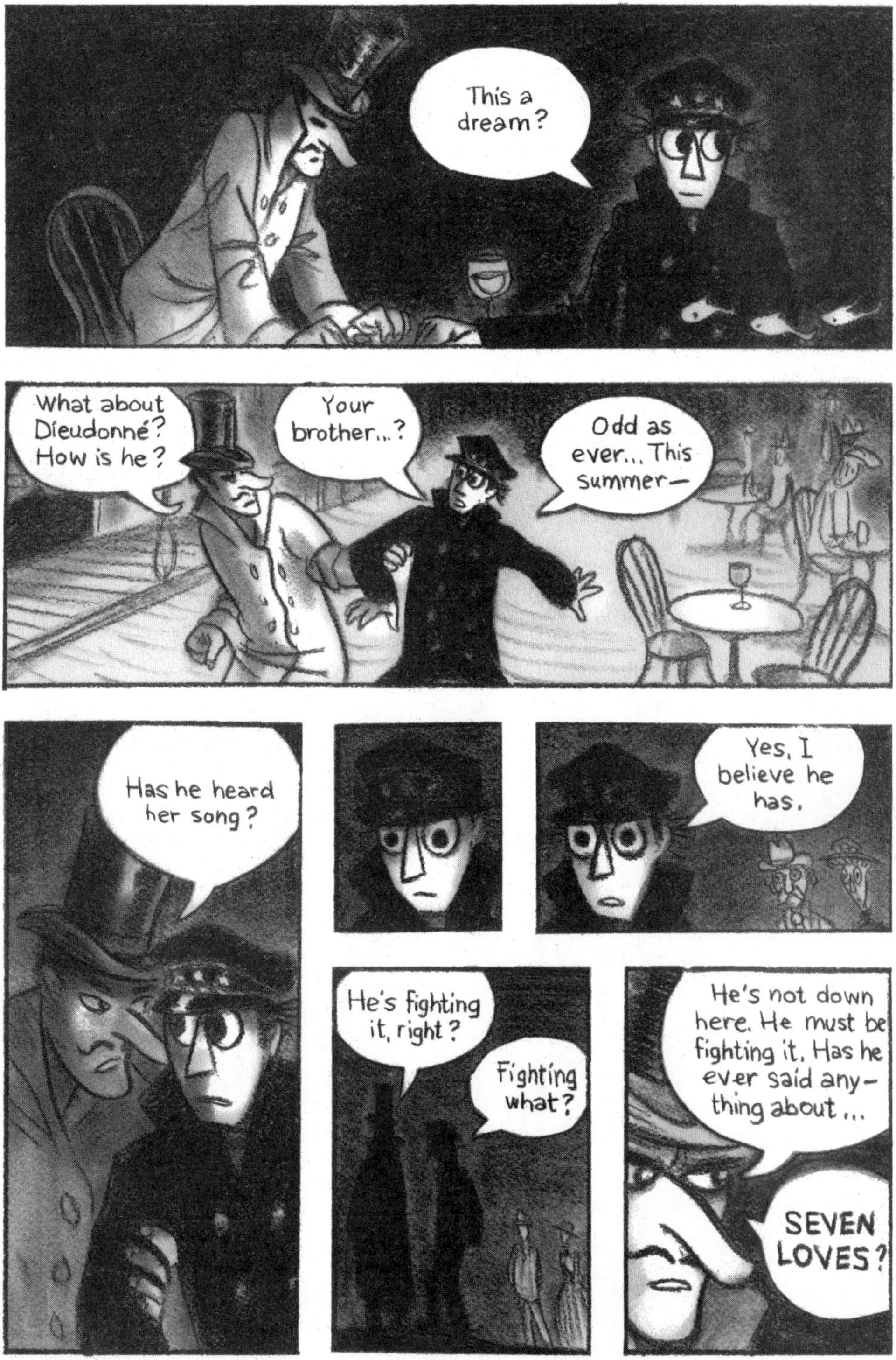
This a dream?
What about Dieudonné? How is he?
Your brother...?
Odd as ever... This summer—
Has he heard her song?
Yes, I believe he has.
He's fighting it, right?
Fighting what?
He's not down here. He must be fighting it. Has he ever said anything about...
SEVEN LOVES?

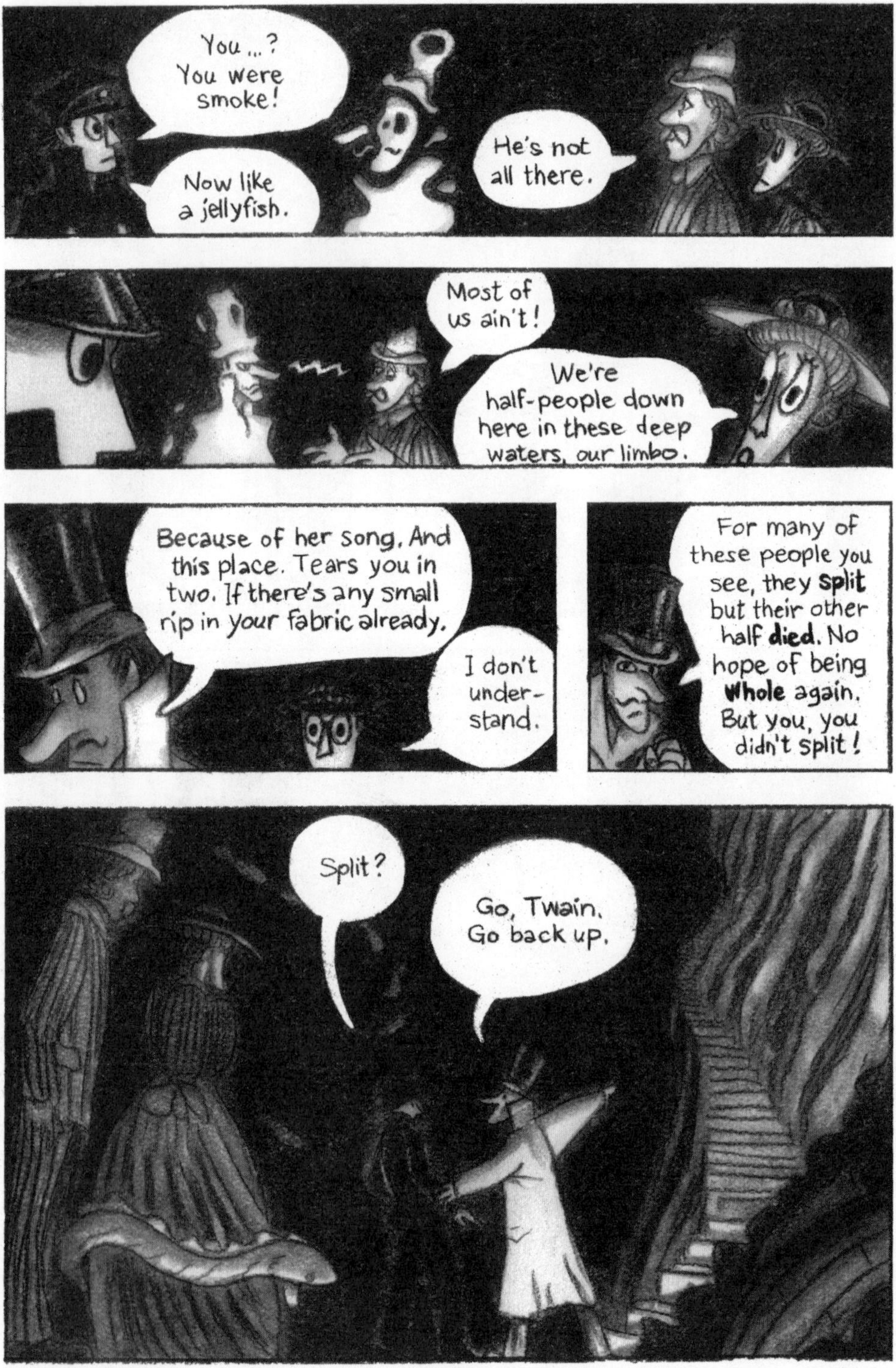
You...?
You were smoke!
Now like a jellyfish.
He's not all there.
Most of us ain't!
We're half-people down here in these deep waters, our limbo.
Because of her song. And this place. Tears you in two. If there's any small rip in your fabric already.
I don't under-stand.
For many of these people you see, they **split** but their other half **died**. No hope of being **Whole** again. But you, you didn't split!
Split?
Go, Twain. Go back up.

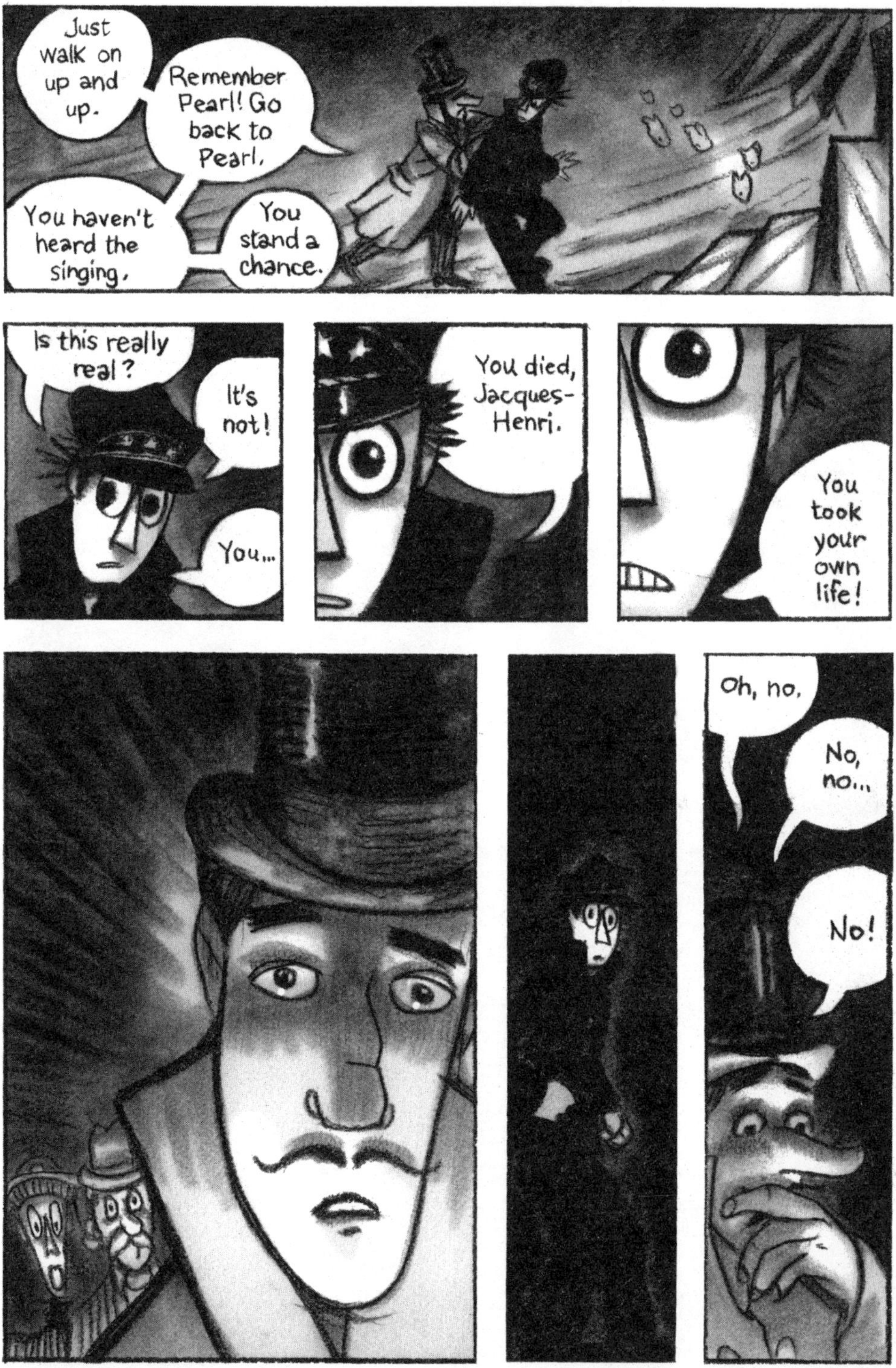
Just walk on up and up.
Remember Pearl! Go back to Pearl.
You haven't heard the singing.
You stand a chance.
Is this really real?
It's not!
You...
You died, Jacques-Henri.
You took your own life!
Oh, no.
No, no...
No!

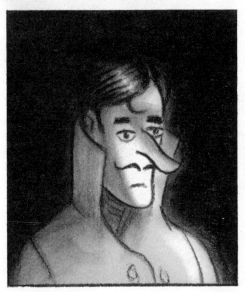

Pt III, Chap. 3

"A LADY BEGUILED"

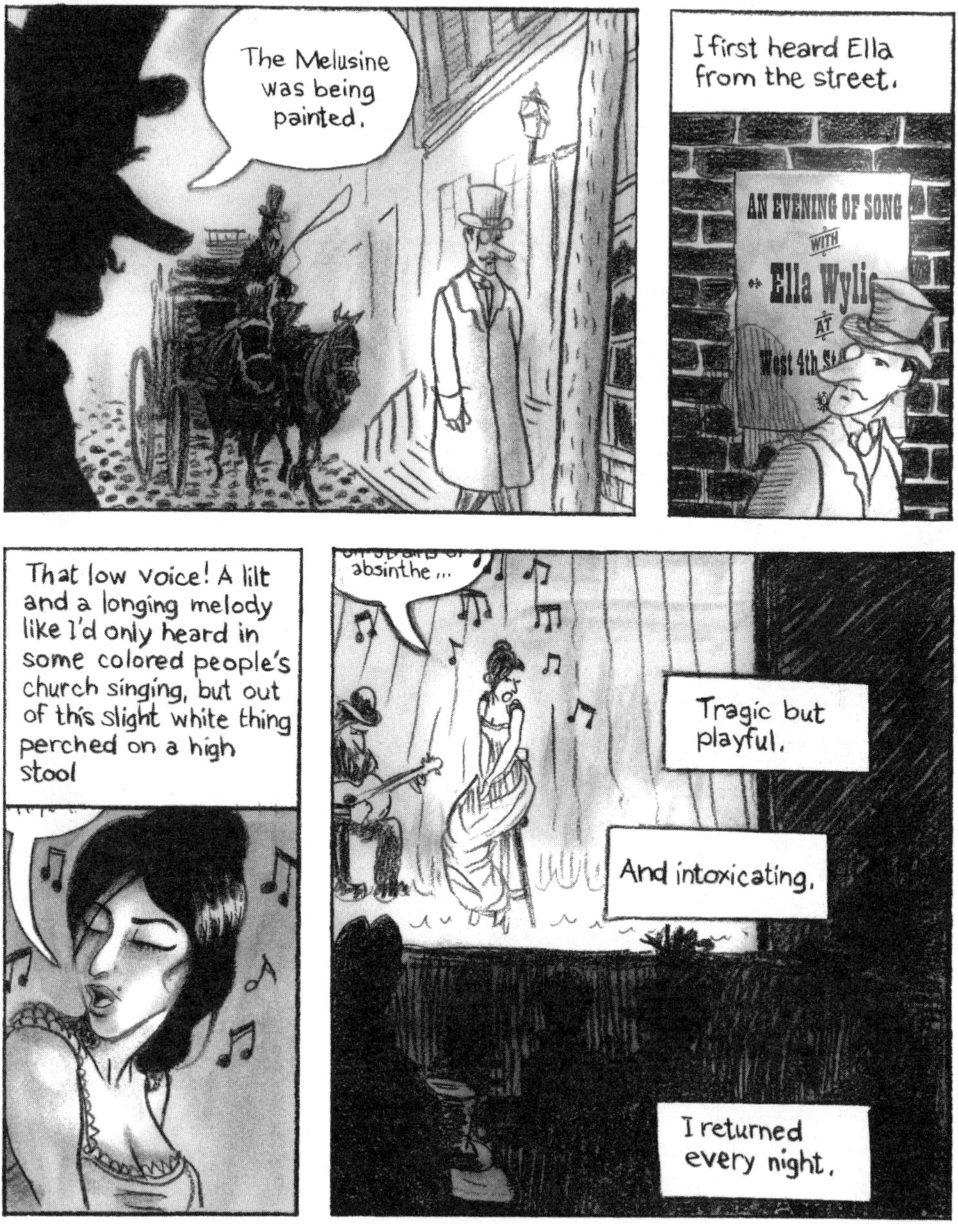
The Melusine was being painted.
I first heard Ella from the street.
AN EVENING OF SONG WITH Ella Wylie AT West 4th St
That low voice! A lilt and a longing melody like I'd only heard in some colored people's church singing, but out of this slight white thing perched on a high stool
absinthe ...
Tragic but playful.
And intoxicating.
I returned every night.

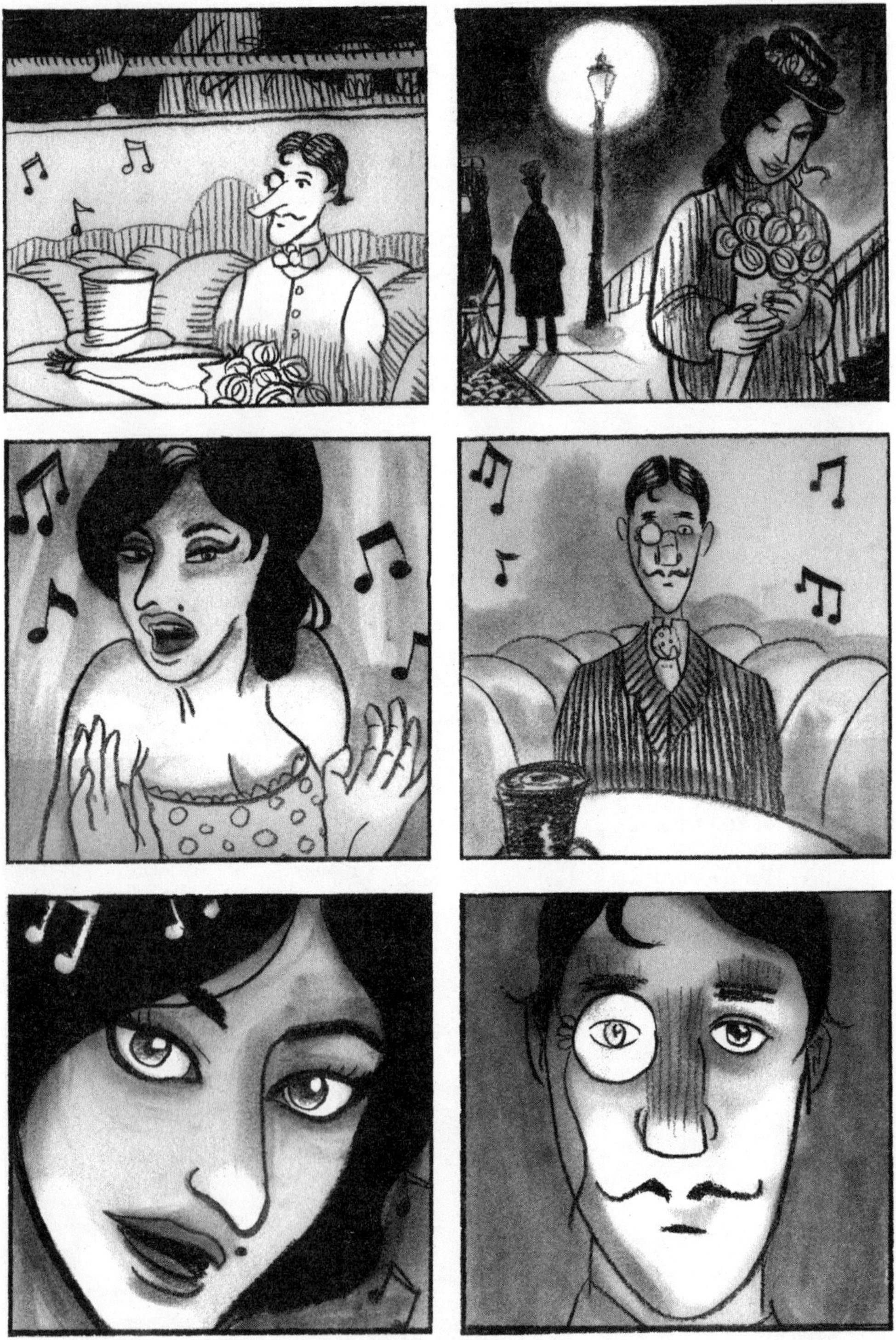

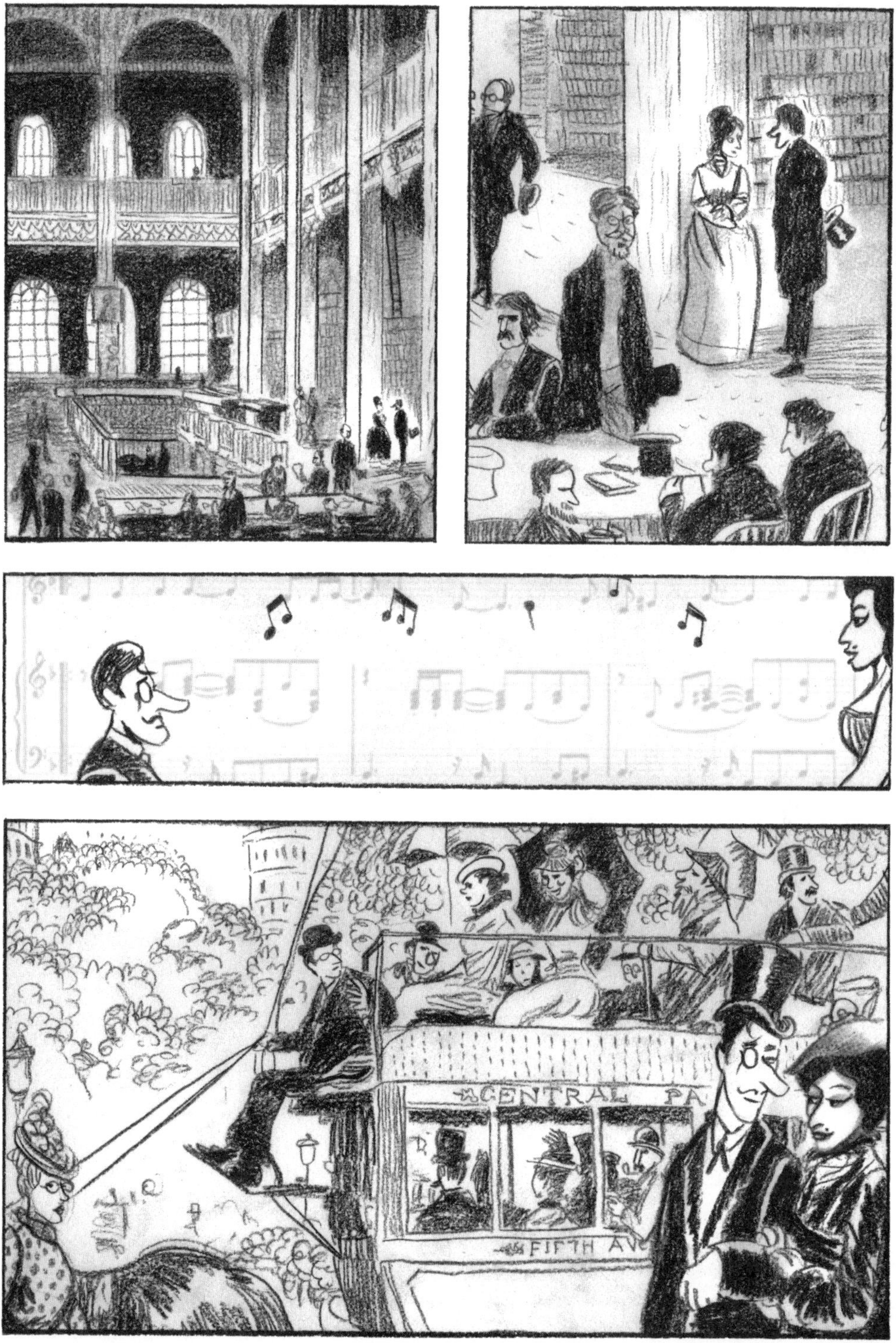
CENTRAL PA
FIFTH AV

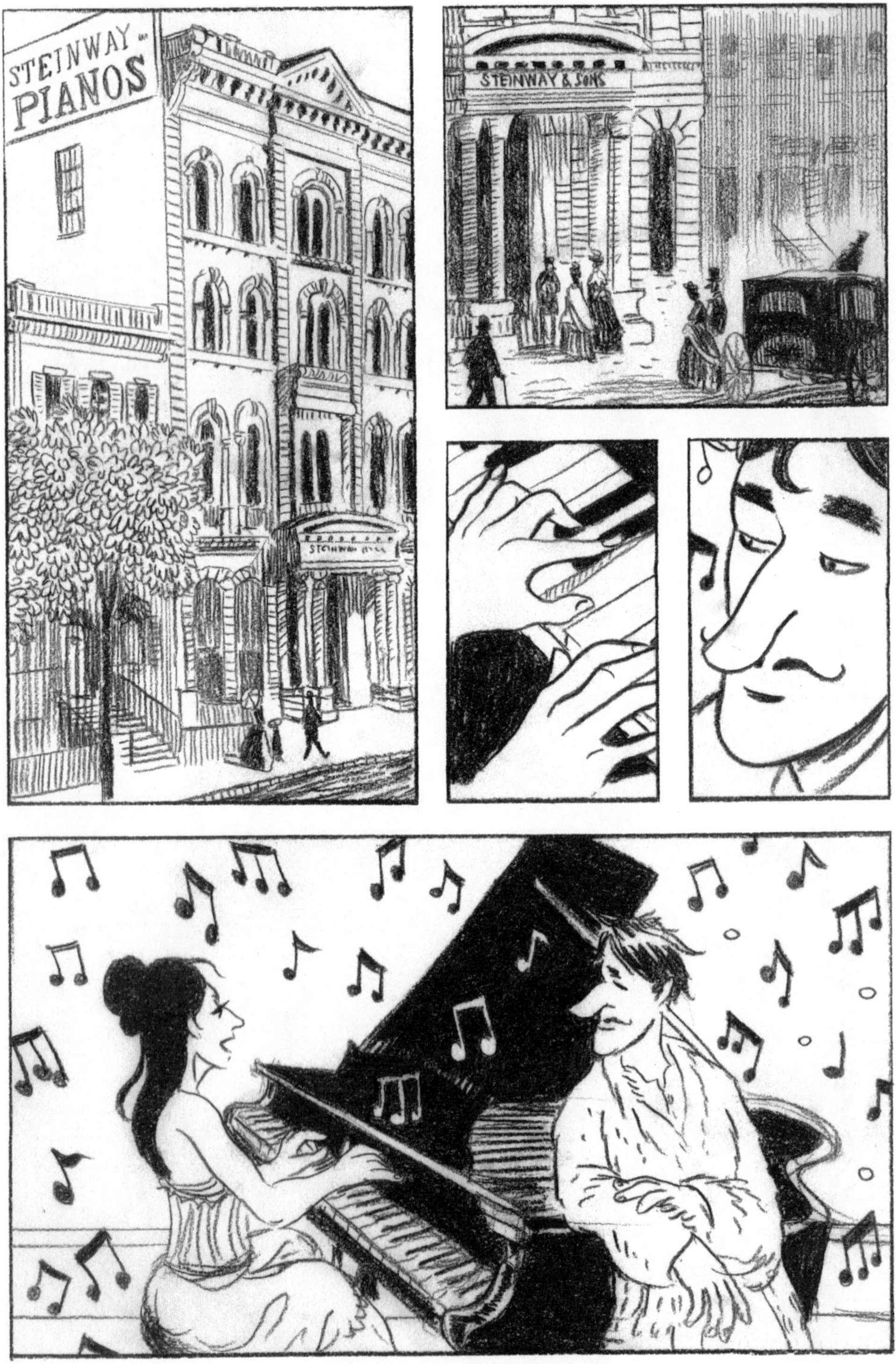
STEINWAY PIANOS
STEINWAY & SONS

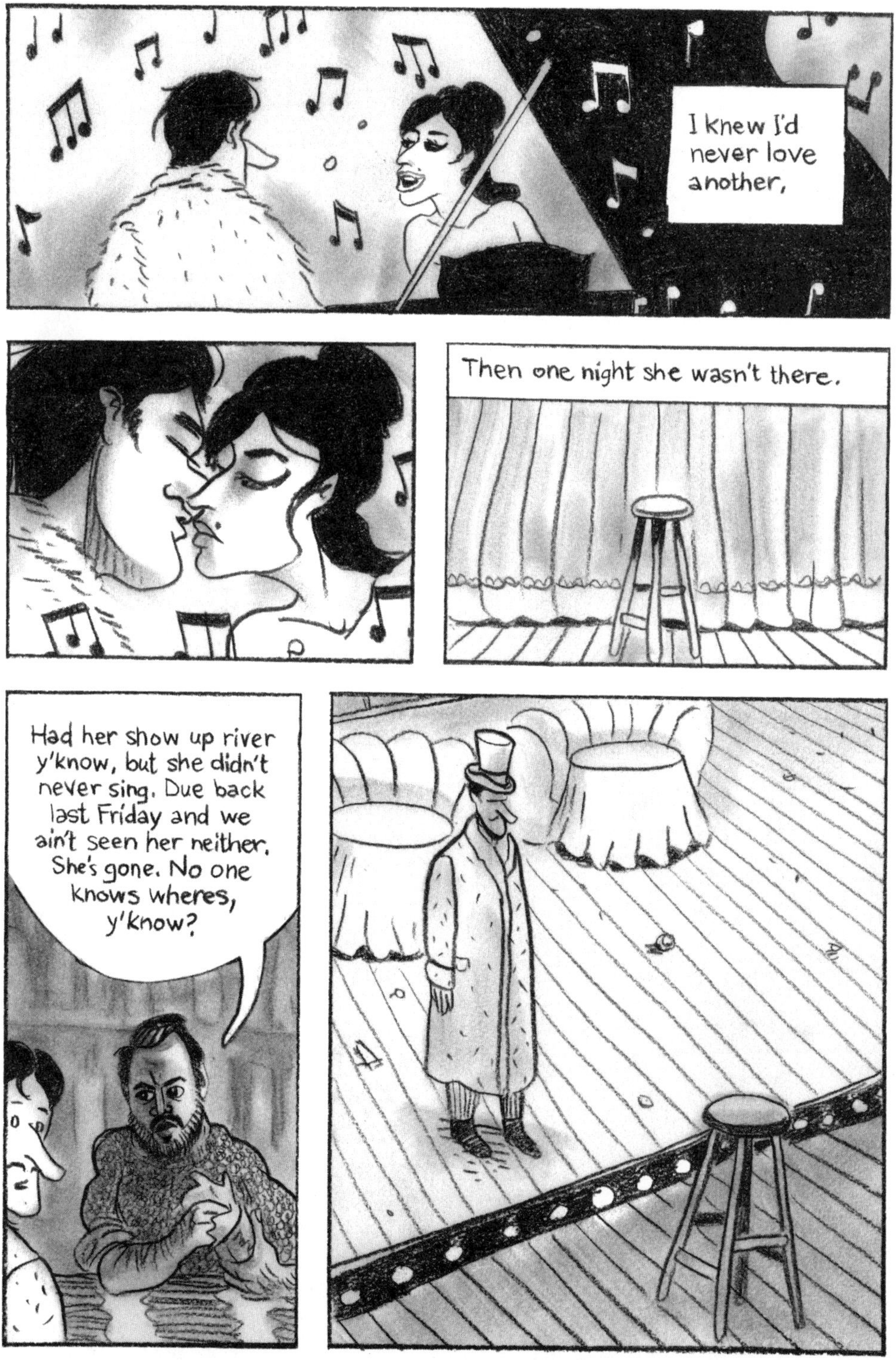
I knew I'd never love another,
Then one night she wasn't there.
Had her show up river y'know, but she didn't never sing. Due back last Friday and we ain't seen her neither. She's gone. No one knows wheres, y'know?

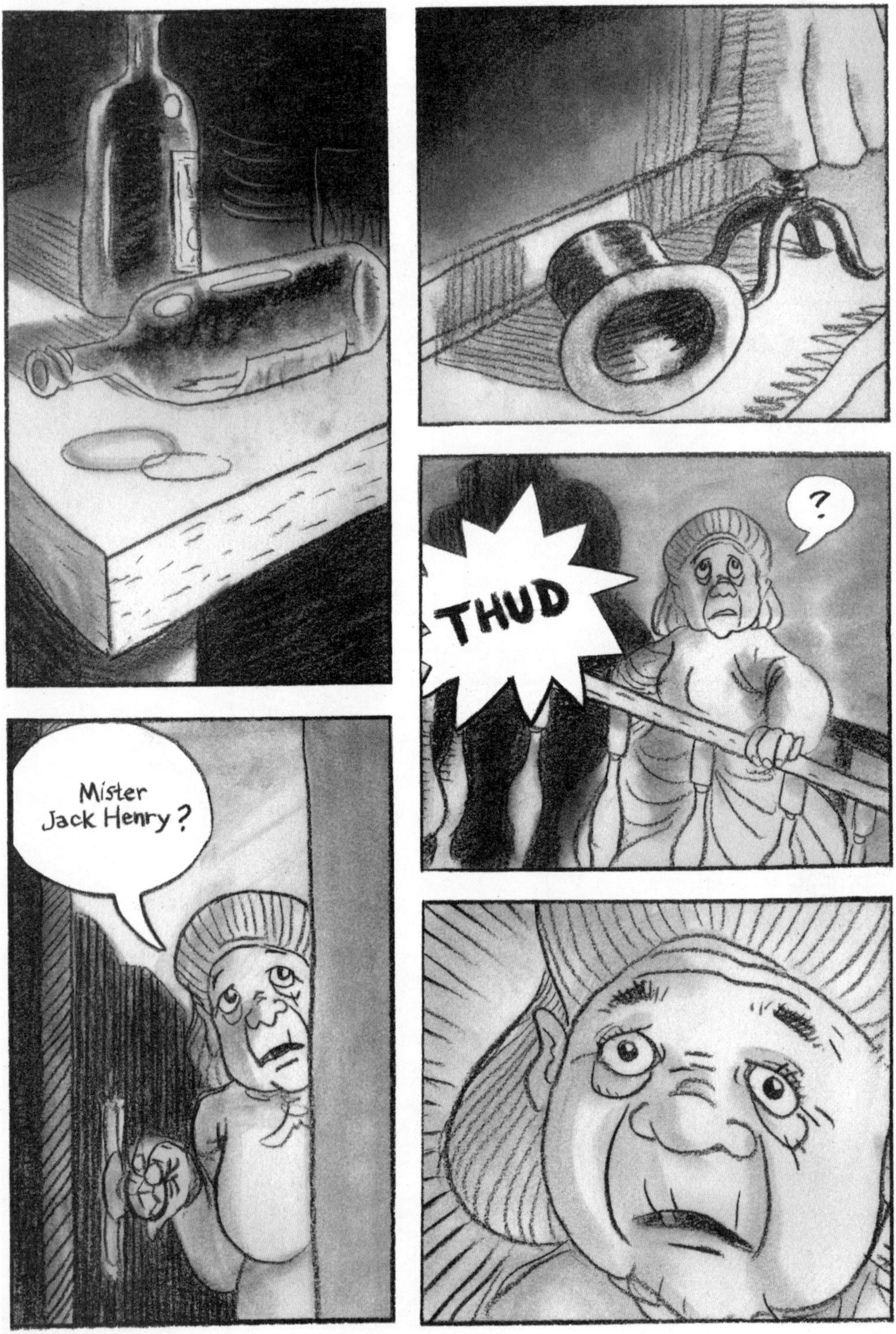
?
THUD
Mister Jack Henry?

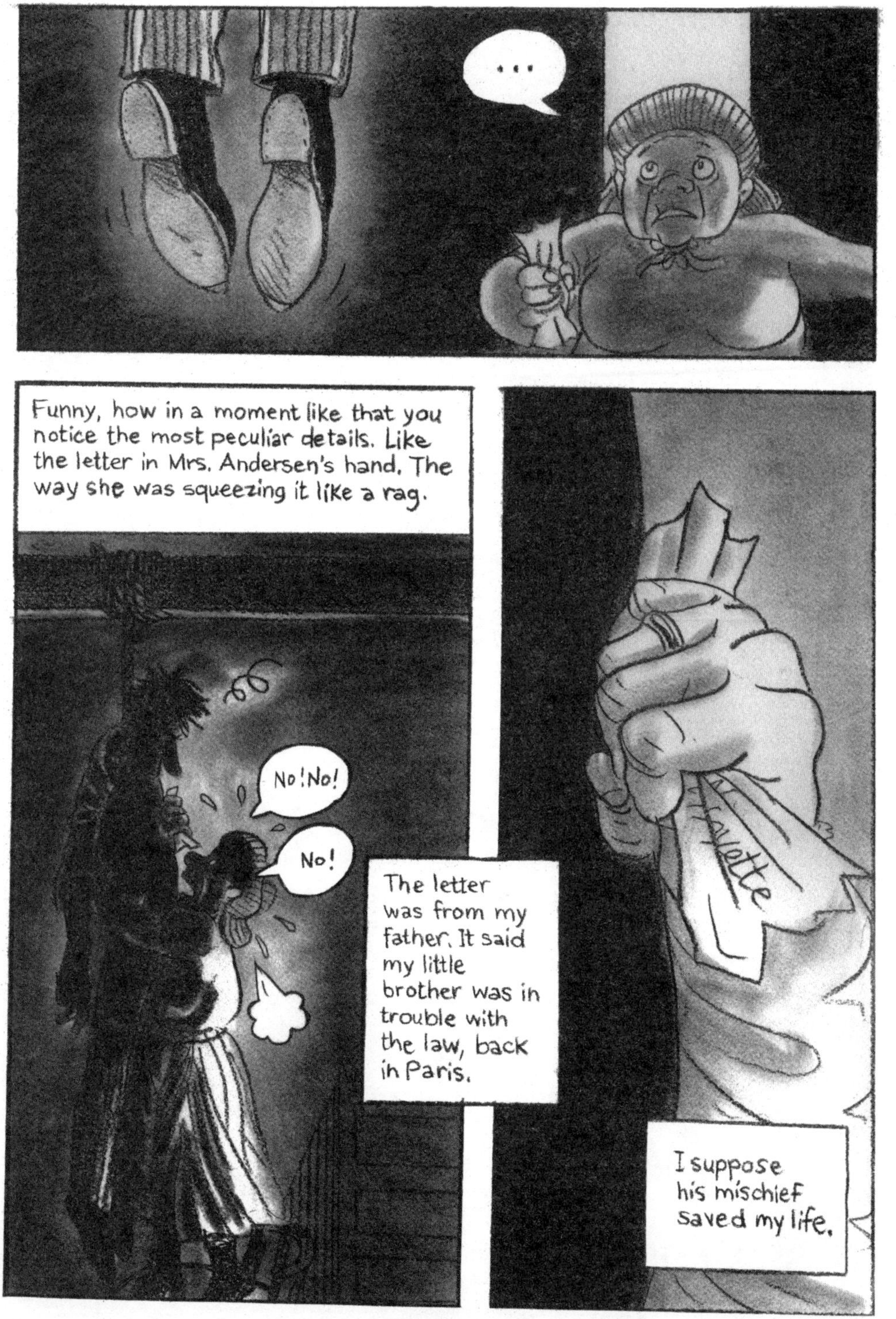
...
Funny, how in a moment like that you notice the most peculiar details. Like the letter in Mrs. Andersen's hand. The way she was squeezing it like a rag.
No! No!
No!
The letter was from my father. It said my little brother was in trouble with the law, back in Paris.
I suppose his mischief saved my life.

320

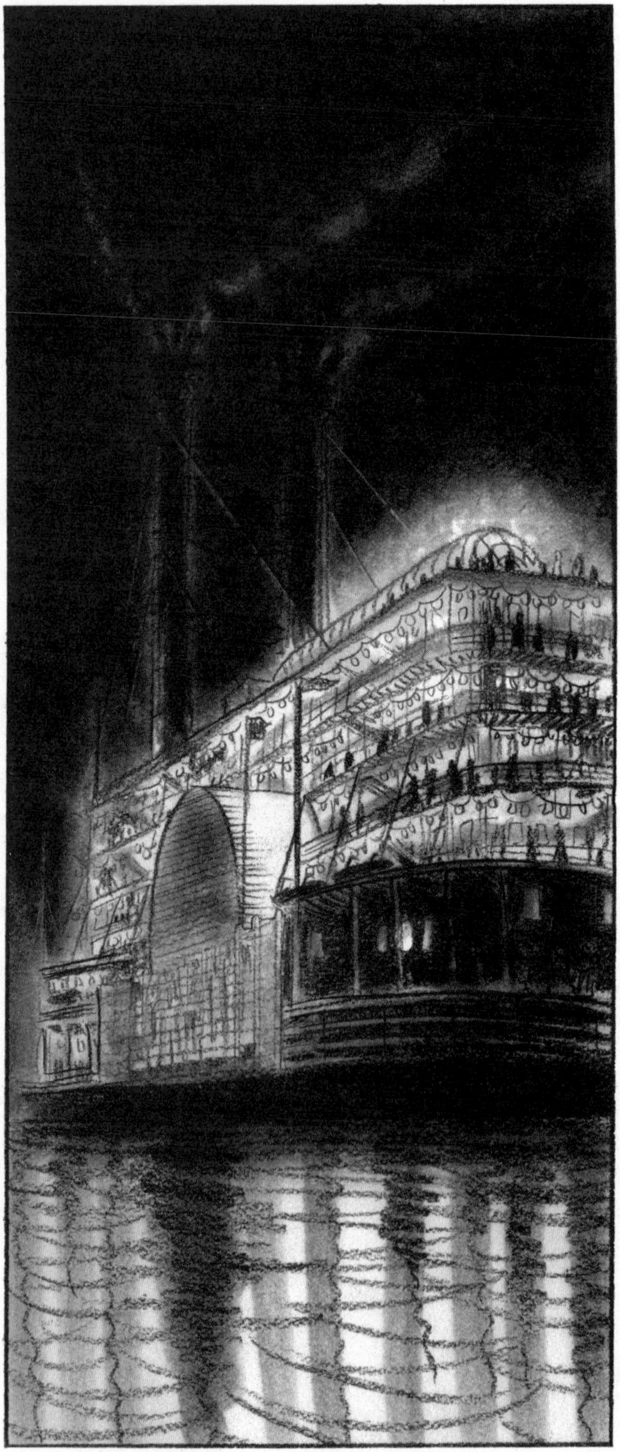

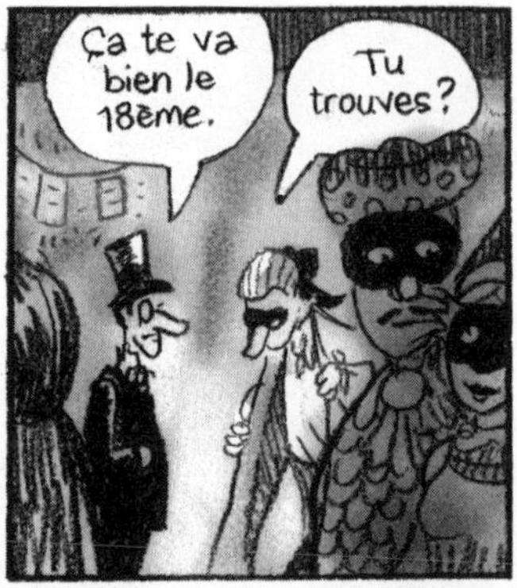
Ça te va
bien le
18ème.
Tu
trouves?

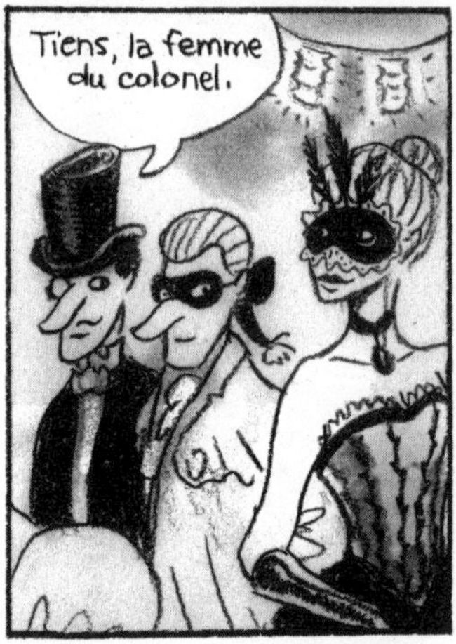
Tiens, la femme
du colonel.

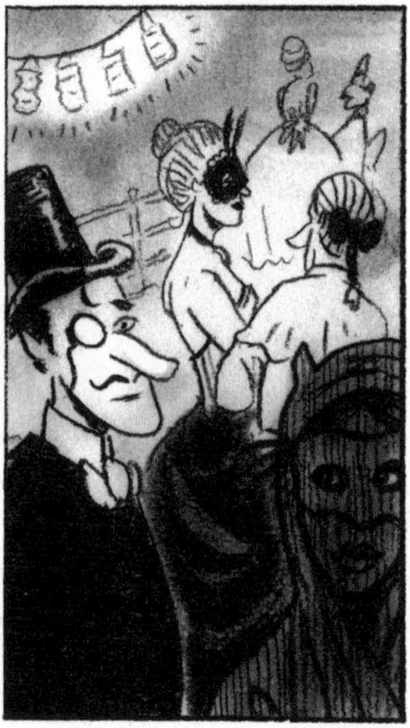

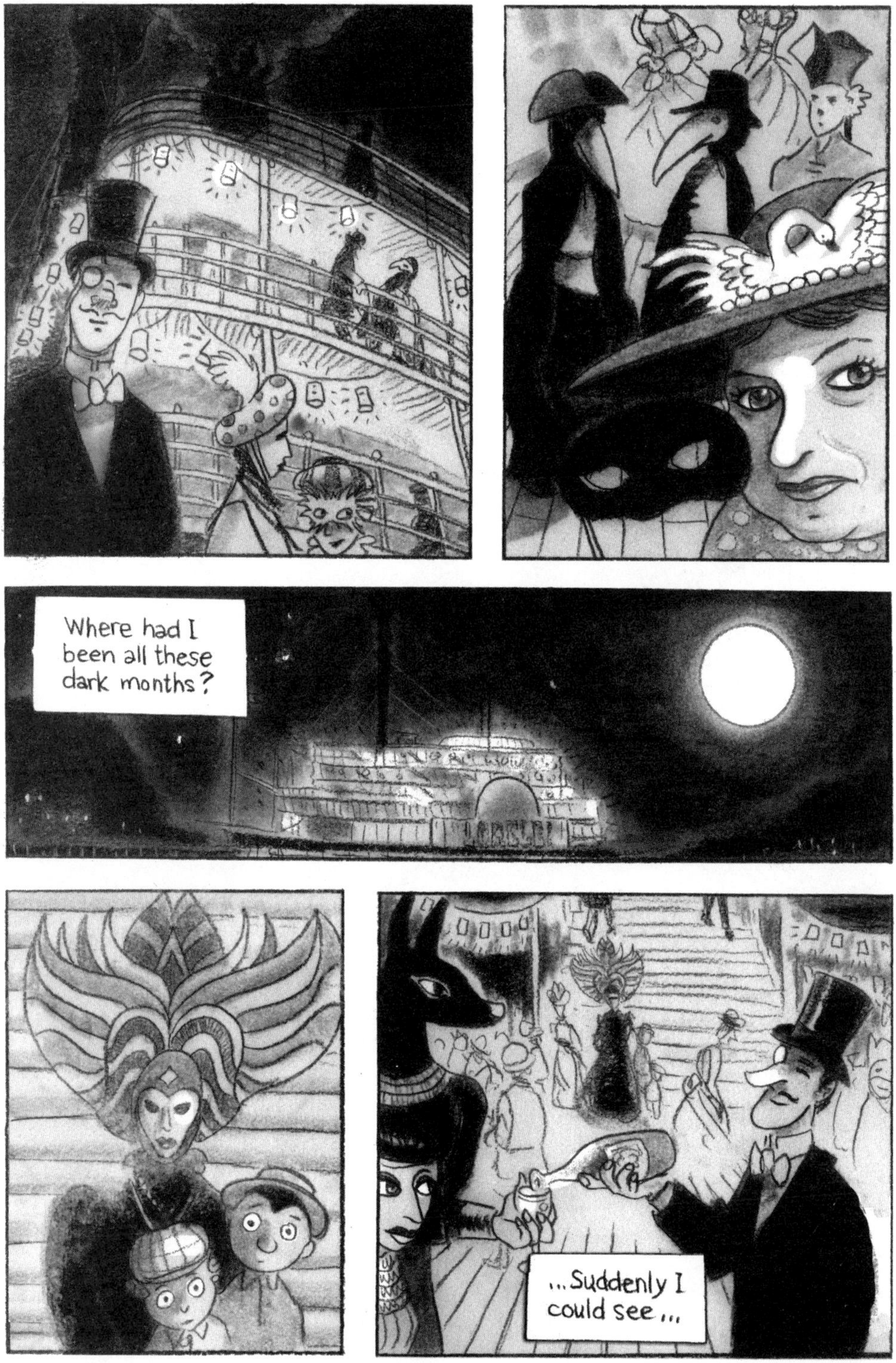
Where had I been all these dark months?
...Suddenly I could see...

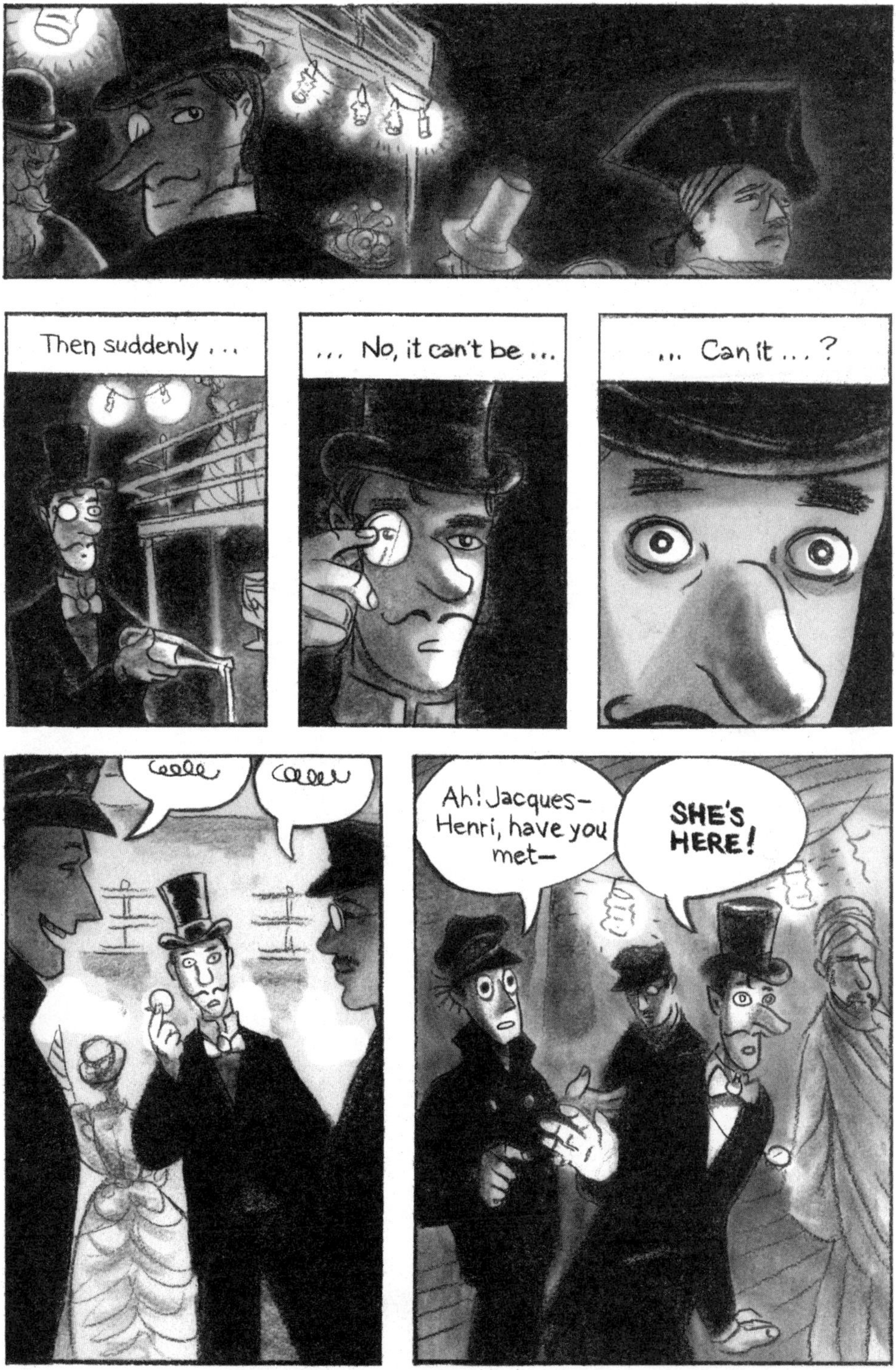
Then suddenly . . .
. . . No, it can't be . . .
. . . Can it . . . ?
Ah! Jacques-Henri, have you met—
SHE'S HERE!

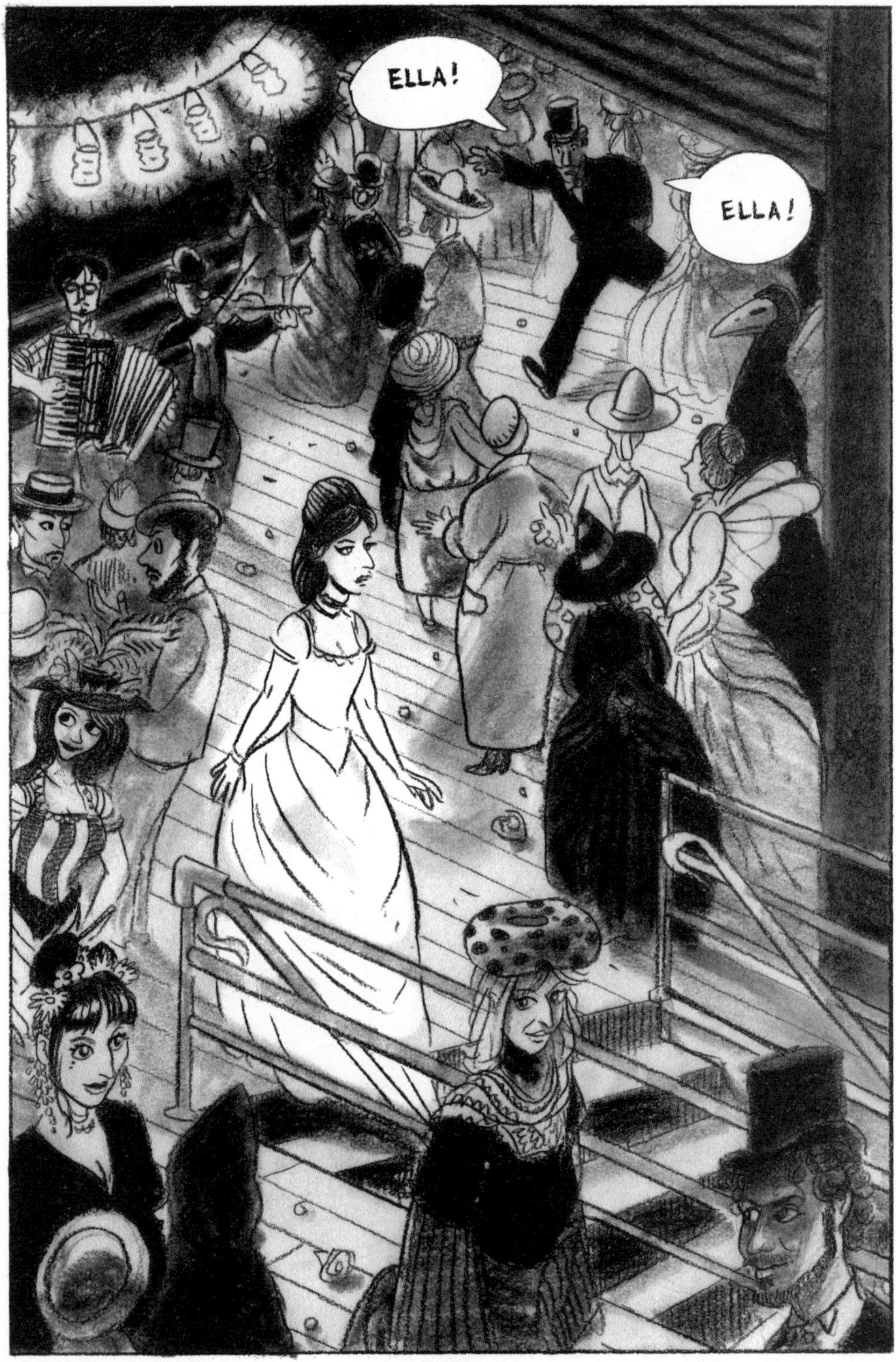
ELLA!
ELLA!

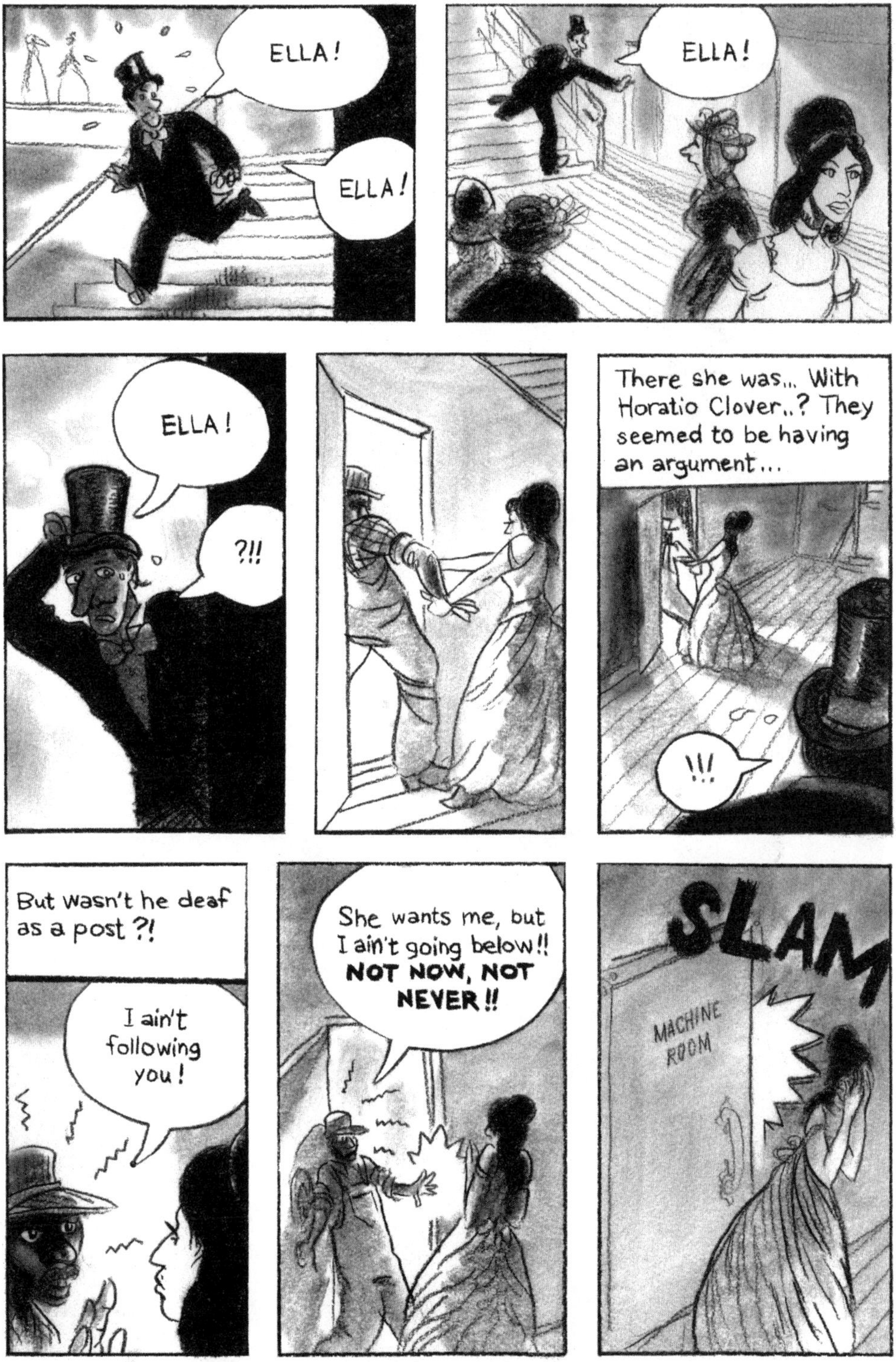
ELLA!
ELLA!
ELLA!
ELLA!
?!!
There she was... With Horatio Clover..? They seemed to be having an argument...
!!!
But wasn't he deaf as a post ?!
I ain't following you!
She wants me, but I ain't going below!! NOT NOW, NOT NEVER!!
SLAM
MACHINE ROOM

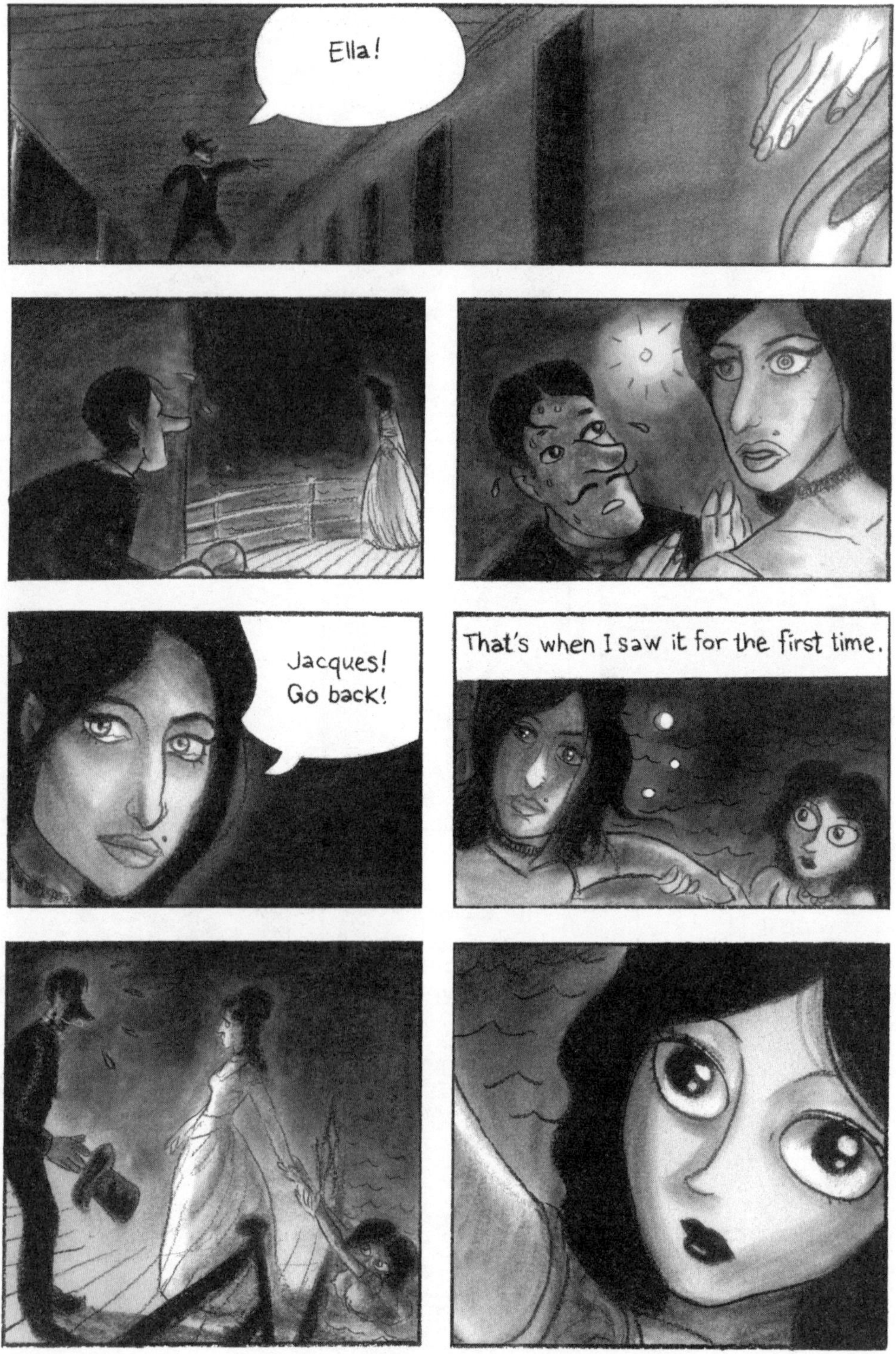
Ella!
Jacques! Go back!
That's when I saw it for the first time.

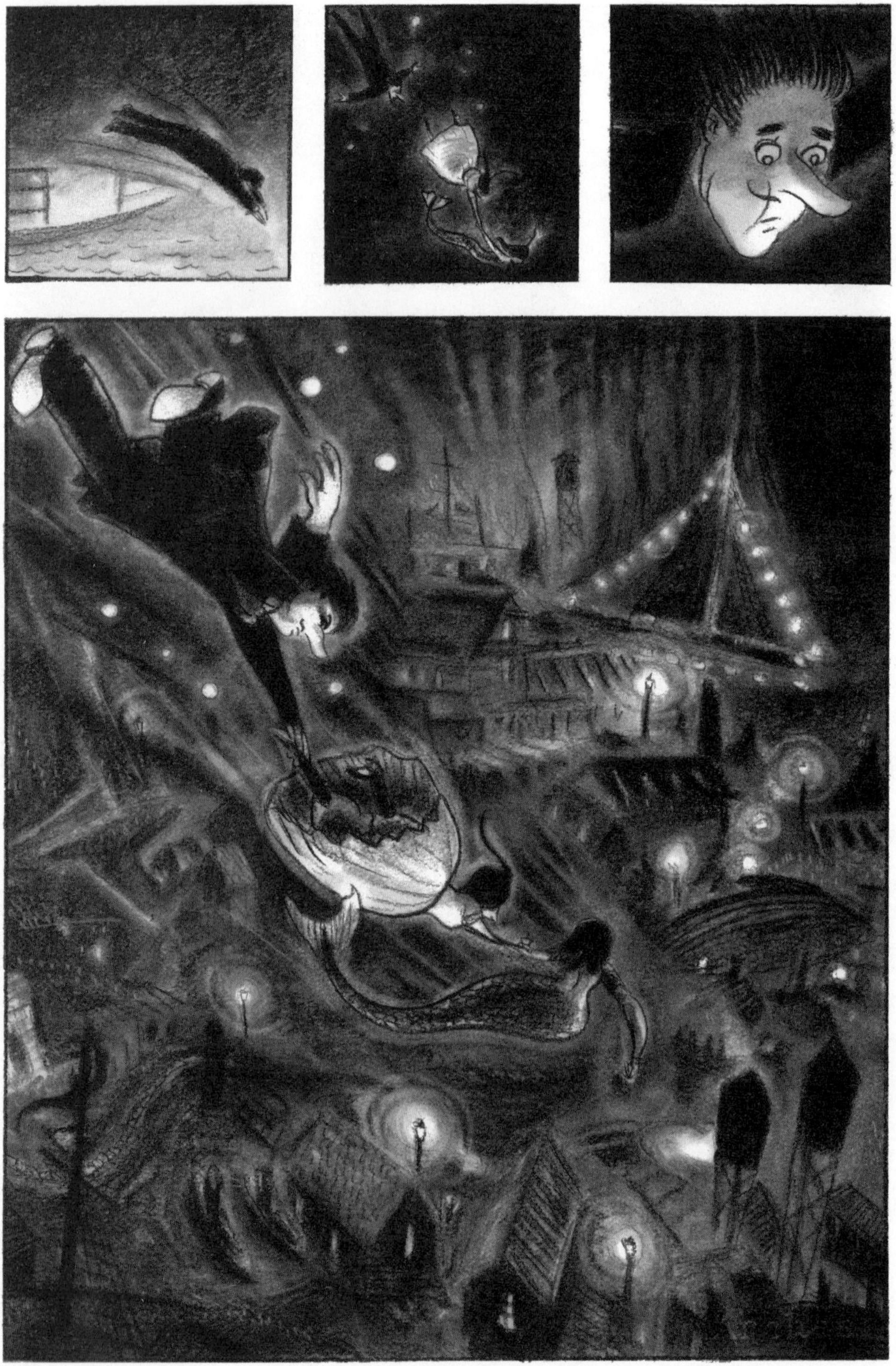

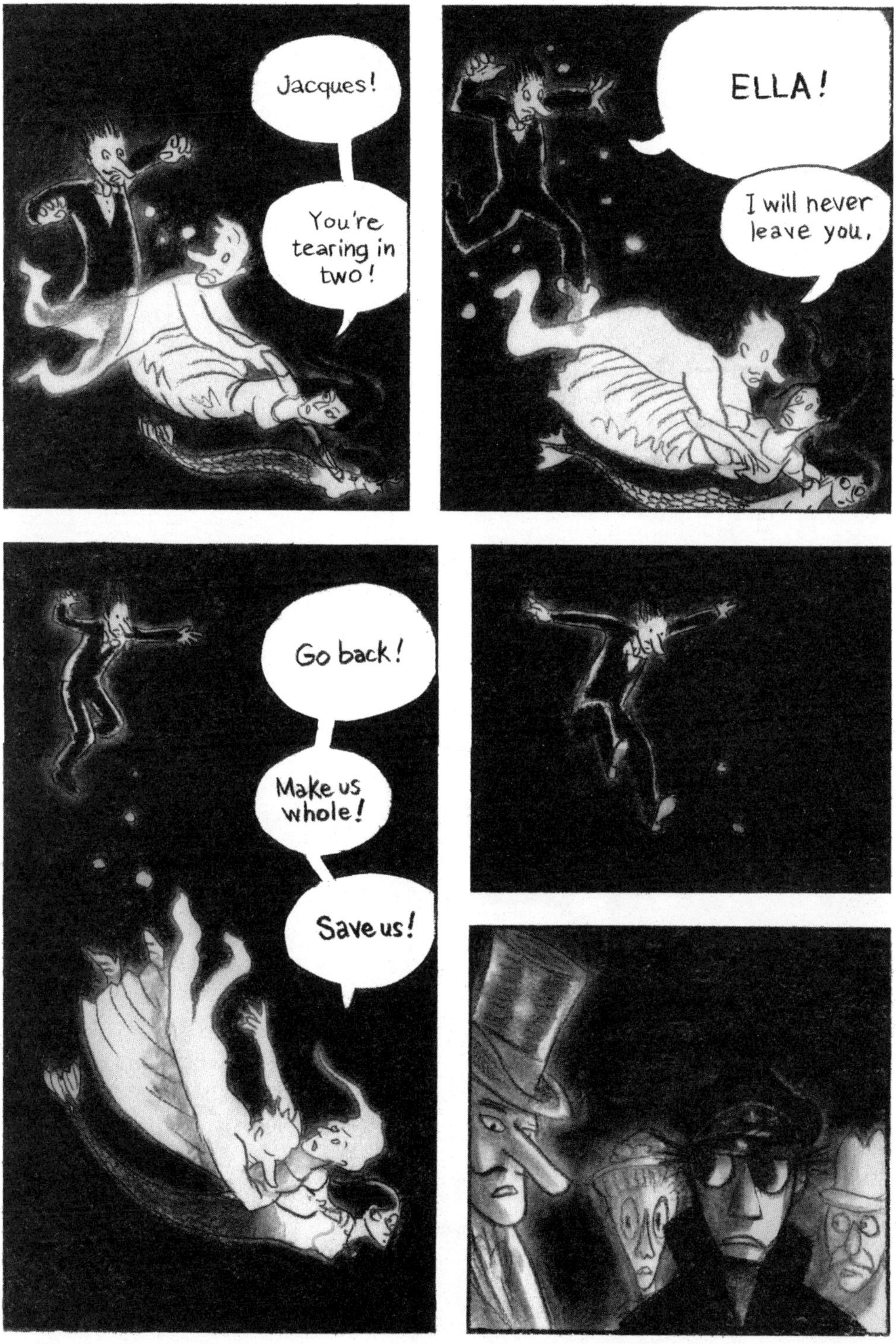
Jacques!
You're tearing in two!
ELLA!
I will never leave you,
Go back!
Make us whole!
Save us!

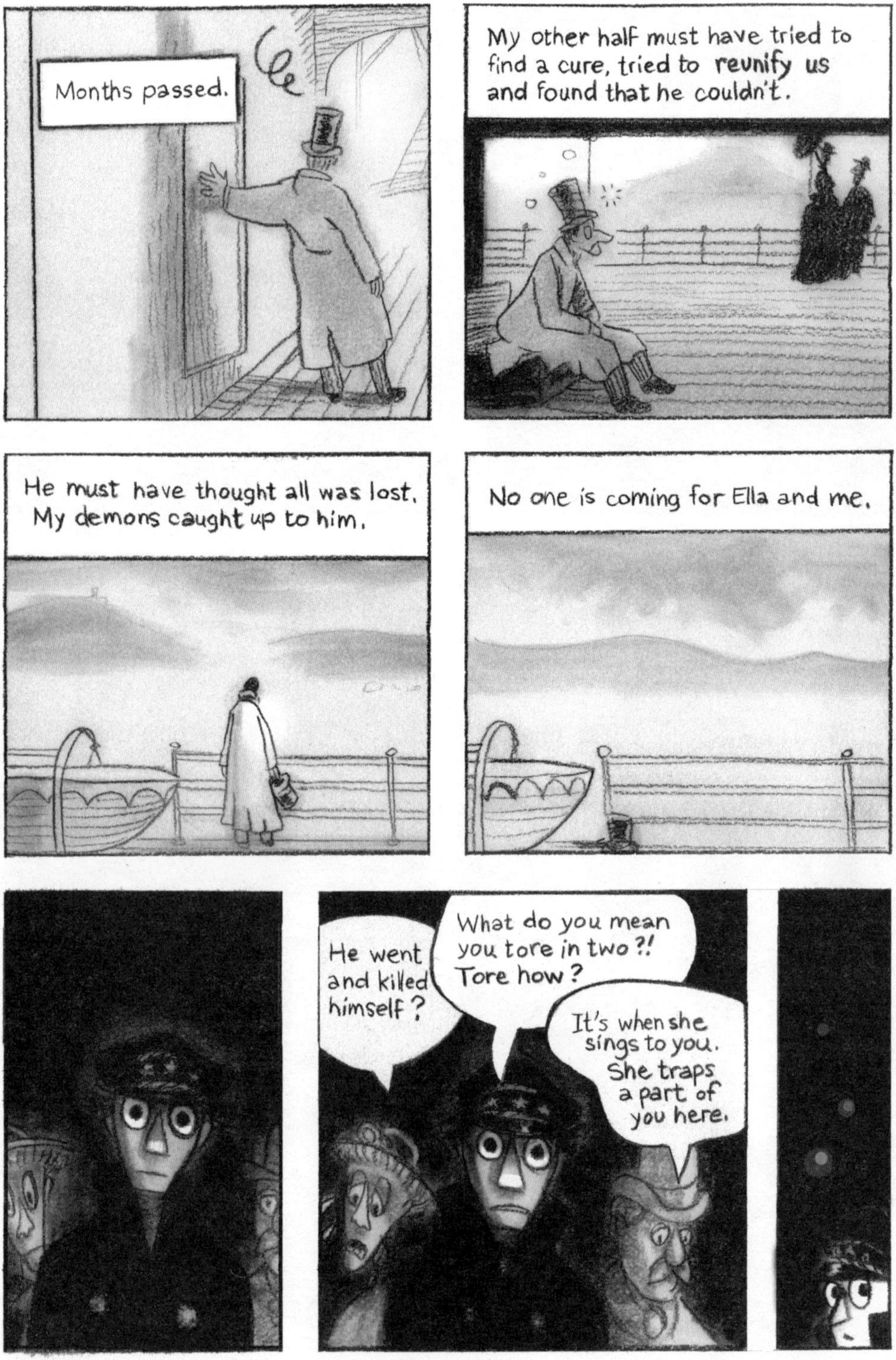
Months passed.
My other half must have tried to find a cure, tried to reunify us and found that he couldn't.
He must have thought all was lost. My demons caught up to him.
No one is coming for Ella and me.
He went and killed himself?
What do you mean you tore in two?! Tore how?
It's when she sings to you. She traps a part of you here.

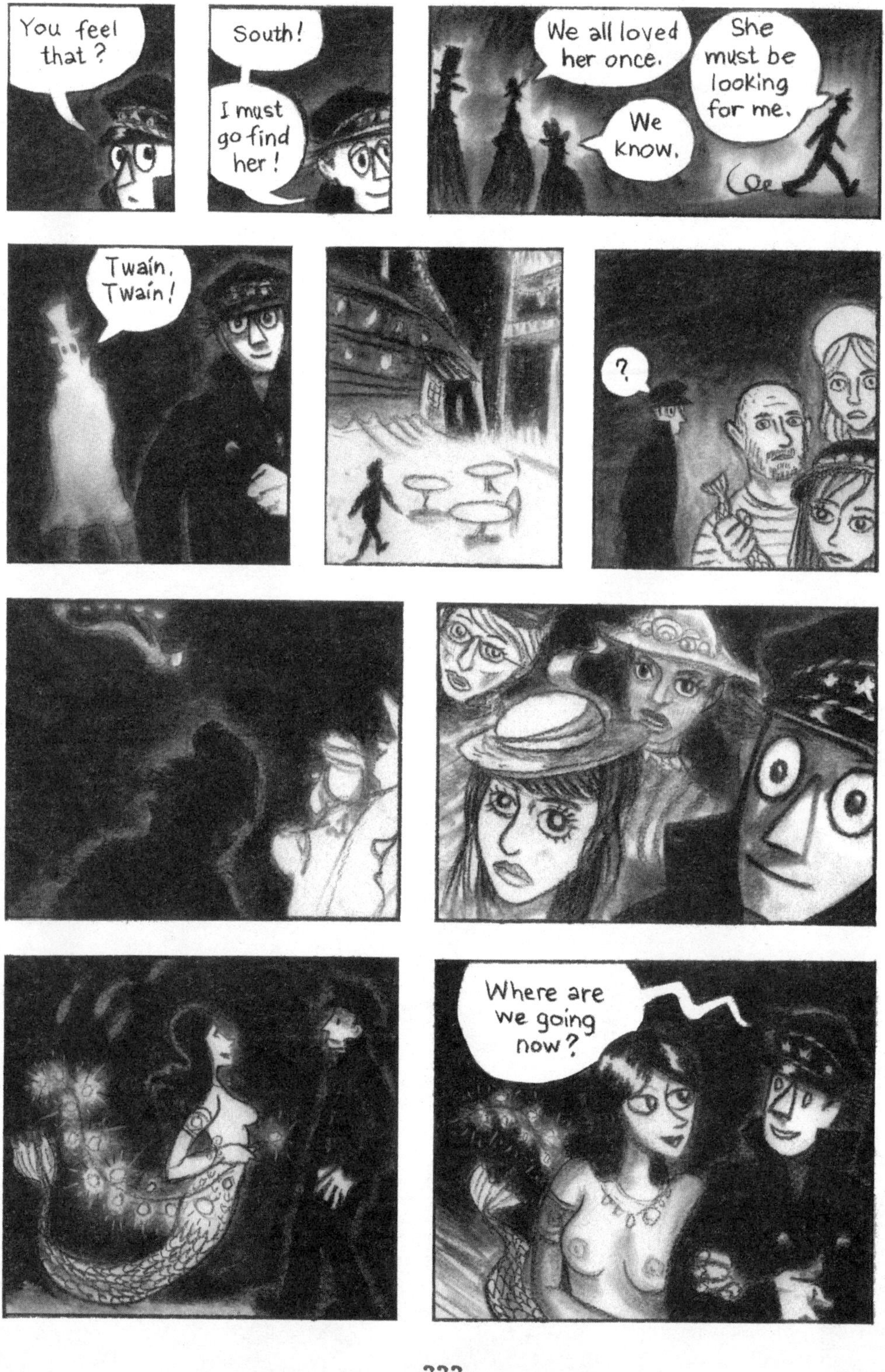
You feel that?
South!
I must go find her!
We all loved her once.
We know.
She must be looking for me.
Twain, Twain!
?
Where are we going now?

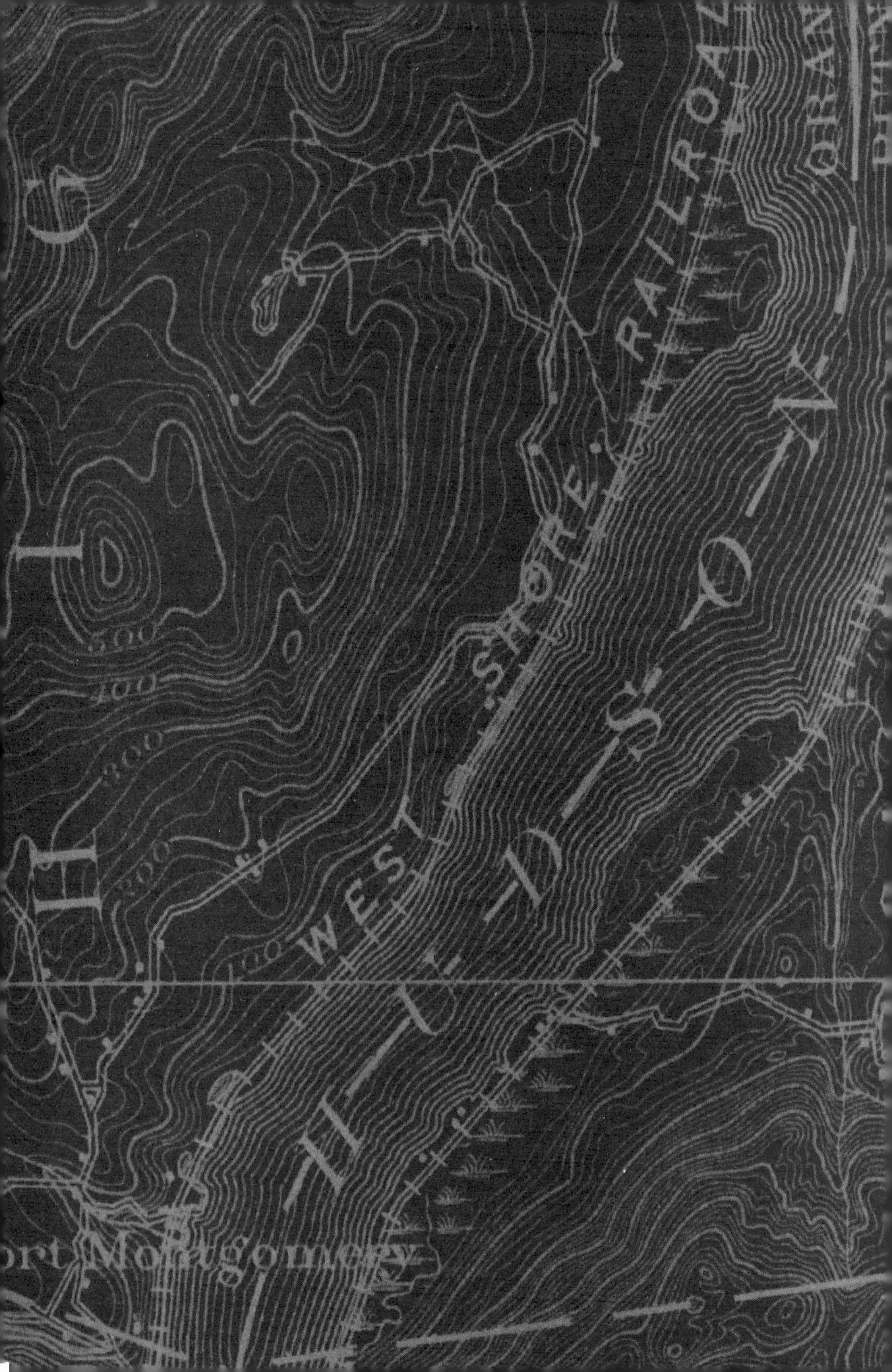
WEST SHORE
RAILROA
HUDSON
ort Montgomery
500
400
300
200
100

Pt III, Chap. 4

"THE CHAINED HEART"

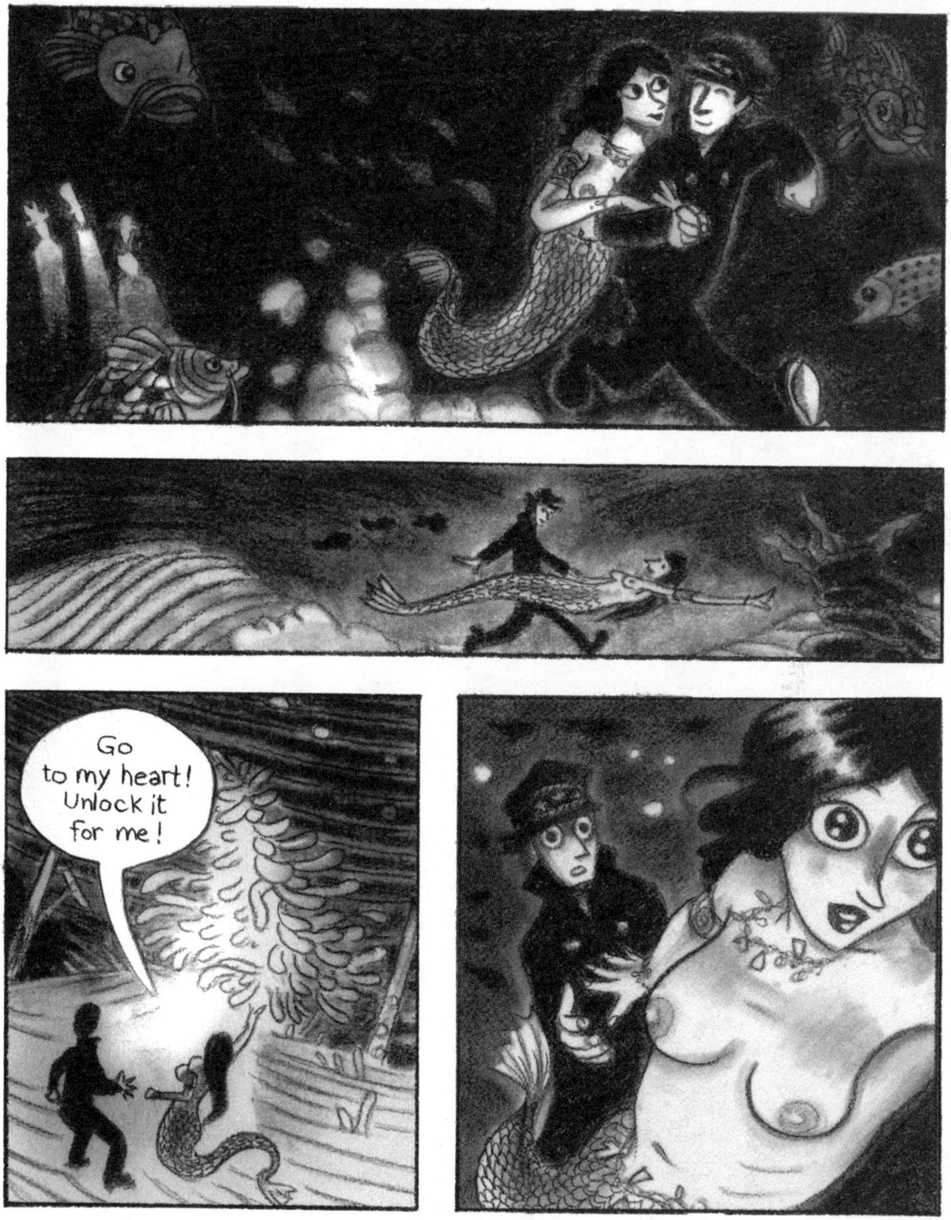
Go to my heart! Unlock it for me!

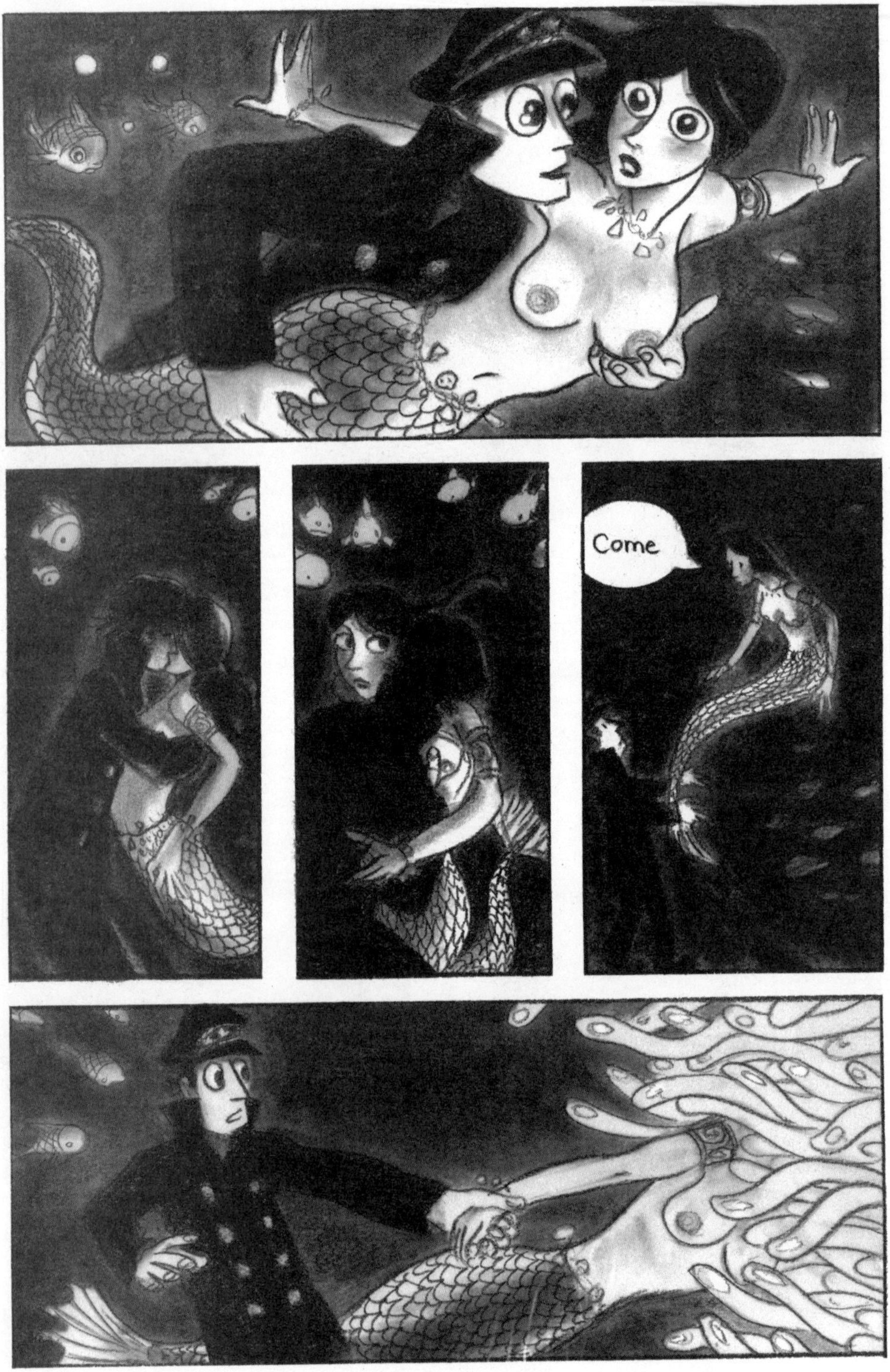
Come

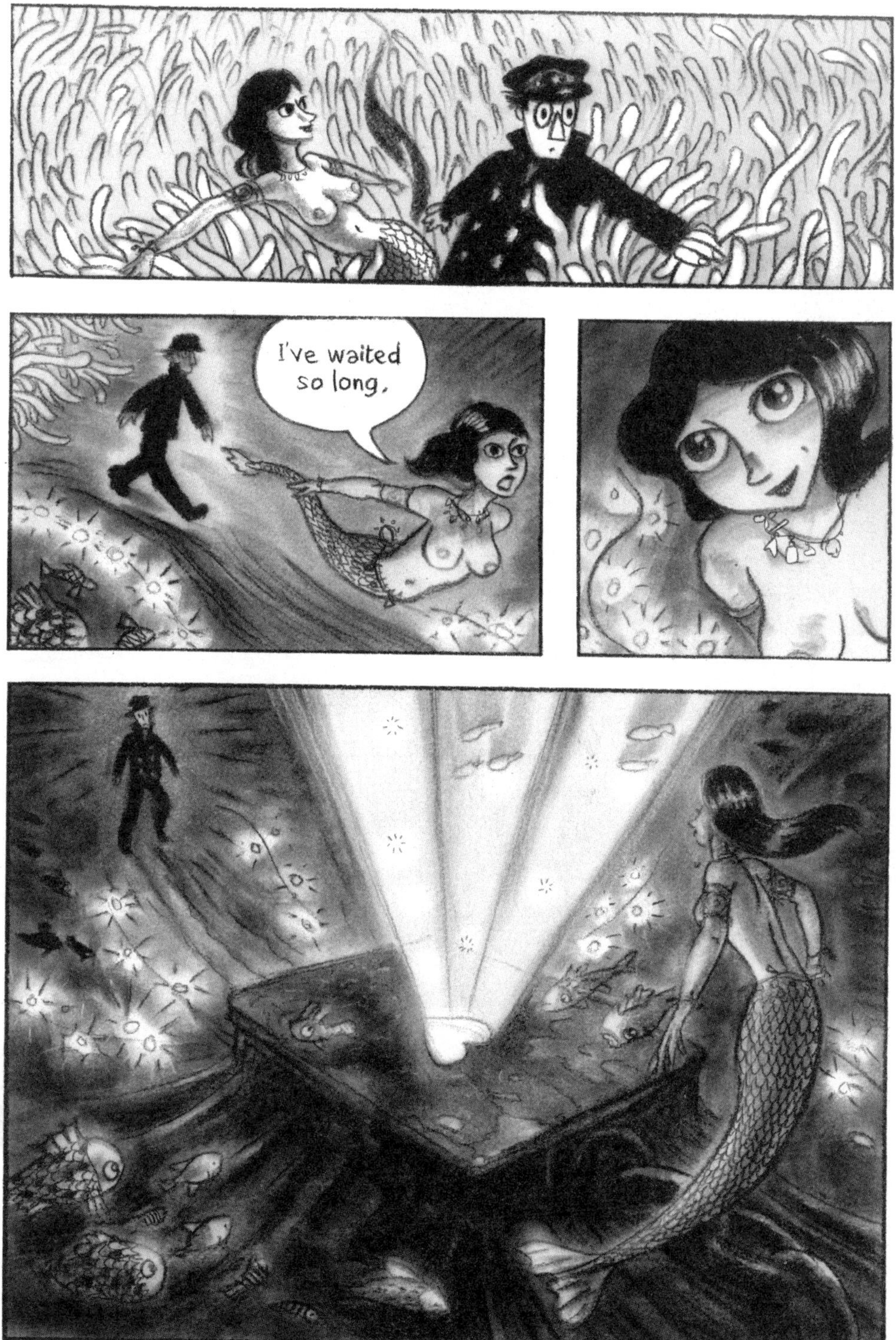
I've waited
so long.

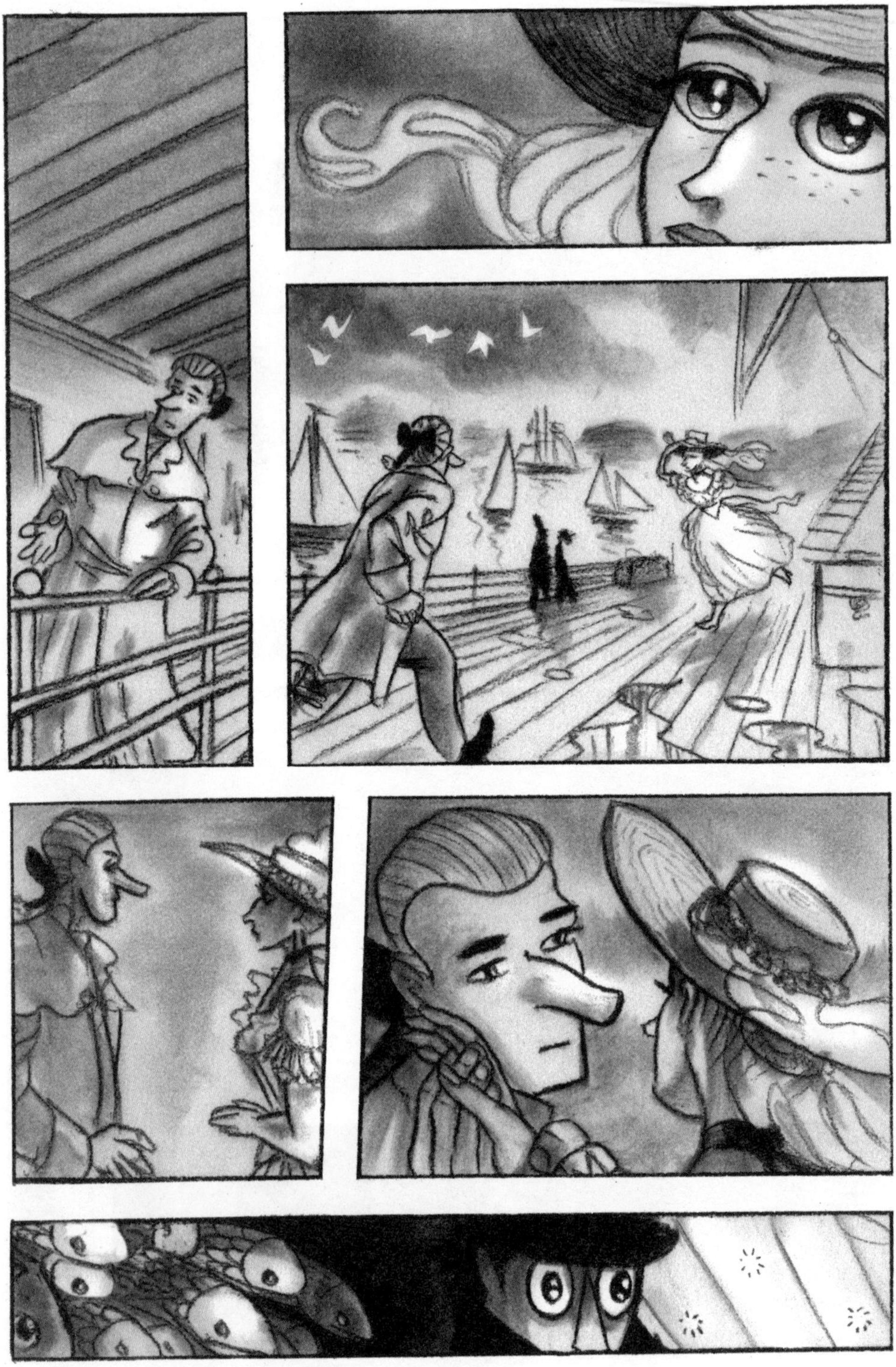

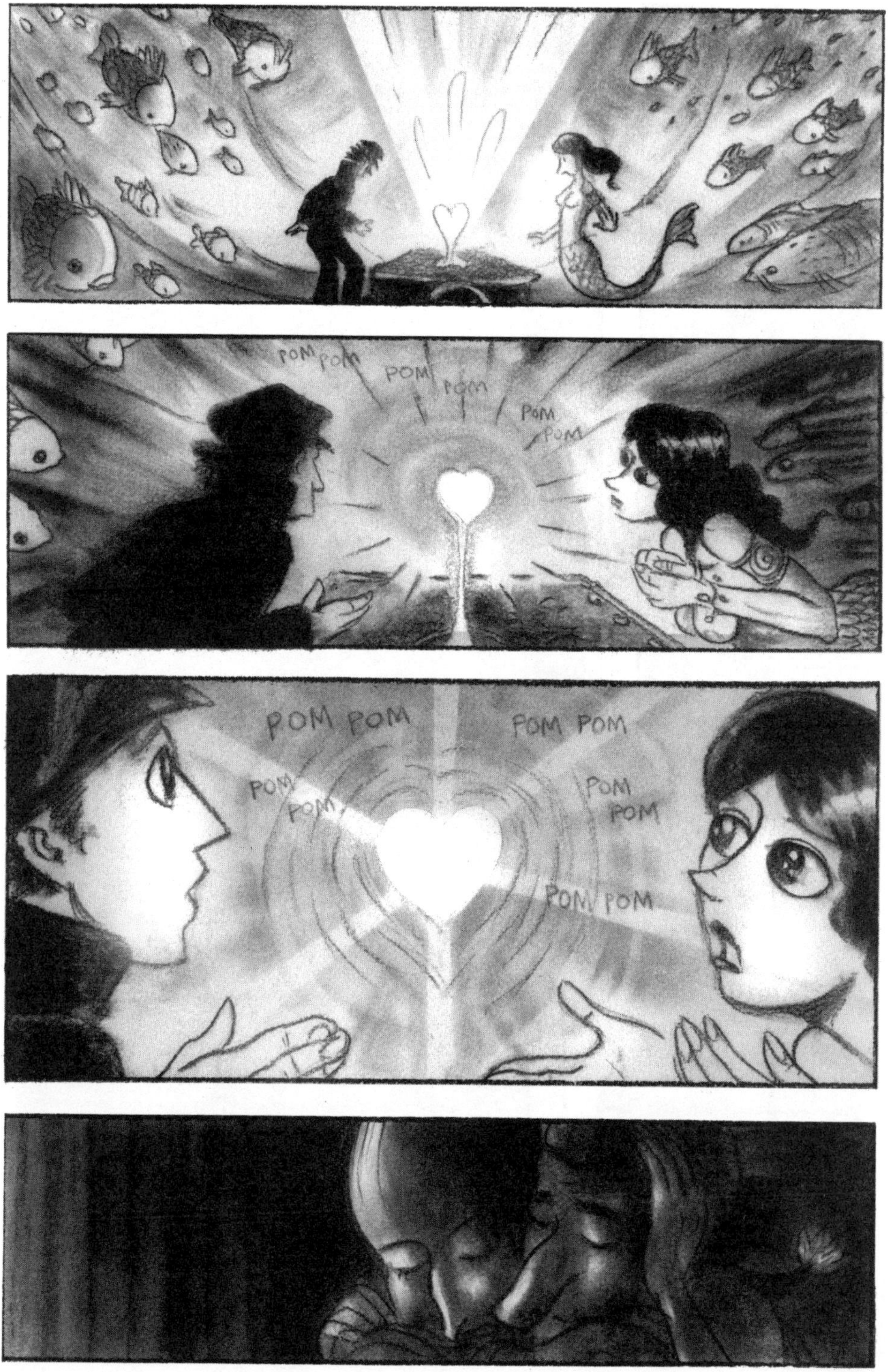
POM
POM
POM
POM
POM
POM
POM POM
POM POM
POM
POM
POM
POM
POM POM

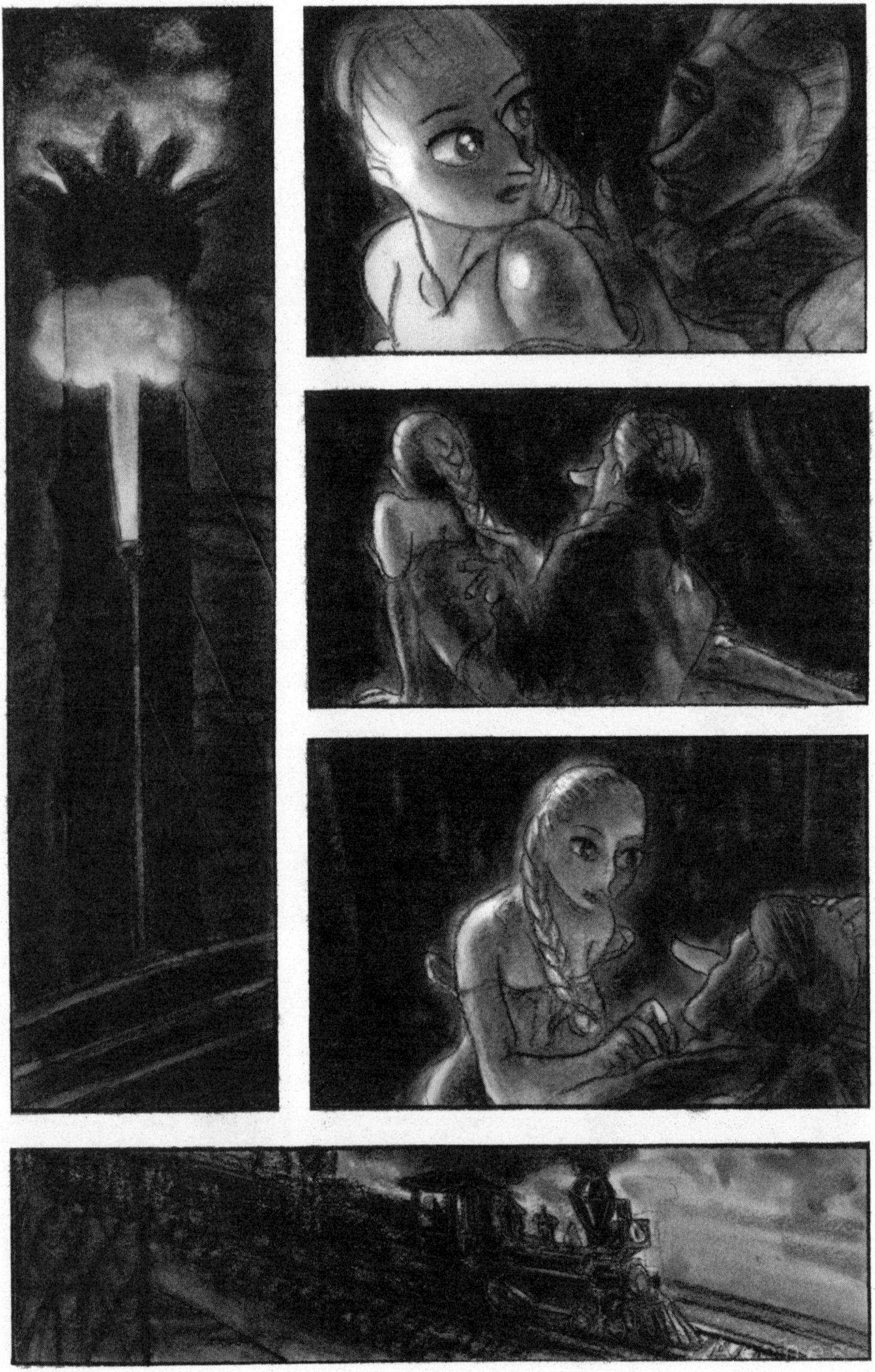

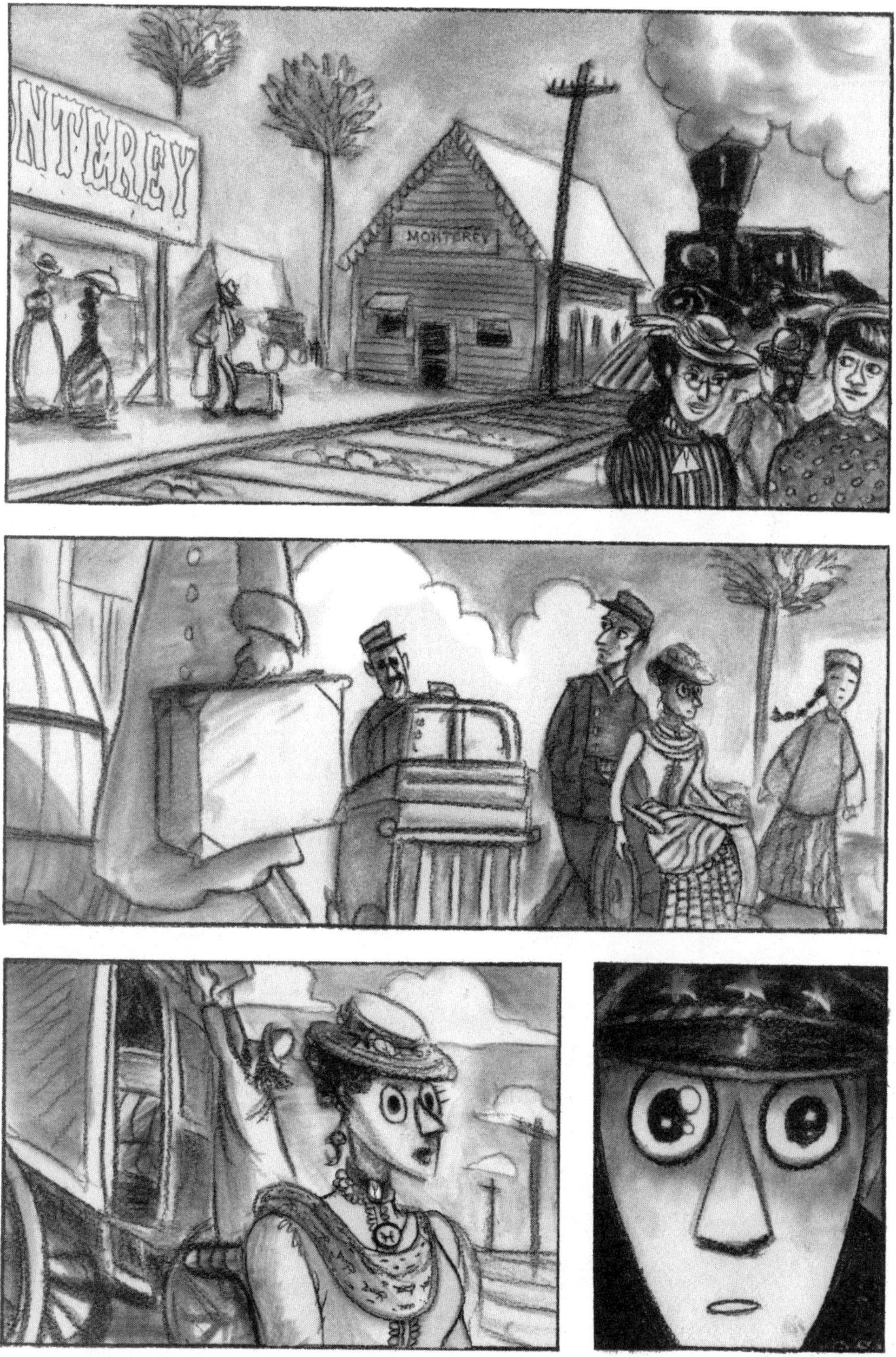
NTEREY
MONTEREY

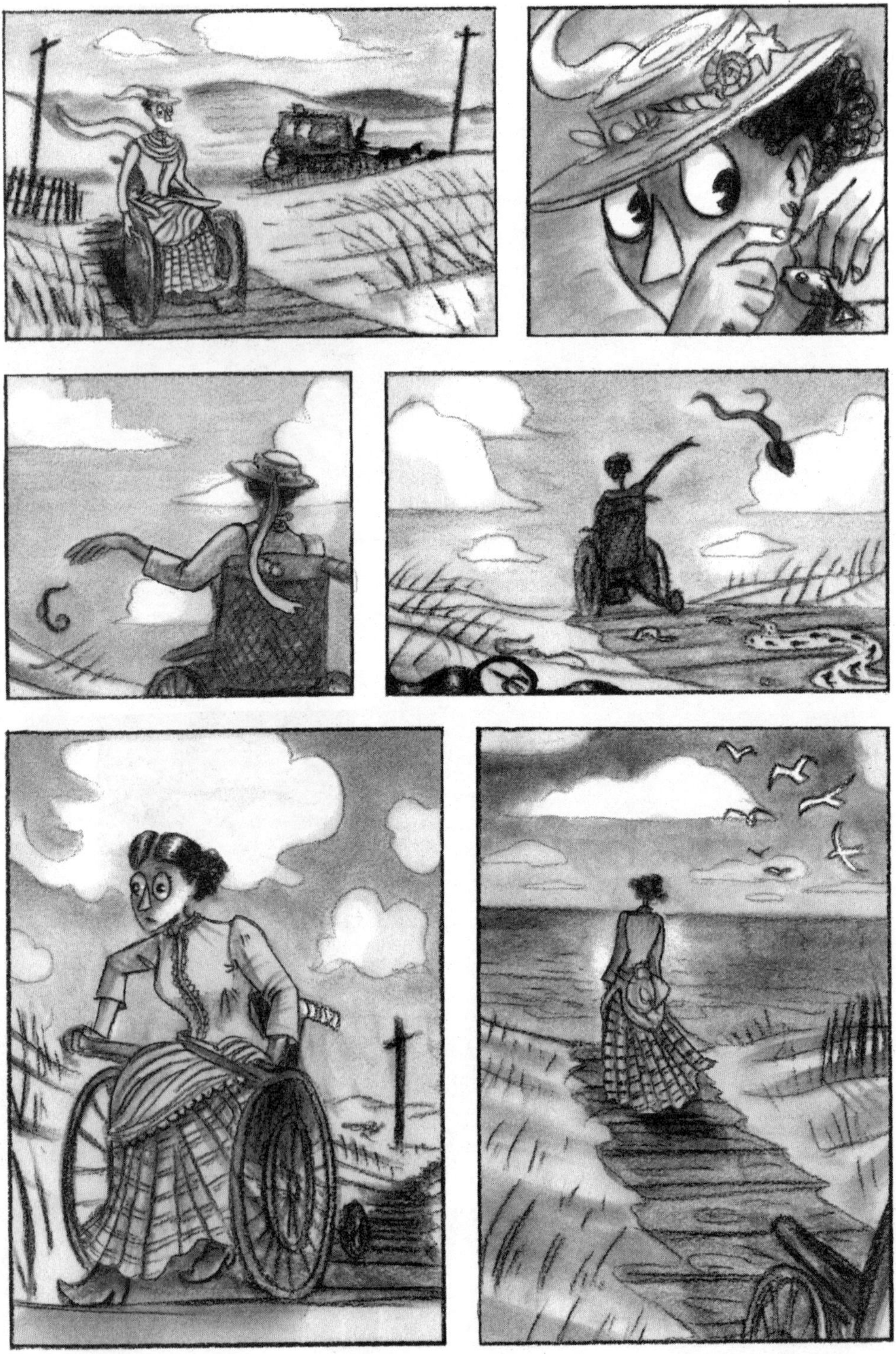

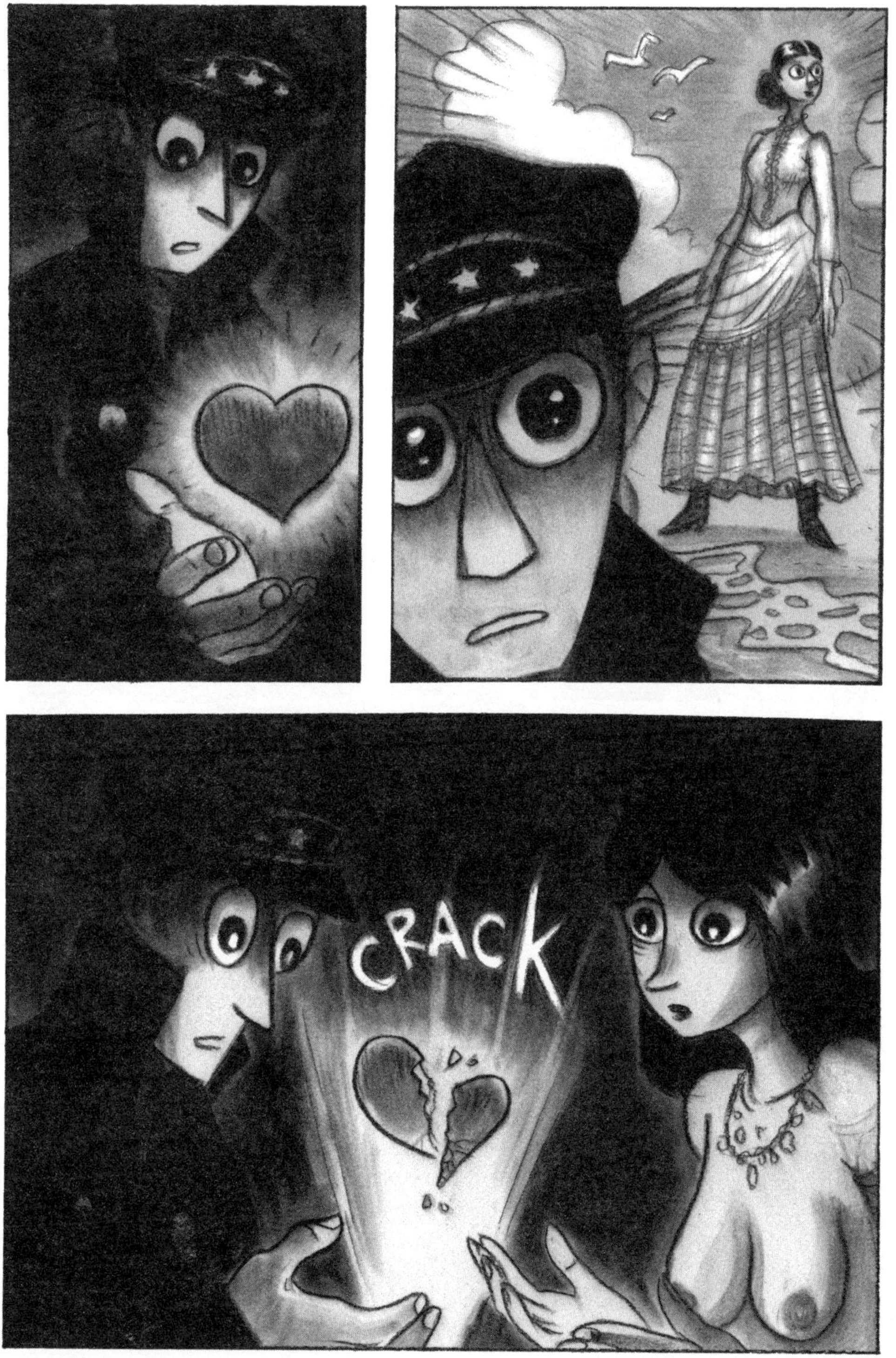
CRACK

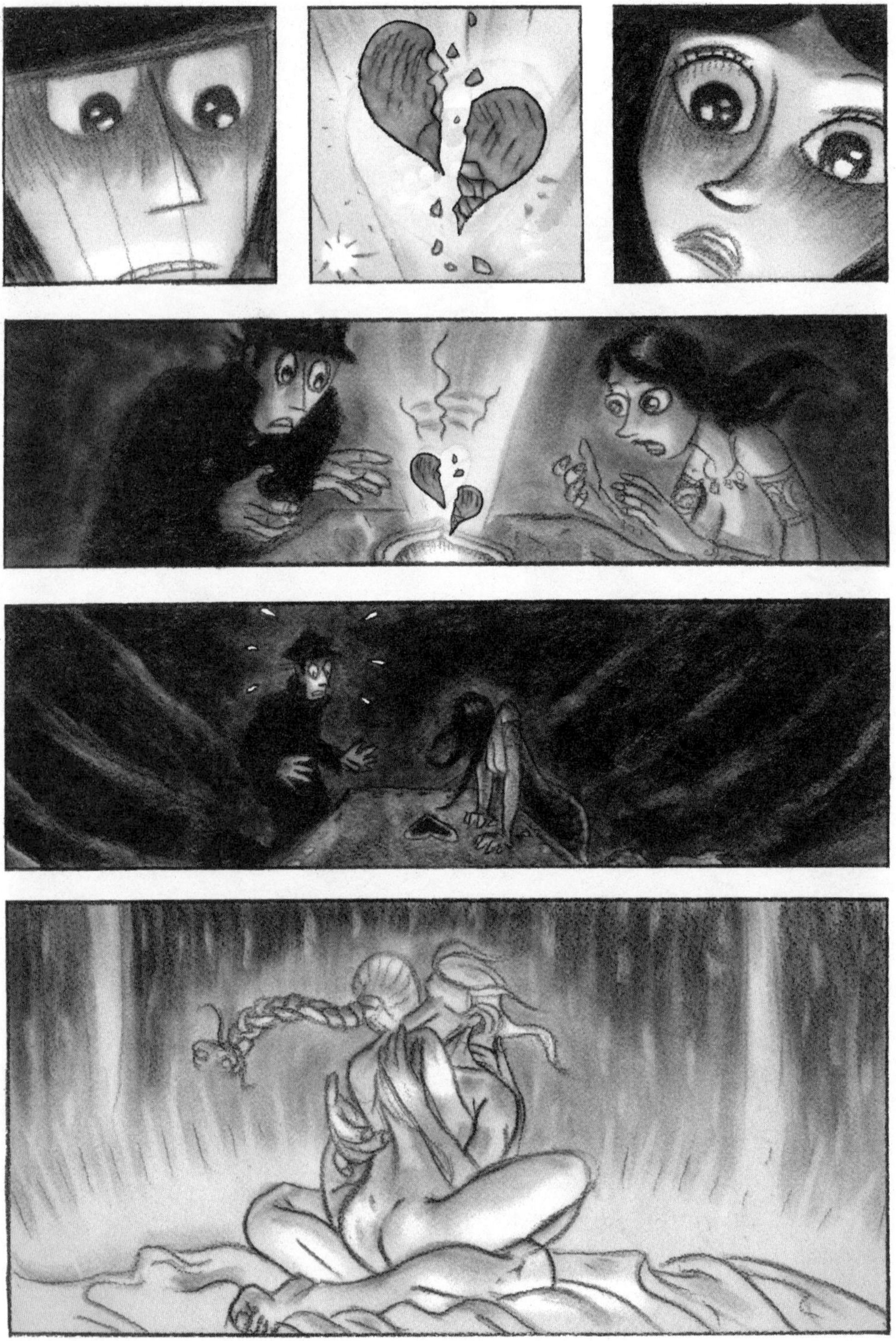

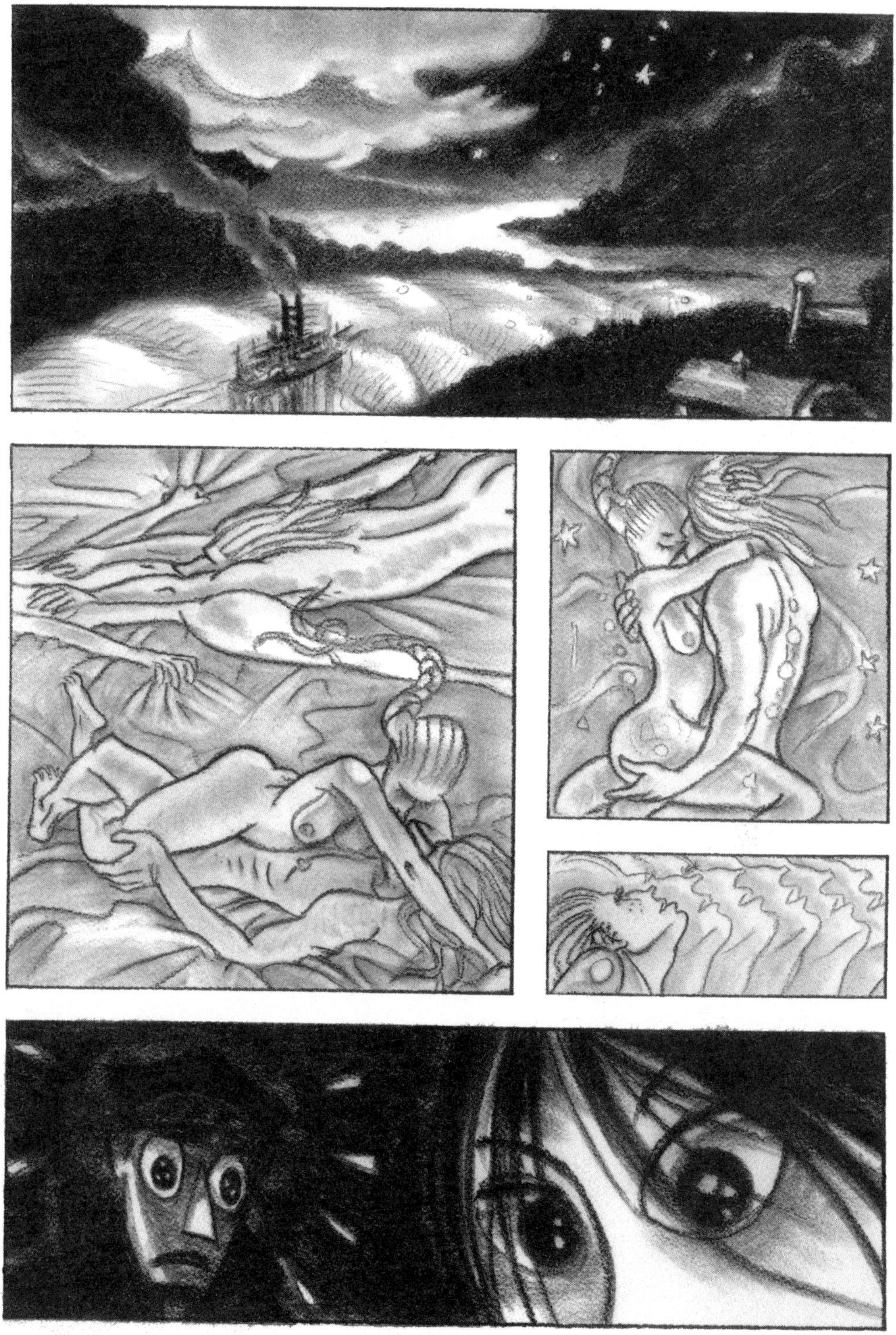

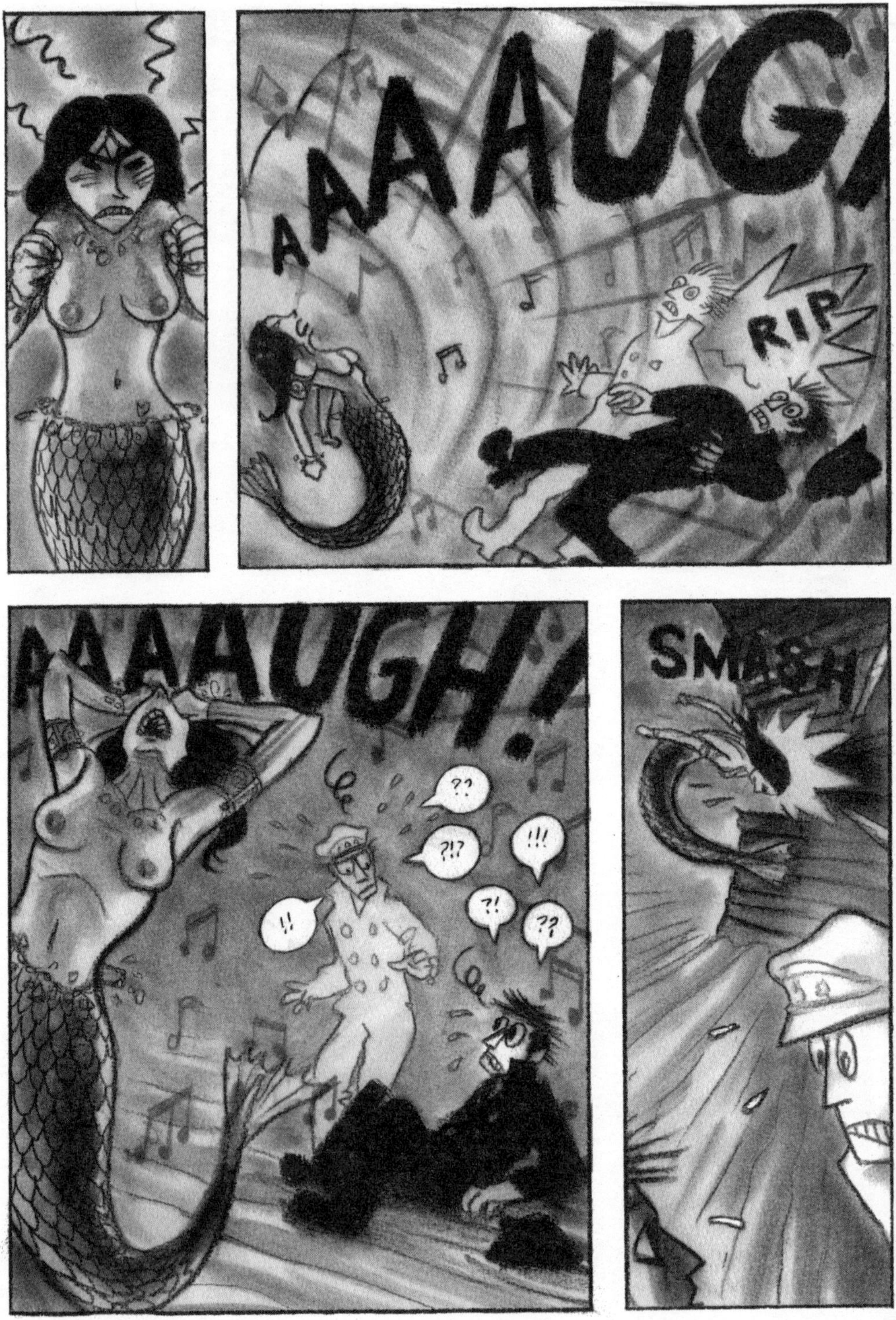
AAAAUG
RIP
AAAAUGH!
??
?!?
!!!
!!
?!
??
SMASH

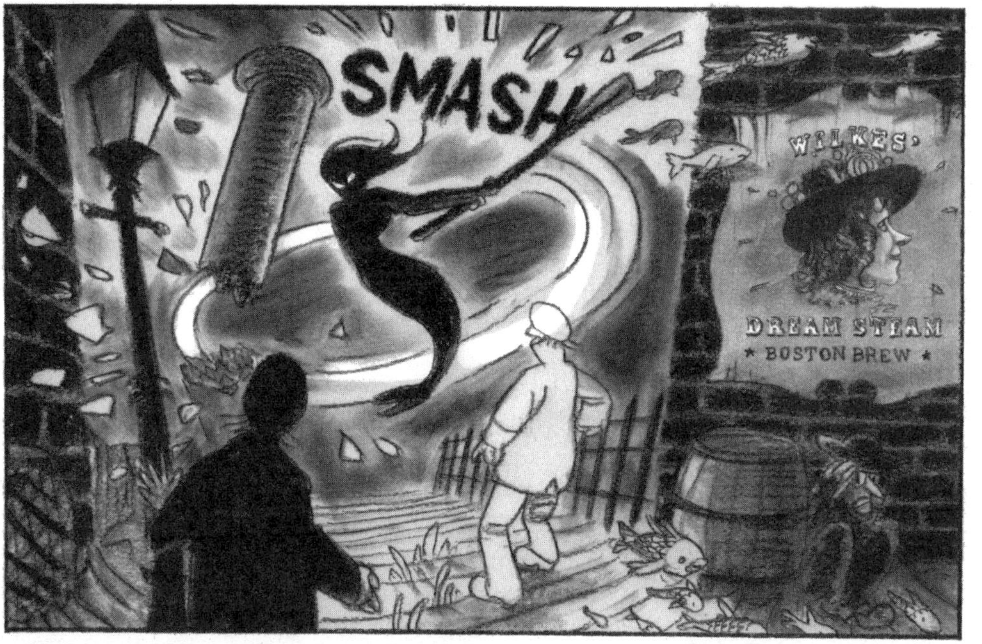
SMASH
WILKES'
DREAM STEAM
★ BOSTON BREW ★

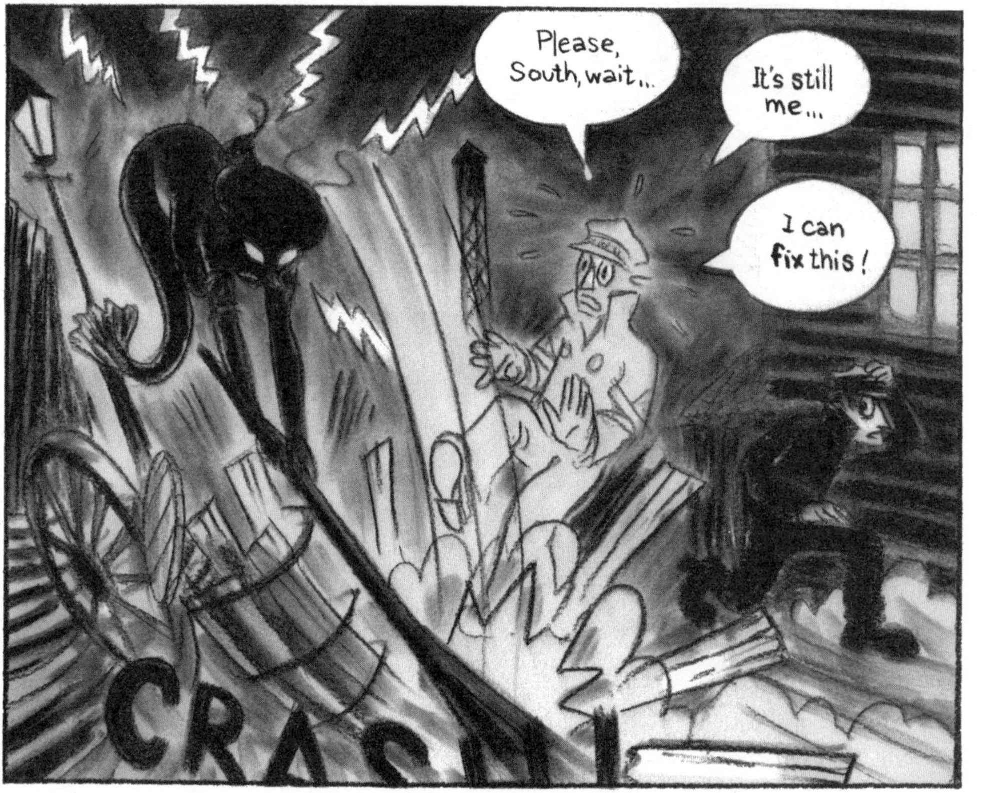
Please, South, wait...
It's still me...
I can fix this!
CRASH

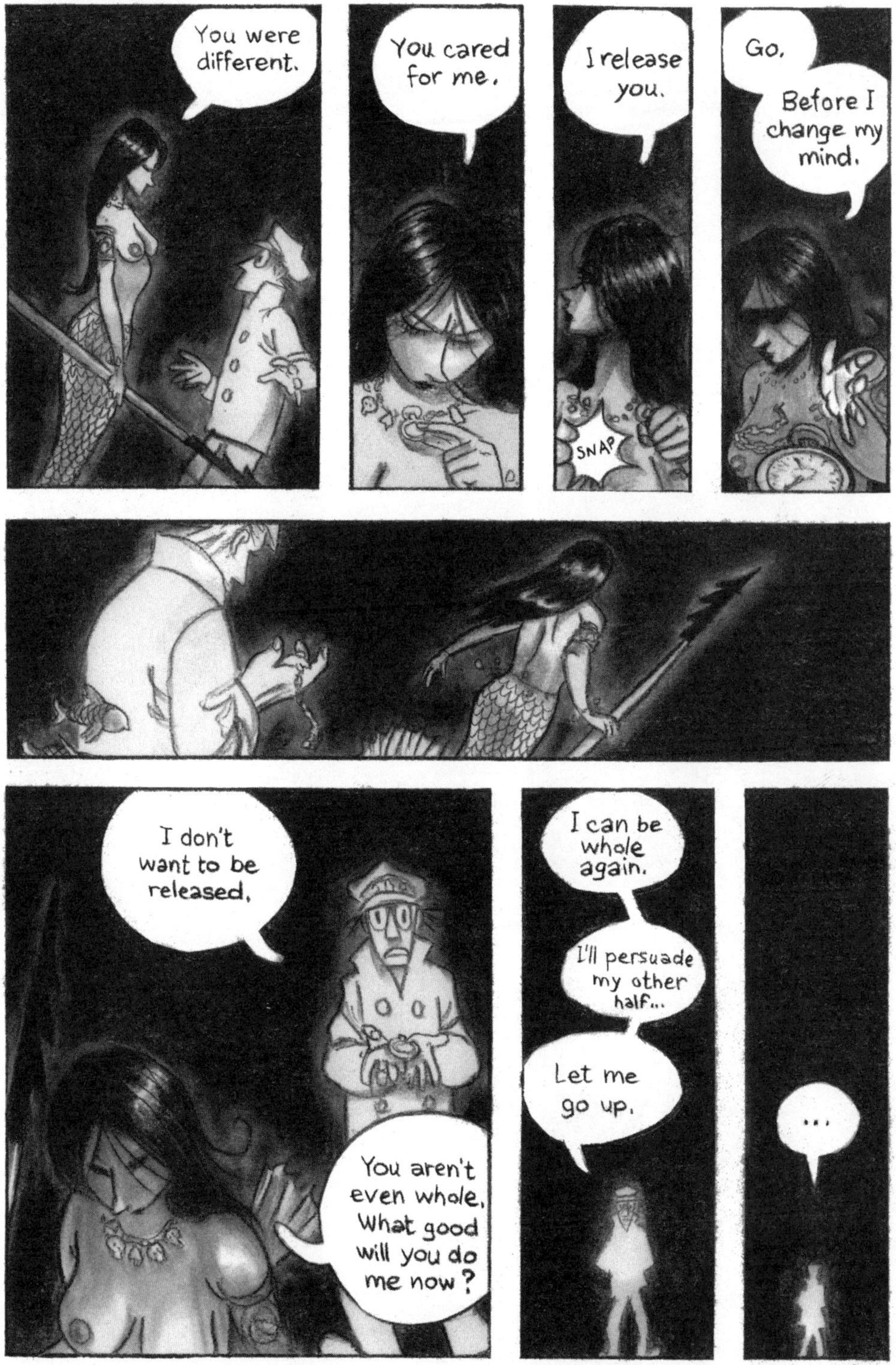
You were different.
You cared for me.
I release you.
SNAP
Go.
Before I change my mind.
I don't want to be released.
You aren't even whole. What good will you do me now?
I can be whole again.
I'll persuade my other half...
Let me go up.
...

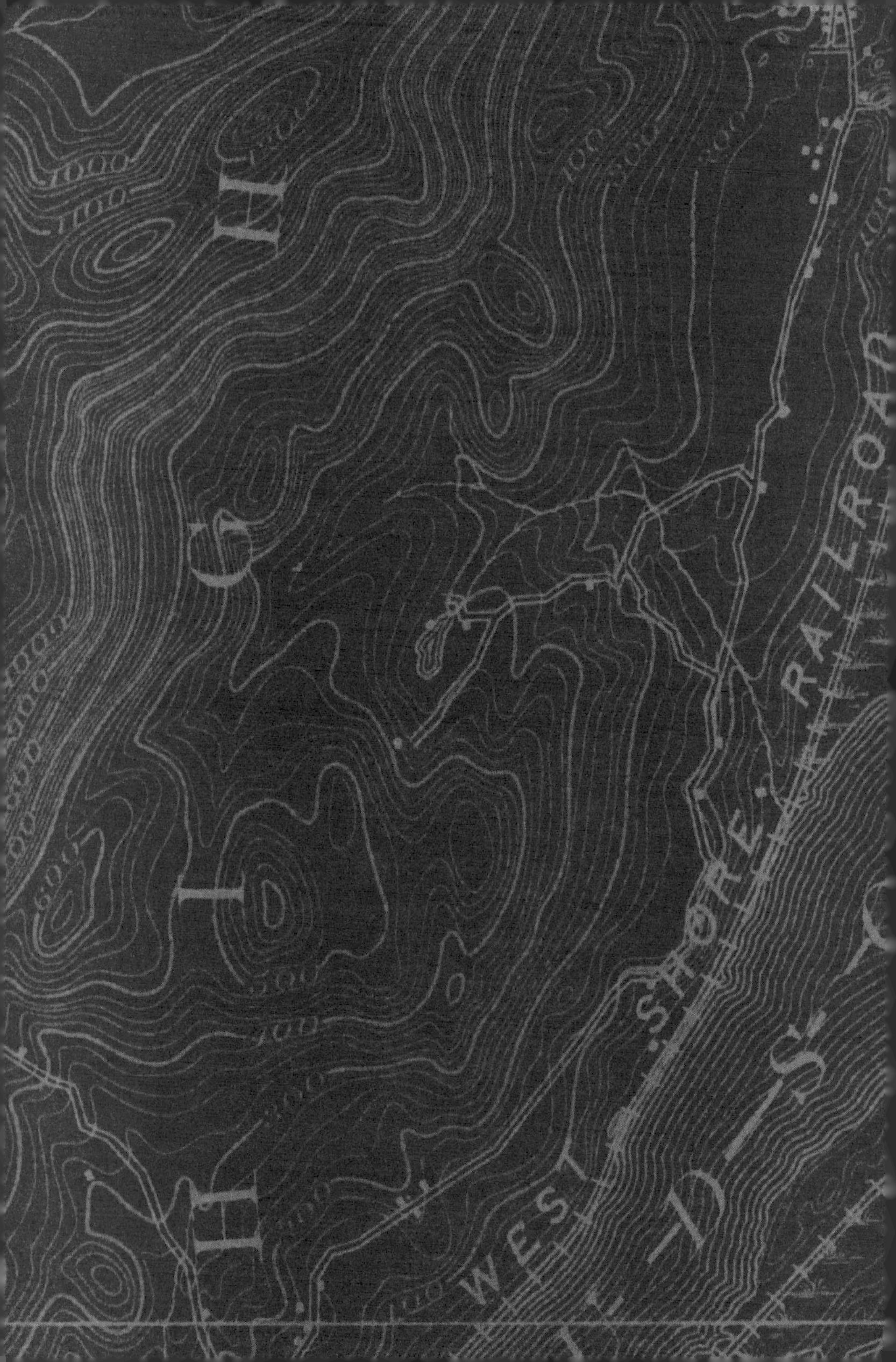

WEST SHORE RAILROAD
H
G
I
H
D
S
1000
1100
500
400
100

SUMMER STORM

by Elijah Twain

...hty river flow...
...housands...

C.G. Beaverton's
CRETS *MYSTERIES
OF THE RIVER HUDSON

. BEAVERTON
AUTHOR OF

CRETS AND MYS
THE RIVER H

A RARE PUBLI
ON SEVERING CRUEL BONDS

Beaverton went on: "...to witness the four
physical cruelty, in our daily news... The
Tennessee lynchings are but the latest...
Have I lured you all here today under false
pretenses? No doubt many of you woul
rather hear about the legends and folktale
of the Hudson, than to be outraged wit
me over the latest ghastly headlines.
But how can we not be trouble
Why does cruelty sedu
Why does it have
...uman fa...

THE END

Part Four
SAILOR TWAIN

A BENEFIT FOR N.A.W.S.A.
WOMEN'S SUFFRAGE ASSOCIATION

WEEKLY.

HARPER'S

New-York Ti

NEW-YORK, WEDNESDAY, NOVEMBER 18, 1887

FOUND GUILT

Stripped of captainc

DISAST
STEAMBO
Survivors not
Explosion rep

Tria concludes in mi

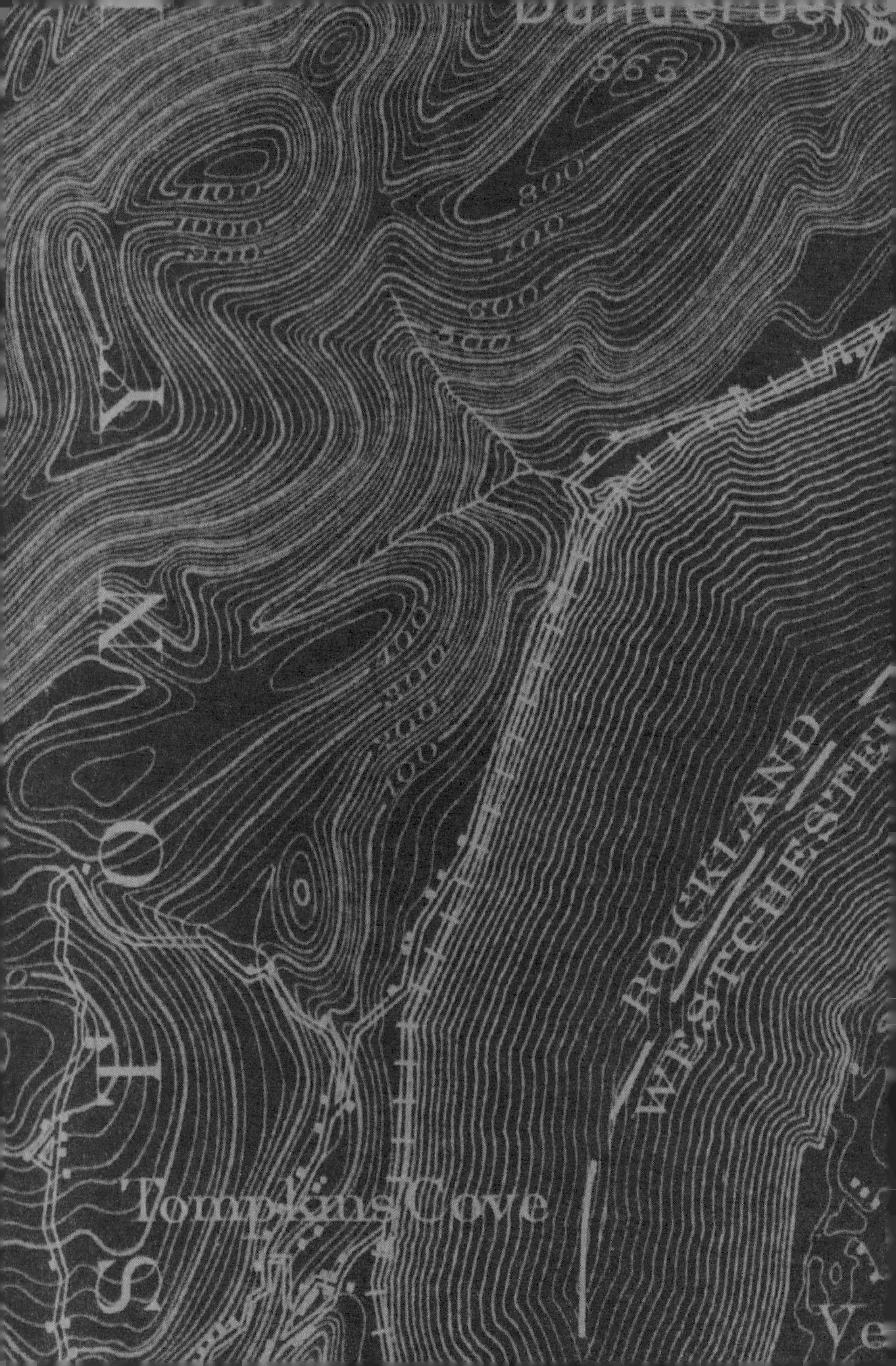

865
1000
800
700
600
500
400
300
200
100
ROCKLAND
Tompkins Cove

Pt IV, Chap.1

"THE TWAIN SHALL MEET"

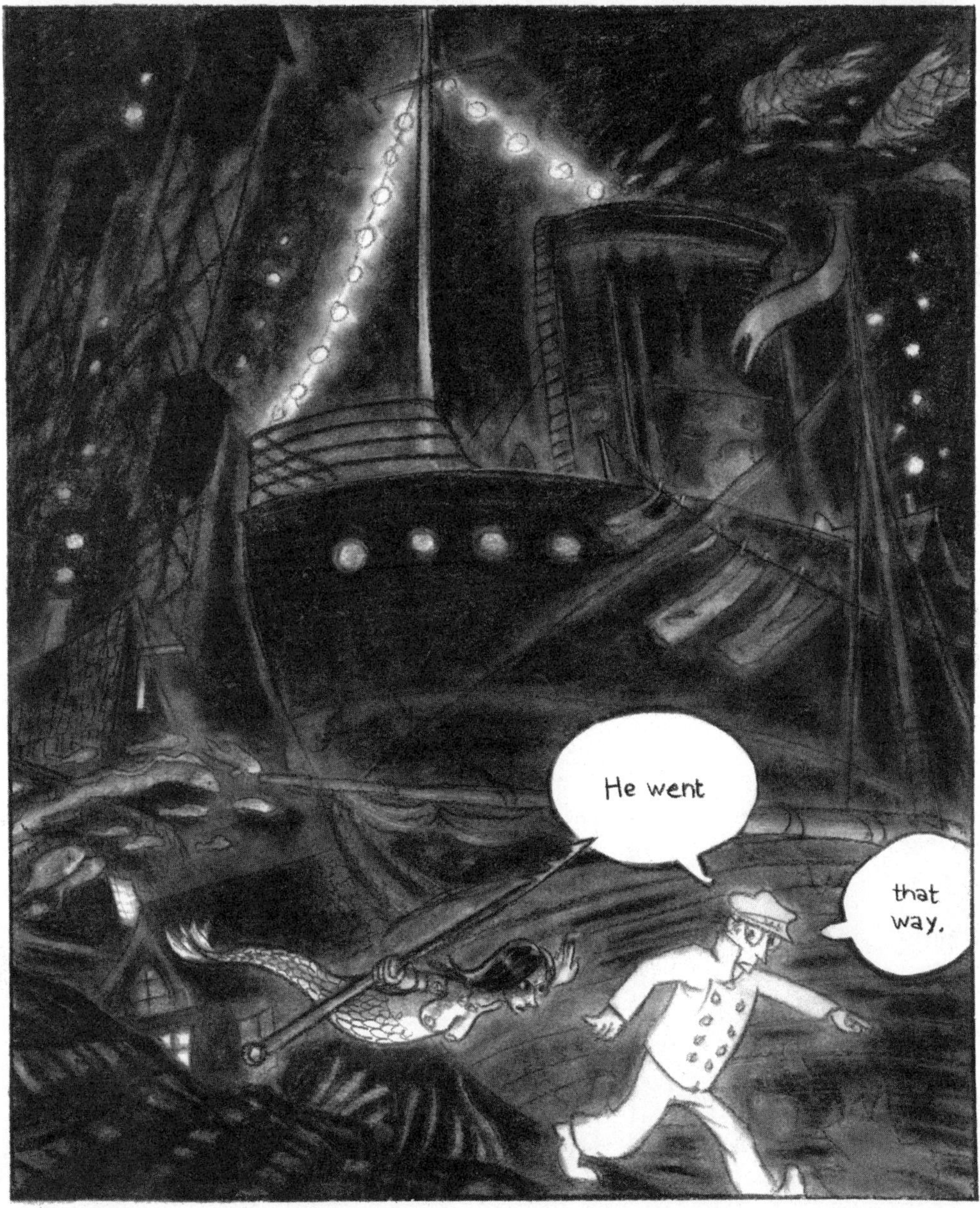
He went
that way.

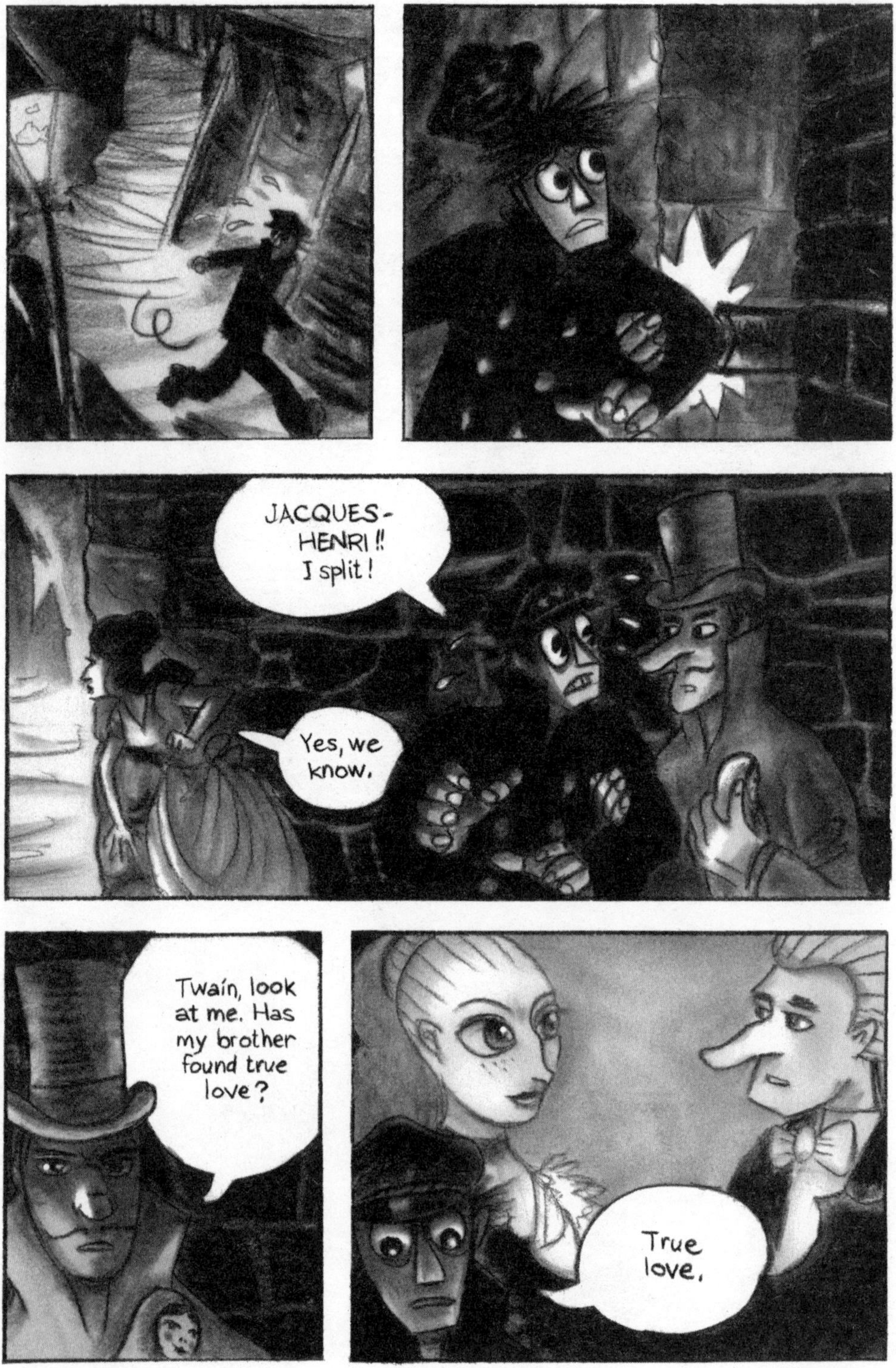
JACQUES-HENRI!! I split!
Yes, we know.
Twain, look at me. Has my brother found true love?
True love.

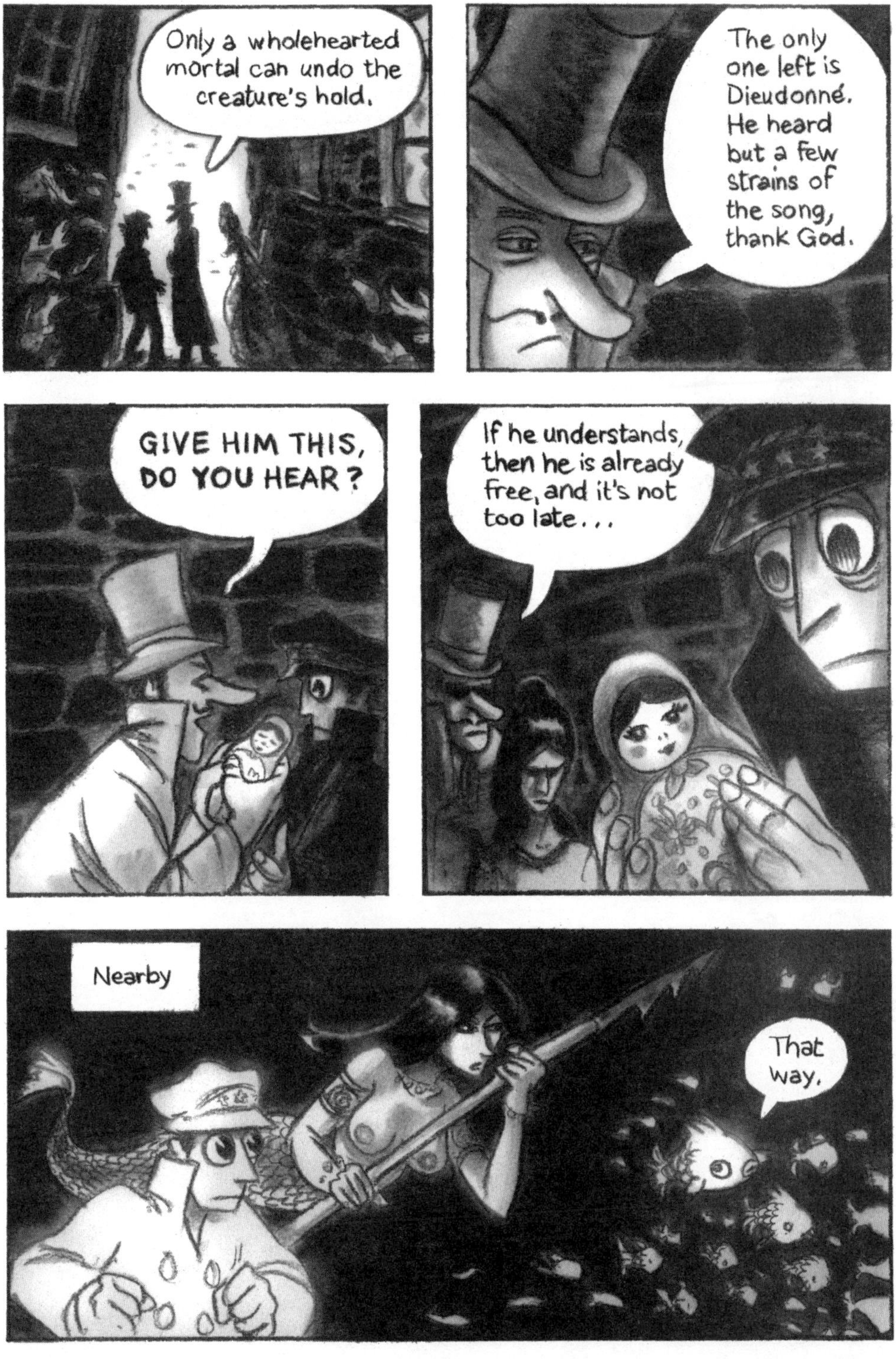
Only a wholehearted mortal can undo the creature's hold.
The only one left is Dieudonné. He heard but a few strains of the song, thank God.
GIVE HIM THIS, DO YOU HEAR?
If he understands, then he is already free, and it's not too late...
Nearby
That way.

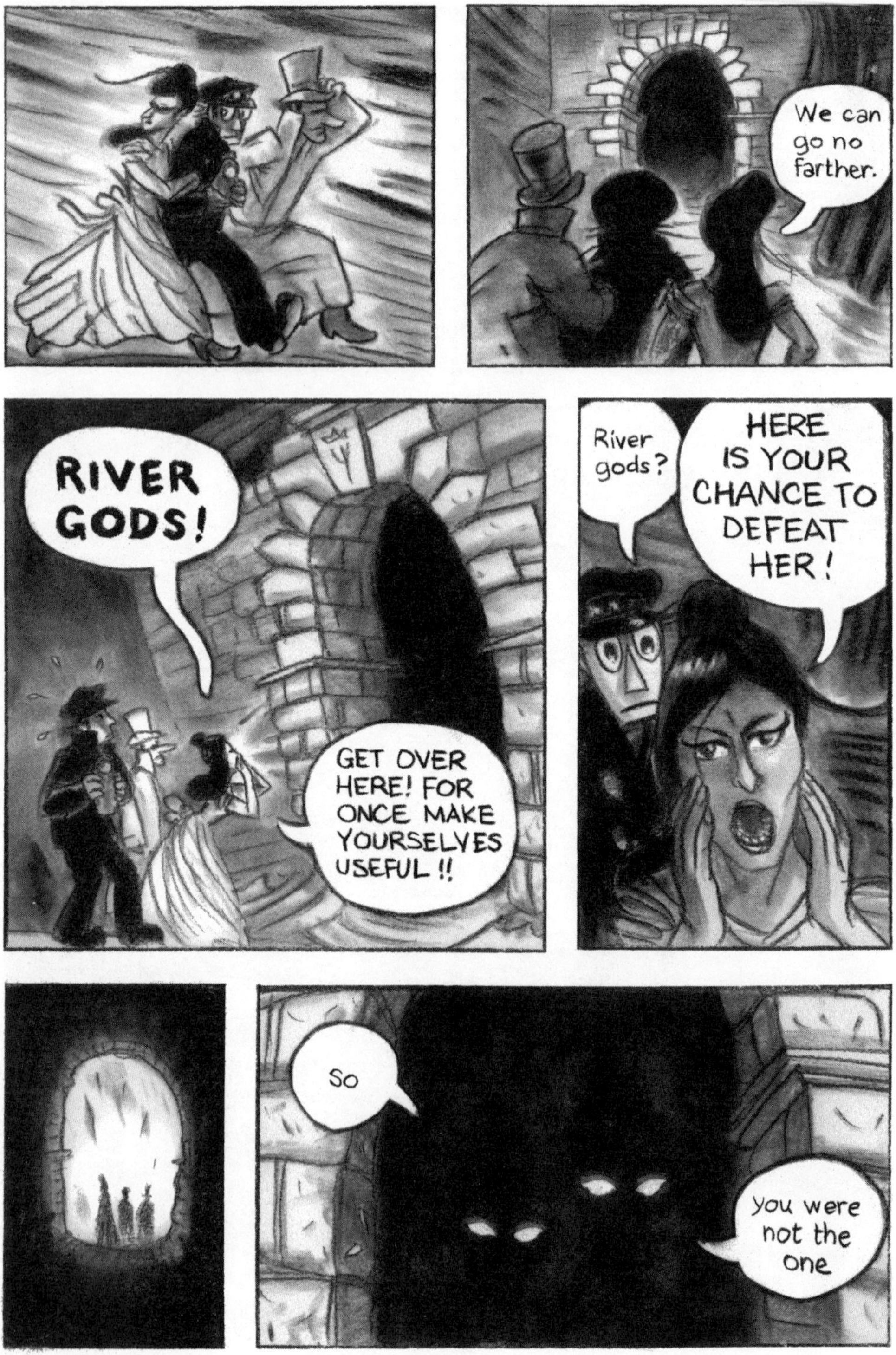

We can go no farther.
RIVER GODS!
GET OVER HERE! FOR ONCE MAKE YOURSELVES USEFUL !!
River gods?
HERE IS YOUR CHANCE TO DEFEAT HER!
So
you were not the one

357

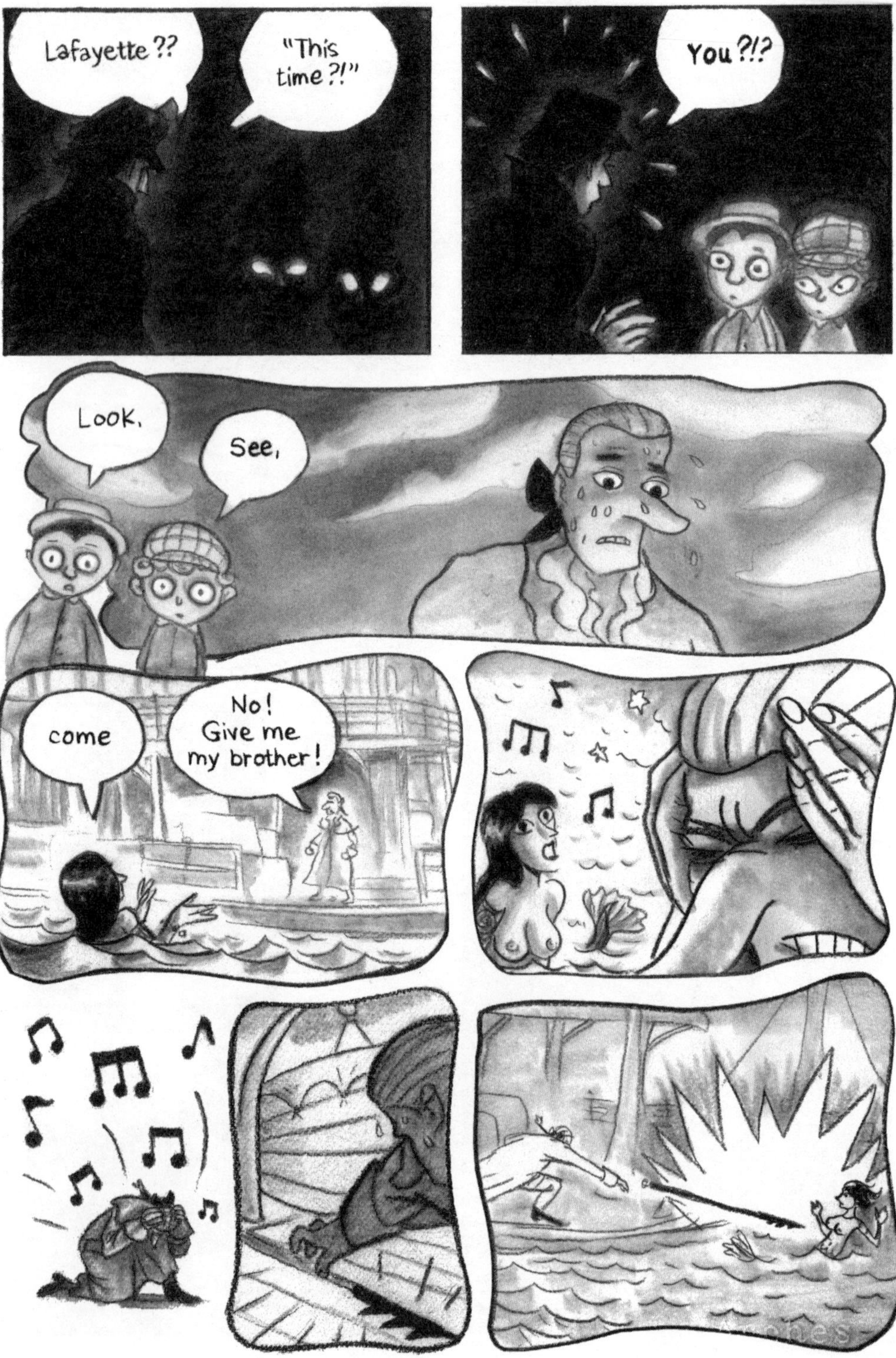
Lafayette??
"This time?!"
You?!?
Look,
See,
come
No! Give me my brother!

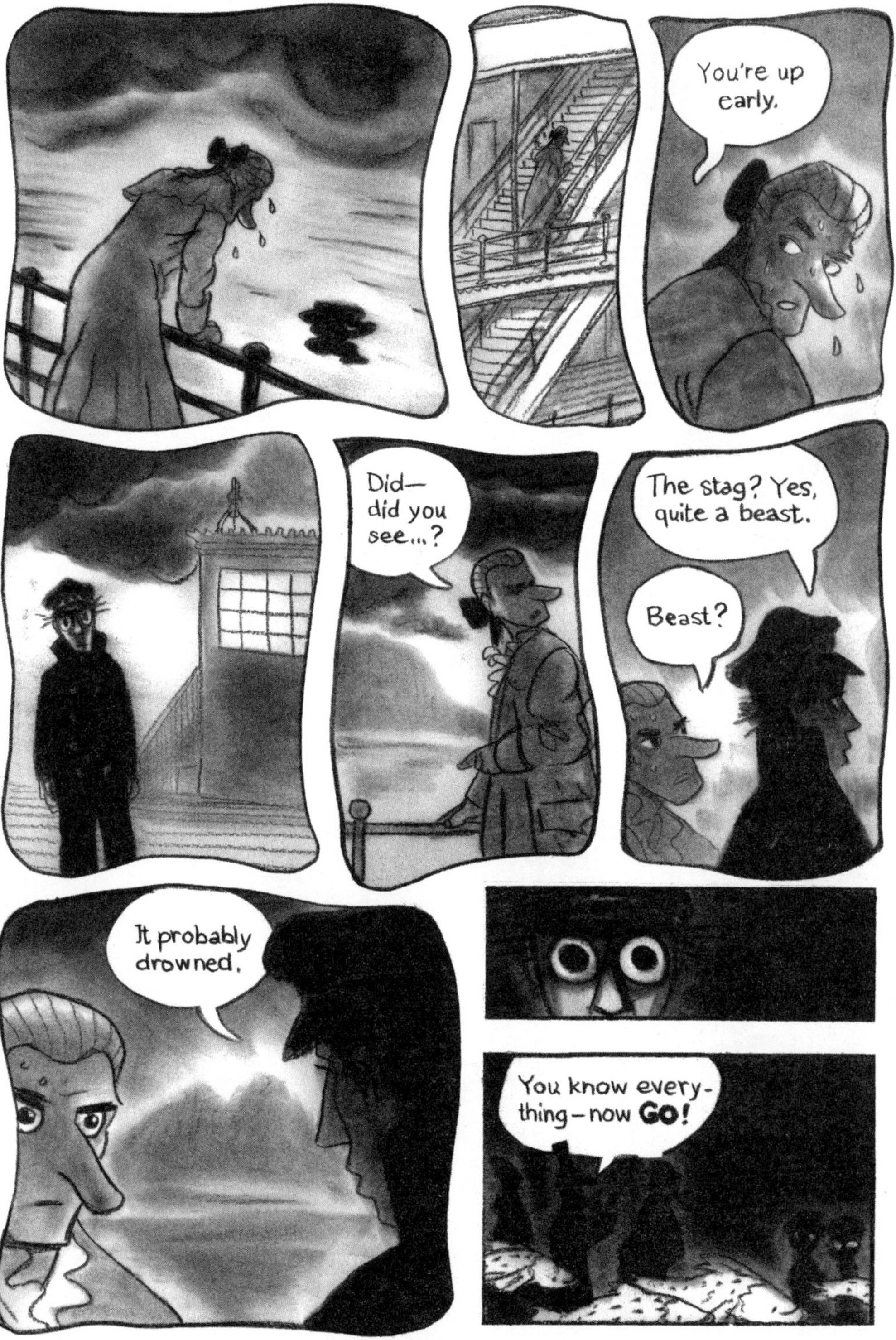
You're up early.
Did— did you see...?
The stag? Yes, quite a beast.
Beast?
It probably drowned.
You know every-thing—now GO!

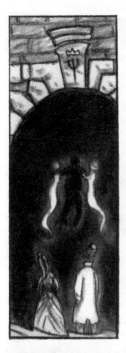

BLOOP

AAAR

WHERE DID HE GO?

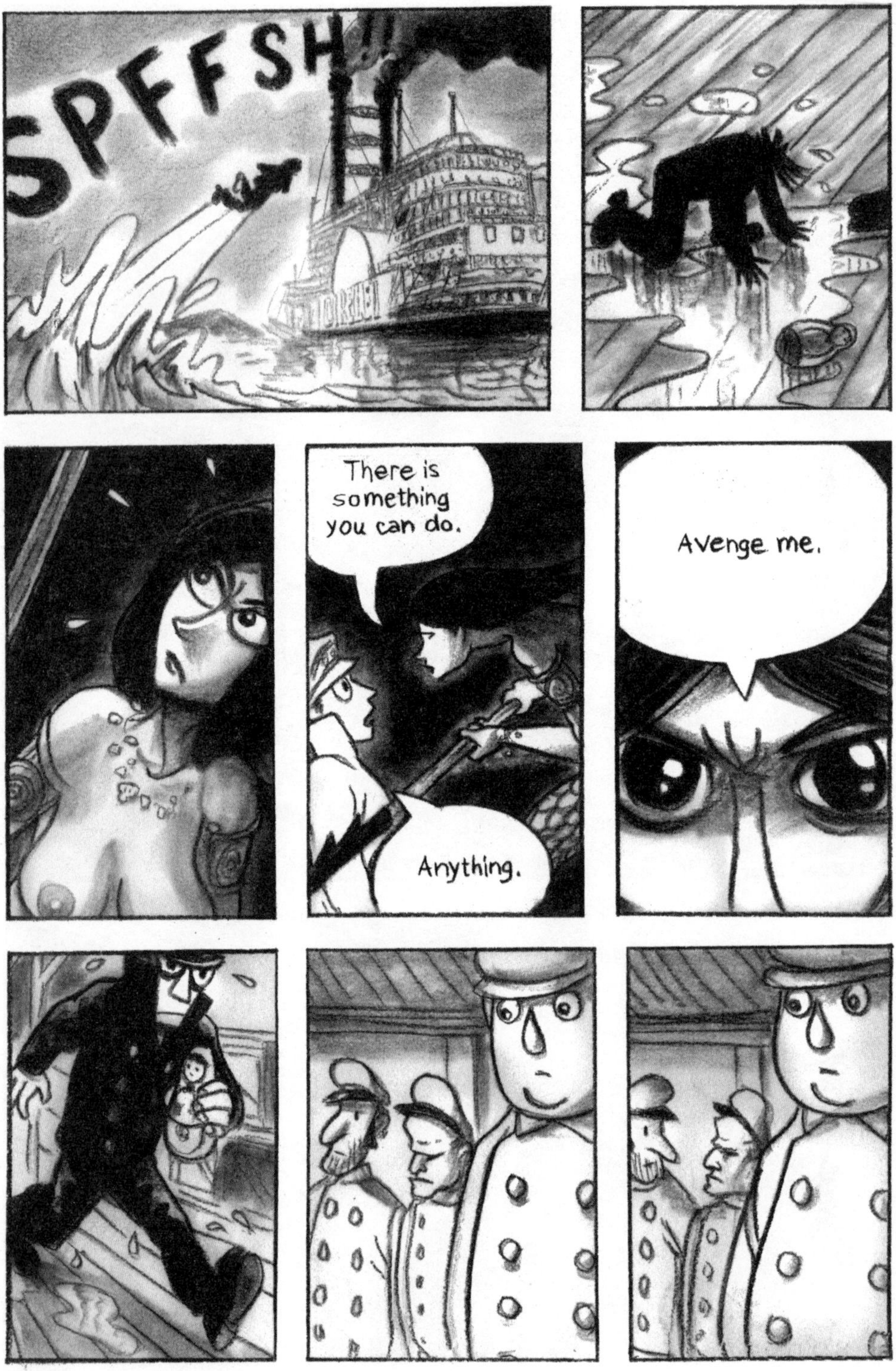
SPFFSH!!
There is something you can do.
Anything.
Avenge me.

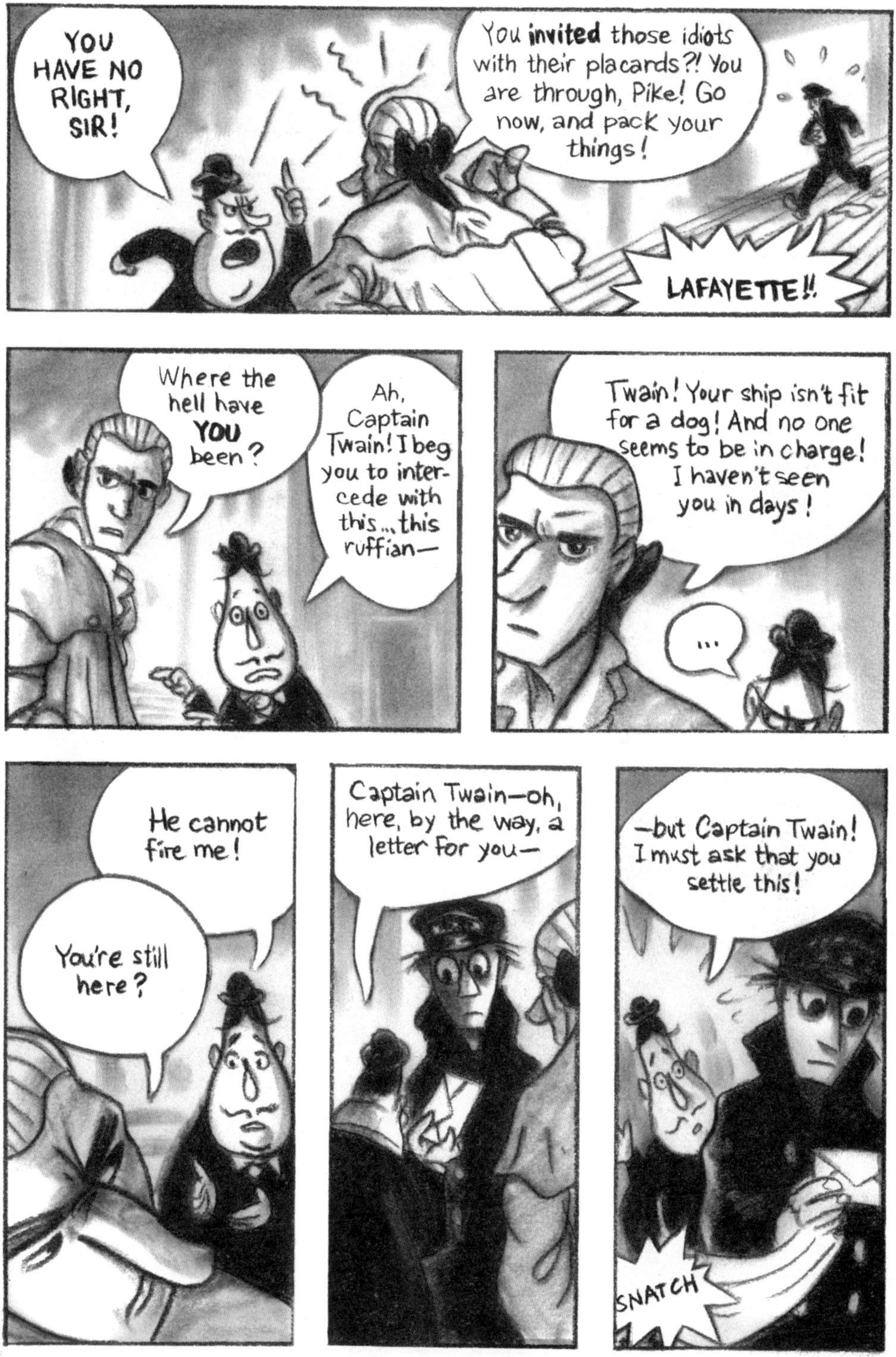
YOU HAVE NO RIGHT, SIR!
You **invited** those idiots with their placards?! You are through, Pike! Go now, and pack your things!
LAFAYETTE!!
Where the hell have **YOU** been?
Ah, Captain Twain! I beg you to intercede with this... this ruffian—
Twain! Your ship isn't fit for a dog! And no one seems to be in charge! I haven't seen you in days!
...
He cannot fire me!
You're still here?
Captain Twain—oh, here, by the way, a letter for you—
—but Captain Twain! I must ask that you settle this!
SNATCH

365

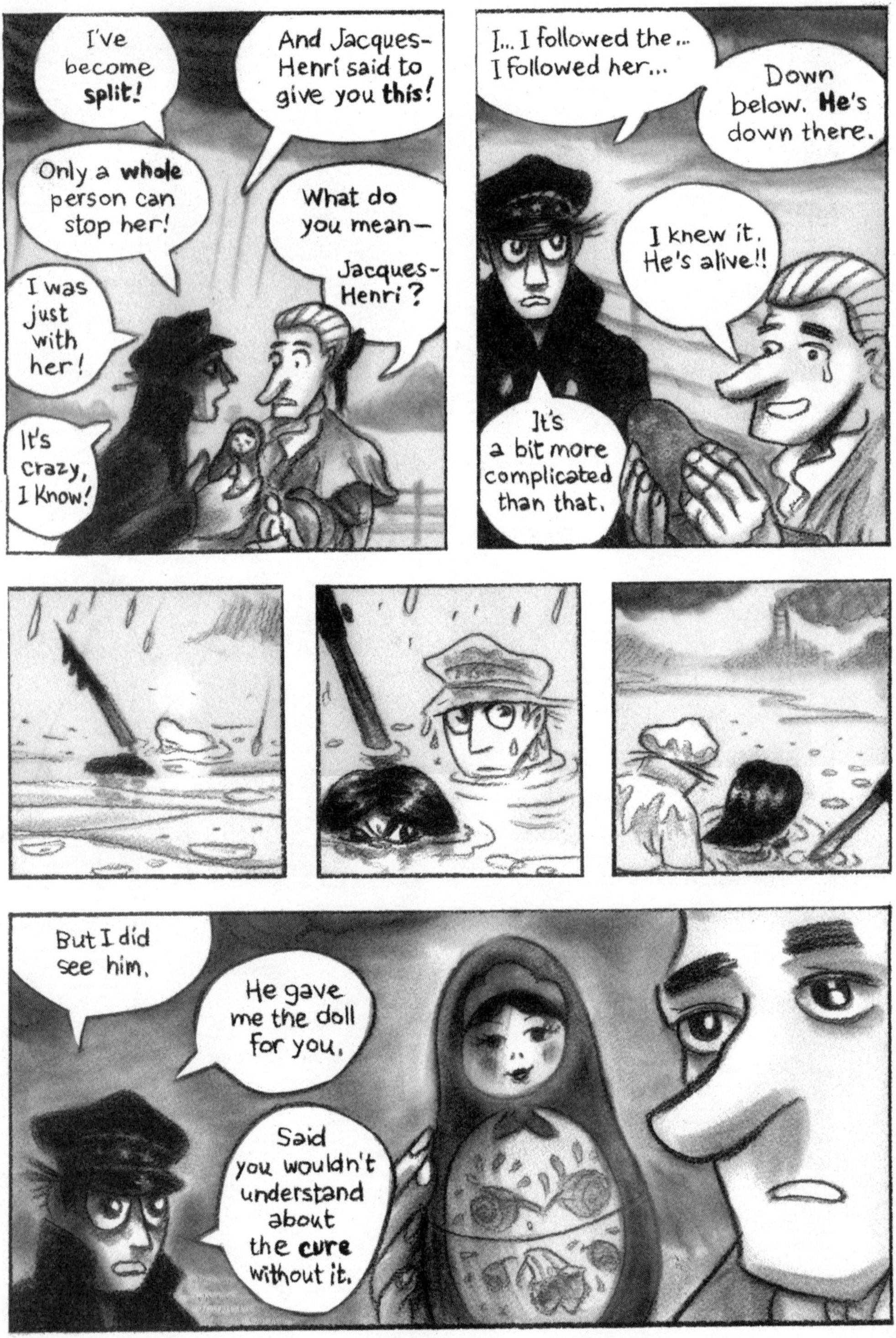
I've become split!
And Jacques-Henri said to give you this!
Only a whole person can stop her!
What do you mean—
Jacques-Henri?
I was just with her!
It's crazy, I Know!
I... I followed the... I followed her...
Down below. He's down there.
I knew it. He's alive!!
It's a bit more complicated than that.
But I did see him.
He gave me the doll for you.
Said you wouldn't understand about the cure without it.

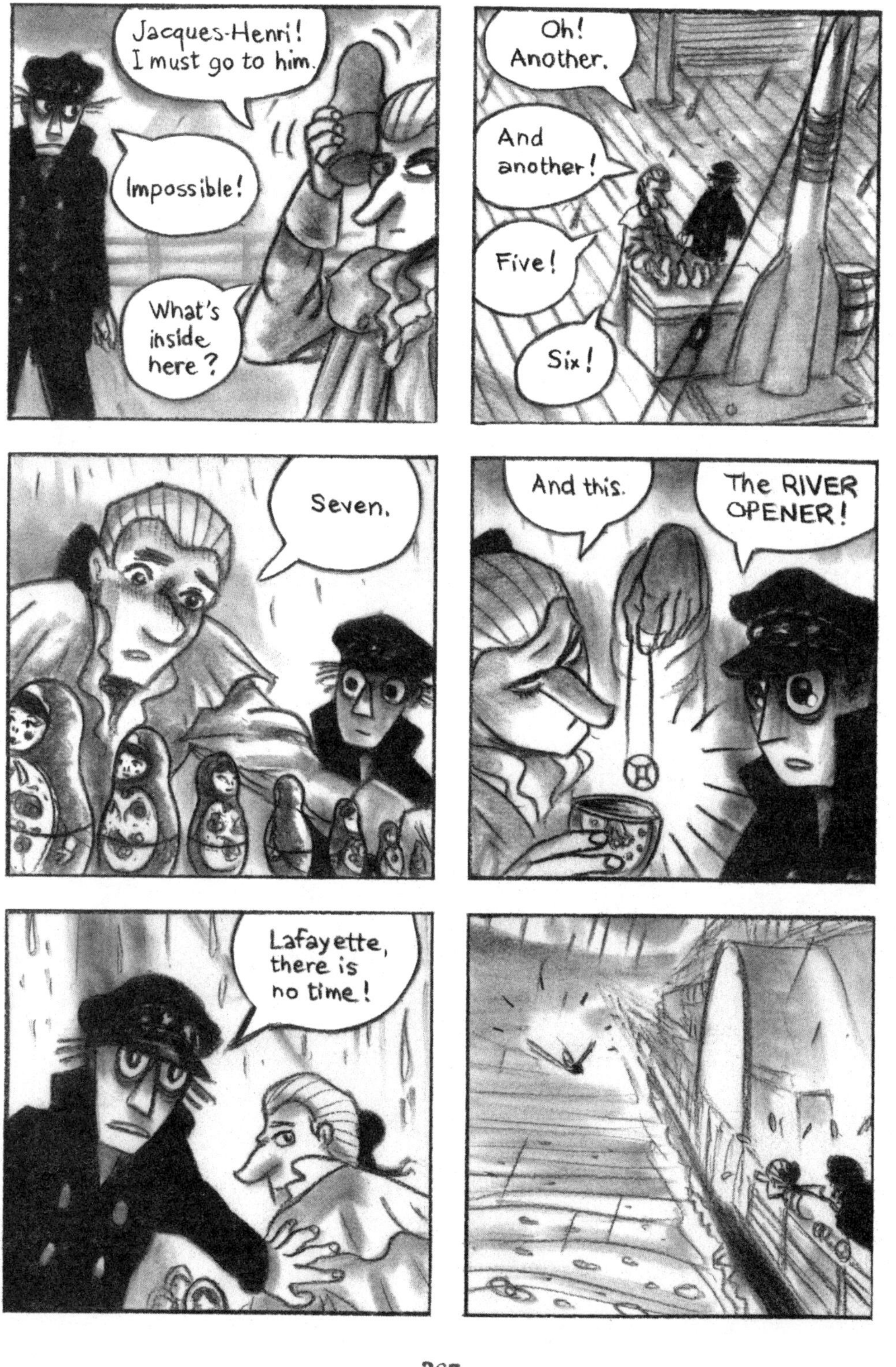
Jacques-Henri! I must go to him.
Impossible!
What's inside here?
Oh! Another.
And another!
Five!
Six!
Seven.
And this.
The RIVER OPENER!
Lafayette, there is no time!

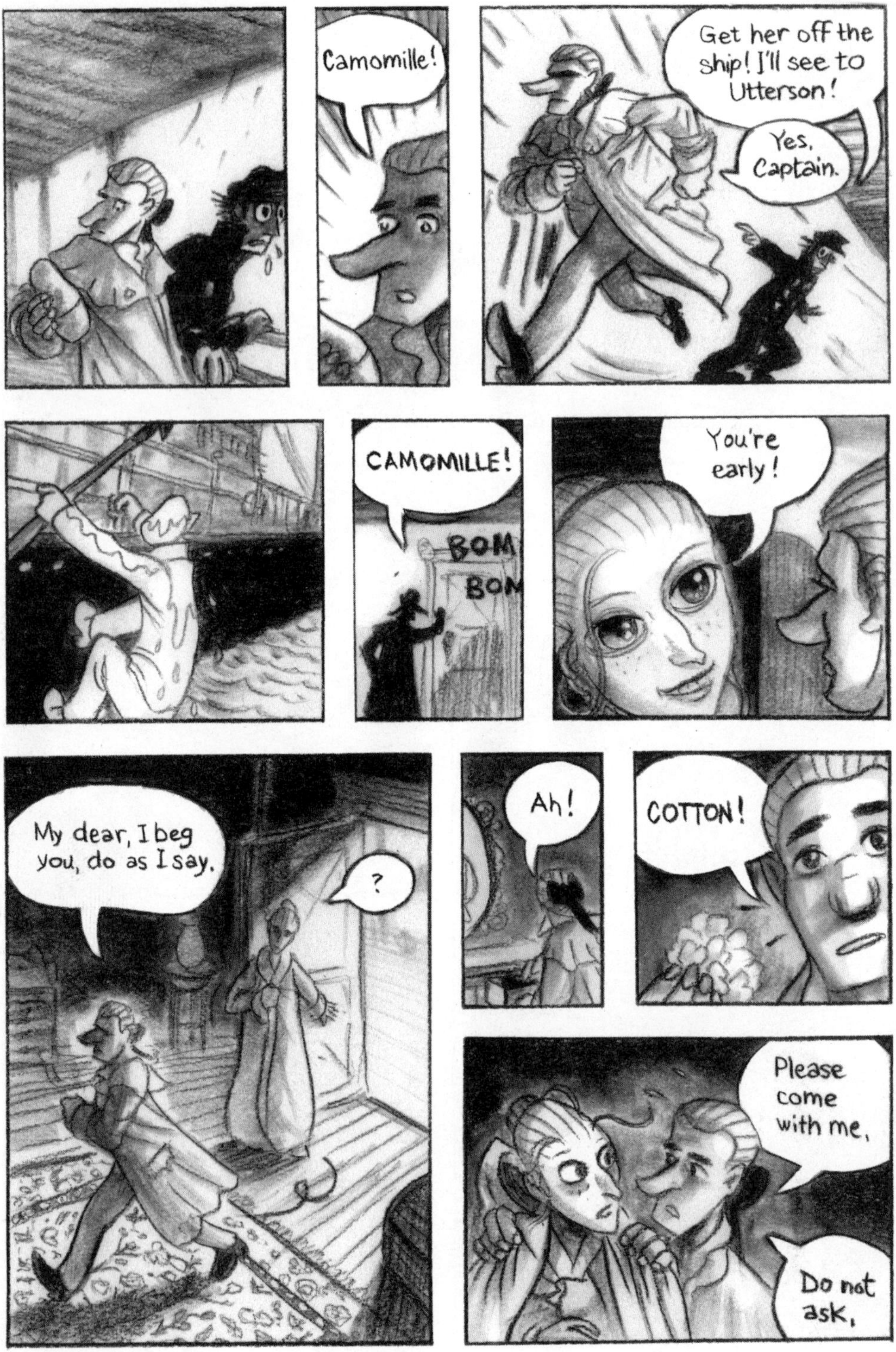
Camomille!
Get her off the ship! I'll see to Utterson!
Yes, Captain.
CAMOMILLE!
BOM
BOM
You're early!
My dear, I beg you, do as I say.
?
Ah!
COTTON!
Please come with me.
Do not ask.

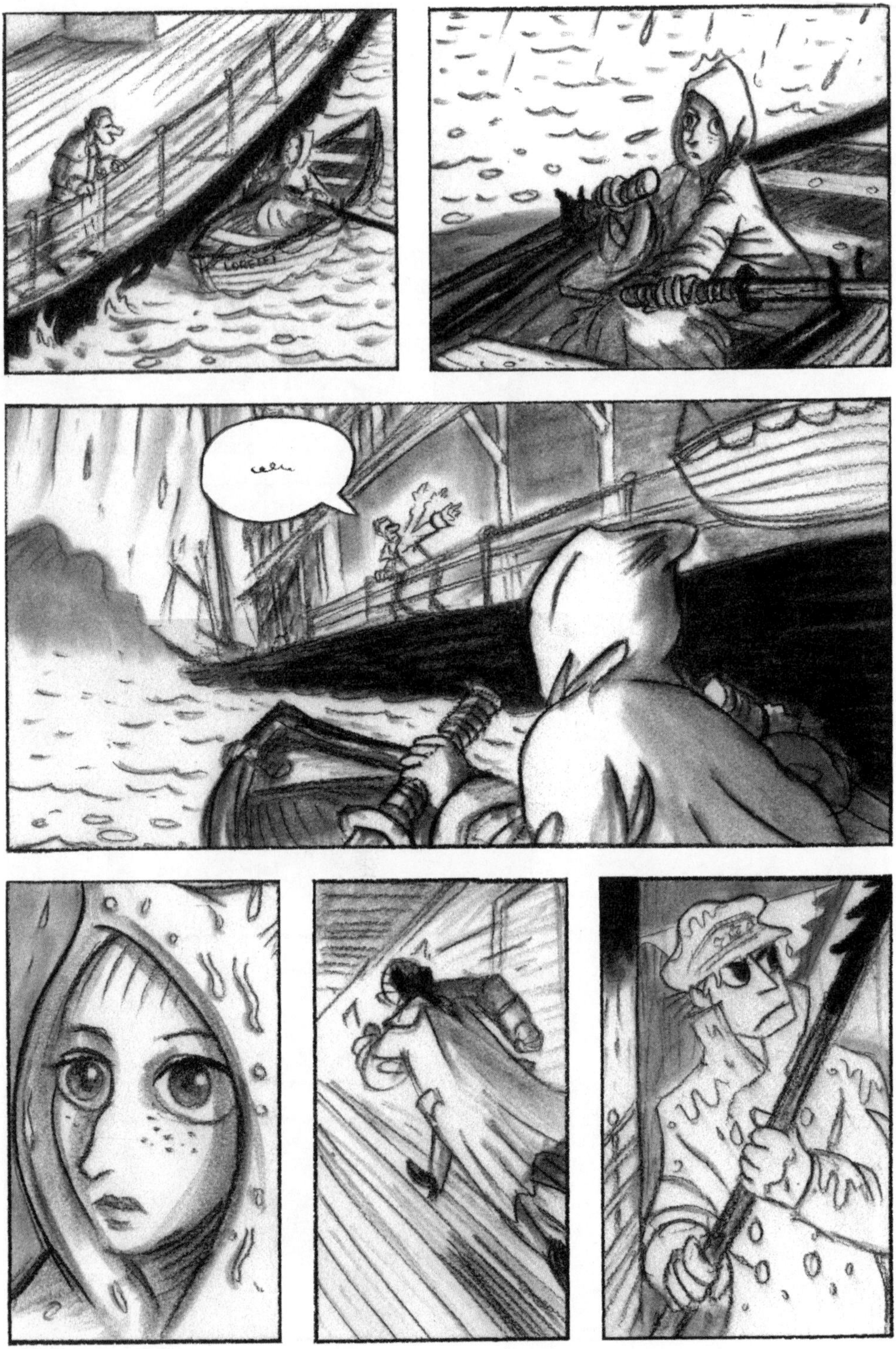

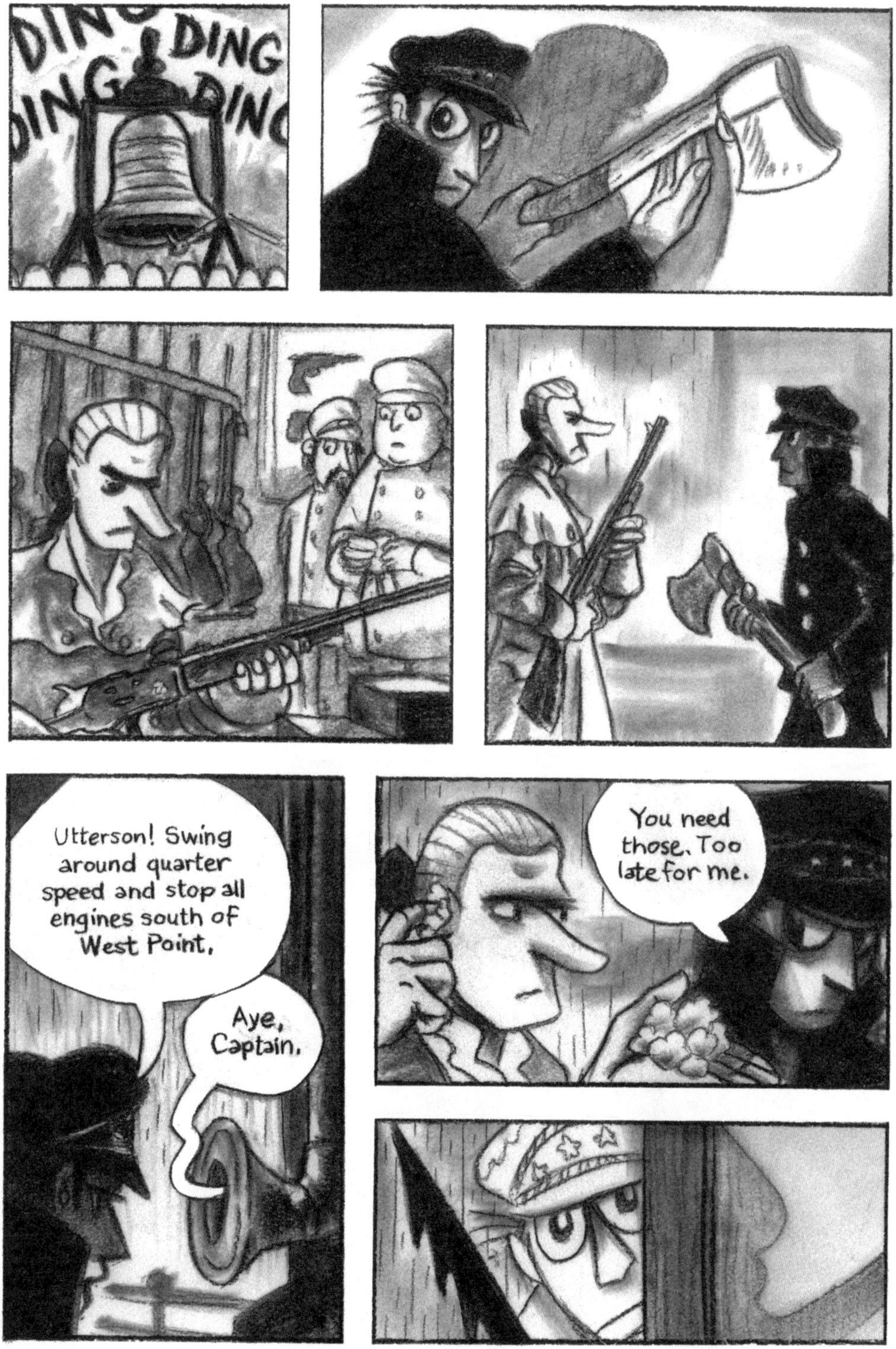
DING DING DING DING
Utterson! Swing around quarter speed and stop all engines south of West Point.
Aye, Captain.
You need those. Too late for me.

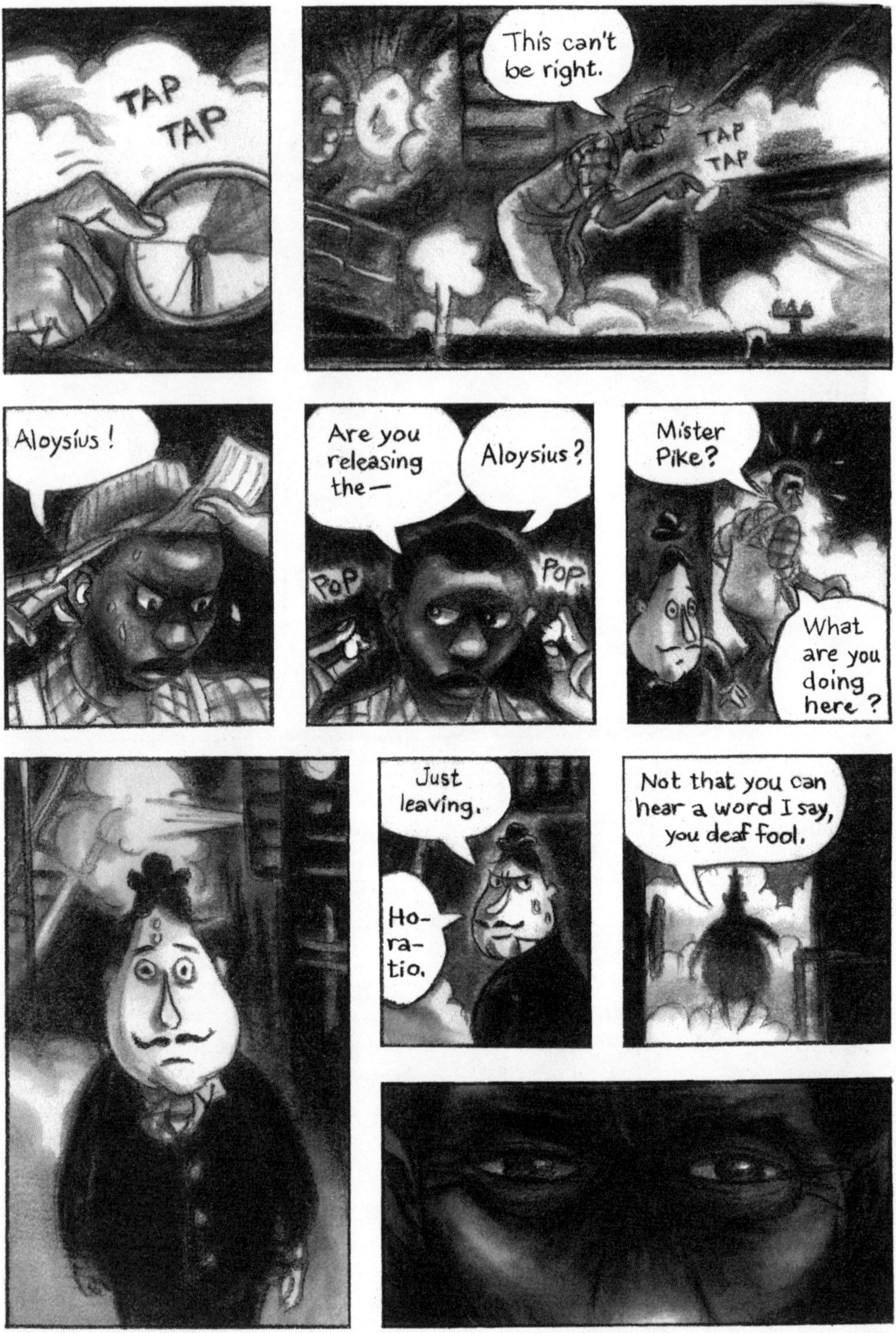
TAP TAP
This can't be right.
TAP TAP
Aloysius!
Are you releasing the—
Aloysius?
POP
POP
Mister Pike?
What are you doing here?
Just leaving.
Ho-ra-tio.
Not that you can hear a word I say, you deaf fool.

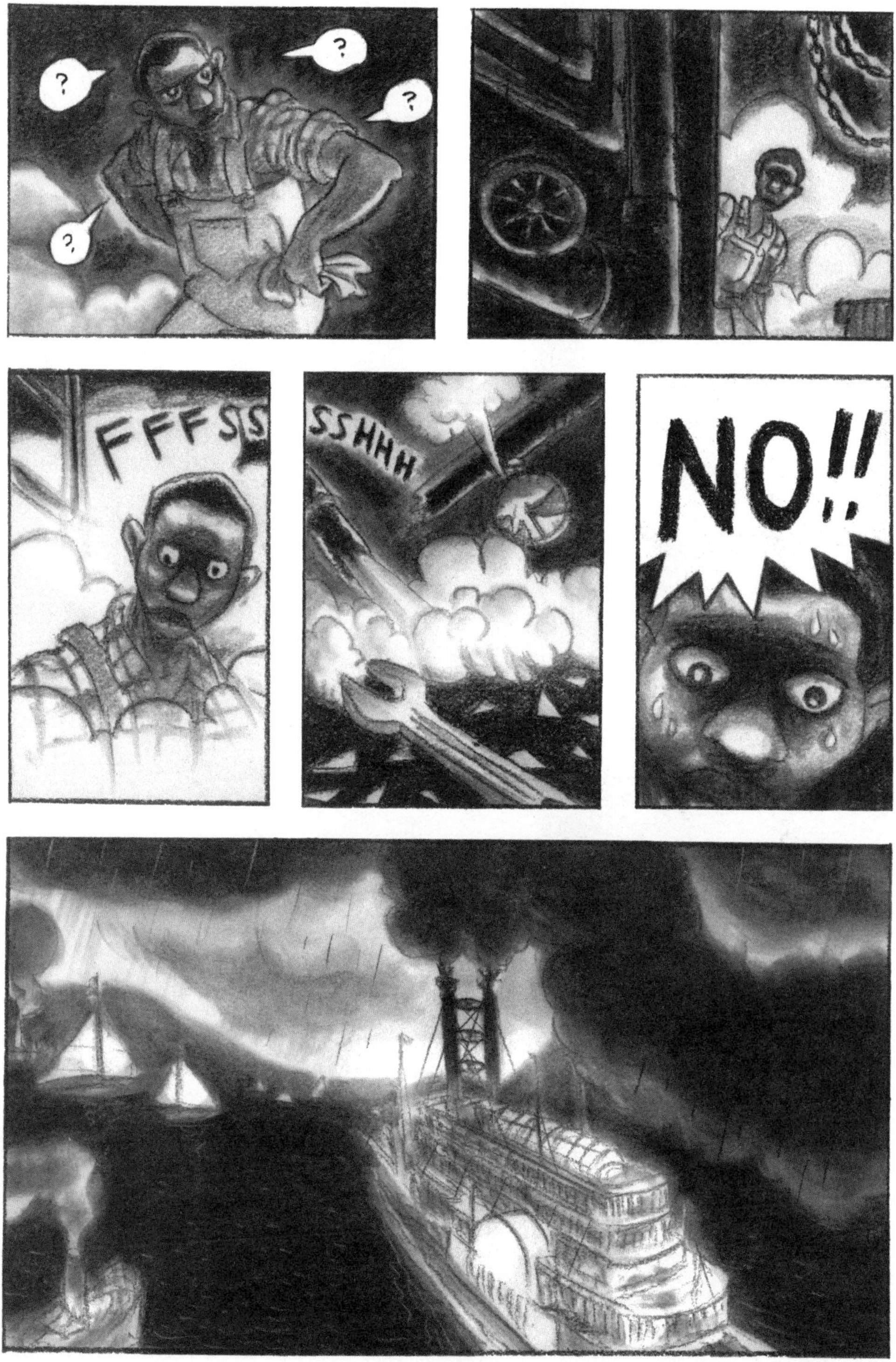
?
?
?
?
FFFSS
SSHHH
NO!!

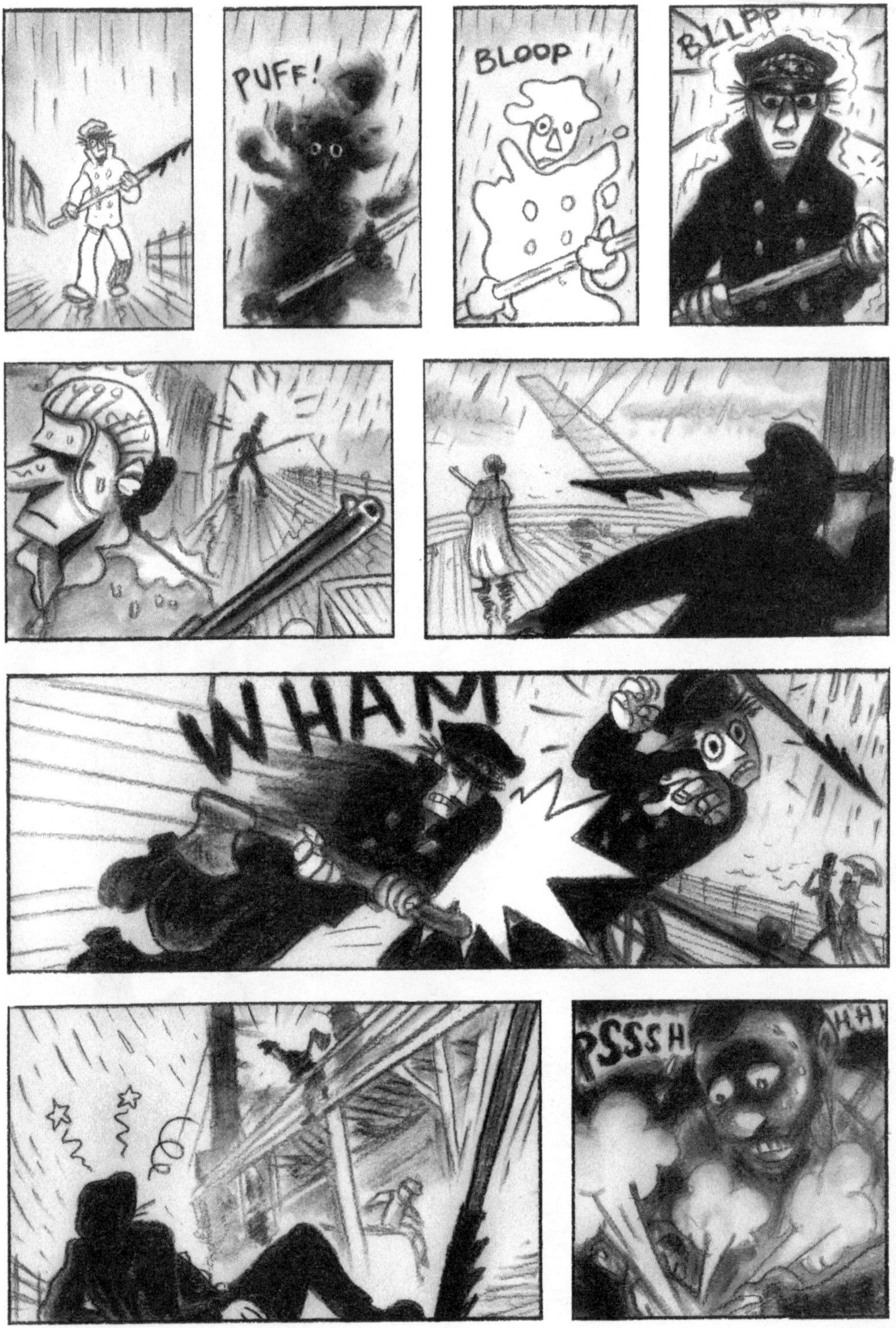
PUFF!
BLOOP
BLLPP
WHAM
PSSSH

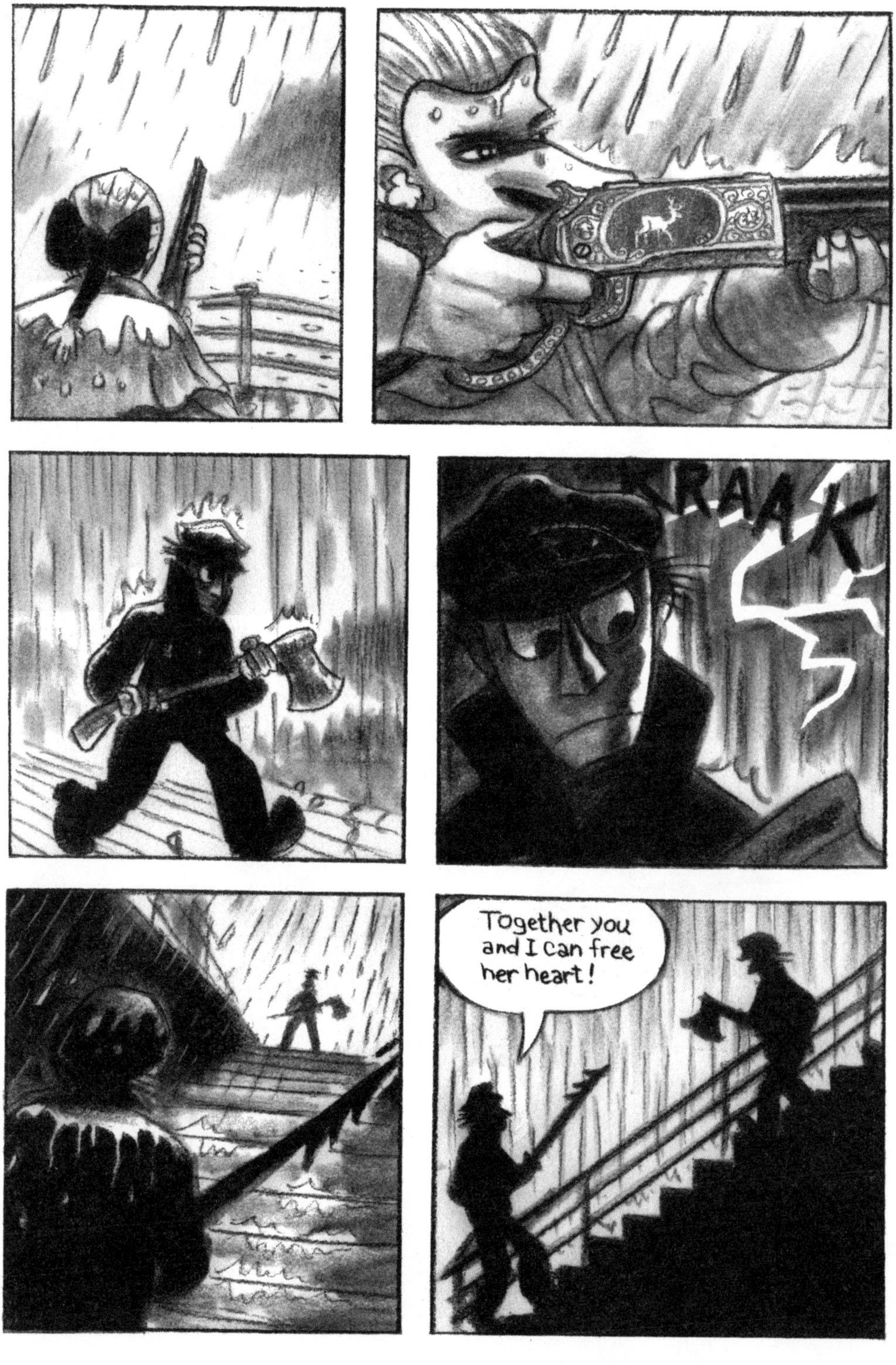
KRAAK
Together you and I can free her heart!

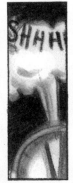

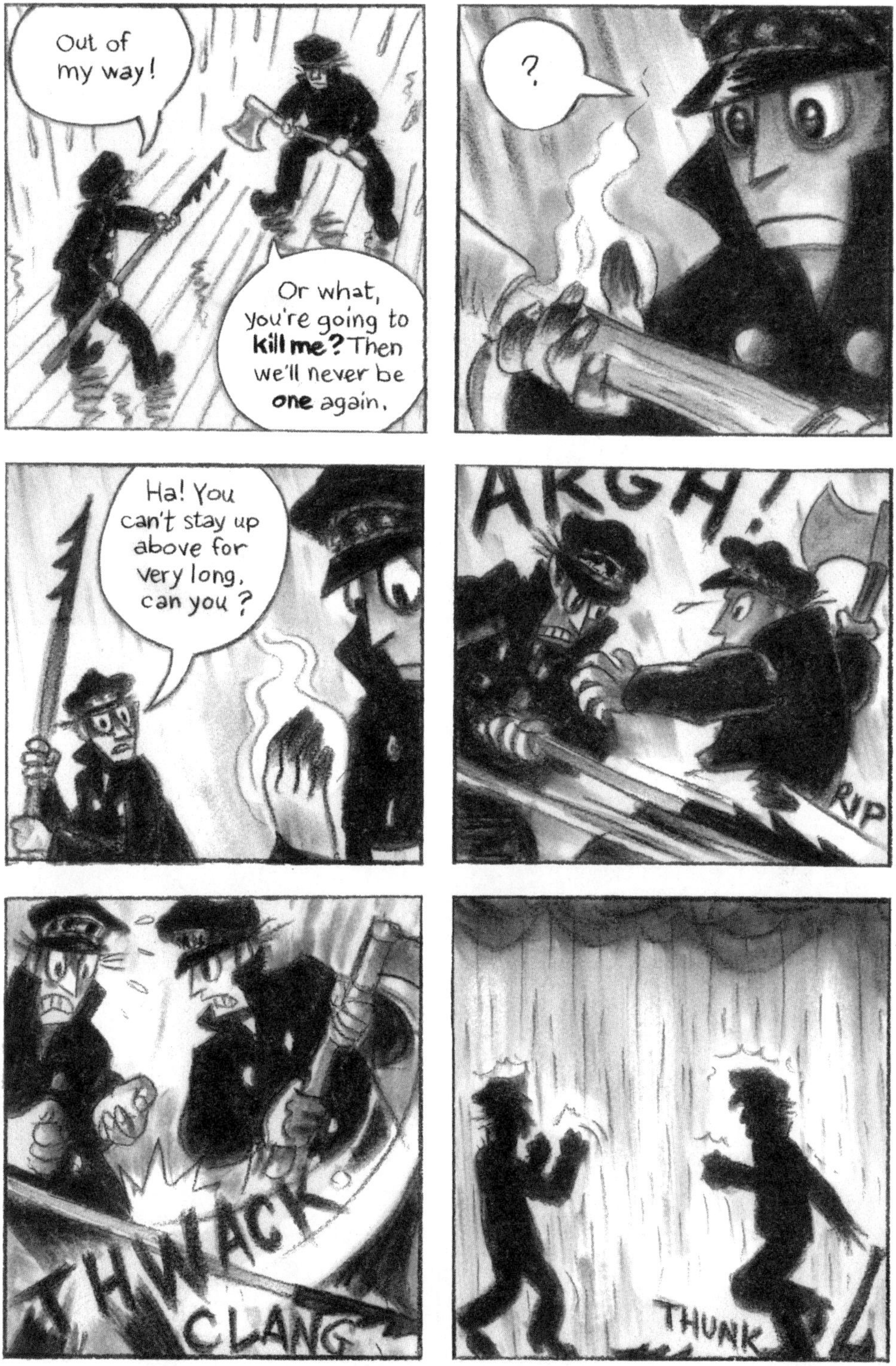
Out of my way!
Or what, you're going to **kill me?** Then we'll never be **one** again.
?
Ha! You can't stay up above for very long, can you?
AKGH!
RIP
THWACK
CLANG
THUNK

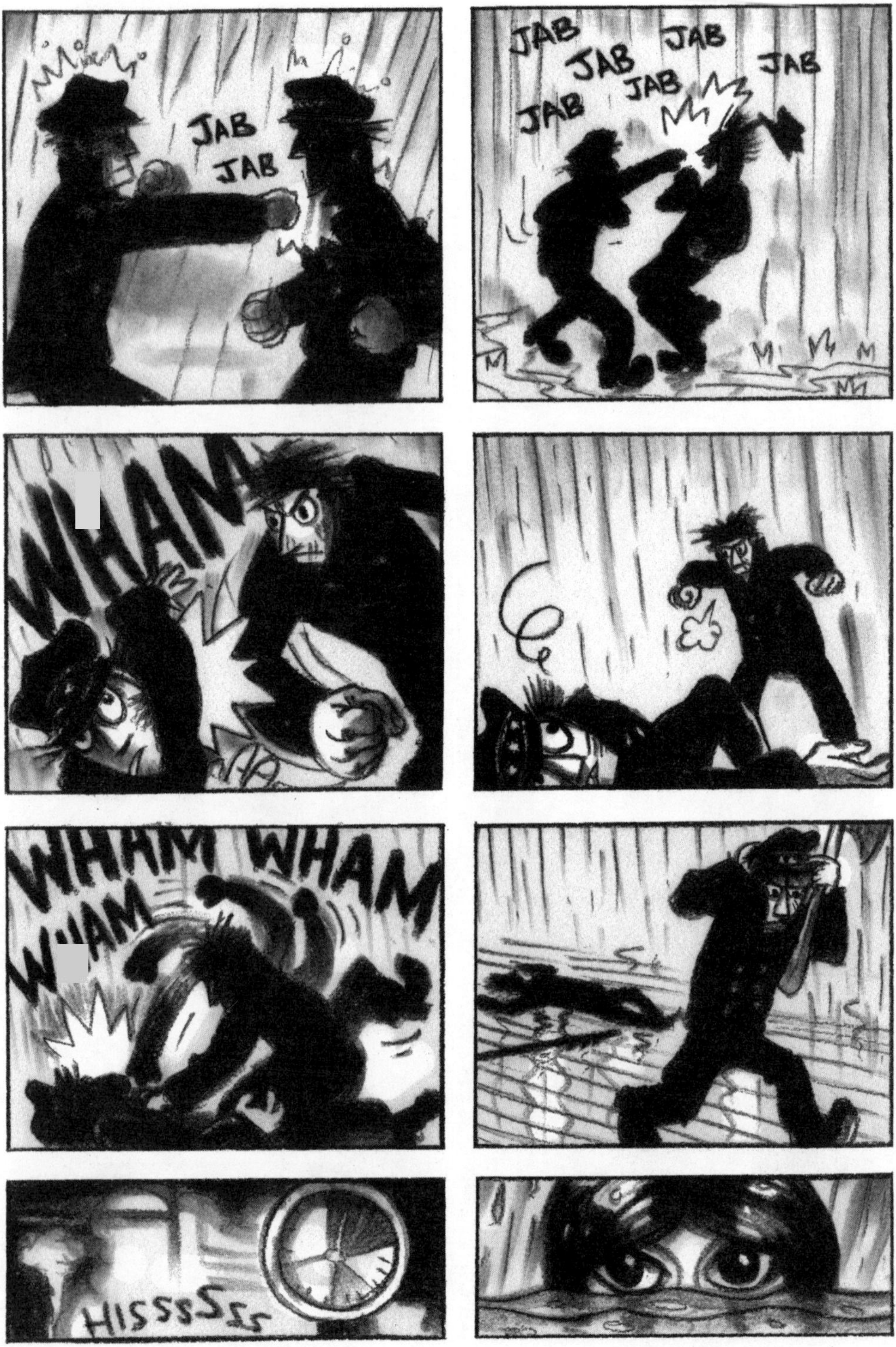
JAB
JAB
JAB
JAB
JAB
JAB
JAB
JAB
WHAM
WHAM
WHAM
WHAM
HISSSSss

Pt IV, Chap.2

"THE SIREN'S WRATH"

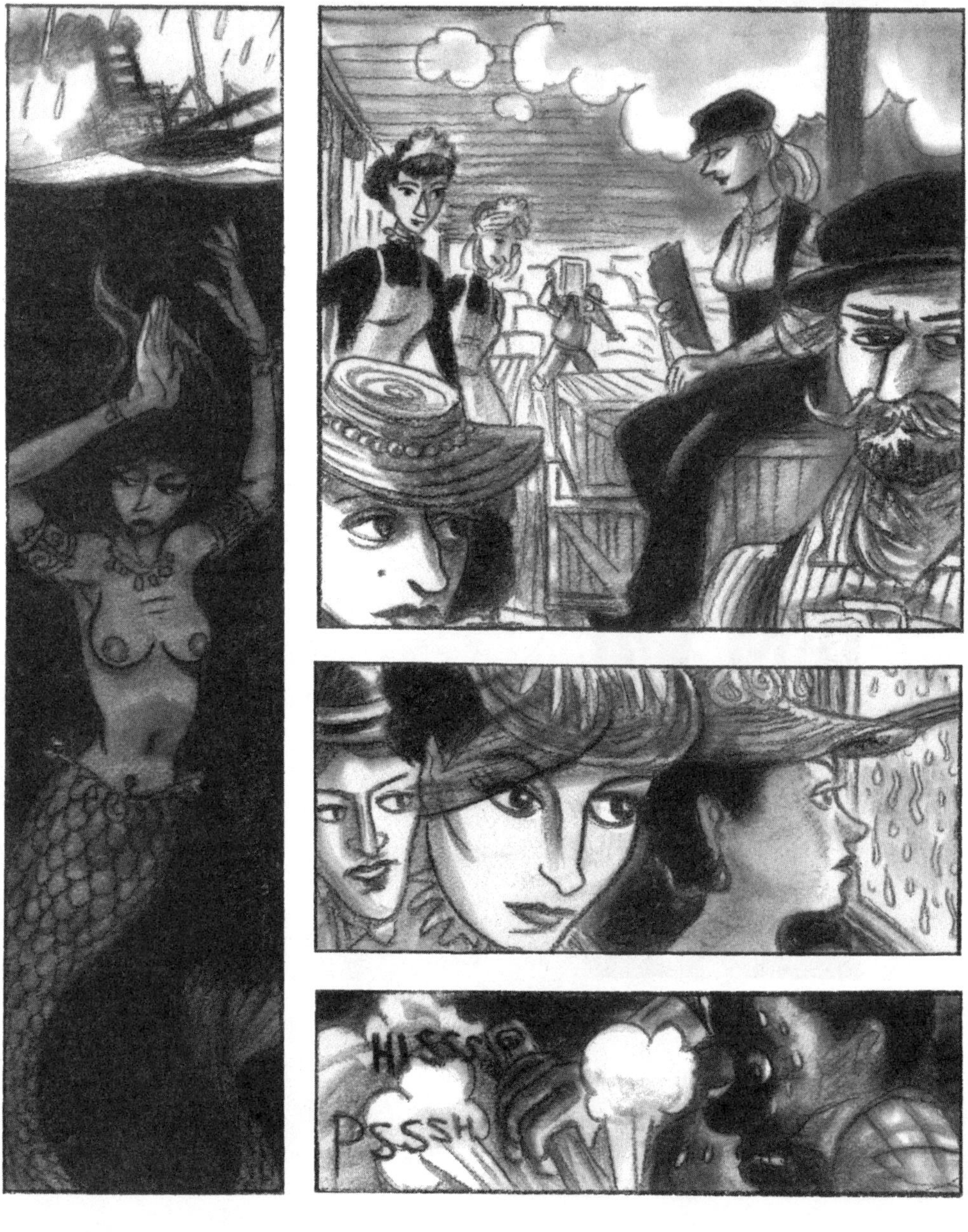
HISSS
PSSSH

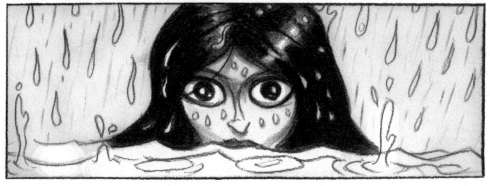

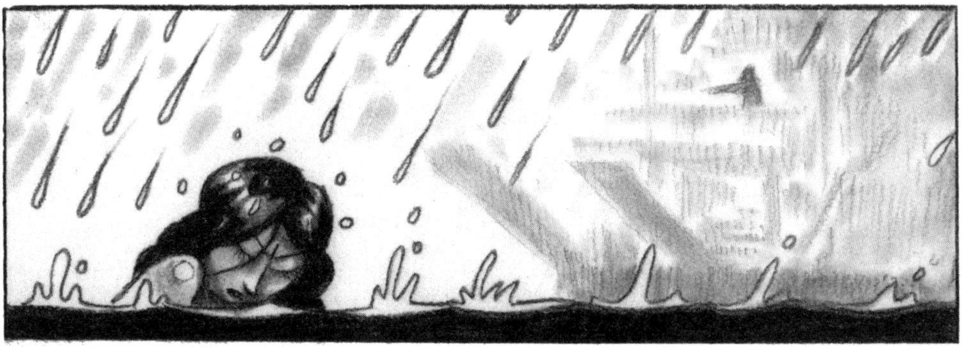

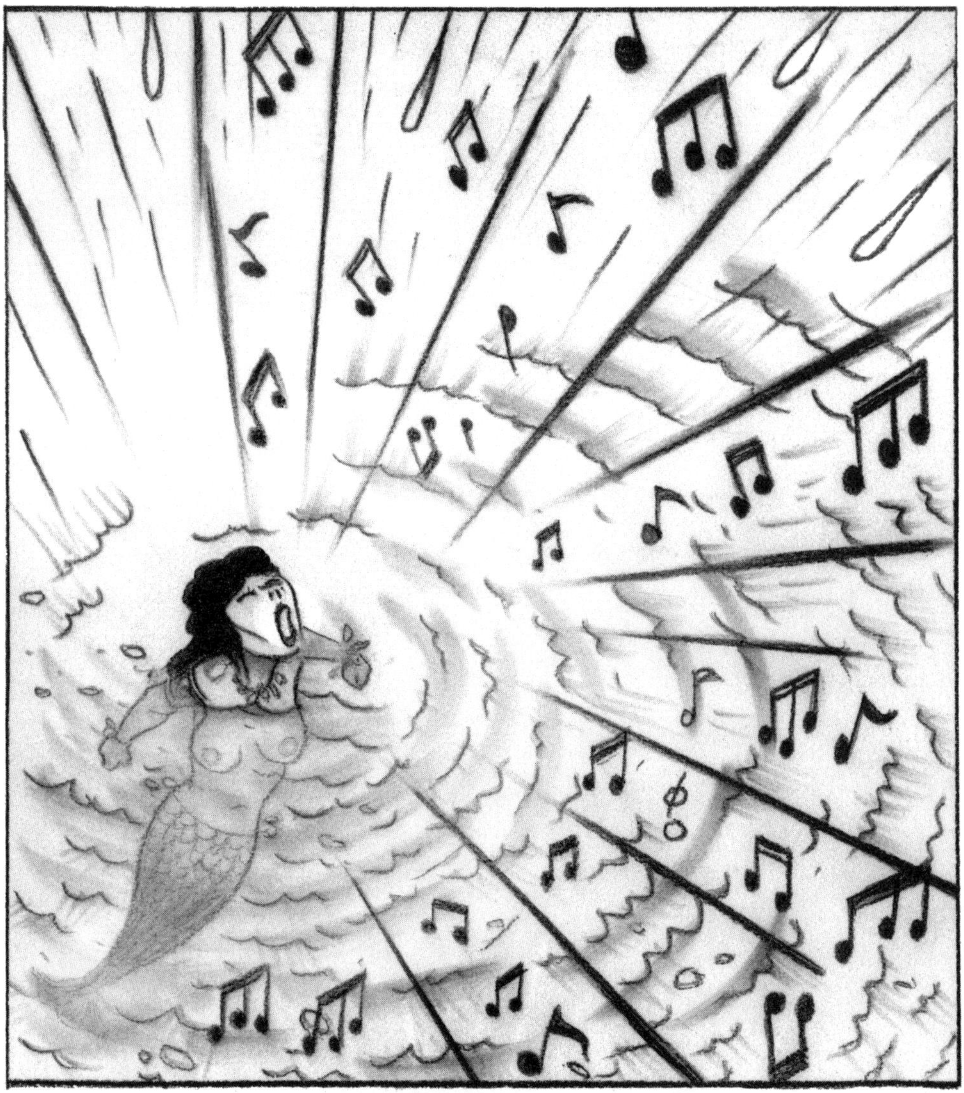

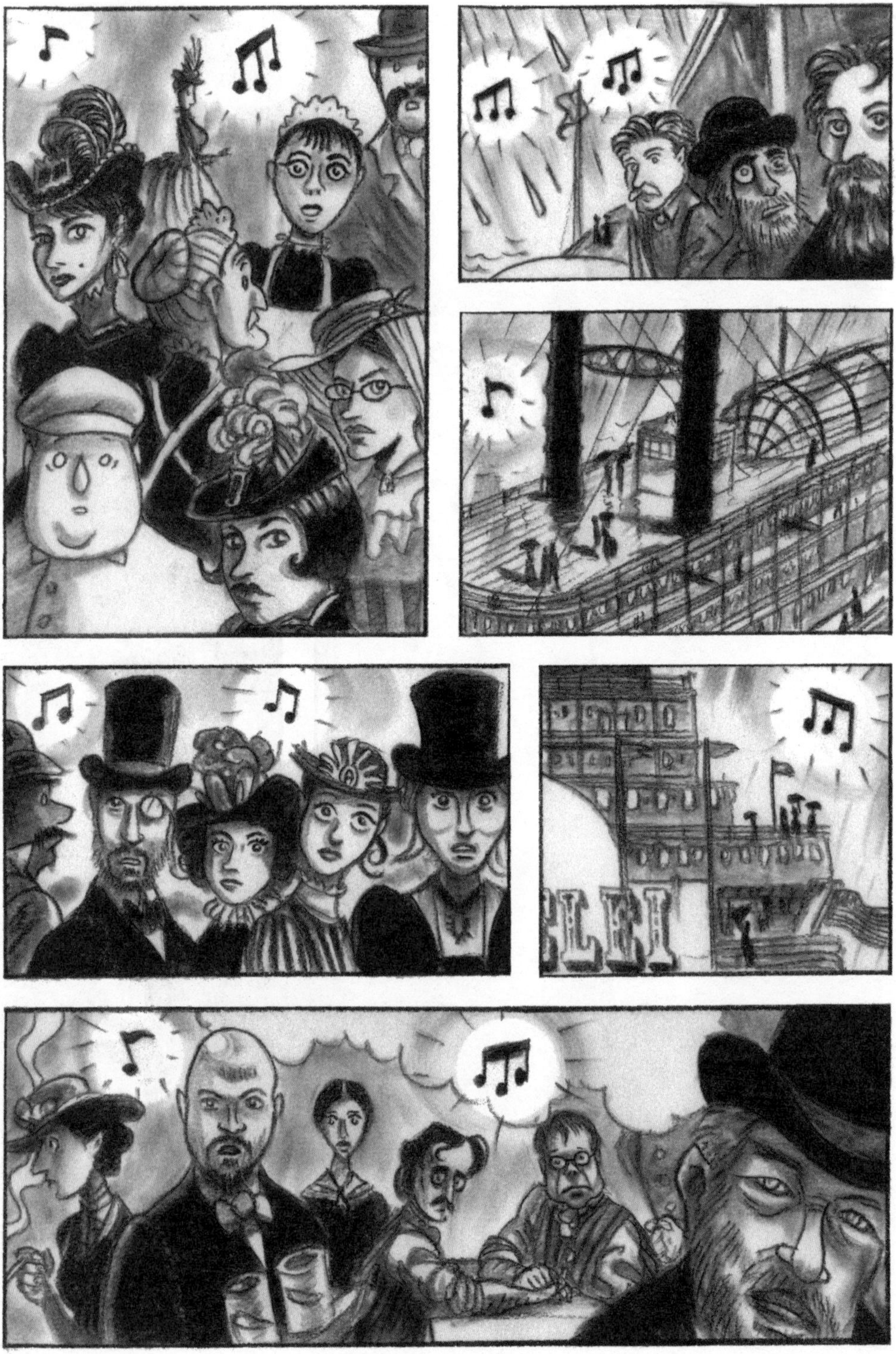

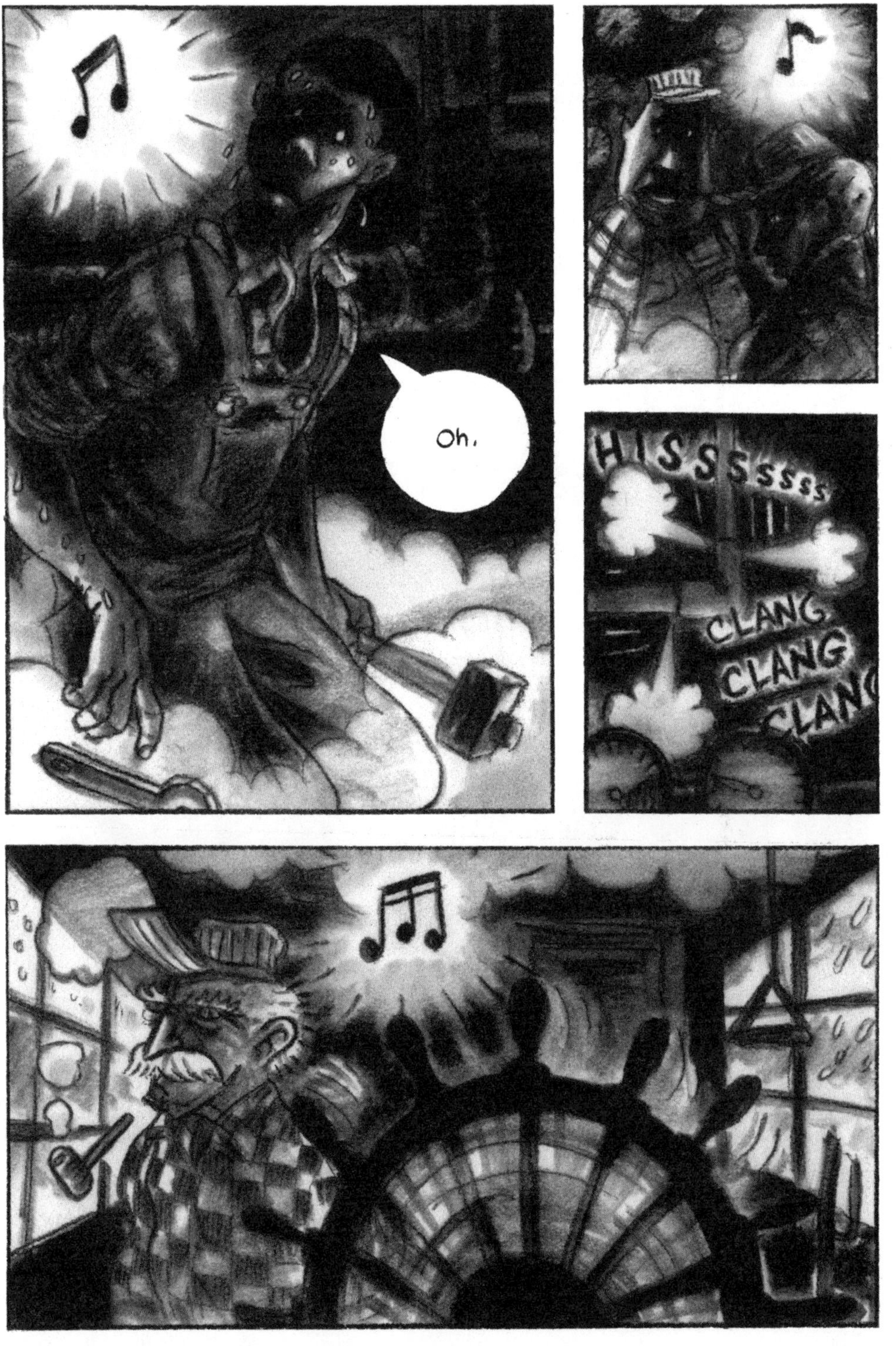
Oh.
HISSSssss
CLANG
CLANG

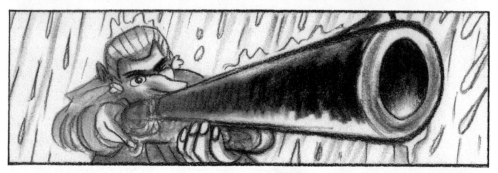

What is he waiting for?

His bullets are useless against her.

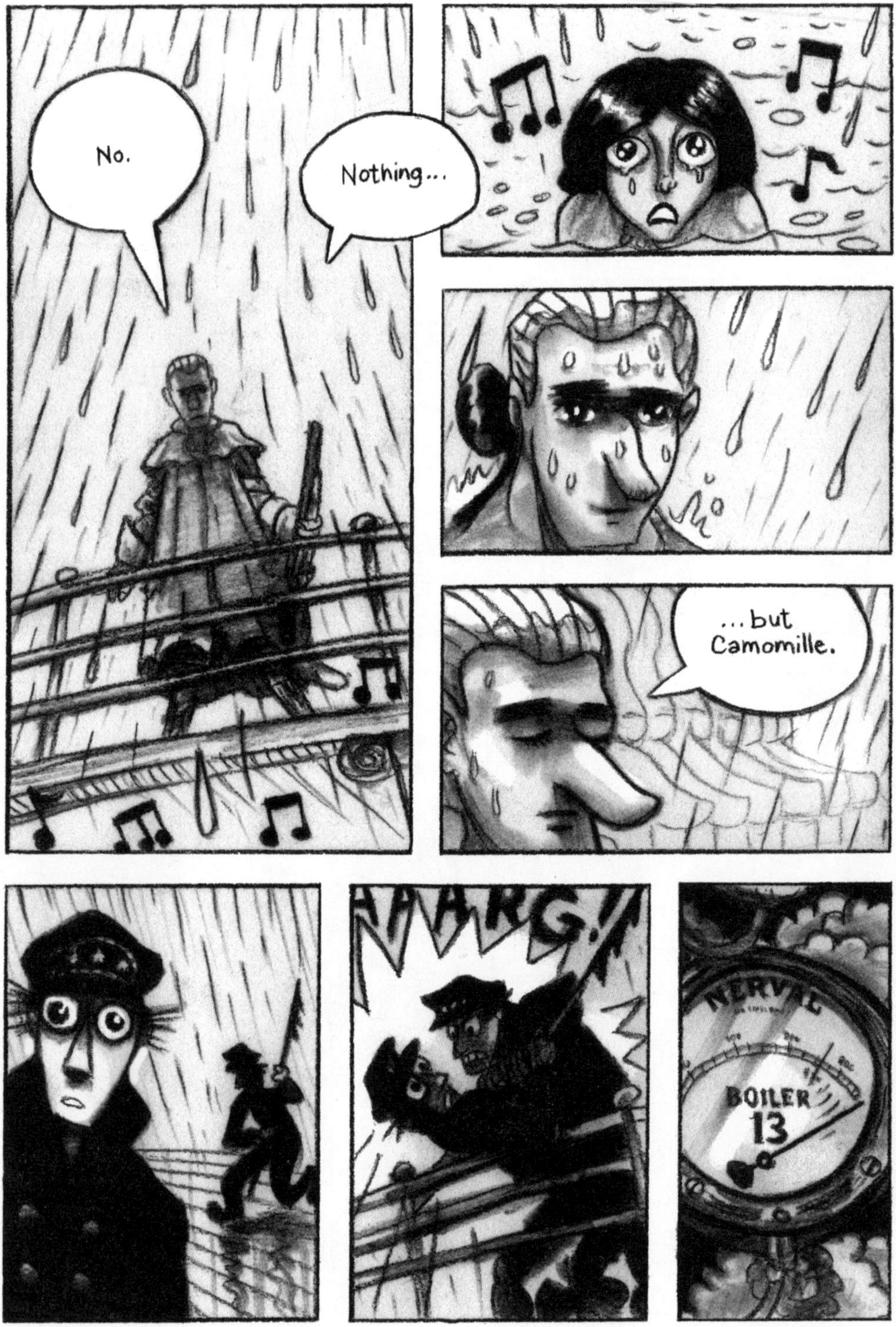
No.
Nothing...
...but Camomille.
AARG!
NERVAL
BOILER
13

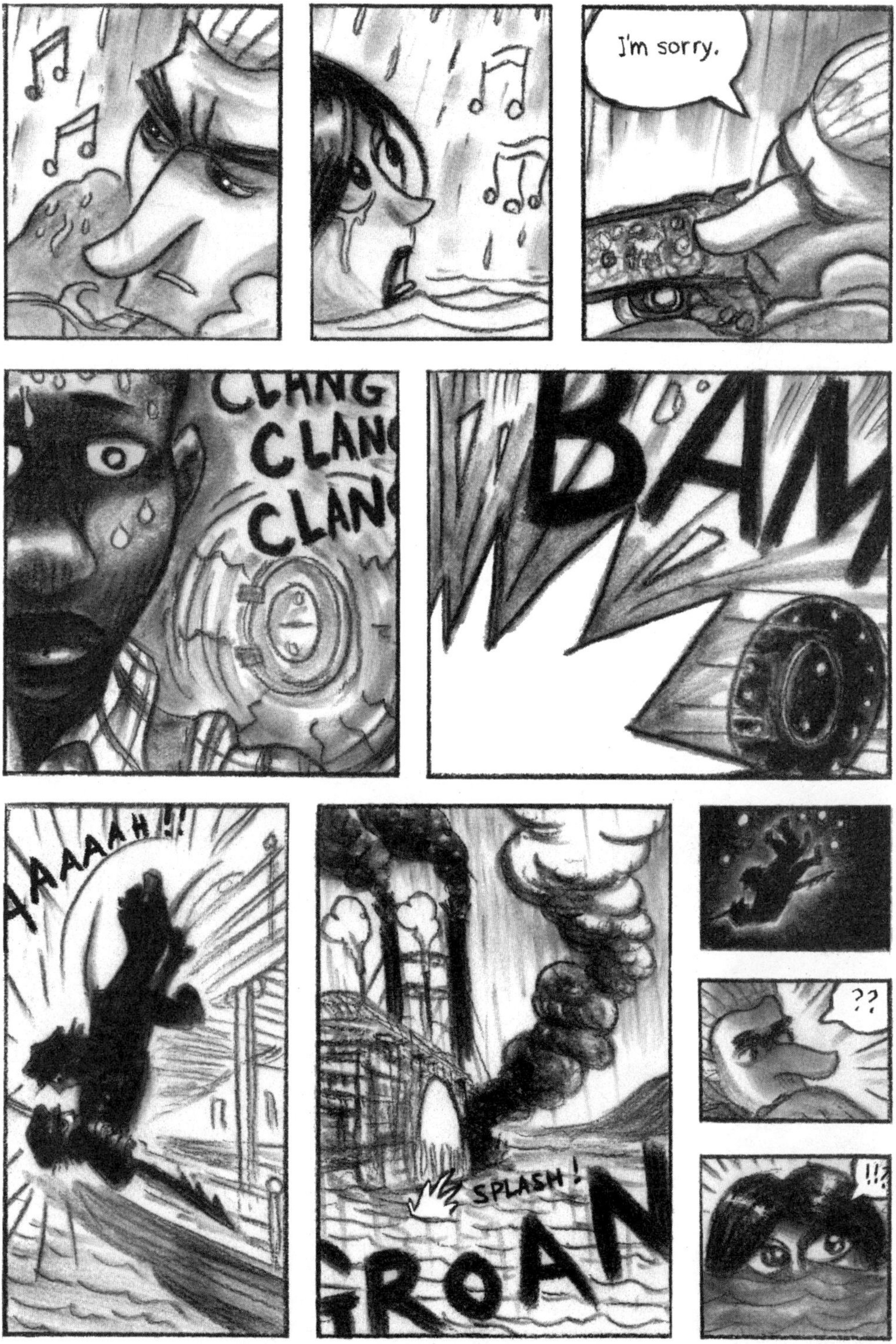
I'm sorry.
CLANG
CLANG
CLANG
BAM
AAAAAH!!
SPLASH!
ROAN
??
!!?

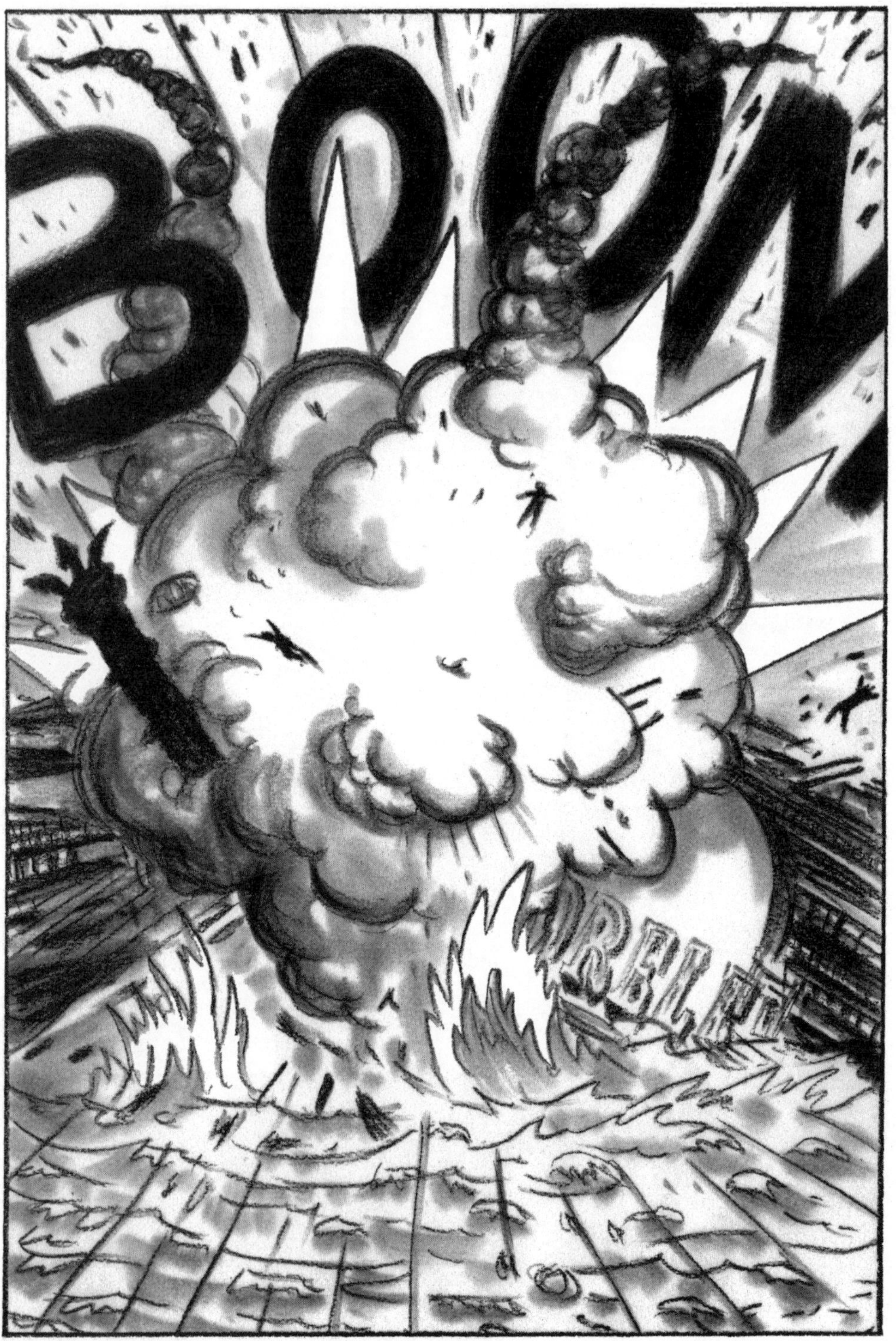
BOOM

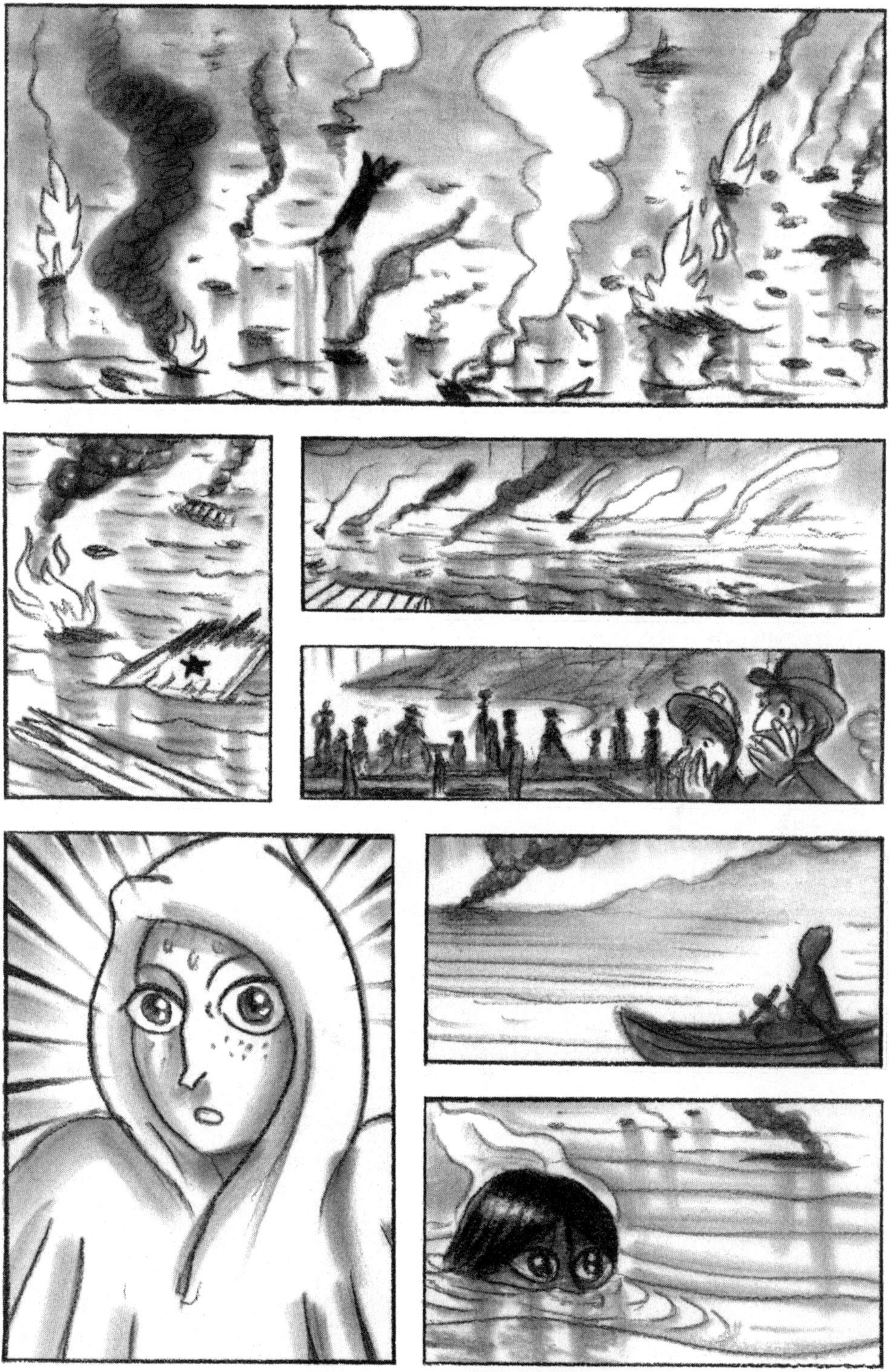

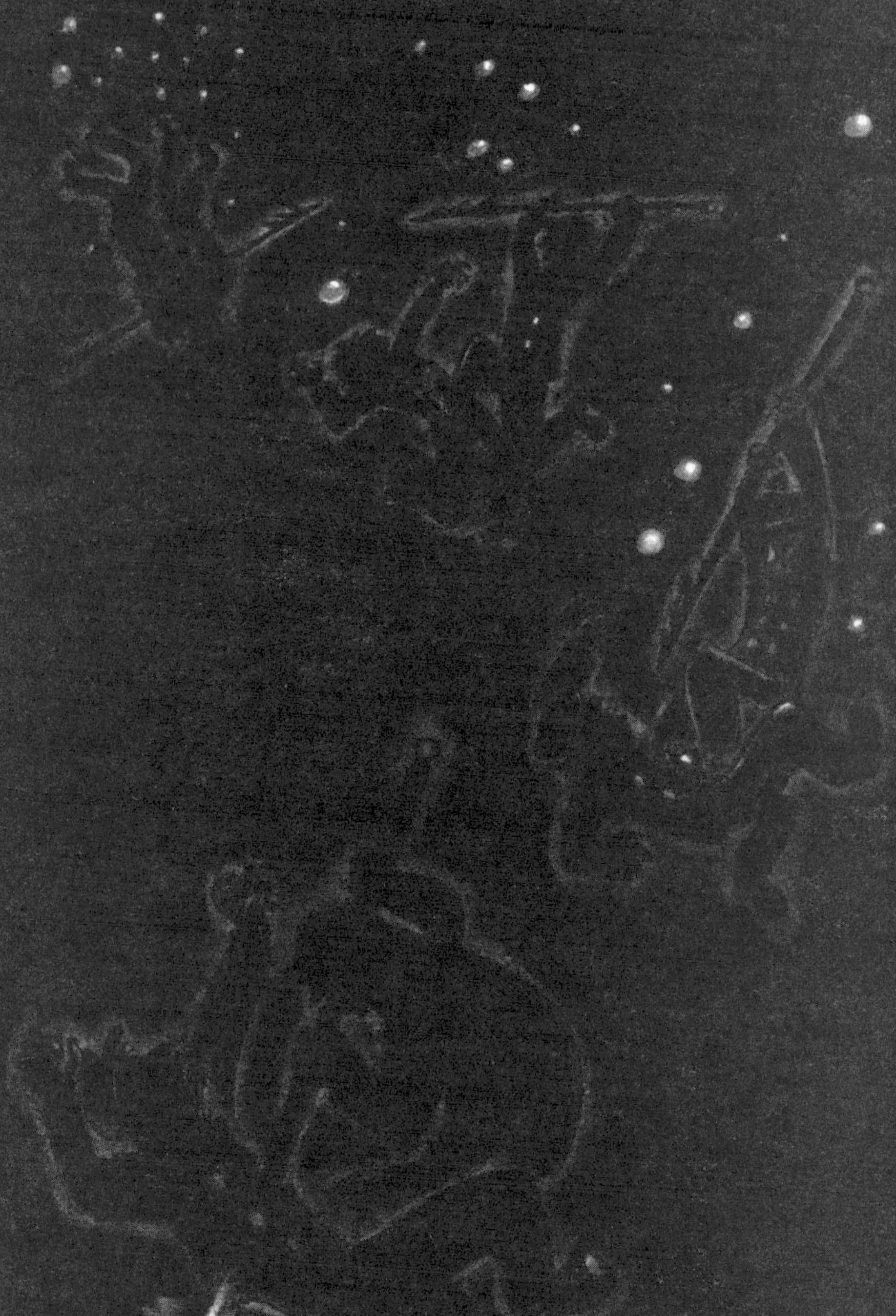

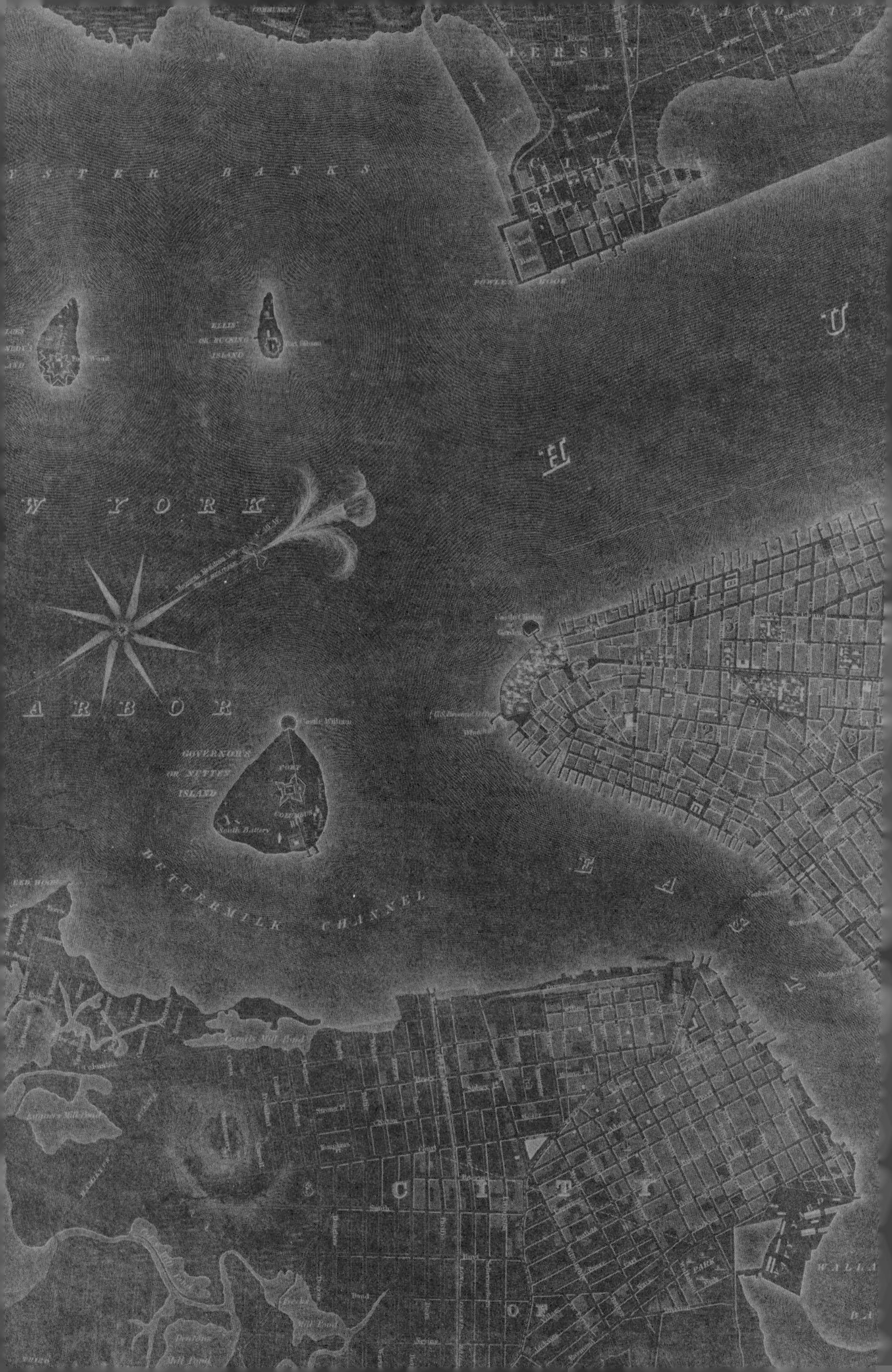

GOVERNOR'S OR NUTTEN ISLAND
Castle William
South Battery
BUTTERMILK CHANNEL

CODA

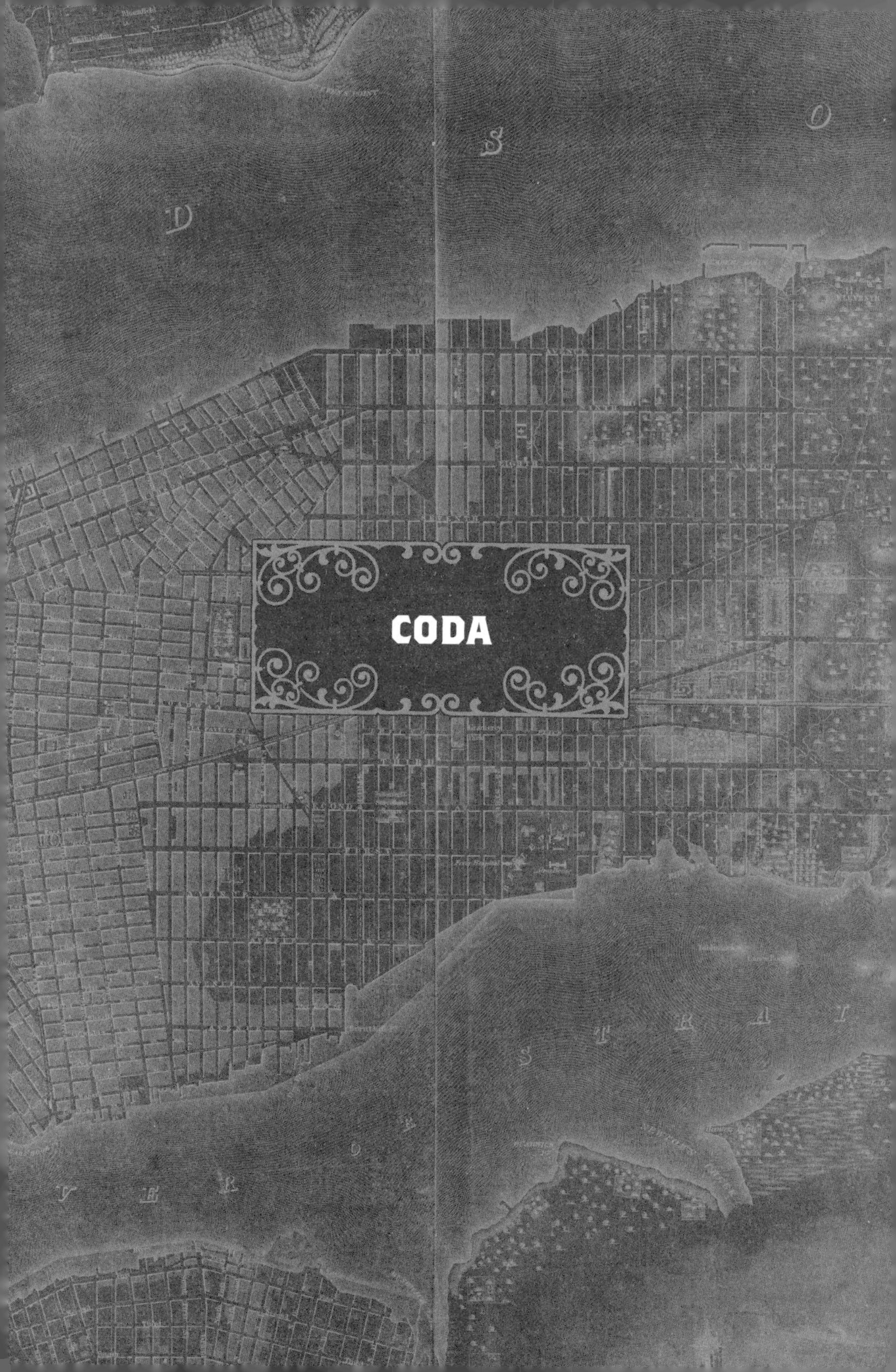

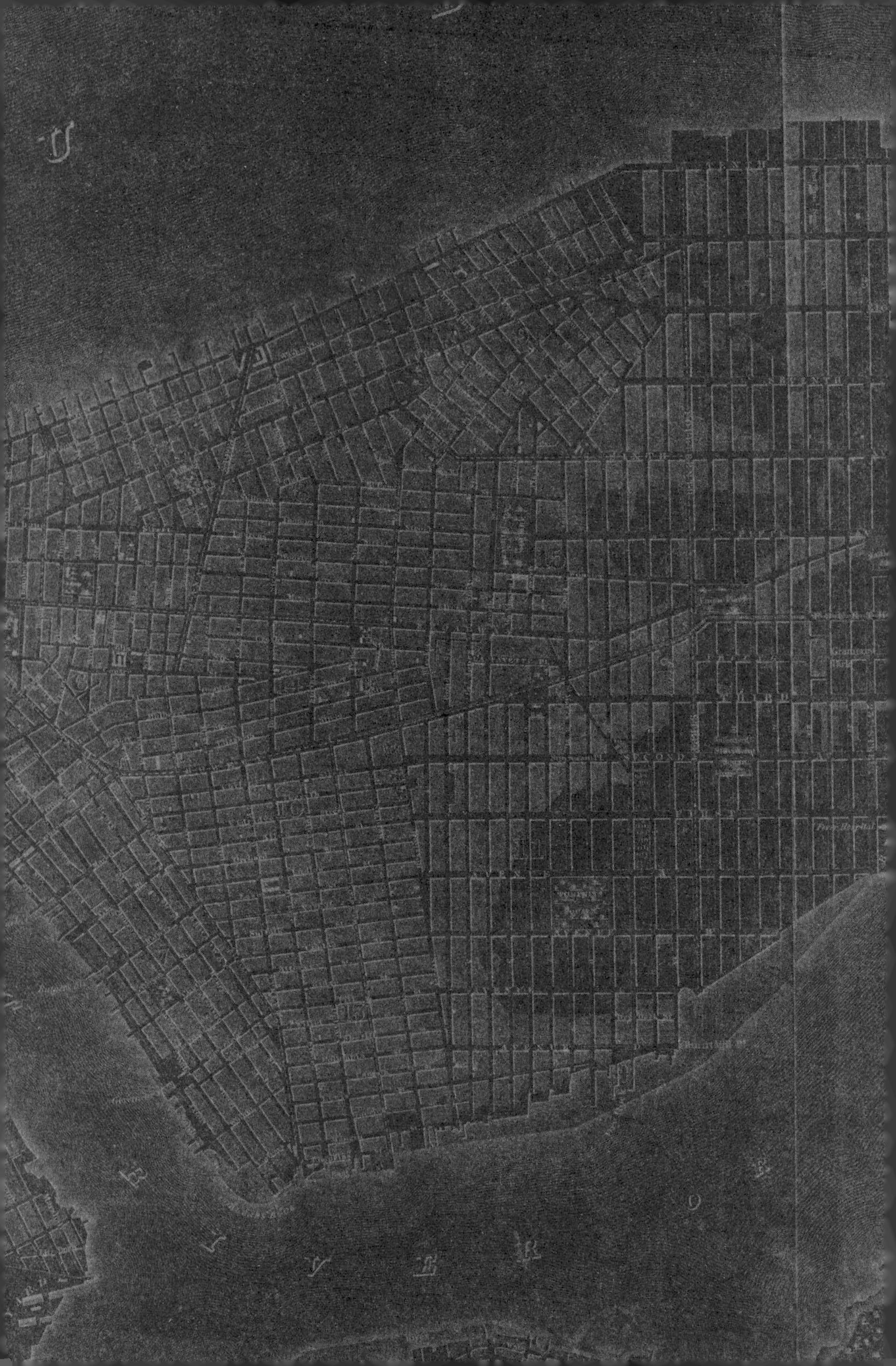

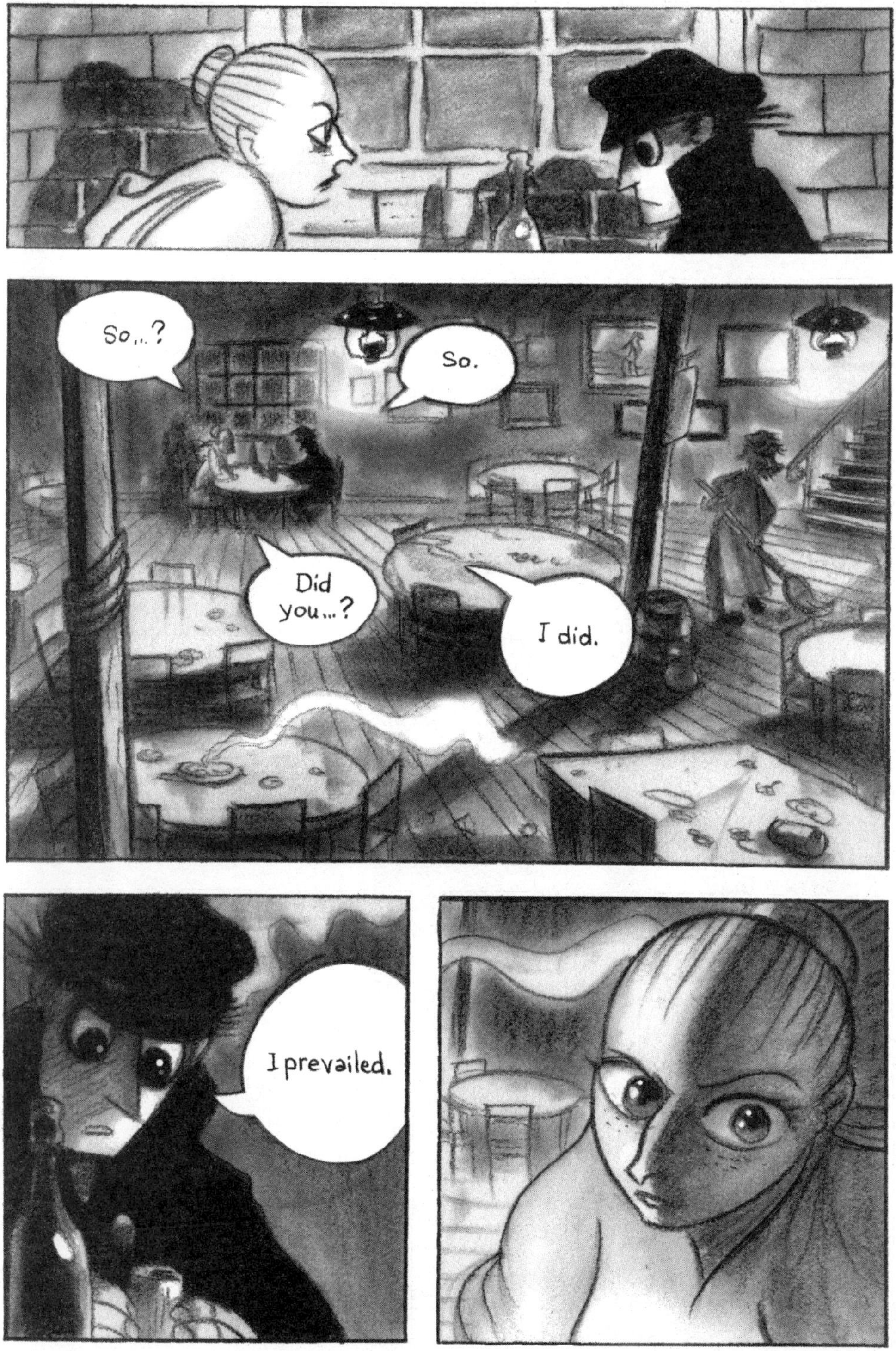
So...?
So.
Did you...?
I did.
I prevailed.

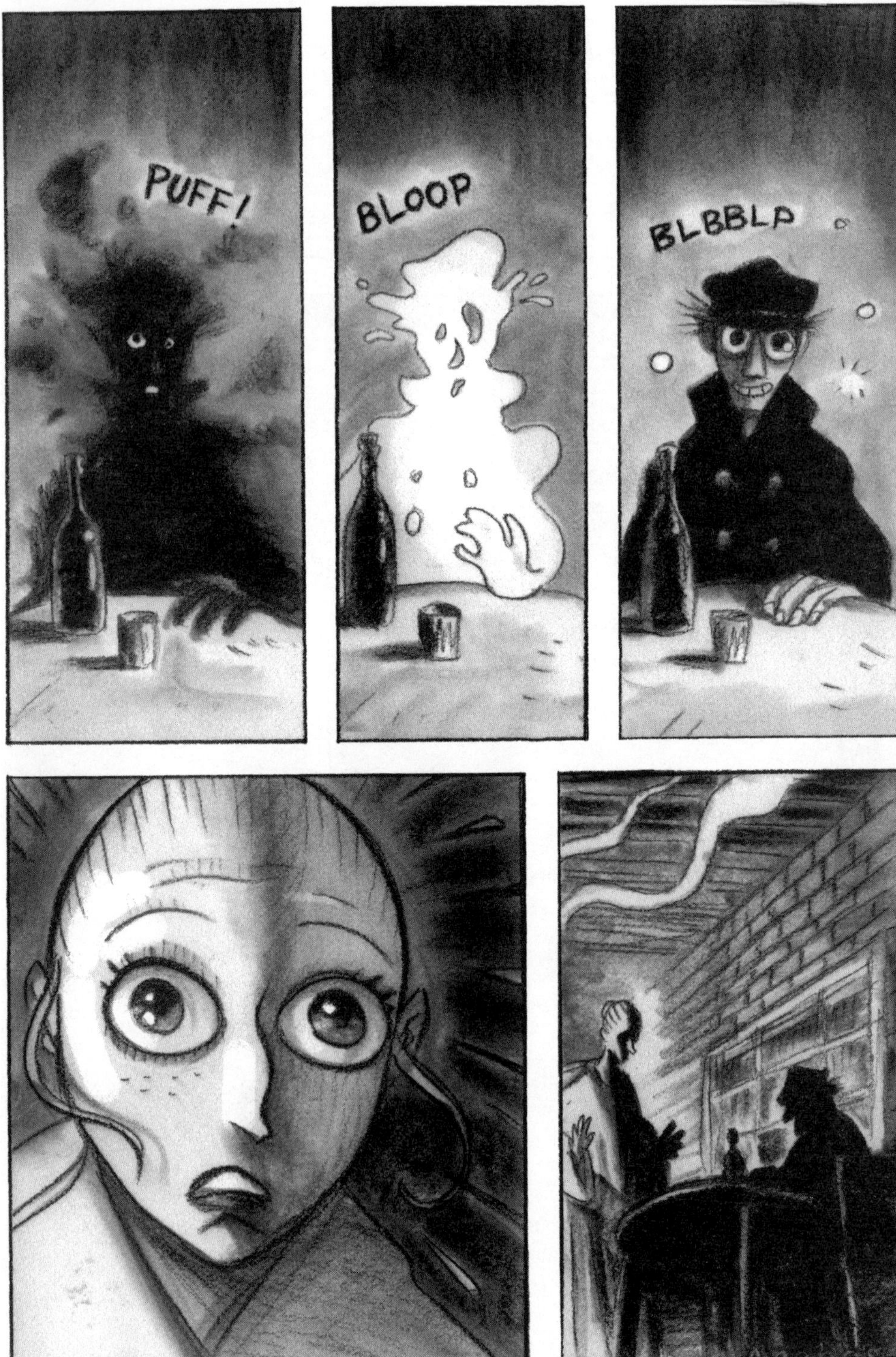
PUFF!
BLOOP
BLBBLP

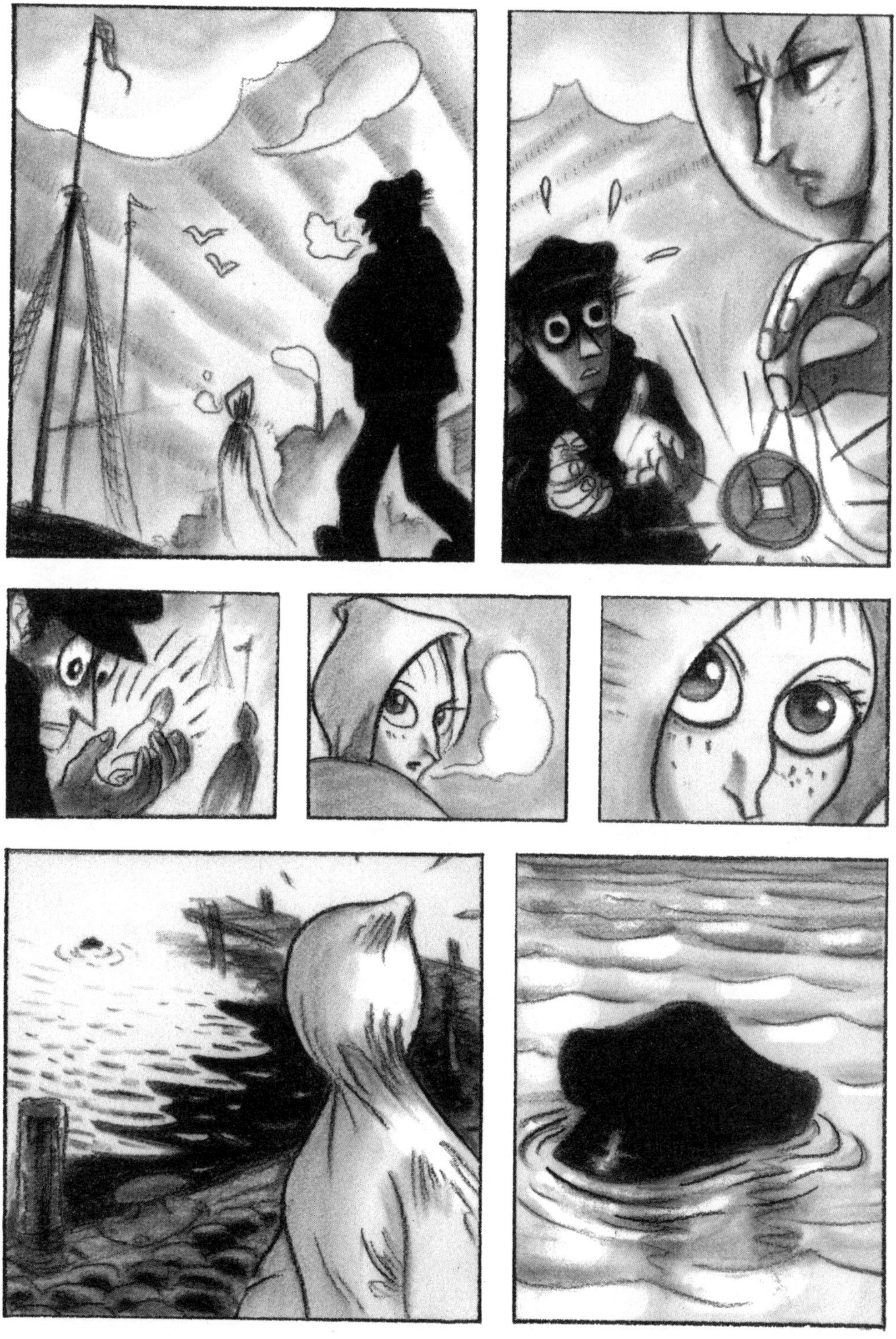

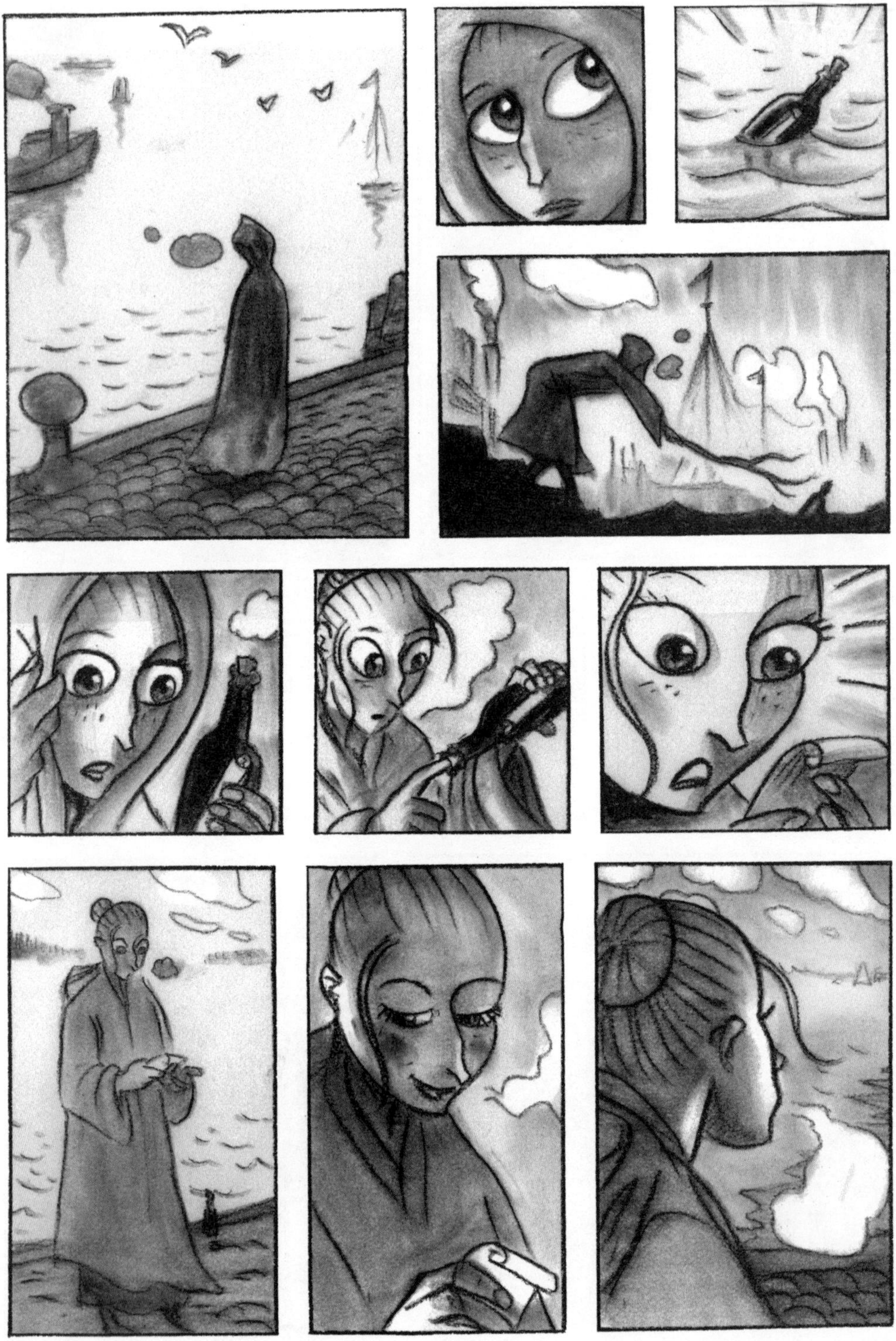

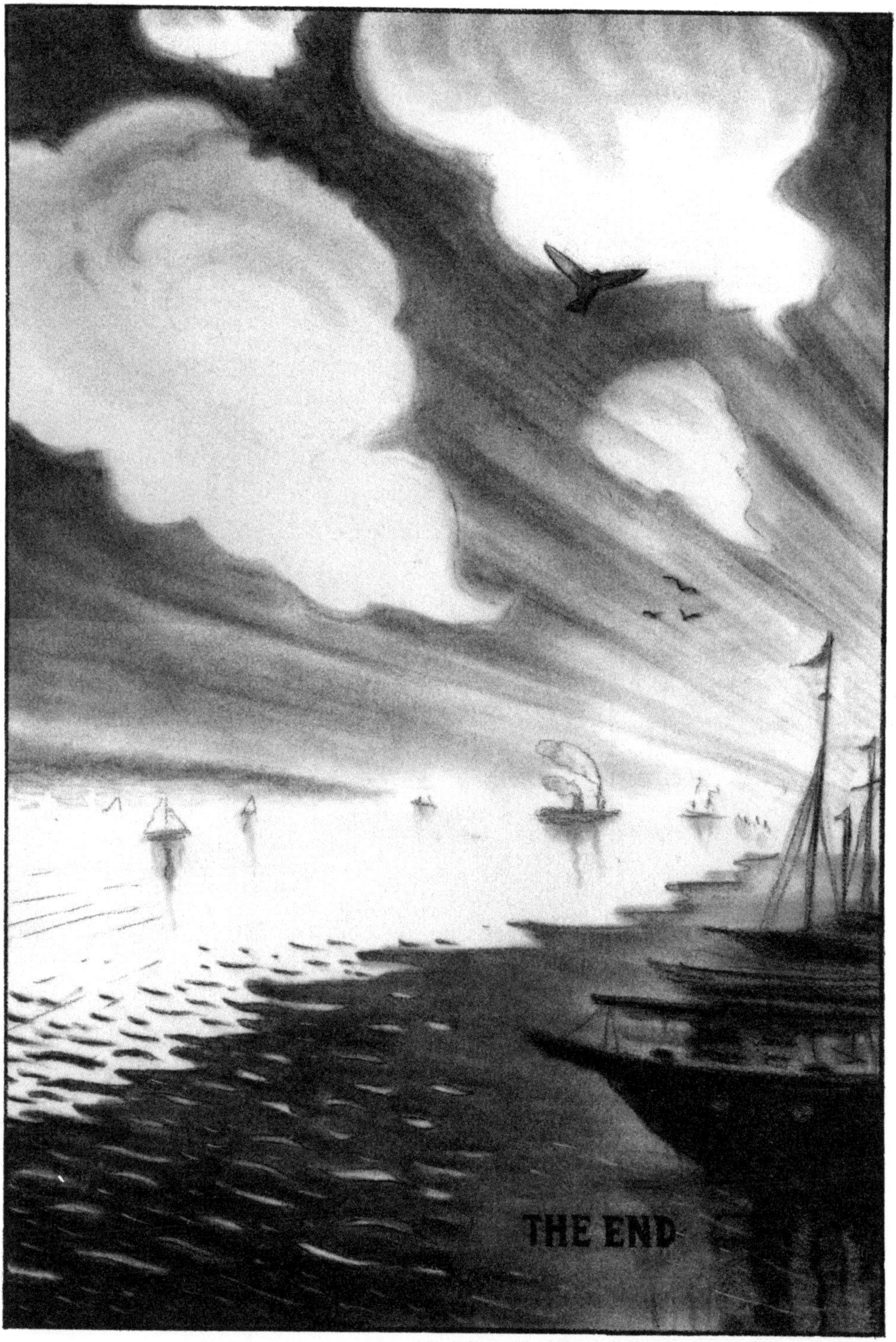
THE END

THANK YOU

My dearest Siena, for the paths we haven't taken.

Tanya McKinnon, for your brilliant and relentless partnership.

Alexis Siegel, mon ami, mon frère, et Sonia, ma petite soeur bien aimée.

Simon Boughton, for your trust and many insights.

Colleen Venable, Calista Brill, Gina Gagliano, Jill Freshney, Alexa Villanueva

Jon Yaged, John Sargent
Lora Fountain, Holly Hunnicutt

Richard Simon, Victoria Sanders

Thierry Laroche, Muriel Chabert, Nicolas Leroy, Caroline Moreau, Raphaël Ventura, and the whole team at Gallimard

Special thanks Joann Sfar

Fellow Twainers! How can I thank you for the weeks and months spent with you in fog and rain aboard the *Lorelei*! I never knew so many friends would join what is normally a lonesome journey.

Extra thanks for help on the Old English, Italian, and Russian: Anne Maclachlan, Filippo Baccino, Lyudmila Kapustina, Konstantin Svist, and Alexey Zaytsev.

Thank you, Pete Seeger and his mighty sloop *Clearwater* and its entire crew, in particular Nina Sanders and Catherine Stankowski.

Susan Kriete and Jillian Pazereckas at the magnificent New York Historical Society

The mighty Matt Knutzen at the New York Public Library's Maps Division

Allison Hourcade of RockLove, for creating the Sailor Twain jewelry!

Joe Monti, for reading a dreadful early script and research help on New York folklore.

Katherine Ramos and Mariana Cardier, partners in crime
Kelly Maguire, web ninja extraordinaire
Joe DiStefano and Andrea Blasich
Evelyn Kriete
Tor.com and HeroesandHeartbreakers.com
Casey Gonzalez

Don and Karen Steinmetz
Jonathan Kruk, for his passion and knowledge of all things Hudson.

Professor Paul Kane at Vassar, for leading me to the river's great poetry.

CREDITS

Pages 62–65: *Sailors of the Firmament* © Laura Senechal. Used by kind permission of the song's author.

Page 219: Valery and Lafayette share *In Cabin'd Ships at Sea*, by Walt Whitman.

Maps on chapter breaks are from nineteenth century surveys courtesy of the U.S.G.S. and Colton's 1836 Topographical Map of New York City is from the David Rumsey Historical Map Collection.

Page 364: Pearl's letter, calligraphy by Jennifer King. *Lorelei* letterhead created by Lissi Erwin, based on steamboat stationery of the late nineteenth century.

First Second
New York

Published by First Second
First Second is an imprint of Roaring Brook Press, a division of Holtzbrinck Publishing Holdings Limited Partnership
175 Fifth Avenue, New York, New York 10010
All rights reserved

Cataloging-in-Publication Data is on file at the Library of Congress.

Hardcover ISBN 978-1-59643-636-7
Paperback ISBN 978-1-59643-926-9

First Second books are available for special promotions and premiums.
For details, contact: Director of Special Markets, Holtzbrinck Publishers.

Book design by Colleen AF Venable
Printed in the United States of America

FIRST
EDITION

First hardcover edition 2012
First paperback edition 2014

Hardcover 3 5 7 9 10 8 6 4
Paperback 1 3 5 7 9 10 8 6 4 2

BY ART WE LIVE